Dictionary of the Place-Names of Wales

DICTIONARY *of the* PLACE-NAMES *of* WALES

Hywel Wyn Owen
Richard Morgan

Gomer

Published in 2007 by
Gomer Press, Llandysul, Ceredigion SA44 4JL
www.gomer.co.uk

Reprinted with corrections in 2008

ISBN 9781843239017
A CIP record for this title is available from the British Library

This book is published with the financial support of the Welsh Books Council

Typesetting and cover design by Almon, Pwllheli

Printed and bound in Wales at Gomer Press, Llandysul, Ceredigion

PRIFYSGOL BANGOR UNIVERSITY 1884

Cyhoeddir y gyfrol hon gyda chefnogaeth ariannol
Cronfa Goffa Ellen Kent, Ysgol y Gymraeg, Prifysgol Bangor

This volume has been published with financial support from the Ellen Kent Memorial Fund, School of Welsh, Bangor University

Based on a research project funded by

Arts & Humanities
Research Council

dedicated to the memory of
Melville Richards
who devoted himself to the study of
the place-names of Wales
and had a vision of such a dictionary

Contents

Foreword

This work fulfils a long-awaited need for an authoritative dictionary of the place-names of Wales and its most important topographical features. Wales has not benefited from a nation-wide survey such as that of the English Place-Name Society in England since 1923 and still in progress. In Wales, reliable information has to be acquired from a widely dispersed corpus of published and unpublished material ranging from a comparatively small number of specific studies to articles and notes in journals and edited versions of literary texts, much of which is not easily accessible to the general reader. Drawing on a distillation of the work of place-name scholars, past and present, together with their own original researches, the authors of this dictionary now present the first accredited compilation of its kind in Wales.

Some constraints have had to be imposed on the range and depth of treatment given to interpretations and etymologies, and some minor names are omitted. This is inevitable in the production of a volume of manageable proportions. But the inclusion of a comprehensive glossary of place-name elements will be of considerable value to the reader who wishes to pursue investigations further. Of particular merit also is the place given to establishing the historical circumstances under which the names were first given, the social significance of settlements and the topography of their locations.

The publication of this dictionary is a milestone in the history of Welsh place-name studies and the authors have proved to be worthy inheritors of a proud tradition in Bangor of those outstanding place-name scholars, Sir Ifor Williams, Professor Melville Richards, Professor Bedwyr Lewis Jones and Tomos Roberts. The Place-Name Research Centre is a notable addition to the profile of the School of Welsh/Ysgol y Gymraeg at Bangor.

Emeritus Professor Gwynedd O Pierce

Introduction

Background

This project was prompted by the need for a dictionary of place-names in Wales which is both scholarly and accessible. In England, several such works have existed for some time in parallel with exhaustive surveys of over thirty counties (in over eighty volumes) conducted by the English Place-Name Society. In Wales, progress has been far slower. The major place-names are fairly well documented but the less well-known names vary considerably in the amount and quality of the evidence available. There is, however, sufficient authoritative information about most place-names in Wales to enable us to collate existing knowledge in one synoptic dictionary, drawing on surveys of certain historic counties and some more limited areas, notes on selected names in academic journals and editions of literary texts, anthologies of scholarly articles for the general reader and unpublished research dissertations. For the very many remaining place-names not discussed elsewhere, or for areas of Wales where little or nothing has been published, we have undertaken the appropriate research necessary to provide a currently reliable exposition of forms, etymology and interpretation.

This publication is intended to be of value to scholars in various disciplines who turn to place-names for toponymic evidence but have hitherto been hampered by the lack of an authoritative dictionary for Wales on this scale. Equally, it will satisfy a remarkable appetite in Wales for knowledge about the names of places.

The project was funded by substantial grants from the Arts and Humanities Research Board (later Council) and the Department of Welsh at Bangor University, together with the support of the Board of Celtic Studies of the University of Wales.

The Melville Richards Archive

Professor G Melville Richards (1910-1973) was a philologist of international repute who devoted most of his research interests to the place-names of Wales, publishing erudite books and articles in Britain and Europe as well as contributing regularly to the media.

During his teaching and research years at the universities of Swansea, Liverpool and Bangor (where he was Professor of Welsh) he amassed an archive of over 300,000 slips containing incomparable research material. This was the source material for his national and international publications, but the vast bulk of historical forms, dates and sources had not, until recently, seen the light of day. Fortunately, his archive material was deposited in Bangor University (in what is now the Place-Name Research Centre within the Department of Archives), and the archive was there transformed into a database (launched in 2005 and accessed as www.bangor.ac.uk/amr) in a project funded by the Board of Celtic Studies and by the Arts and Humanities Research Board (under the Research Enhancement Scheme).

It is very clear from evidence in the archive that Melville Richards was working towards a Welsh onomasticon, some material for which appeared in the weekly column for *Y Cymro* (March 1967 to May 1970) and in his contribution to *The Names of Towns and Cities in Britain* (1970). His untimely death in 1973 frustrated such an ambition. This supplementary material went further than the resource slips themselves in that it proposed etymologies, and has thus been invaluable in preparing this dictionary, particularly for those place-names which had hitherto received scant attention in published works.

This volume is dedicated to the memory of one of Wales's most eminent place-name scholars and in recognition of the posthumous contribution of his research archive.

Selecting the place-names

The principal factor in the selection of these place-names was the publication of a volume which would encompass as many places as possible, and yet remain economically viable.

We have chosen to draw on names appearing on the Ordnance Survey map Travelmaster 7 'Wales and the West Midlands' (1:250 000) 1999 and in several OS digital gazetteers. In order to ensure that this very large body of evidence remained manageable, we have had to make a number of subjective exclusions which some readers may consider unjustifiable. We have generally excluded names of minor locations except those names which are better known nationally; we have omitted names of localities which have become suburbs through the expansion of towns and cities.

Coverage based on any general map inevitably reflects the settlement history of Wales. There are areas which, for geographical, historical and socio-economic reasons, have attracted a more numerous population with a dense settlement pattern; these areas tend to have a high incidence of place-names.

Following the practice of similar publications elsewhere in Britain and Ireland, we have included landscape features such as rivers, mountains and notable coastal features. We are, however, particularly mindful of the fact that there are large tracts of Wales on the Travelmaster map where the majority of the names are streams and hills, and where the toponymic evidence is notably thin. We are of the opinion that detailed interpretation of many of these names is best left to publications specifically dedicated to mountains and hills, to coastal features and to rivers and streams (for which R J Thomas's initial volume set the standard). Inclusion here is based on a subjective selection of those features of the landscape which are perceived to have regional or national significance, those features which the general reader might reasonably expect to find in such a dictionary.

Arrangement of the entries

Each place-name appears as a ***headword*** (in capitals, but in mixed case in the glossary of elements). The form of the headword reflects the orthographic conventions of Welsh in the twenty-first century and is based on the standard reference gazetteers for Welsh place-names, the *Gazetteer of Welsh Place-names* (1957) and *Welsh Administrative and Territorial Units* (1969) but with modifications which reflect subsequent settlement history and, in particular, more recent usage (in the light of the recommendations of the Welsh Language Board's advisory panel on place-name orthography). In collaboration with that panel, counties are currently undertaking a review of their place-names; where that review is complete and a revised list of standardised forms is available we have incorporated such forms as our headwords. Where a place currently has dual names (Welsh and English), the English form is usually cited first in this dictionary in keeping with an English-medium publication (with the Welsh form cross-referenced). However, we have not followed this practice where a less well-known name is evidently Welsh and the English form is a variant differing perhaps by a single letter, and where the standard form is currently a matter of discussion. We are very conscious both of local ownership of names and of evolving attitudes as some names achieve greater currency or prominence, both locally and nationally, especially in the media. The entries for such names will usually include appropriate comment on significant variations. We have also, with considerable reservation, included some non-standard forms which can still be observed on road-signs and some maps, but which we would not wish to advocate as standard orthography. For these reasons, the dictionary should not, in every instance, be regarded as the definitive authority on standard place-name forms.

The headwords are followed by the historical ***county*** names (1536-1974) displaced by new district and county councils which were themselves replaced by the unitary councils in 1996. A list of the counties and their abbreviations are on page xxi. The ***national grid reference*** (NGR) is provided with kind permission of Ordnance Survey (© Crown copyright ED 274194). Whereas the geographer would wish to see NGRs that define the extent of, say, a mountain range, or a river's course from source to estuary, we have normally provided a single four-figure NGR, sufficient to enable the general reader to locate the settlement, mountain, bay or river, usually the position of the name itself on an OS map.

The ***meaning*** of the place-name (in inverted commas) is followed by the ***element(s)*** (in bold italic) which are the component(s) of the name. Since the vast majority of the place-names of Wales are of Welsh origin, each element is assumed to be Welsh unless indicated otherwise. A later section deals with some of the features of Welsh phonology as they apply to place-names. Suffice to say here that Welsh elements are presented in their radical forms as recorded in *Geiriadur Prifysgol Cymru* (GPC), regardless of mutations or dialectal variants (unless specified). For those place-names which are not Welsh in origin, the language of the element is indicated. In accordance with the conventions of English place-name studies, English elements are cited in their Old or Middle English forms (prefixed OE or ME), unless the more recent emergence of a place-name, or uncertainty as to the precise date of adoption, makes it more appropriate to cite the form as it appears in modern English (prefixed E). Personal names and river names, too, are cited in radical forms. Hypothetical elements, those elements which are evident in the place-names but are not independently attested, are marked by an asterisk. Where a settlement is implied or elliptical, that is expressed in such terms as '(settlement by) [stream name]', '(settlement of) [personal name]'.

The historical ***forms*** (in italics) and ***dates*** provide the evidence for the interpretation of the name. In exhaustive local and regional surveys it is also customary to cite the documents from which the forms are taken. Regrettably, to have included them in this dictionary would have drastically increased the bulk of the volume. Where we have drawn on authoritative scholarship (published and unpublished) we have accepted the documentary references and transcriptions obtained there. However, there are very many instances where later research has allowed us to emend a form or date.

The meaning of a river name is given either as a dedicated entry or within the entry for a settlement name which incorporates the river name if that is more appropriate (in which case the river name will be included as a headword but cross-referenced to the relevant place-name). We have not been tempted in the same way with personal names. The actual etymology of a personal name rarely has any bearing on the place-name in which it appears, despite determined attempts to perceive significant links in onomastic folklore and ecclesiastical tradition, and furthered by enthusiastic antiquarians. The term personal name is used to cover both a given name and a surname, and treats the saintly and the secular alike.

The bulk of the entry is devoted to ***interpretation***, which comments on the meaning and significance of the place-name, and sets the name in a historical and environmental context. Attention is drawn to linguistic characteristics and development, with the exception of those phonological changes which are regular modifications in the Welsh language; the section '**Place-names and Welsh sound-changes**' (below) provides a summary of the most commonly found phonological modifications. The modern pronunciation, usually a dialectal variant, is cited where it throws light on the linguistic origin or development of the name. We frequently draw attention to the role of perception, that under-estimated phenomenon which perceives the name to have a particular meaning and gives a phonologically irregular spin to its later development. Where doubt exists as to the precise significance of the name, that is reflected in the designation 'obscure' or 'unclear', in the hope that future research can provide clarification; we have been ready to concede defeat where there is insufficient evidence to warrant venturing into the realms of conjecture.

Interpreting place-names in Wales

Wales has several layers of linguistic contact. The Celtic and Brittonic base, the Roman occupation, Anglo-Saxon settlements, Scandinavian sorties, Anglo-Norman strongholds, English immigration, have all left toponymic footprints. Although we may have some idea of the historical context, the exact significance of a particular event or the identity of the person may now be lost to us. Sometimes, the converse holds true, when a place-name is the sole piece of evidence of otherwise unrecorded history.

Various aspects of Welsh history can be traced in certain place-names. For example, Celtic or Brittonic river names (**Alun**, **Dyfrdwy**); settlements reflecting occupation by Romans (**Gwent**, **Powys**), Irish (**Gwynedd**, **Llŷn**), English (**Shotton**, **Newport**), Scandinavians (**Swansea**,

Fishguard) and Normans (**Malpas**, **Grosmont**); 'new' settlements (**Newborough**, **Newcastle Emlyn**); transferred names (**Montgomery**, **Denbigh**); names whose connotations are religious (**Betws**, **Bethesda** and the *llan* names), industrial (**Porthmadog**, **Morriston**), agricultural (**Cynheidre**, **Talwrn**) and vacational (**Fairbourne**, **Builth Wells**). Settlements of various types are denoted by elements such as *bod*, *-by*, *caer*, *cas(tell)*, *din*, *llan*, *pentre(f)*, *town*, *-ton*, *tre(f)*.

The landscape prompted the majority of place-names which then provide topographic clues to their past which may not be discovered in other historical research. While it is important to stress that we may not always be interpreting particular linguistic terms and elements in quite the same way as they were understood by those who originally coined them, some topographical elements (whatever their precise meaning) are easily identified in settlement names taken from hills (**Harlech**, **Moelfre**), valleys (**Cwmbrân**, **Nant Gwrtheyrn**), rivers (**Aberystwyth**, **Ystradgynlais**), promontories (**Penrhos**, **Penrhyn**), bays and inlets (**Amlwch**, **Porth-cawl**) and islands (**Priestholm**, **Ramsey**). Other features of the landscape are witnessed in place-names containing common elements such as *bala*, *ban*, *blaen*, *bron*, *bryn*, *cefn*, *craig*, *cymer*, *esgair*, *ffridd*, *ford*, *glan*, *glyn*, *hill*, *maes*, *rhyd*, *sarn*, *ton*.

The linguistic heritage of Wales is evident in its place-names, since the history of any language is reflected not only in oral and written communication but in the names given to places in the course of everyday life. Recorded place-names expose both the different layers of our linguistic past and special linguistic features such as non-standard plurals (**Cymau**, **Aber-naint**), dialectal variants (**Pencader**, **Ffrith**), stress shift (**Prestatyn**, **Trefyclo**) and cymricization (**Bagillt**, **Niwbwrch**).

It follows, then, that the study of place-names requires a close examination of the earliest possible evidence. When we are aware from other sources, or suspect, that a place has been in existence long before the appearance of the name in documents, we cannot always be absolutely confident in our interpretation of the name. The reliability of documentary evidence itself is sometimes suspect, possibly adulterated by incremental copying errors in transmission or by attempts to make sense of names communicated in one language and transcribed by a monoglot speaker of another language whose orthographic conventions may have been very different. Some modern place-names may well mean what they say, but many other names defy obvious explanation. In such cases, only a scholarly linguistic analysis of the earliest forms and their subsequent development can illuminate the significance of a name.

In this process, familiarity with the stock of place-name elements is essential. Over many years in Britain, toponymists have been compiling a glossary of place-name elements. The knowledge acquired in this way can help us in the analysis and interpretation of other place-names. The actual topographic significance may vary slightly from place to place, but that in itself adds to our understanding of the range of meanings ascribed to that element. Toponymists in England can draw on very many years' research into the vocabulary of English place-names, experience which has, in recent years, resulted in a reassessment or a refinement of the significance of a considerable number of elements. In Wales, we can draw on that corpus for our interpretation of English names, making allowances for variant meanings in a Welsh context, but the precise understanding of many Welsh elements is an accumulative process. The inclusion in this dictionary of a Glossary of Elements goes some way to setting out our current knowledge, a contribution eventually to a 'Dictionary of Welsh Place-Names Elements'.

The structure of Welsh place-names

This section will demonstrate, somewhat cryptically perhaps, the types of place-names which can be encountered in Wales.

A place-name can be a single generic element and is usually referred to as a simplex name (**Cwm**, **Rhaeadr**). Sometimes, it may be preceded by the definite article (**Y Bala**, **Y Fflint**) which may cause a phonological change (**Y Foel**, **Y Felinheli**), and occasionally be omitted (**Waunfawr**, **Felindre**).

Most place-names comprise a generic element and a qualifying element which specifies or distinguishes a location. Where the syntax is regular, a place-name is frequently described as a name phrase (**Bryn-mawr**, **Llanbadarn**). Extended qualifiers may define the location within another administrative unit (**Llandrillo-yn-Rhos**, **Castellnewydd Emlyn**). Where the word order is irregular (usually with the qualifier preceding), a place-name is frequently described as an inversion compound (**Rhuddlan**, **Moelfre**).

Some of the phonological changes (in addition to lenition of initial consonants referred to below) are assimilation (**Nanmor**, **Lampeter**), dissimilation (**Kinmel**, **Caerdydd**), metathesis (**Marloes**, **Dynfant**), loss of final consonant (**Solva**, **Abermo**), reduction of final syllable (**Brymbo**, **Trefor**), intrusive consonant or semi-vowel (**Plwmp**, **Cricieth**) and metanalysis (**Narberth**, **St Athan**).

Place-names and Welsh sound-changes

This section provides a very basic guide to the phonological characteristics of place-names in Welsh.

In Welsh, adjectives regularly follow nouns (**Maes-gwyn, Bryn-coch, Porth Mawr**) with some exceptions (**Hirwaun, Rhuddlan**). Adjectives such as ***gwyn*** may be feminine ***gwen*** (**Gwendraeth, Wenallt**). Furthermore, adjectives undergo a mutation (called lenition) to the initial consonant if the noun is feminine (**Afon Wen, Craig Goch, Garn Fawr**). Lenition of feminine nouns is also caused by the definite article (**Y Borth, Y Drenewydd**). The same process affects nouns following ***ar*** 'on' (**Argoed, Pontardawe**) or ***am*** 'near, around' (**Amlwch, Castellnewydd Emlyn**) or ***dau/dwy*** 'two' (**Aberdaugleddau, Dwygyfylchi**), or when the following noun indicates possession of some sort (**Beddgelert, Tyddewi** and the ***llan*** names). Another mutation (the nasal mutation) follows *yn, ym* or *yng* 'in' (**Llanfair-yn-Neubwll, Llanfair-ym-Muallt, Llanfihangel-yng-Ngwynfa**).

Broadly speaking, the commonest standard phonological changes in place-names can be summarised thus:

p > b	**Tal-y-bont, Benllech**
t > d	**Pontardawe, Cardiff**
c > g *or* **ch**	**Caergybi, Machen**
b > m *or* **f**	**Llanfair-ym-Muallt, Llanfabon**
d > dd	**Bont-ddu, Llanddewi**
g > ng	**Llanfihangel-yng-Ngwynfa**
gl > l	**Rhuddlan, Rhiwlas**
gr > r	**Rhosllannerchrugog, Ro-wen**
gw > w	**Yr Wyddgrug, Llanwrda**
ll > l	**Amlwch, Carreg-lefn**
m > f	**Llanfair, Y Bont-faen**

These standard phonological changes to elements in place-names cause the greatest frustration for non-Welsh speakers when the place-name element is not immediately recognisable, mainly due to the initial consonant being obscured, and seemingly untraceable in a lexicographic search. In this dictionary, the analysis of each place-name cites the elements in their radical form (with occasional citation of relevant feminine or plural forms). This helps to identify the significant element but does not undertake to explain its commonplace standard variations.

Acknowledgements

Siân Lewis, Melville Richards's daughter and executor to his estate, has provided her personal support over many years and has shown an informed interest in the progress of the dictionary. We are grateful for her permission to make extensive use of his research archive.

The initial paragraphs of the Introduction have made it clear that our methodology has been to draw on authoritative published sources and on selected unpublished material. It is this corpus of received opinion which has made the dictionary possible. Where we have deviated from those views, the revision usually reflects more recent information.

There has been further consultation with scholars who have specialist knowledge of individual names or elements, or who are far more familiar than we are with the history, dialect and landscape of certain areas. They have scrutinised drafts of the entries for individual counties. Their corrections and suggestions have been cheerfully incorporated into the text. We ourselves, however, must accept responsibility for the accuracy or otherwise of the published dictionary.

Staff and colleagues at Bangor University have been particularly helpful and supportive, particularly Dr Glenda Carr, Dr Bruce Griffiths, Gwilym Trefor Jones, Professor Peredur Lynch, Professor Trefor M Owen, Dr Nia Watkin Powell, Professor Huw Pryce, Delyth Prys, Tomos Roberts, Einion Thomas, Professor Gerwyn Wiliams and Emeritus Professor Iolo Wyn Williams. Others consulted, either directly or through correspondence or commentary elsewhere, include Ifor Baines, Gareth Bevan, Duncan Brown, Professor Richard Coates, Murray Ll. Chapman, Bruce Coplestone-Crow, Dr Paul Cullen, Dr Aled Lloyd Davies, E Wendy O Davies, J Barry Davies, J Arwel Edwards, G G Evans, Olwen Idwal Forman, Alan Fryer, Dr Angharad Fychan, Bedwyr Fychan, Dr Margaret Gelling, Ann Griffith, Ken Lloyd Gruffydd, Emeritus Professor R Geraint Gruffydd, Dai Hawkins, Dr Carole Hough, Dr Glyn Tegai Hughes, R Cyril Hughes, Eleanor Imhoff, Brian Ll James, Professor Geraint Jenkins, Brenda Wyn Jones, Deric John, Peris Jones-Evans, Gwenfron Humphreys, Dr D Geraint Lewis, Marion Arthur Jones, Peter Meurig Jones, Arwyn Morgan, Emeritus Professor Prys Morgan, Tim Morgan, E R Morris, R M Morris, Twm Morus, Beryl Orwig, Dr Graham Osborne, Elfyn Owen, Griffith Owen, Dr Oliver Padel, Tom Parry, Emeritus Professor Gwynedd

O Pierce, R F Peter Powell, Derrick Pratt, Curig Pritchard, John Pugh, Professor Patrick Sims-Williams, Douglas Smith, Professor David Thorne, Dei Tomos, Dr Dafydd Wyn Wiliam, Christopher J Williams, Dai and Megan Williams, Dr David Page Williams, Geraint Williams, Dr Iwan Bryn Williams, Mair Lloyd Williams, Wenna F Williams, Dr Iwan Wmffre, Dr Goronwy Wynne and Rosemary Yale.

Particular reference must be made to Emeritus Professor Gwynedd O Pierce who undertook to read the final draft. His encouragement, experience and vast knowledge of Wales, its languages and its place-names, have made an inestimable contribution to the merits of the publication.

Ann Daniels was the research assistant for the original AHRB project (2000-2003) at Bangor. Both of us appreciate her enthusiasm, commitment, efficiency and encouragement. In the later stages of the project, her responsibilities and support were undertaken by Owain L Davies, Gruff Prys and Nesta Roberts.

Professor Peredur Lynch took a keen interest in the dictionary's progress and ensured vital additional funding and facilities at critical times. Others who provided technical or editorial support and advice were Heledd Wyn Owen and Rhiain Wyn Owen.

Robat Trefor and Lowri Morgan prepared the text for publication and subsequently read the proofs. Their labours and interest in the project, as well as timely advice, deserve our praise. On their advice, Bedwyr ab Iestyn admirably took on the technical task of putting the text into proofs. The cover design itself is also Bedwyr's excellent work.

Finally, we must, as always, pay tribute to our respective wives, Rhiain and Verona, who have afforded us support and encouragement over many years.

We are very conscious indeed of the pitfalls of long-term collaborative projects, and the challenges of incorporating most recent scholarship. Dictionaries are prone to such hazards. We accept the volume may on occasion betray signs of exasperated omission or oblivious temerity. Further information, particularly from philologists and local historians, will be gratefully included in a future revised edition.

Hywel Wyn Owen
Richard Morgan

Bibliography

Selected publications relevant to Wales

Not included are the very many notes and articles on specific elements and particular place-names which appear in scholarly journals (such as *Archaeologia Cambrensis, Bulletin of the Board of Celtic Studies, Transactions of the Cymmrodorion, Études Celtiques, Indo-Celtica, Journal of the National Library of Wales, Journal of the English Place-Name Society, Nomina, Studia Celtica,* and in the published transactions of the county historical and antiquarian societies. For example, Melville Richards published authoritative discussions of varying length over many years on elements such as ***dryll, ffridd/ffrith, hafod, hendre, is, march, meifod, lluest, rhyd, sarn*** and ***uwch***. These articles can be accessed by reference to the index of each journal. An extremely useful guide is to be found in Spittal and Field (below).

Charles, B G (1938)
Non-Celtic Place-Names in Wales (University College London)

Charles, B G (1992)
The Place-Names of Pembrokeshire (National Library of Wales, Aberystwyth), 2 vols

Davies, Ellis (1959)
Flintshire Place-Names (University of Wales Press, Cardiff)

Davies, Elwyn (1957, 1967)
Rhestr o Enwau Lleoedd/A Gazetteer of Welsh Place-Names (University of Wales Press, Cardiff)

Eyers, M (1992)
The Masters of the Coalfield: People and Place-Names in Glamorgan and Gwent (Pontypool 1992)

John, D (1998)
Cynon Valley Place-Names (Gwasg Carreg Gwalch, Llanrwst)

John, D (1999)
Notes on some Placenames in and around the Bont (Deric John, Aberdare)

Jones, B L and **Roberts, T** (1979)
'Coastal toponyms of Anglesey' in *Journal of the English Place-Name Society* 11

Jones, B L (1991)
'Place-names: Signposts to the past in Anglesey' in *Transactions of the Anglesey Antiquarian Society and Field Club* 23-37

Jones, B L (1991)
Enwau (Gwasg Carreg Gwalch, Llanrwst)

Jones, B L (1992)
Yn Ei Elfen (Gwasg Carreg Gwalch, Llanrwst)

Jones, G T and **Roberts, T** (1996)
Enwau Lleoedd Môn/The Place-Names of Anglesey (Isle of Anglesey County Council, Research Centre Wales, Bangor University)

Jones, I (1998)
Enwau Eryri: Place-Names in Snowdonia (Lolfa, Tal-y-bont)

Lias, A (1991)
Place-Names in the Welsh Borderlands (Ludlow)

Lias, A (1994)
A Guide to Welsh Place-Names (Gwasg Carreg Gwalch, Llanrwst)

Lewis, D G (2007)
Y Llyfr Enwau: Enwau'r Wlad. A Check-list of Welsh Place-Names (Gomer, Llandysul)

Lloyd-Jones, J (1928)
Enwau Lleoedd Sir Gaernarfon (University of Wales Press, Cardiff)

Mawer, A (1932-3)
A Survey of the Place-Names of Wales (Cardiff)

Morgan, R with **Evans, G G** (1993)
Enwau Lleoedd Buallt a Maesyfed (Gwasg Carreg Gwalch, Llanrwst)

Morgan, R (1998)
A Study of Radnorshire Place-Names (Gwasg Carreg Gwalch, Llanrwst)

Morgan, R and **Powell, R F P** (1999)
A Study of Breconshire Place-Names (Gwasg Carreg Gwalch, Llanrwst)

Morgan, R (2001)
A Study of Montgomeryshire Place-Names (Gwasg Carreg Gwalch, Llanrwst)

Morgan, R (2004). Translated and adapted by **D Hawkins**.
Enwau Lleoedd ym Maldwyn (Gwasg Carreg Gwalch, Llanrwst)

Morgan, R (2005)
Place-names of Gwent (Gwasg Carreg Gwalch, Llanrwst)

Morgan, T J and **P** (1985)
Welsh Surnames (Univerity of Wales Press, Cardiff)

Ordnance Survey. (2004)
A Glossary of the most common Welsh elements used on maps of Wales (Southampton)

Osborne, G and **Hobbs, G** (1998)
The Place-Names of Eastern Gwent (Old Bakehouse, Abertillery)

Osborne, G and **Hobbs, G** (2002)
The Place-Names of Western Gwent (Old Bakehouse, Abertillery)

Owen, H W (1987)
'English place-names and Welsh stress-patterns' in ***Nomina*** XI, 99-114 ed. C Clark, O J Padel, A Rumble, V Smart (Society for Name Studies in Britain and Ireland)

Owen, H W (1991)
Enwau Lleoedd Bro Dyfrdwy ac Alun (Gwasg Carreg Gwalch, Llanrwst)

Owen, H W (1994)
The Place-Names of East Flintshire (University of Wales Press, Cardiff)

Owen, H W (1997)
'Old English place-name elements in Domesday Flintshire' in ***Names, Places and People*** ed. A Rumble and A D Mills
(Paul Watkins, Stamford)

Owen, H W (1998)
The Place-Names of Wales (University of Wales Press, The Western Mail, Cardiff)

Owen, H W (2000)
Cymreigio Enwau Lleoedd yng nghylch Wrecsam (Trafodion Bangor 1, Ysgol y Gymraeg, Prifysgol Bangor)

Owen, H W (2005)
Dehongli Enwau Lleoedd gyda golwg arbennig ar Faldwyn a'r Gororau (Trafodion Bangor 2, Ysgol y Gymraeg, Prifysgol Bangor)

Owen, H W (2007)
Rhai Enwau Lleoedd yng nghymydau Prestatyn a Rhuddlan (Trafodion Bangor 4, Ysgol y Gymraeg, Prifysgol Bangor)

Pierce, G O (1960)
'Enwau lleoedd anghyfiaith yng Nghymru' in ***Bulletin of the Board of Celtic Studies*** 18, 252-65

Pierce, G O (1968)
The Place-Names of Dinas Powys Hundred (University of Wales Press, Cardiff)

Pierce, G O (1973)
'Some aspects of English influence on place-names in Wales' in *Onoma* 17, 173-91

Pierce, G O (1982)
'Mynegbyst i'r Gorffennol' in ***Abertawe a'r Cylch*** ed. I M Williams (Gwasg Christopher Davies, Llandybïe)

Pierce, G O (1984)
'The evidence of place-names' in ***The Glamorgan County History*** 2 ed. H N Savory (Cardiff)

Pierce, G O (1988)
'Place-names' in ***Settlement and Society in Wales*** ed. D H Owen (University of Wales Press, Cardiff)

Pierce, G O (1990)
Dan y Bargod (University of Wales Registry, Cardiff)

Pierce, G O (2002)
Place-Names in Glamorgan (Merton Priory Press, Cardiff)

Pierce, G O, Roberts, T and **Owen, H W** (1997)
Ar Draws Gwlad (Gwasg Carreg Gwalch, Llanrwst)

Pierce, G O and **Roberts, T** (1999)
Ar Draws Gwlad 2 (Gwasg Carreg Gwalch, Llanrwst)

Powell, R F P (1993)
The Place-Names of Devynock Hundred (Pen-pont, Brecon)

Richards, M (1962)
'Norse place-names in Wales' in ***Proceedings of the First International Congress of Celtic Studies***, Dublin, 51-60

Richards, M (1969)
Welsh Administrative and Territorial Units (University of Wales Press, Cardiff)

Richards, M (1998)
Enwau Tir a Gwlad ed. B L Jones (Gwasg Gwynedd, Caernarfon)

Rowlands, J and **S** (1996)
The Surnames of Wales (Federation of Family History Societies, Birmingham)

Thomas, R J (1938)
Enwau Afonydd a Nentydd Cymru (University of Wales Press, Cardiff)

Williams, I (1945)
Enwau Lleoedd (Gwasg y Brython, Liverpool)

Wmffre, I (2004)
The Place-Names of Cardiganshire (BAR British series 379)

Relevant selected publications relating to Britain

Coates, R and **Breeze, A** (2000)
Celtic Voices, English Places (Shaun Tyas, Stamford)

Ekwall, E (1960)
The Concise Oxford Dictionary of English Place-Names (Clarendon Press, Oxford)

Field, J (1980)
Place-Names of Great Britain and Ireland (David & Charles, Newton Abbot)

Gelling, M, Nicolaisen, W F H and **Richards, M** (1970, 1986)
The Names of Towns and Cities in Britain and Ireland (Batsford, London)

Gelling, M (1978, 1988)
Signposts to the Past (J M Dent & Sons, London)

Gelling, M and **Cole, A** (2000)
The Landscape of Place-Names (Shaun Tyas, Stamford)

Jackson, K (1953)
Language and History in Early Britain (Edinburgh University Press, Edinburgh)

Mills, A D (2003)
Oxford Dictionary of British Place-Names (Oxford University Press, Oxford)

Padel, O J (1985)
Cornish Place-Name Elements (English Place-Name Society)

Padel, O J (1988)
A Popular Dictionary of Cornish Place-Names (Alison Hodge, Penzance)

Parsons, D N and **Styles, T** with **Hough, C** (1997)
The Vocabulary of English Place-Names: Á-Box (Centre for English Name Studies, Nottingham)

Parsons, D N and **Styles, T** (2000)
The Vocabulary of English Place-Names: Brace-Cæster (Centre for English Name Studies, Nottingham)

Parsons, D N (2004)
The Vocabulary of English Place-Names: Ceafor-Cockpit (English Place-Name Society, Nottingham)

Rivet, A L F and **Smith, C** (1979)
The Place-Names of Roman Britain (Batsford, London)

Room, A (1983)
A Concise Dictionary of Modern Place-Names in Britain and Ireland (Oxford)

Room, A (1988)
Dictionary of Place-Names in the British Isles (Bloomsbury, London)

Smith, A H (1956)
English Place-Name Elements (English Place-Name Society), two parts, EPNS 25, 26

Spittal, J and **Field, J** (1990)
A Reader's Guide to the Place-Names of the United Kingdom (Paul Watkins, Stamford)

Watts, V (2004)
The Cambridge Dictionary of English Place-Names (Cambridge University of Wales Press, Cambridge)

Relevant online databases and reference resources

Archives Network Wales:
www.archivesnetworkwales.info

Archives of Welsh colleges and universities:
www.archiveshub.ac.uk

Canolfan Bedwyr/Welsh Language Board, list of modern Welsh place-names:
www.e-gymraeg.org/enwaucymru

Domesday Book:
www.nationalarchives.gov.uk/domesday

Geiriadur Prifysgol Cymru:
www.aber.ac.uk/gpcwww (in preparation)

National Archives:
www.nationalarchives.gov.uk

National Library of Wales:
www.llgc.org.uk

Ordnance Survey gazetteer:
www.gazetteer.co.uk

Ordnance Survey first edition six-inch scale maps:
www.oldmaps.co.uk

Ordnance Survey two-inch scale drawings in the British Library:
www.collectbritain.co.uk

Ordnance Survey website:
www.ordancesurvey.co.uk/oswebsite

Ordnance Survey maps:
www.ordnancesurvey.co.uk/oswebsite/getamap

Richards, M (2005)
A database of historical forms for place-names in Wales, created from an archive of over 330,000 research slips on deposit in the University of Wales Archives Department (a project funded by the Board of Celtic Studies and the Arts and Humanities Research Council):
www.bangor.ac.uk/amr

Royal Commission on Ancient and Historical Monuments for Wales historical monuments record:
www.coflein.gov.uk

Abbreviations

Anglesey	Angl	Glamorgan	Glam
Breconshire	Brec	Merionethshire	Mer
Caernarfonshire	Caern	Monmouthshire	Monm
Cardiganshire	Card	Montgomeryshire	Mont
Carmarthenshire	Carm	Pembrokeshire	Pemb
Denbighshire	Denb	Radnorshire	Radn
Flintshire	Flints		

adj.	adjective	OE	Old English
adv.	adverb	OF	Old French
AF	Anglo-French	OIr	Old Irish
AN	Anglo-Norman	ON	Old Norse
Br	Brythonic,	OS	Ordnance Survey
	Brittonic	OW	Old Welsh
c.	circa	pers.n., pers.ns	personal name(s)
cent.	century	pl.	plural
cf.	compare	p.n., p.ns	place-name(s)
dat.	dative	pref.	prefix
def.art.	definite article	prep.	preposition
dial.	dialectal	q.v.	refer to name
dim.	diminutive	r.n., r.ns	river name(s)
E	English	sing.	singular
el., els	element(s)	suff.	suffix
F	French	s.v.	under the name
fem.	feminine	terr.	territorial
gen.	genitive	tnshp	township
Ir	Irish	var., vars	variant(s)
L	Latin	W	Welsh
masc.	masculine	*	postulated form
ME	Middle English	#	form which can
MnW	Modern Welsh		justifiably be
MW	Middle Welsh		considered a
n.	name		radical element
NF	Norman French		in its own right

Glossary of Elements

Unless stated otherwise, each element is Welsh and each element (of whatever language) is a noun. Where the element is prefixed *, it is a hypothetical form. Where an element is prefixed #, GPC does not cite it as a separate element but we consider such a citation is by now justified in the light of the evidence of place-names. Superscript numeration is used to distinguish between elements. The prefixed ? indicates doubt as to the form of an element, its meaning or the inclusion of a name. Alphabetisation follows that of the dictionary, where letter sequence has to accommodate elements with OE, ON, L, F, E and W origin. Consequently such OE digraphs as *-æ-* are treated here as if *-ae-*, and standard W *-ch-*,*-dd-*, *-ll-*, *-ng-* are treated as separate letters rather single digraphs; OE *ð* is treated as *-th-*.

Toponymic dictionaries of England have in the past cited elements in their OE form, for ease of reference. However, it has also become customary to cite them in the OE, ME or MnE form appropriate to the date of the name's first appearance. This dictionary follows that practice. Where different names containing an element occur for the first time in different periods, the names are grouped together, for convenience, under the OE element and cross-referenced from the MnE form. In practice, however, unless the name reveals specific phonological characteristics that can be ascribed to the late ME period, names appearing from the 14cent. onwards have simply been described as E.

Each W element is recorded in its standard form as cited in GPC. However, it should be remembered that this glossary relates to words as they appear in the names of places in this dictionary, and so may cite plurals (for example) which are not features of standard modern Welsh or indeed past literary usage and therefore may not appear in the published volumes of GPC. The same is true of the meanings ascribed to some elements, which may have more specific connotations associated with place-names. It is worth emphasising that the study of place-names has added to Welsh lexicography and, indeeed, is continually adding to the stock of words.

We have resisted the temptation to indicate derivations and cognates of elements in this glossary. The etymological background of elements is available in standard dictionaries such as GPC and the OED and in more specialised p.n. dictionaries and glossaries; admittedly, the general reader may not have ready access to such information but equally may not need such linguistic detail. However, in the entry for certain p.ns within the dictionary proper, we have in fact provided etymological comment on those elements which merit further elucidation.

Where several names start with the same element, they are cited not as individual names but as (for example) **Aber-**, **Caer-**, **Llan-**.

Naturally, this glossary is based on the place-names appearing in this dictionary. A more exhaustive 'Dictionary of Welsh Place-Name Elements' remains a project for the future.

abad	masc. 'abbot' **Tirabad**
aber	masc./fem. 'mouth of a river (into the sea), estuary, confluence of a lesser with a larger river' **Aber-, Barmouth, Berriw, Bronaber, Llanaber, Pont Aber, Pontyberem**
āc	OE 'oak(-tree)' **Broad Oak, Greatoak, Oakdale, Oakford**
-ach	noun suff. of Ir origin; W var. ***–og*** 'river' **Clydach, Clywedog, Solfach**
-ach	dim.suff. **Mawddach**
achub	masc. 'holding, occupancy' **Rachub**
acr	pl. ***acrau***. fem. 'acre' **Acre-fair, Talacre**
-ad	noun suff. **Cwmduad, Tanat**
addug	masc. ?'feat, attack' **Moel Hiraddug**
aderyn	var. ***ederyn***; masc. 'bird' **Penderyn**
æsc	OE 'ash tree' **Cross ash, Monknash/Yr As Fawr, Nash, Nottage/Notais**
ǣwell	OE 'source of a stream' **Ewloe**
afon	fem. 'river' **Afon-wen, Blaenafon, Glan-yr-afon** (2)
aig	pl. ***eigiau***; fem. 'shoal of fish' **?Cwm/Llyn Eigiau**

aith pl. 'furze, gorse'
Mynydd Hiraethog

**al* adj. 'wandering'
Aled, Alun, Alwen

alaf masc. 'herd of cattle'
Penarlâg

alaw masc./fem. 'water-lily'
Alaw

ald OE 'old; former'
Nolton, Oldcastle, Old Castle Head

allt fem. var. ***gallt***
1. 'hill, slope, height'
Allt-melyd, Rhuallt, Y Wenallt
2. 'wooded slope'
Allt-, Gamallt

am prep. 'about, around, near, on; opposite'
Amlwch, Amroth, Newcastle Emlyn, Llandovery, Castellnewydd Emlyn

-an dim.suff.
Aberhosan, Aran Benllyn, Aran Fawddwy, Cennen, Cogan, Crychan, Cymyran, ?Dolanog, Goginan, Llandinam, Llanfihangel Nant Melan, ?Pwllcrochan, Trelogan, Twynllannan

angle ME 'angle, nook'
Angle

ar prep. 'near, at, by, on'
Argoed, Arberth/Narberth, Caernarfon, Casnewydd-ar-Wysg, Pen-y-bont ar Ogwr, Pontarfynach, Clas-ar-Wy, Llanfair-ar-y-bryn, Y Bontnewydd ar Wy, Yr Eglwys Newydd ar y Cefn, Hendy-gwyn ar Daf, Tal-y-bont ar Wysg

âr masc. 'ridge'
Aran Benllyn, Aran Fawddwy

aradur ?fem. 'oratory, house of prayer, chapel'
Radur

ardd masc. 'hill, highland'
Talerddig

argae pl. ***argaeau***; masc. 'weir, dam, sluice; embankment'
Rhydargaeau

arglwydd var. ***arlwydd*** 'lord'
Waunarlwydd

arth masc./fem. 'bear'
Aber-arth, Glynarthen

ash	see ***æsc***
aside	E 'aside' **Stepaside**
askr	ON 'ash(-tree)' **Axton**
athro	masc. 'teacher' **Caeathro**
atten	ME 'at the' **Monknash, Nash, Neyland, Nolton**
aur	masc. 'gold' **Gelli Aur**
-aw	MW, MnW var. **-o**; ?adj. suff. ?'characterised by, featuring' **?Mynytho**
bach[1]	fem. ***bech***, see also ***bychan***; adj. 'little, small' **Cas-bach, Casnewydd Bach, Cwm-bach** (3), **Cwmfelin-fach, Dre-fach** (3), **Dwyfach, Eglwys-fach, Felindre-fach** (2), **Ffair-fach, Fforest-fach, Fforest Fach, Glyder Fach, Gwendraeth Fach, Llandocha Fach, Llandyfaelog Fach, Llundain-fach, Llyn y Fan Fach, Maerdy**[1], **Mynydd-bach, Pentre-bach** (2), **Rhinog Fach**, **Tai-bach**
bach[2]	fem. 'nook, angle, corner, bend' **Eglwys-bach**
bad	masc. 'boat, ferry' **Glan-bad**
?*badfa	fem. ?'place of plague' **Bwlch-y-fadfa**
bae	masc. 'bay' **Bae Cemlyn, Bae Cinmel, Bae Colwyn, Bae Penrhyn**
bâl	fem. 'peak, summit' **Mynydd Pen-y-fâl**
bala	masc. 'route between two lakes or areas of wet ground, passage of dry land amid otherwise impassable wet terrain, neck of land' **Bala**
ban	pl. ***bannau, *benni***; masc./fem. 'top, summit, crest, peak, height, mountain, bare hill, beacon' **Bannau Brycheiniog, Aber-fan, Fan Fawr, Fan Gyhirych, Fan Llia, Llyn y Fan Fach/Fawr, ?Talbenni, Tal-y-fan, Tryfan**
banc	masc. 'bank, breast of a hill, hill' **Bancyfelin, Bancffosfelen, Banc-y-ffordd, Pen-y-banc**

bangor	masc./fem. 'wattle-fence enclosure' **Bangor, Bangor Is-coed, Bangor Teifi, Capel Bangor**
banw	masc./fem. 'young pig, pig' **Banw, Ammanford, Cwmaman, Glanaman, Ogwen**
bar	masc. 'hill, top, summit, crest' **Barry, Y Berwyn, Cefn Berain, Crug-y-bar**
bargod	masc./fem. 'boundary, border' **Bargoed**
baseleg	?fem. 'church' **Basaleg**
baw	masc. 'dirt, mud' **Brymbo**
bay	E 'bay, cove, inlet' **Bull Bay, Cardigan Bay, Church Bay, Colwyn Bay, Kinmel Bay, Penrhyn Bay, Red Wharf Bay, St Brides Bay**
beacon	E 'peak, hill (suitable for a beacon-fire)' **Brecon Beacons**
beau	NF 'fine, fair' **Beaumaris**
bece	OE 'stream, especially in fenland' **Slebech**
bedd	pl. ***beddau***; masc. 'grave, tomb' **Beddau, Beddgelert**
bedwen	pl. ***bedw***; fem. 'birch' **Michaelston-y-fedw, Llanfihangel-y-fedw, Pentre Tafarnyfedw**
bedwos	fem. 'grove of birch trees' **Bedwas**
bendigaid	adj. 'blessed, sacred, holy' **Llanfendigaid, Pontrhydfendigaid**
bere-wīc	OE 'grange, outlying farm' **Ferwig**
#berran	fem. 'short share-land' **?Ystalyfera**
berw	masc. 'foam, boiling; waterfall' **Llyn Berwyn, ?Pentreberw**
berwr	var. ***berw***; collective noun 'cress' **?Pentreberw**
betws	masc. 'house, of prayer, chapel of ease' **Betws-**
beudy	masc. 'cowshed' **Llanboidy**

bill	E 'narrow promontory' **?Strumble Head**
biscop	OE 'bishop' **Bishops and Clerks, Bishopston, Bishton, ?Bistre**
bishop	see *biscop*
black	E 'black, black-haired, swarthy, dark, forbidding' **Blackmill, Black Mountains, Blackpill, Blackwood**
blaen	masc. 'source of a river, headwater; upland; far end' **Blaen-** pl. *blaenau* 'uplands' **Blaenau, Blaenau Ffestiniog**
blow	E 'gust of wind; exposure to wind' **Cold Blow**
bluff	E 'steep cliff, headland' **Hay Bluff**
boat	E 'boat, ferry' **Upper Boat**
boch	fem. 'cheek, mouth' **Bochrwyd, Fochriw**
bod	fem. 'abode, dwelling'; 'church' **Bod-, Bedlinog, Botwnnog, Meifod, Mynydd Bodafon**
bodkin	E 'bodkin' **Pontybodkin**
bol	masc. 'swelling, bulge, hump' **Rhos-y-bol**
bôn	masc. 'base, root, stump, trunk, stock' **Bôn-y-maen**
boncath	masc. 'buzzard' **Boncath**
both	fem. 'hub' **?Trofarth**
bourne	E 'destination, bounds' **Fairbourne**
brād	OE 'broad, wide' **Broadhaven, Broad Oak, Broad Sound, Broadway** (3)
brân	pl. *brain*; fem. 'crow, rook, raven' **Brenig, Cwmbrân, Llys-y-frân, Nant Brân**
bras	adj. 'big, bulky; fertile' **Foel Fras**
bre	fem. 'hill, highland, brae' **Lampeter Velfrey, Llanddewi Velfrey, Moelfre, Penbre**

bref	fem. 'bleating, bray, cry, yearning' **Llanddewibrefi**
breni	fem. 'prow of a ship' **Frenni Fawr**
breuant	pl. ***breuannau***; masc./fem. 'throat, ?gorge' **?Llyn Brianne**
bridge	see ***brycg***
briog	fem. 'high ground' **Friog**
brith	fem. ***braith***; adj. 'variegated, speckled' **Brithdir, Cefn-brith, Pontllan-fraith**
bro	masc. 'region, land' **Penfro, Doc Penfro, Llanbedr-y-Fro, Rhyd-y-fro**
broad	see ***brād***
brōc	OE 'brook, stream' **Brooks, Broughton** (2), **Coalbrookvale, Sudbrook, Whitebrook**
****brog***	Br 'region, land' **Pembroke, Pembroke Dock**
bron	pl. ***bronnydd***; fem. 'breast (of a hill), hill-side, slope' **Bron-, Fron-, Bronydd, Gaufron, Tan-y-fron**
bronwydd	fem. 'wooded hill-side' **Bronwydd**
brook	see ***brōc***
brūn	OE 'muddy, dirty, brown' **Brynford**
brwd	adj. 'warm' **Bridell**
brycg	OE 'bridge' **Briton Ferry, Canaston Bridge, Cowbridge, Devil's Bridge, Four Mile Bridge, Menai Bridge, Merlin's Bridge, Newbridge** (2), **Newbridge-on-Wye, Pelcomb Bridge, Sennybridge**
brych	fem. ***brech***; adj. 'variegated, speckled' **Brechfa**
bryn	pl. ***bryniau***; masc. 'hill' **Bryn-, Bron-gwyn, Brymbo, Brynna, Bryn-gwyn, ?Cledfryn, Glasfryn, Glasinfryn, Llanbryn-mair, Llanfair-ar-y-bryn, Llanfihangel Brynpabuan**
budr	adj. 'dirty, muddy' **Pandytudur**
bugail	masc. 'shepherd, herdsman' **Maen y Bugail**

bugeildy	masc. 'shepherd's hut' **Bugeildy**
burh	dat. ***byrig***; OE 'dwelling(s) within a fortified enclosure; fortified dwelling; estate, manor-house; borough' **Burry Port, Burton, Glasbury, Gwesbyr, Newborough, Worthenbury**
bush	E 'bush, shrub; tree' **Hollybush**
buwch	fem. 'cow' **Castlebythe/Cas-fuwch, Trwyn y Fuwch**
bŵl	masc. 'hollow' **Ynys-y-bŵl**
bwlch	pl. ***bylchau***; masc. 'pass, gap' **Bwlch-, Bylchau, Mynydd Bwlch-y-groes, Tan-y-bwlch**
?***bwn***	pl. ****byn(i)au***; 'bittern' ?**Bynea**
by	E 'near, beside, by' **Ogmore-by-sea**
bych(an)	fem. ***bechan***; adj. 'little' **Dinbych, Dinbych-y-pysgod, Graigfechan, Llanafan Fechan, Llanfairfechan, Morfa Bychan, Pontneddfechan**
byddar	pl. ***byddair***; masc. 'deaf person' **Llanybydder**
byth	adv. 'always, ever' **Aberbythych**
cadair	fem. 'mound or hill shaped like a seat; seat, fort, defensive settlement' **Cadair Idris, Pencader, Trwyn y Gadair**
cadarn	adj. 'strong, mighty' **Crickadarn**
cae	masc. 'enclosed land, field' **Caeathro, Pen-y-cae** (2), **Pen-y-cae-mawr**
caenog	adj. '(lichen-) encrusted' **Clocaenog**
caer	pl. ***caerau***; fem. 'fort, stronghold, fortified settlement' **Caer-, Cardiff, Carew, Carmarthen, Gaerwen, Gelli-gaer, Llanfair Caereinion, Moel y Gaer, Pen-caer, Tregare**
cærse	OE '(water) cress' **Cresswell**
caeth	pl. ***caith***; masc. 'captive, prisoner' **Cricieth**, ?**Llanychâr**

cafn	masc. 'trough, gutter, hollow, dip' **Llangefni, Tal-y-cafn**
cain[1]	adj. 'fair, fine' **Cilcain, Porth-gain**
cain[2]	masc. 'ridge' **?Cilcain, Llanfihangel-yng-Ngheinmeirch**
cald	OE 'cold, exposed, bleak; inhospitable' **Caldicot, Cold Blow**
caled	adj. 'rough, hard' **Cledwen**
cam	adj. 'bent, crooked, curved, winding' **Camros, Cemlyn, Derwen-gam, Gamallt, Pengam**
camas	pl. *cemais*; fem. 'bend, loop (in a river, inlet or bay)' **Cemaes (2), Cemais, Kemeys Commander**
can	adj. 'white; shining, brilliant' **Ganllwyd**
**cān-*	Br 'reeds' **Conwy, Aberconwy, Nant Conwy**
candryll	adj. ?'in pieces, broken into many pieces' **Gelli Gandryll**
cannaid	adj. 'bright, shining' **Abercannaid**
canol	adj. 'middle, centre' **Felinganol**
cant	pl. **ceint*; masc. 'border, edge, rim' **Ceint**
cantref	masc. 'group of commotes; hundred; district' **Cantref**
capel	masc. 'ecclesiastical chapel-of-ease; nonconformist meeting-house or chapel' **Capel-**
câr	masc. 'beloved, dear one' **Ceiriog**
cardinal	E 'cardinal' **Carmel Head**
caredig	adj. 'gentle' **?Nantgaredig**
carfan	masc./fem. 'ridge, row' **Llancarfan**
carn	masc./fem. 'cairn, mound; pile, heap; barrow, tumulus' **Carn Fadrun, Carno, Garn, Garndolbenmaen, Garn Fawr, ?Lacharn, Pen-y-garn, Trefgarn**
carnedd	fem. 'cairn, tumulus, mound' **Penygarnedd**

carreg	pl. ***cerrig***; masc./fem. 'stone, rock' **Castell Carreg Cennen, Carreg-lefn, Carregwastad Point, Cerrigceinwen, Cerrigydrudion, Garreg, Llanbadarn-y-garreg, Penygarreg Reservoir, Pontgarreg, Talgarreg**
carrog	fem. 'torrent, swift-flowing stream; stream' **Carrog, Dolgarrog**
carw	pl. ***ceirw***; masc. 'deer, hart, stag' **Bryncir**
cas	see ***castell***
castel	ME 'castle' **Hayscastle, Little Newcastle, Newcastle, Newcastle Emlyn, Oldcastle, Old Castle Head, Painscastle, Trecastle, Walwyn's Castle**
castell	var. ***cas-***; masc./fem. 'castle, strong-hold; mansion; prominent rock' **Cas-, Castell-, Croes Cas-lai, Casllwchwr, Yr Hengastell, Trecastell, Cas-wis**
cath	pl. ***cathau;*** fem./masc. 'cat' **?Cathedin**
cat-hole	E 'narrow shaft in a mine for raising men or materials' **Cadole**
cau	var. ***cou***; adj. 'enclosed, hollow' **Gaufron, Cwm-cou**
cawell	masc. 'basket; fish-trap, creel' **Llyn Cwellyn**
cawg	masc. 'bowl, basin, dish' **Cogan**
cawl	masc. 'sea-kale' **Porth-cawl**
cawn	see ***cān-***
cawr	pl. ***cewri*** var. ***ceiri***; masc. 'giant' **Tre'r Ceiri**
caws	masc. 'cheese' **Nant-y-caws**
cēap	OE 'market' **Chepstow**
cefn	masc. 'ridge' **Cefn-, Kingcoed, Llan-y-cefn, Yr Eglwys Newydd ar y Cefn, Ty'n-y-cefn**
cefnffordd	fem. 'ridgeway' **Pengenffordd**
cegid	var. ***cegyr***; collective pl. 'hemlock, hex' **Cegidfa**

cegin	masc. 'ridge, hogback' **Goginan**
cegyr	see ***cegid***
cei	masc. 'quay' Cei Connah, Ceinewydd
ceibr	masc. 'rafter, beam, joist' **Penrhiw-ceibr**
ceiliog	masc. 'cock' **Croesyceiliog** (2), **Esgairgeiliog**
**ceint*	fem. ?'border, edge' **Ceint**
cell	pl. ***cellau***; fem. 'hermit's cell; ?stall, booth' **Gell, Dolgellau**
cellan	fem. 'little cell' **Cellan**
celli	pl. ***cellïoedd***; fem. 'grove, copse, woodland' **Gelli-, Pengelli, Drenewydd Gelli-farch**
celyn	pl. 'holly' **Llangattock Lingoed, Llwyncelyn, Llyn Celyn, Tafarnygelyn, Trecelyn**
celynnog	adj. 'abounding in holly' **Clynnog**
cen	masc. 'lichen' **Cenarth, ?Cennen**
cennin	fem. pl. 'leeks; daffodils' **Cilcennen, Llanbedrycennin**
cerwyd	masc. ?'stag' **?Erwood**
cerwyn	fem. 'vat, tub' **Cwm Cerwyn**
cest	fem. 'paunch' **Borth-y-Gest, Brongest**
ceuffordd	fem. 'hollow-way, narrow sunken road' **Geuffordd**
ceulan	fem. '(hollow) river bank, edge, brink' **Cwm Ceulan**
channel	E 'sea channel' **Bristol Channel**
chapel	E 'ecclestiastical chapel-of-ease, nonconformist meeting house or chapel' **Newchapel**
church	see ***cirice***
chwilog	adj. 'abounding with beetles, beetle-infested' **Chwilog**

chwyth masc. 'gust, breeze'
Pentre-chwyth

ci pl. ***cŵn***; masc. 'dog, hound'
Trecŵn

ciaidd adj. 'savage, fierce'
Cwmgïedd

cib pl. ***cibau***; masc. 'husk; hollow'
Bwlch-y-cibau

cil pl. ***ciliau***; masc. 'corner, angle, retreat, nook'
Cil-, Ciliau, Kil-, Gilwern, Killay, Kinmel, Llanycil

cilan var. ****cilian***; fem. 'corner, angle, retreat, nook; inlet of sea'
Cilan, Cilieni

cilfach fem. 'nook, corner, sheltered or secluded spot, retreat'
Gilfach-

cirice OE 'church'
Cheriton (2), **Churchstoke, Church Village, Church Bay, Christchurch, Common Church, Coychurch, Ludchurch, Michaelchurch-on-Arrow, Newchurch** (3), **St Mary Church, Whitchurch** (2)

claer adj. 'bright, shining, clear'
Clyro

claerwyn adj. 'shining bright, radiant'
Llyn Claerwen

clafrdy masc. 'lazar-house'
Rhydyclafdy

clas masc. 'monastic community; cloister'
Glasbury/Clas-ar-Wy

clatter E 'clatter, rattle'
Clatter

clawdd masc. 'dyke, earthwork; ditch, gutter; boundary, hedge, fence'
Clawddnewydd, Clawdd Offa, Pen-clawdd (2)

**clawedog* adj. 'wild; rocky'
Clywedog (2)

cleddyf var. ***cleddau***; masc. 'sword'
Aberdaugleddau, Cleddau

clerk E 'clerk in holy orders, cleric'
Bishops and Clerks

clif OE 'cliff'
Goldcliff

cliff see ***clif***

clochog adj. 'bell-like'
Maenclochog

clog fem. 'rock, cliff, precipice'
Clocaenog

clud fem. 'pile, pack, heap'
Clud

cludair var. *cluder*, *clyder*; masc./fem. 'stack, pile, heap'
Glyder Fawr/Fach

clun masc. 'meadow; moor, brushwood'
Clunderwen

clwt masc. 'patch of land'
Clwt-y-bont

clwyd pl. *clwydau*; fem. 'hurdle, wattle'
Clwyd, Pentreclwydau

?*cnicht* masc. 'peak, cone'
?Cnicht

cniht OE 'follower, soldier; freeman; knight'
?Cnicht, Knighton

cnwc masc. 'hillock, knoll'
Knucklas

cnwch masc. 'swelling, protuberance, mound'
Cnwch-coch

coal E 'coal'
Coalbrookvale

coch adj. 'red, ruddy; brown; ginger (of hair)'
Bont-goch, Bryn-coch, Castell Coch, Cefn-coch (2), **Cnwch-coch, Comins-coch, Cors Goch Glan Teifi, Craig Goch Reservoir, Croes-goch, Dôl-goch, Fron-goch, Gilfach-goch, Llanbedr-goch, Penrhiw-goch, Penrhyn-coch, Rhos-goch** (3), **Traeth Coch**

cock E 'cock'
Three Cocks

cocket[1] E 'hillock'
?Cocket

cocket[2] E. 'customs office or post-house', '?seal'
Cockett

**cocyd* masc. 'customs office or post-house', '?seal'
Cocyd

coed pl. and collective noun. 'trees, woodland'
Coed-, Argoed, Betws-y-coed, Blaen-y-coed, Cefncoedycymer, Cil-y-coed, Coety, Coychurch, Hengoed (2), **Kingcoed, Llangattock Lingoed, Llangoed, Llangoedmor, Melin-y-coed, Capel Coed-y-mynach, Trawsgoed**

coelbren	masc./fem. 'lot, portion, allotted share of patrimony' **Coelbren**
coes	fem. 'leg; long, narrow land with a slight bend' **Croes-erw, Penegoes**
coetgae	var. ***coedcae***; masc. 'land enclosed with a hedge, field, enclosure; park' **Penycoedcae**
cold	see ***cald***
colf	masc./fem. 'branch, bough' **Colfa**
coll	collective noun; sing. fem. ***collen***, pl. ***cyll***; 'hazel' **Llanfair Pwllgwyngyll**
colwyn	masc. 'whelp, puppy' **Colwyn Bay**
comander	var. ***comawndwr***; masc. 'commander, administrator of a commandery' **Cemais Comawndwr**
comandere	OF 'commander, administrator of a commandery' **Kemeys Commander**
comins	masc. pl. 'common, unenclosed land; commons' **Comins-coch**
côr	masc./fem. 'sanctuary, chancel' **Corwen, Llangorwen**
corn[1]	pl. ***cyrn***; masc. 'promontory, point; mountain top or cairn' **?Corndon, Cornelly, Cyrn y Brain, Llanfair-yng-Nghornwy, Llanfihangel Rhos-y-corn**
corn[2]	see ***cron***
corres	fem. 'little one, dwarf' **Corris**
cors	fem. 'fen, bog, swamp' **Cors Goch Glan Teifi, Cors Ddyga, Cors Fochno, Gorseinon, Gors-las, Cwm-gors, Llan-gors**
corun	masc. 'crown, top, summit' **Corntown**
cot	OE 'hut, (temporary) shelter; cottage' **Caldicot, Disgoed, Mancot**
**coth-*	adj. ?'scouring, emptying, washing' **Cothi**
court	ME 'court, manor house' **Southgate**
cow	see ***cū***
cowyn	var. ***cywyn***; masc. 'plague, pestilence' **Cywyn**

crab	E 'crab apple' **Crabtree Green**
crach	pl. fem. 'scabs, scabby eruption' **?Pwllcrochan**
craf	collective noun 'wild garlic' **Aber-craf, Dyffryn Crawnon, Llyn Crafnant**
cragen	pl. *cregyn*; fem. 'shell' **Abergwyngregyn**
crai	adj. 'rough, severe' **Crai**
craig	fem. 'rock, boulder, stone; cliff' **Craig Goch Reservoir, Cregrina, Godre'r-graig, Graig (2), Graigfechan, Pen-y-graig**
crau	fem. pl. *creuau*; masc. 'pigsty, hovel; defensive place, stockade' **Creuddyn, Creunant, Moel-y-crio**
cress	see *cærse*
crib	masc./fem. 'crest, ridge, top' **Cribyn**
crin	pl. **crinau*; adj. 'parched, miserly, shrunk' **?Crinow**
croes	pl. *croesau, crwys* (originally var. sing.); fem. 'cross; cross-roads' **Croes-, Groes-, Bryncroes, Bwlch-y-groes, Cefn-y-groes, Cresselly, Y Crwys, Glyn-y-groes, Llan-y-crwys, Llwyn-y-groes, Mynydd Bwlch-y-groes, Pen-y-groes (2), Pont-rhyd-y-groes, Rhydycroesau, Tan-y-groes, Tre-groes, Tŷ-croes (2), Tyn-y-groes**
croft	E 'croft, enclosure near a house' **Sandycroft**
cron	var. *corn*; OE 'crane' **Caergwrle, ?Corndon**
cros	OE 'cross' **Marcross**
cross	E 'crossroads' **Cross-, Cefn Cross, Ffôr, Four Crosses (3), Hayscastle Cross, Newcross, Robeston Cross, Simpson Cross, Tiers Cross**
croyw	adj. 'clear, fresh' **Ffynnongroyw**
crug	pl. *crugau, crugiau, *crugion*; masc. 'hillock, knoll; cairn, tumulus' **Bryn-crug, Cricieth, Crickadarn, Criggion, Crug, Crug-y-bar, Gwyddgrug, Llanvihangel Crucorney, Maesycrugiau, Yr Wyddgrug**

crundel	OE 'quarry' **Crundale**
crux	L 'cross' **Valle Crucis**
crwbyn	masc. 'little hump' **Crwbin**
crwm	adj. 'bent, curved, bowed, hooked' **Crumlin, Crymych**
crwn	fem. *cron*; adj. 'round, circular' **Cronwern**
crwys	see *croes*
crych	fem. *crech*; adj. 'rippling, bubbling, rough' **Crychan, Ffrwd-grech**
crythor	masc. 'fiddler, crowder' **Rhoscrowther**
cryw	masc. 'weir, fish-trap, creel; ford, causeway' **Crew Green**
cū	OE 'cow' **Cowbridge**
curn	var. *cyrn*; masc./fem. 'heap, mound; cone, spire' **Gurnos**
cuwch	var. *cuch*. 'frown, grimace' **Aber-cuch**
cwm	masc. 'short, bowl shaped valley; deep narrow valley; depression, hollow; valley' **Cwm-, Felin-gwm-uchaf, Foel Cwmcerwyn, Glasgwm, Llanddewi'r-cwm, Llangwm** (2), **Llan-gwm**
cwmwd	masc. 'commote; region, district' **Llansanffraid Cwmteuddwr**
cwmwr	var. *cwmer*; masc. '(narrow) footbridge' **Maesycwmer**
cwrt	masc. 'enclosure, yard, farmyard; grange; court, mansion' **Cwrt, Cwrt Henri, Cwrtnewydd, Pentre-cwrt**
cwys	fem. 'furrow' **Nercwys**
cyff	masc. 'trunk, stump' **Pont-rhyd-y-cyff**
cyffin	masc./fem. 'border, boundary; land near a border, vicinity' **Gyffin**
cyffordd	fem. '(railway) junction' **Cyffordd Llandudno**

cyffyll masc. 'stock, trunk of a tree, stump'
Gyffylliog

cyfylchi fem. 'circular stronghold or fortress'
Dwygyfylchi

cyhyrwch masc. 'strength'
?Fan Gyhirych

cymer pl. *cymerau*; masc. 'confluence of two or more rivers or streams'
Cefncoedycymer, Cymer, Cymyran, Pentrellyncymer, Pontycymer, Rhydcymerau

cymyn masc. 'bequest, legacy, endowment'
Eglwys Gymyn

cŷn masc. 'chisel, wedge'
Ystradgynlais

**cynaeafdref* fem. 'harvest lodging; buildings occupied during harvest'
Cynheidre

cynhordy masc. 'dog-house, kennel; gate-house'
Cynghordy

cysylltau masc. pl. 'junctions'
Froncysyllte

cyw masc. 'chick, young bird; young animal'
Heol-y-cyw

cywarch var. *cowarch*; fem. 'hemp'
Abercywarch

dæl OE 'valley'
?Dale, Ferndale, Oakdale, Wolfsdale

**daf-* adj. 'tame'
Dafen

dale see *dæl* and *dalr*

dalr ON 'valley'
?Dale

dâr pl. *deri*; fem. 'oak-tree'
Aberdare, Bwlch-y-ddâr, Cwmdâr, Darowen, Deri, Nantyderi

dau fem. *dwy*; 'two'
Aberdaugleddau, Bwlch-y-ddeufaen, Cefnddwysarn, Dwygyfylchi, Dwyran, Dwyryd, Llanddeusant (2), **Llanfair- yn-Neubwll, Llansanffraid Cwmteuddwr, Penrhyndeudraeth**

daw pl. *dawon*; masc. 'son-in-law'
Dawn

defod fem. 'custom, practice'
?Devauden

derwen	pl. *derw*; fem. 'oak-tree' **Derwen-, Clunderwen**
derwin	adj. 'abounding in oaks' **Bwlchderwin**
devil	E 'devil' **Devil's Bridge**
dīc	OE 'dyke, ditch' **Disgoed, Offa's Dyke**
diffwys	masc. 'steep slope, cliff, precipice' **Diffwys**
dihewyd	masc./fem. 'affection, devotion' **Dihewyd**
din	masc. 'fort, stronghold; fortified hill' **Dinbych, Dinbych-y-pysgod, Dinorwig, Llandinam, Porthdin-llaen, ?Ruthin, Tintern**
dinas	masc./fem. 'fort, fortress, stronghold' **Dinas-**
#dinlle	masc. 'site of a fort; land around a defensive settlement' **Dinas Dinlle**
diserth	fem. 'hermitage, retreat' **Betws Diserth, Diserth, Dyserth**
**?distentiio*	?Br adj. ?'separating' **Dysynni**
doc	masc. 'dock (for shipping)' **Doc Penfro**
dock	E 'dock, dockyard' **Pembroke Dock**
dôl	pl. *dolau*; fem. 'meadow, dale, field, pasture; bend, ox-bow' **Dol-, Dôl-, Bontdolgadfan, Doly-hir, Melin-y-ddôl, Tre'r-ddôl**
down	see *dūn*
draen	pl. *drain*; masc./fem. 'thorn, bramble, briar' **Ffynnon-ddrain**
dreane	ME 'drain, channel, gutter' **Dreenhill**
drud	pl. *drudion*; masc. 'hero, bold or daring one' **Cerrigydrudion**
dryslwyn	masc. 'tangled bush, thicket, bramble-brake, place full of brambles' **Dryslwyn**

du(f)	adj. 'black, black-haired, swarthy; shaded' **Bont-ddu, Coed-duon, Coety, Cwm-du** (2), **Cwmduad, Dowlais, Dulais, Dulas, Dyfi, Melin Ifan Ddu, Llanddulas, Mynydd Du, Nant-ddu, Parlwr Du, Pwll-du Head, Rhyd-ddu, Ton-du, Traeth Dulas, Tŷ-du, Ynys-ddu**
dūn	OE 'hill, upland expanse' **Corntown, Corndon, Orielton, Snowdon, Snowdonia, Southerndown**
**dūno-*	Br 'fort' **Carmarthen**
Duw	var. *Dwyw*; masc. 'God' **Llan-ddew, Llandow**
dwfn	var. *dyfn*; adj. 'deep' **Dynvant**
dŵr	var. *dwfr*, pl. **dyfri*; masc. 'water' **Abertridwr, Dyfrdwy, Glandŵr** (2), **Gwenddwr, Llandovery, Llansanffraid Cwmteuddwr, Pant-y-dŵr, Pentredŵr** (2)
**dwy(w)*	adj. 'holy, divine' **Dwyfach, Dwyfor, Dyfrdwy, Llanystumdwy**
**dyfadfa*	masc./fem. 'place notable for sheep' **Bwlchyfadfa**
dyffryn	masc. 'valley, vale, bottom' **Dyffryn-, Llanarmon Dyffryn Ceiriog, Llanbedr Dyffryn Clwyd, Llanfair Dyffryn Clwyd, Llangatwg Dyffryn Wysg, Llanfihangel Dyffryn Wysg**
dyfrwr	pl. *dyfrwyr*; masc. 'one who drinks only water' **Llanddowror**
dyke	see *dīc*
dylif	pl. **dylifau*; masc. 'flood, torrent' **Dylife**
**dynn*	masc. 'fortification; height' **Creuddyn, Tre-fin, Treuddyn, Trevethin**
dyrys	adj. 'wild, uncultivated, tangled, thorny, dense' **Llwyndyrys**
dywal	adj. 'fierce, fearful, frightening' ?**Alltwalis, Hirddywel, Tafolwern**
ēast	OE 'east, eastern' **East Mouse, Walton East**
eb-	masc./fem. 'horse' **Epynt**

edwi — 'abate, dwidle, shrink'
Aberedw

ēg — OE 'island; flood plain, land by a river, well-watered land, water meadow, raised land or low promontory jutting out into a loop of a river'
Eyton, Saltney

ēg-land — OE 'low-lying land, marsh land, land liable to flooding, dry ground in marsh'
Neyland

eglwys — fem. 'church'
Eglwys-, Bryneglwys, Cwm-yr-eglwys, Heneglwys, Pentre'r Eglwys, Trefeglwys, Yr Eglwys Newydd

ehed — fem. 'flight'
Moel Hebog

eira — var. ***eiry***; masc. 'snow'
Nant-yr-eira

eirin — fem. pl. 'plums, damsons, sloes, bullace'
Brynrhydyrarian

eisingrug — var. ***singrug, shingrig***; masc. 'chaff-heap, winnowing bank'
Eisingrug

eisteddfa — fem. 'abode, dwelling; seat; shrine'
Eisteddfa Gurig

**el-*[1] — adj. 'thrusting, swift'
Elwy

el-[2] — pref. 'numerous, various'
?Elwy

elain — masc./fem. 'young deer, doe, fawn'
Elan, Elan Village

-ell — dim.suff.
Cwmllynfell

en- — intensive pref.
Ynys Enlli

-en — fem. dim.suff.
?Cennen, Dafen, ?Devauden, Glynarthen, Deiniolen

end — E 'end, limit'
Grovesend

erch — adj. 'mottled, dappled; dark'
Aber-erch, Nannerch, Nercwys

ermid — masc. 'hermit'
Bodermid

erw — fem. 'Welsh measure of land; acre; plot of land, enclosed field; estate'
Croeserw, Nantyr

eryr	masc./fem. 'eagle' **Foel Eryr**
eryres	fem. 'flock of eagles' **Eryrys**
eryri	masc. pl. 'highland' **Eryri**
esgair	fem. 'ridge, mountain spur' **Esgairgeiliog**
ey	ON 'island, raised ground in marshes' **Anglesey, Bardsey, Caldey, Ramsey, Skomer, Swansea**
eyrr	ON 'gravel or sand bank' **Point of Ayr**
fair	E 'fair, fine , pleasant' **Fairbourne**
fall(s)	E 'waterfall, cararact, cascade' **Aber Falls, Swallow Falls**
farmer	E 'farmer' **Ffarmers**
feld	OE 'open land; arable or pasture land' **Bettisfield, Greenfield, Guilsfield, Gwernaffield, Marshfield, Portfield Gate**
fern	E 'fern' **Ferndale**
ferry	E 'ferry' **Briton Ferry, Ferryside, Queensferry**
ffair	fem. 'fair, market' **Ffair-fach, Ffair-rhos**
fferi	fem. 'ferry, ferry-boat' **Glanyfferi**
ffin	fem. 'boundary, border, limit; district' **Ffos-y-ffin**
ffordd	fem. 'road; ford' **Banc-y-ffordd, Bodffordd, Minffordd** (2), **Pen-ffordd, Pen-y-ffordd, Penffordd-las**
fforest	fem. 'forest; park' **Fforest-fach, Fforest Fach, Fforest Fawr, Trefforest**
ffos	fem. 'ditch, dyke, gutter' **Bancffosfelen, Blaen-ffos, Ffostrasol, Ffos-y-ffin**
**ffranc*	pl. **ffrancon*; ?masc. 'spear' **Nant Ffrancon**
ffridd	var. *ffrith*; fem. 'mountain pasture; moorland; recently cleared land' **Ffrith, Bwlch-y-ffridd, Pant-y-ffridd, Ty'n-y-ffridd**
ffrith	see *ffridd*

ffrwd	fem. '(swift-flowing) stream'; 'waterfall' **Aber-ffrwd, Cwm-ffrwd, Ffrwd-grech, Gwenffrwd**
ffwrnais	fem. 'furnace' **Ffwrnais**
ffyll	adj. 'wild, overgrown' **?Tir-phil**
ffynnon	fem. 'spring, well' **Ffynnon-ddrain, Ffynnongroyw, Ffynnon Taf, Pantyffynnon, Swyddffynnon, Treffynnon**
ffyrling	var. *ffyrlling*; fem. 'farthing; small, insignificant, puny one' **Nantyffyllon**
field	see *feld*
fiskr	ON 'fish' **Fishguard**
five	E 'five' **Five Roads**
fjǫrðr	ON 'sea inlet, fjord' **Milford Haven**
flint	ME 'hard rock' **Flint**
florida	L 'in flower' **Strata Florida**
floti	ON 'fleet' **Flatholm**
foot	E 'foot-hill' **Saundersfoot**
ford	OE 'ford; route, road' **Ammanford, Edwinsford, Gresford, Haverfordwest, Marford, Whiteford Point, Whitford**
forge	E 'forge, smithy' **Forge**
four	E 'four' **Ffôr, Four Crosses** (3), **Four Mile Bridge, Four Roads**
furnace	E 'furnace' **Furnace**
**gadfa*	fem. 'exit path, outrake' **Yr Adfa**
gafl	dual pl. *geifl*; fem. 'fork' **Eifl**
galar	masc. 'grief, sorrow, misery' **Pentregalar**

gardd fem. 'garden'
Ardd-lin

garth[1] masc./fem. 'mountain ridge, promontory, hill; wooded slope; woodland; uncultivated land'
Garth-, Cenarth, Gwaelod-y-garth, ?Heniarth, Llan-arth, Llanfihangel-ar-arth, Llannarth, Mynydd Llwydiarth, Penarth, Talgarth (2), Tregarth

garth[2] masc. 'enclosure, close, fold, pen; field; fort'
?Heniarth

garðr ON 'enclosure; fishery, fish-yard'
Fishguard

garw adj. 'wild, rough'
Abergarw, Blaengarw, Garnant, Nantgarw, Ynys Arw

gât fem. 'gate'
Pentregât

gate E 'gate, toll gate'
Crossgates, Portfield Gate, Princes Gate

geard OE 'enclosure, yard'
?Yardro

geat OE 'gate, passage'
Rogiet

gefail dim. *gefeilan*, pl. *gefeilion*; fem. 'smithy, forge'
Efail-isaf, Efailnewydd, ?Gofilon, Tonyrefail

gefel var. *gefail* pl. *gefeilion*; fem. 'pincers, tongs'
Gofilon

geil ON 'ravine, narrow lane, way'
?Newgale

geit ON 'goat'
Gateholm

gelau var. *gele*; masc./fem. 'leech'
Tregele

genau masc. 'pass, entrance to a valley'
Llanfihangel Genau'r-glyn,

ger prep. 'near, close to, in front of, before'
Gerlan

glais var. *glas*, pl. **glasau*; masc. 'stream'
Glais, ?Alltwalis, Dowlais, Dulais, Dulas, Knucklas, Marlais, Pantlasau, Pentregwenlais, Tongwynlais

glan fem. 'river-bank, edge, shore, side; slope, hillside'
Glan-, ?Croes-lan, Gerlan, Llangrwyne, Llanbradach, ?Llancaeo, Llanmorlais, Llansanffraid Glan Conwy, Llan-y-pwll, Rhos-lan, Rhuddlan, Glan-bad

glas[1]	adj. 'green, verdant; blue; clear' **Glas-, Aberglaslyn, Bryn-glas, Dulas, Glasfynydd Forest, Gors-las, Heol-las, Llanddulas, Maes-glas (2), Marian-glas, Nant-glas, Pant-glas, Pentrefoelas, Pwll-glas, Rhiwlas (3), Penffordd-las, Ynys-las**
glas[2]	see *glais*
glasgoed	pl. 'saplings, copse of saplings' **Glasgoed**
glesyn	masc. 'common borage; woad' **Glasinfryn**
glo	masc. 'coal; charcoal' **Cwm-y-glo, Nant-y-glo**
glyn	masc. 'narrow valley, glen, dell, dingle' **Glyn-, Llanfihangel Genau'r-glyn, Llanfihangel Glyn Myfyr, Llansanffraid Glynceiriog, Llawr-y-glyn, Nantglyn, Castellnewydd Emlyn, Glyn-y-groes**
go-	var. MW ***gwo-***; pref. 'under, below' **Gwydir**
**gobann-*	Br 'smith' **Abergavenny**
godre	masc. 'foot, bottom' **Godre'r-graig**
gogerdd	masc. 'step, ledge, terrace' **Gogarth**
golde	OE 'gold' **Goldcliff**
golden	E 'golden' **Golden Grove**
gor-	pref., prep. 'over, exceedingly, very; above, over' **Lanfihangel-ar-arth**
gorffwysfa	masc./fem. 'resting-place, seat' **Pengorffwysfa**
gorlech	fem. 'gritstone' **Abergorlech**
gorsedd	masc./fem. 'mound, knoll, hillock; tumulus' **Gorsedd, Yr Orsedd**
gōs	OE 'goose' **Tre-os**
graban	masc. 'corn marigold' **Llandeilo Graban**

graean	pl. 'gravel, shingle, grit'
	Graianrhyd, Dôl-gran
grǣfe	OE 'grove, copse, thicket'
	Grovesend, Golden Grove, Moylgrove
græs	OE 'grass'
	Gresford
gras	ON 'grass'
	Grassholm
grass	see ***græs***
great	E 'large, big'
	Greatoak, Great Orme
green[1]	E 'grassy spot, village green, common grazing land'
	Burton Green, Crabtree Green, Crew Green, Horseman's Green, Talbot Green
green[2]	see ***grēne***
grēne	OE 'green, verdant'
	Greenfield
grēoten	OE 'gravelly'
	?Gredington
gris	pl. ***grisiau***; masc./fem. 'step, terrace'
	Tanygrisiau
gro	fem. 'shingly beach, shingle bank'; pl. 'gravel, shingle
	Gronant, Ro-wen
gros	OF 'great, big, large'
	Grosmont
grove	see ***grǣfe***
grug	collective noun 'heather, ling'
	Llanrug
grugog	adj. 'heath-covered, abounding in heather'
	Rhosllannerchrugog
grugos	fem. 'heath'
	Rhigos
**guo-*	Br 'wind'
	Wye
gwaelod	masc. 'bottom, base'
	Gwaelod-y-Garth
gwaith	masc. 'works, industrial district'
	Pont-y-gwaith
gwal	var. ***wal***; pl. ***gwaliau***; fem. 'wall'
	Rhosygwaliau
gwales	fem. 'sanctuary, retreat, refuge'
	Gwales

gwas	masc. 'youth, young servant' **Abergwesyn**
gwastad	adj. 'flat' **Carregwastad Point, ?Gwastedyn**
gwaun	fem. 'moor, heath; low-lying marshy ground; meadow' **Gwaun-, Gwaen-, Waun-, Waen-, Abergwaun, Blaen-waun, Bryn-gwyn, Dawn, Hirwaun, ?Minwear, Penisa'r-waun**
gwedd	masc./fem. 'appearance, condition' **?Crynwedd**
gwehelog	adj. 'mottled' **Gwehelog**
gwennol	fem. 'swallow' **Rhaeadr Ewynnol**
gwern	masc./fem. 'alder; alder-grove, alder-marsh, swamp; damp meadow' **Gwern-, Cronwern, Gilwern, Gwyddelwern, Llan-wern, Pengwern, Pont-hirwaun, Tafolwern, Trewern**
gweryn	pl. **gwerynau*; masc. ?'liquid, moisture' **?Grwyne Fawr, ?Tryweryn**
gwig	fem. 'wood, forest, glade' **Melin-y-wig**
gwrach	fem. 'witch, crone, hag' **Blaen-gwrach, Rhyd-y-wrach**
gŵydd	masc. 'prominence; sight, face' **Gwyddgrug, Yr Wyddgrug**
gwyddfa	fem. 'prominent place, eminence' **Yr Wyddfa**
gwyddwal	pl. *gwyddeli*; masc./fem. 'thicket, bush, brake; thorny place' **Gwyddelwern**
gŵyl	adj. 'kind, generous' **Abergwili**
gwyn	fem. *gwen*; adj. 'white; blessed', 'light', 'cleared (land)' **Gwenddwr, Afon-wen, Abergwyngregyn, Alwen, Berwyn, Bron-gwyn, Bryn-gwyn, Bwlch-gwyn, Capel Gwyn, Capel Gwynfe, Cilgwyn, ?Cledwen, Dolwen, Gaerwen, Gelli-wen, Gwendraeth Fach/Fawr, Gwenffrwd, Hendy-gwyn ar Daf, Hirwaun, Llanfair Pwllgwyngyll, ?Llyn Berwyn, Llys-wen, Maes-gwyn, Moelwyn, Pentregwenlais, Rhoshirwaun, Tongwynlais, Wenallt**

gwyndy	masc. 'church, holy house; stone-built church' **?Undy**
gwynfa	fem. 'fair land, blessed land, paradise' **Llanfihangel-yng-Ngwynfa**
gŵyr	adj. 'curved, bent' **Gŵyr, Gwyrfai, Tre-gŵyr**
gwyryf	pl. *gwyryfon, gwryddon*; fem. 'virgin, maiden' **Llangwyryfon**
gwŷs	masc./fem. 'sow, pig' **Gwystre**
hæfen	OE 'haven, harbour' **Broadhaven, Milford Haven**
hæfer	OE 'goat' **Haverfordwest**
(ge)hæg	OE 'enclosure, area within a fence' **Hay-on-Wye**
haf	masc. 'summer' **Howey, Aberhafesb**
hafn	masc./fem. 'gap, cleft, gorge, ravine' **Maeshafn**
hâl	fem. 'moor, down, moorland' **Pennal**
halc	pl. *halcen(a)*; OE. 'cavity, nook' **Halkyn, Pentre Halkyn**
half	E 'half, mid' **Halfway** (2)
halh	OE 'nook; spur of land between rivers' **Halghton, Halton**
hālig	OE 'holy' **Holyhead, Holy Island, Holywell**
hall	E 'mansion, house' **Northophall**
halog	adj. 'dirty, soiled, unclean' **Login, Rhytalog, Talog, Trelogan**
hamm	OE 'land hemmed in by water or marsh, land in a river bend, river meadow' **Bersham, Esclusham, Wrexham**
hand	E 'hand' **Cross Hands** (2)
hardd	adj. 'fine, fair, splendid' **Harlech**
haterel	OF 'crown of the head' **Hatterrall Hill**

hault	NF 'high' **Mold**
haven	see ***hæven***
hawdd	adj. 'pleasant' **Honddu (2), Llanddewi Nant Hodni**
head	see ***hēafod***
hēafod	OE 'head; headland' **Carmel Head, Cemais Head, Holyhead, Old Castle Head, Pwll-du Head, St Anne's Head, St David's Head, St Govan's Head, Stackpole Head, Strumble Head, Worm's Head**
hēah	OE 'high, in a lofty location' **Hawarden**
hedge	E 'hedge' **Newhedges**
heli	masc. 'sea-water; brine' **Felinheli, Pwllheli**
hell	E 'hell' **Hell's Mouth**
helyg	pl.; sing. ***helygen***; 'willow, osier' **Llanfihangel Helygen**
hemm	OE 'border' **Presteigne**
hen	adj. 'old; former' **Hen-, Brynhenllan, Yr Hengastell**
hendref	var. ***hendre***; fem. 'winter dwelling, permanent residence; mansion' **Hendre(f)-, Capel Hendre**
hendy	masc. 'old house, former house, mansion' **Hendy, Hendy-gwyn ar Daf**
heol	var. ***hewl***; fem. 'street, road, way' **Heol-, Pump-hewl, Pedair-hewl, Pen-yr-heol, Rhewl** (2)
herber	masc./fem. 'arbour, bower, orchard, leafy glade, shelter' **Penrherber**
hesb	adj. 'dry' **Aberhafesb**
higher	E 'upper, higher' **Higher Kinnerton,**
hill	see ***hyll***

hir	adj. 'long, extensive; tall' **Hir-, Doly-hir, Fan Hir, Hirddywel, Moel Hiraddug, Mynydd Hiraethog, Pont-hir, Pont-Hirwaun, Rhoshirwaun, Ynys-hir**
hlāw	OE 'hill; artificial hill, tumulus' **Ewloe**
hlið	OE 'slope, concave hillside' **Pilleth**
hnott	OE. 'pollard; bare, bald' **Nottage**
hōh	OE 'projecting ridge, heel-like ridge' **Penhow**
holly	E 'holly' **Hollybush**
holmr	ON 'island, small island' **Burry Holms, Flatholm, Gateholm, Grassholm, Priestholm, Skokholm**
holt	OE 'wood; single-species wood' **Holt**
holy	see ***hālig***
hook	E 'hook, spit of land' **Hook, Wooltack Point**
hop	OE 'remote valley; enclosure in marsh or moor' **Hope, Evenjobb, Northop**
hóp	ON 'small bay, inlet' **Lydstep**
horu	OE 'mud, dirt, filth' **Horton**
house	E 'house' **Horseman's Green, Hundred House, Parkhouse**
hoyw	adj. 'lively, sprightly' **Nant Gwynant**
hrēod	OE 'reed' **Redwick**
hund	gen.pl. ***hunden(e)***; OE 'hound' **Hundleton**
hundred	E '(administrative) hundred' **Hundred House**
hús	ON 'house' **Hasguard**
hwch	fem./masc. 'sow, pig; swine' **Stryt-yr-hwch**

hwīt	OE 'white' **Whitchurch (2), Whitebrook, Whiteford Point, Whitesands, Whitford, Whitland**
hyll	OE, ME ***hull***; 'hill' **Dreenhill, Gwersyllt, Hatterrall Hill, Kenfig Hill, Rhos-hill, Rhyl, St Mary Hill**
hynt	fem./?masc. 'path, route' **Epynt**
hysb	fem. ***hesb***; 'dry' **?Hebste**
-i[1]	terr.suff. '(land) belonging to, territory of' **Kerry, Kidwelly**
-i[2]	r.n. suff. **Abergwili, Cilieni, Cothi, Dyfi, Elái, Llangefni, Llanllyfni, Llynfi, ?Rudry, ?Teifi, Troddi**
iaith	fem. 'language, utterance' **Ieithon**
iâl	fem. 'late-bearing land, unfruitful land' **Llanarmon-yn-Iâl, Llandysilio-yn-Iâl**
iarll	masc. 'earl' **Betws Tir Iarll**
iau	var. ***iou***; masc./fem. 'yoke' **Cwmyoy**
-ig	dim.suff. **Aberbythych, Brenig, Talerddig**
-ing	OE connective particle **Evenjobb, Hyssington**
inn	E 'inn, tavern' **Cross Inn, New Inn, Synod Inn**
-iog[1]	terr.suff. '(land) beonging to, territory of' **Ffestiniog, Pencarnisiog, Tudweiliog**
-iog[2]	adj. suff. **Ceiriog, Gyffylliog**
-ion	terr.suff. '(land) belonging to, territory of' **Castle Caereinion, Ceredigion, Prion**
ir	adj. 'verdant' **?Cwm Irfon**
isaf	adj. 'lower; lowest' **Efail-isaf, Mynyddisa, Penisa'r-waun, Pentre-isaf**
island	E 'isle, island' **Holy Island, Puffin Island, St Tudwal's Island**

junction	E '(railway) junction' **Llandudno Junction**
kald	ON 'cold' **Caldey**
key	E 'key' **Cross Keys**
**kleu*	Celtic ?'strong-flowing; stony; scouring' **Clydach, Clywedog**
lǣs	OE 'meadow-land, pasture' **Summerleaze**
land	E 'land' **Sealand**
lane	E 'lane' **Crosslanes**
lang	OE 'long' **Landshipping**
lark	see *lāwerce*
launde	OF 'glade, open space in woodland, woodland pasture' **Whitland**
lāwerce	OE 'lark' **Lavernock**
le	F/ME 'at, near' **Michaelston-le-pit**
lēac	OE 'leek' **Leighton**
lēah	dat. *lēage*; OE 'woodland clearing, glade; meadow; river-meadow' **Bagillt, Buckley, Caergwrle, Leeswood, Penley, Pylallai, Ridleywood**
legio	pl. *legiones*, gen. pl. *legionum*; L 'legion' **Caerleon**
licksome	E 'agreeabale, pleasant' **Lixwm**
little	E 'little, small, short' **Little Orme, Staylittle**
llachar	adj. 'bright' ?**Lacharn**
llafar	adj. 'babbling, loud, resounding' **Llafar**
#llai	?masc. '(river-)meadow' **Coed-llai, Llay**

llan	fem. 'enclosure, yard; church; parish' **Llan-, Lan-, Llam-, Lam-, Bwlch-llan, ?Croes-lan, Henllan (2), Henllan Amgoed, Landimore, Llawhaden, Penrhiw-llan, Twynllannan, Ynys Llanddwyn**
llandref	var. ***llandre***; 'church village, church farm' **Llandre**
llannerch	masc./fem. 'clearing, glade' **Llannerch-y-medd, Llannerch Banna, Rhosllannerchrugog**
llawd	masc.; adj. 'agitation, tumult, turbulence, heat' **Ynys Lawd**
llawr	masc. 'low ground, floor or bottom of valley' **?Lawrenny, Llawr-y-glyn**
lle	masc. 'place, location, designation, position, site' **Penlle'r-gaer**
llech	var. ****lleg***, pl. ***llechau***; fem. 'slab of stone; rock, boulder; slate' **Llechcynfarwy, Llechryd, Llechrydau, Benllech, Harlech, Talyllychau, Tre-lech, Trelleck**
llechog	adj. 'rocky' **Porth Llechog**
lled	adj. 'half, partial, semi-' **Lledrod**
lliaws	var. ***llios***; masc./fem. 'multitude' **Rhydlios**
llid	pl. ***llidiau*** var. ****llidau***; 'fury, wrath' **?Llyn Llydaw**
llif	masc. 'current, flow' **Ynys Enlli**
llin[1]	pl. ***llinau***; masc./fem. 'line, series' **?Cwmllinau**
llin[2]	pl. ****llinau***; masc. 'flax' **?Cwmllinau, Pen-llin**
llithfaen	masc. 'loadstone' **Llithfaen**
lliw	masc. 'bright, shining' **Lliw, Pont-lliw**
lloc	masc. 'pen, fold, pound' **Lloc**
llogail	var. ***llogel***; masc./fem. 'wattle fence, hurdle' **Pontllogail**
#llong	?masc. 'swamp, bog, quagmire' **Llong, ?Trallong**

llug	masc. 'light, brightness, radiance' **Llugwy**
llumon	?masc. 'stack, chimney' **Pumlumon**
llwch	pl. *llychau*; masc. 'inlet, fjord; lake, pool; marsh' **Amlwch, Llan-llwch, ?Talyllychau**
llwyd	adj. 'grey; pale; russet, brown; muddy; holy, blessed' **Llyn Cowlyd, Mallwyd, Mynydd Llwydiarth, Pentre Llwyn-llwyd**
llwyn-	masc. 'grove, bush' **Llwyn-, Onllwyn, Pentre Llwyn-llwyd,**
llwyth	masc. 'family' **Llanfair Llythynwg**
llychwr	masc. 'brightness' **Casllwchwr**
llydan	adj. 'broad, wide' **Gellilydan, Pontlotyn, Rhydlydan**
llyfn	fem. *llefn*; adj. 'smooth, even; slippery' **Carreg-lefn, Cwmllynfell, Llynfi, Llanllyfni, Rhoslefain**
llyfu	var. *llyo*; 'lick, lap' **?Fan Llia**
llyn	pl. *llynnau*; masc. 'lake; pool' **Aberglaslyn, Aran Benllyn, Cemlyn, Crumlin, Cwm Ystradllyn, Llanfihangel Tal-y-llyn, Llanuwchllyn, Llyn Cwellyn, Maes-llyn, Minllyn, Nantlle, Pentre-llyn, Pentrellyncymer, Pontllan-fraith**
llys	masc./fem. 'court, manor house, hall' **Llys-, Bronllys, Henllys, Lisvane, Scleddau**
loggerheads	E 'dispute'; 'drunkard, blockhead' **Loggerheads**
lôn	fem. 'lane; road' **Groeslon**
long	see *lang*
ma	var. (or pl.) *mai*; masc./fem. 'plain, field; place, spot' **Machen, Machynlleth, Mallwyd, Manafon, Mynydd Mallaen, Bleddfa, Brechfa, Colfa, Cegidfa, Capel Gwynfe, ?Gwyrfai, ?Myddfai**
mab	masc. 'son' **Llanddaniel-fab, Man-moel**
mǣd	OE 'meadow' **Presteigne**

mægden	OE 'maiden; the Virgin Mary' **Maiden Wells**
maen	pl. ***meini, main, mein***; masc. 'stone, slab, standing stone, rock' **Maen-, Bôn-y-maen, Bryn-y-maen, Bwlch-y-ddeufaen, Corwen, Bont-faen, Groes-faen, Lisvane, Llandochau'r Bont-faen, Llangorwen, Llysfaen, Maen y Bugail, Pont-faen (2), Rhos-maen, Rhyd-y-main, Torfaen, Tre-main**
maenor	var. ***maenol***; fem. 'landed estate, demesne; manor-house, mansion' **Maenordeilo, Manorbier, Manorowen, Vaynor**
maerdref	fem. 'demesne, home farm, farm' **Faerdre, Llantwit Fardre**
maerdy	masc. 'dairy farm, home farm' **Maerdy (4), Mardy**
(ge)mǣre	OE 'boundary' **Marcross, Marford**
maes	masc. 'open country, level land, plain; territory; field, land set aside for a purpose' **Maes-, Llan-faes (2), Llanmaes, Miskin**
magwyr	fem. 'wall, fortification; ruin' **Magwyr**
mainc	pl. ***meinciau***; fem. 'bank, ledge, terrace' **Meinciau**
major	E 'main, principal' **Llantwit Major, St Brides Major**
mal	OF 'bad, difficult' **Malpas**
mall	adj. 'rotten, putrid, unwholesome, unhealthy' **Malltraeth**
man	masc./fem. 'place, spot, location, position' **Fan**
marais	NF 'marsh' **Beaumaris**
march	pl. ***meirch***; masc. 'horse, stallion'; adv. 'very'; adj. 'great, large' ?**Marros, Marteg, Pen-marc, Rhos-meirch, Rhyd-y-meirch, Drenewydd Gelli-farch**
marchog	masc. 'knight, nobleman' **Felindre Farchog**
marchwiail	masc. pl. 'large saplings, stout shoots' **Marchwiel**

marian	masc. 'gravel, pebbles, shingle, gravelly bank' **Marian-glas, Llanfarian**
market	ME 'market' **Rosemarket**
marsh	E 'marsh' **Malltraeth Marsh**
marw	adj. 'dead, languid, stagnant' **Marlais**
math	E 'mowing, a day's mowing' **Horseman's Green**
mathr	masc. 'sorrow, distress' **?Mathri**
mawr	adj. 'large, big' **Allt-mawr, Yr As Fawr, Bryn-mawr, Cefn-mawr, Clynnog Fawr, Derwen-fawr, Dwyfor, Fan Fawr, Fforest Fawr, Frenni Fawr, Garn Fawr, Gellifor, Glyder Fawr, Gwendraeth Fawr, Grwyne Fawr, Llanbadarn Fawr, Llandeilo Fawr, Llanfor, Llangoedmor, Llanilltud Fawr, Llannor, Llwyndyrys, Llyn y Fan Fawr, Mynydd Mawr, Nanmor, Penmaenmawr, Pen-y-cae-mawr, Porth Mawr, Rhinog Fawr, Rhos-fawr, Waunfawr, Waun-fawr**
medd	masc. 'mead' **Llannerch-y-medd**
mei-	pref. 'half, mid' **Meidrum, Meifod**
mêl	masc. 'honey' **Llanfihangel Nant Melan**
melin	fem. 'mill' **Melin-, Felin-, Bancyfelin, Banc-y-ffordd, Cwmfelin-boeth, Cwmfelin-fach, Cwmfelinmynach, Dre-felin, Pentrefelin** (4), **Rhydyfelin**
melr	ON 'sand-bank' **Milford Haven**
melyn	fem. ***melen***; adj. 'yellow' **Bancffosfelen, Trefelen, Rhydfelen**
men	fem. 'cart, wagon' **Pont-rhyd-y-fen**
**men-*	Br ?fem. ?'flow, current' **?Menai Strait**
menechdid	fem. 'monastery; monastery grange' **Efenechdyd**

mere	OE 'mere, pond, lake, pool' **Hanmer**
mersc	OE 'marsh' **?Marshfield**
merthyr	masc. 'shrine, sanctified cemetery, church consecrated by saint's bones' **Merthyr-, Martletwy**
meudwy	masc. 'hermit, anchorite' **Ynys-y-meudwy**
micel	OE 'big, great' **Mitchel Troy**
middel	OE 'middle, midway' **Middle Mill, Middle Mouse, Middletown**
middle	see ***middel***
mieri	var. ***meri***; fem. pl. 'blackberry, brambles; briers, thorn bushes' **Cilmeri**
mign	fem. 'marsh, bog, swamp' **Migneint**
mil	?masc. 'lesser celandine, pilewort, figwort' **?Trefil**
mile	E 'mile' **Four Mile Bridge**
mill	see ***myln***
min	masc. 'edge, border, side' **Minffordd (2), Minllyn, Minwear**
minera	L 'mine' **Minera**
moch[1]	pl. 'pigs, swine' **Mochdre (2), ?Llanrhaeadr-ym-Mochnant, Nant-y-moch**
moch[2]	adj. 'swift, rapid' **?Llanrhaeadr-ym-Mochnant**
moel	adj. 'bald, bare, barren'; fem. 'treeless hill, hilltop, summit' **Moel-, Foel-, Felin-foel, Llampeter Velfrey, Llanddewi Velfrey, Man-moel, Marloes, Moelfre, Moelwyn, Nant-y-moel, Pentrefoelas, Rhyd-y-foel**
moelrhon	pl. ***moelrhoniaid***; masc./fem. 'seal' **Ynysoedd y Moelrhoniaid**
momele	ME 'mumble' **?Mumbles**

monk	E 'monk' **Monknash, Monkswood, Monkstone Point**
mont	NF 'hill' **Mold**
morfa	masc./fem. 'sea marsh, salt-marsh' **Morfa Bychan, Morfa Nefyn, Penmorfa**
**mori-*	Br 'sea' **Carmarthen**
mos	OE 'bog, fen, swamp' **Moss, Mostyn**
moss	see *mos*
mote	ME 'moat, protective ditch; castle embankment, mound' **Henry's Moat, New Moat**
mountain	E 'mountain' **Black Mountains, Holyhead Mountain**
mouse	E 'little island' **East/Middle/West Mouse**
mouth	see *mūða*
mūða	OE 'mouth' **Hell's Mouth, Monmouth**
mwyn	masc. 'mineral, ore; mine' **Rhandir-mwyn, Rhyd-y-mwyn**
mwynglawdd	masc. 'mine' **Mwynglawdd**
mydd	masc. 'dish, tub' **?Myddfai**
myln	OE 'mill' **Blackmill, ?Garthmyl, Middle Mill, Milton, New Mills (2), Parkmill**
mynach	var. *manach*; pl. *myneich, meneich*; masc. 'monk' **Cwmfelinmynach, Pontarfynach, Llanymynech, Capel Coed-y-mynach, Ystradmynach**
mynachlog	fem. 'monastery; monastic grange' **Mynachlog-ddu**
mynydd	masc. 'mountain; hill; common, unenclosed land, mountain land, moorland' **Mynydd-, Cilfynydd, Glasfynydd Forest, Llanbadarn Fynydd, Llanfynydd (2), Mynytho, Penmynydd, Eglwys Fair y Mynydd, Trawsfynydd, Uwchmynydd**

nant — pl. ***nentydd, naint***; masc. 'valley'; fem. 'stream'
Nant-, Nan-, Abernaint, Abernant, Bronnant, Creunant, Cwm Nantcol, Dyffryn Crawnon, Dynvant, Garnant, Glyntrefnant, Gronant, Hirnant, ?Llanbythery, Llanboidy, Llancarfan, Llanfarian, Llanfihangel Nant Brân, Llanfihangel Nant Melan, Llantarnam, Llan-teg, Llanthony, Llantrithyd, Llyn Crafnant, Migneint, Nant Brân, Nant Gwynant, Trefnant, Tŷ-nant

new — see ***nīwe***

newydd — adj. 'new'
Betws Newydd, Bontnewydd (3), Bwlchnewydd, Caeriw Newydd, Capel Newydd, Casnewydd-bach, Castell-newydd, Castellnewydd Emlyn, Casnewydd-ar-wysg, Ceinewydd, Clawddnewydd, Cwrtnewydd, Y Drenewydd, Drenewydd Gelli-farch, Drenewydd yn Notais, Eglwys Newydd ar y Cefn, Felin Newydd, Llannewydd (3), Pontnewydd, Tredegar Newydd, Drenewydd Gelli-farch

-ni — r.n. suff.
Rhondda, Rhymni

nigh — E 'near, close'
Llangattock nigh Usk

nīwe — OE 'new, recent'
New-, Carew Newton, Little Newcastle, Shirenewton, Wolvesnewton

norð — OE 'north'
Northop, North Stack, Norton

-nwy — pers.n. suff.
Efyrnwy

-o — see ***-aw***

oak — see ***āc***

odyn — fem. 'lime-kiln'
Rhydodyn

of — E 'of, associated with'
Point of Ayr

ofer — OE 'flat ridge (with a convex shoulder)'
New Radnor

ōfer — OE 'river bank'
Overton

og — adj. 'fast, sharp'
Ogmore-by-sea, Ogwen

-og[1]	terr.suff. '(land) belonging to, territory of' **Defynnog, Gregynog**
-og[2]	MW var. *-awg*; adj. suff. **Dolanog, Moel Hebog, Mynydd Hiraethog, Penarlâg**
ogof	fem. 'cave, cleft' **Dan-yr-ogof**
old	see *ald*
on	E 'on, adjacent to' **Hay-on-Wye, Michaelchurch-on-Arrow, Newbridge-on-Wye, Rhos-on-Sea, Tal-y-bont on Usk**
-on	noun suff. **Ieithon**
onn	fem. sing *onnen*; 'ash tree' **Trefonnen, Onllwyn, Rhydyronnen**
-or	pl. suff. **Croesor, Prysor**
ormr	ON 'snake' **Great/Little Orme**
-os	dim. pl. suff. **Gurnos**
oxa	OE 'ox' **Oxwich**
pabell	var. (sing.) *pebyll*; masc./fem. 'tent, tabernacle; refuge, shelter' **Babell, Cilybebyll**
**pagēnses*	L 'dwellers in a district, province or hinterland' **Dinas Powys, Powys**
pâl	pl. *palau*; masc. 'pale, fence; park enclosed within a pale; post, stake' **Pale, Penrhiwpâl**
pandy	masc. 'fulling-mill' **Pandy (3), Pandytudur, Tonypandy**
pant	masc. 'depression, hollow, dingle; bottom' **Pant-, Cwmsychbant**
parc	pl. *parciau, parcau*; masc. 'enclosed land, field; open land, park' **Cwm-parc, Park Seymor, Penparcau**
park	E 'park' **Parkhouse, Parkmill**
parlwr	masc. 'parlour, inner chamber' **Parlwr Du**
parrog	masc. 'flat land by the sea-shore' **Parrog**

pas	OF 'passage, route' **Malpas**
pastwn	pl. ***pastynod***; masc./fem. 'cudgel, stick, staff' **Pantpastynog**
pedwar	fem. ***pedair***; 'four' **Pedair-hewl**
pelan	fem. 'hillock, tump' **Cwm-belan**
pen	masc. and adj. 'head, top, summit; end; promontory, headland; source, uplands' **Pen-, Ben-, Aran Benllyn, Benllech, Mynydd Pen-y-fâl, Pembrey, Pembroke, Pembroke Dock, Penygarreg Reservoir**
#penllech	masc. 'capstone' **Benllech, Penllech**
penmaen	masc. 'rocky outcrop, promontory; cape' **Dolbenmaen, Garndolbenmaen, Penmaen Dewi, Penmaenmawr, Penmaenpool, Penmaen-pŵl**
pennant	masc. 'upland, (head of) valley' **Pennant** (2), **Pennant Melangell, Llanfihangel-y-Pennant** (2)
pennardd	fem. 'headland, promontory, hillside' **Penarlâg**
****penno-***	Br 'end, headland' **Pembroke**
#penrhos	fem. 'moor headland' **Penrhos** (2), **Penrhosllugwy**
penrhyn	masc. 'promontory, headland' **Penrhyn-**
pentir	masc. 'headland' **Pentir**
pentref	var. ***pentre***; masc. 'hamlet, village; (industrial) settlement' **Pentref-, Pentre-**
perfedd	masc. 'middle, centre; inaccessible' **Treberfedd**
perllan	pl. ***perllenni***; fem. 'orchard' ?**Penperllenni**
perth	fem. 'thicket, brake, copse' **Narberth, Redberth**
perthog	adj. 'abounding in bushes or thickets' **Pantperthog**
pil	masc. 'pill, tidal creek or stream' ?**Pyle**

pill	see *pyll*
pistyll	masc./?fem. 'waterfall; spring' **Pistyll, Pistyll Rhaeadr**
pit	see *pytt*
plwyf	masc. 'parish' **Blaenplwyf**
poeth	adj. 'burnt; scorched, parched, withered' **Coed-poeth, Cwmfelin-boeth, Pentre-poeth, Ynys-boeth**
point	E 'promontory, tip' **Carregwastad Point, Dale Point, Giltar Point, Monkstone Point, Point Lynas, Point of Ayr, Whiteford Point, Wooltack Point**
pollr	ON 'pool' **Stackpole**
pont	fem. 'bridge' **Pont-, Bont-, Clwt-y-bont, Dôl-y-bont, Llanbedr Pontsteffan, Llandochau'r Bont-faen, Pen-pont, Pentre-bont, Pen-y-bont, Pen-y-bont-fawr, Pontrhypont, Tal-y-bont (4), Tal-y-bont on Usk**
pool	E 'pool, river pool' **Penmaenpool, Pontypool, Pool Quay**
port[1]	E 'port, harbour' **Burry Port, Porthmadog, Port Talbot, Port Tennant**
port[2]	OE 'town, market town' **Newport (2), Portfield Gate**
porth	masc. 'door, entrance' **Y Porth, Porth-y-rhyd;** fem. 'cove, bay; ferry' **Porth-, Borth-, Aber-porth, Blaen-porth, Borth, Port Eynon, Portskewett**
post	masc. 'post office' **Post Mawr**
pren	masc. 'tree' **Pren-gwyn, Pren-teg**
prēost	pl. *prēosta*; OE 'priest' **Prestatyn, Presteigne**
prestr	ON 'priest' **Priestholm**
pryf	masc. 'wild animal, hunted animal, quarry' **Rhiwbryfdir**
prysg	var. *prys, pres*; masc.pl. 'copse, grove, thicket' **Preseli, Prysor**
puffin	E 'puffin' **Puffin Island**

pump	var. ***pum***; 'five' **Llanpumsaint, Pumlumon, Pump-hewl, Pumsaint**
pwll	masc. 'pool; pit, hollow' **Pwll-, Llanfair Pwllgwyngyll, Llanfair-yn-Neubwll, Llanfihangel-y-pwll, Llan-y-pwll**
pwmp	var. ***plwmp***; masc. 'pump, village pump' **Plwmp**
pyll	OE 'tidal stream, pool, small stream' **Blackpill, Pilleth**
pysgod	masc.pl. 'fish' **Dinbych-y-pysgod**
pytt	OE 'hollow' **Michaelston-le-pit**
quay	E 'landing place' **Connah's Quay, Newquay**
queen	E 'queen' **Queensferry**
rā	OE 'roe-deer' **Rogiet**
ras	pl. ***rasau***; fem. 'race, watercourse' **Rasau**
rēad	OE 'red' **New Radnor, Red Wharf Bay**
red	see ***rēad***
rhaeadr	masc./fem. 'waterfall, cascade, torrent' **Rhaeadr, Rhaeadr Aber, Rhaeadr Ewynnol, Llanrhaeadr-ym-Mochnant, Llanrhaeadr-yng-Nghinmeirch, Pistyll Rhaeadr**
#rhaglan	fem. 'rampart' **Raglan**
rhan	fem. 'part, share, portion, division' **Dwyran**
rhandir	masc./fem. 'area, portion of land' **Rhandir-mwyn**
rhath	masc. 'earthwork, fortification' **Roath**
**rhawdd*	var. ****rhodd***; masc. 'noise, sound' **Rhondda**
rhedynog	adj. 'abounding with ferns' **Glynrhedynog, Tredunnock**
rheidiol	var. ***rheidol***; adj. 'swift' **Rheidol**
rhes	fem. 'row (of houses)' **Rhes-y-cae**

rhiniog	var. *rhinog, hinog*, pl. *rhinogau*; masc./fem. 'threshold' **Rhinog Fawr/Fach, Rhinogau**
rhisgl	var. *rhisg* pl. *rhisgau*; masc. 'bark' **Rhisga**
rhiw	masc./fem. 'steep slope, hill (side); road on a slope' **Rhiw, Rhiwbryfdir, Rhiwlas (3), ?Carew, Fochriw, Mynydd Rhiwsaeson, Penrhiw-ceibr, Penrhiw-goch, Penrhiw-llan, Penrhiwpâl, Rhiwabon, Trefriw, Troed-y-rhiw**
rhod	fem. 'shield, defence' **Lledrod**
rhos	fem. 'promontory'; 'moor' **Rhos-, Aberhosan, Camros, Ffair-rhos, Llandrillo-yn-Rhos, Llanelian-yn-Rhos, Llanfihangel Rhos-y-corn, Llan-rhos, Llanllŷr-yn-rhos, Marloes, ?Marros, Pen-rhos (2), Red Roses/Rhos-goch, Resolfen, Rhoose, Rosemarket**
rhudd	adj. 'red; brown' **Rhuddlan, Ruthin**
rhuthr	masc./fem. 'rush' **?Rudry**
rhwmp	masc. 'auger, bore, piercer' **Rhymni, Rymney**
rhwyd	fem. 'net, snare' **Bochrwyd**
rhy	adv.; intensive pref. 'extreme, considerable' **Rhuallt**
rhyd	pl. *rhydau*; fem. 'ford' **Rhyd-, Brynrhydyrarian, Y Ddwyryd, Dwyryd, Glan-rhyd, Graianrhyd, Henryd, Llechryd, Pontrhypont, Llanfihangel Rhydithon, Llechryd, Llechrydau, Pontrhydfendigaid, Pont-rhyd-y-cyff, Pont-rhyd-y-fen, Pont-rhyd-y-groes, Pontrhypont, Porth-y-rhyd (2), Redberth, Rhytalog, Talog**
(ge)ryd(d)	OE 'cleared of trees' **Ridleywood**
road	E 'road' **Clarbeston Road, Five Roads, Four Roads**
roche	F 'rock, cliff' **Roch, Rockfield**
saeth	?var. *saith*; 'arrow' **?Tresaith**
saint	see *seint*

Sais pl. ***Saeson***; 'Englishman; one who can speak English, or who lived in England, or who habitually consorts with English people or affects English customs; an anglophile'
Mynydd Rhiwsaeson, Pont-ar-Sais

saltan OE 'salty'
Saltney

salw adj. 'unhealthy, dark, sallow, discoloured'
Solva

sands E 'expanse of sand, sandbanks, dunes'
Cefn Sidan Sands, Lavan Sands, Whitesands Bay

sandy E 'sandy'
Sandycroft

sant var. ***san, sain, saint***; pl. ***saint***; masc. 'saint'
Sain-, Saint-, San-, Llanddeusant (2), **Llanpumsaint, Llan Sain Siôr, Llan-saint, Llansanffraid** (2), **Llansanffraid Cwmteuddwr, Llansanffraid Glan Conwy, Llansanffraid Glynceiriog, Llansanfraid Gwynllŵg, Llansanffraid-ym-Mechain, Llansanffraid-yn-Elfael, Llansan-siôr, Llantrisant** (3)

****santōn-*** Br ?'path'
?Trannon

sarn pl. ***sarnau***; fem; 'causeway, stepping stones, paved way'
Sarn-, Cefnddwysarn, Pen-sarn (3), **Tal-sarn, Talsarnau, Tal-y-sarn**

sbeit masc. 'spite, malice'
Tavernspite

sbens masc./fem. 'buttery, pantry, place where drink is kept'
Rhydspence

scēot OE 'hill, steep slope'
Shotton

scīr-(ge)rēfa OE 'sheriff'
Shirenewton, Twyn-y-sheriff

scypen OE 'cow-shed'
Landshipping

sea E 'sea'
Ogmore-by-sea, Rhos-on-Sea, Sealand

seint ME 'saint'
St-

seven E 'seven'
Seven Sisters

sgathrog	var. *sgethrog*; adj. 'rough, craggy, rocky' **Sgethrog**
shabbed	E 'scabbed' **?Moel Siabod**
sheriff	see *scīr-(ge)rēfa*
sidan	masc. 'silk' **Cefn Sidan**
side	E 'adjacent part' **Penrhyn-side**
siryf	var. *sirydd*; 'sheriff' **Twyn-y-sirydd**
sister	E 'sister' **Seven Sisters**
skáli	ON 'temporary hut' **Scolton**
skálm	ON 'cleft, fissure' **Skomer**
skarð	ON 'pass, gap, opening' **Hasguard**
sker	ON 'rock, reef' **?Skerries, Tusker Rock**
skerry	E 'rugged sea-rock, stretch of rocks, reef' **Skerries**
skot	ON 'projecting piece of land or rock' **Tusker Rock**
**slǣpe*	OE 'muddy' **Slebech**
snāw	OE 'snow' **Snowdon, Snowdonia**
sofl	masc. dim. *soflyn*, fem. dim. ?*soflen*; 'stubble' **?Resolfen**
**sōg*	OE 'bog, swamp, marsh' **Sychdyn**
sound	E 'passage of water, arm of the sea' **Broad Sound**
south	see *sūð*
southern	E 'southern' **?Southerndown**
spitel	ME 'hospice, house of the indigent, hospital' **Spittal**
stack	see *stakkr*
stakkr	ON 'stack, rock in the sea' **North Stack, South Stack, Stackpole**

star	E 'star' **Star**
stay	E 'remain, stay' **Staylittle**
step	E 'step' **Stepaside**
sticil	var. ***sticill***; fem. 'stile' **Pontsticyll**
stoc	OE '(secondary) settlement, outlying farmstead' **Churchstoke, Erbistock, Woodstock**
stokkr	ON 'sound, narrow passage of water' **Skokholm**
stone	E 'stone, rock, crag' **Monkstone Point**
storm	var. ***strom***; E 'storm' **?Strumble Head**
stōw	OE 'place, assembly place, holy place' **Chepstow, Dingestow, Michaelston-le-pit, Wonastow**
strait	E 'narrow passage of water' **Menai Strait**
strata	L 'valley bottom, vale' **Strata Florida**
stryd	var. ***stryt***; fem. 'street, (main) road, highway' **Pen-y-stryt, Stryt-yr-hwch**
**stuctio*	Br; adj. 'winding' **Aberystwyth, Ystwyth**
sugar loaf	E 'conical mass of sugar' **Sugar Loaf**
sumor	OE 'summer' **Summerleaze**
super	L 'on, above' **Peterston-super-Ely,**
sūð	OE 'south' **South Cornelly, ?Southerndown, Southgate, South Stack, Sudbrook**
swallow	E 'swallow' **Swallow Falls**
swtan	masc. 'whiting-pout' **Porth Swtan**
swydd	fem. 'area, district' **Swyddffynnon**
sych	adj. 'dry' **Abersychan, Cwmsychbant, Moel Sych**

synod	E 'council, meeting place for debate, assembly' **Synod Inn**
tafarn	fem./masc. 'tavern, inn, public house' **Pentre Tafarnyfedw, Tafarnygelyn, Tavernspite**
tâl	masc. 'end, extremity, top' **Tâl-, Tal-, Llanfihangel Tal-y-llyn** (2), **Ystalyfera**
talwrn	masc. 'open ground, clearing, grassland; threshing floor; cockpit' **Coed-talon, Tallarn Green, Talwrn** (2)
**tam-*	Br 'flow' **Taff, Tawe, ?Teifi**
tan	var. ***dan***; prep. 'under, below, beneath' **Dan-yr-ogof, Tan-y-bwlch, Tan-y-fron, Tanygrisiau, Tan-y-groes**
tân	masc. 'fire, heat; bright' **Tanat**
**tardder-*	?'bubbling forth' **?Glyn Tarell**
teg	adj. 'fair, fine, beautiful' **Bryn-teg, Llan-teg, Maesteg, Ton-teg**
teml	fem. 'temple' **Tredeml**
tempel	OE 'hospice of the Knights Templars' **Templeton**
**teuā-*	Br ?'swell' **?Tywi**
three	E 'three' **Three Cocks**
throp	OE 'hamlet' **Freystrop**
tir	masc. 'land, earth, ground, territory' **Brithdir, Betws Tir Iarll, Gwydir, Rhiwbryfdir, Tirabad, Tir-phil**
tocyn	masc. 'heap' **Bwlchtocyn**
tom	masc./fem. 'dung, manure, mire; dung-hill' **Domgae**
ton	pl. ***tonnau***; masc./fem. 'unploughed land, lay-land, grassland, sward' **Ton-**
tor[1]	fem. 'slope, flank, hill' **Torfaen, ?Trofarth**
tor[2]	E 'hill, rocky peak' **Giltar Point**

torlan	fem. '(undercut) river bank' **Darland**
tour	ME 'tower' **Tretower**
town	see ***tūn***
tra	adv. 'extremely, exceedingly' **Tryweryn**
traeth	pl. ***traethau***; masc. 'beach, shore, strand' **Traeth Coch, Traeth Lafan, Gwendraeth Fawr/Fach, Llanfihangel-y-traethau, Malltraeth, Penrhyndeudraeth, Pentraeth, Trefdraeth**
trallwng	masc. 'muddy area, boggy spot, dirty pool' **?Trallong, Y Trallwng**
trap	masc. 'trap' **?Pwll-trap, ?Trap**
trawdd	masc./fem. 'route, assault' **Troddi**
traws	adj. 'across, opposite; strong,powerful' **Trawsfynydd, Trawsgoed**
tree	see ***trēow***
tref	var. ***tre***; fem. 'farmstead; dwelling, residence, homestead, estate; hamlet, township; village; industrial settlement; town' **Tref-, Tre-, Tre'r-, Dre-, Felindre**(6), **Glyntrefnant, Gwystre, Mochdre** (2), **Troed-yr-aur**
trēow	OE 'tree; meeting-place' **Crabtree Green, Gladestry**
tri	fem ***tair***; 'three' **Abertridwr, Llan-y-tair-Mair, Llantrisant** (3)
**tri-*	see ***try-***
trindod	masc. 'Trinity' **Eglwys y Drindod, Llandrindod**
troed	masc./fem. 'foot, foot-hill' **Troed-y-rhiw**
trosol	masc./fem. 'crowbar' **Ffostrasol**
tru	adj. 'wretched, miserable' **?Mathri**
trum	var. ***drum***; masc./fem. 'crest, ridge, peak, range' **Drum, Meidrum, Trimsaran**
trwyn	masc. 'headland, promontory, point; spur' **Trwyn Eilian, Trwyn y Fuwch, Trwyn y Gadair**

try- var. Br **tri-*, reinforcing pref. 'conspicuous, outstanding, exceptional'
?Trannon, Tryfan, Tryleg

tuft ME 'cluster of trees; grassy hillock'
?Tufton

tumble E 'tumble, fall'
Tumble

tūn OE 'settlement; farm,manor; homestead; enclosure; village; town'
Allington, Ambleston, Axton, Bishopston, Bishton, Bletherston, Bonvilston, Bosherston, Boverton, Bretton, Briton Ferry, Broughton, Burton, Buttington, Cadoxton, Canaston Bridge, Carew Newton, Castleton, Cheriton, Clarbeston Road, Colwinston, Cosheston, Druidston, Dukestown, Eyton, Flemingston, Forden, Gileston, Gowerton, Gredington, Griffithstown, Halghton, Halton, Haroldston West, Herbrandston, Higher Kinnerton, Hodgeston, Hopkinstown, Horton, Hundleton, Hyssington, Ifton, Ilston, Jameston, Jeffreyston, Johnston, Johnstown, Jordanston, Keeston, Kinnerton, Knelston, Knighton, Lambston, Leighton, Letterston, Michaelston-y-fedw, Middletown, Milton, Morganstown, Morriston, Mostyn, Newton (2), **Newton Nottage, Newtown, Nicholaston, Nolton, Norton, Peterstone Wentlooge, Peterston-super-Ely, Prestatyn, Reynoldston, Robeston Cross/Wathen/West, Rudbaxton, Sageston, Scolton, Shirenewton, Siginston, Sychdyn, Templeton, Tufton, Tylorstown, Uzmaston, Walton, Walton East/West, Waterston, West Williamston, Whitson, Whitton, Wiston, Wolvesnewton, Yerbeston**

twr masc. 'heap, pile'
Mynydd Twr

tŵr masc. 'tower, keep; castle'
Tretŵr

twrch gen. and pl. *tyrch*; masc. 'boar'
Twrch (2), **Cwm-twrch, ?Foel Dyrch, Pen-tyrch**

twymyn masc./fem. 'fever, heat'
Twymyn, Glantwymyn

twyn	masc. 'hillock, mound, dune' **Pen-twyn, Twynllannan, Twynrodyn**
tŷ	pl. *tai*; masc. 'house' **Tŷ-, Hendy-gwyn ar Daf, Maendy, Pentre Tŷ-gwyn, Pontypridd, Tai-bach**
tyddyn	var. *t'yn, tyn*; masc. 'croft, small-holding, homestead, (small) farm, cottage' **Ty'n-, Tyn-, Tŷ-nant**
tylles	fem. 'den, lair' **?Duthlas**
tywyn	var. *towyn*; masc. 'strand, sea-shore; sand-dune' **Llanfihangel-yn-Nhywyn, Pentywyn, Porth Tywyn, Towyn, Tywyn**
uchaf	adj. 'highest, uppermost; tallest; upper' **Felin-gwm-uchaf, Rhyduchaf**
uchel	adj. 'high,tall' **Bontuchel**
uisc	OW 'fish' **Usk**
upper	E 'upper, higher' **Upper Boat**
uwch	prep. 'above, over, on; beyond, on the further side; higher' **Llanfihangel-uwch-Gwili, Llanuwchllyn, Pen-uwch, Uwchmynydd**
vale	E 'vale, valley' **Coalbrookvale, Ebbw Vale, Merthyr Vale**
valley	E 'valley' **Valley**
vallis	L 'valley' **Valle Crucis**
venta	?pre-Br ?'chief place (of a tribe), field; market' **Caer-went, Gwent**
vík	ON 'bay, small creek, inlet' **Gelliswick**
village	E 'village, settlement nucleus' **Church Village**
ville	F 'town' **Rockfield, Wattsville**
wæfre	OE 'restless, wavering' **?Warren**

wælle	OE 'well; mineral well' **Builth Wells, Cresswell, Crosswell, Llandrindod Wells, Llanwrtyd Wells, Maiden Wells, Taff's Well, Walton**
**walis*	'walls, rampart, fortification' **Wallis, Alltwalis**
warth	E 'shore, strand' **Red Wharf Bay**
way	E 'way, road' **Broadway** (3), **Halfway** (2)
weard	OE 'watch, protection' **Gwesbyr**
wearpe	OE 'silted land' **Wepre**
well	see *wælle*
Welsh	E 'Welsh' **Welshpool, Welsh St Donat's**
west	OE 'west, western' **Gwesbyr, Haroldston, Haverfordwest, Robeston West, West Mouse, West Williamston**
-wg	terr.suff. '(land) belonging to, territory of' **Morgannwg**
white	see *hwīt*
wīc	OE 'farm (for a specialised purpose), dairy farm' **Oxwich, Redwick, Wick**
wild	E 'wild, tempestuous' **Wooltack Point**
wood	see *wudu*
worðign	OE 'enclosure' **Hawarden, Worthenbury**
wudu	OE 'wood' **Blackwood, Monkswood, Padeswood, Ridleywood, Wentwood, Woodstock**
-wy[1]	r.n. suff.; 'bending, turning' **Clyro, Elwy, Howey, Llugwy, Tawe, ?Teifi**
-wy[2]	terr.suff. '(land) belonging to, territory of' **Aran Fawddwy, Ardudwy, Deganwy, Dinas Mawddwy, Llanfair-yng-Nghornwy**
wyrm	OE 'snake' **Worm's Head**
-wys	adj. suff. 'characterised by' **Caerwys**

y, yr def.art. 'the'

Y -, Yr -, As Fawr, Bala, Bancyfelin, Banc-y-ffordd, Betws-y-coed, Blaen-y-coed, Bont-faen (2), Bontnewydd ar Wy, Bôn-y-maen, Borth-y-gest, Brynrhydyrarian, Bryn-y-maen, Bwlch-llan, Bwlchycibau, Bwlch-y-ddeufaen, Bwlch-y-ddâr, Bwlchyfadfa, Bwlch-y-ffridd, Bwlch-y-groes, Capel Coed-y-mynach, Cefncoedycymer, Cefnddwysarn, Cefn-y-groes, Cerrigydrudion, Cilybebyll, Cil-y-coed, Clas-ar-Wy, Clwt-y-bont, Cnicht, Coed-llai, Coed-y-Paen, Coed-yr-ynys, Coelbren, Croesyceiliog, Crug-y-bar, Crwys, Cwm-ffrwd, Cwm-y-glo, Cwm-yr-eglwys, Cwrt, Cymer, Cyrn y Brain, Dan-yr-ogof, Ddwyryd, Diffwys, Dinbych-y-pysgod, Dolgarrog, Dôl-y-bont, Domgae, Dre-felin, Drenewydd, Drenewydd Gelli-farch, Drenewydd yn Notais, Efail-isaf, Efenechdyd, Eglwys Fair y Mynydd, Eglwys Lwyd, Eglwys Newydd, Eglwys Newydd ar y Cefn, Eglwys y Drindod, Eifl, Faenor, Faerdre, Fali, Fan, Fan Fawr, Fan Gyhirych, Fan Hir, Fan Llia, Felindre (6), Felin-foel, Felin Ganol, Felin-gwm-uchaf, Felinheli, Felin Newydd, Fenai, Ferwig, Fflint, Ffos-y-ffin, Fochriw, Foel, Foel Dyrch, Foel Eryr, Foel Fras, Frenni Fawr, Friog, Fron, Froncysyllte, Fron-goch, Gaerwen, Gamallt, Ganllwyd, Garn, Garnant, Garndolbenmaen, Garn Fawr, Garreg, Gell, Gelli Aur, Gellifor, Gelli-gaer, Gelli Gandryll, Gellilydan, Gellïoedd, Gelli-wen, Gilfach, Gilfach-goch, Gilwern, Glais, Glan-rhyd, Glanyfferi, Glan-yr-afon, Glyder Fawr/Fach, Glyn-y-groes, Godre'r-graig, Goginan, Gors-las, Graigfechan, Groes, Groes-faen, Groeslon, Groes-lwyd, Gumfreston, Gurnos, Gwaelod-y-Garth, Gwernaffield, Gwernymynydd, Gyffin, Gyffylliog, Hendy, Hengastell, Hengoed, Heniarth, Heol-y-cyw, Llai, Llampeter Velfrey, Llanbadarn-y-garreg, Llanbedrycennin, Llanbedr-y-fro, Llanddeusant (2), Llanddewi'r-Cwm, Llanddewi Velfrey, Llandochau'r Bont-faen, Llandysilio-yn-Iâl, Llanelian-yn-Rhos, Llanfair-ar-y-bryn, Llanfihangel Genau'r-glyn, Llanfihangel Rhos-y-corn, Llanfihangel Tal-y-llyn,

Llanfihangel-y-Creuddyn, Llanfihangel-y-Pennant (2), Llanfihangel-y-pwll, Llanfihangel-y-traethau, Llangwyryfon, Llannerch-y-medd, Llan-saint, Llantwit Fardre, Llanybydder, Llan-y-cefn, Llanycil, Llan-y-crwys, Llan-y-pwll, Llan-y-tair-Mair, Llawr-y-glyn, Llwyn-y-bedw, Llwyn-y-groes, Llyn y Fan Fach/Fawr, Maendy, Maen y Bugail, Maerdy, Maesycrugiau, Maesycwmer, Maindee, Melin-y-coed, Melin-y-ddôl, Melin-y-wig, Migneint, Moelwyn, Moel y Gaer, Môt, Mwmbwls, Mynydd Bwlch-y-groes, Mynydd Du, Mynydd Pen-y-fâl, Mynydd Twr, Mynydd y Fflint, Nant-y-caws, Nantyderi, Nantyffyllon, Nant-y-glo, Nant-y-moch, Nant-y-moel, Nant-yr-eira, Onllwyn, Orsedd, Pant-y-dŵr, Pant-y-ffridd, Pantyffynnon, Parlwr Du, Penegoes, Penffordd, Pengenffordd, Penisa'r-waun, Penrherber, Penrhiw-ceibr, Pen-sarn (3), Pentrefelin (4), Pentre'r Eglwys, Pentre Tafarnyfedw, Pen-y-banc, Pen-y-bont, Pen-y-bont ar Ogwr, Pen-y-bont-fawr, Pen-y-cae (2), Pen-y-cae-mawr, Pen-y-clawdd, Penycoedcae, Pen-y-ffordd, Pen-y-garn, Penygarnedd, Penygarreg Reservoir, Pen-y-graig, Pen-y-groes (2), Pen-yr-heol, Pen-y-stryt, Pont-ar-Sais, Pont-rhyd-y-cyff, Pont-rhyd-y-fen, Pont-rhyd-y-groes, Pontrhypont, Pontybodkin, Pont-y-clun, Pontycymer, Pont-y-gwaith, Pontypool, Pontypridd, Porth-y-rhyd (2), Rachub, Redberth, Rhaeadr Ewynnol, Rhes-y-cae, Rhewl (2), Rhigos, Rhos, Rhos-maen, Rhos-meirch, Rhos-y-bol, Rhosygwaliau, Rhydcymerau, Rhydri, Rhydyclafdy, Rhydycroesau, Rhydyfelin, Rhyd-y-foel, Rhyd-y-fro, Rhyd-y-main, Rhyd-y-meirch, Rhyd-y-mwyn, Rhyd-yr-onnen, Rhyd-y-wrach, Rhyl, Roath, Rossett, Saint-y-brid, Stryt-yr-hwch, Tafarnygelyn, Talgarreg, Talgarth, Tal-y-bont (4), Tal-y-bont on Usk, Tal-y-cafn, Tal-y-fan, Talyllychau, Tal-y-sarn, Tan-y-bwlch, Tan-y-fron, Tanygrisiau, Tan-y-groes, Tonypandy, Tonyrefail, Trallwng, Trefnant, Trefyclo, Tregare, Tregarth, Tre-llech a'r Betws, Tre'r Ceiri, Tre'r-ddôl, Tre'r-llai, Tretŵr, Trevethin, Troed-y-rhiw, Trofarth, Trwyn y Fuwch, Trwyn y Gadair, Twynrodyn, Twyn-y-sheriff, Tŷ-nant,

Ty'n-y-cefn, Ty'n-y-ffridd, Tyn-y-groes, Waun, Waunarlwydd, Waunfawr (2), Wenallt, Wîg, Wyddfa, Wyddgrug, Ynysoedd y Moelrhoniaid, Ynys-y-bŵl, Ynys-y-meudwy, Ystalyfera

-ych adj. suff.
Crymych

-ydd[1] terr.suff. '(land) belonging to, territory of'
Eifionydd, Llyswyrny, Maelienydd, Meirionnydd, Senghennydd

-ydd[2] noun suff.
Dysynni

yn prep. 'in'
Betws-yn-Rhos, Caernarfon, Llanarmon-yn-Iâl, Llanfair-ym-Muallt, Llanfair-yng-Nghornwy, Llanfair-yn-Neubwll, Llanfihangel-yng-Ngheri, Llanfihangel-yng-Ngwynfa, Llanfihangel-yn-Nhywyn, Llanrhaeadr-ym-Mochnant, Llanrhaeadr-yng-Nghinmeirch, Llansanffraid-ym-Mechain, Llansanffraid-yn-Elfael, Llanymawddwy, Llanllŷr-yn-rhos, Llys-y-frân, Narberth, Nercwys, Y Drenewydd yn Notais, Llandrillo-yn-Rhos

-yn masc. dim.suff.
Abergwesyn, ?Berwyn, Cefn Berain, Cribyn, ?Gwastedyn, Login

ynys pl. *ynysoedd*; fem. 'island; river meadow; dry ground in marsh, raised area in wet ground; well-watered land'
Ynys-, Coed-yr-ynys, Llanynys, Skenfrith, Sketty, Skewen, Ystalyfera

ysbyty masc./fem. 'hospice, hospital; lodging house for pilgrims; almshouse'
Ysbyty Ifan, Ysbyty Ystwyth

#ysgeifiog adj. 'sloping'
Ysgeifiog

ysgor fem. 'fortress, stronghold, defence'
Gwaunysgor

ysgubor pl. *ysguboriau*; masc./fem. 'barn, granary, farm building'
Tonysguboriau

ysgwr pl. *ysgyr*; masc. 'stick, staff'
?Ysgir

ystrad	masc./fem. 'valley floor, plain, vale' **Ystrad-, Cwm Ystradllyn, Llanddewi Ystradenni**
ystum	masc./fem. 'bend, curve, meander, corner' **Llanystumdwy, Ystumtuen**
ystyllen	fem. 'shelf, ledge of rock' **Rhostyllen**

A

ABER Brec SN1021

'mouth of the river', ***aber***

Aberclydach 1745, *Aber* 1832

At the confluence of the rivers Clydach (which rises west of the village) and Caerfanell (which then runs into Tal-y-bont Reservoir).

ABERAERON Card SN4562

'mouth of (the river) Aeron', ***aber***, r.n. ***Aeron***

ad ostium Ayron 1184 (1285), *aber aeron* 15cent.

The river Aeron (*Aeron* 12cent. [c.1400], *Airon* 1184 [1285], *Aeron* 1536-9) rises on the moorland of Mynydd Bach above Bontnewydd where it is joined by Afon Ddu formerly *Aeron Ddu* (*ayron du* 1165-82, ***du*** 'black'). The r.n. is the goddess of battle (***aer*** 'battle' and a suff. ***-on*** denoting the divine or mythological association frequently found in r.ns). The L ***ostium*** translates ***aber*** with reference to the estuary itself. The town of Aberaeron derives its importance from the harbour created in 1807 when the breakwaters were built.

ABERAFAN, ABERAVON Glam SS7590

'mouth of (the river) Afan', ***aber***, r.n. ***Afan***

Aven 1208, *(Ecclesia de) Avene* 1291, *Abber[a]uyn* c.1400, *Aber Avon* 1536-9, *Aberavan* 1549, *Aber Afan* 1606

The river (*Auan, Auen* c.1150, *Avennae fluvius* c.1200, see Cwmafan) probably takes its name from the pers.n. Afan or Afen and gave its name to the medieval borough of Avon or Avan at the river mouth. This was later replaced by the fuller form Aberavon or Aberafan. The influence of the W ***afon*** 'river' and the E river Avon is evident from an early period (*ecclesia de Abbona* 1348). The adjoining 19cent. town which developed at Aberafan harbour was Port Talbot (q.v.).

ABERAMAN Glam SO0100

'mouth of (the river) Aman', ***aber***, r.n. ***Aman***

Aberaman 1623, *Aberamman* 1648-9

At the confluence of Aman and Cynon. For the r.n. see Ammanford.

ABERANGELL Mer SH8410

'mouth of (the river) Angell', ***aber***, r.n. ***Angell***

Aberangell 1454

In r.ns ***angell*** has a variety of meanings such as 'arm', 'leg' and 'talon', but can also mean 'appendage, tributary'. It also occurs in *Nant yr angell* 1608-9 Monm, *Nant-yr-angell* Mont. One imaginative interpretation is of two or three tributaries of Angell grasping the enclosed land.

The stream (*Angel* 1610) flows from near Esgair Angell (*Esgair Angell* 1627) and through Cwm Angell (*Come Angell* 1590) to join Afon Dyfi at Aberangell. The modern village probably developed in response to the needs of the Forestry Commission. A similar r.n. is Yrannell (which occurs, for example, in Brec, Caern, Carm, Denb, Pemb) with a different origin as a pers.n. Ar(i)annell, but forms for some of which have fallen in with Angell (such as Yrannell in Pemb as *Blaenyrangell* c.1830); there is no evidence here of Angell ever being called Ariannell.

ABERARAD Carm SN3140
'mouth of (the river) Arad', ***aber***, r.n. ***Arad***
Aberarard 1558, *Aber Arad* 1573, *Abarorarde* 1574, *Aberarad* 1629
At the confluence of the rivers Arad and Teifi. The r.n. is ***ar-*** 'to plough' and noun suff. ***-ad*** to describe the river's furrowing course, or even a reduced form of ***aradr*** 'plough'.

ABER-ARTH Card SN4763
'mouth of (the river) Arth', ***aber***, r.n. ***Arth***
ab ostio Arth 1184 (1285), *Aberarth* 1291, *Aber Arth* 1425, *Aberarth* 1513
The river rises in Pennant, Dyffryn Arth, and flows into Cardigan Bay at Aber-arth, which has always been a convenient port and, in the early 19cent., was a small shipbuilding centre. The r.n. falls into the category of rivers named after animals, in this case ***arth*** 'bear'.

ABERAVON see **ABERAFAN**

ABERBEEG, ABER-BIG Monm SO2102
'mouth of (the river) Big', ***aber***, r.n. ***Big***
Aberbyg 1659, *Aberbeek* 1705, *Pont-aberbyg* 1833
Near the confluence of the rivers Big and Ebwy. The r.n. (*Byg* 1625, *Cwmbyg* 1833) may be a pers.n. comparable with *Buga* in Brynbuga (q.v.).

ABER-BIG see **ABERBEEG**

ABERCANNAID Glam SO0503
'mouth of (the river) Cannaid', ***aber***, r.n. ***Cannaid***
Abercanaid 17cent., *Abernant Cannad* 1783, *Abercannaid* 1795, *Abercaned* 1814
At the confluence of the rivers Cannaid and Taf. The river rises at Blaencannaid (***blaen*** 'headwater'). The r.n. is ***cannaid*** 'bright, shining'.

ABER-CARN Monm ST2195
'mouth of (the river) Carn', ***aber***, r.n. ***Carn***
Habercarne 1535, *Abercarne* 1560, *Abercarn* 1677
The village n. is taken directly from the former Abercarn Ironworks

(*Abercarne Works* 1756) on the north side of the village but properly applies to the confluence of the river Carn (*Nant garn* 1631) and Ebwy near Cwm-carn (q.v.). The village actually occupies the site of *Aberguyddon* (1795 and still in use in 1874) at the confluence of Nant Gwyddon with Ebwy about a mile north of Cwm-carn. The r.n. refers to its location near a ***carn*** 'cairn'. Carn was also the name of a medieval chapel.

ABERCEGIR Mont SH8001

'mouth of (the river) Cegir', ***aber***, r.n. ***Cegir***

Aber y Ceccyr 1757, *Aber-cegir* 1837

At the confluence of the rivers Gwydol and Cegir (*Kegyr* 1570), probably *cegyr*, var. of ***cegid*** 'hemlock'. Only the 1757 form has the def.art. ***y***.

ABER-CRAF, ABERCRAVE Brec SN8112

'mouth of (the river) Craf', ***aber***, r.n. ***Craf***

Abercraven 1680, *Abercraf* 1690

The r.n. Craf no longer appears on maps, but may refer to an unnamed stream on the east side of the village next to Aber-craf farm. Craf is W ***craf*** 'garlic', a plant with medicinal properties and reputed to ward off the devil. Several streams are called Crafnant. Many later spellings with *-crave* represent the dial. pronunciation; cf. Aberdare and Aber-dâr.

ABERCRAVE see **ABER-CRAF**

ABER-CUCH Pemb SN2441

'mouth of (the river) Cuch', ***aber***, r.n. ***Cuch***

Aberkyche 1561, *Aberkeach* 1603, *Abercych* 1791

The river rises at *Blaen Kych* 1602 (***blaen*** 'headwater') and flows through the valley (***glyn***) known as *y glyn Kuch yn Emlyn* 12cent. and *Glynn Cuch* 13cent. The r.n. is probably ***cuwch*** var. ***cuch*** 'frown, grimace', possibly an epithet for someone who lived near the river.

ABERCYNFFIG see **ABERKENFIG**

ABERCYNON Glam ST0895

'mouth of (the river) Cynon', ***aber***, r.n. ***Cynon***

Abercynon 1893

At the confluence of the rivers Taf and Cynon (*Canan* 1253, *Kenon* 1536-9) which is a pers.n. Earlier described as *Navigation*, taken from the name of the railway station (now Abercynon South) opened by the Taff Vale Railway Co. 1840, referring to the *Navigation Counting House* (1797) next to the Glamorganshire Canal (opened 1792). The station's name was changed to Aberdare Junction after the construction of the railway up the Cynon valley branching from the main railway, but *Navigation* survived as the name of the village until 1893.

ABERCYWARCH Mer SH8615

'mouth of (the river) Cywarch', ***aber***, r.n. ***Cywarch***

Aber Cowarch 1624

The river (*Avon Cowarch* 1635) rises in Blaencywarch (*blaen cwm kowarch* 1570), flows through Cwm Cywarch (*Kwm Kowargh* 1532-3) and the area known as Cywarch (*Cowargh* 1561) and into Afon Dyfi at Abercywarch. The r.n. derives from ***cywarch*** (occasionally spelt ***cowarch*** and sometimes locally pronounced ***cŵarch***) 'hemp', the plant which must have characterised a section of the river or which was steeped in the river to extract the fibres used for making ropes and strong cloth.

ABERDÂR, ABERDARE Glam SO0002

'mouth of (the river) Dâr', ***aber***, r.n. ***Dâr***

Aberdar 1203, *Aberdaer* 1348, 1578, *Aberdare* 1528

The town is on the confluence of the rivers Cynon and Dâr. The r.n. is probably ***dâr*** 'oak' (although the el. found in ***cynddaredd*** 'rage' has also been proposed). The form Aberdare represents the dial. narrowing of the long vowel -â-.

ABERDARE see **ABERDÂR**

ABERDARON Caern SH1726

'mouth of (the river) Daron', ***aber***, r.n. ***Daron***

Aberdaron 1252, *Abindarun* 1254, *Aberdaron* 1258

The river Daron rises north of Rhoshirwaun to enter the sea at Aberdaron. Daron was believed to be the goddess of the oak-tree (***dâr*** 'oak' as in Aberdâr q.v.).

ABERDAUGLEDDAU see **MILFORD HAVEN**

ABERDESACH Caern SH4251

'mouth of (the stream and fort) Desach ', ***aber***, ***din***, tribal n. ***Desach***

Aberdaydesach 1626, *Aber Du Desach* 1709, *Aberdûdesach* 1782, *Abar di Desach* 1754, *Aber dudesach* 1770, *Aberdidesach* 1795, *Aberdesach* 1805, *Aberdindesach* 1810, *Aber-dusoch* 1838

In some of these forms, the el. preceding Desach is ***din*** 'fort' (despite the conflicting spellings and its disappearance in later usage). The location of the fort is probably the defensive enclosure on Y Foel a mile-and-a-half to the east, close to the source of Afon Desach. The r.n. appears to have been adopted from the Ir tribal n. Déissech 'members of the Déisi' who occupied the fort.

ABERDOVEY see **ABERDYFI**

ABERDYFI Mer SN6196

'mouth of (the river) Dyfi', ***aber***, r.n. ***Dyfi***

Aberdewi, Aberdiwy, 12cent., *aber dyfi* 14cent., *Aberdeui* 1536-9, *Aberdovi* 1653-4, *Aberdovy* 1690, *Aber Dyfi or Aberdovey* 1795, *Aberdyvi* 1796
The earliest documentary evidence refers to the estuary of river Dyfi (q.v.). In the 19cent. the town developed as a holiday resort. The form Aberdovey is an anglicized spelling now obsolescent.

ABEREDW Radn SO0847
'mouth of (the river) Edw', ***aber***, r.n. ***Edw***
Aberedo 1291, *Abereduwy* 1293, *Aberedwy* 1375
The river Edw(y) rises near Blaenedw farm (SO 146594) (***blaen*** 'source') and reaches the Wye just below Aberedw. The r.n. may be ***edwi*** 'shrink, dwindle, abate' perhaps referring to the river's flow in summer. There was a small castle here described as *Aberhedon Castel* 1536-9.

ABER-ERCH Caern SH3936
'mouth of (the river) Erch', ***aber***, r.n. ***Erch***
Abher 1254, *Aber* 1291, *Abererch* 1349, *Y bererch* 1441-50, *Eberch* 1495
The village of Aber-erch is now a mile from the sea, but up to the 16cent. the river Erch (***erch*** 'dappled, dark' or possibly a pers.n.) entered the sea directly at this point. The sand dunes of Morfa Abererch (***morfa*** 'sea marsh') and the drained land (along which the railway runs) send the river south-west into Pwllheli harbour. A common colloquial pronunciation is Y Berch where the medial syllable of Aber-erch has been lost and the initial vowel taken as the def.art. ***y***. The church was referred to as Llangawrda (*Abererch. ll. gowrda* c.1566) from its dedication to Cawrdaf.

ABER FALLS, RHAEADR ABER Caern SH670
'falls of Aber', E ***falls***, W ***rhaeadr***, p.n. ***Abergwyngregyn***
Rhaiadr Mawr 1814, *Cascade* 1841, *Rhaiadr Fawr* 1891, *Falls* 1898
A waterfall where Afon Goch becomes Afon Rhaeadr-fawr (*Afon-fawr* 1838) to flow through the village of Abergwyngregyn (q.v.) colloquially contracted as Aber. Recently the waterfall has taken the name of the village (in W and in E) since tourist access to the falls is principally through the village. The older alias Rhaeadr Fawr (***mawr*** 'big') is in contrast to the adjacent Rhaeadr Fach (*Rhaidr Fâch* 1891).

ABER-FAN Glam SO0700
'mouth of (the stream) Fan', ***aber***, r.n. ***Fan***
Teyr Aber-van 1536, *Tir Abervann* 1612, *Aber y van* 1623, *Aber-fan-fawr,* ~ *-fach* 1833, *Aberfan* 1898
The village n. is taken from two former farms distinguished by ***mawr*** 'big' and ***bach*** 'small' near the confluence of the stream Fan (***ban*** 'crest, height') with the river Taf. The first forms cited above have ***tir*** 'land, territory'. The industrial village developed near Perthigleision farm and *Perthigleision Pit* (1884).

ABERFFRAW Angl SH3568

'estuary of (the river) Ffraw', ***aber***, r.n. ***Ffraw***

Aberfrau c.1191, *aberffrav* c.1200, *Aberfraw* 1281, *Aberffraw* 1582-3

The river Ffraw (***ffraw*** 'brisk, lively, strong') flows from Llyn Coron (q.v.). The final diphthong -aw regularly becomes -o in Aberffro. The pronunciation and spelling Y Berffro is common, with the unaccented first syllable of Aberffro being interpreted as the def.art. ***y***. The commoner modern spelling, Aberffraw, preserves the r.n. but has led to the (regressive) pronunciation of 'Aber-ffraw' with final stress.

ABERFFRO see **ABERFFRAW**

ABER-FFRWD Card SN6878

'mouth of the waterfall stream', ***aber***, (***y***), ***ffrwd***

Aberiffrwd 1592, *Aberffrwd* 1684-5, *Aber y ffrwd* 1716,
Aber y Ffrwd 1803, *Aber' ffrwd* 1834

The stream now called Nant yr Aber or Ffrwd-ddu (*y Ffrwd Ddu* 1684/5) flows through a narrow valley into Afon Rheidol near Aber-ffrwd. ***ffrwd*** usually refers to a rapidly flowing stream as this is, but dialectally ***ffrwd*** is also used of a waterfall. Several such names are found in the area, and there is a considerable waterfall close to this stream's source, an association which is reinforced by the occasional form with the def.art. ***y***. Possibly Aber-(y)-ffrwd originally signified 'the stream flowing from the waterfall' before it was later associated with its confluence with Afon Rheidol.

ABERGARW Glam SS9184

'mouth of (the stream) Garw', ***aber***, r.n. ***Garw***

Abergarw 1631, *Abergarrow* 1754

A modern village near the confluence of Nant Garw with the river Ogwr (Ogmore). The r.n. is thought to be ***garw*** 'wild, rough' as in Nantgarw (q.v.) near Taff's Well. The river rises near Blaengarw (q.v.) and has a tributary Garw Fechan (*Blaen Garw Fechan* 1711, ***bechan*** 'small, lesser').

ABERGAVENNY, Y FENNI Monm SO2914

'mouth of (the river) Gafenni', ***aber***, r.n. ***Gafenni***

Gobannio(n) 4cent., *Bergaveni* 1103-4, *Abergevenni* c.1191,
Bergeni c.1327, *Evenni* c.1400, *(tref) gevenni* 15cent. (1556-64),
Gyveni 1569, *Y Fenni* 1778

Gobannio(n) was the location of a Roman fort meaning 'place by the (river) Gafenni' from *Gobannia* 'river of the blacksmiths' or 'river of the ironworks' (Br **gobann-* 'smith' and seen in W ***gof*** 'blacksmith') probably a reference to iron minerals and ironworking in this area. The town of Abergavenny developed at the confluence (***aber***) of the river Gafenni with the river Usk. Gefenni seems to be the more authentic form of the r.n. (*Gebenni, Geuenni* 1136-54) showing vowel affection of *Gobannio(n)* with -o-, -a- > -e-, -e-. Gafenni seems to be a var. of Gefenni with dissimilation of the first -e- > -a-. The W name for the town Y Fenni (*a thre Venni* 1455-85, *o Dref Fēni* 1606) derives from Efenni the lenited form of Gefenni with the unstressed initial syllable taken as the def.art. *y*. This was reinforced by association with the name of the area around the river (*Bro Venni* 1460-80, *Swydd Efenni* 1565-1616).

ABERGELE Denb SH9477

'mouth of (the river) Gele', ***aber***, r.n. ***Gele***

Opergelei 9cent., *Abergel'* 1254, *Abergele* 1257, *Abergeleu* 1310

The r.n. Gele (r. *Geley* 1460, *Gele* 1517-8) is a dial. form of ***gelau*** 'spear, blade, lance', one of a number of W r.ns describing the action of cutting through or piercing the land, such as Cleddau (q.v.) and Nodwydd (***nodwydd*** 'needle' Angl and Mont). It has also been suggested that these rivers are named because their waters flash brightly. Significantly, the river, which rises on the foot-hills south of the town, does not now flow into the sea to form an ***aber***, since it was diverted east across Morfa Rhuddlan into the river Clwyd as a result of the Rhuddlan Marsh Embankment Act 1794 and the building of the Holyhead-Chester railway (1845).

ABERGLASLYN, Afon Caern SH5942

'river of the estuary of the green (or blue) lake', ***afon, aber, glas, llyn***

Aberglasselyn 1338, *Aberglasslyn* 1432, *Aberglaslyn* 1578

The estuary of the river is now south-west of Porthmadog (q.v.) but the original ***aber*** was in the upper reaches of the estuary (*Morva Havod y Llyn* 1756, *havod y llyn* 1561-2, *Havod y llyn* 1612, *Hafodllyn* 1883, ***morfa, hafod***), an area reclaimed after the building of the Cob at Porthmadog. The lake Glaslyn (*Glesse Llinne, gleslin* 1536-9, *Glaslyn* 1838) is within the Snowdon massif, and the river Glaslyn flows through Llyn Llydaw (q.v.), Nant Gwynant (q.v.) and Beddgelert to the bridge of Pont Aberglaslyn (*Pont aberglaslyn* 1816). The original name of the lower part of the river was *Ferlas* (*ferlas* 13cent. [14cent.], ***ffêr*** 'strong, lively', ***glas***). Ynys Fer-las (*Ynys y ferlas* 1883, ***ynys***) is still the name of a hillock on the bank of the river.

ABERGORLECH Carm SN5833

'mouth of (the river) Gorlech', ***aber***, r.n. ***Gorlech***

Abergorluch 1411, *Abergorlewch* 1544, *Abergorlech* 1567, *abargorlech* 1741, *Abergorlech* 1831

At the confluence of Afon Gorlech (*Gorluch* 1411, *r. gorlech* 1541, *r.gorlych* 1589) and Afon Cothi. The r.n. is ***gorlech*** 'gritstone' characteristic of the river bed.

ABERGWAUN see **FISHGUARD**

ABERGWESYN Brec SN8552
'mouth of (the river) Gwesyn', ***aber***, r.n. ***Gwesyn***
Abergweffyn 1273 (16cent.), *Abergwessyn* 1344-9, *aber gwesyn* c.1566
At the confluence of the rivers Gwesyn and Irfon. The r.n. is probably ***gwas*** 'youth, young servant' and ***-yn***, perhaps in the sense of a minor river in contrast to the major river Irfon.

ABERGWIDOL Mont SH7902
'mouth of (the river) Gwydol', ***aber***, r.n. ***Gwydol***
Aber gwidol 1573, *Abergweidol* 1627, *Abergwidol* c.1633, (bridge) *Pont Aberguydol* 1640
The r.n. *Gnedall* [= *Guedall*], *Gwedall* 1578, also occurring in *Roswidaul* 1199 (***rhos***) and *mynyd Gwidawl* c.1222 (***mynydd***), may be a pers.n. Gwidol; some forms may have been influenced by ***gwydol*** 'wicked, corrupt'.

ABERGWILI Carm SN4321
'mouth of (the river) Gwili', ***aber***, r.n. ***Gwili***
Aber Gwyli 1022 (c.1400), *Aberguili* 1222 (14cent.), *Aberwilli* 1278, *Abergwyli* c.1300, *Abergwylly* 1331
Near the confluence of Gwili and Tywi. The r.n. Gwili (*Guili* 12cent. [c.1300], *Gwyly* 1400) may be connected with ***gŵyl*** 'kind, generous' and the r.n. suff. ***-i***.; the falling diphthong -ŵy- became a rising diphthong -wŷ- and then represented by -i-.

ABERGWYNFI Glam SS8996
'mouth of (the river) Gwynfi', ***aber***, r.n. ***Gwynfi***
Aber Gwyn Viewe 1570, *Abergwnfyw* 1601, *Aber-gwynfy* 1833
The r.n. is the pers.n. Gwynfyw. The modern form with -fi has probably been influenced by r.ns such as Llynfi. The village takes its name from a farm which lay near the Tunnel Hotel close to the confluence of Nant Gwynfi with the river Afan.

ABERGWYNGREGYN Caern SH6572
'estuary of white shells', ***aber***, ***gwyn***, ***cragen*** pl. ***cregyn***
Aber 1254, *Aberguynne Gregin*, *paroche Aber o. Llan Boduan* 1536-9, *Abergwyngregin* c.1700
The river, Afon Aber, enters the sea near a bank of shingle (a departure point for medieval and later ferries) a mile from the present village (frequently referred to as Aber) which was an important medieval settlement. A quarter-of-a-mile south of the village is the confluence (at Bont Newydd) of two rivers (Anafon and Afon Rhaeadr Fawr). Occasional references suppose the river to be *Gwyngregyn* (1811).

ABERGYNOLWYN Mer SH6706

'mouth of (the river) Gynolwyn', ***aber***, r.n. ***Gynolwyn***

Abergwen Olwyn 1592, *Abergwynlwyn* 1672, *Aber Gynolwyn* c.1700, *Abergarnolwyn* 1764, *Abergyrnolwyn* 1796

The earlier forms suggest a r.n. *Gwenolwyn* possibly with the el. ***gwennol*** 'a swallow, a swift' to denote the speed of the river. Later (inconsistent) forms suggest association with the pers.n. Gynolwyn seen in Bodynolwyn in Angl. The stream, the present Nant Gwernol, flows into Afon Dysynni near the village.

ABERHAFESB Mont SO0792

'mouth of (the river) Hafesb', ***aber***, r.n. ***Hafesb***

Aberafh' 1254, *Aberhauesp* 1330, *Aber Hafais* 15cent., *Aberhaves* 1577

The r.n. is *Hawes* 1578, *Hafhesb* 1764 and also appears in the names of two commotes in Cedewain called *Comm. Huchaues, Comm. Hisaues* 1536-9 'commote above (the river) Hafesb' (***uwch***) and ' below the (river) Hafesb' (***is***). The r.n. is ***haf*** 'summer' and ***hysb*** fem. ***hesb*** 'dry', with *Hafes* and *Haffes* as common vars. probably influenced by the fem. suff. ***-es*** (as in the river Haffes (*Haffes* 1744, 1819) Brec, a tributary of the river Tawe.

ABERHONDDU see **BRECON**

ABERHOSAN Mont SO8097

'mouth of (the river) Rhosan', ***aber***, r.n. ***Rhosan***

Aber Rhossan 1573, *Aber Rossan* 16cent.

The r.n. is ***rhos*** and a r.n. suff. ***-an*** 'river rising on a moor' or a dim.suff. 'little moor', both referring to its source on the ridge (***cefn***) Cefn Rhosan (*Keven Rhossan* 1573, *Cefn'r-hosan* 1837). Rhosan joins Nant Cymddu here to form Afon Carrog.

ABERKENFIG, ABERCYNFFIG Glam SS8983

'mouth of (the river) Cynffig', ***aber***, r.n. ***Cynffig***

Aberkenfyg 1590-1, *Aberkenfigg, Aberkinfigg* 1590-1, *Aber Cenfig* 1775

An industrial village which developed near the confluence of Nant Cynffig (now unnamed on OS maps) with the river Ogwr. The r.n. may be identical in meaning to the river Cynffig (see Kenfig) which lies only three miles west of Aberkenfig.

ABERLLEFENNI Mer SH7709

'mouth of (the river) Llefenni', ***aber***, r.n. ***Llefenni***

Lloyveny 1558-1603, *Llyveni* c.1700, *Aber Llyveni* 1600-20, *Aber Lluwyfeni* 1650, *Lhyveni* c.1700

The river rises in Waunllefenni, and flows through Cwm Llefenni, past Craig Hen-gae (probably the former *Kraig Lloyveny* 1558-1603) and into

Afon Dulas at Aberllefenni. The r.n. is ***llwyfen*** 'elm' and the adj. suff. ***-i*** or the pl. ***llwyfenni***. Llyfenni and Llefenni are vars. The village (and the area) took its name fron the local mansion (*Aberllyveni* 1795).

ABERLLYDAN see **BROAD HAVEN**

ABERLLYNFI see **THREE COCKS**

ABER-MAD Card SN6076

'mouth of (the river) Mad', ***aber***, r.n. ***Mad***

Aber maed 1540-77, *Abbermayte* 1558, *Aber Maed* 1569, *Abermadd, Abermayde* 1598-9, *Abermaed* 1610-1, *Aber Mâd* 1834

The river flows into Afon Ystwyth at Aber-mad. The earlier form of the r.n. was *Maed*, probably a pers.n. Maed which also appears in the historical forms of the nearby Rhos-mad (*Roysmayde* 1280-1306, *Rodmayed* 1618, *Rhod maede* 1632, *Rhos Mâd* 1834). The length of the later single vowel is indicated in *Aber Mâd* 1834 and *Afon Fâd* 1906.

ABERMAW see **BARMOUTH**

ABERMENAI see **MENAI STRAIT**

ABERMEURIG Card SN5656

'mouth of (the river) Meurig', ***aber***, r.n. ***Meurig***

Abermeirig 1692-8, *Abermeurig* 1735, *Abermeyrig* 1737, *Abermeyrick* 1760, *Abermoyrig* 1758

The river Meurig (*Meuric* 1184 [1285]) flows into Afon Aeron at Abermeurig and was probably a pers.n.

ABER-MIWL, ABERMULE Mont SO1694

'mouth of (the river) Miwl', ***aber***, r.n. ***Miwl***

Aberunhull c.1211-44 (1291), *Abrunol, Aber Miwl* 1273, *Aber Miwl* 1263 (c.1400), *Abermule* 1535, *Abermoyle* 1562, *Abermole alias Abermoile* 1568

Early forms show scribal confusion of -m- as -un-. The river flows into the Severn at this point. The r.n. is *Mule Brook* 1566-7, *Mule* 1610 of obscure meaning. It is unlikely to be ***moel*** 'bald' though that seems to have influenced the forms with *-moyle* and *-moile*. Forms with *-mule* probably arose through association with E ***mule***.

ABERMO see **BARMOUTH**

ABERMULE see **ABER-MIWL**

ABER-NAINT, ABERNANT Mont SJ1221

'mouth of streams', ***aber, nant*** pl. ***naint***

Abernaint 1658, *Abernant* 1837, *Aber-naint* 1891

The name is taken from a farm located near the point where Nant y Clawdd and an unnamed tributary flow into Nant Ffyllon.

ABER-NANT Carm SN3423

'mouths of the stream', ***aber*** pl. ***ebyr, nant***

Hebernat 1264, *Obernaund* 1266, *Ebernant* 1290, *Ab'nant* 1535, *ebyr nant* c.1566

Three small streams meet near the hamlet. The unusual pl. form has been replaced by the sing. ***aber***.

ABEROGWR see **OGMORE-BY-SEA**

ABERPENNAR see **MOUNTAIN ASH**

ABER-PORTH Card SN2651

'estuary in the bay', ***aber, porth***

Porthotny 1180-97 (1324), *Porth Hodni* c.1200, *Porthodeni* 1241, *Aberporth* 1254, *aber porth* c.1566

The ***porth*** is the bay or haven into which the river Howni, Hoddni or Hoddnant (*Hotnant* 1180-97 [1324]) flows. Hoddni (found also in Aberhonddu) is ***hawdd*** originally 'quiet or pleasant', MnW 'easy' (with -d- for -dd- in several forms).

ABERRIW see **BERRIEW**

ABER-SOCH Caern SH3128

'mouth of (the river) Soch', ***aber***, r.n. ***Soch***

Abersogh 1350-1, *Avon Soch* 1598

The river (*Avon Soch* 1598) follows a meandering route from the middle of the Llŷn Peninsula, flowing west of Carn Fadrun to enter the sea at Aber-soch. The r.n. Soch is considered to be Ir ***socc*** (cf. the river Suck in Connacht) related to W ***hwch*** 'sow', and in the category of rivers named after animals that burrow through the land (such as Banw, Ogwen, Aman, Hwch and Twrch). The Ir connection in the peninsula is apparent in a number of p.ns including Llŷn (q.v.).

ABERSYCHAN Monm SO2603

'mouth of (the stream) Sychan', ***aber***, r.n. ***Sychan***

Abersechan 1614-15, *Abersychan* 1634

The stream (*Sychan* 1616) joins Afon Llwyd at Abersychan where the industrial village developed in the 19cent. The r.n. is ***sych*** 'dry' and the dim.suff. ***-an*** probably suggesting a river which dried up in summer, disappearing underground through its limestone bed.

ABERTAWE see **SWANSEA**

ABERTEIFI see **CARDIGAN**

ABERTELERI see **ABERTYLERI**

ABERTILLERY see **ABERTYLERI**

ABERTRIDWR Mont SJ0319
'confluence of three streams', ***aber*, *tri*, *dŵr***
Abertridwr 1946
Previously *New Inn* 1831, *Dafarn Newydd* 1832-3, *Dafarn-newydd* 1891, this modern name is identical with Abertridwr Glam (*Abertreedwr* 1708, *Abertridwr* 1833). It lies near the junction of the rivers Marchnant, Efyrnwy and with a very small stream on the south-east side of the village which rises on Boncyn Celyn.

ABERTYLERI, ABERTELERI, ABERTILLERY Monm SO2104
'mouth of (the brook) Teleri', ***aber***, r.n. ***Teleri***
Aber-Tilery 1779, *Abertillery* 1856
Located where Tyleri joins the river Ebwy Fach. The r.n. is *Teleri* 1332, from a pers.n. Teleri (***ty-*, *Eleri***) and also recorded in the name of a former forest Glyn Tyleri (*Glenteler* 1257, ***glyn***) probably referring in the valley now called Cwm Tillery (*Cwm Tilery* c.1790, *Cwm Telerau* c.1800, ***cwm***).

ABERTYSWG Monm SO1305
'mouth of (the river) Tyswg', ***aber***, r.n. ***Tyswg***
Abertowsowe 1570, *Aber Towssoge* 1583, *Abertwssog* 1630
At the confluence of the rivers Tyswg and Rhymni. The r.n. is also found in *Blaen nant tussocke* 1631 (***blaen*, *nant***). The earlier form seems to have been ***Tywysog*** 'prince, leader' but it is unclear whether it refers to an actual prince or was a pers.n.

ABERYSTWYTH Card SN5881
'mouth of (the river) Ystwyth', ***aber***, r.n. ***Ystwyth***
Aberescud c.1194, *Aber Ystwyth* 1166 (c.1400),
aber Ystwyth 1206 (c.1400), *Aberestuuth* 1232-3, *aber ystwyth* c.1400
The original Norman castle was built in 1110 at the old estuary of the river Ystwyth (q.v.) near Rhydfelin about a mile-and-a-half south of the modern town. In 1211 a new castle was built, possibly at Plas Crug near the estuary of the river Rheidol (probably on the site of an earlier castle (*Aber Redival* 1164 [late 13cent.], *Aber Reidawl* 1164 [c.1400]) and the older name was transferred to it and ultimately to the present castle (constructed in 1277) and its adjoining borough. As a p.n.

Aberystwyth, however, did not become the fixed name until the late 14cent., alternating with Llanbadarn Fawr (q.v.).

ACRE-FAIR Denb SJ2743

'Mary's acres', ***acer*** pl. ***acrau*** dial. var. ***acre***, pers.n. ***Mair***

Yr Acrefair 1795, *Acre-fair* 1838

The tithes from these fields were for the support of the church of St Mary at Ruabon, the mother church of a very large parish. The dial. pl. ***acre*** was reinforced by the supposition that it was the E sing. ***acre***. Cf. Talacre.

ACSTYN see **AXTON**

ADFA, YR Mont SJ0601

'the exit path, outrake', ***yr***, ***gadfa***

Adfa 1811, *yr Adfa* 1818

A ***gadfa*** was an area in which animals were released from the confines of a farm or enclosure. The village is near an old route, possibly a drovers' road, running west from Llanwyddelan.

AERON, Afon see **ABERAERON**

AFON-WEN Flints SJ1371

'white river', ***afon***, ***gwyn*** fem. ***gwen***

Avon wen 1768-9, *Afonwen* 1780, *Avon Wen* 1796, *Yr Afon-wen* 1838, *Afon-wen* 1878

The hamlet of Afon-wen takes its name from the river Afon Wen which flows into Afon Chwiler (Wheeler) near Caerwys. An earlier name for the river was Afon Galchog (*Kalchawk* 1297, *Calchok* 1309, *Calghok* 1357, *Avon Galchog* c.1700), with ***calchog*** 'containing lime', a reference to limestone quarries, the demise of which probably caused the substitution of Afon-wen which was directly associated with the hamlet. It has been claimed that this river, under yet another name, was the river from which Caerwys (q.v.) took its name.

ALAW, Afon, Llyn Angl SH3987, SH3483

'water lily river, lake', ***afon***, ***llyn***, ***alaw***

llynn alaw 14cent., *Avon Alaw* 1536-9

The valley associated with the upper reaches of river Alaw and the surrounding Cors-y-bol (*Cors y Bol* 1818, ***cors*** 'bog', and see Rhos-y-bol) were submerged in 1966 to create Angl's largest reservoir. The river becomes tidal near Valley and in medieval literature was frequently called *Aberalaw* (*Aboralew* 1291, *Aberhalowe* 1294, *Aberalaw* 1562, ***aber*** 'estuary') and *Aber Glaslyn* (*Aber Glaslyn, blew poole* 1536-9, *y glaslyn* 1549, ***glas*** 'blue, green').

ALED, Afon Denb SH9260-9567

'winding (river)', ***afon***, ****al***, suff. ***-ed***

Alet 1527, *Aled* 1578, *Alett* 1589

The river's source is Llyn Aled (*Llin Aleth* 1536-9, *Llynaled* 1645, *Llyn Alet* 1777, *Llyn Aled* 1839), adjacent to Llyn Alwen, but flowing north through Aled Isaf Reservoir and Dyffryn Aled (*Dyffrin Aled* 1656, ***dyffryn*** 'valley') to join the river Elwy. For the significance of ****al***, see Alwen and Alun. However, Aled was also a pers.n. in Denb (such as *Allet* 1334, *Alet* 1466) suggesting the r.n. is much older than hitherto recorded or that the pers.n. was transferred to the river which is less likely given the incidence of ****al*** as a river el. The r.n. also became a district name.

ALLINGTON see **TREFALUN**

ALLT-MAWR Brec SO0746

'big wooded slope', ***(g)allt***, ***mawr***

gallt-mawr c.1566, *Alltmawr* 1615

gallt or ***allt*** is usually fem. but the name is appropriate to the location above the Wye. Cf. nearby Henallt.

ALLT MELYD see **MELIDEN**

ALLTWALIS Carm SN4431

'wooded slope near ?walls', ***allt***, ?****walis***

Allt dwalais 1624, *Allt y wallis* 1765, *Allt Wallis* 1831, *Alltwalis* 1875

A name of uncertain and conflicting interpretations. The village takes its name from a farm. The closest comparison is Wallis Pemb (q.v.) which is ME ***walles*** 'walls, rampart' adopted into W as ****walis***. The existence of such a cymricized form is borne out by its late (post ME) appearance in several separate sites in Pemb and Carm. The hilly area around the original farm and the village is *Mynydd Gall Walis* 1754 and *Glyn-Wallis* 1891 (***glyn***) and ****walis*** here may refer to a medieval settlement near the head of Nant Alltwalis. There is also a Glyn Wallis (*Glyn Walis* 1725, ***glyn***) at Llanedi Carm, a Clun Walis at Gwernogle Carm and perhaps a field name *Parc y Wallis* 1753 at St Clears Carm. The prevalence of the el. elsewhere eliminates an unidentified person and an unrecorded r.n. Dwalais (with els ***dywal*** 'fierce, furious', cf. Tafolwern and the river Tyweli Carm and ***glais*** 'brook'). The 1624 form can be explained as ***allt*** > colloquial *alld* with -d- transferred scribally to *dwalais*.

ALLT-WEN, YR Glam SN7203

'the white wooded-slope', ***yr***, ***(g)allt***, ***gwyn*** fem. ***gwen***

Alltewen 1493, *Yr Allt Wen* 1610, *Gallt-wen* 1729

The village is named from its location on hill-slopes above the river Tawe. Cf. Wenallt, (***gwen***, ***(g)allt*** 'the white hill') and Y Wenallt near

Cardiff which is named after the thorn blossom, still in evidence, and Thornhill for virtually the same area.

ALLTYBLACA Card SN5245

?'hill of the plagues', ***allt, y***, ?***plag*** pl. ***plagau***

gallt y Placca 1681, *Allt y placa* 1760, *Alltyblacka* 1767, *Allt y Placca* 1803, *Allt-y-placa* 1834, *Alltyblacka* 1843

The final el. is problematic. The name of a smallholding (*ddydyn pris blackey* 1550, ***tyddyn, pris*** 'price. rent') may be relevant if *blackey* could be shown to be the name of a coin. If it is ***plaga(u)***, the plague, pestilence or affliction need not have been medical. The unvoiced var. ***placa*** is not recorded elsewhere and a suggestion that it may be a var. of ***plwca*** 'dirt, mud, mire, clay' is not convincing although it could have been influenced by ***llaca*** 'mud, mire'. The later -blaca development is influenced by ***blac*** 'black'.

ALUN, Afon Denb/Flints SJ1950-3756

'meandering one', ***afon***, Br pers.n. ***Alaunos***

Aluni (fluvius) c.1191, *Alun* 1337, *Alyn* 1478-9, *Alen* 1489, *Allyn* 1637, *Allen* 1645, *Alin* 1672, *Alen, Alyn* c.1700

The r.n. (as *Alauna*) also occurs in Glam, twice in Pemb and is related to r.ns in Scotland as Allan (several) and in England as Aln and Allen (Northumberland), Alne (NYorkshire), and Ellen (Cumberland). *Alaunos* is traditionally a Celtic god corresponding to Mercury, but the precise significance of the river name *Alauna* is unclear, perhaps 'flowing' but in Wales meandering, wandering characteristics have been ascribed to the rivers. For the possibility that it gave rise to an el. ****al*** 'wandering' see Alwen and Aled. This river rises in Cyrn-y-brain north of Llangollen, following a circuitous route, passing Cilcain where it disappears in dry weather into the limestone river bed at Hesb Alun (*Hespalen* 1536-9, *hesp Alyn* c.1700, ***hysb*** fem. ***hesb*** 'dry'), Ystrad Alun (*Stradalun* 1327-8, *Ystrad Alun* c.1435-70, *Ystrat alun* c.1450, ***ystrad*** 'wide, shallow valley, river-meadow') and into the Dee south of Holt. The form *Alyn* (which probably developed by analogy with other Flints p.ns such as Mostyn, Prestatyn and Sychdyn) has had some prominence, partly due to its appearance on maps and partly because of its adoption as the name of (post 1974) unitary authorities of Alyn and Deeside and (in a derived blend) Delyn.

ALWEN, Afon, Llyn, Reservoir Denb SH9056-SJ0343

'white wandering (river)', ***afon, llyn***, ****al, gwyn*** fem. ***gwen***

The river (*Alwen* 1425) flows from Llyn Alwen (*llynalwen* 13cent. [14cent.], *Lhyn Alwen* c.1700), into the Alwen reservoir, past Pont ar Alwen (*Pont ar Alwen* c.1700) and then follows a long course to join the

Dee at Aberalwen (*Aberalwen* 1277, *Aber Alwen* c.1700). Afon (and Llyn) Alwen are adjacent to Afon (and Llyn) Aled (q.v.), which suggests that ***al*** was once a name for a river in this area though its precise significance can only be deduced from other r.ns such as Alun (q.v.).

AMBLESTON, TREAMLOD Pemb SN0025

'Amelot's farm', pers.n. ***Amelot***, OE ***tūn***, W ***tref***

Villa Amenols, Villa Amlot ?1175-6 (16cent.),
ecclesiam de Almenolfestuna 1176-98 (17cent.), *Amleston* 1230,
Amelotiston 1325, *tre amlod* c.1566

The first documentary form has L ***villa*** conventionally translating OE ***tūn***, as indeed the later cymricization shows the substitution of W ***tref*** for ***tūn*** and an adaptation of the pers.n. *Amelot* has been explained as a double dim. of OF Amé, perhaps the name of an AN settler (cf. a *Thomas Amblott* 1634) but the *Amenols* and the first part of *Almenolfestuna* suggests a slightly different name.

AMLWCH Angl SH4493

'around the inlet', ***am***, ***llwch***

Anulc 1254, *Hamloth* 1291, *Amelogh* 1352, *Amloch* 1547,
Amlough 1639-40

The ***llwch*** was probably the creek which later became the harbour of Porth Amlwch (*Porth Amlwch* 1763). It has been argued that the alternative meaning of ***llwch*** 'pool, mud, swamp' is relevant here, probably referring to the area near the present church, formerly swampy and now drained.

AMMANFORD, RHYDAMAN Carm SN6212

'ford on (the river) Aman', r.n. ***Aman***, E ***ford***, W ***rhyd***

Ammanford 1880, *Rhydaman* 1890

Formerly known as *Cross Inn* (1807) from a tavern on the road between Swansea and Llandeilo. The town developed as a consequence of the coal industry in the late 19cent. and the name Ammanford was formally adopted in 1880 with reference to its location near a ford over the river Aman (*ammen* 1222, *Amman* 1538, the *-mm-* of which appears to have survived in Ammanford) possibly to avoid confusion with other places called Cross Inn particularly one in Carm. Although Rhydaman was in use from 1890 it was not widely adopted until after 1930. The r.n., probably *Aman(a)w* in its original form, is a var. of ***banw*** 'pig' or 'piglet', in the category of r.ns describing rivers which burrow and root their way through the ground.

AMROTH Pemb SN1607

'near (the river) Rhath', ***am***, r.n. ***Rhath***

Amrath c.1145, *Ambrud* 1176-98 (16cent.), *Amerath* 1330, *Amroth* 1513

The river is also recorded in *glann rath* c.1145 (***glan*** 'bank of a stream'), the lost name of the stream entering Carmarthen Bay. The r.n. also occurs in Coedrath and other p.ns in this area, and is probably ***rhath*** 'fort', a reference to the fort near the church *(Lanrath, Lannrath, ecclesia Radh* c.1145).

ANGLE Pemb SM8602

'(land in) the angle, nook', ME ***angle***

(*de*) *Angulo* 1291, *le Angle* 1272-1307, *le Nangle, Angle* 1325, *nangel* c.1566

The name refers either to the bay or to the headland. The el. ***angle*** also occurs in *Goldsmethes angle* 1362, now lost, thought to have been located in Loveston or Carew Pemb. A suggested alternative derivation is ON ***ǫngull*** 'fish-hook', again a topographic allusion. Forms such as *Nangle* derive from ME ***atten angle*** 'at the angle'; cf. Narberth Pemb and Nash Glam.

ANGLESEY, YNYS MÔN Angl SH3994-4461, 2882-6581

'island of ?Mon-', 'island of Ǫngull', ON pers.n. ***Ǫngull***, ON ***ey***, W ***ynys***, ?***Mon-***

Mona 1cent.BC, 1cent. AD, *Mōνα* 2cent., *ynys uon* 815, *Anglesege* 1098, *Anglorum insula* 12cent., *Ongulsey* 13cent., *Angleseye* 1248, *Angliseie, Angliseye* 1304-5, *Engleseye* 1353

Wales's large northern island. The older name is consistently Môn and (in its latinized documentary form) Mona but its origin defies satisfactory interpretation. In addition to confusion with the Isle of Man, attempts have been made to link what is probably a pre-Celtic root with a Br ****men-*** and W ***myn-*** (as in ***mynydd*** 'mountain'), supposedly 'high, prominent island' with reference to the landmark of Mynydd Twr or Holyhead Mountain (q.v.). Mona has survived in antiquarian and commercial usage. The ON name (which is first recorded in a Norse text) can be ascribed to Scandinavian coastal forays whose names transferred to the general stock of maritime names. The identity of *Ǫngull* is unknown. The form of the name has long been influenced by association with Angles.

ARAN BENLLYN Mer SH8624

'little ridge in Penllyn', ***âr***, dim.suff. ***-an***, p.n. ***Penllyn***

Aran-benllyn 1686, *Aren Benllyn* 1722, *Aren Bennllyn* 1819, *Aran Benllyn* 1838

A ridge in the commote of Penllyn (*penllin* 1191, *Penllyn* 1315, ***pen***, ***llyn*** 'end of the lake' [Llyn Tegid q.v.]). See also Aran Fawddwy and Eryri.

ARAN FAWDDWY Mer SH8521

'little ridge in Mawddwy', ***âr***, dim.suff. ***-an***, p.n. ***Mawddwy***

yr arann 1599, *Aren Voudhwy* 1722, *Aren Mawddwy* 1796, *Arran Fowddy* 1795, *Aren Mowddwy* 1819, *Aran mouddwy* 1839

The higher of two distinctive adjoining ridges called Aran (the other being Aran Benllyn q.v.) located in the commote of Mawddwy (see Dinas Mawddwy). The 1599 form (with ***yr*** 'the') may well indicate both ridges being seen as one mountain called *Yr Aran;* there may be another reference to it in *Raranuawr hill* 1645 (***mawr*** 'big'). There are several mountains called (Yr) Aran and Aren(n)ig (dim.suff. ***-ig***), as well as the related 'ridges' of Eryri (q.v.).

ARBERTH see **NARBERTH**

ARDDLEEN, YR ARDD-LIN Mont SJ2615

'the flax garden', ***yr, gardd, llin***

yr ardd lin 1569, *Arthleen* 1688, *Gardd-llîn or Arleen* 1836

Flax, used in the manufacture of linen, was formerly grown extensively in the Severn valley.

ARDD-LIN, YR see **ARDDLEEN**

ARFON see **CAERNARFON**

ARGOED Monm ST1799

'woodland', ***argoed***

Argoyd 1476, *Argoed* 1653, *Argoed Vawr* 1756

The name of several farms in a former wooded area near the river Sirhywi.

ARTHOG Mer SH6414

'(place near the river) Arthog', r.n. ***Arthog***

Arthog 1821

The village takes its name from an older chapel-of ease Capel Arthog. On the river Arthog, a saint's name, are a pool (*Pull Arthoge* 1592, *Pullarthog* 1748) at the foot of the waterfall east of Arthog, and a mill (*Melin Pwll arthog* 1592, ***melin, pwll***).

ARTRO, Afon Mer SH6230-5723

'river of Artro', ***afon***, pers.n. ****Arthro***

Arthro c.1191, *Artro Fawr* 14cent., *Artro* 1536-9

The river rises in Llyn Cwm Bychan, flows past Llanaber and into the sea between Mochras and Llandanwg. It formerly divided the cantref of Dyffryn Ardudwy (q.v.) into Uwch Artro and Is Artro. The earliest form suggests an unrecorded **Arthro*, one of several pers.ns with the el. ***arth*** 'bear', rather than tentative attempts to see it as 'winding river' (***ar*** 'on', ***tro*** 'bend'). *Artro Fawr* probably distinguished it from a smaller tributary which joined it at Aberartro.

AS FAWR, YR see **MONKNASH**

AXTON, ACSTYN Flints SJ1080

'ash-farm', ON ***askr***, OE ***tūn***

Asketone 1086, *Axton* 1242, *Agyston* 1291-3, *Axtyn* 1569,
Axton, Actston, Actstyn c.1700

Another Scandinavian coastal name is Point of Ayr (q.v.) three-and-a-half miles away. A cymricized Axtyn or Acstyn has had some currency following the pattern of Prestatyn and Mostyn a few miles away.

B

BABEL Carm SN8335
biblical chapel n.
Babel 1891
The name of the Congregational chapel established near farms Beili-bedw (*Beilibedw* 1819) and Beili-helyg (1891) (***beili, bedw, helyg***).

BABELL Flints SJ1573
biblical chapel n.
'(the) tabernacle, tent', (*y*), ***pabell***
Pabell 1838, *Babell* 1878
The name of the Calvinistic Methodist chapel erected c.1819. Pabell, Y Babell, is an uncommon chapel name.

BAE ABERTEIFI, BAE CEREDIGION see **CARDIGAN BAY**

BAE COLWYN see **COLWYN BAY**

BAE PENRHYN see **PENRHYN BAY**

BAGILLT Flints SJ2275
'Bacca's clearing or pasture', pers.n. ***Bacca***, OE ***lēah*** 'clearing, pasture'
Bachelie 1086, *Backelegh* 1325, *Bakele* 1408, *Bacley* 1444, *Bagyllt* 1306, *Bagild* 1368, *Bagill* 1682, *Bagilht* c.1700, *Backley alias Bagillt* 1577, *Backley or Bagillt* 1624
The identity of Bacca is unknown but he was probably one of the Mercian settlers on the Flints Dee coast. The later history of the p.n. reveals two parallel developments. One was the regular E development to *Backley* which did not survive. The other was the cymricized development to Bagillt in which E stress on the initial syllable was treated as W penultimate stress resulting in a loss of the last syllable and subsequent change of -l- to -ll- (cf. E ***mackerel*** and ***riddle*** as W ***macrell*** and ***rhidyll***) and then to -llt (cf. ***bwyall*** as dial. ***bwyallt*** 'axe'). This phonological development features in several Flints p.ns such as Gwersyllt (q.v.), *Hendre Figill* as Hendre Figillt (see Hendre), and Coleshill as *Cwnsyllt*.

BAGLAN Glam SS7592
'(place at the church of) Baglan', pers.n. ***Baglan***
Bagalan 1186-99, *Bagelan* 1199, *Baglan* c.1262
The now disused church at Baglan (which stands in the churchyard of the modern St Catherine's church) was dedicated to Baglan. There is no record of a 'Llanfaglan' (as in Llanfaglan, Caern). There are other places in Wales which simply preserve a saint's name, such as Ceidio and Gwytherin.

BALA, Y Mer SH9236

'isthmus, route between two lakes or areas of wet ground', ***bala***

bala c.1191, *Bala* 1278-82, *la Bala* 1331, *y bala* 14cent., *the Bala* 1482, (*o*) *vala Lhyn Tegid c.* 1700

Traditionally ***bala*** has been defined as an 'outlet (from a lake)'. However, it is evident that the ***bala*** sites are all between two lakes or between a lake and potentially (or formerly) very wet ground, both situations requiring a specific crossing point or route. Here, the river Dee from Llyn Tegid (*Thlintegit* 1285) and Afon Tryweryn (q.v.) flow into extensive wetlands east of Bala, which all major north-south routes traverse via the dry ground of Bala. The consistent use of the def.art. (in W, E and F) in the historical forms reinforces the view that the ***bala*** was a recognizable topographic feature. The later sense of 'outlet' is probably a semantic shift to the actual river which flowed from the lake at that point.

BALA LAKE see **LLYN TEGID**

BANCFFOSFELEN Carm SN4911

'hill of the yellow ditch', ***banc, ffos, melyn*** fem. ***melen***

Bank ffoesfelen 1861, *Banc-ffos-felin* 1891, *Bankffosfelen* 1903

The 1861 document also refers to a house or cottage called *Ffoesfelen*, which seems to have been characterised by a stream or gutter which was muddy. Nearby is Trallwm; cf. Trallwng. The village developed around crossroads on a hill on the Pontyberem-Carmarthen road. The 1891 form interprets it as ***melin*** 'mill'.

BANCYFELIN Carm SN3218

'the mill bank', ***banc, y, melin***

Bankyfelin 1767-8, *Banc-y-felin* 1831

Located on the slopes of a low hill above Afon Cywyn. The village had a woollen mill and a corn mill in 1891.

BANC-Y-FFORDD Carm SN4037

'the road bank', ***banc, y, ffordd***

Banc-y-ffynnon 1831, *Bank* 1875, *Banc-y-ffordd* 1947

The modern name has apparently replaced an older p.n. meaning 'the well bank' (***ffynnon***). Llwynffynnon (*Llwynffynnon issa, ucha* 1811, ***llwyn***) is about a mile to the north. The road runs between Llanpumsaint and Llandysul.

BANGOR Caern SH5771

'wattle-fence enclosure', ***bangor***

Benchoer 634 (9cent.), *Bangor* c.1191

Bangor is a common word for an ecclesiastical or secular enclosure protected by a wattled fence strengthened by a distinctive plaited top called a ***bangor***, and is still an agricultural term. There was a monastic site at Bangor. There is a Bangor in Brittany, in Ulster and in Flints.

BANGOR IS-COED, BANGOR-ON-DEE Flints SJ3945
'wattle-fence enclosure below the trees', ***bangor, is, (y), coed***
Bancor, Bancornaburg 8cent., *Bankerbur* 1270, *Bangor* 1277-8, *Bonkerbury* 1278-81, *Bankeburw* 1291, *Bangor* 1309, *Bangor monach'* 1607, *Bangor otherwise Bangor Monachorum* 1677, *Bangor monachorum vulgo Bangor is-y-Koed* c.1700
For the meaning and frequency of ***bangor*** see Bangor. The monastery is said to have been founded by Deiniol and the monks to have been massacred in 615 by Æthelfrith of Northumbria. Before very long, it had been destroyed completely. The *Bancornaburg, Bankerbur, Bonkerbury* and *Bankeburw* forms contain OE ***burh, byrig*** which usually means 'stronghold' but in this case can be taken to signify an enclosure for the inhabitants of a small settlement which grew up around the monastery; the *-na* probably represents a gen. pl. ***-ena***. *Bancornaburg* therefore means 'the protected enclosure of the people of Bangor'. How much local currency such a form had is difficult to judge. *Bangor monachorum* 'Bangor of the monks' may also have existed primarily in literary, ecclesiastical or antiquarian usage. Bangor's location 'lower than' (***is***) trees to the south-east seems to have been later adopted as a parish name in the form Is-coed. The very recent adoption -on-Dee reinforces the distinction between it and Bangor in Caern and locates the village on the east bank of the river Dee (q.v.).

BANGOR-ON-DEE see **BANGOR IS-COED**

BANGOR TEIFI Card SN3840
'wattle-fence enclosure on river Teifi', ***bangor***, r.n. ***Teifi***
bangor esgor c.1170 (c.1400), *Bangor* 1326, *Bangor ar Deifi* 1869, *Bangor Teifi* 1950
See Bangor. The land belonged to the bishop (***esgob***) of St David's and the church is dedicated to that saint. The reference to its location beside the river Teifi was a later addition to distinguish it from other Bangor sites.

BANNAU BRYCHEINIOG see **BRECON BEACONS**

BANW, Afon Mont SH9612-SJ1207
'young pig (river)', ***afon, banw***
Banw 1574, *Banwy* 1796
Several rivers are called Banw, including Aman (see Rhydaman) and

Ogwen (q.v.) to describe a furrowing course. The form Banwy found commonly on maps is influenced by the popular notion that there was a generic suff. *-***gwy*** denoting a river (cf. Wye) and possibly by analogy with Efyrnwy. From Glanbanw Bridge some maps call the river *Banw* or *Einion*, a form derived from Llanfair Caereinion (q.v.).

BARDSEY, YNYS ENLLI Caern SH1221

'strong current', 'Barðr's island', ***ynys***, ***en-***, ***llif***, ON pers.n. ***Barðr***, ON ***ey***
insula Enli 1154-75,
insula Enthli kambrice vocatur, et lingua Saxonica Berdeseie c.1191,
Bardesey 1277, *Bardsey* 1315, *Enisenthle* 1536-9,
Ynis-Enlli or Bardsey-Island 1795, *Ynys Enlli or Bardsey Island* 1840
The intensive pref. ***an-*** or ***en-*** describes the particularly strong current (***llif*** with loss of final -f) in Bardsey Sound (*Bardsey Sound* 1805) or Swnt Enlli (*swnd enlhi* c.1700, ***swnt*** 'sound') between the island and the mainland. The island has long been venerated as an ecclesiastical settlement and place of pilgrimage. Although the identity of *Barðr* is unknown, the two ON els are additional evidence of Scandinavian contact in the coastal toponyms of Wales. Modern maps frequently add the tautologous Island (as in Isle of Anglesey); in fact, national and local usage tends to be Bardsey and Enlli.

BARGOD see BARGOED

BARGOED Glam ST1499

'boundary', ***bargod***
Bargoed 1799
The name is taken from the stream Nant Bargod Rhymni (*Bargau Remni* c.1170) which flows from the hill Mynydd y Fochriw into the river Rhymni at Aberbargoed (*Aber Bargoed* 1578, *Aberbargod* 1729). The r.n. Rhymni distinguishes it from Bargod Taf (*Berkehu Taf* c.1170), a tributary of the river Taf, which rises on the same hill. Nant Bargod Rhymni seems to have marked off the land at Brithdir from other land in the commote of Senghennydd Uwch Caeach. With industrial and urban development in the 19cent., the settlement on the eastern side of the river Rhymni became Aberbargoed (*Aberbargod* 1729, *Pontaber Bargoed* 1794), while that on the western side around Bargoed (railway) Junction took the name Bargoed. The modern form Bargoed, recorded from the 16cent. onwards, has been influenced by ***coed*** 'trees, wood', a change reinforced by the proximity of Penycoed and Argoed and the perception that the second syllable of Bargod represents the regional pronunciation of ***coed*** and therefore needs correcting to -coed.

BARMOUTH, ABERMO Mer SH6115

'mouth of (the river) Mawdd', ***aber***, r.n. ***Mawdd***

Abermau 1284, *Abermowth* 1410, *The Mowth of Maw Ryver* 1536-9, *Bermo* 1587, *Abermouthegh* 1695, *Barmouth* 1714, *Barmouth o. Abermowthech* 1741, *'Bermaw or Abermawddach* 1795

Originally, the r.n. was Mawdd (probably a pers.n.) and seen in the name of the area Mawddwy 'the territory of Mawdd' (the river or the pers.n.); cf. Dinas Mawddwy. The estuary was 'Aber Mawdd', which, with loss of final -dd, became Abermaw (which has recently been restored on some signs) and then Abermo and Y Bermo (where the first syllable of Abermo is taken to be the definite article *y*). An anglicized version 'Aber Mawdd' (similar to the 1410 form) became Barmouth, possibly influenced by the ***mouth*** of the river. Today the river is called Mawddach (q.v.), but originally that was the name of a tributary of the Mawdd (with the dim.suff. -***ach***, 'the little Mawdd').

BARRI, Y, BARRY Glam ST1168

?'hill brook', ?***bar(r)***, suff. -***en*** or -***enn***

Barren ?11cent. (early 13cent.), *Barri* c.1180-90

The name is probably taken from a small stream (*the Barrie* 1586) rising above the town in the Buttrills and flowing into Barry harbour (*Aberbarrey* 1536-9, ***aber***). The r.n. may have developed from an earlier *Barren* to *Barre*, *Barri*, anglicized as Barry, with loss of final -n (cf. Penally Pemb and Rhosili Glam). The name was then apparently extended to Barry Island (*island of Barre* 1485). The def.art. *y* seems to be a late addition.

BARRY see **BARRI, Y**

BASALEG Monm ST2787

'church', ***baseleg***

Basselec 1102, *Bassalech* 1146-7, *Basselek* 1318, *Massalec* c.1562, *bysaleg* c.1566, *Massalec* c.1569, *Baslecke* 1570

The name derives from L ***basilica***, a rare el., also recorded in early names of the rivers Afon Seilo and Afon Stewi Card (respectively *Salek fluvius*, *Massalek fluvius* 1578). The nasal mutation (b- > m-) seen in some forms and the similarity in local pronunciation of *Mas*- and ***maes*** accounts for the supposition that the p.n. contained this el. Local E pronunciation generally stresses the first syllable (as 'baze'-). The dedication of the church to St Basil was drawn from the p.n.

BATEL see **BATTLE**

BATTLE, Y BATEL Brec SO0031

'(place named after) Battle', p.n. ***Battle, y***

(*de*) *Bello* 1222-4, *Battle* 1527, *y battel* c.1566

Named after Battle Abbey Sussex (which held the advowson of the church), itself named from the battle of Hastings 1066. The cymricized ***batel***, here preceded by the def.art. ***y***, probably referred to the popular tradition associating the p.n. Battle with the battle in which Bernard de Neufmarché slew Rhys ap Tewdwr, a prince of south Wales, in 1093.

BEAUFORT, CENDL — Monm SO1611

'place named after Beaufort' (and) 'Kendall', pers.n. ***Beaufort***, pers.n. ***Kendall***

Beaufort Furnace 1785, *Beaufort Works* c.1790, *Kendle, Cendle* 1839, *Beaufort* 1854, *Cendl* 1867

The ironworks was established by Edward Kendall, Jonathan Kendall and Joseph Latham under lease from the Duke of Beaufort in 1779 (who had an iron ore and coal mine there in 1769). It was generally known as *Beaufort Furnace* or *Works* before c.1847 or as *Kendle* and *Kendall* (active down to about 1854) giving rise to the W form Cendl, also found in the name of a wood Coedcae Cendl about three miles lower down the river Ebwy.

BEAUMARIS, BIWMARES — Angl SH6076

'fair marsh', NF ***beau, marais***

(villa de) Bello Marisco 1284, *Beaumaris* 1296, *Beaumareys* 1301, *(villa) Belli Marisci* 1304-5, *Bewemarras* 1489, *Bumares* 1536-9, *Bewmaris* 1610, *Bewmares* 1612, *Blwmoris* 1761

The castle and town of Beaumaris were built after 1294 as an English royal stronghold on the open marshland beside the Menai Strait. The W pronunciation has always been very close to *Bewemarras* and *Bewmares*, with occasional local vars *Duwmares* and *Bliwmaras* (with common intrusive -l- after b-; cf. Plwmp and Plynlimon). Before Beaumaris was established, the name of the location was Cerrig y Gwyddyl 'Irishmen's rocks' (*Carrekgwoythel* 1301-2, *Carrikuthel* 1352, *Kerrykwythell* 1409) and seems to have retained some currency.

BEDDAU — Glam ST0685

'graves', ***bedd*** pl. ***beddau***

Beddau 1875

An industrial village which developed after c.1860, taking its name from Heol y Beddau (*hewl y Bedda* 1804) 'street of the graves' which is probably the road running north-south through the village. The name is recorded as that of a house (*Heol y Beddan* 1833) at the crossroads Croes Heol-y-beddau (*Croesyrheol-y-Beddau* 1875, ***croes, heol***) which has been explained as the site of a battlefield or place of execution but there is no corroborative evidence. Cf. Pen-bont Rhydybeddau.

BEDDGELERT Caern SH5948

'Celert's grave', ***bedd***, pers.n. ***Celert***

Bekelert 1258, *Bedkelerd* 1269, *Bethkelerd* 1284, *Bethkelert* 1286, *Beddgelert* 1737

The identity of Celert is not known, but he was certainly a man and not a dog. From at least the 16cent., the village came to be associated with the legend of Gelert, the faithful hound of Prince Llywelyn (in a W version of an international folk-tale). In the 18cent., the tradition was further popularized when a commemorative stone was erected on the supposed site of the dog's grave.

BEDLINOG Glam SO0901

?'house near (the stream) Llwynog', ?***bod***, r.n. ***Llwynog***

Gwayne Vedlinog 1604, *Bodlwynog* 17cent., *Bedloynog alias Tir Coli* 1688, *Beddyllwynog* 1813, *Bedllwynog* 1833

An industrial village which developed near Bedlinog and Bedlinog Fach farms and Gwaun Fedlinog (***gwaun*** 'moor'). The forms are late and equivocal but it is likely that the first el. is ***bod*** 'house, homestead' with the stream name here recorded as *Nantyllwynog* 1813. This is probably ***llwynog*** 'fox' and is likely to belong to the category of rivers with animal-names. The 1688 alias *Tir Coli* (with ***tir*** 'land' and a pers.n.) survives in the name of two farms Coly Isaf (*Colly-isaf* 1842) and Uchaf; there is evidence that the village was 'popularly called Colly' (19cent.). The p.n. seems to have been influenced by ***bedlwyn*** 'birchgrove' with adj. suff. ***-og***. ***bod*** also became *Bed-* in Bedwellte Monm. The 1813 form interprets it as ***bedd*** 'grave'.

BEDWAS Monm ST1789

'grove of birch trees', ***bedwos***

Bedewas c.1102 (1330), *Bedewas* 1254, *Bedeways* 1263

bedwos was associated with a profusion of undergrowth and young hazel and birch trees (***bedw***), usually on a slope; cf. *Bedwes, a birche grove* 1536-9. Variation of -os, -as, and -es is common.

BEDWELLTE Monm ST1700

'abode of Mellteu', ***bod***, pers.n. ***Mellte(u)***

Bedwellte 1411, *Bodwellllte* 1457, *Bedwellty* 1584, *bod mellde* c.1566, *Bodwellte* 1606, *Bedwelltie* 1667, *Bedwellty* 1833

The identity of *Mellte* is unknown, although a 13cent. genealogy has such a name for one of the daughters of Brychan Brycheiniog, and a r.n. Mellte occurs in Ystradfellte (q.v.). ***bod*** also occurs as Bed- in Bedlinog (q.v.) although some have argued for the influence of ***bedw*** 'birch' here. A common modern var. (seen as early as 1584) is Bedwellty probably influenced by ***tŷ***.

BEGELI see **BEGELLY**

BEGELLY, BEGELI Pemb SN1107
'territory of Bugail', pers.n. ***Bugail***, terr.suff. ***-i***
Urgely, Beg'geby 1291, *Bekeli* 13cent., *Begely* 1362, *Castelbigili* 1365-6, *Bigelly* 1411, *bigeli* c.1566
The pers.n. (from ***bugail*** 'shepherd') occurs in a lost p.n. *Merthir buceil* 1129, probably near Bridgend Glam. The name may also appear in *Wiliiam de Barry of Bekeli* 13cent. The solitary form *Bigelydd* found in a W source 1606 might also suggest a terr.suff. ***-ydd*** as in Llanfugeilydd, a grange of Margam abbey Glam. The 1366 form has E ***castle*** but there seems to be no evidence of one here.

BEGUILDY see **BUGEILDY**

BENLLECH Angl SH5182
'(the) capstone', (*y*), ***penllech***
Penclegh 1352, *y penllegh* 1453, *y Benllech* 1483, *Penllech* 1732, *Benllech* 1753
The el. ***llech*** 'stone' is also found in ***cromlech*** (***crwm*** fem. ***crom*** 'curved') 'the circular stone' and in ***penllech***, the flat capstone of a cromlech. This particular cromlech had a distinctively large capstone which gave its name to a mill (*mol. Penclegh* 1352, *melyn y penllegh* 1453), a fulling-mill (*Pandû-r Benllech* 1718/19) and a croft (*Tythyn y penllach* 1639, *Tythyn y Benllech* 1691). It was the latter (also known as *Tythyn-iolyn* 1718/19) which gave the 18cent. village the name of (Y) Benllech.

BEREA Pemb SM7929
biblical chapel n.
Berea Meeting House 1832, *Berea Chapel* 1843
Named from the Congregational chapel.

BERMO, Y see **BARMOUTH**

BERRIEW, BERRIW Mont SJ1800
'mouth of (the river) Rhiw', ***aber***, r.n. ***Rhiw***
Eberrw c.1100, *Aberrw* c.1253, *Aberyw, Eberreu* 1291, *Abberyw* 1390, *Beriw* 1540-77, *or beryw* 1579, *the Berow* 1620
The village is west of the confluence of the river Rhiw (*Riu* 1185, *Ryu, Ryw* 1263, *Rhiwe* 1608-9, *Rue* 1698) with the river Severn. The forms of the r.n. point to an association with ***rhiw*** 'slope' but it has been suggested that it a Br ****riu*** 'stream' here simply describing 'river'. Berriw has the lost initial A- (except in the literary form *Aberriw*), probably through confusion with the def.art. ***y*** (as in the 1579 spelling *or beryw* for *o'r Beryw* 'from the') and imitated by ***the*** in the English context of 1620); cf. Abermaw (q.v.) > Y Bermo.

BERRIW see **BERRIEW**

BERS see **BERSHAM**

BERSHAM, BERS Denb SJ3049

'Bers's river-meadow', pers.n. ****Bers***, OE ***hamm***

Berertessha' c.1201 (1295), *Bercessham* 1202, *Bersham* 1315, *Bers* 15cent.

The ***hamm*** was a meadow within a bend in Afon Clywedog. The identity of ***Bers*** is unknown and the pers.n. itself is conjectural, but the etymology fits a pattern of OE pers.ns in combination with ***hamm*** found in the area (such as Borras or *Borasham* 1315, Esclusham or *Esclus*, and Wrexham). These OE p.ns were adopted as W p.ns and then lost the final syllable, here as Bers, the W form of Bersham. It has been suggested that the first el. is not a pers.n. but ME ***berse*** 'pleached hedge'.

BERWYN, Y Denb/Mer/Mont SJ1139

'white summit', ***bar***, ***gwyn***

Berwyn 1165 (late 13cent.), *berrwin* c.1191, *Berrwyn* 1279,
Berwyn 1450-1500

Extensive highlands (*the berwyn hills* 1814-13) between Llandrillo and Llanarmon Dyffryn Ceiriog, one of the highest peaks being Cadair Berwyn (*Kadair Verwyn* 1568, *Cader Berwyn* 1838, ***cadair*** 'seat') which may have been the original snow-capped peak. W usage retains the def.art. Several other peaks in Wales are called Berwyn. The -a- > -e- is caused by the following -y-.

BETHANIA[1] Caern SH6250

biblical chapel n.

Bethania 1851

Named after the Calvinistic Methodist chapel.

BETHANIA[2] Card SN5763

biblical chapel n.

Bethania 1809

Named after the Calvinistic Methodist chapel built on Mynydd-bach.

BETHEL Caern SH5265

biblical chapel n.

Bethel Chapel 1816, *Bethel* 1838

Named after the Congregational chapel, whose registers date from 1815.

BETHESDA Caern SH6266

biblical chapel n.

Bethesda 1820

Named after the Nonconformist chapel built in 1820 on the site of what was earlier *y wern uchaf* 1820. The village developed mainly in response to the slate quarries in the 18 and 19cent.

BETHLEHEM Carm SN6825

biblical chapel n.

Bethlehem 1851

A small hamlet near *Dolgoy* and *Bancyfedwen* 1834 which took the name of the Congregational chapel erected in 1800. Bethlem is the usual pronunciation.

BETTISFIELD Flints SJ4635

'Bēda's field'; pers.n. ***Bēda***, OE ***feld***

Beddesfeld 1086, *Bedusfeld* c.1280, *Bettisfield* 1388, *Bettesfeld* 1391, *Bettisfyld* 1496, *Bettysfeld* 1551, *Bettisfield* 1653, *Betsfield* c.1700, *Bettisfield al's Betchfield* c.1700, *Llysvaesbedydd* 1356, *Llisbedith* 1427, *Llys Bedyth* 1486-7, *Llys beduth* 1500, *Llysvedyth* 1507

Bēda's identity is not known. The W Maesbedydd interpreted *Beddes-* and *Bedus* as ***bedydd*** 'baptism', and the addition of ***llys*** (referring to the manorial court held at the old Bettisfield Hall) precipitated the loss of ***maes***. There is evidence of a farm in the tnshp called *Coed-y-llys-bedydd* in 1879. *Llysbedydd* may possibly have had some medieval local currency but it did not otherwise survive except in antiquarian and literary usage.

BETWS[1] Carm SN6311

'prayer-house', ***betws***

Betwse 1536, *y betws* c.1550, *Betws* 1767, *Bettus* 1804, *Bettws* 1830

Probably once a chapel-of-ease of the adjoining parish Llandybïe, and now a parish in its own right.

BETWS[2]**, BETWS TIR IARLL** Glam SS9086

'prayer-house', ***betws***, p.n. ***Tir Iarll***

Bethouse 1545, *Bettus* 1591, *Bettws* 1749, *Bettws Gwayr* 1584-5 (c.1700)

The name is thought to refer to a chapel-of-ease recorded 'on the east side of the (river) Llynfi' (*Leueni* 1153-83). Some late sources call it *Betws Gwair*, associating the name with Gwair ab Aron, reputed lord of this area. This is also called *ll. ysbyttel* c.1566 (but otherwise unattested) with ***llan*** and ****ysbytel*** 'hospice'. Betws lies in the ancient lordship of Tir Iarll (*Tyriartlh alias Tyryartlh* 1296, *Tyearlth* 1335-6, *Erleslande* 1460) 'earl's land' (W ***tir***, ***iarll***, OE ***eorl***, OE ***land***), reputed to take its name from the 12cent. Robert the Consul, later earl of Gloucester.

BETWS[3] Monm SO2919

'prayer-house', ***betws***

Bettous c.1544-45, *Bettus chappell* 1586, *Bettus* 1600-7, *the Bettus* 1657, *Bettus Chapell* c.1700

A former chapel-of-ease in Llandeilo Bertholau parish. This is probably identical to Gwerngochen (*Werngozhyn* 1348, *Gwerne Gochyn* 1562, *Bettus warrin alias Gwerne gouchyn* 1600-9) and the ruinated chapel of *Wern gochen Chapell* c.1700 (***gwern***, ***?cochyn*** fem. ***cochen*** 'the red-haired one').

BETWS[4], Y Monm ST2890

'prayer-house', (*y*), ***betws***

Bettus 1476, *Bettws* 1604, *Bettus Chapell* 1695

Probably once a chapel-of-ease in the parish of Basaleg.

BETWS BLEDRWS Card SN5952

'chapel of Bledrws', ***betws***, pers.n. ***Bledrws***

Bethus Bledrus 1284, *Betus Bledrus* 1299, *Betus Bledrus* 1348, *Bettous Bletherous* 1399, *Bettws* c.1566, *Bettus Bledrws* 1746, *Bettws* 1798, *Bledrws* 1808

Probably a chapel of Llangybi. Originally the church itself was dedicated to Mihangel (*Lanvihangel Betws* 1507) in 1398, and to Bledrws in 1808. However, it has been argued that the church had concurrent dedications, to Bledrw(y)s as a Celtic saint and to Mihangel in the Roman tradition.

BETWS CEDEWAIN Mont SJ1296

'prayer-house in Cedewain', ***betws***, cantref n. ***Cedewain***

Bettws 1254, *Bettus* 1365-6, *Bettous* 1377, *y betws* c.1566, *betws Kydewain* 1534-80

A chapel-of-ease in Berriw parish. The cantref n. Cedewain (*Kedewyng* 12cent., *Keddewein* late 12cent., *Kedewing* 1273, *Kedewen* 1250) is probably a pers.n. Cadaw and terr.suff. ***-ein***.

BETWS DISERTH Radn SO1156

'prayer-house in Diserth (parish)', ***betws***, p.n. ***Diserth***

The Bettus 1546, *y bettws* c.1566, *Betws yn elfel* c.1562, *Bettus Dissard* c.1700

The absence of early forms supports the interpretation of ***betws*** as 'chapel-of-ease'. The use of the def.art. in W and E suggests an identifiable building. It is now a separate parish. Elfael was the cantref name (see Diserth below).

BETWS GARMON Caern SH5456

'prayer-house of Garmon', ***betws***, pers.n. ***Garmon***

Betous Carmon 1303-4, *Bettus Garmon* 1306-7, *Bettws Garmon* 1838

The prayer-house or chapel was dedicated to Garmon (the saint Germanus of Armorica who became bishop of Man).

BETWS GWERFUL GOCH Mer SJ0346

'prayer-house of Gwerful Goch', ***betws***, pers.n. ***Gwerful Goch***

Betos 1254, *Bettus* 1535, *Bettus Guervyl* 1291, *Bettws gwyrfyl goch* c.1566, *Bettws Gwerfyl Goch* 1730
Early genealogies identify the patron of this chapel as Gwerful Goch, daughter of Cynan ab Owain Gwynedd, who lived at the beginning of the 13cent.

BETWS IFAN Card SN3047

'prayer-house of Ifan', ***capel***, pers.n. ***Ifan***
Sancti Johannis de Betuskarleugi pre-1227 (1308), *Bettos* 1513, *Bettus Ievan* 1543, *bettws ifan* c.1566, *Bettus Ievan* 1557, *Bettus Euan* 1586, *Bettus Evan* 1692, *Bettws Ifan* 1804, *Bettws Efan* 1834
The forms record W vars of Johannus as Ieuan, Evan and Ifan. The second el. of the 1227 form is obscure.

BETWS LLEUCU Card SN6058

'prayer-house of Lleucu', ***betws***, pers.n. ***Lleucu***
Bettos 1513, *bettus Llyky* c.1546, *Capel bettus lekye* 1578, *Bettws Lleyky* 1592, *Bettus Lleiky* 1669, *Capel Bettws Lickys* 1762-3, *Bettws Leicy* 1763, *Bettws-Leiky* 1804, *Capel Bettws Lleici* 1834, *Bettws-Leiki* 1851
The history of the female Lleucu is obscure, and some doubt has been expressed as to whether she was actually a saint. Earlier references, not satisfactorily explained, identify the place as *Betus Bydonith* 1281, *Betous Bydonith* 1299, *Betus Bydyonith* 1348. This was a chapel-of-ease for the extensive parish of Llanddewibrefi but modern maps have applied the name to the Nonconformist chapel (frequently referred to as Capel Betws).

BETWS NEWYDD Monm SO3605

'new prayer-house', ***betws, newydd***
Bettus Aythan 1432, *Bethouse Newithe* 1452, *Bettehouse filiorum Aythen* 1468-9, *y bettws newydd* c.1566
Early forms associate the ***betws*** with Aeddan and his sons traditionally identified as Aeddon ap Gwaethfoel, lord of Cleidda (Clytha) in 1188 but the evidence for this is unreliable.

BETWS TIR IARLL see BETWS[2]

BETWS-Y-COED Caern SH7956

'prayer-house in the wood', ***betws, y, coed***
Betus 1254, *Bettus* 1352, (*o*) *vetws y koed* 1545-53, *Bettws y Coed* 1675
The chapel-of-ease was also known as as Llanfihangel y Betws (*ll. V'el y bettws* c.1566) and Betws Wyrion Iddon (*Bettus Seyrion ython* 1645-62, *Bettws Wyrion Iddon)* 'the descendants or family (***wyrion***) of Iddon' who built the church at Betws-y-coed.

BETWS-YN-RHOS Denb SH8974

'prayer-house in the hundred of Rhos', ***betws***, ***yn***, hundred n. ***Rhos***

Bettws 1291, *le bethows* 1530, *Bettus in Rhos* 1630

One alias for the chapel-of-ease at Betws-yn-Rhos was *Betus wyrion gwgon* 1545-53 'the descendants of Gwgon' (***wyrion***, pers.n. ***Gwgon***); another was *Bettus Abergeley* 1652, *Bettws Abergele* 1839 from its mother church in Abergele.

BEULA see **BEULAH**[1]

BEULAH[1]**, BEULA** Brec SN9251

biblical chapel n.

Beulah 1851

Named from the Congregational chapel established here in 1821-2.

BEULAH[2] Card SN2846

biblical chapel n.

Bwla 1875, *Beulah Chapel* 1891

Named from the Congregational chapel built in 1860. The village was formerly *Blaen Pant Trei* 1651, *Blaen-pantrefy* 1834, *Blaen-pant-arfi* 1891, possibly from its location at the junction of six roads leading from several villages (***pentref*** pl. ***pentrefi***) but given the consistency of the forms it is more likely to be ***pant*** 'hollow' and ***tref*** pl. ***trefi***.

BIDNO, Afon Mont SN8881

'(river associated with) Budno', ***afon***, pers.n. ***Budno***

Buduo, Byduo [=*Budno, Bydno*] 16cent., *Bidno R.* 1795, *Afon Bidno* 1836

The unrecorded pers.n was probably originally **Buddno* with -ddn- > -dn-; cf. Old Breton *Budnou*. Local dialect later has *i* for *u*. The area where the river meets the river Wye is *Aber Budno* 16cent., *Aber Bidno* 1742-3.

BINIE see **BYNEA**

BIRCHGROVE Glam SS7098

'birch-grove', E ***birch***, E ***grove***

Birch-grove 1832

Named from a farm recorded as *Birchgrove* 1775 and *Tir y Bedw or Birchgrove* 1808.

BISHOPS AND CLERKS Pemb SM6725

'(rocks likened to a) bishop and his clerks', E ***bishop***, E ***clerk***

The Bisshoppis and his clerkis 15cent., *The Bushopp and his Clarkes* 1578, *Bushop and his Clerckes* 1603, *The Bishop and his Six Clerks* 1728

A group of seven islands west of Ramsey (q.v.) also called Bishop and his Clerks. The perceived bishop may properly have applied to North Bishop and the collective name arising from a bishop leading his line of clerks, a name possibly prompted by association with St David's (q.v.) and the cathedral. The southernmost island (which now has a lighthouse) is South Bishop or Emsger (*Emskyr* c.1600, *Emskir* 1602, *Carreg Emskar* 1717), probably ON ***eimr*** 'mist', ON ***sker*** 'rock, reef'. For a possible 2cent. reference, see St David's Head.

BISHOPSTON, LLANDEILO FERWALLT Glam SS5789
'bishop's farm', 'church of Teilo belonging to Merwallt', OE ***biscop***, OE ***tūn***, W ***llan***, pers.n. ***Teilo***, pers.n. ***Merwallt***
Sancti Teilaui de lann merguallt 1119 (1160-90),
villae Sancti Teliawi de Lanmerwalt 1131, *villa episcopi* c.1230,
Bisschopiston' 13cent., *Bisshopeston* 1299, *ll. deilo ar ferwallt* c.1566
A farm or settlement which belonged to the bishops of Llandaf around a church dedicated to Teilo. Merwallt is recorded as the name of a former *principe*, perhaps abbot, of *Lann Merguall* c.695 (1136-54).

BISHTON, LLANGADWALADR Monm ST3887
'bishop's farm', 'church of Cadwaladr', OE ***biscop***, OE ***tūn***, W ***llan***, pers.n. ***Cadwaladr***
Lann Catgualatyr 1136-54, *Bishton manor of Lankaderwader* 1290,
Bishopiston 1504, *tre esgob* c.1566
A manor held by the bishops of Llandaf till 1650. The c.1566 form (***tref***, ***esgob***) is a W translation and probably had no currency as a p.n.

BIWMARES see **BEAUMARIS**

BLACKMILL, MELIN IFAN DDU Glam SS9386
'mill of Ifan the dark', E ***black***, E ***mill***, W ***melin***, pers.n. ***Ifan***, ***du***
Blackmill 1584-85 (c.1700), *Melin Evan ddu* 1729,
Melin-Evan-Ddu 1744, *Black Mill* 1787, *Melin-du* 1833
Blackmill is probably a translation of an earlier unrecorded *Melin-du* a contracted form of *Melin Ifan Du*. The mill was originally associated with an unidentified Ifan Ddu (***du*** 'black-haired' or 'swarthy') whose name survives in Mynydd Ifan Ddu (*Mynydd Evan Du* 1650, *Mynydd Jevanddy* 1700) and Dolau Ifan Ddu (*Dola Evan Du* c.1840).

BLACK MOUNTAIN, THE, Y MYNYDD DU
Brec/Glam SN6515-8423
'black mountain', E ***black***, E ***mountain***, W ***y***, ***mynydd***, ***du***
ymynyd du 1136-54 (14cent.), *y mynyd du* 1375-80,
o'r Mynydd Ddu 15cent., *Y Mynydh duy* 1584, *the Blake Montaine, Munnith du, the Blake Montaine* 1536-9, *the Blacke Mountaines* 1559,
the blacke mounteines in Brecknockshire, ~ of Carmardineshire 1586,
Mynydd Dû or Black mountain 1760
A very rugged range of mountains notable for deep valleys and cliffs,

often in shadow. The peaks are centred on Bannau Sir Gaer and Y Fan Frycheiniog.

BLACK MOUNTAINS, THE, MYNYDD DU

Brec/Monm SO1932-2732, 1925-3225

'black mountains', E ***black***, E ***mountain***, W ***mynydd, du,***
Atterel Hylles … in Walsche Meneth e Cadair 1536-9,
Black-Mountaine 1612, *Mynydd Du* 1839, *Mynyd du* c.1700,
Mynyddy Gader 1754, *the Black mountains* 1801,
the Black Mountains of Talgarth 1814, *y Mynydd-du* 1839

Early references to the Black Mountains as such are rare and may derive from the 1536-9 notes which described *Blak Montayne* as stretching from near Monmouth to near Carmarthen, incorporating these mountains with the Black Mountain Brec/Carm, and the Brecon Beacons (q.v.). Hatterrall Hill (q.v.) is at the south-east corner of the range of mountains on the border with Herefordshire. Mynydd y Gadair (or Gader) 'mountain shaped like a chair' (***mynydd, y, cadair***) properly applies to Y Gader Fawr and Pen y Gader-fawr. Occasional modern instances of Y Mynyddoedd Duon represent a translation of Black Mountains but have no historical basis.

BLACKPILL, DULAIS

Glam SS6190

'black or dark stream', OE ***blæc***, OE ***pyll***
Blakepulle 1153-84, *la Blakepulle* 1319, *Black Pill* 1729

The stream is *dubleis* 1136-54 ('black stream', ***du, glais***) possibly a stream which runs over coal-measures or is overshadowed by trees. ***pyll*** is generally applied to small streams flowing over marshland into the sea and into tidal creeks.

BLACKWOOD, COED-DUON

Monm ST1797

'black trees', E ***black, wood***, W ***coed, du*** pl. ***duon***
Coed-duon, Blackwood 1822, *Black Wood, Coed-dduon* 1833,
Coed-duon 1839

Other p.ns in the Sirhywi valley suggest that it was formerly heavily wooded. Perhaps 'dark, forbidding' is an appropriate interpretation, but a small part of the wood Coed-duon survived on the darker, south-west side of the village in 1886. The village developed around a model settlement established in the 1820s by J H Moggridge, landowner and social reformer.

BLAENAFON, BLAENAVON

Monm SO2509

'headwaters of the river', ***blaen, afon***
Blaen Avon 1532-3, *Blaen-afon* 1750

Near the upper reaches of Afon Lwyd (*Blaen Cwm yr Afon Lwyd* 1834), often simply recorded as Afon. The river was also reputed to have been called *Torvaen* 1792, *Torfaen* 1801, *Blaen yr Afon Torvaen* 1834. Whatever its authenticity, it gave its name to Torfaen District Council 1974-96 and its successor Torfaen County Borough Council. It has been interpreted as 'rocky slope' (***tor*** 'slope', ***maen*** 'stone').

BLAENANNERCH Card SN2449

'source of (the river) Annerch', ***blaen***, r.n. ***Annerch***

Blaynanarwith, Blaynaunerbigh 1291, *Blaynannerch* 1537-9, *Blayenannerth* 1559, *Blayne Annarche* 1577, *Blaen Annerch* 1697, *Blaenannerch* 1819

The 1291 forms are probably the result of miscopying. However, they may be representations of what appears to be earlier name for the river, *Ithenerth, Ithnerth, Blainhitheneh* 1242 (var. of the pers.n. Idnerth or Iddnerth). The stream flows into Nant Arberth. There is another Cwm Annerch in Cards.

BLAENAU FFESTINIOG Mer SH7045

'uplands of Ffestiniog', ***blaenau***, p.n. ***Ffestiniog***

Blean y Ffestiniog 1818, *Y Blaenau* 1861, *Blaenau Ffestiniog* 1891

Blaenau Ffestiniog, the centre of an 18-20cent. slate industry, is some two miles to the north of Ffestiniog (q.v.).

BLAENAU GWENT Monm SO1908

'uplands of Gwent', ***blaenau***, p.n. ***Gwent***

Blaynawe 1397, *blayne guent* c.1566, *Blaynegwent* 1570, *Aberystrwyth Blaeney Gwent* 1590, *Blaenau gwent* 1821

Blaenau Gwent referred formerly to the upper, hilly part of the ancient territory of Gwent (Caer-went q.v.) and was employed as an alternative name for Aberystruth parish (*Aberstrewyth* 1391, *Aberustithe* 1535, *Aberystrwyth* 1738), 'mouth of (the (river) Ystrwyth' (***aber***, r.n. Ystrwyth, *Blaen yr ystruth* 1638, *Blaen Istrwyth* 1832); Ystrwyth is a pers.n. The name was revived for the District Council of Blaenau Gwent in 1974. Blaenau (or earlier Blaina) is used of the town.

BLAENAVON see **BLAENAFON**

BLAENDULAIS see **SEVEN SISTERS**

BLAEN-FFOS Pemb SN1937

'top of (the) ditch', ***blaen***, ***ffos***

Blaneffosse 1724, *Blaenfose* 1782, *Blaen-y-foes* 1819, *Blaenyffos* 1839

The name applies to a hamlet on the Narberth-Cardigan road and is taken from Blaen-ffos farm (*Blaen-y-ffôs* 1843) to the north-west. The ditch may be one of three small tributaries (***tri***, ***nant***) of the river Trinant.

BLAENGARW Glam SS9092

'headwater of (the river) Garw', ***blaen***, r.n. ***Garw***

Blayne Garo 1582, *blaen garw* 1630, *Blaen-garw* 1833

An industrial village which developed near the Garw Ocean Colliery in the late 19cent. near the head of the river Garw (*Garowe* 1586-7), a tributary of the river Ogwr. The valley is *Glyn Garu* 1261 (***glyn***); for the r.n. see Abergarw.

BLAEN-GWRACH Glam SN8605

'headwater of (the river) Gwrach', ***blaen***, r.n. ***Gwrach***

Bleinwrach 1208, *Bleinwrac* 13cent., *Blaen Gwrache* 1574, *Blaengwrach* 1738

The name properly applies to the area around Blaen-gwrach Fawr at the head of the stream Nant Gwrach which gave its name to the ***parsel*** or subdivision of Blaen-gwrach in the north of Glyncorrwg parish. The r.n. is ***gwrach*** 'hag, crone, witch', a reference to such a person associated with the river, or feasibly, used of a weak, slow river.

BLAENGWYNFI Glam SS8996

'headwater of (the river) Gwynfi', ***blaen***, r.n. ***Gwynfi***

Blaengwnfy 1813, *Blaen-gwynfy* 1833

Named from a farm near the river Afan about a mile from the actual source of Nant Gwynfi. See Abergwynfi .

BLAENPENNAL Card SN6264

'uplands of Pennal', ***blaen***, p.n. ***Pennal***

Blaynpennal 1326, *Blaine Pennial* 1536-9, *Blayne Pennall* 1680, *Blaenpenal or Hendre* 1788, *Lanpenal* 1801, *Llan Penal* 1834

This village is on high ground on the banks of the upper reaches of Afon Aeron. Pennal (*Pennal* 1181-2 [1285]) is probably ***pen*** 'top' and ***hâl*** 'moorland promontory' on either side of Afon Aeron. The alias of 1788 refers to the present farm to the south-east while the 1801 and 1834 forms refer to the church (***llan***) south-west of the village.

BLAEN-PLWYF Card SN5775

'(at the) far end of the parish', ***blaen***, ***plwyf***

Blain Plwy 1821, *Blaenblwy* 1826, *Blaen Plwyf* 1834, *Blaenplwy* 1851

Blaen-plwyf is on fairly high ground in the upper part of the parish of Llanychaearn on the border with Llanddeiniol parish, and may have been the name of the location of the first chapel (built in 1802) slightly south-west of the present village. There is evidence to suggest that until the resiting of the chapel within the village in 1878-80 the village was called Pentre-parc (*Pentre'r-parc* 1843, *Pentre Park* 1864), a reference to nearby Parc (*Parcmawr* 1814, *Parc* 1821). Another alias Pontllanio (*Pont*

Lanio 1891, *Pont-lanio* 1906) and also used of another nearby location (*Pontlanio* 1828) seems to be a reference to a Pont Llanio near Llanddewibrefi (a var. of the pers.n. Llonio), but the connection is obscure.

BLAEN-PORTH Card SN2648

'uplands of (the) bay', ***blaen, porth***

Blaen Porth Hodnant 1116 (c.1400), *Blaenporth* 1197 (1424), *Blainport* 1241, *Blaenporth* 1284, *Bleynporthe* 1424, *Blaen Porth* 1590

The brook Nant Howni (formerly *Hoddni*) rises near Blaen-porth (or Blaen Porth Howni) flows through Cwmhowni (*Cwm Howny* 1813) and Dyffryn Howni (*Dyffrin Porth Hoffni* 1651, *Dyffrin Howni* 1760) into the sea at Aber-porth (or Aber Porth Howni). Evidently, from the earliest records onwards, there has been a perception that Porth or Porth Howni was the name of the brook. The r.n. is ***hawdd*** 'pleasant' and r.n. suff. ***-ni***; cf. Honddu.

BLAENRHONDDA Glam SS9299

'headwaters of the Rhondda (Fawr)', ***blaen***, r.n. ***Rhondda***

blaen Ronthe 1479, *Tir blaen Rhothni* 1552, *Blaen Ronthey* 1666, *Blaen-rhondda* 1833

A farm which gave its name to the village which developed near a coalpit sunk in 1868-9. See Rhondda.

BLAEN-WAUN Carm SN2327

'top of the moor', ***blaen, (y), gwaun***

Blaenwaun 1811, *Blaen-y-waun* 1839, *Blaen-waun* 1843, *Blaenwain* 1895

A small settlement which developed around a Baptist chapel on moorland near Waun Fawr and Waun Fach farms (*Waun-fawr, Waun-fach* 1843).

BLAEN-Y-COED Carm SN3427

'top of the wood', ***blaen, y, coed***

Blaen-y-coed 1754, 1831

Named from a farm at the head of a heavily wooded valley.

BLAINA see **BLAENAU**

BLEDDFA Radn SO2068

'wolf's nook', ***blaidd, bach***

Bledwach 1195-6, *Bledvach* 1262, *Bleddfach* 1600-7

Located in a small valley which could have been the lair of wolves. The first el. may also be the pers.n. Blaidd. The ending *-ch* has been lost, probably through E influence (as with Solfach q.v.). Compare Wolfpits (*Wolfpitt* 1548, *Wolfpits* 1828) Radn and Wolfsdale Pemb.

BLETHERSTON, TREFELEN Pemb SN0721

'Bleddri's farm', ?'the yellow farm', pers.n. ***Bleddri***, OE ***tūn***, W ***y***, ***tref***, ***melyn*** fem. ***melen***

Blethiston' 1326 (16cent.), *Bletherston* 1489, *Bledderston* 1597, *y dre felen* c.1566, *Trevelen* 1573

Bleddri or Bledri was the name of a 12cent. bishop of Llandaf. The pers.n. is anglicized as Blethery; a parallel form occurs in Tremblary Cornwall. The W name has not been satisfactorily explained. In addition to 'yellow' ***melyn*** has a range of other meanings such as 'golden', 'brown' and 'deadly, unpleasant'. However, it has been asserted that Trefelen represents *tref Elen* (***tref***, pers.n. ***Elen***) since there is an *Elen's Well* in the parish of Llawhaden in which Bletherston was a chapelry.

BLOREIS see **BLORENGE**

BLORENGE, BLOREIS Monm SO2611

Obscure

Bloreys 1256-7, *Bloreis* 1263, (*ym*) *Mlorens* late 15cent., *Blorench hill* 1577, *Blorenge Hill* 1695

There seem to be no obvious parallels with this name. The suggestion of W ***blawr*** 'grey' and ***ais*** 'ribbed' is difficult to link to the topography. The p.n. Blore in Staffordshire seems to have OE ***blōr*** of uncertain meaning but is possibly linked with ME ***blure*** 'blister' and W ***plôr*** 'pimple' used of a hill. Later forms with intrusive -n- could tentatively be ascribed to influence of the Italian city of Florence and an anglicized substitution of final -ch- and -g- (possibly influenced by ***orange***).

BOCHRWYD see **BOUGHROOD**

BODEDERN Angl SH3380

'church of Edern', ***bod***, pers.n. ***Edern***

Bodedern 1343

The same saint (or the same name) occurs in Edern and Edeyrnion (Caern) and Llanedern/Llanedeyrn (Glam). In a p.n. with ecclesiastical associations, ***bod*** 'abode' often has the connotation of 'church' or 'chapel'.

BODELWYDDAN Flints SJ0075

'abode of Elwyddan', ***bod***, pers.n. ***Elwyddan***

Bodylwyddan 1422, *Bodylwyddon* 1426, *Boedelwyth* 1439, *Bodelwethan* 1524, *Bodlwiddon* 1550-62, *Bodelwydhen*, *Bod elwydhan* c.1700

Neither the identity of this Elwyddan nor the exact location of his residence is known, although a 5cent. Elwyddan does appear in W heroic literature, with a brother allegedly associated with the area around Bodelwyddan.

BODERMID Caern SH1525

'abode of a hermit' ***bod, ermid***

Bodermitt 16cent., *Bodermid* 1731

The location may be associated with the pilgrim route to Bardsey and the nearby Porth Meudwy ('hermit bay', ***porth, meudwy***).

BODEWRYD Angl SH3990

'church of Gewryd', ***bod,*** pers.n. ***Gewryd***

Borheurit 1254, *Bodewryt* 1294, *Bodewryd* 1460

Gewryd, Iewryd or Ewryd was supposedly the uncle of St David. The church is now dedicated to St Mary.

BODFARI Flints SJ0970

'abode of the revered Barre', ***bod, ty-,*** pers.n. ***Barre*** or ***Baru***

Boteuuarul 1086, *Batavari* 1093, *Bottewaru* 1254, *Botevarro* 1292, *Botyvarru* 1332, *Botuarre* 1334, *Botvarri* 1534, *Bodvarrie* 1660, *Bot Varri* c.1700, *Bodvarry* 1721, *Bodfari* 1839

A difficult p.n. to explain satisfactorily, made all the more frustrating by the ample evidence. The first el. is probably ***bod*** but the rest is obscure. Much was once made of the supposed identification with the Roman station of *Varae* or *Varis* whose location is now considered to be near St Asaph. With the historical forms consistently recording -t- in the initial syllable, the first consonant of the second el. could be one of several. The hypocoristic or honorific pref. ***ty-*** followed by a pers.n. such as *Baru, Barre* or *Marre* to produce **ty-Farre* meets most requirements. There was an Ir saint Barre and the name exists as a r.n. in Card, but there is no corroboration of such a person here. An unrecorded version of the church's patron saint's name Dier or Deufer (cf. Ffynnon Ddier not far from the church) such as *Deufaru, might also be a consideration. The W -f-, faithfully recorded in earlier forms as -v-, was later taken to be the E -f- (as if W -ff-) and is the pronunciation commonly heard today. It is also interesting to observe ***bod*** restored in modern spellings, but local pronunciation still retains the *Bot-* of the early forms (cf. Bodffordd).

BODFFORDD Angl SH4276

'abode by a ford', ***bod, ffordd***

Botford 1346, *Botforde* 1352, *Botfford* 1406, *Botforth ddeyniell* 1408-9, *Bodforde* 1478, *Bodffordd Ddeiniel alias Bodffordd Esgob* 1688, *Bodffordd* c.1737, *Bodffor* 1838, *Bod-ffordd* 1891

W ***ffordd*** meant 'ford' (cf. OE ***ford***) before taking on the exclusive meaning of 'road'. It is therefore possible that 'ford' is the meaning of the second el. in Bodffordd rather than 'road' since several fords are recorded near the present village, two of them on the route of the old Post Road from Chester to Holyhead. The tnshp belonged to the bishop (***esgob***) of Bangor cathedral which was dedicated to Deiniol. The colloquial vars Botffor and Botffordd are still very common, the latter particularly so even in documents.

BODORGAN Angl SH3867

'abode of ?Corgyn', ***bod***, pers.n. ?****Corgyn***

Bodgorgyn 1335, *Bodgorging* 1534, *Bodgorgan* 1565-87, *Bodorgan* 1647, *Bodorgan alias Bodgorgan* 1749

The second el. is probably an unknown pers.n. *Corgyn. It has also been suggested that it is an unrecorded el. ****corgyn*** with ***côr***[3] 'boundary, limit' since the area overlooks the estuary of Afon Cefni at Malltraeth which formed the boundary of the commote of Malltraeth and the hundred of Aberffraw. The railway station was called Bodorgan which helped to consolidate the area name as a p.n.

BODUAN Caern SH3237

'abode of Buan', ***bod***, pers.n. ***Buan***

Bodanen [?=*Bodauen*] 1177-87 (late 15cent.),
Bothenav [=*Botheuan*] 1177-c.1190 (late 15cent.),
Bothwian 1194-1200 (late 15cent.), *Bodunan* 1284, *Bodevean* 1330, *Bodvean* 1423, *Bodvyan* 1548, *Bodean* 1795, *Boduan* 1838

Buan is recorded as a pers.n., including the name of the grandson of Llywarch Hen, and a name still preserved in the civil parish Buan. Some of the forms also survived in a non-standard form Bodfean.

BONCATH Pemb SN2038

'buzzard', ***boncath***

Boncath 1777, *Boncath isaf* 1841, *Boncath uwchaf* 1852

Probably from an inn Tafarn y Boncath (*Tafarn Boncath* c.1772, *Tavern y Boncath* 1787, *Boncath Tavern* 1875), 'the buzzard tavern' (***tafarn***), referring to its sign. There is another Boncath (locally Y Bwncath) in St David's which also had a *Bwncath* (1875) inn.

BONT, Y Monm SO3819

'the bridge', *y*, ***pont***

Bont 1813

Near a bridge carrying a small lane from Llangatwg Lingoed over a small tributary of the river Troddi.

BONT-DDU Mer SH6618

'(the) dark bridge', ***(y)***, ***pont***, ***du***

Bont Ddu 1763, *Bontddu* 1765, *Pont-ddû* 1798

The bridge carries the Llanelltyd-Barmouth turnpike road across Afon Cwm-llechen just before its confluence with Afon Mawddach. The river flows through a fairly narrow defile here between wooded cliffs which explains several p.ns in the locality which are dark or shaded (such as Cae-du, Ffridd-ddu and Tyddyn-du). The road was probably linked to gold and copper mining.

BONTDOLGADFAN Mont SH8800
'bridge at Dolgadfan', ***(y)***, ***pont***, p.n. ***Dolgadfan***
Dolgadfan Bridge 1683-7, *Bont, Melin Dolgadfan* 1833,
Pont Dolgadfan 1836
A bridge over the river Twymyn near Dolgadfan farm. Dolgadfan (*Dolgadvan* 1573, *Dolegadvan* 1573) is ***dôl*** + pers.n. Cadfan).

BONT-FAEN[1]**, Y** see **COWBRIDGE**

BONT-FAEN[2]**, Y** see **PONT-FAEN**[2]

BONT-GOCH Card SN6886
'(the) red bridge', *(y)*, ***pont***, ***coch***
Pen y Bont Goch 1747, *Bont Gôch* 1767, *Penbontgoch* 1778,
Y Bont Goch 1803
Nant Llynloyw passes under the minor road at this point, which also had a ford *Rhyd-goch* 1747. An older name Elerch (*Eleirch* 14cent., *Elerch* 1570-1, *Elyrche* 1617) is associated with the area (as in Bont-goch/Elerch on modern maps), which is possibly a fem pers.n. Elerch (influenced by ***eleirch*** 'swans'). Some maps locate Bont-goch south of the stream and Elerch to the north.

BONTNEWYDD[1] Caern SH4859
'(the) new bridge', *(y)*, ***pont***, ***newydd***
Bontnewith 1536-9, *y Bont Newydd* 1582, *Pontnewydd* 1704
The major route between Caernarfon and the Llŷn peninsula crosses the river Gwyrfai across *the new bridge* 1552, *Pontnewydd Bridge* 1735; the present bridge was built in 1840.

BONTNEWYDD[2] Denb SJ0170
'(the) new bridge', (y), pont, newydd
novi pontis de Eloy 1439, *y bont nevyth* 1549, *y bonte Newyth* 1562,
Pont Newydd 1659
The road between Henllan and Cefn Meiriadog crosses Afon Elwy here.

BONTNEWYDD-AR-WY, Y see **NEWBRIDGE-ON-WYE**

BONTUCHEL Denb SJ0857
'(the) high bridge', *(y)*, ***pont***, ***uchel***
Pont vchal 1573, *y bont vchel* 1598, *y Bont vchel* 1605, *Pont uchel* 1737
The bridge is over the river Clywedog.

BONVILSTON, TRESIMWN Glam ST0674

'farm of Boneville', 'farm of Simon', pers.n. ***Boneville***, OE ***tūn***, W ***tref***, pers.n. ***Simwn***

Bonevilestune, Boleuileston' 1173-83, *Bonevilla, Bonevilestune* late 12cent., *Bolstonne'* 1517, *Tresimon* 1536-9, *tre simwnt* c.1566, *Bonvilston ... for shortness Bowlson* 1591, *Tresymwnd* 1740

Named from the family of *de Boneville* recorded in this area in the late 12cent. who may have taken their name from Bonneville-sur-Touques, Normandy. Many forms show that Bonvilston was contracted by local E speakers to Bolston but this has now given way to the restored longer form. The W name, with its cymricized form *Simwn(d)*, is probably *Simon de Boneville*, a witness in charters c.1230-62.

BÔN-Y-MAEN Glam SS6895

'base of the rock', ***bôn***, ***y***, ***maen***

Bone y Mane 1650, *Bon-y-maen* 1832

The rock is a prehistoric stone on the roadside near the centre of the village. Cf. an identical farm name *Bon y maen* 1783 in Merthyr Tudful (and recalled in Rocky Road).

BORTH, Y Card SN6089

'the harbour', ***y***, ***porth***

borthe 1565, *Y Borth* 1602, *Borth* 1738-9, *Porth* 1798, *Borth* 1837

Once the location of a ferry to Aberdyfi. An alias is reputedly Porth Wyddno (*Porth Gwydno* c.1233 [14cent.]) after the Gwyddno Garanhir of legends but lacks early documentary evidence and may refer to an entirely different place.

BORTH-Y-GEST Caern SH5637

'harbour of the paunch', ***porth***, ***y***, ***cest***

Borth y Gest 1791

The dominant feature of the landscape north of the harbour and the Glaslyn estuary is the hill called Gest (*Gest* 1303-4), modern Moel y Gest (*Moel-y-gest* 1838, ***moel*** 'bare hill'), whose shape prompted the comparison with a paunch or big belly and which gave its name to a fairly extensive medieval tnshp called Gest. However, it has been argued that the belly could allude figuratively to a vast bog which swallows everything. There was such a *Cest* near Tremadog; Moel y Gest overlooks this bog. A modification of this is that ***cest*** may refer to the undulating belly-like hills and hollows of low-lying moorland (cf. Rhos-y-bol Angl). Whatever the precise significance of ***cest***, the p.n. is Borth-y-Gest rather than 'Porth-y-Gest' probably because it was customary to refer to it as 'Y Borth' or simply 'Borth', or the persistence in speech of lenited forms following ***i*** 'to' and ***o*** 'from'. The emergence of the nearby Porthmadog in the mid-19cent. necessitated the addition of a distinguishing identification since Porthmadog reduced Borth-y-Gest's importance as a harbour (*Gest harbour* 1748) at the entrance to the estuary.

BOSHERSTON Pemb SR9694

'Bosher's farm', pers.n. ***Bosher***, OE ***tūn***
Stakep' bosser 1291, *Stakepole Bosser* 13cent., *Bosseston* 1502, *Bocherston* 1543, *Stackpole Bosherston* 1564
The 1291 form refers to Stackpole Elidor (q.v.). A *William Boscher* lived here in the 13cent.

BOTWNNOG Caern SH2631

'church of Tywynnog', ***bod***, pers.n. ***Tywynnog***
Bottywynawc c.1291, *Botwynnok* 1352, *Bottwnnog* 1658-9
Although this may be an example of ***bod*** 'abode' signifing 'church', the church itself is dedicated to Beuno.

BOUGHROOD, BOCHRWYD Radn SO1239

?'jaw-shaped net', ***boch***, ***rhwyd***
Bouret 1205, *Bocred* 1242-3, *Boghred* 1234, *Bochroed* 1291, *Boghroyde* 1513, *bochrwyd* c.1566
Possibly ***boch*** 'cheek, jaw' and ***rhwyd*** 'net, snare' in the sense of 'jaw-shaped net' for a fish-trap in the river Wye. The present spelling -rood and the occasional Bochrwd show reduction of -wy- > -w-.

BOVERTON, TREBEFERED Glam SS9868

'farm of Bo(u)vier', pers.n. ***Bo(u)vier***, OE ***tūn***, W ***tref***
Bovyareston 1296, *Boverton* 1330, *Bovyarton* 1375, *Berton alias Boverton* 1559, *Trer Bwferaid* a6cent., *Trebofered* 1756, *Tref Beferad*, *Trebefred* c.1800
Nothing is known of anyone here with this name but it is well-authenticated elsewhere. The W name is poorly documented and its correct modern form is certainly not clear. It must have derived directly from Boverton but its development is somewhat irregular. The replacement of -tūn by ***tref*** is common but the forms with *-bofered*, *-befered* presumably derive from *Bovert-* (not *Bover-* as one might expect) and retain the E stress and the E initial B- (rather than b > f). Forms with -ad for -ed may be dial. substitution of -a- for - e- (cf. Cymar for Cymer).

BOW STREET Card SN6284

'Bow Street', p.n. ***Bow Street***
Bow Street 1782, *Bowstreet* 1792, *Boulstreet* 1803, *Bow-Street* 1813, *Bow Street* 1851
A fanciful name in imitation of the London street, possibly in connection

with the turnpike road in common with several London names in Card such as Piccadilly, Chancery, Tyburn, Newgate, Temple Bar and Llundain Fach. However, Bow Street in particular, it is believed, arose from the habit of a London businessman who had moved to a nearby farm in the late 18cent. and, on being made a magistrate, frequently used the roadside tavern as his office for signing warrants. Attempts have also been made to link Bow with Cwm Bwa (***bwa*** 'bow') some distance away. Evidence is slight for both explanations.

BRAINT, Afon Angl SH5478-4463/5371

'(goddess) Brigantia', ***afon***, Br ****Brigantia***

breint 1200, *Braint* 1400, *Avon Braynt* 1477-8, *Afon Vraint* 1757

The river rises in Llyn Llwydiarth (on Mynydd Llwydiarth) and later forms two branches, both of which flow into the Menai Strait, one at Pwll Fannog, the other at Traeth Melynnog, Aber Menai, both locations being called Aber Braint (*aber breint* 1200, *Aber y Braint* 1400). The name reflects divine associations in r.ns, and the phonological development was Br **Brigantia* > OW **Bryeint* > MW **Breint* > MnW *Braint* (a word which is also cognate with ***brenin*** 'king' and ***braint*** 'status'). Because of its length, various sections have had at some time or other some half-a-dozen names usually reflecting its location. Braint has also been used as a pers.n. (such as *Myler ap Breynt* 1334 Gwytherin Denb).

BRÂN, Nant Brec SN9731

'brook dark like a crow', ***nant, brân***

Bran 1326 (1516), *Bran flu.* c.1570, *the Brane* 1586, *Nant-bran* 1832

Since the r.n. is common, the second el. is unlikely to be a pers.n. Brân (cf. Dinas Brân near Llangollen and see Llyn Brenig). An alternative interpretation is that ***nant*** is 'valley', one which was the haunt of the raven. There was also a grange called *Brane* 1326 (1516) and a manor *Braan* 1379 at Aber-brân where Nant Brân joins the river Usk (*Aberbram* 1503, *Aberbraine* 1568, *Aberbrayne* 1578, *Aberbraen* 1600-1).

BRAWDY, BREUDETH Pemb SM8524

?'(church of) Breudeth', ?pers.n. ***Breudeth***

Breudi, Brewdi 1204-14, *Bre'udy* 1293, *Brewdy* 1399, *Browdy* 1437, *Brodi* 1565, *breydeth* c.1566

A difficult p.n. of very uncertain etymology. Brawdy is possibly an anglicization of the W pers.n. Breudeth with loss of final -th. Breudeth has been explained as a W adaptation of the Ir saint's-name Brigid, which normally became Ffraid in W, but there are phonological problems with this explanation and it would require early loss of ***llan*** (cf. Llywel Brec). The church is dedicated to David.

BRECHFA
Carm SN5230

'speckled place', ***brych*** fem. ***brech***, ***-ma***
Brechua 1235-65 (1324), *Brechya Cothy* 1281,
Brechva in Strateuwy 1288, *Brechva* 1321-2, *Brechnagothy* 1535,
Brekagothy 1559, *brechfa gothi* c.1566

The name probably refers to the variegated nature of the soil and ground near the river Cothi. The 1288 form has the name of its district Ystrad Tywi (***ystrad***, r.n. Tywi).

BRECON, ABERHONDDU
Brec SO0428

'land of Brychan', 'mouth of (the river) Honddu', ***aber***, r.n. ***Honddu***
Brecch' 1120-48, *Brechonia* 1254, *Brechon'* 1291, *Aberhotheni* c.1200,
Aberotheny 1231 (13cent.), *Brekon'* 1516

The E name Brecon is taken from an abbreviated latinized form *Breconia* for the ancient *gwlad* and lordship of Brycheiniog (*Bricheniauc* 895 [c.1000], *bricheinauc* 12cent., *Brechyeniok, Brekhnok* 1241). The county formed in 1536-42 included the whole of Brycheiniog and adjoining areas, and, in E usage, took the name of Breconshire or Brecknock (also derived from Brycheiniog) with Brecon reserved for the town as administrative capital for the county; cf. Cardigan. Brychan was reputedly a king of Brycheiniog in the 5cent. Aberhonddu refers to the town's location at the confluence of the rivers Usk and Honddu[1] (q.v.).

BRECON BEACONS, BANNAU BRYCHEINIOG
Brec SN9820, 9920

'peaks of Brecon', E ***beacon***, p.n. ***Brecon***, W ***ban*** pl. ***bannau***,
p.n. ***Brycheiniog***
the Banne Hilles, Banne Brekeniauc 1536-9,
The Vann or Brecknock Beacons 1754,
the Breconshire Van, as well as that of Carmarthenshire 1809,
Y Fan Brycheiniog, Beacons 1832

The Beacons or Bannau extend in a line from Bannau Sir Gaer to Fan y Big and include Fan Gyhirych (q.v.), Fan Fraith, Fan Nedd, Fan Dringarth, Fan Hir (q.v.), Fan Llia (q.v.) and Fan Fawr (q.v.) reaching their highest point at Pen y Fan. The latter is probably *Kaerarthur dictus, id est cathedra Arthuri* 1188, *Artures Hill* 1536-9 and *Arthur Cadahir* c.1570 (possibly standing for Cadair Arthur) (***caer***, ***cadair***). Pen y Fan is also likely to be *o uann uwch deni* late 15cent., *Mynydd Bannwchdêni (which some call) Bann Arthur* 1592, *Monuchdenye hil* 1578, and *Manuchdenny Hill or Cader Arthur* 1720. The authenticity of some of these is difficult to judge since the forms feature in the work of antiquarians and maps of varying reliability. For example, *-deni* may be in error for ***-benni*** (see Y Fenni). Certainly their currency as local or colloquial forms must be in doubt.

BRENIG, Llyn Denb SH9755

'lake (of the river) Brenig', ***llyn***, r.n. ***Brenig***

Brenic 1100, *brenic* 13cent. (14cent.), *Brennig* 1536-9, *Brenig* 1838

The river Brenig (***brân*** 'raven', dim.suff. ***-ig***, and also a pers.n. Brân) took its name from the lake Llyn Brân (*llynbren* 1598, *Lhyn-bren* c.1700, *Llyn Llymbren* 1795, *Llyn-llymbran* 1840), whose forms suggest that the lake's name had become (colloquially at least) *Llymbran* with the addition of the tautologous ***llyn***. The river formerly flowed into Afon Alwen at Pentrellyncymer (q.v.) but most of the intervening valley was flooded (1979) to became the reservoir now called Llyn Brenig, two miles south-east of Llyn Brân. Brân has popularly been interpreted as the name of a legendary king (mentioned in the medieval Mabinogi) whose seat (***gorsedd***) was at Gorsedd Brân (earlier, significantly, *Gorsedh y vrân* c.1700 'seat of the raven'). The association with a raven in several rivers called Brân may refer to the colour of the water or perhaps, more likely, to sources in the remote upland haunts of ravens.

BRETTON Flints SJ3563

'farm of the Britons', ON ***Bretar*** gen. pl. ***Breta***, OE ***tūn***

Edritone 1086, *Brecton* 13cent., *Bretton* c.1310

The 1086 form is believed to be a miscopy of 'Britone', while the solitary *Brecton*, although possibly OE ***brēc*** 'land broken up for cultivation', could also be a miscopy of *Bretton*. The more usual names given by the Mercians to distinctively Welsh settlements were either Comberton or Walton. The Scandinavians, however, used *Bretar* of the British and Welsh (as in Bretby, Derbyshire and ON *Bretland* 'Wales'). There was an extensive settlement of Scandinavians in north Wirral and it is known that Norse settlers were granted land near Chester and that the Scandinavians had in their army Welsh or north of England Britons. The inhabitants of Welsh Bretton may have been distinctively scandinavianized in dress, custom or speech.

BREUDETH see **BRAWDY**

BRIDELL, (Y) Pemb SN1742

'(place near the river) Bridell', (*y*), r.n. ***Bridell***

Bridell 1357, *Brydelth* 1390, *Bridellys* 1399, *Brydell'* 1535, *y briddell* c.1566, *Bryddillth* 1618

Possibly a r.n. incorporating ***brwd*** 'warm' and a dim.suff. ***-ell***; there was a lost Pemb r.n. *Brydellach*. Later the name was replaced by Afon Plysgog (*Plisgogk*, *Pliskogg*, *Pliskoge* 1669, ***plisg*** 'shells', adj. suff. ***-og***). Several r.ns are preceded by the def.art. Forms such as *Bridellys* 1399, *Bridellis* 1411 and *Bredellorth* 1786 suggest that it was once divided into two tenements *Bridell-llys* and *Bridell-gordd* distinguished by ***llys*** 'court' and ***(g)ordd***, probably ***cordd*** 'tribe, family, troop'.

BRIDGEND, PEN-Y-BONT AR OGWR Glam SN1745
'end of the bridge (over the Ogwr)', E ***bridge***, E ***end***, W ***pen***, ***y***, ***pont***, ***ar***, r.n. ***Ogwr***
Bryggen Eynde 1444, *Brugeende* 1452, *Pennebont*,
Pont Newith on Ogor 1536-9, *Brygend* 1542, *(o) benn y bont* 1550-1600,
(tua) Phen-pont-ar-ogwyr 1778
The town developed on the east bank of the river Ogwr (q.v.) next to the bridge (thought to have been built c.1425) midway between Oldcastle also called Nolton ('old settlement', OE ***āld***, OE ***tūn***), and Newcastle on the west bank. The W form has *ar Ogwr* 'on (the river) Ogwr' to distinguish it from other places with the same name but appears to be a very late addition.

BRISTOL CHANNEL, MÔR HAFREN, ABER HAFREN
Monm ST3073
'sea channel leading to Bristol', 'Severn sea', p.n. ***Bristol***, E ***channel***, W ***môr***, r.n. ***Hafren***
Severn Se 1536-9, *the sea of Sevarne at Chepestowe, for so they calle More Hafren the sea which separeth Wales from Somerset, Devenshire and Cornwall* 1559, *De Canael van Brosto* 1584, *the Sea called Seaverne* 1625, *Bristol Channel* 1728, *the Bristol Channel, the Severn sea* 1805
The name is now applied to the large area of sea between south Wales and the English counties of Somerset and Devon but appears to derive specifically from the sea channel leading from the area near Flatholm between sand banks or 'grounds' to the mouth of the river Avon Bristol (*The chanell between the groundes* 1595).

BRITHDIR Mer SH7719
'variegated land', ***brithdir***
Brythtyr 1326, *Brithdir* 1563
brithdir is fairly common for land which is not particularly good or inconsistent in quality, or mottled or speckled, or dotted with stones.

BRITON FERRY, LLANSAWEL[2] Glam SS7394
'ferry at the farm near the bridge', 'church of Sawel', OE ***brycg***, OE ***tūn***, E ***ferry***, W ***llan***, pers.n. ***Sawel***
Brigtune 1193-9, *Ponte* 1208, *Brigetone, Ponte* 1254, *Brittone* 1281,
Passag' de Brytton 1315, *Lanysawelle* 1479,
Britan Ferry caullid in Walsche Lanisauel 1536-9
There seems be no evidence of a bridge here over the river Nedd. Gerald of Wales 1188 records only quicksands at the mouth of the river and William of Worcester 1479 noted only 'a ferry with a boat that goes to Swansea'. Any bridge may have been destroyed or have been over the small stream which descends from Ynysymaerdy towards Briton Ferry.

BROAD HAVEN, ABERLLYDAN Pemb SM8613

'broad haven', 'broad estuary', E ***broad***, E ***haven***, W ***aber***, ***llydan***

Brode Hauen 1578, *Broade haven* 1602, *Broad hauon* 1603

A bay which is contrasted with the adjacent cove Little Haven (*the Lytel hauen* 1578, *Little Haven* 1671). In recent years, the W translation Aberllydan has had some currency.

BROAD OAK, DERWEN-FAWR Carm SN5722

'wide-spreading oak', E ***broad***, E ***oak***, W ***derwen***, ***mawr***

an Oake 1675, *Broad Oak* 1760, *Dderwen-fawr* 1831, *Broadoak* 1891

A notable tree was a feature near one of the junction of several lanes with the Llandeilo-Carmarthen road.

BROAD SOUND Pemb SM7307

'broad strait', E ***broad***, E ***sound***

Broad Sound 1748

The area between Skokholm Island (q.v.) and Skomer Island (q.v.).

BROADWAY[1] Carm SN2910

'broad road or way', E ***broad***, E ***way***

Broadway 1675, *Broad-way* 1831

A stretch of the Laugharne-Pendine road, contrasted with *Stonyway* 1891 which was that part of the same road leading directly down to the middle of Laugharne.

BROADWAY[2] Carm SN3808

'broad way', E ***broad***, E ***way***

Broadway 1814

Apparently a late name referring to its location on the ancient portway running from Kidwelly to Ferryside. Broadway Farm is known to be medieval but documentary references to it are lacking.

BROADWAY[3] Pemb SM8713

'broad way', E ***broad***, E ***way***

Broadway 1815

Located on the Broadhaven-Haverfordwest road. There is another Broadway (*Broadway* 1711) near Llawhaden Pemb on a lane running from Gelli to Plain Dealings.

BRONABER Mer SH7132

'hill-side at the confluence', ***bron***, ***aber***

Bronaber 20cent.

The original hamlet (Rhiw-goch) is situated on a gentle slope overlooking the confluence of Afon Eden and a stream (which flows past Aber farm). The existence of a military training camp here gave greater prominence to the name Bronaber, although occasional local usage referred to 'Tin Town' from the corrugated sheets used to build some of the houses.

BRONGEST Card SN3245

'rounded hill-side', ***bron, cest***

Brongest c.1600, *Bron-gest* 1891

There are several distinctive hills with and slopes reminiscent of a paunch (***cest***) to the east and south- east of Brongest. There was another *Brongest* 1697 near Lampeter.

BRON-GWYN Card SN2843

'white hill', ***bryn, gwyn***

Brongwyn 1559, *y bryngwyn* c.1566, *Brynn Gwynn* 1811, *Brongwyn* 1851

It would appear that the name was first Bryn-gwyn but supplanted (though not exclusively) by Bron-gwyn (which would otherwise have been 'Bron-wen' since **bron** 'hill-side' is fem.), a substitution which was probably influenced by the nearby Bron-glyd and preserving a distinction from another Bryn-gwyn a mile-and-a-quarter to the north-east. Another alias was Betws Ithel (*Bettws Ithell* 1554, *Bettws ythel* 1617, ***betws***, pers.n Ithel) whose name is also recorded in *Kaer ithel* 1617 (the Parc y Castell fortification). Because of the existence of the ***betws*** in this location it is conceivable that ***gwyn*** signified 'blessed'.

BRONLLYS Brec SO1435

?'court of Brwyn', ?pers.n. ***Brwyn, llys***

Brendlais c.1200, *Brenleis* 1210-12, *Brenthles* 1299,

(*hyd*) *Vrwynllys* 15cent.

The first el. might also be ***brwyn*** 'rushes'. The modern form may have originated with reduced forms of the diphthong -wy- and finally confused with **bron** 'hill-side, slope'. The pers.n. Brwyn has been identified with the 12cent. *bruin o bricheinauc* (Brycheiniog). In medieval documents *Bren* frequently represents ***bryn***.

BRONNANT Card SN6467

'hill-side above the brook', ***bron, nant***

Bronant 1851, *Bron-nant* 1891

It would appear that the name of the village was originally Briwnant (*Briwnant* 1843, ***bryw*** 'lively vigorous', ***nant*** 'stream'), a name still preserved as a house-name near the chapel. In local usage Bronnant emerged when the Nonconformist chapel was built in the 1830s (*Bronant* 1851). It is not known whether the congregation felt it more appropriate to avoid the connotations of ***briw*** 'injury, sore'. The village has Afon Talfryn to the west and Afon Hirfain to the south and the river Camddwr to the east.

BRONWYDD Carm SN4123
'wooded hillside', ***bronwydd***
Bronwydd 1831
Named from a public house Bronwydd Arms (not recorded as such until 1875). On late 19cent. maps it was *Bronwydd Station*.

BRONYDD Radn SO2245
'(the) hills', *(y)*, ***bron*** pl. ***bronnydd***
y Bronnydd 1682, *Bronydd* 1832
bron generally means 'hill-side' but frequently describes hills. The hamlet stands immediately below a hill near the river Wye.

BROOKS Mont SO1499
'(area characterised by) brooks', E ***brooks***
Brookland 1725, *the Brook otherwise Brooksland* 1736, *Brooks* 1817
Applied on maps to a scattered village near the confluence of river Llifior with several tributaries. There are other E p.ns in the area, all apparently late.

BROUGHTON[1], BRYCHDYN Flints SJ3463
'farm by the brook', OE ***brōc***, OE ***tūn***
Brochetune 1086, *Brocton, Broghton, Broughton* 1283-4, *Brocton* c.1300, *Brochton* 1331, *Broughton als Brockton* 1675
The brook itself is the Broughton Brook (*r. Broghton* 1484, *Broughton Brooke* 1629-30). Although there is no historical evidence in this area for the cymricized form Brychdyn which has recently emerged (especially in the media), it is in keeping with other similar p.ns in Flints (such as Sychdyn, Golftyn, Mostyn and Prestatyn) and is analogous with another Broughton (*Brochtyn* c.1700) near Wrexham. Cf. the development of Broughton Glam with -twn in south Wales rather than -tyn .

BROUGHTON[2], BRYCHDWN Glam SS9271
'brook farm', OE ***broc***, OE ***tūn***
Broughton 1501, *Broughtowne* 17cent., *Brychton* 1757, *Brychdwn* 1888
Named from Nash Brook. The W form is recorded very late but is likely to be much older since it preserves the early E aspirate -gh- as -ch- and the final vowel is close to the OE -ū-. Cf. the development of Broughton Flints with -tyn in north-east Wales rather than -twn.

BRYCHDWN see **BROUGHTON[2]**

BRYCHDYN see **BROUGHTON[1]**

BRYMBO Denb SJ2953
'hill of dirt', ***bryn, baw***
Brynbawe 1391, *Brinbawe* 1412, *Brymbo* 1416, *Brimbo* 1620, *Brymbow* 1658, *Brumbo* 1707

Brymbo has been associated with the steel, iron and coal industries, and early references could suggest a spoil heap produced by medieval mining. However, since similar names occur elsewhere with no evidence of industrial excavation (as in Brymbo near Eglwys-bach, Denb and Cwm Baw near Llanllugan, Mont), ***baw*** may simply have described dirty, muddy conditions underfoot, possibly associated with steep hills. The change from -n- to -m- is influenced by the following -b- (cf. Lampeter); the change from -aw to -o is regular in the unaccented final syllable (cf. Y Bermo).

BRYN[1] Carm SN5400

'(the) hill', (*y*), ***bryn***

le Bryn 1446, *y brynn* 1554, 1594, *Bryn* 1854

The modern hamlet is located around *Bryn Coal-pit* near *Bryn-bach* (1833).

BRYN[2] Glam SS8192

'hill', ***bryn***

Bryn 1885

Named from *Bryn Navigation Colliery* opened 1841. The village developed between the farms Bryn-gurnos (*Brynygyrnos* 1813, *Bryn-gyrnos* 1833, ***bryn***, ***y***, ***gurnos***; cf. Gurnos Brec) and Bryntroedgam Isaf (*Bryntrotgamisaf* 1813), near Bryntroedgam Uchaf (*Bryn-troedgam-uchaf* 1813, ***bryn***, ***troed*** 'foot', ***cam*** 'crooked' probably alluding to the shape of the hill between them).

BRYNAMAN Carm SN7114

'hill near (the river) Aman', ***bryn***, r.n. ***Aman***

Bryn-amman 1834, *Bryn Amman* 1844,

Brynaman, neu'r Gwtter Fawr 1874

Named after Brynaman House. The r.n. also occurs in Rhosaman (***rhos*** 'moor'), the valley Cwm Aman (***cwm***) and Ammanford (q.v.). The name was chosen in 1864 when the Swansea Vale Railway station was built here. Earlier called Y Gwter Fawr 'great channel' (*Guter vaur* 1805, *Guterfawr* 1810) the name of a channel used in scouring coal; a coal-mine *Pwll y Gwter* was sunk in 1855. Both names were in use for some time.

BRYNBERIAN Pemb SN1035

'pool in (the river) Byrian', ***llyn***, r.n. ***Byrian***

Pont llin birian c.1600, *Llynbyrians bridge* 1611, *Llwyn berrian* 1796,

Brynberian 1743

The r.n. could be Byrian or Pyrian, possibly a pers.n. The two early references apply to a bridge (***pont***) over the river now called Afon Bryn Berian (earlier *Llyn byrian alias Clydach* 1605, *Biran R* 1729).

BRYNBUGA see **USK**

BRYNCIR Caern SH4844

'hill of deer', ***bryn***, ***carw*** pl. ***ceirw***

Brynnkeirw 1550-62, *Bryn y Ceirw al's Brynkyr* 16cent., *Brinkir* 1611, *Brynker* 1741, *Brynkir* 1838

In common with several other p.ns, the final unaccented syllable was lost following a stress shift to the penultimate syllable. Since there is no record of a deer-park here, the hill is more likely to have been the habitual location of wild deer.

BRYN-COCH Glam SS7499

'red hill', ***bryn***, ***coch***

Brincoch 1729, *Brincoch Furnace & Tenement* 1772, *Bryn-coch* 1832

An industrial village named from a farm just above the village.

BRYNCROES Caern SH2231

'cross hill', ***bryn***, ***croes***

Bryncroes 1252, *Bryncrois* 1535, *Bryncroes* 1659

There are several ecclesiastical sites in the vicinity (including Ffynnon Fair 'Mary's well'). The church is situated on a slight hill but the precise significance of the cross is still to be established.

BRYN-CRUG Mer SH6003

'cairn hill', ***bryn***, ***crug***

Bryncrug 1801, *Bryn Crug* 1837, *Bryn-y-crug* 1851

Little is left today of the cairn on the hill overlooking the Dysynni valley and its estuary. An alias seems to have been *Pontfathew* (1820) from the bridge in the village and a pers.n. Mathew.

BRYNEGLWYS Denb SJ1447

'church hill', ***bryn***, ***eglwys***

Breneglus 1284, *Bryn Eglwys* 1291, *Bryneglwys* 1348

The church, dedicated to Tysilio, is on a hill beside the main Bala-Afon Morwynion road. The valley floor between Llandegla and Corwen has a considerable number of drumlins.

BRYNFFORDD see **BRYNFORD**

BRYNFORD, BRYNFFORDD Flints SJ1774

'mud ford', OE ***brūn***, OE ***ford***

Brunford 1086, *Brunneford* 1317-18, *Brunford* 1341, *Brynforthe* 1433, *Brynfforthe* 1507, *Brynford* 1532,

Brinford, Bryn fordh, Brynford Brit. Brynfordh c.1700

There is no evidence of a ford or stream here but ***ford*** here is likely to have the sense 'causeway', an interpretation reinforced by the existence of the Roman road which passed through Brynford. Subsequently, two W words ***bryn*** 'hill' and ***ffordd*** 'road' influenced the cymricized development to Brynford and Brynffordd.

BRYN-GLAS Mer SH6203

'verdant hill', ***bryn, glas***

y Bryn glase 1592, *y Bryn glas* 1633, *Bryn Glas* 1690

A hill overlooking Dolau-gwyn ('white meadows') beside Afon Fathew which has given its name to the Bryn-glas Station of the Tal-y-llyn Railway.

BRYNGWRAN Angl SH3577

'hill of Gwran', ***bryn***, pers.n. ***Gwran***

Bryngwran 1740

The identity of Gwran is unknown.

BRYN-GWYN[1] Monm SO3909

?'moorland hill', ?***bryn***, ?***gwaun***

Brengwein 1254, *Brongwayn* 1291, *Brangwayne alias Bryngweyne* 1313, *Bryngwyn* 1349, *y bryn gwyn* c.1566

Despite the modern form as if 'white hill' (***bryn, gwyn***) the village does not stand on a hill (unless it refers to the small hill about a mile to the north). The early forms are inconclusive on the first el. and could also be ***bron*** 'slope' or ***brân*** 'crow, raven' (possibly in the sense 'dark').

BRYNGWYN[2] Radn SO1849

'white hill', ***bryn, gwyn***

Brewen 1231, *Bringwyn* 1291, *ll. V'el y bryngwyn* c.1566

Located on the east side of Bryngwyn Hill. The church is dedicated to Michael/Mihangel as in the c.1566 form.

BRYNHENLLAN Pemb SN0039

'hill by the old church', ***bryn, hen, llan***

Brinhenllan ?13cent. (c.1600), *Brynhenllan* 1580

Nothing is known of an old church here, unless it refers to the ruined, former parish church of Dinas in Cwm yr Eglwys (q.v.) about half-a-mile away.

BRYNHOFFNANT Card SN3351

'hill of Hoffnant', ***bryn***, r.n. ***Hoffnant***

Bryn-Hoffnant 1891

The village is at the junction of five roads, two of which lead in the direction of Blaenhoffnant, the river Hoffnant and Dyffryn Hoffnant (*dyffryn hoffnant* 1635, *Hofnant* 1651) which was earlier *Hodnant* 1331 (***hawdd*** 'fair, pleasant', ***nant*** 'valley' but later interpreted as ***hoff*** 'pleasant, favourite'). The r.n. is locally pronounced Hownant. At the crossroads was a tavern (*New Inn* 1798, *Bryn-Hoffnant Inn* 1891).

BRYN-MAWR Brec SO1811

'big hill', ***bryn, mawr***

Brin Maure 1587, *Bryn Mawr* 1769, *Brynmawr* c.1814, *Bryn-mawr* 1832

An industrial town which developed in the early 19cent. (providing workers for the *Nantyglo Ironworks*) around Bryn-mawr farm (*Brin Maure* 1587, *Bryn Mawr* 1769) and the *Prince of Wales* inn on Gwaun yr Helygen moor (*Waun r Ellygon* 1794, *Gwayn yr Helycen* 1801, *Gwaun-helygen* 1832, ***gwaun, yr, helygen***).

BRYNNA Glam SS9883

'hills', ***bryn*** pl. ***bryniau***

Named from a colliery (*Brynau-gwynion Colliery* 1885) worked in the 1870s by the *Brynna Coal & Steel Co. Ltd.* which took its name from the common Brynnau Gwynion (*Bryna gwynnon Isha* 1740, *Brynagwynon* 1784, *Brynau-gwynon* 1833, ***gwyn*** *pl.* ***gwynion***). Brynna represents the dialect var.

BRYNRHYDYRARIAN Denb SH9567

'hill of the ford of plums', ***bryn, rhyd, yr, eirin***

Rhydyreirin 1614, *Rhyd-yr-eirin* 1915, *Bryn-rhŷd-yr-arian* 1880,
Bryn Rhyd-yr-arian 1915

Rhydyreirin itself is a farm west of the village. The ford took the route between Henllan and Llansannan through Afon Deunant. A bridge (Pont Deunant) was later built here while a new bridge (*Rhyd yr arian New Bridge* 1915) was also built across the adjacent Afon Aled. The ford was notable, it appears, for plum trees. The modern form for the hamlet appears to favour the change from ***eirin*** to ***arian*** 'silver', perhaps in contrast to the copper and lead works in the valley, or simply with reference to the clarity of the water.

BRYNSIENCYN Angl SH4867

'hill of Siencyn', ***bryn***, pers.n. ***Siencyn***

Bryn sienkyn 1587, *Brynshinkin* 1662, *Bryn Shenkin* 1725,
Bryn-Siencyn 1891

The owner of the croft called *Bryn sienkyn* (1587) testified that his grandmother was *Mallt ferch Siencyn*.

BRYN-TEG[1] Angl SH4982

'fair hill', ***bryn, teg***

Bryn-têg 1890

The older name of the area was Rhos-fawr (*y ros vaure alias hen hendre*

1553-4, *rhos fawr* 1582-3, ***rhos, mawr***). The post office established here at the Llangefni and Benllech crossroads adopted the name Bryn-teg from a farm name and in time this displaced Rhos-fawr as the name of the hamlet.

BRYN-TEG[2] Denb SJ3052

'fair hill', ***bryn, teg***

Bryn Teg, Bryn têg 19cent., *Bryn Têg* 1900

Originally the name of a farm, it was adopted for one of several hamlets which developed in the wake of industrial exploitation in the Moss valley north-west of Wrexham.

BRYN-Y-MAEN Denb SH8376

'hill of the stone', ***bryn, y, maen***

Bryn y maen 1608

The village lies in the valley called Nant y Groes. The cross (***croes***) was possibly pulled down and replaced by an unidentified stone. There are several quarries nearby.

BUCKLEY, BWCLE Flints SJ2764

'the wood of Bocca', OE pers.n. ***Bocca***, OE ***lēah***

Bocleghe 1198, *Bokkeley* 1294, *Bukkelee* 1301-2, *Bokele* 1302-3, *Boucle, Bukele* 1326, *Bocle* 1331, *Bookley* 1622

A troublesome p.n. whose historical forms show early confusion of -o- and -u-. One proposal had been ***bucca*** the gen. pl. of OE ***bucc*** 'buck', supported by evidence of a deer park created here by *Roger de Mohault* (Mold) sometime after 1241 and destroyed by Llywelyn ap Gruffudd in 1257. However, the date of the 1198 form argues against that as does the dominance of -o- spellings in early medieval documents (in comparison with other genuine ***bucc*** p.ns in England). Another explanation (one generally favoured by scholars) had been ***bōca*** gen.pl. of ***bōc*** 'beech'. It has been shown the beech tree was not introduced into north Wales until the 18cent. when it was extensively planted in large estates. However, there are examples of ***bōc*** names (such as Great Boughton) recorded in Cheshire from 1086. The explanation which answers most of the difficulties is an (obscure) pers.n. ***Bocca***, but conceding that from an early period the development was strongly influenced by ***bucc*** and the existence of the deer park. The W pronunciation Bwcle preserves the medieval pronunciation ***bucc*** (which had already been adopted into W as ***bwc*** side by side with ***bwch*** 'he-goat') and almost certainly played a part in later development. The modern local pronunciation is 'Bookley' (as in the 1622 form) possibly reflecting W pronunciation but most certainly reinforced by migration from the north of England (particularly Merseyside).

BUGEILDY, BEGUILDY Radn SO1979

'shepherd's house', ***bugail, tŷ***

Bugelte 1259, *Bugeylde* 1291, *Bygyldy* 1392-3, *ll. V'el y bigil dy* c.1566

The valley west of the village is Cwmbugail (*Cwmbbogle* 1729, *Coom bigail* 1752, *Cwmbugail* 1832, ***cwm***) but it may be a contracted form of Cwm y Bugeildy. The c.1566 form has the church dedication to Michael/Mihangel.

BUILTH (WELLS), LLANFAIR-YM-MUALLT Brec SO0350

'cow-pasture', 'church of Mary in Buallt', ***bu, g(w)ellt, llan,*** pers.n. ***Mair, yn,*** cantref n. ***Buallt***

Lanveyr 1254, *Lamueyr Buelth* 1282, *Buelte* 1304-5, *Beult* 1533-8, *Buelth upon Wy* 1536-9, *lan fair y myellt* c.1566

Builth was the anglicized form of *Buellt* (*buellt* c.1100-3, *Buelth* 1176-1188, (*am*) *Vuellt* c.1400, *kantref byellt* c.1566), the name of the ancient cantref in which the town of Llanfair stands. The els are ***bu*** 'cow' (as in MnW ***buwch*** 'cow' and ***buarth*** 'cow yard') and ***gellt*** which appears in MnW as ***gwellt*** 'grass'. The form Buallt may have arisen under the influence of ***allt***. The name also occurs in Domesday Book 1086 as *Calcebuef*, possibly an attempt at spelling *Cantrefbuelt* (***cantref***) or at translating ***bu*** 'cow' as *boeuf*. The parish is still officially Llanfair in Builth, a translation of Llanfair-ym-Muallt. Wells was added to the p.n. in the 19cent. with reference to its mineral wells at Park Wells and Glannau Wells.

BULL BAY, PORTH LLECHOG Angl SH4393

'bay of the bull (pool)', 'harbour of Llechog', E ***bull***, E ***bay***, W ***porth***, commote n. ***Llechog***

Bull Bay c.1742, *Port llechog* 1790, *Bull Bay* 1805, *Bull-bay* 1813, *Porth llechog* 1838, *Bull Bay* 1878

One of the medieval townships of Twrcelyn commote was Llechog (*Leckow* 1291-2, *Lechog* 1317-18, *Lleghoc* 1500-1, *llechog* 1549, ***llechog*** 'rocky') referring to the nature of the coastal terrain. The bay itself is still used extensively as a landing-place. On the shore is a deep distinctive pool called, for some unrecorded reason, Pwll y Tarw (***pwll*** 'pool', ***y*** 'the', ***tarw*** 'bull') which is also recorded as *Pwll-y-Tarw* c.1742 together with *Bull Bay* on the same navigational chart.

BURRY HOLMS Glam SS3992, 4092

'islands near Burry', r.n. ***Burry*** or ***Byrri***, ON ***holmr***

Holmes 1398, *Le Holm, Insula Holmys* 1478, *the Holmes* 1583, *Holmes I.* 1777, *Holmes Isle* 1813, *Burry Holmes* 1832

A small island and rocks at the west end of Gower. Burry is a late qualifier taken from the Burry River formerly applied to part of the Loughor estuary close to Burry Port (q.v.) which itself derives from the small stream Burry Pill (*aqua de Borry* 1318) more than three miles to the east. Burry was transferred from this to the whole of the Loughor estuary (*the Creeke of Burrey* 1566, *Ost. Barry or Burra* 1695, *Burry River* 1805). References to *Burrieshed* 1399, *Burished* 1590 have occasionally been taken to refer to Burry Holms but apply to the general area at the source of the Burry Pill.

BURRY PORT, PORTH TYWYN Carm SN4401

'port on the Burry (estuary)', 'bay of the sandune', r.n. ***Burry***, E ***port***, W ***porth***, ***tywyn***

Berry Port 1833, *Burry Port Harbour* 1836, *Burry Port* 1841, *Porth Tywyn* 1870

Burry is taken indirectly from the river Burry (*Borry* 1318, *Burry* 1323, *Byrri* 14cent., *Burraie* 1586, *arme of the sea called Burrye* 1609, *Burry River* c.1900) of uncertain meaning, but possibly OE ***byrig*** 'fort', a small fort at North Hill Tor. The name was extended from the river to the deeper sea-water channel (*North Burry* 1531), the islands Burry Holms (q.v.) and the estuary. Burry Port probably arose in the 1820s with the construction of the New Pembrey Harbour with the port opening in 1836. Locally, the town was *Twyn-bach* (1911, ***twyn***, ***bach***). Porth Tywyn probably reflects the supposition that Burry Port contains E dial. ***burrows*** 'sand-dunes' commonly found on the south Wales coast (with vars ***bury*** and ***burry***) and influenced by the dunes variously known as Kidwelly, Pembrey and Towyn Burrows (now largely obliterated by an airfield and forestry) and reinforced by the existence of ***tywyn*** in *Towyn Bach* 1812, a small sea inlet and sandbanks now occupied by a dock and industrial buildings, and two farm names (*Towyn-canol*, *Towyn-mawr* 1833).

BURTON Pemb SM9805

'farm near a fortified manor', OE ***burh***, OE ***tūn***

Burton 1291, *Borton* 1307, *Bourton* 1316-31

There appear to be no traces of a fortification here. The village is located on a low hill above the river Daugleddau. A *Richard of Burton* was a canon of St David's cathedral in 1253.

BURTON (GREEN) Denb SJ3458

'farm of the fortified manor', OE ***burh***, OE ***tūn***, E ***green***

Burton 1315, *Bourton* 1397

The village of Burton is in a strategic location on a bend of Afon Alun between Marford and Rossett, while the parish is enclosed by Afon Alun, Stringer's Brook and Wat's Dyke. Additionally, the boundary between the tnshp of Burton and Shordley was formed by the seven to nine feet wide Town Ditch. Some have argued that the promontory hillfort at Rossett was re-used as a motte-and-bailey administrative centre of Marford commote. Alternatively, the farm itself may have been fortified in some way, perhaps by a palisade or even flood embankment to protect against Afon Alun. The present day Llyntro Farm in Burton is known to have been a moated farmhouse but only from c.1350. Burton Green, just over a mile to the north-east, was the tnshp's grazing land.

BUTTINGTON, TAL-Y-BONT Mont SJ2508
'Bōta's settlement', 'end of the bridge', pers.n. ***Bōta***, OE ***tūn***, W ***tâl***, ***y***, ***pont***
Butinton 1166-7, *Botinton* 1245, *Botington* 1278, *Butyngton* 1312, (*i*) *Dal-y-bont* 1440-93, (*o*) *dal y bont* c.1580-90
Bōta has not been identified. A bridge is recorded here over the river Severn from the 13cent.

BWCLE see **BUCKLEY**

BWLCH Brec SO1422
'pass', ***bwlch***
bulche yr arloys 1524, *Bwlch yr arlloys* 1618, *Bwlch* 1720, *Bwlch'r allwys* 1832, *Bwlch Arllwys* 1840
The p.n. refers to the gap through which a Roman road and the A40 pass, and the location for an inn (recorded 1755). The full name was Bwlchyrarllwys (***yr***, ***arllwys***, 'the downpour'), probably a place periodically flooded by streams; cf. a farm *yr Arllwys* 1779, *Arllwys* 1832 in Twyn Allws, Monm.

BWLCHDERWIN Caern SH4646
'pass abounding in oak-trees', ***bwlch***, ***derwin***
Bwlchderwin 1795, *Bwlch derwen* 1812, *Bwlch Derwen* 1838
The pass is between Y Foel and Mynydd Cennin. The 1812 and 1838 forms are influenced by ***derwen*** 'oak-tree'.

BWLCH-GWYN Denb SJ2653
'white pass', ***bwlch***, ***gwyn***
Bulch Gwyn 1649
The 1649 document describes it as a 'common'. The road between Wrexham and Ruthin passes through this gap in the hills flanked by several outcrops of limestone. The same feature appears in several local p.ns (such as Plas Gwyn and Gwynfryn).

BWLCH-LLAN Card SN5758
'gap of the church', ***bwlch***, ***y***, ***llan***
Bwlch y Llan 1836, *Bwlch Llan, Bwlchllan or Penuel Chapel* 1851, *Capel Bwlch-llan* 1891
The parish name Nancwnlle (*Nangwenleu* 1281, *Nantgwynlle* 1326,

Nant gwnlle 1541, *Nantcwnlle* 1834, 'valley of Gwynlleu') was used of the settlement (until at least the end of the 19cent.) but the Calvinistic Methodist chapel (erected in 1846) eventually provided a separate identity. Several minor roads converge on a pass from which a steep hill leads down to Cynllo's church.

BWLCHNEWYDD Carm SN3624

'new pass', ***bwlch, newydd***

Bwlchnewydd 1831

Named from its location near a house Bwlchnewydd and the Bwlch inn on a lane leading northwards towards Cynwyl Elfed. The house may be new in contrast to a predecessor, but there is also another hamlet Bwlch two miles to the south.

BWLCHTOCYN Caern SH3026

'pass of the heap', ***bwlch,*** (*y*), ***tocyn***

Bulche y tockyn 1609, *Bwlch y Tocin* 1783, *Bwlch-tocyn* 1838

The name of the pass appears to refer to the steep road down to the bay of Borth Fawr. *Tocyn* may have been the name of one of the hills near Porth Tocyn a mile from Bwlchtocyn. The inclusion of the def.art. *y* in the earlier forms suggests it was a distinctive feature.

BWLCHYCIBAU Mont SJ1717

'pass of the husks', ***bwlch, y, cibyn*** pl. ***cibau***

Bwlch y Kibbe Gate 1764, *Bwlch-y-cibau* 1836

An elliptical reference to the wooded nature of the pass. The third el. could possibly be ***cib*** pl. ***cibau*** 'vessel, bowl, cup' referring to hollows in the local topography; cf. Pwll-y-cibau farm near Betws-yn-Rhos Denb which lies at the head of two valleys and between two hills. *Gate* apparently refers to a turnpike gate at the crossroads.

BWLCH-Y-DDÂR Denb SJ1622

'pass of the oak-tree', ***bwlch, y, dâr***

Bulch y Ddare, bwlch y thare 1568

The road between Llangedwyn and Llanfyllin passes through several gaps, and here several roads come together at a point probably marked by the oak-tree. It is also alleged that the tree was later a focal point for meetings held by itinerant preachers.

BWLCH Y DDEUFAEN Caern SH7171

'pass of the two stones', ***bwlch, y, dau, maen***

Bulch y dday vaen 1561, *Bwlch y Ddeyvaen* 1616, *bwlch y dheyvan* c.1700, *Bwlch y ddaufaen* 1772, *Bwlch-y-ddeufaen* 1838

A pass on the route of the Roman road from Caerhun (q.v.) marked by two large standing stones.

BWLCHYFADFA Card SN4349

'gap near Y Fadfa', ***bwlch, y,*** p.n. ***Y Fadfa***

Bwlch y Vadva 1652, *Vadva als Bwlch y Vadva* 1728, *Bwlch y Fadfa* 1834

The road between Talgarreg and Pontsiân passes between several hills here. Half a mile west of the settlement is a farm called Fadfa (*Vadva* 1737) and to the north is Foel y Fadfa. There are a number of possible explanations for Y Fadfa, but the likeliest is *****dyfadfa*** (***dafad, -ma***) 'place notable for sheep' as in Y Ddyfadfa Caeo Carm, with the unaccented initial syllable da- taken as dy- (cf. ***dafaty*** 'sheep-fold > Dyfaty Llansannor and Swansea Glam) and then taken as the def.art. ***y***. Here, it is possible to postulate an unrecorded *Bwlch Dyfadfa > Bwlch y Vadva*.

BWLCH-Y-FFRIDD Mont SO0695

'pass near the moor-land', ***bwlch, y, ffridd***

Bwlchyffridd 1800, *Bwlch y Ffridd* 1836

There is moorland about a mile north of the village around Waun-y-pant and Bryn y Fawnog. The settlement was already in existence when the Congregational chapel was established here in 1800. Nearby is Bwlch-cae-haidd (*Bwlchcaehaidd* 1741, *Bwlch-cae-haidd* 1836, ***cae, haidd*** 'barley').

BWLCH-Y-GROES Pemb SN2436

'gap near the crossroads', ***bwlch, y, croes***

Bwlch y Groes 14cent.

The crossroads lie between two small hills.

BYLCHAU Denb SH9762

'gaps', ***bwlch*** pl. ***bylchau***

Bylchau 1795

Four roads converge here, each having passed through gaps between prominent hills.

BYNEA Carm SS5499

?'the bitterns', ?***bwn*** pl. *****byniau***

Baine 1607, *Binie* 1772, *y Bynie* 1786, *Binyea* 1813, *Binea Farm* 1814, *Bynye* 1821, *Binie* 1825

A difficult name, commonly recorded as Y Binie. A not entirely convincing attempt has been made to interpret it as ***bynie***, a dial. var. of an unrecorded ***byniau***. The name was transferred from the farm to Bynea colliery in 1837, later to the railway station, and then extended to incoprate the formerly distinct hamlet of Cwmfelin (*Cwm-felin* 1891, ***cwm, melin***) before 1939.

C

CADAIR IDRIS Mer SH6913

'fort of Idris', ***cadair***, pers.n. ***Idris***

Cadderydris 1578, *Kader ydris* 1592, *Cadeir Idris* c.1600, *Cader Idris* 1656-7, *Kader Idris* c.1700

Occurring regularly in hill-top names, ***cadair*** 'chair, seat' occasionally refers to a hill shaped like a chair but more commonly extended to include 'fortress, fortified settlement'. Here, legend accredits the unidentified Idris with being a lost prince or giant. The regional pronunciation is regularly Cader (retained in the name of the local secondary school Ysgol y Gader) which formerly led to the (now discredited) belief that the word for 'fortress' (and spelt Cader) had a different origin.

CADOLE Flints SJ2062

'cat-hole', E ***cat-hole***

Catshole 1795, *Cat hole Mine* 1840, *Cat Hole Mine (Lead)* 1878, *Cadole* 1959

The term ***cat-hole*** was used of the machinery for raising an anchor, specifically the hole through which the chain or hawser passed, here applied to a contrivance to lift men or buckets through a narrow entrance of the shafts in the lead mine. However, a popular belief alleges that a member of one of the lead-smelting families of Flints was granted the lease in 1737 and found a cat in an old shaft of the Thorntree Rake, whereupon he named the mine *Cathole*. The (deliberate) change to Cadole was probably prompted by respectability.

CADOXTON, TREGATWG Glam ST1269

'settlement of Cadog', pers.n. ***Cadog***, OE ***tūn***, W ***tref***

Caddokeston 1254, *Kadogestona, Caddokestona* 1263, *Caddockeston* 1291, *Tre Gadrock* 1780, *Tregattwg* 1795

Cadog is often Catwg in south Wales. The significance of the E name is uncertain and may be elliptical for 'farm or settlement near church dedicated to Cadog'. Cf. Peterstone Wentlooge/Llanbedr Gwynllŵg and Peterstone-super-Ely/Llanbedr-y-fro. Unlike Cadoxton-juxta-Neath (q.v.), there appears to be no reliable evidence that it was ever called *Llangadog* or *Llangatwg* but the church is dedicated to the same saint. The W translated name appears to be fairly late.

CADOXTON-JUXTA-NEATH, LLANGATWG NEDD
Glam SS7598

'settlement of Cadog near (the river) Neath', pers.n. ***Cadog***, OE ***tūn***, L ***juxta***, W ***llan***, r.n. ***Nedd*** (*de*) *Sancto Caddoco* c.1205, *Sancti Caddoci* 1254, *Caddokston* 13cent., *ll. gattwc glynedd* c.1566, *St. Cadoc's-juxta-Neth* 1571, *Langattoge juxta Nethe* 1556, *Cadoxston juxta Neath* 1582, *Llangattog by Neath* 1890

Cadoxton is identical to Cadoxton/Tregatwg (q.v.) and is probably drawn from an original Llangadog or Llangatwg despite the late occurrence of recorded forms of the W p.n. Nedd refers to the valley of the river Nedd (*glynedd* c.1566) while Neath in this p.n. probably refers directly to the river rather than the town. Catwg is the usual form of the saint's name and is recorded in the name of a spring *Pistŷl Catuc* c.1200 (***pistyll*** 'spring') in this parish.

CAEATHRO Caern SH5061

'teacher's field', ***cae***, ***athro***

Kay yr athro 1558, *Caer Athro* 1770, *Cae Athro* 1761

The ***athro*** has not been identified earlier in person or in role. He need not have been associated with a school but could have been an educated man renowned for his erudition and local influence or widely regarded as a bardic or music teacher. One intriguing suggestion is that the name refers to a descendant of a 14cent. *yr Athro* whose daughter (***merch***) Gwenllian *mergh Erathro* appeared in court in Caernarfon in 1364.

CAEO Carm SN6739

'land of Caeo', pers.n. or commote n. ***Caeo***

Kenwell Cayo 1291, *Kunwillgaeo* 1396, *Caio* 1439, *kynwyl gayo* c.1566

The village name, earlier Cynwyl Gaeo, was taken from a church dedicated to Cynwyl in the commote of Caeo (*kemmoto ... de Kaeoe* c.1191, *Cayo* 1257, pers.n. Caeo). This location may also be *caircaiau* 1160-85, *kaiarcaiau* late 14cent., ***caer***) between Pumsaint and Pentywyn.

CAERAU[1] (near Cardiff) Glam ST1375

'forts', ***caer*** pl. ***caerau***

la Kayre 13cent., *Kayre* 1386, *Caire* 1536-9, *Kayrey* 1578, *Cayra* 1762

Named from the hill-fort and castle ring-work around the church, or a specific description of the multivallate nature of the hill-fort.

CAERAU[2] (near Maesteg) Glam SS8594

'(the) forts', ***caer*** pl.***caerau***

Kaire c.1700

Identical in meaning to Caerau[1] but the identity of forts is uncertain; perhaps they were the prehistoric tumuli on Mynydd Caerau (*y Cayra* c.1700). Nearby is the farm *Blaencaerau* 1813, *Blaen-caerau* 1833. The village developed around the confluence of the stream Caerau and afon Llyfni near *Caerau Colliery* from c.1893.

CAERDYDD see **CARDIFF**

CAERFARCHELL Pemb SM7926

'Marchell's fort', ***caer***, pers.n. ***Marchell***

Cayrvarchell 1341, *Kayrvarghell* 1485, *Caervarchell* 1579

Traditionally associated with the saint Marchell, daughter of Tewdrig ap Teithfall and mother of Brychan, who sailed from Porth Mawr to Ireland. The same pers.n. also occurs in Llanfarchell, the old name for Denbigh church, *Capel Marchell* (lost) in Llanrwst Denb, and in Ystrad Marchell abbey Mont.

CAERFFILI see **CAERPHILLY**

CAERFYRDDIN see **CARMARTHEN**

CAERGEILIOG Angl SH309785

'fort of Ceiliog', ***caer***, pers.n. ***Ceiliog***

Carceilogh 1666, *Caer Geiliog* 1683, *Caergeiliog* 1686, *Cae'r-ceiliog* 1838, *Cae'r-geiliog* 1890

The word ***ceiliog*** 'cock' has been generally accepted as a feasible explanation although its significance is entirely obscure. Some historical forms reveal the extent of that confusion, with ***caer*** being interpreted as if ***cae'r***, 'field of'. Another explanation is of an (albeit unrecorded) adj. ****ceiliog***, based on ***cail*** 'sheepfold' and an adj.suff. ***-iog***, 'characterised by sheepfolds'. The derivative pers.n. Ceiliog presents fewer problems. The fort is probably the Roman site Caer Helen (now Caer Elen farm) a mile south-east of Caergeiliog.

CAERGWRLE Flints SJ3057

'fort at Corley', ***caer***, p.n. ***Corley***

?*Kaierguill* 1277-8, *Caergorlei* 1327-8, *Caergorley* 1331-2, *Gaergwrlai* c.1450-90, *Kaergorley* 1580, *Caergurley* 1601-2, *Caergwrley* 1614, *Kargwrle* 1628, *Caer Gwrle* c.1700, *Caergwrle* 1793

The Mercian settlement on the banks of the river Alun is deduced to have been called **Corley* (from OE ***corn*** or ***cron*** 'crane' and OE ***lēah*** 'wood' or 'clearing' or 'river-meadow'). The Edwardian castle built c.1278 was referred to by W speakers as a ***caer*** which was prefixed to the E *Corley* which had been cymricized as **Cwrlei*, **Cwrle* or **Gwrle*, a form variously interpreted as ***cawr*** 'giant' and ***lle*** 'place' or as L ***legio*** (a reference to the Twentieth Legion based at Chester). The most enduring interpretation was the creation of a legendary giant Gwrle (said to be buried at the neolithic burial mound of nearby Cefn-y-bedd). There is still a distinct difference between the standard W pronunciation (as Caergwrle) and the local E pronunciation (represented closely by *Caergurley* 1601-2).

CAERGYBI see **HOLYHEAD**

CAERHUN Caern SH7770
'fort of Rhun', ***caer***, pers.n. ***Rhun***
Caerun 1254, *Kaerun* 1284, *Caer Run* 1391, *Caer Hûn* 1795, *Caerhun* 1838
The late 1cent. Roman auxiliary fort of *Canovium* (four miles up-river of the present Conwy) overlooking a narrow crossing point on Afon Conwy. It was destroyed c.200 and abandoned in the 4cent. It was later associated in W history with an unidentified Rhun, but popularly believed to be Rhun Hir son of the 6cent. king Maelgwn Gwynedd.

CAERIW CHERITON see **CAREW CHERITON**

CAERIW NEWYDD see **CAREW NEWTON**

CAERLEON, CAERLLION Monm ST3390
'fort of the legions', ***caer***, ***llion***
carleion, *Carlion* 1086, *Kaerlegion* c.1130-44, *Karliun* 1154-8, *Karleun Legionum urbs* c.1191, *Karleon* 1200, *Caerlleon* c.1000 (1225-50), *caerllion* 13cent., *Kairllon* 1314
The site of a Roman legionary fortress Isca (*Iskalis* [= *Iska leg.*] c.150, *Isca leg. II Augusta* 4cent.) occupied by the II Augusta legion and named from the river Usk/Wysg (q.v.). ***caer*** refers either to the fortress or the town which developed on the site and ***lleon***, ***llion*** is a development of L ***legionum*** 'of the legions'. The connection with the Roman legions was well known, hence its description as *(in) urbe Leogis, que Britannice Cairlion dicitur* c.1140. From the mid 15cent. it was accorded the occasional antiquarian qualifier 'on the (river) Usk' (such as *Caerlhion upon Wyske* 1569).

CAERLLION see **CAERLEON**

CAERNARFON Caern SH4862
'fort in Arfon', ***caer***, ***yn***, cantref n. ***Arfon***
Cairnarvon c.1191, *Kaer yn Arvon* 1258, *Kaer in Arvon* 1284, *Caernarvon* 1345, *Caernarfon* 1795
The cantref of Arfon (*Aruon* 1269, *Arvan* 1284) took its name from its location 'ar Fôn' ('opposite or facing Môn', ***ar***, ***Môn*** Anglesey). Caernarfon was also the location of the Roman stronghold of *Segontium*, a name based on the British r.n. **Segont-* (***seg-*** 'strong, powerful'). The r.n. became *Seynt* (1284) and eventually Saint. The var. Seiont (*Seiont flu.* 1570) is an antiquarian restoration.

CAERPHILLY, CAERFFILI Glam ST1586

'fort of Ffili', ***caer***, pers.n. ***Ffili***

Kaerfili 1271, *Kaerphilly* 1314

Ffili's identity is unknown. The fort may be the small Roman auxiliary fort adjoining the castle (the building of which was begun by a lord of Glamorgan in 1268).

CAERSŴS Mont SO0392

'fort of Swys', ***caer***, pers.n. ***Swys***

Kairesosse 1470-1, *Kaersoys* 1478, *Kaer Sws* 1545-53

This was the site of a Roman fort (***caer***) but Swys is unidentified. Tradition maintains she was a queen, Swys Wen (***gwen*** 'fair'), and that the fort was once called *Caer Swys Wen* (*a Chaerswys wen* late 15cent., *Caer Souse or Dinas Southwen* [= Swyswen], ***dinas***).

CAER-WENT Monm ST4690

'fort of Gwent', ***caer***, terr.n. ***Gwent***

Cair Guent c.800, *Caruen, caroen* 1086, *Chaeruuent;*
Cairguent, urbs Guenti 1163-83, *Kaerwent* 1234

The name of the Roman fort and town here *Venta Silurum* (3cent. and *Ventaslurum* c.700) is Br ***venta*** with a Br tribal name *Silures*. The el. ***venta***, of uncertain etymology and meaning, believed by some to mean 'field' with an extension of the meaning to include 'market', is also found on the continent and in Winchester (*Venta Belgarum*) and Caistor St Edmund Norfolk (*Venta Icenorum*) with Br tribal names Belgae and Iceni. The name *Venta* was transferred to the town, and the surrounding area subsequently became known as Gwent; for Cas-gwent see Chepstow.

CAERWYS Flints SJ1272

'fortified place', ***caer***, suff. ***-wys***

Cairos 1086, *Kayroys* 1242, *Cayrois* 1242, *Karoys* 1242-3, *Kayrus* 1254, *Kerwys* 1284, *Kaerwys* 1297

Despite the lack of any historical record of a fort, the mound in the field called Erw'r Castell (*erw'r Castell* c.1700, ***erw*** 'acre', ***castell*** 'castle') is adequate support for a fort of some kind. The adjectival suff. ***-wys*** denotes a place characterised by a particular feature, in this case a ***caer***. The second el. has been ascribed to the river which runs east of Caerwys. One writer alleged it was once called 'Afon Gwŷs' (***gwŷs*** 'pig', a reference to a burrowing river as in Afon Gwŷs near Ystalyfera); however, there is no independent evidence to substantiate the assertion. Certainly Lhuyd knew the river only as Afon Galchog (*Avon Galchog* c.1700). In medieval W poetry an adj. ***caerwys*** appears at least twice (13 and 15cent.) meaning 'fair, beautiful', but the connotations are far from clear and could even be an adj. derived from the p.n. Caerwys.

CALDEY, YNYS BŶR Pemb SS1496

'cold island', 'Pir's or Pyr's island', ON ***kald***, ON ***ey***, W ***ynys***, pers.n. ***Pir*** or ***Pŷr***

insula Pyrus 864 (12cent.), *Caldea alias insula Pyr* 1100-35, *Insula Caldei quam Kambri Enispir, id est Insulam Pirri* c.1191, *Kaldey, Caldey* 1291, *Insula Caldey* c.1485, *kaldey yw ynys pyr or pur hwnnw y kauas kastell Maenawr pyr y enw* 15cent., *Inis Pir i.e. Insula Pirrhi alias Caldey* 1536-9, *the Ieland of Cauldey* 1566

A small, exposed island projecting into Carmarthen Bay; the same pers.n. (and probably the same person) is found in Maenor-bŷr (q.v.) about four miles to the west on the mainland (*or pur hwnnw y kauas kastell Maenawr pyr y enw* 'from that Pŷr the castle of Maenor Bŷr tooks its name' 15cent.). Recent usage has tended to favour Caldey rather than Caldy.

CALDICOT Monm ST4788

'cold hut', OE ***cald***, OE ***cot***

Caldecote 1086, 1336, *Caldicote* 1148-55, *Calecote* 1381, *Calcote* 1478, *Caldecott* 1535, *Calecoyth* 1536-9, *Calycott* 1541

OE ***cot*** (related to E ***cottage*** and W ***cwt***) sometimes indicates a hut some distance away from a farm or village which could be used as a store or as a refuge in bad weather, here exposed to the winds of the Severn estuary. Many of the forms are identical to those for similar p.ns in England such as Caldecote, Caldecott or Calcott. A very recent innovation is a W coinage Cil-y-coed, probably of local provenance, perhaps influenced by -cot taken as ***coed***. Intriguingly, some recent maps show a misprinted Caldicot/Cil-y-cold.

CAMROS see **CAMROSE**

CAMROSE, CAMROS Pemb SM9220

'crooked peninsula', ***cam***, ***rhos***

Kamros 1188, *Camros* 1291, 1539, *Kameros* 1323, *Camrose* 1578

The name probably refers to its location on a curved projection of land between Camrose Brook, the Western Cleddy and a small tributary of the latter. E influence is to be detected in the -rose forms which in turn probably influenced the church's former dedication to Ambrose (now Ismael).

CANASTON BRIDGE Pemb SN0615

'bridge near Canaston', p.n. ***Canaston***, E ***bridge***

Caneston bridge 1602, *Canaston Gate* 1844, *Canaston Bridge* 1843

Canaston itself is 'Canan's farm' (*Cananyston* 1413, *Cananeston* 1572, *Cannestone* 1609, pers.n. ***Canan***, OE ***tūn***) and lies a short distance south of the bridge over the river Eastern Cleddy. There was a toll-gate at the junction of the Canaston road and the Haverfordwest-St Clears road.

CANTREF Brec SO0525

'cantref', ***cantref***

Cantr' 1372, *Cantref* 1402, *Cantref al' Llankenedre* 1404, *p(lwyf) y kantre* c.1566

The parish derives its name from Cantref Tewdos (pers.n. Tewdos), which made up most of Brycheiniog south of the river Usk but later came to apply to a much smaller area centred on Pencelli; the remainder was called Cantref Mawr, 'big, larger cantref' (possibly in contrast to Cantref Selyf on the north side of Usk). The alternative name of the parish Llangynidr (pers.n. Cynidr) recalls the former dedication of the church (***llan***), later replaced by Mary/Mair.

CAPEL BANGOR Card SN6580

'chapel at Bangor', ***capel***, p.n. ***Bangor***

Capel Bangor 1834

Bangor is to be associated with other p.ns involving ***bangor*** 'enclosure within a hedge'. This ***bangor*** had the connotations of a religious enclosure (see Bangor Caern) as did the nearby Cefnbangor (*Keven Bangor* 1692) and Maesbangor (*Maes-e-Bangor* 1607), referring to a lost church. The temptation to identify the lost church with nearby Bron Llangwrda should be resisted since that appears to be ***glan*** later substituted with ***llan*** (*Bron Glan Gwrda* 1736, *Bron Llangowrda* c.1757, *Bron Lan Gwrda* 1747). A Nonconformist chapel was called *Capel Pen-llwyn* (1790-91) from the name of an area called Pen-llwyn (*Pen Lwyn* 1732) west of the current village, and Pen-llwyn was used of the village until the Anglicans created a chapel-of-ease here (*Capel Bangor* 1834) and then a church in 1839 (*Maesbangor Church* 1843, *St David's Church* 1982) adopting the name Capel Bangor from Maesbangor. Capel Bangor came to dominate usage although Nonconformists favoured Pen-llwyn, which still has considerable currency especially for the western end of the village; Pen-llwyn has also been retained for the primary school.

CAPEL BETWS see **TRE-LECH A'R BETWS**

CAPEL COED-Y-MYNACH see **MONKSWOOD**

CAPEL CURIG Caern SH7258

'Curig's chapel', ***capel***, pers.n. ***Curig***

Capel Kiryg 1536-9, *Gurik* 1543, *Capel Kerig* 1578, *Cirick Chappel* 1680, *Cappel Cerrig* 1736, *Capel Currig* 1795, *Capel Curig* 1838

This chapel-of-ease was originally associated with Llandygái. Some early forms are influenced by ***cerrig*** 'stones', a pronunciation still heard locally.

CAPEL CYNON Card SN3849
'Cynon's chapel', ***capel***, pers.n. ***Cynon***
Capel Kenog 1570, *Capel Kenon* 1578, *Cappel Cynon* 1612,
Capel Cynon 1834
This was a chapel-of-ease to Llandysilio Gogo (q.v.). Cynon, allegedly a son of Brychan, had another dedication at Tregynon (q.v.). The stream here is Nant Cynon.

CAPEL DEWI[1] Card SN4542
'Dewi's chapel', ***capel***, pers.n. ***Dewi***
Dewi Chapel, St David's Chapel 1836, *Capel Ddewi* 1851
Several ***capel*** locations in Card are dedicated to Dewi /David. This was a chapel-of-ease rather than a Nonconformist chapel despite the late date, and became a church (built 1835) with the same dedication.

CAPEL DEWI[2] Card SN6282
'Dewi's chapel', ***capel***, pers.n. ***Dewi***
Capel Ddewi 1823, *Dewi Chapel* 1851, *Capel Dewi* 1851
The Calvinistic Methodist chapel (now demolished) was erected in 1813. Nearby is Llwyn-ddewi (***llwyn*** 'grove'). The older alias of the village was Tafarnfagl (*Tavarn y Vagal* 1681) with ***tafarn*** 'inn', ***magl*** 'snare' (cf. Tafarn Trap) or ***bagl*** 'crozier', a reference to Cyrwen the holy relic of Llanbadarn Fawr whose ecclesiastical territory ended at Tafarnfagl.

CAPEL DEWI[3] Carm SN4720
'Dewi's chapel', ***capel***, pers.n. ***Dewi***
Cappel dewy 1710, *Cappel Dwy* 1731, *Capel Ddewi* 1811,
(farms) *Capel Dewi-isaf, -uchaf, -ganol* 1831
This may also be *chappell Dewie* 1586. There was a chapel (in the parish of Llanarthne) dedicated to David here, said to be in ruins in 1811 and a well *Ffynnon Dewi* 1831 (***ffynnon***).

CAPEL GARMON Denb SH8155
'Garmon's chapel', ***capel***, pers.n. ***Garmon***
Capel Garmon 1578, Garmon *Chappell* 1680, *Cap(p)el Garmon* c.1700,
Garth-Garmon or *Capel-Garmon* 1851
The chapel-of-ease (for Llanrwst) was built in the tnshp of Garth Garmon (*Gacrd Karmon* 1284) by the Anwyl family of Plas-yn-Rhos.

CAPEL GWYN Carm SN4622
'white chapel', ***capel***, ***gwyn***
Capel Gwyn 1812, 1891
Taken from a Calvinistic Methodist chapel registered in 1800.

CAPEL GWYNFE Carm SN7222

'chapel at the white ?field', ***capel***, ***gwyn***, ?***mai***

Gwynvey alias Wynvey 1316, *gwynvaye* 1600-7, *Gwynvey Chapel* 1757, *Capel Gwynfe* 1831

Possibly *Wlfry* 1288. A chapel-of-ease in Llangadog parish.

CAPEL HENDRE Carm SN5911

'chapel at Hendre', ***capel***, (***yr***), ***hendref***

Capel-`r-hendre 1831, *Hendre*, *Hendre Chapel* 1891, *Capel-hendre* 1947

A former chapel-of-ease in Llandybïe parish and the location of a Calvinistic Methodist chapel erected 1812 near two farms *Hendre-sigle* (***siglen*** 'marsh') and *Hendre-wen* (***gwen*** fem. of ***gwyn***) 1831.

CAPEL ISAAC Carm SN5826

'Isaac's chapel', ***capel***, pers.n. ***Isaac***

Chapelisac 1742, *Cappell Isaac* 1772, *Capel Isaac* 1806

Named from an Independent meeting-house established in 1650 on land donated by Isaac Thomas and alternatively known as Eglwys Mynydd Bach (*y mynydd Bach* 1715, *common Mynydd bach* 1719) 'little mountain' (***mynydd***, ***bach***) though the name is now obsolete.

CAPEL IWAN Carm SN2936

'Iwan's chapel', ***capel***, pers.n. ***Iwan***

Saynt John is Chaple 1552, *Capeleuan* 1578, *Cappel Joan* 1757, *Capel Evan* 1760, *Capel-efan* 1831, *Capel-Ifan* 1891

The dedication shows several W vars of John, Ifan, Evan, Ioan and Iwan.

CAPEL LLANILLTERN Glam ST0979

'Illteyrn's church', ***llan***, pers.n. ***Illteyrn***

Lanriltern 13cent., *Lanilthern* c.1348, *Lanultern* 1351, *Capel Llanilton* 1729, *Chappell Laniltern* 1745

The pers.n. was earlier *Ellteyrn*. ***capel*** was added at a late date to indicate its status as a chapel-of-ease in St Fagans.

CAPEL NEWYDD see **NEWCHAPEL**

CAPEL SEION Card SN6379

'Seion chapel', ***capel***, p.n. ***Seion***

Sion 1792, *Capel Sion* 1834, *Sion Chapel* 1838

The 1792 reference is to a meeting house which preceded the Nonconformist chapel built in 1825. The normal expectation would be for the hamlet to have taken the name of the biblical chapel n. (as in Moriah a mile west and Pisgah two-and-a-half miles south-east). However, in this instance Capel has been prefixed possibly under the influence of Capel Dewi and Capel Bangor some two miles north-west and one-and-a-half miles north-east.

CAPEL ULO Caern SH7476

'Ulo's chapel', ***capel***, pers.n. ***Ulo***

Capel Lilo 1838

Despite the extremely late record, the chapel was probably a medieval chapel of ease (sited at the location of the roadside cottage in the village at the foot of the Sychnant pass) dedicated to a saint whose name could have been Ulo, Ilo or Lulo and also commemorated in a Capelulo in Holyhead Angl.

CARDIFF, CAERDYDD Glam ST1876

'fort on (the river) Taf', ***caer***, r.n. ***Taf***

Kard' c.1102, *Kairdif* 1106, *Cardythe* 1555, *o gaer dydd* c.1566

The earlier form was *Caerdyf* in which *-tyf* is derived from the gen. sing. of the original Br word which gave the r.n. Taf (*Taf* c.1102, *Thaph* 1291). The anglicized form Cardiff has developed directly from *Caerdyf* substituting -ff for W -f [v]; cf. Taf/Taff and Llandaf/Llandaff. Both Cardiff and Llandaff have the additional modification of stress shift to the first syllable, while Caerdydd and Llandaf retain final stress. The W form Caerdydd displays the colloquial alternation of W -f and -dd. The r.n. Taf is also found in *Tamion* (8cent.) which may be a reference either to the river or to the Roman fort here.

CARDIGAN (CEREDIGION), ABERTEIFI Card SN1746

'territory of Ceredig', 'mouth of (the river) Teifi', pers.n. ***Ceredig***, terr.suff. ***-ion***, ***aber***, r.n. ***Teifi***

Karadigan 1130, *Cardygan*, *Cardigan* 1165-97 (15cent.), *Kerdigan* 1194, *Abertewy* 1136 (late 13cent.), *Aberteiui* 1171,

Aberteivi, id est, casum Teivi fluminis in mare c.1191 (c.1214)

Cardigan is the anglicized form of Ceredigion (*Coritciana regio* c.1191 [11cent.], *Cereticiaun* 807 [c.954], *Keredicíaun* c.1100 [c.1200]), corresponding closely in area to the modern county of Ceredigion. Ceredig himself was popularly believed to be one of the sons of Cunedda, the legendary 5cent. leader from the north of Britain who reputedly established the dynasty of Gwynedd. The E form Cardigan originally referred to the location of the town as the chief administrative centre in the original shire of Cardigan (*Kaerdigan sub' Hyrewen* 1242, *Kardigansyre* c.1244 *Kardiganshire* 1292), a small area corresponding with part of the commote of Iscoed west of the river Hirwern or Hirwen. The W name Aberteifi refers to its location on the estuary of the river

Teifi, while Sir Aberteifi is used of the county. The meaning of the r.n. is obscure although it has been suggested it derives from the same root as Taf (see Cardiff and Llandaf) with the r.n. suff. *-i*.

CARDIGAN BAY, BAE ABERTEIFI, BAE CEREDIGION

Card/Mer SN5000-0042

'bay near (town of) Cardigan', p.n. ***Cardigan***, E ***bay***, W ***bae***, p.n. ***Aberteifi***

The greate bay early 16cent., *Cardigan Bay* 1768, *Bai Aberteifi* 1899, (*dros*) *Fae Ceredigion* 1972

The major bay off the west coast of Wales. The W name varies between association with Aberteifi/Cardigan (q.v.) the county town, and Ceredigion the county of Cardigan (also known as Sir Aberteifi).

CAREW CHERITON, CAERIW CHERITON

Pemb SN0402

'settlement around the (parish) church of Carew', ME ***chirche***, ME ***-ton***

Churcheton 1346, *Chyrcheton* 1382, *Cheriton* 1418

ME ***-ton*** was the small settlement around Carew parish church (*ecclesie de Karreu* 1231-47, *Careu* c.1325-7) distinguishing it from Carew (*Olde Caryewe* 1544, *Olde Cayrew* 1545) and Carew Newton (q.v.).

CAREW NEWTON, CAERIW NEWYDD

Pemb SN0404

'new settlement in Carew (parish)', 'new Carew', E ***new***, E ***-ton***, W ***newydd***

Newcarrewe 1476, *Newe Cayrewe* 1543, *Newton* 1592, *Newton alias New Carew* 1619

Earlier forms show that this was the new settlement in contrast to the older settlement near the castle. The settlement around the parish church is Carew Cheriton (q.v.). Carew itself is *Kaereu, Kerreu* c.1200, *Kairreu* c.1208, (*o*) *Gaer Riw* 1257 (late 14cent.), *Kaeriu* 1280 (late 14cent.), *Caerewe* 1543, *Kaeriw* c.1566, *Oldecarrewe* 1476. This evidently has ***caer***, probably a fort on which the castle was built. The second el. has not been satisfactorily explained since the relatively flat area here does not favour ***rhiw*** 'slope'. Some forms are reminiscent of Aberriw (q.v.). and it is possible that *Rhiw* is an unrecorded name for Carew River which does have some gentle slopes on either bank.

CARMARTHEN, CAERFYRDDIN

Carm SN4120

'fort at Moridunum', ***caer***, p.n. ***Moridunum***

Chaermerthin 1126-53, *Cairmerdin* 1158-9, *Kaermerdyn* c.1191, *caer uyrtin* 13cent, *Kaervirddhyn* 1440, *kaer fyrddin* c.1566

The Roman fort *Maridunum, Moridunum* (2cent.) is Br ****mori-*** 'sea' and ****dūno-, dūnon*** 'fort' (influenced in several versions of the fort's name by L ***mare***). Later development was by way of OW **morddin* to *merddin* and *myrddin* and then prefixed with ***caer*** when the significance of *-ddin* had been obscured (although ***caer*** is also recorded in early sources in the sense 'town' as well as 'fort'). *-myrddin* was then reinterpreted as a pers.n. Myrddin by Geoffrey of Monmouth (c.1090-1155), drawing on older tales and the Colloquy of Myrddin and Taliesin, who incorporated Myrddin, latinized as Merlinus, in the legend of King Arthur.

CARMEL[1] Caern SH4954
biblical chapel n.
Carmel 1826
Named after the Calvinistic Methodist chapel (built in 1826) whose name was selected to reflect the hill location.

CARMEL[2] Carm SN5816
biblical chapel n.
Charmel 1851, *Carmel* 1891
From a Baptist chapel erected in 1833.

CARMEL[3] Flints SJ1776
biblical chapel n.
Carmel 1814
Named after the chapel in an elevated position and which replaced a chapel called *Penucha'r Golch* (***penuchaf*** 'upper end', ***golch*** 'pool for washing lead ore').

CARMEL HEAD, TRWYN Y GADAIR Angl SH 2993
'cardinals' headland', 'headland of the fort' E ***cardinals***, E ***head***; W ***trwyn***, ***y***, ***cadair***
Cardinals 16cent., *(o) drwyn y gadair* 1750,
Carnel's Point, Carnells Pt. 1805, *Carnel's Point* 1813,
Carnels Point or Y Gadair 1818, *Carmels Points or Trwyn-y-gadair* 1838
The north-west headland of Angl. In 1478 it was recorded as *le Fouleforeland* (F ***le***, E ***foul*** 'dangerous, rocky, unsafe with reefs', E ***foreland*** 'cape, headland') probably a reference to the passage or roads between the headland and reefs of Skerries q.v. (*The Roode of Cardinals betwixt the Skerres and the Shores* 16cent.). The name changed to Carnells and then to Carmels and finally to Carmel influenced by the biblical name appropriate for a prominent hill. There was also an ecclesiastical settlement here and a fort Cadair Mynachdy.

CARNEDD DAFYDD Caern SH6662
'cairn of Dafydd', ***carnedd***, pers.n. ***Dafydd***
Karnedh Dhavydh c.1700, *Carnedh David* 1700, *Carnedh Dhavydh* 1719, *Carnedd David* 1795, *Carnedd Dafydd* 1813
Believed to commemorate Dafydd ap Llywelyn (d. 1246) son of

Llywelyn ap Iorwerth (see Carnedd Llywelyn). The more strictly correct Carnedd Ddafydd is now limited to literary usage.

CARNEDD LLYWELYN Caern SH6864

'cairn of Llywelyn', ***carnedd***, pers.n. ***Llywelyn***

Carnedh Llewellin 1700, *Carnerh Llewellin* 18cent.,
Carnedh Lyüelyn 1719, *Carnedd Llewelyn* 1795

Believed to commemorate Llywelyn ap Iorwerth (d. 1240) whose son is commemorated in Carnedd Dafydd (q.v.). The twin peaks are collectively referred to as Y Carneddau.

CARN FADRUN Caern SH2835

'cairn of Madrun', ***carn***, pers.n. ***Madrun***

Karnmadrun c.1191, *Carne vadryn* 1542, *Carn Madryn*, *Carn Fadryn* 1778

Frequently referred to as Garn Fadrun; alternation between -un and -yn is common. The pers.n. does occur elsewhere, but tradition holds that this hill commemorates *Matrona* a river goddess (certainly in Gaul). Cf. *Matryn Issa* (1777) farm.

CARNO Mont SO9696

'(place beside the river) Carno', r.n. ***Carno***

(battle of) *Carno* 950 (c.1100), *Carno* c.1216, *Carnowe* 1293,
(manor of) *Carno alias Crano* 1545, *Blainkarno* 1206

Probably derived from the r.n. *Nant Carno* (1143-51), possibly 'river in an area characterised by cairns' (***carn***, adj. suff. ***-o***); carn is also found in the name of its tributary Cerniog (adj. suff. ***-iog***). Carno may, however, have been a pers.n. ascribed to the river. This was a place of pilgrimage and the location (perhaps within the earthworks of Caer Noddfa) of a community of Knights Hospitallers.

CARREG CENNEN, CASTELL Carm SN6619

'castle on a rock next to (the river) Cennen', ***castell***, ***carreg***, r.n. ***Cennen***

Carec Kennen 1248 (c.1400), *Karrekennen* 1257, *Carakenin* 1277,
Karakenny 1280, (castle) *Carregkennen* 1282 (late 13cent.),
castell Carec Kennenn 1248 (c.1400), *Kerikennen* 1536-9

In some historical sources, ***caer*** is substituted for ***carreg*** (*Kaerkenny* 1280, *Kaerkenyn* 1455-7, *Caerkennen* 1760). The present castle, located above the river Cennen (q.v.), is late 13cent./early 14cent. but an earlier castle is recorded in 1248.

CARREG-LEFN Angl SH3889

'slippery rock', ***carreg***, ***llyfn*** fem. ***llefn***

Y Garreg lefn 1736-7, *Carreg lefain* 1744, *Carreg lefan* 1838,
Careg-lefain 1890

This rock's smooth slippery surface seems to have been distinctive in an area which is particularly stony. The historical forms show the fairly uncommon fem. adj. form ***llefn*** with an intrusive vowel (cf. ***fferm*** var. ***fferam***) possibly reinforced by ***llefain*** 'cry out, weep'.

CARREGWASTAD POINT Pemb SM9340

'flat stone point', ***carreg, gwastad***

Carreg Gwastad Point 1814, *Cerrig Gwastod Pt.* 1815, *Carreg Gwastad Point* 1819, *Garreg-gwastad Point* 1843

The 1815 form has a dialectal -od for -ad and has a pl. ***cerrig***. Recorded as the landing place of the French in 1797.

CARROG Mer SJ1143

'swift flowing stream; torrent', ***carrog***

Carrau 1278 (?=*Carrac* or *Carrauc*), *Carrok* 1292-3, *Carrocke* 1549, *Karrog* 1608, *Carrog* 1865

The river was one of two streams flowing down the southern slopes of the Dee valley past the farmsteads of Carrog Uchaf and Carrog Isaf, giving its name, originally, to a tnshp over a mile to the south-east of the present village, on the south side of the Dee, and which may well have been the caput of the Lordship of Glyndyfrdwy and one of Owain Glyndŵr's ancestral seats. The present village of Carrog was formerly known as Llansanffraid Glyndyfrdwy (*villa de Lansanfreyt* 1292-3, *ll. ffyred ynglyn dyfrdwy* c.1566, *Llansant fraid Glyn Dyfrdwy* 1691); cf. several Llansanffraid p.ns and cf. Glyndyfrdwy. However, the railway station (on the Ruabon-Barmouth line) built in 1865 to serve the village was called Carrog to ease pronunciation for travellers, eventually replacing Llansanffraid Glyndyfrdwy as the village name (which was retained as the name of the civil parish until 1974).

CARWAY, CARWE Carm SN4606

'(place by the brook) Carwed', r.n. ***Carwed***

Carwed 1565, *Carowed* 1578, *Carway* 1834

This may be *Kylycarwe* 1578; the r.n. also occurs in the area as land called *Cwyn Carwed* 1565. Taken directly from a farm near the small stream Carway which rises at Dan-y-quarry above the farm Blaencarway (*Blaen-carway* 1834) to flow into the Gwendraeth Fawr. Carwed is also recorded as a pers.n. in Tregarwed (Llangaffo) Angl and Carwedfynydd Denb. The loss of the final consonant in Carwe led to the anglicized form Carway. The village developed near *Carway Drift Mine* opened in 1863.

CARWE see **CARWAY**

CAS-BACH see **CASTLETON**

CAS-BLAIDD see **WOLF'S CASTLE**

CAS-BWNSH see **PUNCHESTON**

CAS-FUWCH see **CASTLEBYTHE**

CAS-GWENT see **CHEPSTOW**

CAS-LAI see **HAYSCASTLE**

CASLLWCHWR see **LOUGHOR**

CAS-MAEL see **PUNCHESTON**

CASMORYS see **CASTLEMORRIS**

CASNEWYDD(-AR-WYSG) see **NEWPORT**[1]

CASNEWYDD-BACH see **LITTLE NEWCASTLE**

CASTELL CAEREINION Mont SJ1605
'castle in Caereinion', E ***castle***, W ***castell***, cantref n. ***Caereinion***
(chapel of) *Castell* 1254, *castellum Kereiniaun, Castel', le Castul* 1309, *Castelkereignon* 1344, *Kastell yn ynghaer Einion* c.1544-50, *Castell Caereinion* 1728
Some early forms may not apply here but could refer to some other important castle in Caereinion, e.g. *gastell yGhaer Einawn yn ymyl Kymer* 1156 (late 13cent.) is likely to refer to Mathrafal near the junction (***cymer***) of the rivers Efyrnwy and Banwy. Although Caereinion (*Kereinavn* 1200, *Kereinnyaun* 13cent.) probably ***caer*** and a pers.n. ***Einion*** it has been suggested that it could be pers.n. ***Ceraint*** and a terr.suff. ***-ion***.

CASTELL COCH Glam ST1382
'red castle', ***castell, coch***
Rubeocastro 1307, *Castelle Gogh* 1536-9, *Cast: coch* 1578, *Red Castle, Castle Coch* 1578-84, *Red Castle upon Taf* 1591, *kastell Koch* 1609
The original medieval castle and the late 19cent. reconstruction were built of red sandstone. There are architecturally identical examples near Cowbridge, St Donat's and Llangynwyd.

CASTELL GWALCHMAI see **WALWYN'S CASTLE**

CASTELLHENDRE see **HENRY'S MOAT**

CASTELLHYWEL Card SN4447
'castle of Hywel', ***castell***, pers.n. ***Hywel***
castello Hoeli 1154 (late 13cent.), (*o*) *gastell howel* c.1500, *Castell Howell* 1736
The village takes the name of the castle (now a large farm) said to be named after Hywel ab Owain Gwynedd (d.1170) but the pers.n. was

very common. It has also has been identified with *Castello Humfredi* 1137 (c.1286), *Gastell Hwmffre* 1151 (c.1400), supposedly named from a Humphrey reputedly an Anglo-Norman conqueror of Ceredigion in the early 12cent. but the evidence for this and even the location is disputed. Modern preference is for Hywel rather than Howell.

CASTELLMARTIN see **CASTLEMARTIN**

CASTELL-MEIRCH see **NEWCASTLE**

CASTELL-NEDD see **NEATH**

CASTELL-NEWYDD see **NEWCASTLE**

CASTELLNEWYDD EMLYN see **NEWCASTLE EMLYN**

CASTELL-PAEN see **PAINSCASTLE**

CASTLEBYTHE, CAS-FUWCH Pemb SN0229
?'cow castle', ***castell, buwch***
(*de*) *Castro Pulch'* 1291, *Castelh borth* 1316, *Castelbugh* 13cent. (c.1600), *Castellbuch* 1513, *Castell beoch* 1543, *Castlebythe* c.1545, *Castlebeigh* 1549, *kastell y fywch* c.1566
Possibly one of a number of derogatory names applied to abandoned fortifications or small hills thought to resemble castle-sites (such as Castell-y-dryw Glam, ***dryw*** 'wren' and Castell-moch Mont, ***moch*** 'pigs'). ***castell*** is reduced to ***cas-*** in a number of p.ns in south Wales.

CASTLEMARTIN, CASTELLMARTIN Pemb SM9198
'castle of Martin', ME ***castel***, W ***castell***, pers.n. ***Martin***
(*de*) *Castro Martini* , (*de*) *Castro Sancti Martini* 1291, *Castlemartin* 1341, *Castelmartyn* 13cent. (1382), *kastell marthin* c.1566
Apparently from the former dedication of the church to Martin (or Marthin in the regular W form), but it is possible that it refers ultimately to a secular individual. The dedication is now to Michael. Traces of an early earthwork castle lie on the north side of the main crossroads.

CASTLEMORRIS, CASMORYS Pemb SM9031
'castle of Maurice', ME ***castel***, W ***castell***, pers.n. ***Maurice***
(*de*) *Castro Mauricii* 1256-60, *Castle Maurice* 1256-72, *Castell Morys* 1587, (*o*) *Gastell Morus* 1591, (*i*) *Gastell-moris* 1778
The village takes its name from the castle, possibly named from Maurice fitz Gerald, brother of David, bishop of Llandaff, who had a grant of land at Priskily c.1174-6 about a mile south-east of the village. ***cas-*** is a late reduction for ***castell***.

CASTLETON, CAS-BACH Monm ST2583
'castle settlement', 'little castle', E ***castle***, E ***-ton***, W ***castell***, ***bach***
Lutyll Castell 1466, *Castelle Behan* 1536-9, *Castell towne* 1570, *Castelton* 1652, *y Castell-bychan (a elwir yn gyffredin Cas-bach)* 1778, *Castell bychan, Trecastell Wenllwg* 1838
The site of a small castle. The W name has ***cas-*** the reduced form of ***castell***. *Trecastell* 1838 is an otherwise unattested translation.

CAS-WIS see **WISTON**

CATHEDIN Brec SO1425
?'cats' fort', ***cath*** pl. ***cathau***, ***din***
Kethedin 1143-54, *Kethedyn* 1331, *Myghaleschurch in Kethedyn* 1382, *Llanuihengle (Michael) Kethedine* 1536-9, *ll. V'el gythedin* c.1566
The etymology is uncertain. Association of forts with animals is not unknown usually in a derogatory sense; cf. Castlebythe. If there is a pers.n. here, it may be Cathed or Cethed. The 1382 form referring to 'Michael's church' is otherwise unattested and may simply represent a clerk's interpretation of Llanfihangel. There seems to be little evidence that Llanfihangel Cathedin was widely used.

CEDWELI see **KIDWELLY**

CEFN BERAIN Denb SH9969
'ridge of the little crest', ***cefn***, ***bar***, dim.suff. ***-yn***
Keven berayne 1583, *Kevn Beren* c.1700
A difficult p.n. since there is no record of ****beryn*** (from ***bar*** 'top, crest' and the dim.suff. ***-yn***). The later forms may have been influenced by the pl. ending ***-ain***. The name of the mansion, Berain (*Berryng* 1256, *Beryn* 1335, *Beryng* 1368, *Berayne* 1589, *Berain* c.1700), may well have been older than Cefn Berain.

CEFN-BRITH Denb SH9350
'mottled ridge', ***cefn***, ***brith***
y Keven brith 1574, *y Kefn brith* 1593
This ridge of variegated soil, stone and vegetation is a spur on the southern slopes of Mynydd Hiraethog and was common land.

CEFN-COCH[1] Denb SJ1351
'red ridge', ***cefn***, ***coch***
Keven goch 1568-9, *Keven Kôch* c. 1700, *Kefn Coch* 1718, *Cefn-côch* 1838
This ridge is on the westerly slopes of Mynydd Cricor above Afon Hesbin.

CEFN-COCH[2] Mont SJ0402

'red ridge', ***cefn*, *coch***

Kenyncoch' 1310, *Kevencoch* 1322, *Keven Coch* 1577, *Keven Goz* 1587

Located on a low ridge between two arms of the river Rhiw. A house Fron-goch Hall lies on the north side of the hamlet (***bron*, *coch***). The redness probably refers to the geology; cf. Cefn Coch (hill) near Darowen (*Keuencohc, Cumcoch* 1187, *Keuenchoch* 1226, *Keuen Coch* 1420, *Cefn-coch* 1836), and Cefncoch (*Cefn-coch* 1836) at Llanllugan Mont.

CEFNCOEDYCYMER Brec SO0307

'wooded ridge at the confluence', ***cefn*, *coed*, *y*, *cymer***

Coed y Cummar 1798, *Coed y Cymer* 1813, *Cefn-coed-y-cymmer* 1832

The village occupies a promontory between the rivers Taf and Taf Fechan near their confluence recorded as *cymer* 1136-54. The village developed during the 19cent. as an industrial suburb of Merthyr Tudful and was transferred to it from Brec in 1974.

CEFNCRIBWR Glam SS8582

'ridge of ?the wool comber', ***cefn*, *cribwr***

La Rugge 1303, *Kevencribur* 1329, *la Rugge* … *Keven Cribour* 1360, *Kevan* 1782

Some forms have OE ***hrycg*** **'ridge',** identical in meaning to ***cefn*** (which also appears as the dial. ***cefen***). The significance of the second el. is obscure but may be ***cribwr*** 'wool comber' (cf. Bwlch y Cribwr near Llangywer Mer) or a derivative pers.n. Cribwr. This el. may also be recorded in *Castellum Kibur* late 12cent., probably in error for *Kribur*, known to have been near Kenfig, and possibly located at a defended enclosure or reputed hill-fort near Penycastell farm.

CEFN CROSS, CEFN-Y-GROES Glam SS8682

'crossroads near Cefncribwr', ***cefn*, *y*, *croes***, E ***cross***

Cefn Cross 1914

A crossroads immediately east of Cefncribwr (q.v.). Both Cefn Cross and Cefn-y-groes appear to be very late p.ns but there are several standing stones in the area and it is possible that one of these was identified as a cross.

CEFNDDWYSARN Mer SH9638

'ridge of the two causeways', ***cefn*, (*y*), *dwy*, *sarn***

Keven dhwy sarn c.1700, *Cevyn y Ddwysarn* 1795, *Cefn-ddwysarn* 1838

The former road between Corwen and Bala (now the route of the main road) had to cross two rivers (Cors y Sarnau and Afon Meloch) through pavemented fords (hence ***sarn*** 'causeway' rather than ***rhyd*** 'ford'). The ridge is the prominent slope of Bryn Banon to the south of the village on which stand the ruins of a settlement.

CEFNI see **LLANGEFNI**

CEFN-MAWR Denb SJ2842
'big ridge', ***cefn, mawr***
Cefn y mawr 1808, *Cefn-mawr* 1838, *y Cefnmawr* 1867
Cefn-mawr was one of two ridges overlooking the river Dee. The village emerged alongside industrial developments in the early 19cent. The other ridge is Cefn-bychan (*Cefn-bychan* 1835); see Newbridge.

CEFN SIDAN SANDS Carm SN3405
'silk bank', ***cefn, sidan,*** E ***sands,*** E ***point***
Cefn Sidan 1811, *Cefn Sidan Sands* 1891
Extensive sands and sandbanks in the Tywi and Gwendraeth estuary. Sidan may refer to the silky, glossy appearance of the sands. The colloquial pronunciation shidan makes it unlikely to be ***sidan*** a dial. var. of ***sydyn*** 'sudden, fast, unexpected' referring to the treacherous tidal inlets within the sands.

CEFN-Y-GROES see **CEFN CROSS**

CEGIDFA see **GUILSFIELD**

CEI CONNAH see **CONNAH'S QUAY**

CEINEWYDD see **NEWQUAY**

CEINT Angl SH4874
'(place near) Ceint', *r.n.* ***Ceint***
Gynt flu. 1578, *Avon Keynte* 1629, *r. Keint* 1710, *Ceint* 1795
The location and the district take the name of Afon Ceint, which is probably related to ***cant*** 'edge, border' possibly in an unrecorded pl. form. The river was the boundary between two parishes and two commotes (Menai and Dindaethwy).

CEIRIOG, Afon Denb SJ 1433-1966
'beloved (river)', ***câr,*** adj. suff. ***-iog***
Keiryawc 14cent., *Keiriog* 1568-9, *Ceiriog* 1795
The tributaries of Afon Ceiriog come together at Llanarmon Dyffryn Ceiriog (q.v.) and flow through Glyn Ceiriog (***glyn*** 'narrow valley'), under the aqueduct of the Shropshire Union Canal near Chirk (q.v. as a possible anglicization of Ceiriog) and then into the Dee. The r.n. may originally have been the pers.n. Ceiriog.

CELLAN Card SN6149

'little cell', ***cellan***

Kethlen 1229, *Kellan* 1284, *Kelh Lhan*, c.1700, *Cellan* 1834

The monastic cell here was a parish church by 1284. Cellan was later taken to be the female saint Callwen to whom the church was dedicated and whose name is also commemorated in the spring Ffynnon Callwen (*Fynnon Calhwen, ffynon Callwen* c.1700) located near the church. The c.1700 *Kelh Lhan* seems to offer an interpretation as ***cell*** and ***llan***.

CEMAES[1] Angl SH3693

'bends', ***camas*** pl. ***cemais***

Kemeys 1238 (1295), *Kemmeys* 1291-2, *Kemmes alias Kemmays* 1461, *the crike of Kemmeys* 16cent., *the creke of Kemeys* c.1566, *Cemmaes* 1757, *Cemmaes Bay* 1797

The bends or inlets refer to the bay and adjacent coastline at Cemaes or to bends in the river Wygyr (*Gwegyr* 1451) just before it reaches the sea at Porth Wygyr *(portu yoiger in Monia* 1194, *porth wygyr* 15cent., pers.n. ***Gwygyr***) which appears to have been an earlier name for Cemaes. The form Cemais (advocated by some) has long been supplanted in general usage by Cemaes which is influenced by the perception that it is ***maes*** 'field' (*Cemmaes comes from cefn and maes* 1757). Cemaes Bay is a form which emerged to attract tourists and is still used in some contexts.

CEMAES[2] Mont SH8306

'river-bends', ***camas*** pl. ***cemais***

Kemeys 1254, *Kemmeys* 1293, *Kemes* 1545, *Y Kemais* 16cent., *Cemmes* c.1679, *Cemmaes* 1836, *Y Cemes* 1852

Adjacent to the river Dyfi. Cf. Cemaes Angl.

CEMAES ROAD, GLANTWYMYN Mont SH8204

'road leading to Cemaes'; bank of (the river) Twymyn', E ***road***, p.n. ***Cemaes***, W ***glan***, r.n. ***Twymyn***

Glan twymin 1710, *Cemmaes Road* 1871

Located on the banks of the river Twymyn (q.v.) a quarter-of-a-mile to the east. The railway station for the *Newtown & Machynlleth Railway* was opened in 1863 beside the road to serve the Cemaes area.

CEMAIS COMAWNDWR see **KEMEYS COMMANDER**

CEMAIS HEAD, PEN CEMAIS Pemb SN1349

'headland of Cemais', terr.n. ***Cemais***, E ***head***, W ***pen***

Penkemas poynt 1578, *Kemes hed* 1589, *Kemes head called Pen Kemes pointe* 1603, *Kemaes head* 1748

Cemais is the name of the commote and hundred comprising the north-east part of Pemb, probably referring to the 'bends' (***camas*** pl. ***cemais***) of the coast between the Teifi estuary and Afon Gwaun, or perhaps a particular location which has become generalised for a larger area. Cf. Cemaes (q.v.).

CEMLYN Angl SH3393

'curved lake (bay)', ***cam*, *llyn***

Kemelin 1291, *Kemlyn* 1352, *The Crike of Kemlyn* 16cent., *Porth Kamlyn (croked poole)* 16cent., *Cemlyn* 1669-70, *Kemlyn Bay* 1805, *Camlyn Bay* 1818, *Cam Lyn* 1830

The lake Cemlyn, which gave its name to the medieval tnshp and harbour, is now part of a nature reserve, consisting of a brine lagoon enclosed by a shingle bar (Ysgar Gemlyn, ***esgair*** 'ridge') within a fairly narrow bay.

CENARTH Carm SN2641

'lichen ridge', ***cen*, *garth***

Cenarth maur 1136-54, *Kenarthmaur* c.1191, *Canartmaur'* 1221-9, *Keniarth Vaur* 1315, *kenarth* c.1566, *Kenarth* 1760

Located on a steep bank above the river Teifi. Cf. Cenarth Radn (*Kennerth* c.1545, *Kenarth* c.1546), with similar characteristics in Clocaenog (q.v.). The church is dedicated to Llawddog (*Sancti Leudoci* c.1191); cf. Llanllawddog. Early forms have ***mawr*** 'great' distinguishing Cenarth from Cenarth Bychan.

CENDL see **BEAUFORT**

CENNEN, Afon Carm SN6418

?'little lichen river', ?***cen***, dim.suff. ***-en***

(*o*) *Gennen* 15cent., *Kennenn Riveret*, *Cennen* 1536-9, *Kennen* 1558-9, *Cennen River* 1831

The r.n. may be ***cen*** 'lichen' (frequently found on the local limestone; cf. Cenarth Card) and the dim.suff. referring to the river (rather than to ***cen***). However, it could also be a pers.n. *Cennen*. The river rises above Blaen Cennen farm on Black Mountain and meets Afon Tywi near Ffairfach, formerly Abercennen (*Aberkennen* 1332, ***aber***), and gave its name to the medieval commote Is Cennen (*Deyskennen* [= *De Is Cennen*] 12cent., *Iskennen* 1303-4, *Is Kennen* late 14cent., ***is***). See also Carreg Cennen.

CEREDIGION see **CARDIGAN**

CERI see **KERRY**

CERRIGCEINWEN Angl SH4273

'the stones of Ceinwen', ***carreg*** pl. ***cerrig***, pers.n. ***Ceinwen***

Kareckeynweyn 1254, *Carrykkynweyn* 1352, *Karickywen* 1535, *Cerrig-ceinwan* 1746-7, *Cerrig Ceinwen* 1753, *Cerrigceinwen* 1890

The church is dedicated to the female saint Ceinwen whose other church was Llangeinwen, Newborough (*Llan Keynwen* 1535) in contrast with which Cerrigceinwen was occasionally called *Llangeinwen Vechan* 1536-9 (***bychan*** fem. ***bechan***). It is sheltered on its west side by a prominent rock called locally Pigyn Siw ('fine peak', ***pigyn***, ***syw***). The earlier forms (in ***carreg***) refer to this single rock while later forms (in ***cerrig***) refer to the lesser rocks nearby.

CERRIGYDRUDION Denb SH9548

'stones of the heroes', ***carreg*** pl. ***cerrig***, ***y***, ***drud*** pl. ***drudion***
Kerricedrudeon 1199 (1232), *Kericdrudion* 1254, *Kerrye Edrudeon* 1291, *kerricedrudeon* 13cent. (14cent.), *keric y drydion* c.1566, *Cerig-y-Drudion* 1594, *Cerrig y Druidion* 1673, *Kerrig y Drydion, Kerrig Druidion c.* 1700

This was a common enough name (six in Angl, two in Caern, for example), adopted usually by a croft or cottage, possibly referring to the fortitude of the inhabitants. The local significance of the allusion here is lost. By the 16cent. there is clear evidence in the historical forms that some antiquarians perceived the name somehow to be an adaptation of E ***druid***. Cf. *id est Lapides Druydarum* (1594, L ***lapides*** 'stones') and *Kerrig Druidion A gavas i enw, hyd yr ydys yn i vedhwl odhiwrth y Drydion neu'r Derwydhon* (c. 1700, ['...which got its name, as far as we can tell, from...], ***derwydd*** pl. ***derwyddon*** 'druid'). This perception of druidic association was reinforced by the existence of several tumuli and forts in the area.

CHANCERY Card SN5876

'Chancery', p.n. ***Chancery Lane***
Chancery-lane 1751, *Chancery* 1775

The hamlet is on the main Aberystwyth-Aberaeron road and the name is probably a fanciful one for a busy highway; cf. other Card places with London names (such as Bow Street and Temple Bar). Also called (Ffos)Rhyd(y)galed at one time.

CHEPSTOW, CAS-GWENT Monm ST5393

'market-place', 'castle in Gwent', OE ***cēap***, OE ***stōw***, W ***castell***, p.n. ***Gwent***
Shepstowe 1306, *Chepestowe* 1308, *Chapestowe* 1338; *castellguent* 1128 (1160-85), *kastell gwent* c.1566, *Kaswent or Castelh Gwent* 1722

An older name *Striguil* (*Estrighoiel* 1086, *Striguil* 1170) is obscure, despite tentative attempts to link it with L ***striga*** 'furrow' and its derivative ***ystre*** 'border' referring to the course of the river Wye around the town and the Norman castle. The growing importance of the town and its markets may account for its gradual replacement by Chepstow. Cas- is the reduced form of ***castell***. On Gwent see Caer-went.

CHERITON[1] Glam SS4593

'church settlement', OE ***cirice***, OE ***tūn***

Cheriton 1387, 1578, *Cheryton* 1535, *Chiriton* 1601

The church distinguished this settlement from the many other places in Gower with -ton settled by E people in the Middle Ages.

CHERITON[2], **STACKPOLE ELIDOR** Pemb SM9897

'church settlement', OE ***cirice***, OE ***tūn***

Cherriton 1794, *Cheriton* 1813

This is the part of Stackpole where the parish church is located, as with Carew Cheriton (q.v.). Stackpole Elidor (*Stakepol* 1176-98 [17cent.], *Stakepol* 1230, *Stakepol Elidur* 1256, *Stacpole Elider* 1488) is 'pool or bay near the stack' (ON ***stakkr***, ***pollr***) with a W pers.n. ***Elidir***; a monument in Cheriton church has a dedication to *Eliodorus de Stokepole* c.1191. The stack is Stack Rock (*the Stacke* 1594, *The Stack Ro(c)ke* 1610) at the entrance to Broad Haven while the pool may be Broad Haven itself or perhaps Bosherston Mere which is linked to it. Recently, the cymricized Ystagbwll has had some limited currency.

CHIRK, Y WAUN Denb SJ2937

'(the river) Ceiriog', 'the moorland', r.n. ***Ceiriog***, ***y***, ***gwaun***

Chirc 1164-5, *Chyrk(e)* 1295, *Cheyrk* 1309, *Cherk* 1422, *Churk* 1540, *Ewevn* 1291, *Y Waun* 1368

Chirk appears to be an early anglicization of the r.n. Ceiriog (q.v.) which flows past Chirk (which became the centre of the lordship of Chirkland, *Castelli de Chirc* 1164-5). In the light of the obscure phonological difficulties of Ceiriog > Chirk, several have proposed OE ***cirice*** 'church' for Chirk on the basis of forms such as *Chirchelanda*, *Chirchelande* 1163, later Chirkland, and a reference to the castle being at *Chirch* 1166. The W name (referring to the moorland near the castle) appears in the name of the lordship Swydd y Waun, the town Y Waun, and the church (*Eccl'ia de Ewevn* 1291), and was still in later use (*Waen issa* 1549, *Y Wayne Issa* 1552).

CHRISTCHURCH, EGLWYS Y DRINDOD Monm ST3489

'church dedicated to Christ', 'church dedicated to the Holy Trinity', OE ***crist***, OE ***cirice***, W ***eglwys***, ***y***, ***trindod***

ecclesiam Sancte Trinitatis 1154-58, *sancte Trinitatis* 1204, ~ *iuxta Karlion* 1230-40, (*de*) *Christi Ecclesia* 1233, *Christchurch in the Wode* 1349, *Christ Church or Holy Trinity by Kaerlion* 1408, *eglwys y drindod* c.1566

The church is dedicated to the Holy Trinity which sometimes replaced earlier dedications to Christ and to God e.g. Llandrindod Rad and Llanddew Brec. The 1349 form must refer to what was once very wooded countryside, perhaps even to Wentwood, once a much more extensive area between Usk and Wye.

CHURCH BAY see **PORTH SWTAN**

CHURCHSTOKE, YR YSTOG Mont SO2794

'church settlement', OE ***cirice***, OE ***stoc***

Cirestoc 1086, *Chirstoke* c.1190, *Chircstok* 1291, *Churchstoc* 1542, *Churstoke* 1577, *Churstocke* c.1679, *yr Ystog* 1447-89, *yr ystoc* c.1566, *Trerustock* 1552, *The Rustock* c.1600

Chirbury Shrops, only three miles away, has OE ***cirice*** with ***byrig*** 'fortified place'. The W forms are late. *Yr Ystog* seems to have developed from ***stoc*** with the addition of initial *Y-* (as with words such as ***ystrad*** and ***ysgol***) together with the def.art. ***yr*** (which is also recorded as the E ***the*** in at least one form). The 1552 and c.1600 forms suggest the development of a by-form *Rystog* (as with Rhewl and Rhyl q.v.). The 1552 form has W ***tref*** in its sense of 'settlement'.

CHURCH VILLAGE, PENTRE'R EGLWYS Glam ST0886

'(the) church village', E ***church***, E ***village***, W ***pentref***, ***yr***, ***eglwys***

Church Village Sta. c.1898, *Church Village* 1902

A village which developed in the late 19cent. around *Church Village Halt* on the *Llantrisant & Taff Vale Junction Railway* c.1885 near Llantwit Fardre church and may have been coined by the owners of the railway. The name may have arisen because the area around the church was sometimes described as the Village (*Villa* 1794, *Village* 1814). Pentre'r Eglwys appears to be a recent translation of Church Village arising from residential developments, but *Pentre Eglwys* 1941 suggests it could be older. Gartholwg 'hill view' (***garth***, ***golwg***) has also had some currency as the W form, probably because of the location here of the former Gartholwg Children's Home and a hospital which appears to have been taken from a house Gartholwg overlooking the Taf valley at Gwaelod-y-garth (***gwaelod*** 'bottom' of the hill of *the Garth* 1638) about two miles south-east, and which is now preserved in the name of an educational campus.

CHWILOG Caern SH4338

'abounding in beetles', ***chwilog***

Wylok 1352, *Whelock* 1535, *Chwilog* 1684

The adj. ***chwilog*** was probably first applied to the river (or a section of it) and then to the tnshp and village which developed in the early 19cent. near the mill where the turnpike road crosses the river, which had for some time been known as Afon Wen (*Yr Avon Wen* 1719, *Avonwen* 1766, ***afon***, ***gwyn*** fem. ***gwen***) which in turn gave its name to the nearby hamlet of Afon-wen (*Afonwen* 1780).

CHWITFFORDD see **WHITFORD**

CILÂ see **KILLAY**

CILAN Caern SH2924

'corner, angle', ***cilan***

Kilan 1307-27, *Kylan* 1352, *Celen* 1488-9, *Cilan* 1838

cilan has a variety of meanings all of which are also appropriate to the topography of this hilly promontory, such as 'retreat, nook', 'back', 'ridge'. The name is also preserved in Mynydd Cilan (***mynydd***) and Trwyn Cilan (***trwyn*** 'headland').

CILCAIN Flints SJ1765

'fair corner', ***cil, cain***

Kilkein 1202 (1295), *Kilkeyn* 1254, *Kilkyn* 1284, *Kylleyn'* 1291, *Kilken* 1463, *Kilkayn* 1465

The significance of the second el. cannot be determined with any certainty. The river is Nant Gain (a tributary of Afon Alun) and was probably taken to be the origin of Cilcain (*Kilken so called from ye Brook Kain quasi Kîl Kain* c.1700). However, Cain could also be a pers.n. or ***cain*** 'ridge' (of the dominant Moel Fama).

CILCENNIN Card SN5260

'nook of leeks', ***cil, cennin***

Kilkennin 1210 (c.1400), *Kil Kennin* 1375-80, *Kilkennyn* 1550, *Cilcennin* 1834

The church is dedicated to the Holy Trinity despite later antiquarians postulating saints such as Cenwyn, Cannen and an unrecorded Cennin. There is a Nant-y-drindod nearby (***trindod*** 'trinity'). In the 17cent. the church was incorporated into the adjacent parish of Llanbadarn Trefeglwys as Llanbadarn Cilcennin (*Lanbaderne Kylkenyng* 1361, *Llanbaderne Kilkennyn* 1696-97) and occasionally as *Llanbadarn Fach* (1727).

CILFÁI see **KILVEY**

CILFYNYDD Glam ST0892

'mountain nook', ***cil, mynydd***

Kilfynidd 1730, *Kilvyunidd* 1754, *Kilfonydd* 1766, *Cil-fynydd* 1833

The village developed around the Albion Colliery from c.1884 and was known for a short period as *Albion Town*, a name preserved in the Albion Industrial Estate. Villagers petitioned the Postmaster-General for the retention of Cilfynydd, a name taken from a farm in a small valley above the village.

CILGERRAN Pemb SN1941

'nook of Cerran, ***cil***, pers.n. ***Cerran***

Kilgerran 1165 (late 14cent.), *Kilgerann* 1166 (c.1400), *Kilgarran* c.1191, *Kylgaren* 1241

The pers.n. may be an unrecorded Cerran probably found in *castell cerran* 1136-54 thought to have been near Tenby Pemb. The spellings with *-gar(r)an* may have been influenced by ***garan*** 'crane' found in r.ns. The original Cilgerran has been identified as Cenarth Bychan (*Chenarth Bechan* 1107 [13cent.], *Kenartvechan* 1222, *Kengarth Vachan* 1108 [15cent.]) but that may actually have been at Cefn-garth where there is a tumulus near Pont-y-ceirt; see Cenarth.

CILGETI see **KILGETTY**

CILGWYN Carm SN7429

'fair nook', ***cil***, ***gwyn***

y kilgwyn 1540-77, *Kilgwyn* 1627, *Cilgwyn* 1831

Located in a narrow, wooded part of the valley of Afon Ydw. ***gwyn*** could be 'white' used of vegetation.

CILIAU AERON Card SN5058

'nooks of (the river) Aeron', ***cil*** pl. ***ciliau***, r.n. ***Aeron***

Killev 1273, *Killeu* 1284 (c.1400), (church of) *St. Michael, Kylieu* 1361, *Kyllyhayron* 1543, *Kilie ayron* c.1566, *Ciliau-Aeron* 1834

Probably the several small valleys and hollows to the south, but there are some distinctive bends in the river Aeron at this point.

CILIENI Brec SN9134

?'river rising in a small nook' , ?***cilan*** var. ****cilian-*** , r.n. suff. ***-i***

nant cilieni 1136-54, *Killieny* 1556, *Kyllyeny* 1571, *Cilieni* 1838

The first el. is probably the unrecorded var. ****cilian*** (a dim. of ***cil*** 'nook') a reference to the source of the river in a small hollow between the ridges of Mynydd Epynt (the ***nant*** 'valley'of the c.720 form).

CILMERI Brec SO0051

'nook of brambles', ***cil***, ***mieri*** dial. var. ***meri***

Kilmery 1712, *Cilmeri* 1820-1

The name is taken from a farm half-a-mile west of the village. Cilmeri appears in earlier records as Cefnybedd (*Keuenebeht* 1277, *Keven y Bedh* 1600-7, *Cefn-y-bedd* 1833, 'ridge of the grave' ***cefn***, ***y***, ***bedd***). Reputedly the place where Llywelyn ap Gruffudd, prince of Wales, was killed in 1282, and commemorated by a monument placed here in 1956, but the 1277 reference shows that the 'grave' is earlier, and locally associated with a prehistoric grave. The antiquity of *Cwm Llywelyn* 1833 (Llywelyn's valley) is unknown. Meri may have been a pers.n.

CILYBEBYLL Glam SN7404

?'nook of the shelter', ?*cil*, *y*, *pebyll*

Killebebit 1254, *Kilthibebilth* 1281, *Kilbebill* 1468, *kil y bebyll* c.1566

It is by no means certain that the first el. is ***cil*** since many early forms such as *Kilth-*, *Kylth-* and *Kell-* may well stand for W ***celli*** 'grove, copse' as in Gelligeiros (***ceirios*** 'cherries') and Gelli-nudd (?***nudd*** 'haze, mist') on the south-west side of the village. The second el. is the old sing. ***pebyll*** (which was later taken to be an analogous pl. in MnW). It referred to a temporary shelter, arbour, refuge or sanctuary (as well as tent).

CIL-Y-COED see **CALDICOT**

CINMEL, KINMEL Denb SH9880

'nook of Mael', ***cil***, pers.n. ***Mael***

Kilmayl 1311, *Kilmeyl* 1331, *Kilmayl* 1334, *Kynmayll* 1515-16, *Kynmell* 1535, *Kynmell' alias Kilmaill'* 1579, *Kinmel* 1680

The identity of Mael is unknown leading some to argue that it is ***mael*** 'prince'. The change from -l- to -n- is probably caused by the following -m-; -ae- became -e- in the final unaccented syllable. The anglicized form Kinmel has retained its popularity due to Kinmel Hall, the nearby army training base of Kinmel Camp and the resort of Kinmel Bay.

CITY DULAS see **DULAS**

CLARBESTON Pemb SN0521

'Clarenbald's settlement', pers.n. ***Clarenbald***, OE ***tūn***

Clarebaldestun 1159-63, *villa Clarenbaldi* 1176 (17cent.), *Clarebaston* 1338

The identity of Clarenbald is unknown.

CLARBESTON ROAD Pemb SN0121

'road leading to Clarbeston', E ***road***, p.n. ***Clarbeston***

Cross Inn Station c.1850, *Clarbeston Road* 1856

Named from a railway station on the Fishguard-Carmarthen railway about two miles west of Clarbeston (q.v.). The *Cross Inn* was a tavern.

CLAS-AR-WY see **GLASBURY**

CLATTER Mont SN9994

'gate that clatters', E ***clatter***, E ***gate***

Clatter-gate 1836, *Clatter* 1891

The location of a former turnpike gate (at the inn *Templebar* 1817) which appears to have been known for its noise. Attempts to interpret it as an unidentified stream name *Cletwr* 'rough water' (***caled***, ***dŵr***) are not supported by the forms. Local pronunciation is 'Clêtyr'.

CLAWDDNEWYDD Denb SJ0852

'new dyke', ***clawdd, newydd***

Clawdd Newydd 1635-6, *Klawdh Newydd* c.1700

The dyke possibly marked a terr. boundary (possibly Mer and Denb). However ***clawdd*** can signify 'ditch, gutter' in reference to drainage; the nearby Sarnau 'causeways' supports this explanation.

CLAWDD OFFA see **OFFA'S DYKE**

CLEDDAU Pemb SN0313, SM9912

'sword river', ***cleddyf***

aber yr auon a elwir Cledyf 1108 (14cent.), *duo Cledeu* c.1194, *Deu Gledyf* 1220 (c.1400), *avon Gleddyf* 1220 (15cent.), *ad fluminis Cledyf* 13cent., *Gladius* 13cent., *aque de Clethi* 1326, *Gledy* 1394, *Gleddau Wen* 1460-80, *Cleetheddy* 1602, *Clethe dduy*, *Cledde niger* c.1600, *Clethe wen*, *Cleetheddy*, *both Cleddies* 1603

Two adjoining rivers bear the name ***cleddyf***, locally pronounced Cledde and Cleddy (with loss of final -f), from a fancied resemblance to the manner in which they cut like a sword through the landscape; the 13cent. form may well be a conscious substitution with the cognate L ***gladius*** 'sword'. The Eastern Cleddau or Cleddau Ddu (***du*** 'black') rises on Wauncleddau above Mynachlog-ddu while the Western Cleddau or Cleddau Wen (***gwen*** fem. of ***gwyn*** 'white') rises at Llygadcleddau (***llygad*** 'eye; source') near Scleddau (q.v.). Sometimes, Cleddau was used indiscriminately for both without qualifiers. The rivers come together below Picton Point to form the major channel at Aberdaugleddau/ Milford Haven (q.v.). The emergence and later predominance of the var. Cleddau, at least in written forms and in Aberdaugleddau, can be ascribed to the perception of Cleddau as a plural to encompass both rivers.

CLEDWEN, Afon Denb SH8964

?'rough hill' (river)', ***afon***, ?p.n. ***Caledfryn***

fluvium Kaletwyn 1333, *Cledwyn* 1483, *Cledwen* 20cent.

The river's principal tributary is Nant Caledfryn (***nant*** 'stream' or 'valley', ***caled*** 'rough', ***bryn*** 'hill') which, as the modern Cledwen, flows past Llangernyw to be joined by Afon Gallen to become Elwy. Cledwen seems to be a very recent form, influenced by the expectation of a regular fem. ***gwen*** associated with a river. However, the historical forms all seem to show a problematic masc. ***gwyn***. One hypothesis, lacking any documentary corroboration, is that it was originally 'afon Cledfryn' from its tributary, which then became *Cledwyn* and eventually regularised as a r.n. to Cledwen under the further influence of the nearby Afon and Llyn Alwen.

CLEIRO see **CLYRO**

CLOCAENOG Denb SJ0854

'lichen-encrusted rock', ***clog, caenog***

Colocaynauc 1254, *Clocaynauc* 1266, *Clocaenok* 1349

There are several steep rocks here with extensive uplands (*Maes Clocaynoke* 1556, *Parc Glocaenawc* c.1600, *Clockaynocke Parke* 1603) between the village of Clocaenog and Mynydd Hiraethog (q.v.) now largely afforested. The adj. ***caenog*** 'encrusted' occurs several times in the area (*Caenog, Nant Caenog* 1652/3, *Llidiart Caenog* 1765). The noun ***caen*** is used of crust on a rock, almost certainly the lichen from which dye was produced.

CLUD see **RADNOR FOREST**

CLUNDERWEN Carm SN1219

'oak meadow', ***clun, derwen***

Klin Derwidd 1760, *Clynderwen* 1765

clun is a common el. in south Wales and is sometimes confused with ***glyn***. The first form is ***derwydd*** 'oak-trees' replaced by ***derwen*** 'oak-tree'.

CLWT-Y-BONT Caern SH5762

'patch (of land) at the bridge' ***clwt, y, bont***

Clwt y bont 1828, *Clwt y Bont* 1854

The name was originally associated with a 17cent. house near one of the bridges crossing the stream Caledfffrwd. The hamlet which developed in the early 19cent. was probably associated with the slate industry of Dinorwig quarry; Dinorwig Terrace is the name of a row of houses built 1855-65 in Clwt-y-bont.

CLWYD, Afon Denb SJ0549-0178

'hurdle river', ***afon, clwyd***

Cloit 1086, *Cloid* 1191, *Cloyt* 1284, *Cloyd* 1334, *Clwyd* 16cent.

The river's source is in the uplands of Clocaenog, and then through Nantclwyd (*Nancloid* 1481, *Nantecloyd* 1627) and Dyffryn Clwyd (*Dyffryncloyd* 1206, *Dyffryn Klwyd* 15cent., ***dyffryn*** 'vale') to enter the sea at Rhyl. The hurdle was probably associated with a particular ford somewhere along its length, with hurdles set on either side of the ford or along the river bed to ensure a safer crossing. The ford may even have been at Y Foryd west of Rhyl (*Forryd* c.1490, *Vorryd* 1609, ***môr, rhyd***, 'sea ford') accessible at low tide. Another suggestion is that the hurdle formed a weir or fish-trap. Dyffryn Clwyd was also the name of the medieval cantref and Clwyd itself became an administrative regional name. Cf. Baile Átha Cliath (Dublin) with Ir ***baile*** 'town', ***átha*** 'ford', ***cliath*** 'hurdle' (and cognate with ***clwyd***).

CLYDACH[1] Brec SO2213

'(place near the river) Clydach', r.n. ***Clydach***

Clidagh ddye 1583, *Clydach Dee, Coyd Clydaugh* 1605-23, *Clydach Iron Works* 1813

The river was described in the 1583 and 1605-23 forms as ***du*** 'black, dark' perhaps because it flows over coal measures. An industrial village developed next to the late 18cent./early 19cent. ironworks. The name is now applied to settlements on both sides of the river but until recent times that on the north side was called *Cheltenham* (probably a name imported by migrant workers) which itself replaced *Ffynnon-y-coed* (1832, ***ffynnon, y, coed***). For the r.n. see Clydach[2].

CLYDACH[2] Glam SN6801

'(place near river) Clydach', r.n. ***Clydach***

Clydach Mill 1650, *Clydach* 1691, *Cledach* 1729

The village stands next to the river Clydach Isaf (*Clydach* 1695, *Lower Clydach* c.1700, ***isaf***) a tributary of the river Tawe. Several rivers in Glam and adjoining areas are called Clydach such as near Cadoxton-juxta-Neath (*Cloeda* 1289, *Cleudach* 13cent.), Clydach (Uchaf) near Resolfen (*Aberclaudac* c.1200, *Cludach* 1289) and Clydach Vale (*Cleudac* early 12cent., *Blaen Cladach* 1547, *Cwm Clydach* 1799). Derivation is possibly from a Celtic ****klou-*** (or ****kleu***) found in W ***clau*** 'swift, ready' and in several r.ns in Ireland with the sense of 'stony river' and 'the one who washes' or 'the strong-flowing one'. Certainly, the suff. ***-ach*** is of Ir origin in other r.ns in south Wales, and Clydach may therefore be a W adaptation of an Ir r.n. It has been argued that the north and mid Wales development corresponding to Clydach is *Clawedog* > Clywedog (q.v.).

CLYNNOG FAWR Caern SH4149

'principal church in a place abounding in holly', ***celynnog, mawr***

Kelynnokvawr, Kelymaukvaur' 1291, *Kelynnawc, Y Gelynnawg* 13cent., *Clynnog Vaur* c.1305, *Kellynnawc* 1346, *Clennok* 1352, *Clennok Vaur* 1392, *Clynnok* 1538, *Clynnog-fawr* 1838

celynnog is an adj. derived from ***celyn*** 'holly' which seems to have grown here in profusion. The description Clynnog Fawr (***mawr*** 'big, major') refers to its role as the principal church established by and dedicated to the 5cent. Beuno. There was a *Clynnog Bâch* (1840) 2 miles south-east, while *Clynnog Fechan* was at Llangeinwen in Angl, so called because Clynnog Fawr owned the parish land at Llangeinwen.

CLYRO, CLEIRO Radn SO2143

'(place near the river) Cleirwy', r.n. ***Cleirwy***

Cliro 1482, *Gleirwy* 1447-89, *Clereho* 1536-9, *Clyro* 1502, *kylirw* c.1566

Named from the river flowing through the village. The r.n. is possibly ***claer*** 'clear' and the suff. ***-wy***, frequently found in r.ns, and often reduced to -w, particularly in areas subject to E influence as in Ebbw (q.v.). An earlier name for the location appears to be *Ruyll* 1232, *Royl* 1283 and *la Royl* 1334 possibly containing ***rhwyl*** 'court, palace' but this is a very rare el. in W p.ns.

CLYWEDOG[1], Afon Denb SH0257-0962

'wild, rocky (river)', ***afon***, ****clawedog***

Cluedog 1536-9, *Klywedog* 1598, *Clewedog* 1637, *Clywedog* 1795

There are several rivers called Clywedog in north and mid Wales; cf. in particular the Clywedog which flows near Wrexham into the Dee (*Clawedoc* 1325-6, *Clowedog* 1550, *Clywedog* 1620) and Clywedog Mont (*Clewedauc* 1201, *Clawedauc* 1206, *Clawedock* 1558, *Clywedog* c.1700). The generally held view has been that the name is derived from ***clywed*** 'hear' with the adj. suff. ***-og*** to signify a noisy river. However, such a perceived derivation, although it influenced the later development of the name, is not borne out by the historical forms for the north and mid Wales rivers. The name is believed to be a north Wales var. of the group of south Wales rivers called Clydach (q.v.).

CLYWEDOG[2], Afon Mont SN8592, 9486

'wild, rocky river', ***afon***, ****clawedog***

Clawedauc 1201, *Clowedok* 1578, *Clawedauce* 1588, *Afon Clywedog* 1836

A tributary of river Dyfi, Mont it was later called Nant y Dugoed. The river gives its name to Llyn Clywedog (q.v.) reservoir constructed in 1964. On the r.n. see Clywedog[1].

CNICHT, Y Caern SH6446

'(mountain named after) Knight', ***y*** 'the', pers.n. ***Knight***

Cnicht 1480-1535, *Pen Kynycht, Y Kynycht, Y Gynhycht* c.1700, *the Knicht* 1810, *Cynicht* 1838

The name has long been recognised as a cymricization of OE ***cniht*** 'knight, feudal tenant', which retained the OE cn-, the monophthong -i- and the velar fricative [x] represented by -gh-. Several forms have an intrusive vowel in Cyn-. However, in the past, the difficulty has been in interpreting an OE ***cniht*** as the name of a distinctively shaped hill overlooking Cwm Croesor where there are very few E let alone OE names. The W word ***cnicht*** 'peak, cone' is recorded, but despite the def.art. (in W and E) it is difficult to ascertain whether that word is derived from the hill. Recently, it has been suggested that the reference is probably to the family name Knight, merchants of Caernarfon who held land in the area; the letter K is still retained as a sheep mark.

CNWCH-COCH Card SN6775
'red hillock', ***cnwch, coch***
Cnwch Coch 1798, *Cnwch* 1815, *Cnwch-goch* 1834, *Cnwch-coch* 1891
A fairly low hillock of possibly reddish soil as in the nearby Allt Goch, but since it was once a common (certainly until the end of the 19cent.) bracken may have been the distinctive feature.

CNWCLAS see **KNUCKLAS**

COALBROOKVALE Monm SO1909
'coal brook valley', E ***coal***, E ***brook***, E ***vale***
Coal-brook-vale 1836, *Coalbrook Vale* 1859, *Coalbrookvale* 1871
Probably named directly from the *Coalbrook Vale Company's* ironworks which had collieries here including the *Coalbrookvale Colliery* 1878 (later called Deep Pit). The company's name may be a deliberate translation of the older p.n. Nant-y-glo (q.v.) a mile further up the valley.

COCKETT, Y COCYD Glam SS6294
?'customs office', E ?***cocket***
le Cockett 1583, *the Cockett* 1650, *the Cocket on the Town Hill* 1749, *Cockit* 1799
The same name occurs in Pentyrch Glam (*the Cockyd* 1570, *ye Gockett* 1670, *Y Gockett* 1683, *Gockid Isa, Gockid Ycha* 1825), in *the Cockit* 1773-8 in Tre-graig Brec, in *the Gocket* 1630 in Llandogo Monm, and elsewhere. A number refer to inns or buildings next to old highways prompting the suggestion that there is a connection with E ***cocket*** cymricized as ****cocyd***, a type of seal, a certificate of customs, and used in the specific sense of a customs office which was located at an inn or post-house. The prominent locations could suggest an E ****cocket*** 'small heap'.

COCYD see **COCKETT**

COED-DUON see **BLACKWOOD**

COED-ELÁI see **COEDELY**

COEDELY, COED-ELÁI Glam ST0185
'wood by (the river) Elái', ***coed***, r.n. ***Elái***
Coydylai 1784, *Coedylay* 1814
Named from a farm on the western side of the river Ely or Elái (q.v.) There are other 'wood' names in the area.

COED-LLAI see **LEESWOOD**

COED-POETH Denb SJ2851
'burnt trees', ***coed, poeth***
Coid poch 1391, *Coed Poeth* 1412, *Coyde Poyth* 1564-5, *Coed Poeth* 1620

There was considerable industrial exploitation of the surrounding area (in Minera, Bersham and Brymbo). However, the early occurrence of Coed-poeth suggests that the area was cleared by burning, possibly in order to facilitate mining, well before the major industrial developments.

COED-TALON Flints SJ2658

'trees around open ground', ***coed, talwrn***

Talur, Talwr c.1700, *Coed Talwrn* 1810, *Coed Talurn* 1844, *Coed-talwrn* 1875, *Coed-Talon* 1914

While ***talwrn*** can mean a 'threshing floor' or a 'cockpit' here it refers to open ground on a slope with several plantations of trees; cf. *Coyd y talwrn* 1670-1, *Coed y Talwrne* 1646-7 in Llanfair Dyffryn Clwyd. The village is at a road junction near Pontybodkin. The migration of non-Welsh speaking workers to Coed-talon and nearby Pontybodkin probably influenced the change from *-talwrn* to -talon and is so pronounced today by in E and W speakers. From about 1860-1890 the village was also referred to as *Black Diamond* or *the Black* from the local inn, named after a huge lump of cannel coal mined there and exhibited in London in 1851.

COED-Y-PAEN Monm ST3398

?'wood belonging to Payn', ***coed, y***, pers.n. ***Payn***

Payneswode 1314, *Coed mab paen* 1558-9, *Coed mab paen comon* 1709-10, *Coed y Pan* 1832

The pers.n. is also found in Pentrebane/Pentre-baen (*Kentrebane* 1536-9, *Pendrebaen* 1578-84, *Keven Tre Payne* 1595 with ***cefn, tref*** replaced by ***pentref***) at St Fagans Glam. Many later forms include 'son of Payn' (***mab*** 'son'). Some later forms shows association with ***paun*** 'peacock' which may explain the def.art. ***y***. The area is still wooded.

COED-YR-YNYS Brec SO1520

'wood at the water-meadow', ***coed, yr, ynys***

Coyde Er Enes 1552, (common) *Coed yr Innis* 1704-7, *Coed yr ynis* 1745, *Coed-yr-ynys* 1832

The water-meadow is in the Usk valley. Many of the adjoining hills are still wooded.

COELBREN Brec SO8511

'lot, portion', ***coelbren***

Tyre y Kolbren 1503 (1553), (torrent) *Nant ye Keylbren* 1555, *Capel Coyelbryn* 1578

A former chapel (***capel***) to Ystradgynlais. ***coelbren*** which has several meanings including 'lot, omen-stick' and 'inscribed piece of wood'. The first reference 'land of the coelbren' (***tir, y***) indicates the sharing of land or patrimony by drawing lots (a meaning which is independently recorded); cf. Dob in Caern, where, allegedly, the allocation of houses was determined by the process of *tynnu dob* 'draw lots'.

COETY, COITY Glam SS9281

'black or dark wood', ***coed, duf***

Coitif 1173-83, *Coytif* 1254, 1349, *Coity* 1411, *y koyty* c.1566

The early forms appear to indicate the unusual survival of the adj. ***duf***. Subsequent forms with ***du*** have regular loss of -f encouraging the belief that the second el. is ***tŷ*** 'house'. In spoken W, the combination of -d + d- produces -tt- (-t- in standard orthography). There are other p.ns in the area which suggest that there were once extensive woods in this area.

COGAN Glam ST1772

'small bowl-shaped hollow', ***cawg***, dim.suff. ***-an***

Cogan c.1139-49, 1254, *Coggan* 1577, *Cogan Vach* c.1678

The p.n. now refers to an urban area, next to Penarth, adjoining a small (once partly tidal) stream Cogan Pill (*Crokonpile* 1479, *Cogan Pylle* 1492) (***pill***). However, the original Cogan was probably the area around the old parish church and Old Cogan Hall a mile south of modern Cogan. Old Cogan lies in a hollow and adjoins a small stream, prone to flooding, which flows about a mile southwards to join Sully Brook near Cog Bridge (*Cokbryge* 1455) on a lane leading to Cog (*Kock* c.1566, *Cog* 1578) in Sully parish. The relationship, if any, between Cogan and Cog is obscure, but the latter, seen in Cog, Cog Bridge and the lost *Kouggewod* 1465-7, may be abbreviations.

COITY see **COETY**

COLD BLOW Pemb SN1212

'cold, exposed place', E ***cold***, E ***blow***

Cold Blow 1764, *Cold Blow House* 1784,
Hoares Wood alias Cold Blow 1834

At crossroads on a low exposed hill. The name occurs elsewhere in Pemb and in Carm.

COLFA (COLVA) Radn SO2053

?'place characterised by tree branches', ?***colf, ma***

(*i*) *golua* 1447-89, (*a*) *cholva* c.1541, *Colva* 1544

colf is sing. which makes interpretation difficult. The name Colfa or Y Golfa also occurs in Card, Denb and Mont, possibly for a place littered with branches, perhaps with some specialised meaning such as a 'place where branches were cut and stored'. An alternative explanation is that it refers to a well-wooded area.

COLVA see **COLFA**

COLWINSTON, TREGOLWYN Glam SS9475

'Colwine's farm', pers.n. ***Colwine***, OE ***tūn***, W ***tref***

Colvestone 1141, *Colwinestune* 1141-49, *Colwinestone* 1149-83,

Colwinston 1564, *Colston* 1544-7, *tref golwyn* c.1566, *Tregolwin* 1766
One of a number of E p.ns in the Vale of Glamorgan consisting of pers. n. + ***-ton***. The contracted form *Colston* is matched in other p.ns in this area, e.g. Bonvilston (*Bolston*) and Boverton (*Berton*).

COLWYN BAY, BAE COLWYN Denb SH8678
'bay near (the river) Colwyn', E ***bay***, W ***bae***, r.n. ***Colwyn***
Coloyne 1334, *Colwyn* 1587-8, *Colwyn Bay* 19cent.
There are several brooks named after ***colwyn*** 'a young animal, a whelp, a pet dog'. The river Colwyn (*Avon Colloine* 1638, *Avon Golwyn alias Avon Benmen* 1684-5) flows from near Llanelian-yn-Rhos into the sea to the west of Penmaen Rhos, through the original tnshp of Colwyn (*Colwyn Village* 1847). From 1870, land became available westwards for development as a seaside resort, which saw the addition of the marketable Bay (cf. *Colwyn Bay Hotel* c.1870 and its use for the railway station in 1872) to create the modern town of Colwyn Bay, emulated by the W Bae Colwyn. Although *New Colwyn* (c.1880) was also in use for only a short time for the town, it did become customary to refer to the former Colwyn village as Old Colwyn/Hen Golwyn (*Colwyn (Old Colwyn)* 1898).

COMINS-COCH Card SN6182
'red commons', ***comins***, ***coch***
Cwmmins Coch 1824, *Comins Côch* 1828, *Commons coch* 1829, *Cwmynscoch* 1851, *Comminscoch* 1903
The upland region above Aberystwyth whose common land was covered in bracken, although it has been suggested that it is a reference to clayey soil. Cf. Comins-coch Mont.

COMMON CHURCH, EGLWYS GYMYN Carm SN2210
'endowed church', ***eglwys***, ***cymyn***
Egluscumin 1248-55, *Egluskymin* 1307, *Egloiscymyn* 1488, *eglwys gymyn* c.1566, *The Communion Church* 1831, *Eglwys-cymmyn* 1843
cymyn means 'gift made by will, bequest' but some forms show confusion with ***cymun*** 'communion' hence the 1831 form. Very late forms show E ***common*** in the sense of 'in communion' or 'in common'. The farm Parcummin (*Parc-gymmyn* 1843, *Parc-y-cymmyn* 1891) has ***parc*** 'enclosure, field'.

CONNAH'S QUAY, CEI CONNAH Flints SJ2969
'quay of Connah', pers.n. ***Connah***, E ***quay***, W ***cei***
Connas Quay 1791, *Connar's Quay* 1801, *Connah's Quay* 1818
The silting of the Dee and the creation of the New Cut in 1737 gave rise to several new dock systems to sustain commerce. One such quay was

the *New Quay* (*a very handsome pier* 1773) and the associated area was referred to as Connah's Quay. Recent research has shown the Connah in question to be James Connah (1732-87) who lived at the *Quay House*. It has become customary for Welsh-speakers to refer to Connah's Quay as Cei Connah.

CONWY Caern SH7777

'(place on the river) Conwy', r.n. ***Conwy***
Cunewe c.1191, *Conewey* 1290-2, *Conwy* 13cent. (14cent.), *Coneway* 1393, *Conwey* 1530, *The havyne of Conwey* 16cent., *Conway als Aberconway* 1698
The Roman fort of *Canovium* was at Caerhun (q.v.), four miles south of the present town and close to the river Conwy (***cawn*** either 'reeds' or 'full' and the river suff. ***-wy***). The town of Conwy developed on the estuary (***aber***) of the river Conwy (q.v.) and was originally called Aberconwy (*aberconuy* 12cent., *Abberconewey* 1252, *Aberkonwy* 1247, *Aber conwy* 13cent., *Aber Conway* 1316) restored as the name of an administrative district between 1974 and 1996. During the last three hundred years the town has been referred to as *Conway* (now officially obsolete) and as Conwy (also the name of the former district authority).

CORNDON HILL Mont SO3096

Uncertain
Corendon 1275, *Cornedon* 13cent., (forest of) *Corndone* c.1324, *Korundon* 1378, *Cornedon fforest'* 1424-5, *Corndon* 1612, *Corndon Hill* 1836
Possibly 'hill of cranes' from OE ***corn*** gen.pl. ***corna***, OE ***dūn***; cf. Cornhill Northumberland, Cornforth and Cornsay Durham. Unlike other ***corn*** p.ns in England, cymricized stress on the medial syllable resulted in forms such as **Cornatun* or **Cornatyn* (as if it were OE ***tūn*** 'settlement') which survived in the pers.ns *Iorwerth Coronetton* 1253 and *Adam Loyt Cornattun* 1327. However, an equally persuasive case can be made for a hybrid p.n., with W ***corun*** 'summit, head, crown' and OE ***dūn***, influenced in later forms by W ***corn*** 'horn'; Corndon Hill has a distinctive conical shape with a slightly flattened, tilted summit. See Corntown Glam where forms are very similar.

CORNELI see **CORNELLY**

CORNELLY, CORNELI Glam SS8281

?'promontory of Eli', ***corn***, pers.n. ***Eli***
Corneli 1147-83, *Cornhely* 1208, *Corneli Boreali*, *Corneli Australi* 13cent., *Cornely* late 13cent., *Northe-*, *Southcornelye* 1597, *North, South Cornelly* 1729
A difficult name of uncertain etymology. South Cornelly adjoins Whitecross Down at the western end of a low projection of limestone

hills and the older part of North Cornelly is about half-a-mile north of South Cornelly. This may have been the promontory in question although such usage is not documented for ***corn***; it is equally difficult to see the topographical significance of a point or cairn on elevated ground. The pers.ns Eli and Heli are well documented in 12cent. records and in p.ns such as Cresselly (Pemb), Gartheli (Card) and the river name Meheli (Mont). The relative obscurity of the meaning probably contributes to it being influenced later by W ***cornel*** 'corner' var. pl. ***corneli***.

CORNTOWN, CORTWN Glam SS9177

'rounded hill', W ***corun***, OE ***dūn***

Corendon 1210-19, *Corundone* 1226-9, *Corndune* 1262, *Coryndown* 1459, *Corntoun* 1459, *Cornetoun*, *Cornton* 1536-9, *Corndon* 1538-44, *yng Hortwn* c.1700, *Corntown* 1813, *Cortwn* 19cent.

A hybrid W and E p.n. The first el. is probably ***corun*** 'summit, head, crown (of the head)' which also occurs elsewhere to describe a rounded hill. It was eventually taken, presumably, to be the cereal ***corn***. The second el. ***dūn*** was later re-interpreted as -ton ; its ME pronunciation is shown in *Corntoun* and the W form Cortwn.

CORRIS Mer SH7507

'little one', ***corres***

Corrous 1292-3, *Coris* 1585, *r. Corys* 1592, *Avon Gorys* c.1700, *Afon Corys* 1837, *Aber Corys* 1592, *Aber Korys* c.1700, *Abercorris* 1750

corres is the fem. of ***cor*** 'dwarf'. Corris was originally the name of the river which flows through the narrow valley between Corris Uchaf (***uchaf*** 'upper') and Corris. The river is the 'little river' compared with the Afon Dulas into which it flows at Aber Corris. It is unlikely to be a reference to a woman of small stature living near the river. The name of the mountain to the east of the valley is was Mynydd Abercorris (*mynyth Korys* 1592).

CORS DDYGA, MALLTRAETH MARSH Angl SH4572

'marsh of Dygai', 'marsh inland of Malltraeth', ***cors***, pers.n. ***Dygai***, E ***marsh***, p.n. ***Malltraeth***

Corse Tygai 1536-9, *Cors-ddygai* 1674, *Malltraeth Marsh* 1818

The marsh through which Afon Cefni (see Llangefni) flows to Malltraeth (q.v.). The identity of Dygai is unknown. The 1536-9 form associates the pers.n. with Tygái (see Llandygái) but stress on the initial syllable argues against this.

CORS FOCHNO Card SN6391

'marsh of Mochno', ***cors***, pers.n., ***Mochno***

(*dra*) *Chors Vochno* c.1150 (c.1400), *Cors Mochno* c.1250, *Nghors Uochno* c.1485, *Cors Fochno* 1748, *The Great Bog* 1790, *Cors Fochno* 1834

A roughly triangular former marsh, now largely drained, between a broad sand bar bordering Cardigan Bay, the estuary of Afon Dyfi and the low hills extending from Glan-y-wern to Tre'r-ddôl and Glandyfi Castle. A local alternative (at least for the area near Borth) was *Y Figyn* 1885 (***mign*** 'bog').

CORS GOCH GLAN TEIFI, CORS CARON Card SN6863
'red marsh on Teifi bank', ***cors, coch, glan***, r.n. ***Teifi***, p.n. ***Caron***
Gors Glan Teify 1777, *Gors Goch* 1803, *Gors Goch Lan Teifi* 1834, *Cors Garon* 1904, *Y Gors Goch neu Gors Caron* 1966, *Cors Tregaron* 1980, *Cors Caron* 1995, *Cors-goch Glan Teifi* 1966
A large marsh, red from its peat, extending around the course of Afon Teifi. Cors Caron or Cors Garon 'marsh in (the tnshp of) Caron' (see Tregaron) appears to be modern, now applies to a nature reserve (although a large part of the marsh lies in the adjoining parish of Lledrod).

CORTWN see **CORNTOWN**

CORWEN Mer SJ0743
'sanctuary stone', ***côr, maen***
Cornain 1206, *Coruain* 1207, *Corvaen* 1254, *Corvain* 1278, *Coruan* 1292-3, *Coruayn* 1309-10, *Korvaen* 14cent., *Corwen* 1443
The church in Corwen has a reputedly ancient stone called Carreg-y-big 'the pointed stone' built into the porch, which may formerly have been a standing stone, a long-stone or a menhir. 'Sacred stone' would be appropriate perhaps with reference to ecclesiastical or pagan ritual. However, it has been argued that the first el. is ***cor*** 'small' the significance of which is obscure as well as making Carreg-y-big irrelevant. The earliest forms can be interpreted either way. Corwen is a natural enough development (with -f- changing to -w- and -ae- to -e- in an unstressed final syllable) and begins to appear in the 15cent. probably influenced by *-wen* as if the lenited form of ***gwen*** 'white'.

COSHESTON Pemb SN0003
'Constantine's farm', pers.n. ***Constantine***, OE ***tūn***
Vill Costentini 1268, *Villa Constantini* 1283, *Villa Costyn* 1291, *Costyneston* 1324, *Custyneston* 1353, *Cossheston* 1543, *Constington or Coustington* 1543-4, *kostestown* c.1566, *Cosheston* 1584
The pers.n. was probably the OF Co(n)stantin. Some of the forms may represent the parallel W pers.n. Cystennin. Cf. Cosmeston Glam (*Constantinestun* c.1262, *Costyneston* 1314, *Cosmeston* 1320, *Coston* c.1503).

COTHI, Afon Carm SN6948, 5020
?'scouring stream', ?****coth-***, r.n. suff. ***-i***
cothi c.600 (1136-54), *Gothi* 1370-90 (c.1400), *Cothey* 1536-9, *Kothi* 1541, *Kothye* c.1577 (1730), *the Cothie* 1586, *Cothy* 1612

The name is also found in Glyncothi (*Glyncothi* 1302, *Glencothi* 1312, *Glyncothy* 1356 (***glyn*** 'valley'). The meaning is uncertain but *****coth-*** is almost certainly found in ***cothi*** 'throw out, expel, empty' and ***ysgothi*** 'clear the throat, defecate, scour' with the likely sense of a fast stream which sweeps or washes away . Cf. Nant Cothi Glam. The river rises near Blaencothi (*Blaen-y-cothi* 1772, *Blaen Cothy* 1795, ***blaen***) and joins Afon Tywi at Abercothi (*Abercothy* 1645/6, *Aber cothi* 1760, ***aber***).

COWBRIDGE, Y BONT-FAEN Glam SS9974

'bridge used by cows', 'the stone bridge', OE ***cū***, OE ***brycg***, W ***y***, ***pont***, ***maen***

Covbruge c.1262, *Coubrugge* 1263, *Bontvaen* c. 1500

Cowbridge lies on the line of an important medieval portway and Roman road running between Cardiff and Neath. Reference in both languages are to the bridge (*Pont Vain, alias Cowbridge of Stone* 1536-9) over the river Thaw (Ddawan) at the east end of the medieval borough, perhaps one habitually used by cattle being driven to market. Cowbridge was notably elongated, hence its description in 1421 (from a source dated 1254) as *longa villa*. The town lies on the site of a Roman settlement which has been identified with *Bovium* 'cow-place' (with Br ****bou-*** rather than L ***bos***, ***bovis***), thought to have been in this area, but the occurrence of 'cow' in both p.ns may be a coincidence. The matter, however, has been complicated by references to a 'cow bridge' (*Cowe-bridge* 1630, *Pont y fywch* 1657-60 ***pont***, ***y***, ***buwch***) specifically identified with a very small bridge over a tributary of the river Thaw beyond the west gate of the medieval borough. The evidence is so far inconclusive but it is possible that for W-speakers this was 'the cow bridge' (an unrecorded Pont y Fuwch) in contrast to 'the stone bridge' (Y Bont Faen) over the river Thaw. A few 15cent. W sources have the cymricized Cwbris.

COYCHURCH, LLANGRALLO Glam SS9379

'church near a wood', 'church of Crallo', OE ***cirice***, W ***coed***, ***llan***, pers.n. ***Crallo***

Totchirch' (= *Cotchirch'*) 1200, *Cohytchirche* 1247, *Coychurch'* 1254, *Llangrallo* 1535, *ll. grallo* c.1566

A hybrid W and E p.n. ***coed*** p.ns are common in this area (such as Coety and Pen-coed). Nothing certain is known of Crallo, but a local well, Ffynnon Grallo, is dedicated to him.

CRABTREE GREEN Denb SJ3344

'green at a crab-apple tree' E ***crab tree***, E ***green***

Crabtree Green 1838, *Crabtree Green* 1879

This modern name probably replaced an *Eyton Green*, the common pasture belonging to the nearby Eyton. It is likely that the area was noted for several stands of crab-apple trees.

CRAI, CRAY Brec SO8924

'(place near the river) Crai', r.n. ***Crai***

Crey 1454, *Cray flu:* 1578

The river rises above Crai Reservoir; the upper part of the Crai valley is Blaen Crai (*ymlaen Crai* late 15cent., *Blaen Kraye* c.1547, *Blaen-crai* 1832, ***blaen***). The r.n. may be ***crai*** 'rough, severe' to describe an untamed mountain stream.

CRAIG GOCH Reservoir Radn SN8969

'reservoir at the red rock', W ***craig***, ***coch***, E ***reservoir***

A contracted form of Craig yr Allt-goch (*Craig yr allt goch* 1833, *Craig yr Allt-gôch* 1889-91), a steep, wooded slope (***allt***) near the reservoir and the house Allt-goch (*Alltgoch* 1820). There is a rocky outcrop (***craig***) at the south-east end of the slope.

CRAY see **CRAI**

CREGRINA Radn SO1252

'rock of Muruna', ***craig***, pers.n. ***Muruna***

kreicvuruna c.1180 (14cent.), *kreic urna*, ~ *vuruna* c.1200, *Crugrima* 1291, *(yn) Nghraig Runa* 1447-89, *Crugryna* 1513

The original form seems subsequently to have lost the unstressed second syllable > *Craig'runa*, *Cregruna*. Some forms associate the first el. with ***crug*** 'mound' and ***carreg*** pl.***cerrig***. Locally pronounced as if it were 'Cregraina'.

CRESELI see **CRESSELY**

CRESSELLY, CRESELI Pemb SN0606

?'cross of Eli', ***croes***, pers.n. ***Eli***

Crossely 1521, *Croshelly* c.1550, *Crosselie*, *Crossely*, *-e* 1572, *Cressely* 1628

It is not clear whether the pers.n. is Eli or Heli. An 'Eli the priest' was recorded c.1148-76, and Eli or Heli appears in the lost *Crughelly* 1326, *Crugely* 1535 in Haverfordwest Pemb.

CRESSWELL Pemb SN0507

'cress spring', OE ***cærse***, OE ***wælle***

Carssewelle 1326, *Carswell* 1331, *Cristeswell* 1390, *Cristwell* 1535, *Cressewell* 1547

Some forms suggest association with Christ, probably because of the chapel which formerly stood here. Cresswell Quay (*Cresswell Key* 1745) is on the river Cresswell. Cf. Caswell (Bay) Glam (*Carswell* 1650).

CREUNANT see **CRYNANT**

CREW GREEN Mont SJ3215

'open land near Crew', E ***green***, p n. ***Crew***

Crewe Grene 1583

The W name, no longer in use, was Maes-y-crew (*Maes y Crewe* 1599, *Messa Crew* 1747, ***maes, y, cryw***). The green or ***maes*** is an area extending between the rivers Efyrnwy and Severn around the village. The original *Crew* 1265, *Crewe* 1594, *Kryw* 1654 may have formerly applied to the modern village of Crew Green or more probably some other specific location near to a 'creel, weir' (***cryw***) across one of the rivers, but ***cryw*** was also used for a 'ford' or 'causeway'. The area is subject to flooding.

CRIBYN Card SN5251

'little ridge', ***cribyn***

Cribin 1811, *Crybin* 1815, *Cribb Inn* 1825, *Cribyn* 1834

The name was in existence in the 18cent. as the name of a house *Cribyn Bettws* 1792 (1905). The village of Cribyn seems to have taken its name from a hill a mile away called Cribyn Clota or Clottas (*Cribyn Clottas* 1803, *Cribin Clotas* 1843), probably a hill characterized by rough habitations roofed with earth (***clotas*** 'sods') or perhaps with ridges of sods (while the rest of the roof had rushes). Hence, ***cribyn*** could be interpreted as 'roof-ridge', and Cribyn Clotas be seen as a pejorative name for a style of poor habitations with turf-crested roofs. Some historians believe the one metre high, six metre wide earth bank of the circular medieval settlement of Gaerfoel on Cribyn Clotas prompted the association with ***clotas***.

CRICIETH Caern SH5038

'mound of captives', ***crug, caeth*** pl. ***caith***

Kruceith 1235 (14cent.), *Cruket* 1286, *Crukeith* 1273, *Cruckeyth* 1350, *krikieth* c.1566, *Krickieth* 1680, *Criccieth* 1838

The castle was located strategically on the hill (***crug***) above the sea and it was certainly used as a prison. The modern pronunciation as Cricieth began to emerge in the 15cent. (with the intrusive -i- commonly found after -c-, particularly so in the Mer dial.). The occasional local form Criccieth seeks to perpetuate some earlier spellings but has no basis in standard W spelling; cf. Crucadarn.

CRICK, CRUG Monm ST4890

'mound', ***crug***

uilla crucou morcan, crucou morcant 1136-54, *Cric* 1165-83, *le Crick* late 13cent., *Crik* 1307, *Crick* 1583

The mounds (of the earlier records) are prehistoric grave mounds, in particular one Bronze Age barrow west of the village. Morgan is unidentified.

CRICKADARN, CRUCADARN Brec SO0942

'mighty mound', ***crug, cadarn***

Crukadan 1443, *kruc kadarn* mid 16cent., *kraic kadarn* c.1566, *Crickadarne* 1578, *y Cerygcadarn* 1839

On -gc- > -c- cf. Cricieth. The church is built on a sharp point of rock. A few forms show association with ***craig*** (*kraic kadarn* c.1566) and ***carreg*** pl. ***cerrig***.

CRICKHOWELL, CRUCYWEL Brec SO2118

'Hywel's mound', ***crug***, pers.n. ***Hywel***

Crikhoel 1263, *Crukhowell, Krichowel* 1281, *Crukehowell* 1287, *Cerrig Howell* 1584

The mound is generally identified with the prehistoric fort (*Crug Howel* 1813) on Table Mountain (*Table Hill* 1886) but local people called this *Mynydd y Begwn* 1806 (***mynydd, y, begwn*** 'beacon'), *Beacon* 1814, and it is possible that the reference properly refers to the castle mound in the town. Hywel has not been positively identified. The anglicized form is also seen in Crick Monm and Crickadarn Brec (q.v.). A few forms show misassociation with ***carreg*** pl. ***cerrig*** pl. 'stone'; Cerrig Hywel is said to have been the local form in W-speaking parts of Brec.

CRIGGION, CRUGION Mont SJ2915

?'cairns', ***crug*** pl. ****crugion***

Kregeon 1289, *Cregeon* 1305, *the Cruggyon, the Crugion* 1503, (*villa de*) *Crugion 1543, Treykregion* 1545, *Cryggin, alias Cruggeon* 1600

This seems to be an unrecorded pl. of ***crug*** 'hillock, cairn' or perhaps a pers.n. (such as Curig) with the terr.suff. ***-ion***. A *Geoffrey de Crugyon* was ordained deacon in 1343 at Alberbury priory Shrops (about 5 miles to the east). There is a prehistoric grave mound called Back Lane barrow north-east of the village.

CRINOW, CRYNWEDD Pemb SN1214

?'sere lands', ?***crin*** pl. ?***crinau***

Crino 1513, *Crony* 1544, *krynwedd* c.1566, *Creynowe* 1587, *Crinow* 1594, *Crynow* c.1640, *Crynwydd* 1842

An obscure name. The first forms may conceivably represent an unrecorded ***crinau*** of the adj. ***crin*** 'dry, parched'. The form *Crynwydd* 1842 suggests ***crinwydd*** 'dry brushwood', but is at odds with *Crynwedd* which may be ***crin*** 'dry, sere' and ***gwedd*** 'appearance, condition' but that too is far from satisfactory. A tentative suggestion is identification with *Lann teliau tref icerniu* 1136-54, 'Llandeilo Tref y Cernyw', one of several churches disputed between the bishops of St David's and Llandaff, but this is very doubtful and Crinow church has no known dedication.

CROES CAS-LAI see **HAYSCASTLE CROSS**

CROESERW Glam SS8795

'acre shaped like a leg', ***coes, erw***

Coeserowe 1556-8, *Koeserw* 1578 (1697), *Cors Erw* 1813, *Croes-erw* 1833, *Groes-erw* 1884

The name of a village taken from a farm. Similar names occur as field-names such as Leg of Mutton from some fancied resemblance to shape; cf. Penegoes. Later forms, including the modern name, show popular association with ***croes*** 'cross' and 'crossroads' and with ***cors*** 'marsh'.

CROES-GOCH Pemb SM8230

?'red crossroads', ***croes, coch***

Croes-coch 1813, *Croesgoch* 1846

An unlikely description, leading to the suggestion that the earlier name may have been Cors Goch or perhaps Rhos Goch found in nearby *Llain gors goch, Park rhos goch* 1845, *Park bach Rhosgoch (Croescoch)* 1859 (***rhos, cors, llain, parc***).

CROES HYWEL Monm SO3314

'cross of Hywel', ***croes***, pers.n. ***Hywel***

Kae Croes Howell 1557-8, *Croes heol* 1813, *Croes-hywell* 1832, *Croes-Hywel* 1886

Probably a reference to a medieval wayside cross at the junction of roads leading to Abergavenny, Llanddewi Rhydderch and Llanvapley. Nothing appears to be known of Hywel.

CROES-LAN Card SN3844

'parish crossroads', ***croes, llan***

Crosslan 1891, *Croes-lan* 1904

The village is at a crossroads (hence an earlier name *Pant-teg Cross* and *Pant-têg Cross Road P.O.* 1906) and is on the boundary of the parishes of Llandysul, Llangynllo and Orllwyn Teifi (hence ***llan***). However, it is also just west of the bank (***glan***) of Nant Ythan, with Pen-lan farm nearby. Another suggestion is that it is the 'higher crossroads' (dial. ***lan***) as opposed to the lower crossroads at Horeb.

CROES NEWYDD see **NEW CROSS**

CROESOR Mer SH6344

'several crosses', ***croes***, pl. suff. ***-or***

Croisor 1578, *Afon Groyssor* 1591-2, *Croysor* 1655, *Y Kroesôr* c.1700, *Croesor* 1810

Afon Croesor rises in Llyn Croesor north of Moelwyn Mawr and flows through Cwm Croesor to its confluence with Afon Glaslyn at Pont Croesor. The river and the valley appear to have been a boundary which was demarcated by several crosses between the counties of Caern and

Mer and between the parishes of Llanfrothen, Ffestiniog, Dolwyddelan and Beddgelert. The river then gave its name to the hamlet.

CROESYCEILIOG[1] Carm SN4016

'the cock's cross', ***croes*, *y*, *ceiliog***

Crosyceilog 1744, *Pont Groes y ceilog* 1792, *Croes Ceiliog* 1804, *Croes-ceiliog* 1831

The name of a tavern located near a crossroads. There is another Croesyceiliog in Llanedi parish (*Kroes y keilog* 1613) and in Caern (*Croes y ceiliog* 1744-5, *Cross y Kilog* 1760). Cf. Croesyceiliog[2].

CROESYCEILIOG[2] Monm ST3096

'the cock's cross', ***croes*, *y*, *ceiliog***

Crose y kylocke 1628, *Gwayn Croes y Kyloge* 1653, *Cross Ceylog* 1787, *Croes-y-Ceiliog, The Cock* 1833

Cf. Croesyceiliog[1]. This is taken from the name of an inn variously called *The Cock* and *Croes y Ceiliog* on the road to Pant-teg bearing the sign-board *Dyma dafarn Croes y Ceiliog* ('This is the Croes y Ceiliog inn'). The village had two inns, *The Upper Cock* and *The Lower Cock* (1871). The ***croes*** and ***cross*** may refer to a medieval cross in contrast to Croesymwyalch Monm about 3 miles to the south (*Groesyngualch* 1622, *Croes Imwlch* 1665, *Croes-y-mwyalch* 1833) 'the blackbird's cross' (***y*, *mwyalch***) which is ***croes*** 'crossroads'. Cf. Croesyceiliog Caern (*Croes y ceiliog* 1744-5, *Cross y Kilog* 1760).

CRONWERN see **CRUNWEAR**

CROSS ASH Monm SO4019

'ash at the crossroads', E ***cross***, E ***ash***

the Cross Ash 1801, *Cross Ash* 1831

Trees frequently replaced crosses at road junctions.

CROSSGATES Radn SO0864

'crossroads with gates', E ***cross***, E ***gates***

Cross-gate 1833, *Cross gates* 1875

A village which developed around a toll-gate marked in 1833 at the junction of the Builth-Newtown and New Radnor-Rhayader roads. W names of the village have recently been given some prominence as Y Groes ('the cross', ***y*, *croes***) seen on some road signs and Y Crwys ('cross' with later var. pl. ***crwys***).

CROSS HANDS[1] Carm SN5612

'(place near the) Cross Hands', p.n. ***Cross Hands***

Cross Hands 1831

From a public house (near Llan-non) and the site of a former toll-gate. The village developed near an anthracite mine 1869-1962.

CROSS HANDS[2] Carm SN1922

'(place near the) Cross Hands', p.n. ***Cross Hands***

Cross Hands 1906, 1947

Taken from the name of a public house (near Llanboidy). The village was earlier *Cefn-briallu* 1891 'primrose ridge' (***cefn, briallu***).

CROSS INN Card SN3957

'(place near the) Cross Inn', p.n. ***Cross Inn***

Cross Inn 1803

A village taking its name from the Cross Inn at one of the crossroads on the road to New Quay.

CROSS KEYS Monm ST2291

'(place near the) Cross Keys', p.n. ***Cross Keys***

the Cross Keys 1859, *Cross Keys* 1871, *Cross Keys Inn* 1885

An industrial village which developed in the mid and late 19cent., named from an inn recorded in 1822.

CROSSLANES Denb SJ3747

'intersecting lanes', E ***cross***, E ***lanes***

Cross Lane 1805, *Cross Lanes* 1838

The minor road between Bowling Bank and Bedwell crosses what is now the main road between Wrexham and Bangor Is-coed.

CROSSWELL, FFYNNON-GROES Pemb SN1236

'(place near the) Crosswell', p.n. ***Crosswell***, W ***ffynnon, croes***

Crosswell Inn 1841, *Crosswell* 1891

Taken from the name of a tavern *Crosswell Inn* (1838, later *Cwmgloyne Arms* 1891) on crossroads on the Cardigan-Haverfordwest road. The name replaced *Spitewell* (1810, ***sbeit*** 'spite') occurring several times for an inn especially one which was a cause of contention. The original Crosswell was near Hendre spring recorded as *Hendra Gate* 1829 on the road to Haverfordwest adjacent to a group of houses described as *Pen-y-ffordd* 1838, *Pen-ffordd* 1891 (***pen, y, ffordd***) near the crossroads at Iêt-goch ('red gate', ***iêt, coch***). By 1891, *Pen-ffordd* had shifted to the site of the modern Crosswell. The modern W name Ffynnon-groes translates Crosswell.

CRUCADARN see **CRICKADARN**

CRUCYWEL see **CRICKHOWELL**

CRUG[1] Radn SO1972

'mound', ***crug***

Crug 1833, *Crûg* 1891

There appears to be no obvious mound here; ***crug*** is often applied to castle-mounds but no castle is recorded. There have been miscellaneous minor prehistoric finds in the area.

CRUG[2] see **CRICK**

CRUGION see **CRIGGION**

CRUG-Y-BAR Carm SN6537

'mound of the summit', ***crug, y, bar***

Greke Bar' 1503, *y Tyr ynghrygbarr* 1564, *Cryg y Bar* 1739, (*a*) *Chrugybar* 1778, *Cerrigbar* 1831

The name is taken from a farm, possibly applying to a small hill immediately north-east.

CRUMLIN, CRYMLYN Monm ST2198

'curved pool', ***crwm, llyn***

Crymlin 1630, *Crumlyn's bridge* 1631, *Pont Grymlyn* 1710, *Crumlin Bridge* 1810, *Crumlin* 1833

From a farm and bridge across the river Ebwy situated below a bend in the river. Compare Crymlyn near Swansea (*Crimelyn* 1203, *Cremelyn* 1334, *Cremline, -e* 1536-9, *Gwern vawr, or Crymlyn poole* 1705).

CRUNDALE, CRYNDAL Pemb SM9718

'quarry', OE ***crundel***

Crundale 1450, *Crondall, Crondale* 1592

The name properly refers to a small group of houses close to Crundale Hook (*Crundalhoke* 1419, *Crundall Hooke* 1557, OE ***hōc*** 'tongue or spur of land') at Wiston Pemb. At least four quarries are recorded in the immediate area in 1891, one immediately north-west of the village. The name is not thought to exist anywhere else in Wales, but it occurs in south and south-west England (as in Crundale Kent and Crundall Worcester) across the Bristol Channel.

CRUNWEAR, CRONWERN Pemb SN1910

'round alder-marsh', ***crwn*** fem. ***cron, gwern***

lann cronnguern 1136-54, *Cronwerr* 1407, (*ecclesia*) *Sc'i Telion de Cronwer* 1486, *Cronweare* 1553, *Cronwern* 1586

The earliest form refers to the church (***llan***). Later forms show loss of the final -n of ***gwern***, possibly through misassociation with OE ***wer*** 'weir, dam', but the feature is found in other p.ns in south Wales. The church was formerly dedicated to Teilo, now to Elidyr.

CRWBIN Carm SN4713

'hillock', ***crwbyn***

Crwbin 1793, *Crwban* 1831, *Crwbyn* 1875

crwb has a number of relevant meanings such as 'lump, hump' (as well as 'hunchback') and so the dim. ***crwbyn*** refers to a small outcrop. The village lies on the slopes of a steep hill above the river Gwendraeth Fach.

CRWYS, Y see **THREE CROSSES**

CRYCHAN FOREST Carm SN8439

'forestry near (river) Crychan', r.n. ***Crychan***, E ***forest***

Afon Crychan 1831, *River Crychan* 1891

The meaning of the r.n. is uncertain but is probably ***crych*** 'furrowed, wavy, rippling' and the dim.suff. ***-an***. The river rises near the border of Brec and Carm and flows through Cwm Crychan to reach Afon Brân near Abercrychan (*Aber Krychan* before 1559, *Abbercrychan* 1756, ***aber***) below Glancrychan (***glan***). The name is applied to a large forest plantation.

CRYMLYN see **CRUMLIN**

CRYMYCH Pemb SN1833

'crooked stream', ***crwm***, adj. suff. ***-ych***

Crummuch 1468, *Crymmych* 1584, *Nant Crymich* 1652

The r.n. is *Crymmych* 1584, *Nant Crymich* 1652 'crooked stream' (***crwm***, ***-ych***) for its meandering course as a minor tributary of the river Nevern. The village itself appears to have taken its name more directly from the tavern called the Crymych Arms established at the roadside.

CRYNANT, CREUNANT Glam SN7904

?'(place near the river) Creunant', r.n. ***Creunant***

Croynant 1296, 1662, *Capel Krenant* 1578, *Crynant* 1703

The meaning of the r.n. is possibly 'stream by the pigsty' (***crau***, ***nant***).

CRYNDAL see **CRUNDALE**

CRYNWEDD see **CRINOW**

CWM[1] Flints SJ0677

'valley', ***cwm***

Cum 1254, *Kwm* 1284, *Combe* 1608, *Kwm* c.1700, *Cwm* 1795

The valley is flanked by Moel Hiraddug, Marian Ffrith and Mynydd y Cwm. There was a farmhouse Pentre Cwm (built 1636) and a farmstead Cwm.

CWM[2] Monm SO1805

'valley', ***cwm***

Cwm 1839

Taken from Cwm Merddog (*Cwm Rhwdog* 1813, *Cwm-merddog* 1833, *Cwmmyrddarch* 1871, *Cwmyrdderch* 1903), a small valley and farm immediately north of the village, with the stream recorded as

Abermurthyach 1807, *Aber Merddog* 1833 but whose correct form and meaning are uncertain, unless it be ***merdd*** 'weak' (cf. ***merddwr*** 'stagnant water') and an adj. ***-og***.

CWMAFAN Glam SO2607

'valley of (the river) Afan', ***cwm***, r.n. ***Afan***

Cwm Avon 1832, *Cwmavon, Cwmafan* 1851, *Cwm-avan* 1884

The river Afan rises on Mynydd Blaenafan and flows through the valley of Cwm Afan to enter the sea at Aberafan (q.v.). Cwmafan has replaced the parish name Michaelston-super-Avan or Llanfihangel Ynys Afan (*de Sancto Michaele* 1186, *Myzchaelsttowne* 1535, *Lanmighangell Ynys Avan* 1537, 'church of Michael in Ynys Afan' (pers.n. ***Michael/Mihangel***, OE ***tūn***, L ***super***, W ***llan***, ***ynys***, r.n. ***Afan***).

CWMAMAN Glam ST0099

'valley of (the river) Aman', ***cwm***, r.n. ***Aman***

Cwm-Amman 1778, *Cwmaman* 1833

An industrial village which developed around *Cwmamman Colliery* opened in 1851. For the r.n. see Ammanford.

CWM-BACH[1] Carm SN2526

'little valley', ***cwm***, ***bach***

Cwmbach 1811, *Cwm-bach* 1831, *Cwmbach* 1895

In the narrow valley of Afon Sïen (probably related to ***sïo*** 'ooze' or 'babble').

CWM-BACH[2] Glam SO0201

'little valley', ***cwm***, ***bach***

Cwmbach 1788

The name of a farm in the valley of Nant y Groes and transferred to the village which appeared after the construction of the Aberdare Canal in 1812.

CWM-BACH LLECHRYD Radn SO0254

'little valley', 'stone ford', ***cwm***, ***bach***, ***llech***, ***rhyd***

Llechryd early 16cent., *Court Llechridd* c.1755, *Cwm bach* 1820-1

The names of two distinct places combined for the parish created in 1887. Llechryd refers to a slab or paved ford through the river Dulas near Court Farm (*Tir y Courte in Lleghred* 1616, *Cwrt* 1820-1, ***y***, ***cwrt*** 'court'). Cwm-bach is about half-a-mile further up the Dulas valley and takes its name from a farm. This area is now generally called Builth Road from the railway station serving Builth Brec (*Builth Road Sta.* 1898).

CWMBELAN Mont SN9481

'valley with a hillock', ***cwm***, ***pelan***

Cwmmy-Bellan 1802, *Cwm Belan* 1833

Belan is the name of a farm on the hill west of the hamlet. Cf. Belan (*Bellane* 1663, *y Bellan Ucha, ~ Issa* 1680, *Bellhen* 1721, *Belan* 1836) near Welshpool, Mont and Belan Fort, Caern.

CWMBRÂN Monm ST2995

'valley of (the river) Brân', ***cwm***, r.n. ***Brân***

Cwm-brain 1707, *Cwmbran* 1755, *Cwm Braen* 1760, *Cwm Brân* 1833

The name of a new town created in 1949 under the New Towns Act 1946 taking the name of the older village located in the valley of Cwm Brân which had developed around tinplate works and forges of the *Cwmbran Iron Co*. The stream Nant Brân is *Nant brane* 1634, *Nant Braen* 1760 (***nant***, with *Brane* and *Braen* representing the dial. pronunciation; cf. Aberdare). The meaning of ***brân*** is 'crow, raven', probably referring to dark waters rather than a brook frequented by crows; it could be a pers.n. ***Brân***.

CWMCARFAN, CWMCARVAN Monm SO4707

'valley of (the river) Carfan', ***cwm***, r.n. ***Carfan***

Concauvern 1148-86, *Concaruan* 1193-1218, *Cumkarvan* 1307, *kwm karfan* c.1566, *Cwmcarvan* 1831

The early forms with *Con-*, *Cun-* are probably miscopied. The r.n. is also found in Llancarfan (q.v.).

CWM-CARN Monm ST2193

'valley of (the brook) Carn', ***cwm***, r.n. ***Carn***

Cwm Carn 1709, (stream) *Nant Carn, Cwm Carn* 1833, *Cwmcarn* 1903

The valley through which the brook Carn flowed as far as Aber-carn (q.v.).

CWMCARVAN see **CWMCARFAN**

CWM CEULAN Card SN6990

'valley of (river called) Ceulan', ***cwm***, r.n. ***Ceulan***

Cwm-ceulan 1891

The r.n. is *Kaylan* 1570, *Caylan* 1654, *River Caulan* 1765, *Ceulan* 1808, with ***ceulan*** 'hollow river-bank, brink' probably because of its steep river-banks.

CWMCEWYDD Mer SH8713

'valley of (the river) Cewydd', ***cwm***, r.n. ***Cewydd***

Cuwwythe 1543-4, *Cwmkewth* 1563, *Com Kewith* 1607-8, *Cwmcewydd* 1787

The valley takes its name from the brook Nant Cwm Cewydd which flows from the northern slopes of Mynydd Copog into Afon Cleifion where the hamlet is sited. Cewydd is a pers.n. found in Cilcewydd Mont and Llangewydd Glam.

CWM-COU Card SN2941

'enclosed valley', ***cwm***, ***cau*** dial. var. ***cou***

Cwm 1811, *Cwmcoi*, *Cwmcoy* 1818, *Cwmcoy* 1860

Several valleys or hollows in Card are called Cwm-cou, each characterized by a fairly narrow entrance and steep sides. In this case two minor roads pass through the ***cwm***, which is north-east of the confluence of the rivers Teifi and Ceri. It is believed that this was the location of an earlier name *Abergwenffrode* 1554, *Abergwenffrwd* 1651 (***aber***, r.n. *Gwenffrwd*).

CWMDÂR, CWMDARE Glam SN9803

'valley of (the river) Dâr', ***cwm***, r.n. ***Dâr***

Cwmm daer c.1600-25, *Tir Kwmdaer* 1638, *Cwmdare* 1778

An industrial village which developed around a colliery opened in 1867 taking its name from the valley and a notable house. There is another Cwmdâr (*Cwmdare* 1845) and stream Nant Dâr above Cwm-parc. For the r.n. see Aberdare.

CWMDARE see **CWMDÂR**

CWM-DU[1] Brec SO1823

'dark valley', ***cwm***, ***du***

Sancti Michaelis late 12cent., *Miheleschurche* 1331,
St. Michael de Stradewy c.1234, *Cwmde* 1383,
Sci' Michis' de Come Duy 1407

The full p.n. is Llanfihangel Cwm-du. The modern form refers to the narrow valley of the river Rhiangoll but the p.n. also had an earlier qualifier Ystrad Yw (*Estrateu* 1130, *Stradewi* 1215-29, *Stradewy* c.1234, ***ystrad*** 'valley' and possibly ***yw*** 'yew-tree' but early forms favour the pers.n. ***Dewi***) the name of the cantref in which it lay. This may also be *Lann mihacgel meibion gratlaun* 'sons of Gradlon' (***meibion,*** pers.n. ***Gradlon***) and *Lann Michacgel trefceriav* 1136-54 'farm of Ceirio' (***tref***, pers.n. ***Ceirio***).

CWM-DU[2] Carm SN6330

'dark valley', ***cwm***, ***du***

Cwm Duy 1647, *Cwm Du* 1760, *Cwm-du* 1831

From its location in a small eastward-facing valley of Afon Dulais ('dark stream', ***du***, ***glais***).

CWMDUAD Carm SN3731

'valley of (the river) Duad', ***cwm***, r.n. ***Duad***

Cwm-Duad 1769, *Cwm-duad* 1831

The village takes its name from Cwm Duad at the south end of the village next to Afon Duad (*dyad* 1646, *dead R* 1760, *Afon Duad* 1831), probably ***du*** 'black', noun suff. ***-ad***, rising in Blaenduad (***blaen*** 'source').

CWM EIGIAU, LLYN EIGIAU Caern SH7265

'valley/lake of ?shoals', ***cwm***, ***llyn***, ?***aig*** pl. ***eigiau***

Eigyeu 13cent., *eigyen* 13cent. (14cent.), *Comeyge* 1352, *Come eigie* 1589, *Cwm Eigiau* 1775, *llyn eige* 1534-5, *Lhyn Eigie* c.1700, *Llyn Eigiau* 1818

An obscure name. Several tributaries in Cwm Eigiau flow into what is now a reservoir in a deep valley. ***eigiau*** 'shoals of fish' is possible but ***eigion*** 'depths' is appropriate for the lake and also for the valley (to which the first forms refer) in terms of altitude and its location in the heart of a mountainous region.

CWM EINION Card SN6994

'valley of (the river) Einon', ***cwm***, r.n. ***Einion***

Cwm Eynion 1727, *Cwmeinion* 1760, *Cwm Eynon* 1803, *Cwm Einion* 1834

The r.n. Einion (*Eynniaun* 1201, *Euniaun* 1226, *Eynon* 1284, *Einon River* 1790, *Afon Einon* 1834) is a pers.n.

CWMFELIN-BOETH Carm SN1919

'valley of the burnt mill', ***cwm***, (***y***), ***melin***, ***poeth***

Cwmfelinboeth 1819, *Cwm-felin-boeth* 1843

The stream Nant Cwmfelin-boeth takes its name from the former mill.

CWMFELIN-FACH Monm ST1891

'valley of the little mill', ***cwm***, (***y***), ***melin***, ***bach***

Cwm-felin-fach 1813, 1833

A mill (*Melin* 1833) is shown spanning the stream Nant y Draenog at its confluence with the river Sirhywi. A village was constructed for workers at *Nine Mile Point Colliery* 1900-1.

CWMFELINMYNACH Carm SN2224

'valley of the monk's mill', ***cwm***, (***y***), ***melin***, ***mynach***

Cwm-y-Felin-monach c.1720, *(yng) nghwm melin-mynych* 1778, *Cwm-felin-mynach* 1843, *Cwmfelin-monach* 1839

The name appears to be taken from a water-mill demolished in 1976 and identified with Cilgryman mill which belonged to the abbey of Whitland.

CWM-FFRWD Carm SN4217

'valley of the swift-flowing stream', ***cwm***, (***y***), ***ffrwd***

Cwm y froode 1609, *Cwm-ffrwd* 1831

Located where the Carmarthen-Llanelli road crosses Nant Cwmffrwd.

CWMFORGAN see **CWM-MORGAN**

CWMGÏEDD Brec SN7811

'valley of (the river) Gïedd', ***cwm***, r.n. ***Gïedd***
Cwm giadd c.1814, *Cwm-giaidd* 1831
The river is *Gyedd* 1795, *Giaidd* 1831 (possibly ***ciaidd*** 'cruel, savage, fierce', to describe a rough, turbulent river). The village is a 19cent. development near coal and iron works.

CWM-GORS Glam SN7010

'valley of the marsh', ***cwm***, (***y***), ***cors***
Cwm y Gorse 1764, *Cwm-y-gors* 1831, *Cwmgorse* c.1880
A former colliery village which developed after the opening of a mine c.1880 by the *Cwmgorse Colliery Co. Ltd.*, named from a farm in the boggy upper reaches of the river Clydach Uchaf. The unstressed def.art. ***y*** has been lost, while several forms interpret ***cors*** as E ***gorse***.

CWM-IOU see **CWMYOY**

CWM IRFON Brec SN8549

'valley of (the river) Irfon', ***cwm***, r.n. ***Irfon***
Cwm Yrfon 1820-1
The river is Irfon (*Yrvon* 12cent., *Iruon* 1202, *Irwon flu.* c.1570, *Irvon* c.1612, *Irfon* c.1700) possibly related to ***ir*** 'verdant'.

CWMLLINAU Mont SH8407

'valley of (the river) Llinau', ***cwm***, r.n. ***Llinau***
Cwm llyney late 16cent., *Cymh Aberlline* 1573, *Cwm-llyn'e* 1836
The river takes its name from its source on Waun Llinau (***gwaun***). The etymology of the r.n. is difficult. It may well be ***llin*** pl. ***llinau*** 'line' (usually in a genealogical sense as in ***llinach*** 'lineage') but here transferred to a topographic feature of 'lines of pits or pools'. It has also been suggested that Waun Llinau might have been the location of several sites where ***llin*** 'flax' grew which might then prompt an otherwise unrecorded pl. ***llinau***. The dial. var. Cwm Lline is in common use.

CWMLLYNFELL Glam SN7412

'valley of (the river) Llynfell, ***cwm***, r.n. ***Llynfell***
Cwmllynfell 1690
The r.n. contains ***llyfn*** 'even, smooth' and the dim.suff. ***-ell*** to become Llynfell by metathesis (*Llyvenell* 1562, *Llynfell* 1610). There was another Llynfell (*Nant llynvell* 1605) in Llansamlet. The village developed in the late 19cent. and early 20cent. near anthracite coal mines.

CWM-MORGAN, CWMFORGAN Carm SN2934

'Morgan's valley', ***cwm***, pers.n. ***Morgan***
Cwmforgan 1748-9, *Cwmvorgan* 1757-8, *Cwm-morgan, Pont-morgan* 1831
The identity of Morgan is uncertain.

CWM NANTCOL Mer SH6162-6426

'(valley of the) brook of Coel', ***cwm, nant,*** pers.n. ***Coel***
Nancoel 1283, *Nancoyl* 1285, *Nankoel* 1582, *Nancol* 1795,
Cwm Nancoll 1796, *Cwm Nantcol* 1838
The river rises in Cwm Nantcol and, as Afon Cwmnantcol, flows into Afon Artro near Coed Aberartro. This particular Coel has not been identified.

CWM OGWR see **OGMORE VALE**

CWM-PARC Glam SS9596

'valley containing enclosed land', ***cwm, parc***
Cwmpark 1875, *Cwm-parc* 1914
parc has several meanings including 'game park' but the sense here is probably 'enclosed land' in contrast to the open land of adjoining hills. A former coal village developed in the mid 19cent. near the Park Colliery (*Park Colliery* 1875) located above Parc Uchaf and Parc Isaf farms (*Parc Ucha, Parc-isa* 1833).

CWMSYCHBANT Card SN4746

'valley of the dry hollow', ***cwm, sych, pant***
Cwm-sychpant 1891
There are several springs in the locality and ***pant*** features in several names such as Blaenhirbant (*Blaen-hirbant* 1834) and Blaenpant. This ***pant,*** in which stood the original house *Sych-pant* (1834), *Sych bant* (1843), *Sychpant* (1840), was above two small streams which may also have been dry in summer.

CWMTILLERY, CWMTYLERI Monm SO2105

'valley of (the river) Tyleri', ***cwm,*** r.n. ***Tyleri***
Cwm Tilery c.1790, *Cwmtelere* c.1800, *Cwm Tilerau* 1832
The source (***blaen***) of the river is above *Blaen-tilerau* 1832 and Abertillery (q.v.). The village developed after the opening of *Cwmtillery Colliery* c.1850.

CWM TUDU Card SN3557

'?Tudi's valley', ***cwm,*** ?pers.n. ****Tudi***
Cwm tydy 1595, *Cwmtidy* 1632, *Cwmntydyr* 1769-70, *Cwm Tudur* 1808,
Cwm Tydi 1891, *Cwm Tudu* 1950
A bay and valley west of Cross Inn. There are corresponding pers.ns in Brittany and Cornwall. It has been argued that the pers.n. was *Tudur* with loss of final -r but the early forms do not support this, despite being recorded regularly in the 18-19cent. reflecting the persistent local tradition connecting the place with Henry Tudor and commemorated in the nearby Tudor Hall (*Tudor Hall* 1902).

CWM-TWRCH UCHAF Glam SN7511

'upper valley of (the river) Twrch', ***cwm***, r.n. ***Twrch***, ***uchaf***, E ***upper***
Tyr Cum Turch 1729, *Cwm Twrch* 1831
The upper village in contrast to Cwm-twrch Isaf 'lower Cwm-twrch' (***isaf***). Twrch (*Twrch* 1516, *Turch or Torch* 1586) joins the river Tawe at Aber-twrch (*Abertwrch* 1573, ***aber***). The r.n. is ***twrch*** 'boar' belonging to a group of rivers bearing the names of burrowing animals; cf. Aberaman.

CWMTYLERI see **CWMTILLERY**

CWM-Y-GLO Caern SH5562

'charcoal valley', ***cwm***, ***y***, ***glo***
Cwm-y-Glo 1770, *Cwm Glo* 1777
A local charcoal industry (possibly supplying the various quarries in the area) was situated in a narrow valley leading from the present village of Cwm-y-glo towards Bwlch. The pit in which the charcoal was burnt was probably *Pwll y glo* 1597-8, *Pwll y Glo in Rug* 1622 (see Llanrug).

CWMYOY, CWM-IOU Monm SO2923

'valley of (the river) Iou', ***cwm***, r.n. ***Iou***
Comyon 1281, *Cwmyoy* 1513, 1739, *Comyow* 1540s, *kwm Jay* c.1566
This may also be *Cunnou* (?= *Cumiou*) 1131 and *Connuouir* 1147. The r.n. is probably ***iau*** 'yoke' in its dial. var. ***iou*** alluding to the shape of the hills around the valley. The river rises above *Blaenyoy* farm (1832) on Hatterrall Hill.

CWMYREGLWYS Pemb SN0140

'valley of the church', ***cwm***, ***yr***, ***eglwys***
Cwm-yr-eglwys 1826
This probably refers to the ruins of the old parish church dedicated to Brynach at Dinas[2] (q.v.). The modern church of St Brynach is near Brynhenllan.

CWM YSTRADLLYN, Llyn Caern SH5644

'lake in Cwm Ystradllyn', ***llyn***, p.n. ***Cwm Ystradllyn***
llyn ystrallwyn 1631-2, *Llyncwmstrathlyn* 1795, *Llyn Cwmystrad llyn* 1901
Now a reservoir (built in the 1950s), the lake (whose original name does not seem to be recorded) lay in Cwm Ystradllyn (*Cwm ystrallen* 1511, *Cwm Strallyn* 1600, *Cwmystrallyn* 1624, *Cwm Ystrallyn* 1838, ***cwm*** 'valley', ***ystrad*** 'valley bottom', ***llyn***), a name which itself incorporates a reference to the lake. Colloquially Cwmstrallyn, as evidenced in several of the historical forms.

CWRT Mer SH6800

'the court', (***y***), ***cwrt***
Y Cwrt 1795

The farm which gave the hamlet its name was possibly the court or grange of the nearby mansion today called Talgarth.

CWRT-HENRI, COURT HENRY Carm SN5522
'Henry's mansion', ***cwrt***, E ***court***, pers.n. ***Henry***
Court Henry 1596-7, *Cwrt-henry* 1754, *Cwrt Henry* 1831
A name taken from a large house, possibly medieval, reputedly referring to a *Henry ap Gwilym* (c.1474).

CWRTNEWYDD Card SN4847
'new grange', ***cwrt***, ***newydd***
Court Neweth 1729, *Court Newydd* 1762, *Cwrt-newydd* 1834, *Court* 1851
The original grange or small mansion was probably the modern Fferm y Cwrt (*Court Farm* 1891) a half-mile north-east of the present village. In the 17cent., according to some historians, the court was called *Llysnewydd*, while the old court was located at Rhuddlan Teifi.

CYDWELI see **KIDWELLY**

CYFFORDD LLANDUDNO see **LLANDUDNO JUNCTION**

CYMER, Y (CYMER AFAN) Glam SS8696
'confluence (of the river) Afan', ***y***, ***cymer***
Cymmerglyncorrwg 1799, *Cymmer* 1832
The confluence is of the rivers Afan and Corrwg (see Glyncorrwg). For another Cymer see Porth.

CYMER AFAN see **CYMER, Y**

CYMYRAN Angl SH3074
'little confluence', ***cymer***, dim.suff. ***-an***
The Crike of Kemyran' early 16cent., *Cymmyran* 1795, *Cymmeran Bay*1839
The tidal channel south of Four Mile Bridge into which several streams and rivers flow. The beach here is Traeth Cymyran (*Traeth Cymmer* 1838, ***traeth***).

CYNCOED see **KINGCOED**

CYNFFIG see **KENFIG**

CYNGHORDY Carm SN8039
'gate house', ***cynhordy***
Kynhordy 1615, *Kynghordy* 1611, *Cynghordy* 1760, *Cynhordy* 1832
Named from Cynghordy railway station, a name taken from Cynghordy farm. Early medieval documents indicate that ***cynhordy*** had several meanings including 'dog kennel, dog-house' and 'gate house, gateway; porch', and the name does occur elsewhere in Wales (such as Cynhordy

and Cynghordy both in Glam). It is unclear which meaning is relevant here, unless it referred to a farm which had kennels for hunting. Later forms show confusion with ***cynghordy*** 'council chamber, chapter house'.

CYNHEIDRE Carm SN4907

'harvest lodging', ****cynaeafdref***

Kynhaydre 1583, *Y gynheydrey* 1596, *Ginhaydre* 1648, *Kanavdrey* 1660, *Gynhawdref, Gynhafdre, Kunhafdref* 1690, *Cynhidref, Cynhidref-fach* 1831, *Cynheidre* 1920

The unrecorded ****cynaeafdref*** (***cynhaeaf, tref***) is similar in form and meaning to ***cynaeafdy*** var. ***cynhaefdy*** 'autumn-house', connected with the practice of transhumance, presumably a house or small farm (***tref***) conveniently occupied during harvesting (***cynhaeaf***). The modern form has probably resulted from stress shift in ****cynaeáfdref*** > ****cynháefdref*** (with intrusive -h- before the stressed diphthong) > ***Cynhawdre*** (cf. Y Gynhawdre in Card). and ***Cynheidre***. The industrial village developed around Pen-y-maes in the 1920s as a result of the opening of a coal-mine near Cynheidre Fawr farm.

CYNIN, Afon Carm SN2622

'river near Garthgynin', ***afon***, p.n. ***Garthgynin***

Garthkiny River 1536-9, *the Carthkinnie, or Barthkinnie* 1586, *Garthkeny* 1610, *Carthkeny* R. 1695, *Carthginning, Garthginning* c.1700, *Cathgenni* 1814, *Afon Cynin* 1831

The r.n. is probably taken from a particular, unidentified place *Garth Gynin* 'ridge of (man called) Cynin' (***garth***), which gave rise to p.ns such as Llangarthginning (*Llan-garth-gynin* 1831 with ***glan*** 'bank' being replaced by ***llan***). The pers.n. is also found in Llangynin (q.v.).

CYNWYD Mer SJ0541

'(place associated with) Cynwyd', pers.n. ***Cynwyd***

Kowryt 1292-3, *Kynnwyt Vawr* 1470, *Kynnoyd Vaur* 1545, *Kynwyd Vawr, Kynwyd Vechan* 1597, *Cynwyd* 1838

The identity of ***Cynwyd*** is unknown but the name also appears in Llangynwyd in Glam and in Allt Gynwyd Llancarfan. Cynwyd Fawr (***mawr*** 'large') and Cynwyd Fechan (***bechan*** 'little') were the names of the two adjacent tnshps.

CYNWYL ELFED Carm SN3727

'(church of) Cynwyl in Elfed', pers.n. ***Cynwyl***, terr.n. ***Elfed***

Kenewell 1290, *Conwyl* 1395, *Kynwyl Elvet* 1546, *Conwil-in-Elvet* 1549-51, *kynwyl elfed* c.1566, *Conwil Elvet* 1831

Distinguished from Cynwyl Gaeo (see Caeo) through its location in the commote of Elfed (originally a pers.n.).

CYRN Y BRAIN Denb SJ2149

'cairns of the ravens', ***corn*** pl. ***cyrn***, ***y***, ***brân*** pl. ***brain***

Cyrn Y Brain 1835, *Cyrn-y-Brain* 1838

Several prominent peaks north-west of Eglwyseg mountain, characterised by ravens. ***corn*** can mean 'horn, point' or, perhaps more appropriately here in the pl., it refers to several cairns.

CYWYN, Afon Carm SN3116

'pestilence (river)', ***cowyn*** var. ***cywyn***

Couin 12cent.,*(ar) gowyn* 1375-80, *the Gowen or Gow streame* 1586, *Cowyn* 1670

The river rises near Blaen-pant and flows into the estuary of Afon Taf near Llandeilo Abercywyn and Llanfihangel Abercywyn church (*St Michael Abercowyn* 1352, *Sancti Mich(ael)is de Ab(er)cowyn* 1535, *ll.V'el aber kowyn* c.1566, *Abercowyn* 1536-9, *Abercowin* 1660, **llan**, **Mihangel**, ***aber***). The significance of ***cowyn***, ***cywyn*** 'pestilence, plague' is uncertain but the river may have marked the limits of an area of isolation for sufferers.

D

DAFEN Carm SN5201

'(place near the river) Dafen', r.n. ***Dafen***

Davan 1543-4, *Daven* 1552, *Dafen River* 1833

Named from its location on the stream Dafen. The r.n. appears to be ***daf-*** (as in ***dafad*** 'sheep') and the dim.suff. ***-en***, perhaps in the sense of 'river which wanders like a sheep'. It flows through low-lying, formerly marshy, land (*Morva Maes ar Daven* 1609). There was a house nearby described as *Lan Daven* 1555 (***glan*** 'bank').

DALE Pemb SM8005

'(the) valley', OE ***dæl***

(de) Valle 1207, 1366, *Val* 1290, *Dale* 1293 (16cent.), *Ladale* 1307, *le Dale* 1423, *the Dale* 1539

Located in a small valley running from Dale to Westdale Bay. The early forms suggest that the first name was *Vale* (OF ***val***) influenced by Norman French settlers and Latin documents, and that Dale was the local name (probably E but possibly influenced by ON ***dalr*** of Scandinavian settlers). Interestingly, the def.art. is evident in the later forms.

DALE POINT Pemb SM8205

'headland near Dale', p.n. ***Dale***, E ***point***

the Dale Poynte alias the Dale-word or castle-word, Dale worde 1595, *Dale Point* 1839

A narrow headland a mile east of Dale (q.v.). The older name appears to have been *Dale-word* (although earlier evidence is lacking) with ME ***worde*** a var. of OE ***ord*** 'point', an el. found several times in Pemb such as Small Word Point in Caldey Island and Mowingword by Stackpole Head Pemb. Remains of a fort (E ***castle***) were recorded in 1595.

DAN-YR-OGOF Brec SN8316

'(place) below the cave', ***tan*** var. ***dan***, ***yr***, ***ogof***

Tyr dan yr Ogove 1729, *Tyr Dan yr Ogof* 1774, *Tan yr ogof* 1832

The name refers to caves on the land (***tir***) of a former farm just below the cave Ogof yr Esgyrn 'cave of the bones' (***asgwrn*** pl. ***esgyrn***) recorded as *Daren yr Ogof* 1809 and *Tarren yr Ogof* 1814 (***tarren***, 'cliff, knoll').

DARLAND Denb SJ3757

'river bank', ***torlan***

Darland grene 1578, *Darland Green* 1641, *Y Dorlan Gôch* c.1700, *Darlan Green* 1714-5

On low-lying land between the river Alun (q.v.), Pulford Brook and Llyndir (***llyn*** 'lake', ***tir*** 'land'). On ***coch*** 'red' in the c.1700 form, cf. the nearby Rossett. Despite the chronology of the recorded forms, the evidence suggests dual names, an original W form *Y Dorlan Goch* (*Y Dorlan Gôch is a notable high bank above the River Allen* c.1700) and an anglicized form Darland (influenced by E ***land***). However, the present Darland is scarcely *a notable high bank* and is a half mile from the river Alun, suggesting that the name was earlier associated with a site closer to the river. ***torlan*** can also signify 'undercut river bank' appropriate to the undulations of the river in this area. Green refers to 'common pasturage'.

DAROWEN Mont SH8301

'Owain's oak-tree', ***dâr***, pers.n. ***Owain***

Dareweyn 1254, *Darowein* 1394, *Darowen* 1545, *y drowen* c.1566

Owain's identity is unknown. The name appears several times in the area (such as in the bard's description of travelling '*Trwy Ddarowain i Drefowain/trwy Gedowain*' 'through Darowain to Tref-Owain through Cedowain' (c.1461)). *Cedowain* is the former commote of Cedewain Mont.

DAWN Denb SH8673

'(moor of the) sons-in-law', ***gwaun***, ***daw*** pl. ***dawon***

Gwendawn c.1700, *gwaendawn* 1733, *Down* 1795, *Dawn* 1839

This perplexing name seems to suggest moorland inhabited by sons-in-law, though the legal, social or family implications remain obscure. Interestingly, there is a *Gwayne y dawnes* 1605 (***dawnes*** 'daughter-in-law') in Cilcain. The c.1700 reference is to a stream (*avon Gwendawn*) and the 1733 reference is to a small-holding (*Tyddyn gwaendawn*). The reduction of ***dawon*** to Dawn (and the loss of ***gwaun***) was probably influenced by ***dawn*** 'talent' and (in 1795) by the topographically appropriate E word ***down***.

DDWYRYD, Y Mer SJ0443

'the two fords', ***y***, ***dwy***, ***rhyd***

y ddwyryd 1543, *y ddwy Rud* 1628, *dwyryd* c.1700, *the Ddwyryd* 1666, *Dwyryd* 1796, *Druid* 1826, *Druid Inn* 1838

Two major roads and one minor road meet at this point close to Afon Alwen and a lesser stream, but the precise location of the two fords is still uncertain. As travel increased, a bridge was built (*Pont y Dhwyryd, Pont ar Dhwyryd* c.1700, ***ar*** 'on', later *Pont Barker* 1871), and an inn was located here which adapted Dwyryd to Druid (*at the sign of the Druid* 1826). 20cent. maps variously use *Druid, Dwyryd* and *Y Ddwyryd.*

DEE, River, Afon DYFRDWY Denb/Flints/Mer SH8227-SJ4057
'holy one' or 'divine water' or 'water of the goddess', E ***river***,
W ***afon***, ***dwfr***, Br ***Dēuā***, W ***dwy(w)***
Deoua c.150 (1200), *Dee* 1043, *Dubr duiu* 1140, *Dee* 1043,
De 1086, *Deiae fluvio*, *Deverdoeu* 1189, *Deiae fluvio=Devedoeu* c.1191,
Deverdoe=Deiam 1194, *Deverdiw*, *Deverdue* 1234, *Deverdui* 1236,
Dyfrdwy 1314, *De* 1316-7, *Dourdue* 1391, *Dyfrdwy als Dee* 1568-9,
Dowrdwy c.1700, *Dyvrdwy* 1796
A national boundary for its later sections, the river rises west of Llanuwchllyn, flows through Llyn Tegid (q.v.) and Glyn Dyfrdwy (*Glyndeuerdoe* c.1214 [1400], *glynndyfrdwy* 1279, *Glyndowerdwe* 1334, *Glyndyverdwy* 1414, *Glyn Dyfrdwy* 15cent., *Glyndowrdwy* 1695, ***glyn*** 'narrow valley'), through Chester, thereafter canalised (in 1737) to reach the sea in the Dee estuary. The name is bound up in the divine associations attributed to rivers; cf. Dwyfor and Dwyfach and other Dee rivers in Scotland. The original name probably denoted 'divine one' and in its Br form ***Dēuā*** was recorded as the name of the Roman fort *Deva* (*Deoua* 150, *Deva* 4cent.) at Chester and in the Mercian adaptation as **Dēw*, *Dē* and Dee before the W phonological development to ***dwy(w)***. The first el., added later, is probably ***dwfr*** (the older form of modern ***dŵr***) in a reduced form Dyfr- (rather than being the var. pl. ***dyfr***). The actual name of the goddess is purported to be have been *Aerfen*; see Llyn Tegid.

DEFYNNOG Brec SN9227
'territory belonging to Dyfwn', pers.n. ***Dyfwn***, terr.suff. ***-og***
Deuannoc 1202-14, *Devennoc* 1254, *de Vennok* 1372, *Devennock* 1406,
y ddyfynoc c.1566, *y Ddyfynnog* 1778
The pers.n. is found in 12cent. manuscripts but no one with this name has been linked to Defynnog. ***Dyfwn*** and ***-og*** would produce Dyfyn(n)og and the first unstressed vowel -y- might have been confused with -e-, possibly reinforced by association with F ***de*** (seen in some forms). There seems also to have been a belief that it was a fem. noun preceded by the def.art. ***y*** resulting in lenition of -D- > -Dd-. The parish church is dedicated to Cynog (cf. Merthyr Cynog Brec) and some antiquarians fancifully proposed that Defynnog derived from 'Tref Cynog' 'Cynog's farm' (***tref***).

DEGANWY Caern SH7779
'territory of (the) Decantae', tribal n. ***Decantae***, terr.suff. ***-wy***
Arx Decantorum 812 (c.1100),
arcem detantorum (*l. decantorum*) 822 (12cent.), *Dugannu* c.1191,
castrum de Gannoch' 1211, *Diganwy* 1254, *(villa) de Ganneu* 1303-4,
de Ganogh 1304-5, *Diganwy* 1722
Arx Decantorum refers to 'the fortress of the Decantae', a Br tribe who would

have called the hill-fort and castle site something like **Decantouion*. In medieval W texts, the tribe is *Dygant*, and the settlement *Caer Ddygant* (***caer***). The forms cited show that some medieval scribes treated it as a F name with ***de*** (with Gannock surviving as a road-name). The later *Degannwy* (with the terr.suff. ***-wy***) encompassed the surrounding area and then specifically referred to the town of Deganwy. Although *Degannwy* is the spelling advocated on linguistic grounds, Deganwy prevails in modern usage.

DEINIOLEN

Caern SH5763

'(settlement named after) Deiniolen', pers.n. ***Deiniolen***
Deiniolen early 20 cent.
The original name of this village near the Dinorwig quarry was *Ebenezer* (1891), from the name of the Congregationalist chapel built there in 1823 (*Capel Ebeneser* 1891) and still to be seen as the name of the chapel. After 1922, *Ebenezer* or *Ebeneser* was replaced by Deiniolen for the village, a name coined from the parish name Llanddeiniolen, the ***llan*** commemorating the saint Deiniolen, the son of Deiniol of Bangor (see Llanddaniel-fab). Another local name was Llanbabo, from migrant workers from Anglesey parishes such as Llanbabo (q.v.) who came to the Dinorwig slate quarries. Before industrial expansion, the area was called Gwaun Gynfi (*Waun-gynfil* 1838, ***gwaun***, pers.n. ***Cynfil***) a name retained for the local school.

DENBIGH, DINBYCH

Denb SJ0566

'little fort', ***din***, ***bych***
Dunbeig' 1211, *Tynbey* 1230, *Dinbych* 1269, *Dymbygh* 1304-5, *Dynebegh* 1311, *Denbigh* 1536-9, *Denbigh Brit. Dimbech* c.1700
The original fort was possibly in the northern corner of the commote of Cinmeirch c.1230 on land Llywelyn ap Iorwerth granted to his daughter Gwenllian. The mound-castle was known for a long time as Llys Gwenllian (*Llesguenllean* 1536-9, ***llys*** 'court') and still as Llys, and also as Hen Ddinbych (***hen*** 'old, former'). In 1283, Edward I ordered the building of the new castle and town of the present, larger, Denbigh three-quarters-of-a-mile north of the former site. In the anglicized spelling -gh represented the W -ch and was so pronounced in early medieval E. In time, the final -gh disappeared as at the end of other E words to give a modern anglicized pronunciation of 'Denby' (cf. Tenby Pemb). Some of the historical forms show the -nb- > -mb- (cf. Brymbo) regularly heard in W and E pronunciation, and the dial. var. ***bech***.

DERI

Glam SO1201

'oak-trees', ***dâr*** pl. ***deri***
Deri 1881
Named from a farm Deri Newydd (*Derie* 1744, *Derry nawydd* 1814, *Derry-newydd* 1833) (***newydd*** 'new') on the north side of the village.

DERWEN Denb SJ0750

'oak-tree', ***derwen***

Derinney 1254, *Derwen* 1291, *Ll.derewenenyall* 1392, *Derven yn yale* 1499, *Derwenynial* 1535, *Derwen ynial* 1606, *Derwen-ynnial* 1686, *Derwen* 1795

Several minor roads converge on the hamlet of Derwen which at one time was presumably marked by a prominent oak-tree. The fuller name (and that of the parish) was Derwen Anial in which ***anial*** 'desolate, wild' probably refers to the location. Variants of ***anial*** were ***enial*** and ***ynial*** both of which are evidenced in the recorded forms; it was ***ynial*** that gave rise to it being interpreted as 'yn Iâl', 'in Yale' commote possibly in a misleading attempt to distinguish this Derwen from Derwen Llannerch in Llanfair Dyffryn Clwyd.

DERWEN-FAWR see **BROAD OAK**

DERWEN-GAM see **OAKFORD**

DERWEN-LAS Mont SN7299

'green oak-tree', ***derwen, glas***

Derwenlass 1794, *Derwenlas* 1835, *Derwen-lâs* 1837

Named after an oak-tree near close to the entrance of the old port on the river Dyfi.

DEVAUDEN Monm ST4898

?'custom land', ?***defod***, ?dim. suff. ***-en***

(*...de*)*vaudeñ* late 13cent., *Devawden* 1464, *Tee ir Vawden* 1506, *the Vawden* 1567, *the Ddevawden* 1619, *dyfawden* 1677

An obscure name. Also recorded in the unlocated p.n. *y dyfawden* 1677 known to have been about seven miles west of Devauden as well as in a field name *Devaudens aker* 1583 in Basaleg, Monm. The forms all conform with the medieval ***defawd*** (> modern ***defod***) and the dim.suff. ***-en*** though what ***defod*** 'manner, custom, fashion, character' signified is a mystery, unless it be an obscure legal term. The name seems to have resisted the change from ***defawd*** to ***defod*** and the forms reveal several interpretations such as the F ***de***, W ***y*** and E ***the***.

DEVIL'S BRIDGE, PONTARFYNACH Card SN7376

'devil's bridge', 'bridge over (the river) Mynach', E ***devil***, E ***bridge***, W ***pont, ar***, r.n. ***Mynach***

Pont ar Vynach 1629, Pen pont ar vynach 1690, *the Devil's Bridge* 1734, *Pont ar Vunach vulgo The Devils Bridge* 1760, *Pont ar Fynach als Devil's Bridge* 1803, *Pont ar Fynach alias The Devil's Bridge* 1811

The river Mynach (*Munach R.* 1699) possibly took its name from the cell of a monk (***mynach***) somewhere on its banks; one of several waterfalls is Mynach Falls. However, the monks of Strata Florida are known to have owned two properties in the area and the river may have been a boundary. Giraldus Cambrensis records crossing on a wooden structure in 1188; the first stone bridge was built a hundred years later, the second in 1753 (and improved in 1814) and the third in 1901. The desire to attract tourism probably prompted the E name, which variously suggested the devil's need to avoid the a river with holy associations, or the sheer challenge of erecting bridges in such a precipitous location. A later W name of the bridge occurring in folk-tales is Pont y Gŵr Drwg (recorded from 1813), translating Devil's Bridge. A similar commemoration also occurs in the name of another waterfall, the Devil's Punchbowl (a common enough epithet for a waterfall in a confined area).

DEWI FAWR, Afon Carm SN3022

'great (river called) Dewi', ***afon***, pers.n. ***Dewi***, ***mawr***

Duddey riveret 1536-9, *Devy* c.1700, *Dewi-fawr* 1831

The first form probably represents *Duwey*. The stream rises near Godredewi (***godre*** 'outskirts') and Glyn Dewi, and flows into the Taf estuary south of St Clears.

DIFFWYS, (Y) Mer SH6623

'(the) steep slope', (*y*), ***diffwys***

y Dyfoys c.1592, *y diffwys* 1678, *Difws* 1796, *Diphwys* 1838

A precipitous ridge between Dyffryn Ardudwy and Ganllwyd. The use of the def.art. is now less common.

DIHEWYD Card SN4855

'desirable place', ***dihewyd***

Dyewyt 1376, *Diheoit* 1390, *Dyhewyde (alias Betous Bidywyt)* 1415, *Dehewid* 1578, *Dihewid* 1590, *Dihewyd* 1742-3

The reference is probably to a location which is desirable and pleasant. However, it has been argued that the word means 'a rising, a height' since Dihewyd is on a low hill and the hill to the east is Moel Dihewyd. The unusual name, however, also occurs in Doldihewydd Tywyn Mer, in Dihewyd Cwm Rheidol Card and in Dyhewid (*Y Thehewyd* c.1600-25, *Dwyhewid* 1813), a former farm in Llantwit Fardre Glam located on the slopes of a hill Foel. The church was Llanwyddalus or Llanwddalis (*Llanvidales in Dyhewed* 1570, *Ll. Vitalis* 1606) dedicated to a person variously described as Vitalis, Fidalis or Gwyddalus whose name survives in Heol Gwyddalis and Ffynnon Dalis (*Ffynnon Ffidalis* 1651). Another name was *Betus Bydonith* 1284, *Betus Bydoynith* 1348, *Dyhewyde (alias Betous Bidywyt)* 1415, *Bettus Bidowith commonly called Dyhevid* 1674, from ***betws*** and a pers.n. *Bidofydd*. A 16cent. calendar refers to the saint's day as being dedicated to *Fidalis a Bidofydd*. On Bydywydd see Betws Lleucu.

DINAS[1] Carm SN2730

'fort', ***dinas***

Dinas 1819, Dinas 1831, (public house) *Dinas Vale, Dinasfach* 1895

Dinas Foel, possibly a hillfort, is immediately south of the village.

DINAS[2]**, DINAS CROSS** Pemb SN0138

'fort', ***dinas***

Dinas 1264, *Dynas* 1291, *Dinas Cross* 1819

The fort may be the fort at Castell or more probably that on Dinas Island (*Ynys y dinas* 1694, *Island* 1754) close to the old parish church in Cwm yr Eglwys (q.v.). Dinas Cross came from its location near the crossroads, which also gave rise to *Y Cross* as the name of a house and post-office. There was a *Cross Inn* 1844 here at Bwlch-y-groes (***bwlch, y, croes***).

DINAS DINLLE Caern SH4356

'fort at Dinlle', ***dinas***, p.n. ***Dinlle***

Dinas Dinllef 1300-25, *Dynlleu* 1303-4, *Dynthle* 1352, *Dynlle* 1456, *Dinas Dynlle* 1578, *Dinlley* 1727, *Dinas Dinlle* 1769

The el. ***dinlle*** 'site of a fort; land around a defensive settlement' (***din*** 'fort', ***lle*** 'place') is evidenced in 9cent. poetry. However, in popular and literary traditions, the unfamiliar ***dinlle*** was reinterpreted as ***din*** and the pers.n. ***Lleu***, associating the coastal hill fort and settlement with Lleu, a central character of the Fourth Branch of the Mabinogi. Eventually, Dinlle, colloquially Dinlla, became the tnshp name, and the tautological ***dinas*** was prefixed to refer to the actual fort.

DINAS HEAD Pemb SN0041

'promontory near Dinas', p.n. ***Dinas***, E ***head***

Dinas heade 1578, *Dinas headd* 1603, *Ddinas Pt.* 1777

A large promontory in Dinas parish (q.v.). However, this may have been the location of the actual fort (***dinas***).

DINAS MAWDDWY Mer SH8514

'fort of Mawddwy', ***dinas***, commote n. ***Mawddwy***

Dynas mowthoy 1391, *Dinas Mowthwey* 1662, *Mouthey City* c.1666, *Dinas Mowddwey* 1684, *Dinas Mowddwy* 1795

This strategic location where several valleys meet and where two rivers (Cywarch and Cerist) flow into Afon Dyfi was one of the military strongholds of the commote of Mawddwy (see Mawddach), and is flanked by two prominent hills Foel Benddin (***din***)and Foel Dinas. The idiosyncratic c.1666 form interprets ***dinas*** in the modern W sense of *city*.

DINAS POWYS Glam ST1571

'fort in Powys', ***dinas***, district n. ***Powys***

Dinaspowis 1187-1202, *Dinaspois* 1243, *Denispowys* 1218, *Dynaspowys* 1376
A fortified settlement occupied between the Iron Age and early Middle Ages near the castle north-west of the village. The second el. may be identical to Powys (q.v.), the name of an ancient kingdom and modern county, which may derive from L ***pagēnses*** 'dwellers in the district or province (L ***pagus***)'. Quite what this might signify in relation to Dinas Powys is contentious.

DINBYCH see **DENBIGH**

DINBYCH-Y-PYSGOD see **TENBY**

DINGESTOW, LLANDDINGAD Monm SO4510
'church of Dingad', pers.n. ***Dingad***, OE ***stōw***, W ***llan***,
merthirdincat 1129 (1160-80), *Landinegath* c.1191, *Denstowe* 1290, *Dyngarstowe* 1395
W ***merthyr*** 'shrine, church containing bones of a saint' was replaced by ***llan*** in the 12cent. and in E sources by ***stōw***. Various pedigrees attempt to identify Dingad as the saint commemorated in Llanddingad Carm, or as one of the sons of the 5cent. Brychan Brycheiniog or perhaps a son of the legendary Nudd Hael.

DINORWIG Caern SH5961
'fort of ?', ***din***
Dynorwek 1306-7, *Dynorwik* 1352, *Dinorwec* 1430, *dynnorwik* 1505
The fort itself was called Llys Dinorwig (*Lles yn Dynorwik* 1536-9, *Llys Dinorddwig* 1810, *Llys Dinorwig* 1839). Since the second, obscure, el. could be a pers.n., the fort has popularly been associated with the Ordovices tribe in some form such as '*Din-orddweg*'. The village's development is linked to the Dinorwig quarry and Port Dinorwig (see Felinheli, Y).

DISCOED see **DISGOED**

DISERTH Radn SO0358
'deserted place', ***diserth***
Dyssard , *Dysserch* 1291, *y ddiserth* c.1566
diserth also means 'hermitage, asylum' etc. but 'deserted place' seems more appropriate here as there is no village around the actual church. Cf. Dyserth Flints and Diserth Mont (*Disserth* 1309, *Ddisserth* c.1606).

DISGOED, DISCOED Radn S02764
'cottage by the dyke', OE ***dīc***, OE ***cot(e)***
Discote 1086, *Dichcote* 1328, *Discot* 1380, *Discoide* 1553, *Discoide alias Ditchcote* 1591-2, *Discoyt* 1616-20, *Discoed, y disgoed* c.1700
From its location near Offa's Dyke (***dīc***). AN influence is responsible for

the change from ***dīc*** to Dis- (as in Diss Norfolk). Later developments show the influence of W ***dis*** (a var. of ***oddis*** 'below, under') and ***coed*** 'wood, trees'.

DOC PENFRO see **PEMBROKE DOCK**

DOLANOG Mont SJ0612

?'area of small water-meadows', ?***dôl***, ***-an***, *adj. suff.* ***-og***

Dolanog 1633, *Doleanoge* 1654-55, (bridge) *pont y ddolanog, Pont Ddolanog* 1588, *Pont Dolanog* 1836

The area is located next to the river Efyrnwy and a bridge (***pont***). The forms with -an- seem to rule out ***dolennog***, 'winding, meandering, crooked'.

DOLAU Radn SO1467

'water-meadows', ***dôl*** pl. ***dolau***

Doley Gwenfroid 1563, *the Dolley* 1575, *Dolau* 1789

The name properly applies to a very small, scattered group of houses located on meadows close to a stream formerly called Gwenffrwd ('white stream', ***gwen***, ***ffrwd***) near the railway station, but the name has effectively replaced Llanfihangel Rhydithon (q.v.). Sometimes confused with Dolau (*Doley* 1563, *Dole Dylase* 1716) near Nantmel named from its proximity to the river Dulas (***du***, ***glais***) alias Black Brook.

DOLBENMAEN Caern SH5043

'water-meadow of the prominent outcrop', ***dôl***, ***penmaen***

Dolbeddmaen 1284, *Dolbenmaen* 1304-5

The rocky hillside of Craig-y-llan overlooks a strategic crossing of Afon Dwyfor, and the motte referred to in the 1284 document is believed to be the site of the royal residence for the princes of Eifionydd (before it was moved to Cricieth).

DOLFOR Mont SO1087

'water-meadow of Môr', ***dôl***, pers.n. ***Môr***

Doluor' 1281-2, *Dolvaur* 1291, *Dolvor* 1577

Although the second el. has been interpreted as ***mawr*** 'big', Dolfor is located near the head of a narrow valley with a very small stream and a few patches of flat land (rather than water-meadows as such).

DOLGARROG Caern SH7767

'water-meadow of the torrent', ***dôl***, ***(y)***, ***carrog***

Dolgarrog 1534, *Dole y Garrog* 1666, *Dôl y Garrog* 1746, *Dolgarrog* 1851

The water-meadows are between the river Conwy, Afon Porth-llwyd and Afon Ddu. There is an escarpment here down which several streams tumble to the meadows beside the river Conwy. On the nearby river

Dulyn is a waterfall and at Dolgarrog itself there was a hydro-electric scheme. Although it appears in 1534 as *Dolgarrog* the 1666 form suggests that an earlier form was probably 'Dôl y Garrog' (*y* 'the').

DOLGELLAU Mer SH7217

'water-meadow of cells', ***dôl***, ***cell*** pl. ***cellau***

Dolkelew 1254, *Dolgethleu* 1294-5, *Dolgethly* 1292-3, *Dolgelle* 1437, *Dolgelley* 1552, *Dolgella* 1769, *Dolgelly* 1837

The ***dôl*** was a meadow enclosed within a bend at the confluence of the rivers Wnion and Aran. The precise significance of ***cellau*** is obscure, but could refer to monastic cells or merchants' stalls or booths.

DÔL-GOCH Mer SH6404

'red meadow', ***dôl***, ***coch***

Y ddol Gogh 1592-3, *Dhol goch* c.1700, *Dôl-goch* 1837

The village developed near the two houses Dôl-goch Uchaf and Isaf (*Y ddol Gogh vcha, yssa* 1592-3) which were located in the meadow beside the lower end of a brook flowing into Afon Fathew. The adj. ***coch*** refers to the colour of the soil; not far is Craig Goch (***craig***).

DÔL-GRAN Carm SN4334

'gravel meadow', ***dôl***, ***graean***

Dol-grain 1831, *Dolgran* 1875, *Dol-graean* 1891

From its location next to a stream Nant y Gregyn and a farm *Nantygregen* 1811 (***y***, ***cregyn*** 'shells'). The 1875 and modern forms have the dial. long -a- for the diphthong -aea-.

DOLWEN Denb SH8874

'fair meadow', ***dôl***, ***gwyn*** fem. ***gwen***

Dolwen 1546, *y ddol wenn* 1661, *Dôl-wen*, *Dol-wen*, *Dolwen* c.1700, *Dolwen* 1839

The village is between two tributaries of Afon Dulas one of which was *Avon Dhôl wen* (c.1700). Modern stress falls on the first syllable as in the early Dolwen, although *Dôl-wen* is found in some documents.

DOLWYDDELAN Caern SH7352

'water-meadow of Gwyddelan', ***dôl*** , pers.n. ***Gwyddelan***

Doluythelan 1254, *Dolwydelan* 1269, *Doluidelan* 1284, *dol wyddelan* c.1566, *y Nolydd Elen* 17cent., *Dolyddelan* 1748, *Dolwyddelan* 1838

Gwyddelan is also commemorated at Llanwyddelan Mont. Later developments betray the antiquarian obsession with the ubiquitous Elan or Elen and her Roman connections (see Sarn Helen), leading to the conclusion that the first el. was ***dolydd*** (fortuitously the pl. of ***dôl***) beside Afon Lledr. The local holy well was Ffynnon Elan.

DÔL-Y-BONT Card SN6288

'meadow of the bridge', ***dôl, y, pont***

Dol-y-bont 1834, *Dolybont* 1835

In a bend of Afon Leri which passes under a minor road, adjacent to Pen-y-bont or Penbont (*Pen-y-Bont* 1608-9, *Pen y Bont* 1772). The village grew in response to the lead mines.

DOLY-HIR Radn SO2458

'long water-meadows', ***dôl*** pl. ***dolau, hir***

the Dole-hir Lime Kilns 1833, *Dolyhir* 1890

The ***dolau***, widely pronounced 'doli' in Radn, are meadows near Cynon Brook and Gilwern Brook.

DOMGAE, DOMGAY Mont SJ2719

'dung-field', (*y*), ***tom, cae***

Domgey 1543-4, *Domgei* 1546, *y Domgay* 1560, *y domgen* c.1550-62, *Domgay* 1567, *Domgey* 1571

The early forms retain the def.art. *y* which caused the lenition to Dom-.

DOMGAY see **DOMGAE**

DOVEY see **DYFI**

DOWLAIS Glam SO0707

'black brook', ***du, glais***

Dowlais Furnace 1799, *Dowlais* 1832

The village developed around the Dowlais ironworks located near a common or waste called *Tyle Dowlais* 1748 and *Tilla Dowlas* 1757 (***tyle*** 'slope, ascent') and the brook Dowlais (*Dowlais* 1650) which was black perhaps because of rock measures in its river-bed or because it was shaded in parts of its course. There are rivers in other parts of south Wales called Dulais but in this case and with other r.ns such as Dywlais, Dywlas and Diwlas there seems to have been an early development from ***du-*** to ***dyw-***. In south Wales, ***glais*** is a common word for a brook.

DOWNING Flints SJ1578

'Downing', p.n. ***Downing***

y Dwning 1550-62, *Downing* 1639, *Dooning* 1636, 1640, *Downing* 1636, *Dunning* 1651, *y Dwnyn* c.1700

Downing was probably transferred from one of the many places called Downing in Ireland. Downing Hall was notable as being the residence of the Pennant family (from c.1626), a family known to have connections with Ireland. There does not seem to be any archaeological significance for Ir ***dúnán*** 'little fort' (anglicized as *dooneen)* in this location (although the topography is appropriate). The W def.art. *y* in two of the forms however suggests that *Dwning* did have some local topographic significance. Because the name was unfamiliar, Downing has long been assumed to be a deliberate adaptation of the tnshp name Tre-eden-owen or Trefednywain (*Trewednewen* 1248, *villa de Ednewen* 1289, *Tredenewayne* 1302, *Trefednyweyn* 1311) from ***tref*** and an unidentified person Ednywain.

DREENHILL Pemb SM9214

'drain hill', ME ***dreane***, OE ***hyll***

Dreynhill 1416, *Treenhill* 1433, *Dreinhill* 1592, *Dreenehill* 1618

Earlier forms of E ***drain*** are *dreane, drayne, drein*. Dreenhill stands on hill-slopes adjoining a small stream, possibly the 'drain, channel for carrying water'. It also occurs as a surname (*John Drinhill* of Haverfordwest c.1300, *Richard Drinhille* 1313) which may derive from an earlier record of the p.n., or, feasibly, have given rise to the p.n. itself.

DRE-FACH[1] Card SN5045

'(the) little hamlet', (*y*), ***tref, bach***

Trevach 1744, *Dre fach* 1803, *Trefach* 1811, *Drefach* 1861

The village is located at the junction of several roads in the Teifi valley, and the site of mills associated with the textile industry.

DRE-FACH[2] Carm SN3538

'(the) little hamlet', (*y*), ***tref, bach***

tre vach in … Penboyr 1738, *Drefach* 1789, *Trefâch* 1831

The village was perhaps contrasted with Drefelin (q.v.), about half-a-mile up Nant Bargod.

DRE-FACH[3] Carm SN5213

'(the) little hamlet', ***tref, bach***

Trefach 1813, *Tre-fâch* 1831, *Trefach* 1875, *Dre-fach* 1891

Possibly in contrast to larger farms in the area such as Cwm-mawr. Now a large, former coal-mining, village.

DREFELIN Carm SN3638

'(the) mill village',(*y*), ***tref, melin***

Trefelin 1811, *Pentre-felin* 1831, *Pentre-dre-felin* 1891

There were several woollen mills around the village as well as Felindre[4] (q.v.) about half-a-mile lower down the valley (where ***tref*** may have the specific sense of 'mill farm'). It was this which may have prompted the prefixing of ***pentref*** 'village' in some of the forms.

DRENEWYDD (OYSTERMOUTH) see **NEWTON**[1]

DRENEWYDD, Y see **NEWTOWN**

DRENEWYDD GELLI-FARCH see **SHIRENEWTON**

DRENEWYDD YN NOTAIS see **NEWTON NOTTAGE**

DRUID see **Y DDWYRYD**

DRUIDSTON Pemb SM8616
'settlement of Drue', AN pers.n. ***Drue***, OE ***tūn***
Villa Dryw 14cent., *Drewyston* 1393, *Drewiston* 1535, *Druson* 1793, *Druidston* 1811
The modern form has been influenced by an antiquarian belief that the p.n. was connected with a supposed Druidic circle removed c.1740. An *Alfred Drue* occurs as a grantor of lands to religious houses in Dyfed 1174-6. A local pronunciation is 'Drusn'.

DRUM Caern SH7069
'ridge', ***trum*** var. ***drum***
Drym 1816, *Drum* 1841
A long ridge in a series of prominent peaks between Dyffryn Ogwen and Conwy. The existence of the var. ***drum*** is evidence that it need not be the def.art. Y Trum > (Y) Drum.

DRURY Flints SJ2964
'Drury Lane', p.n. ***Drury Lane***
Drurey Lane 1785, *Drury Lane* 1790, *Drury* 1820
A hamlet to the north-west of Drury was called Drury Lane (*'Little Pentre als Drury Lane'* 1790) now Burntwood Pentre. Drury Lane had probably been bestowed because of its London association with places of dubious moral reputation, but was subsequently interpreted as a lane which led to a place called Drury, conveniently preserving the inhabitants' respectability.

DRYSLWYN Carm SN5520
'bramble brake', ***dryslwyn***
Droysloyn 1257, *Drouslant* c.1287, *Drosselan* 1294-5, *Drosloun* 1327, *y Dryslwyn* 1271 (c.1400)
The name of a prominent medieval castle beside the river Tywi which belonged to the princes of Deheubarth, and still the names of two farms, Dryslwyn Fach and Dryslwyn Uchaf ('little', ***bach***, 'upper', ***uchaf***).

DUAD, Afon see **CWMDUAD**

DUKESTOWN Monm SO1410
Dukes Town 1832, *Dukestown* 1886
An industrial village developed on land of the Duke of Beaufort (see Beaufort).

DULAIS[1] Glam SN7802

'black, dark stream', ***du, glais***

Dyueleys 1289 (1336), *Dyveleys* 1289 (1468), *Dulyshe Flu*: 1578, *the Dulesse* 1586, *Dulas* 1612

Perhaps a reference to the dark shadows characteristic of the river's narrow valley.

DULAIS[2] see **BLACKPILL**

DULAS[1] Angl SH4789

'black stream', ***du, glais*** var. ***glas***

Dulas 1536-9

The second el. is ***glas*** 'stream' (found more commonly in south Wales as ***glais***) but has understandably been interpreted as ***glas*** 'blue' (*Avon Dulas i.e. niger cereleus, Duglessus, a brooke* 1536-9). It gave its name to the tnshp and hamlet, the estuary at Traeth Dulas (*Traeth Dulas* 1536-9) and the bay Bae Dulas. Another occurrence is City Dulas (*Citty Dulas* 1763, *City Dulas* 1811, 1838) which seems to be have been a facetious name for the hamlet of *Dulas Village* (1748) associated with the mills on the river, in contrast to Llys Dulas (*Thistulas* 1291-2, *Lisdulas* 1352, *Llysdulas* 1463, *Llŷs dulas* 1838, ***llys*** 'manor house, court') once the home of the rulers of Twrcelyn commote, or with the nearby Din Llugwy with ***din*** deliberately taken to be ***dinas*** 'city'. Cf. minor places also called City in Glam and Mont. Another explanation is that *City Dulas* was the name of a ship then taken as a tavern name. From the beginning of the 19cent. the river which rises in Gors Goch east of Mynydd Parys (q.v.) came to be called Afon Goch Dulas (***coch*** 'red') and then Afon Goch from its contamination from the drainage of the Parys copper mines.

DULAS[2]**, Afon** Mont SN8195-7699

'black stream', ***afon, du, glais*** var. ***glas***

Dulas 1185, *Dywlas* 1569

The river rises between Foel Fadian and Tarren Bwlch Gwyn and flows through Dyffryn Dulas (*Dyffryn Dywlas* 1566, *Dyffryn Diwlas* 1573) into Afon Dyfi (q.v.) east of Machynlleth. On ***glais*** var. ***glas*** see Dulas[1].

DULAS BAY see **TRAETH DULAS**

DUNVANT, DYNFANT Glam SS5993

'deep valley', ***dwfn, nant***

Dyffnant 1652, *Dyvnant* 1736-65, *Dynvant, Dyfnant* 1764, *Dunvant* 1833

Immediately south of the village is a fairly deep valley (through which the river Clyne flows). An identical name occurs for the brook *Dovenant* 1650 in Ilston Cwm about four miles south-west of Dunvant. Cf. Dynfant Card (*Dyffnant* 1798, *Dyfnant* 1799, *Dynfant* 1814).

DUTHLAS Radn SO2177

?'den, lair', ?***tylles***

Dulthlare 1752, *Dothless* 1814, *Duthlis* 1828, *Dothlass* 1862, *Duthlas* 1888

The 1752 form may be an error for *Duthlase.* W -ll- appears to have been preserved as -thl- in speech and in the modern form. There are places called Y Dyllas in Aberdare and Tarren y Dyllas in Rhondda Glam..

DWYFACH, Afon Caern SH4742

'little holy river', ***afon***, ***dwy(w)***, ***bych*** fem. ***bech***

Dwyfech 1495, *Dwyvegh* 1528, *Dwyvech* 1589-90, *Dwyfech* 1622, *Dwyfach* 1838

Cf. Dwyfor. It rises between Pant-glas and Bryncir to join Afon Dwyfor at Llanystumdwy (q.v.). Modern usage has replaced ***bych***, ***bech*** with the more common ***bach*** 'little'.

DWYFOR, Afon Caern SH4940

'big holy river', ***afon***, ***dwy(w)***, ***mawr***

dwynaur 13cent., *Dwyfor* 1450-1500, *dwyvor* 1495, *Dwyfawr* 1838

Cf. Afon Dwyfach. It rises in Cwm Pennant and joins Afon Dwyfach at Llanystumdwy (q.v.).

DWYGYFYLCHI Caern SH7377

'two circular forts', ***dau*** fem. ***dwy***, ***cyfylchi***

Duygeuilby 1254, *Dwykyuelchy*1284, *Doiguoilchi* 1310, *Dwygyvylchi* 1413, *the Doygovylchy* 1558, *Y ddwy gyfylchi* c.1566

The word ***cyfylchi*** appears almost exclusively in p.ns to signify a circular stronghold or fortress; other examples are in Glam and Monm. There are several fortifications on the surrounding hills.

DWYRAN Angl SH4465

'two parts', ***dau*** fem. ***dwy***, ***rhan***

Dwyran 1335, *doranbeuno* 1473-4, *Dwyran beyno* 1590,
Dwyran Fevno 1646-7, *doyran escobe* 1517, *Dwyran Escob* 1737

The church of Beuno at Clynnog Fawr held land in the parish of Llangeinwen as did the bishop of Bangor. The two shares or parts are reflected in the name Dwyran and in the additional distinction between townships as Dwyran Feuno (Beuno) and Dwyran Esgob (***esgob*** 'bishop'). A var. (still heard today) is Dwyrain, seen in historical forms as *Dwyrain beyno* and *Dwyrain Esgob* 1737 (as if ***dwyrain*** 'east'), which may be ascribed to Dwyran being east of Rhosyr and later Newborough, centre of the commote of Menai.

DWYRYD, Afon Mer SH6439

'river of two fords', ***afon***, ***dau*** fem. ***dwy***, ***rhyd***

Drwryd fl. 1645, *Dwyryd* 1838

The river flows through the vale of Ffestiniog to the estuary near

Penrhyndeudraeth. The location of the two fords is uncertain but is possibly in the area of Felinrhyd-fawr (***melin***, ***rhyd***, ***mawr***).

DYFED

'territory of the Demet-', tribal name *****Demet-***

Demetae 2cent., *demeti* 6cent., *Dimetorum*, *Demetorum* 9cent., *Deomedum*, *Deomodum* 918, *Dimet* 10cent., *Devet* 1298, *Dyuett* 1603

The name appears to be a Br tribal name based on **Demet-* but whether that was taken from a pers.n. is untestified. The territory in south-west Wales, which varied in size over the centuries, originally extended from the rivers Teifi (q.v.) and Tywi (q.v.) west to the sea, encompassing Pemb and west Carm, probably with its administrative centre at Carmarthen (q.v.). The 1974 administrative county of Dyfed included Pemb, Carm and Card.

DYFFRYN[1] Glam SS8593

'valley', ***dyffryn***

Diffrin Lleueny 1536-9, *Duffrynllunfy* 1813, *Dyffryn llynfy* 1833, (village) *Dyffryn* 1884

A common el. (comprising ***dwfr*** 'water' and ***hynt*** 'course'). From a farm near Llangynwyd on the south side of Nantyffyllon. The r.n. Llynfi distinguished this Dyffryn from Dyffryn[2] in the adjoining valley but the addition is no longer used.

DYFFRYN[2] Glam SS8395

'valley', ***dyffryn***

Dyffryn 1910, *Duffryn Rhondda* 1926

Named from a coal mine in the Afan valley sunk some time before 1906 probably by the *Duffryn Rhondda Colliery Co*. The mine was held in 1910 by *Imperial Navigation Collieries Ltd* but returned to *Duffryn Rhondda* before 1914 and closed in 1966. The village was largely constructed during the 1920s near Tŷ Isaf farm.

DYFFRYN ARDUDWY Mer SH5823

'valley of Ardudwy', ***dyffryn***, terr.n. ***Ardudwy***

Dyfryn Ardudwy 1796

Ardudwy (*Ardudwy* 12cent., *Ardudwe* 1263) is the pers.n. *****Ardud*** and the terr.suff. ***-wy***. The cantref was divided by the river Artro (q.v.) into Ardudwy Is Artro and Ardudwy Uwch Artro (*Ardudwy Vchartro*, *Ardudwy Issartro* 1419-20). The identity of Ardud is not known, but there is considerable evidence of early and medieval settlements in the hills around the present village of Dyffryn Ardudwy. The original ***dyffryn*** may have been the broad stretch of fertile land between the hills, the sea and Morfa Dyffryn (***morfa*** 'sea-marsh'). Dyffryn Ardudwy also became the name of the railway station despite official preference for *Dyffryn-on-Sea*, a coinage which disappeared in the early 1960s.

DYFFRYN CLWYD see **CLWYD**

DYFFRYN CONWY see **CONWY**

DYFFRYN CRAWNON Brec SO1217
'valley of (the river) Crawnon', ***dyffryn***, r.n. ***Crawnon***
the Duffrin 1744, *Dyffryn-crawnon* 1832
The r.n. is found in *nant crafnant* 12cent. (***nant*** 'valley', ***craf*** 'wild garlic', ***nant*** 'stream'), *Abercrawnon* 1558 (***aber***), *Blaen Crawnant* 1784 (***blaen***) and *Cwm Crawnon* 1605 (***cwm***) with later development of -f- to -w- and loss of final -t . Cf. Crafnant (Trefriw) Caern.

DYFFRYN NANTLLE, LLYN NANTLLE
Caern SH5253-4743, SH5153
'valley, lake at Nantlle', ***dyffryn***, ***llyn***, p.n. ***Nantlle***
See also Nantlle. Afon Drws-y-coed flows from Drws-y-coed (*Druscoyt* 1370-1, *Drws y coed* 1640, ***drws*** 'pass', ***y***, ***coed***) into Llyn Nantlle or Llyn Nantlle Uchaf, formerly the upper (***uchaf***) of two lakes (*deu lenn* 1300-25, *Llynniau Nantlle* 1795, *Lluniau Nantlle* 1818, *Llyniau-Nant-y-llef* 1838, pl. ***llynnau***) with a route (***bala***) between them at Baladeulyn (*Baladeulyn* 1303-4, *Baladulyn* 1338, *Ballardeuelyn* 1398, *Bala'r Dheulyn* c.1700, *Bala-daulyn* 1838, ***dau*** 'two'). The lower lake was filled in by the spoil of 19cent. quarrying and by drainage into Afon Llyfni (see Llanllyfni). Dyffryn Nantlle, now encompassing more than the original ***nant*** of Nantlle, comprises the valley from Drws-y-coed to Pen-y-groes, with the area around Tal-y-sarn (q.v.) frequently called Y Nant.

DYFFRYN OGWEN see **OGWEN**

DYFFRYN TYWI see **TYWI, Afon**

DYFI, Afon Mer/Mont SH8916-SN6696
'black river', ***afon***, E ***river***, W ***du(f)***, suff. ***-i***
Deui 1141 (1216), *Dywi* c.1180, *Deui* 1201, *Devi* 13cent., *Dyui* 1278-81, *Diuy* 1491, *Deuy* 1371, *Dyfi* 1375-80, *Douye* c.1600
The river rises in Creiglyn Dyfi near Aran Fawddwy, and flows through Dyffryn Dyfi, past Glandyfi to the sea at Aberdyfi (q.v.). The waters or the river bed are perceived to be dark; ***duf*** later became ***du*** 'black' in MnW. The anglicized Dovey, now largely obsolescent, may have been influenced by Dove, the name of several rivers in England.

DYFRDWY see **DEE**

DYLIFE Mont SN8694

'torrents, floods, place liable to floods', ***dylif*** pl. ***dylifau***

Deleaven alias Dolyve 1641, *Dylyveu* 1625/49, *y dylifeu, delife* 1683-7, *Dylifau* 1811, *Delive* 1835

The forms show the dial. var. -e for -au. The first 1641 form probably represents *Deleaveu* and the second an association with ***dôl*** 'water-meadow'. The village is near Afon Twymyn and its tributaries.

DYNFANT see **DUNVANT**

DYSERTH Flints SJ0579

'hermitage, retreat', ***diserth***

Dissard 1086, 1258, *Dissarth* 1241, *Dissart* 1280, *Disard, Disserth* 1284, 1346, *Dyssard* 1315, *Dyssart* 1320, *y dissert* 1329, *y disserth* 1375-80, *Dysserth* 1458-9, *y ddiserth* c.1566, *Y Ddiserth* 1590, *Disserth, Diserth, Disart* c.1700, *y Ddisart* 1772

The L ***desertum***, vernacular L ***disertum***, for the remote hermit's cell, appears in several places (variously Desert, Dysart, Diserth, Dyserth) in Ireland, Scotland and Wales (here and in Radn, Denb, and Mont); it does not seem to feature in the p.ns of England. The perception of an actual location is reinforced by the use of the def.art. ***y*** preceding the fem. noun (as in *Y Ddiserth*). In Flints the spelling Dyserth has generally prevailed, possibly because its location at the foot of Moel Hiraddug reinforced the perception that Dyserth was the intensive pref. ***di-*** or ***dy-*** and ***serth*** 'steep'.

DYSYNNI, Afon Mer SH5903

'?separating river', ***afon***, ?****distentiio***, suff. ***-ydd***

Dysenyth c.1191, *Dissennyth* 1194, *Dysynni* 1345-80, *Dissynnhi, Dissynny* 15cent., *Disinny* 1592, *Dysynny* 1592, *Dyssynni* c.1700

The river flows from Llyn Tal-y-llyn through Dyffryn Dysynni and Morfa Gwyllt to the sea at Aber Dysynni (*Aberdysyni* 1796, *Aberdysnwy* 1795, *Abersynwy* 1814, *Aber Dysynni* 1837). The origin of the name is obscure. The tentative suggestion is that it is an otherwise unrecorded word perhaps related to the L ***distineo, distentus*** 'separate', because it separates two commotes (Ystumanner and Tal-y-bont). The final -dd of the agent suff. was eventually lost in the unstressed syllable. The initial unstressed syllable (where the original -i- became -y- under the influence of -y- in the following syllable) was occasionally omitted in local speech as Synni (as in *Abersynwy* 1814). Some forms also show the -wy which frequently appears in r.ns.

E

EASTERN CLEDDAU see **CLEDDAU**

EAST MOUSE see **YNYS AMLWCH**

EBBW VALE, GLYNEBWY Monm SO1609

'valley of (the river) Ebwy', ***glyn***, r.n. ***Ebwy***, E ***vale***,

Ebwy Vale Furnace c.1790, *Ebbw Vale (Ironworks)* 1796, *Ebbw Vale* 1813

The name is taken from *Ebbw Vale Ironworks* begun in 1789. The industrial town was alternatively known as Ebbw Vale and Pen-y-cae (one of the estates on which it developed) down to c.1836. Located in the upper part of Glyn Ebwy (*Glynebbboth* 1314, *Glenebo* c.1593-5, *Glyn Ebwy* 1839). The r.n. Ebwy (*Eboth* 1101, *Ebwy* 1631) is an earlier *Ebwydd* with loss of final -dd to Ebwy and then anglicized as Ebbw It is ***eb-*** 'horse' (as in ***ebol*** 'colt') and ***gŵydd*** 'wild', falling into the category of r.ns based on animals. The r.n. also occurs in the names of the manors of *Eboth alias Greenfield* lower down the river near Newport, and the rivers Ebwy Fechan and Ebwy Fawr (*Ebwythvaghan* 1349, *Ebouthvaur, Ebouthvaghan* 1354) (***bychan*** fem. ***bechan***, ***mawr***).

EDERN Caern SH2739

'(church of) Edern', pers.n. ***Edern***

Edern 1194-1200 (late 15cent.), 1254, *Edern* 1291, *Edarn* 1646, *Edeyrn* 1838

One of a number of churches which retain only the saint's name; contrast Llanedern Glam and Bodedern Angl. The 1646 form records the local pronunciation, while the 1838 form reflects a common interpretation influenced probably by ***teyrn*** ('monarch') seen also (from the Middle Ages) in some vars such as Edeirnion/Edeyrnion Caern 'territory of Edern' and Llanedern/Llanedeyrn Glam.

EDWINSFORD, RHYDODYN Carm SN6334

'lime-kiln ford', ***rhyd***, ***odyn***

Ridodyn 1393-4, *Ridodyn* 1526, *Rhyd Odyn* 1542, *Rhyd Odwyn* 1649, *Edwins foord formerly called Rhydodwyn* 1712, *Edwinsford* c.1730-40

The ford was through the river Cothi. Lime-kilns are recorded in several local p.ns (such as Pantyrodyn and Llwynyrodyn). For some reason, *-odyn* was interpreted as a pers.n. *Odwyn* and then perceived to be an E pers.n. Edwin prompted by antiquarian association with Edwin (d. 956), a son of Hywel Dda, and with Hywel ab Edwin, a lord of Deheubarth defeated in battle in 1041 at Pencader, about thirteen miles west of Edwinsford. There may also be an association with Llanbadarn Odwyn

Card which shows a similar development (from *Lampadern Odyn* 1284, *Llanpadurnodyn* 1390, *Castle Odwyn in llanbaderne Edwyn* 1600-7).

EFAILISAF Glam ST0884

'(the) lower smithy', ***(yr)*, *gefail*, *isaf***

Evel 1729, *Evelisaf* 1799, *Efelisaf* 1814

A smithy is recorded here in 1885.

EFAILNEWYDD Caern SH3535

'(the) new smithy', ***(yr)*, *gefail*, *newydd***

yr Evell newydd 1688, *Efail-newydd* 1838

The village was reputedly a place where the drovers shod their cattle.

EFENECHDYD Denb SJ1155

'the monastery (grange)', ***y*, *menechdid***

Wenechdit 1254, *Venitghit* 1324, *Veneghted* 1530, *y fenechdid* 1530, *Eveneghtid* 1660, *Venechtid*, *Vynechtyd* c. 1700, *Efenechtyd* 1838

menechdid (***manach*** 'monk' and the suff. ***-did***) has been equated with a monastery (or even a nunnery according to some), known to have belonged to Valle Crucis abbey which by the 16cent. was a vaccary or dairy farm (*vaccury and dairy house* 1545). That there was an identifiable monastic building here is reinforced by the def.art. ***y*** which eventually became absorbed in the p.n. as Efenechdyd but for some today, the preferred form is still Y Fenechdyd or Y Fenechtid. The alternation between ***-did*** (the historical form), *-tid*, *-tyd* and *-dyd* reflects a common variation of sound and spelling, with the preference for *-yd* probably by analogy with the common adj. ending ***-yd***.

EFYRNWY, Afon, River VYRNWY Mont SJ0315-1312

'(river associated with) Ebur', pers.n. ?****Ebur***, suff. ***-nwy***

Ev(er)envy, *Evernoy* 1185, *Ewernoe* 1200, *Y vyrnwy* 1201, *evernow* 1226, *Ewernwy* early 13cent., *Evernow* 1226, *Efyrnwy* c.1400, *Vyrnwy* 1455-85, *Y Vyrnwy* 1584

OW ***ebur*** (Br ****eburo-***) seems to have meant 'yew-tree' and is later found in ***efwr*** 'cow-parsnip, hogweed'. ***-nwy*** is also found in pers.ns and suggests a derived pers.n. or a river deity ****Ebur*** or older ****Eburos***; cf. **Eburacon*, *Eburacum*, W Efrog, E York. Vyrnwy now applies to the river formed by the union of the streams Eiddo, Nadroedd, Eunant and Cedig (where Lake Vyrnwy reservoir was created in 1880-1892, drowning Llanwddyn q.v.), and which once formed the south and west sides of the former cantref of Mechain (*virnewy mechen* 1588); it flows into the River Severn. Efyrnwy was also used of what later became the rivers Gam (*Ev(er)envy*, *Evernoy* 1185) and Banw (q.v.) which formed part of the boundary with the cantref of Caereinion (*Vurnuey gerenyo* 1578, *Vurnwye Kereignion* 1588, *River Virniew* 1762).

EGLWYS-BACH Denb SH8070

'church in a nook', ***eglwys, bach***

Egliswach 1254, *Eglwys-y-vach* 1284, *Ecclesie de Vach* 1284, *Eglewys Ewach'* 1291, *Rectoria de Vach* 1535, *ll. eglwys fach* 1566, *Eglwys Vâch* c.1700, *Eglwysfach* 1720, *Eglwys Fach* 1795, *Eglwys Bach* 1838

The church is in the nook or corner of land between two tributaries of Afon Conwy; the early forms provide evidence of the def.art. ***y*** (as well as the F ***de***). The noun ***bach*** 'nook' is fem. and so the mutation to ***fach*** conveniently fell in with several other genuine examples of the adj. ***bach*** fem. ***fach*** 'little' (cf. Eglwys-fach) precipitating the loss of ***y***. There was also a tradition that a local chieftain, Bach ap Carwed, lived near the church and that his name is commemorated here. The modern form is an unlenited restoration of ***bach*** 'nook' or even Bach (ap Carwed).

EGLWYSEG Denb SJ2247

'church of ?Begel', ***eglwys***, pers.n. ?****Begel***

Eglesfegel 1277-8, *Egloisegle* 1391, *Eglossecle* 1467, *Eglwyseg* 15cent., *Eglussegle* 1575, *Eglwyseg* c.1700

Now the name of a mansion (*Plâs yn Eglwyseg* c.1700), river (*Afon eglwysegl* 1640/1), hamlet and rocky upland between Esclusham Mountain (q.v.) and Llangollen. The second el. is obscure. It may be an unrecorded pers. n. **Begel* or **Megel*. The later development of the name resulted in loss of the reduced final syllable and stress shift.

EGLWYS-FACH Card SN6895

'little church', ***eglwys, bach***

ll. eglwys fach c.1566, *Eglwsvach* 1721, *Eglwy Vach* 1760, *Eglwys fach* 1763, *Eglwysvach* 1792, *Eglwys-fach* 1837

The church (established in 1623 by John Lloyd of Ynys-hir) was also referred to as Llanfihangel Capel Edwin (*Little Chapel* 1760, *Eglwys Fâch, or Llanfihangel Capel Edwin* 1811, *Eglwys-vach chapel, or Llanvihangel-Capel-Edwin* 1851), because Capel Edwin, the name of the former chapel-of-ease (associated with an unknown Edwin), became linked to that of the parish of Llanfihangel Genau'r-glyn before itself becoming a church (also dedicated to Mihangel/Michael). Until about 1904, the actual village was known as *Banc-llan* (***banc*** 'hill, upland', ***llan***).

EGLWYS FAIR Y MYNYDD see **ST MARY HILL**

EGLWYS GYMYN see **COMMON CHURCH**

EGLWYS LWYD, YR see **LUDCHURCH**

EGLWYS NEWYDD see **WHITCHURCH**

EGLWYS NEWYDD AR Y CEFN, YR see **NEWCHURCH**[1]

EGLWYS NUNYDD Reservoir Glam SS7984

'reservoir near Eglwys Nunydd', p.n. ***Eglwys Nunydd***, E ***reservoir***

Eglwys Nunnid 1966

The largest reservoir in Glam, constructed in the early 1960s in association with Margam steelworks. Eglwys Nunydd 'church dedicated to Nynid' (*Egloose Nunney* 1543, *Eglwys nynnid* 1543-53, *Eglwys Nunyd* 1733, *Eglwsnunyd* 1746, *Eglwysnynydd* 1799, *Eglwys Nynyd* 1832) was a former chapelry of the parish of Margam dedicated to **Nynid** once believed to be a var. of the pers.n. **Non** mother of St David (as if L **Nonnita**), leading to the belief that it was 'church of nuns'. However, the name is perhaps more likely to be the masc. pers.n. **Nynnid**.

EGLWYSWRW Pemb SN1438

'church of ?Erow', ***eglwys***, pers.n. ?***Erow***

Clefferouw, Cleserouw 1291, *Egloisserou* 13cent. (c.1600), *Egloysyrow* 1315, *Egloserowe* 1357, *eglwys irw* c.1566

The 1291 forms probably represent *Eclesserouw*. The correct form of the pers.n. is uncertain but most forms suggest *Erow* or *Erw*. There is record of a chapel in the churchyard called *Capell Erow* c.1600 containing the tomb of a saint. Other sources attribute the church dedication to *Urw Forwyn* (***morwyn*** 'virgin') 16cent.; it has also been suggested that the pers.n. may be *Gwro* or *Gwrw* or similar derivative.

EGLWYS WYTHWR see **MONINGTON**

EGLWYS Y DRINDOD see **CHRISTCHURCH**

EIFIONYDD Caern SH5844-4039

'territory of Eifion', pers.n. ***Eifion***, terr.suff. ***-ydd***

Evionyth c.1191, *Eyfionydd* 1269, *Eyvynonyth* 1304-5, *eidyionydd* 14cent., *Eifionydd* 16cent.

The commote between Llŷn and Arfon. The particular Eifion is reputed to be Eifion son of Dunod son of the 5cent. Cunedda. The 14cent. form shows the occasional interchange of -f- and -dd-.

EIFL, YR Caern SH3645

'the two forks', ***yr***, ***gafl*** dual pl. ***geifl***

(or) Eiffyl c.1550, *(o'r) Eifl* 16cent., *Yr Eifl* 1757, *Rivel* 1795, *'R Eifl or the Rivals* 1809-11, *the Eifl* 1810

The extensive massif consists of three distinct peaks with two passes or shoulders between them (*Boulchryvel* 1536-9, ***bwlch*** 'pass'). The form ***geifl*** is a residual dual pl. used of pairs. The colloquial contraction Reifl has become The Rivals in E popular use, significantly as a pl.

EINSIOB see **EVENJOBB**

EISINGRUG, SINGRUG Mer SH6134

'winnowing-bank', ***eisingrug***

Singrig 1838, *Eisingrug* 1890-1

The bank beside the river was regularly used as a winnowing-bank for the corn from the nearby mill, and gave its name to the river itself (Afon Eisingrug). Singrug (with vars Singrig and Shingrug) commonly found throughout Wales, results from stress shift and loss of the initial unstressed syllable.

EISTEDDFA GURIG Card/Mont SN7984

'abode of Curig', ***eisteddfa***, pers.n. ***Curig***

Eisteddva Girric 15cent., *Aisteddfa Giric* c.1530, *eisteddfa Giric* 16cent., *Eisteddfa Gurig* 1742-3

Marking the west edge of Llangurig parish (q.v.) the name is perhaps used elliptically for 'abode in Llangurig', possibly in the sense 'shrine'. ***eisteddfa*** 'seat, stool, chair' is commonly used for hills or rocks in the shape of a chair, and is often associated with saints and legendary heroes. This was one of the traditional boundary points of medieval Powys, and it has been suggested that ***eisteddfa*** may have been associated with border meeting places. Some other forms such as *Steddfa Gerrig* 1795, *Eisteddfa Gerrig* 1798, show association with ***carreg*** pl. ***cerrig*** 'stone, rock'; the former, together with *Stethva* 1705, are evidence of the local form *Steddfa*.

ELÁI see **ELY**

ELAN VILLAGE Radn SN9365

'village at (the river) Elan', E ***village***, r.n. ***Elan***

The village was built below Caban Coch dam during the construction of reservoirs for Birmingham Corporation 1892-1904 to house people employed to maintain the dams and filtration systems. The name is taken from the river Elan (*Eleyn* 1241-50, *Alen, Alan* 1563-9, *Glan Elan* 1184, *Driffryn Elan* 1426) probably ***elain*** 'hind, fawn' and very likely referring to its rushing, bounding course.

ELWY, Afon Denb SH0071

'thrusting river', ***afon***, ****el-***, suff. ***-wy***

Elgu 12cent., *Elwey* 1241, *Elwy* c.1300

The river flows from west of Llanfair Talhaearn, following a meandering course into the river Clwyd at Rhydyddauddwr (***rhyd*** 'ford', ***y*** 'the', ***dau*** 'two', ***dŵr*** 'water'). There is a difference of opinion on the meaning of the pref. ****el-***. It is probably the el. found in a verb like *elwyf* 'go' and signifies 'drive, push' and therefore 'thrusting' or 'swift'. However, an equally plausible argument has been made for ****el-*** 'many, diverse, various' which appears in pers.ns; in combination with the **gŵy* found in *gŵyr* 'curved, bent', Elwy could be 'the river of many bends'; cf. Llanelwy.

ELY, River, ELÁI, Afon

Glam ST0284-1872

'river associated with *Eleg', pers.n. **Eleg*, suff. *-i*

(strat) Eléi 1136-54, *eleý* c.1126, *Ely* 1146, *Elei, Eley* c.1150,
Helei c.1179, *Ely* 1314, *Eleewater* 1479,
Ley River, of sum in Englisch caullid Ele, Lay 1536-9,
The Laie, or Ele riuer 1586, *Ely* 1596-1600

The river rises near Cilely farm (*cil*) and runs south through Tonyrefail, Llantrisant, Peterston-super-Ely, St Georges-super-Ely, St Fagans and Ely to the modern harbour of Cardiff, with *Strat Eléi* c.748 (*ystrad*) referring to the area near the Cardiff suburb of Ely. Other references are at Ely Bridge (*Eleebrygge* 1479, *Pont Lay* 1536-9). The pers.n. is unknown leading some to suggest a Br el. **leg-* 'drip, move slowly' since much of Ely's course is through marsh now drained. The W form Elái is stressed on the final syllable, hence forms such as *Lay* 1536-9, *Lai* 1559, with loss of initial E-, perhaps through confusion with the def.art. *y*. The river is recorded as *Y Lai* in a farm Lan-y-lai (*Llan y llaye* 1604, *Glanylay, Glanney lay* 1656, *Lhan Elai* 1695-1709, *Lanlay* 1784, **glan** 'bank' with occasional influence of **llan**) and by a W-speaking local historian in 1899 where the initial syllable of Elái is taken as the def.art. *y*. Ely (now a modern housing estate) is commonly Trelái to W-speakers ([*o*] *dref lai* 1601, *Trelai or Ely* 1833, ***tref***). The E form Ely is the result of anglicized stress on the initial syllable, possibly reinforced by association with the Cambridgeshire Ely.

ENLLI see BARDSEY

EPYNT see MYNYDD EPYNT

ERBISTOCK

Denb SJ3541

'Erp's place', pers.n. ***Erp***, OE ***stoc***

Erpestoch 1086, *Embestok* 1254, *Erbystok* 1291, *Erbistoc* 1391,
Arbistock 1588-9, *Arbistog* 1590, *Erbistok, Erbistock* c. 1700,
Arbistock alias Erbistock 1763

The identity of ***Erp*** is unknown and his name, deduced from the historical forms, is not found elsewhere. The el. ***stoc*** is very common in England (as Stoke) and is frequently qualified by another distinguishing feature but the precise significance is difficult to ascertain as it has a range of meanings including 'place, hamlet, dependent or secondary settlement, a dairy farm, an outlying farm, a religious place, a monastic cell, a meeting place'. From its location enclosed within a loop of the river Dee it could well have been a dairy farm or a secondary settlement associated with Eyton (q.v.) to the north-west, since there is reference in 1268 to land within the enclosure of the park of Eyton which had belonged to the family of Erbistock. Erbistock reveals several characteristics of E p.ns in north-east Wales. One is in having an E pers.n. combined with a habitative name. The other is in the cymricization of an E name involving the voicing of -rp- to -rb- and (in the W form Erbistog) the voicing of the final consonant as -g. A shift of stress from the first to the penultimate syllable, also in keeping with the W system, consequently preserved the possessive -es- as a second syllable and led to a variation in the unstressed first syllable (seen in the forms *Arbistock* and *Arbistog* and in W *Y Bistog*).

ERWD see **ERWOOD**

ERWOOD, ERWD Brec SO0943
?'stag land', ?***cerwyd***
Erwood 1616-20, *Gerwood* 1739, *Gerwd* 1742, *Errwd* 1747, *Erwd* 1822
The name is very perplexing and defies a satisfactory explanation. It is possibly the very rare ***cerwyd*** 'stag', following a now lost fem. el. such as ***coedlan*** 'copse' or ***llannerch*** 'glade, clearing', which would cause lenition to (for example) *coedlan gerwyd* and then further lenition to *erwyd*. Anglicization may then have reinforced the topographical or hunting association to ***wood*** while the 1739 and 1742 forms show the continued existence of *Gerw(y)d*. Paradoxically, the modern Erwood has then been cymricized as Erwd.

ERYRI see **SNOWDONIA**

ERYRYS Denb SJ2057
'flock of eagles', ***eryres***
Erreres 1391, *Erryres* 1565, *Erryris* 1570, *Eryrys* c.1700
The village is on high ground overlooking Afon Alun. Eagles must once have frequented the prominent outcrops here. The final -es (signifying a collective noun) had probably been influenced by the adj. ending ***-us*** or *-ys*.

ESCLUSHAM Denb SJ2550
'Æscel's river-meadow', pers.n. ***Æscel***, OE ***hamm***
Esclesham 1315, *Esglessham* 1325, *Esclusham* 1522,
Esclus ywch y clauth 1554,
Esklysham Ywch & Îs Klawdd, Esklys … Brit. ystlys c.1700, *Ystlys* 1838
The name is now associated with the uplands of Esclusham Mountain but the location of the original ***hamm*** is probably on the banks of Afon

Clywedog which rises north of the mountain. The W form *Esclus* (which did not survive, despite being interpreted c.1700 and 1838 as ***ystlys*** 'side') replicates the characteristic shift of stress and loss of final syllable seen in several p.ns in north-east Wales, such as, within a few miles, Borras or *Borasham* and Bersham/Bers (q.v.). The E Esclusham retains medial stress. The 1554 and c.1700 forms refer to the divisions below (***is***) and above (***uwch***) the ***clawdd*** of Offa's Dyke (q.v.).

ESGAIRGEILIOG Mont SO7506

'cock's ridge', ***esgair, ceiliog***

Eskergeyliog 1542, *esgyr geilioc* c.1562, *Esgergeilioge* 1577, *Eskergylogge* late 16cent.

Perhaps from a fancied resemblance of the ridge to a cock's comb, referring to Pencraig Rocks; cf. Caergeiliog Angl.

EVENJOBB, EINSIOB Radn SO2662

'Emma's remote enclosed valley', pers.n. ***Emma***, OE connective particle ***-ing-***, OE ***hop***

Emynghop 1304, *Evyngeopp* 1544, *Einsiop* 16cent.

Palatalisation of -ing- to -inj- occurs elsewhere (such as Burlingjobb Radn), and may be a product of the influence of the following -h-. W influence is probably responsible for the change from Em- to Ev- comparable with the mutation of -m- to -f- as if it were y M- > y F- , and for the voicing of the final -p to -b. The W form Einsiob is not well attested but probably derives from colloquial contraction.

EWENNI, EWENNY Glam SN6901

'(place near the river) Ewenni', *r.n* ***Ewenni***

Aventio post c.700, *Ewenny* 1130-9, 1382, (r.) *Euenhi* 1136-54, *Ewennith* c.1191, *Eugenni* 12cent., *Wenny* 1536-9

The r.n. Ewenni is probably Br **Auentios* with an el. meaning 'to moisten, to flow'. There are a number of r.ns on the continent such as Avance (France and Switzerland) and Avenza (Italy) thought to derive from *Aventia*, possibly a goddess of springs. *Ewennith* c.1191 suggests a by-form *Ewennydd*.

EWENNY see **EWENNI**

EWLOE Flints SJ2966

'hill at the source of a stream', OE ***ǣwell***, OE ***hlāw***

Ewlawe 1281, *Ewelawe* 1283-5, *Eulawe* 1293, *Ewlowe* 1331, *Ewloe* 1322, *Ewlowe otherwise Yewlowe* 1611

Just below Ewloe Castle hill is the confluence of the Alltami Brook and the New Inn Brook to form the Wepre Brook.

EYTON Denb SJ3444

'farm overlooking a flood plain', OE ***ēg***, OE ***tūn***

Eytune 1268, *Eyton'* 1270, *Eyton* 1315, *Eytoun, Eyton (Vachan), (Vaur), Eutun* 1391, *Eutwn* 15cent., *Eytyn (Ychaf)* 1536-9, *Eutyn* 1565-87, *Eutun* 16cent.

Several places associated with Eyton (such as Eyton Bank, Eyton Hall Farm, Eyton Grange, Eyton Park) are spread over a fairly extensive area. There is reference in 1268 to the park of Eyton associated with the Erbistock (q.v.) family. The el. ***ēg*** has a variety of meanings such as 'land by a river', 'well-watered land', 'water-meadow', 'raised land or a low promontory jutting out into a loop of a river', and there are several places called Eyton in nearby Cheshire and Shropshire. Here Eyton is north and west of a wide loop in the river Dee, but outside, rather than within, the loop. There is a pattern of OE p.ns in the area (such the adjacent Overton and Erbistock) many of which were cymricized. The forms provide evidence of a W Eutun or Eutyn which does not appear to have survived except in literary usage, although it still finds some favour. There was even a literary translation as *Trefwy* (***tref***, r.n. suff. ***-wy*** a suff. found in some r.ns) taking Eyton to mean 'river-farm' (as Allington became Trefalun which did survive). The reason for less prominence for a W form is possibly Eyton's eventual perceived English association with Eyton Hall and Eyton Park (*Eyton parcus* 1473) rather than with a village (such as Overton and Erbistock).

F

FAENOR, Y see **VAYNOR**

FAERDRE Glam SN6901

'(the) demesne', (*y*), ***maerdref***

Vairdre 1322, *le Vayrdreve* 1408, *Vard(r)e* 1764, *Fardre* 1832

It is likely that this was a farm held by a seignorial officer or ***maer*** of the administrative division of Parsel Rhyndwyglydach in the manor of Gower Supraboscus or Gŵyr Uwch Coed.

FAIRBOURNE, (Y) FRIOG Mer SH6113

'fine destination', 'the high ground', E ***fair***, E ***bourn(e)***, W *y*, ***briog***

Y Vriog 1586-1613, Y *Friog* 1838; *Fairbourne Sta.* 1898, *Fairbourne* 1901

Although Briog is found as a pers.n. (as in Llandyfrïog Card, and in St Brieuc Brittany) this is the noun ***briog*** 'high ground' (occurring also in Foel Friog near Corris Mer and Dôl Friog near Nanmor Caern); the village is sited on the steep slopes above the Mawddach estuary. It has also been argued that Y Friog is from ***merïog*** var. of ***meirïog*** 'full of brambles, thorny'. Fairbourne is a resort between Y Friog, the coast at Ro Wen ('the white shingle-beach') and the railway station. The name appears to have been coined in 1898-9 as a name for the station designed to attract holiday-makers (supplanting the 'South Barmouth' rejected by locals), despite the further protest that the site was known as Ynys-faig.

FALI, Y see **VALLEY**

FAN, Y, VAN Mont SN9587

'wet ground', ***man, llaith***

Manfleyth 1293, *Manlleth* 1577, *Manleth* 1606, *Manleoedd* 1813, *Manledd* 1836, *Y Fan, Van Pool, Van Hill* 1956

In the 1293 form *-fl-* represents -ll-. The early forms suggest W ***ma-***, ***man*** with ***llaith*** var. ***lleth*** 'damp, soft, wet' probably referring to Fan Pool; on the var. ***lleth*** for ***llaith*** cf. Machynlleth. ***lledd*** 'level land' has also been suggested. The 1836 spelling is influenced by ***lleoedd*** 'places'. Now also the name of two farms occupying a flat area, partly covered by Fan Pool, called Y Fan (or Van) where there are relics of lead-mining. *Bwlch-y-fan* appears on an 1836 map and Fan Hill is applied to the main hill. These modern forms are all influenced by ***ban*** 'peak, point, beacon', a very common el. in hill names. However, the chapel at Y Fan is still called Manledd.

FAN FAWR, (Y) Brec SN9619

'(the) big peak', (*y*), ***ban*, *mawr***

the Vann 1777, *Ban Fawr* 1813, *Fan Fawr* 1890

A prominent peak in the Brecon Beacons.

FAN GYHIRYCH, (Y) Brec SN8818

'(the) peak near (stream called) Gihirych', (*y*), ***ban***, r.n. ***Gyhirych***

Van Gyherech 1819, *Bangiherych* 1813, *Y-Fan-giharach* 1832

The r.n. is *Nant Gyherech* 1819, which may be related to ***cyhyr*** 'muscle, sinew, flesh', ***cyhyrwch*** 'strength' and ***cyhyrog*** 'brawny, strong'.

FAN HIR, (Y) Brec SN8320

'(the) long peak', (*y*), ***ban*, *hir***

Ban Hir 1813, *Fan-hir* 1832

A long ridge with a sharp scarp on its eastern side, in contrast to *Bangron* 'round peak' (***ban*, *cron***) a name no longer current. It is part of the Black Mountain south-east of Y Fan Brycheiniog (*Y Fan Brycheiniog* 1832, *Brecknock Van* 1886) also recorded in the adjoining pool Llyn Y Fan Fawr (*Llyn y fan fawr* 1813, ***llyn*, *mawr***). Fan Brycheiniog lies in Brec (Brycheiniog) in contrast to the adjoining peaks Bannau Sir Gaer in Carm (Sir Gaerfyrddin).

FAN LLIA, (Y) Brec SN9318

'(the) peak near (stream called) Llia', (*y*), ***ban***, r.n. ***Llia***

Ban Llai 1813, *Van Llia* 1819, *Y-Fan-llia* 1832

The stream is on the western side of the Brecon Beacons and is recorded as *lleya* 1510, *llya* 1599, *Llea* 1754, *Afon Llai* 1813, *Llia Brook* 1819, *Llia* 1832, probably the ***lly-*** found in ***llyfu*, *llyo*** 'lick, lap' but influenced by ***lleiaf*** 'smallest'. It rises north of Blaen Llia (*blaen llya* 1567, *Blaen Llea* 1760) and flows into the river Mellte (see Ystradfellte) at Aber Llia (*aberlya* 1590, *Aberllia* 1608). There is a prehistoric stone Maen Llia (*Maen Llia* 1815, ***maen***) near its source. The 1813 forms for the peak and the river interpret it as ***llai*** 'less' while the other forms seem to be perceive it as ***lleiaf*** colloquially ***llia*** 'least'.

FARGOED see **GILFACH**

FELINDRE[1], VELINDRE Brec SO1836

'(the) mill farm' (*y*), ***melin*, *tref***

(Capel) y felindra, (Pentre) y felindre c.1700, *Velindre* 1744, *y Felindref* 1839

No mill is shown on 19cent. maps but the village lies next to Felindre Brook. The village (***pentref***) had a chapel-of-ease (***capel***) of Glasbury until c.1695, later in ruins.

FELINDRE[2] Carm SN7027

'(the) mill farm', (*y*), ***melin, tref***

Melindreth 1284, *Melindressathney* 1318, *Velindrefe Sawddey* 1591-2, *Velindre* 1777, *Felindre-sawdde* 1831

The mill near Llangadog was close to the river Sawdde. The r.n. is *Sawddai* 1455-85, *Sawdde* c.1700, with ***sawdd*** 'sinking' a reference to fissures and pot-holes, although ***Sawddai*** may be a pers.n.

FELINDRE[3] Carm SN5521

'(the) mill farm', (*y*), ***melin, tref***

Velindre Mill 1752, *Felindre* 1831

The mill was beside Afon Dulas near Llangathen. A corn mill and a large house (Milton Court) are recorded here in 1891.

FELINDRE[4] Carm SN3538

'(the) mill farm', (*y*), ***melin, tref***

Y Velyndree 1545, *Velindre Jenkin* 1587, *Velindre* 1752, *Felindrejenken* 1811, *Felindre-siencyn* 1831

The mill on the stream Nant Esgair near Penboyr was formerly distinguished by the addition of *Jenkin* or *Siencyn*, presumably a former owner or tenant. There were several woollen mills here.

FELINDRE[5]**, Y** Glam SN6302

'the mill farm', *y*, ***melin, tref***

Veheud'r (= ?*Velendr'*) 1319, *Velyn dre* 1512,*Velyndre* 1573, *Sythen Velyndre* 1573, *Y Velindrey* 1596, *Velindra* 1729, *Felindre* 1832

Located on the river Lliw near a water-mill recorded in 1596 and flour mill in 1883. Forms such as *Velindra* represent the dial. final -a (as if it were pl. -au).

FELINDRE[6]**, FELINDRE FARCHOG** Pemb SN1039

'(the) mill farm (of the knight)', (*y*), ***melin, tref, marchog***

Velindre Melinmarchoge 14cent. (1580), *Melyn Marchock* 1419, *Molend' militis* 1488, *Melin y marchogg* 1600, *Knightes Mylle* 1583, *Melindre Marchogg* 1586

The names refer to the village and may be interpreted as 'mill farm (or settlement) around the knight's mill' which is specifically the mill belonging to the knight, probably College Mill in the village. Felindre lies in the parish and knight's fee of Bayvil and was owned by the lord of Cemais . The mill is fed by Afon Nyfer and the small stream running down through Cwmgloyne.

FELINDRE FARCHOG see **FELINDRE**[6]

FELIN-FACH[1] Brec SO0933

'(the) little mill' (*y*), ***melin, bach***

Velin Vach Inn 1798, *Felin fach* c.1817

On the river Dulas, 'little' is in contrast to Trebarried mill two miles downstream or perhaps in contrast to 'the new mill' of Felin-newydd about three miles away (*Velyn Newith* 1513, *y Velyn newyth* 1546, *New Mill* 1625).

FELIN-FACH[2] Card SN5255

'(the) little mill', (*y*), ***melin, bach***

Velin vauch 1685, *Y Velin Ystrad o. Y Felin-Vach* 1704, *Y Velin Ystrad als.Y Velin Vach* 1746, *Felin-fach* 1834, *Felin-fach-ystrad* 1891

The mill was beside Afon Gwili in the valley (***ystrad***) of Ystrad Aeron, and smaller than Melin Llanllŷr less than a mile to the east.

FELIN-FOEL Carm SN5202

'(the) bare mill', (*y*), ***melin, moel***

mill voele 1499-1504, *Y velyn voel* 1532, *Melin-voele, y Felin-foel* 1778, *Felin-foel* 1833

A mill, located on Afon Lliedi, which had subsequently lost its roof or vanes. The suggestion that it could have been named from an unidentified hill known as *Y Foel* does not fit the forms.

FELINGANOL see **MIDDLE MILL**

FELIN-GWM-UCHAF Carm SN5023

'(the) upper mill in the valley', (*y*), ***melin, cwm, uchaf***

Felin gwm 1752, *Velin-Gwm* 1753, *Melin-y-cwm* 1831

The present village developed around the mill which had to be distinguished from a lower mill on the same stream Cloidach. The lower mill *Felin-gwm-isaf* (1831) at *Pen-y-bont-bren* (1831) still had a fulling mill and a small bridge over the stream in 1891.

FELINHELI, Y Caern SH5267

'the tidal mill', *y*, ***melin, heli***

Porth Aber Bwll or Melin heli 1822, *Felin-hely* 1838

There are several tidal mills on the Menai Strait. During the late 18cent., the Dinorwig quarries built an extensive harbour for the export of slate, transported to the quay on a purpose-built narrow gauge railway (1824-5). It was this industrial expansion which gave Y Felinheli the alternative name of Port Dinorwig or Port Dinorwic (*port of Dinorwic* 1851, *Port Dinorwig* 1859, *Port Dinorwic* 1891). The demise of the slate industry (with the last export from Port Dinorwig in 1941) and the development of the harbour for recreational sailing have recently caused the community to deem the name Port Dinorwig as redundant.

FELIN NEWYDD see **NEW MILLS**[2]

FENAI, Y see **MENAI STRAIT**

FENNI, Y see **ABERGAVENNY**

FERNDALE, GLYNRHEDYNOG Glam SS9997

'valley characterised by ferns', E ***fern***, E ***dale*** , W ***glyn***, ***rhedynog***

Ferndale 1862, *Glynrhedynog* 1875

Ferndale seems to have first applied to one of the coal-pits near Blaenllechau farm sunk by David Davies of Blaengwawr between 1857 and 1862. The precise origin of the name Ferndale is obscure, but it may have been taken in translation from *Glynrhedynog Inn* 1875 (but known to have been in existence in 1862) a former hotel, in Blaenllechau village on the east side of the valley, less than half-a-mile from the pits. Ferndale was transferred c.1862 to the new industrial village which developed on the west side of the valley of Rhondda Fach near the Ferndale pits. Both Welsh and English speakers initially referred to the village solely as Ferndale and the W name for the village (rather than the inn) did not come into widespread use until the early 20cent.

FERRYSIDE, GLANYFFERI Carm SN3610

'(place) beside a ferry', ME ***ferry***, ME ***side***, W ***glan***, ***y***, ***fferi***

Ferya 1283, *villa de Passagio in Landesteffan* 1317, *la Ferye* 1326, *la Verie* 1462, *Boatside (Llanstephan Ferry)* 1740, *Llanyferey* 1811, *Ferry-side or Lan-y-ferry* 1831

The ferry connected the east side of the Tywi estuary with Llansteffan on the west, probably the earlier *passagium de Tewy* 1176-98 (17cent.). Ferryside itself is shown as the *Blue Anchor* 1798. The 1811 and 1831 forms show confusion of ***glan*** and ***llan***. The village developed as a health resort in the 19th cent.

FERWIG, Y Card SN1849

'(the) outlying farm', W ***y***, OE ***bere-wīc***

Berwik pre 1197 (1424), *West Berewic'* 1228, *Berwic* 1271 (1332), *Berwik* 1291, *Berwyk* 1405, *Y Verwic* c. 1470, *Verwicke* 1513, *Berwicke* 1535, *y ferwic* c.1566, *Verwig* 1804

In E p.ns Berwick originally meant 'barley farm', but was later used for 'grange' and 'farm on the edge of an estate'. Here, there was a grange belonging to the abbey of St Dogmael's which was established as an independent priory by the monks of Tiron but followed the rules of Benedict. The cymricized Y Ferwig (and Berwig near Llanelli, Carm) are influenced by ***byr*** fem. ***ber*** 'short', ***gwig*** 'woodland; hamlet'.

FFAIR-FACH Carm SN6221

'little fair', ***ffair*, *bach***

Ffair fach yn Llandilo 1612, *Fair vach* 1726, *Ffair-fâch* 1757, *Ffair-fach* 1831

The name contrasts with the larger fairs held at Llandeilo half-a-mile to the north on the opposite side of the river Tywi. The village developed next to the fairground, Llandeilo Bridge and Ffair-fach railway stations and the Union workhouse.

FFAIR-RHOS Card SN7468

'moor fair', ***ffair*, *rhos***

Rose feyre 1541, *Rosseffayres* 1561, *Rossefaire* 1578, *Ffair Ros* 1612, *Rossefair* 1734, *Ffair Rhos* 1834

The village is on a crossroads (with its *Cross Inn* 1906) while the moorland is north-east of Pontrhydfendigaid. Fairs were frequently held on open spaces, sometimes between parishes (cf. Merthyr Tudful's Marchnad y Waun, *the heath Market* 1696, *Marchnad y Wayn* c.1700). Three fairs were known to be held here, at least one of which was probably associated originally with the sheep farming of the Cistercian Strata Florida and later with the drovers; the biggest, the Easter fair, was moved to Pontrhydfendigaid.

FFARMERS Carm SN6544

'(place near the) Farmers', p.n. ***Farmers***

Farmers 1891

Named from the *Farmers' Arms* public house though only the *Drovers' Arms* is shown on the 1891 map.

FFESTINIOG Mer SH7041

'territory of Ffestin', pers.n. ***Ffestin***, terr.suff. ***-iog***

Festinioc 1292-3, *Festynyok* 1393, *ffestynyock* 1499, *ffestiniog* 1590

The identity of Ffestin has not been established. Because of the growth of quarrying at Blaenau Ffestiniog (q.v.) two miles north along Dyffryn Ffestiniog and the development of a large village there, the original Ffestiniog village is frequently distinguished as Llan Ffestiniog.

FFLINT, Y see **FLINT**

FFÔR, Y Caern SH3939

'crossroads', E ***four***, E ***crosses***, W ***y***

Four Crosses 1859

At the junction of a minor road with the Caernarfon-Pwllheli road was an inn called the Fourcrosses, a name which has long been adapted into W as Y Ffôr. A solitary *Pedair Croes* 1870 (***pedwar*** fem. ***pedair*** 'four', ***croes*** 'cross') is probably an antiquarian translation. The former name was *Uwchgwystl* (***uwch*** 'over, beyond') from its location west of the ford of Rhyd-y-gwystl (*Rydygwystyll* 1437/8, *rrydygwystyl* 1526) which is probably the pers.n. ***Egwystl*** but taken as ***y gwystl*** 'the hostage'. The term ***four crosses*** presumably indicates the intersection of four roads marked by four directional signposts which replaced crosses.

FFORDUN see FORDEN

FFOREST FACH[1] Brec SN9026

'little forest', ***fforest, bach***

Forest Vahan 1326, *parue foreste* 1372, *the litle forest and great forest of Brekenok* 1536-9, *the little forest* 1540-50, *le litle forest of Brecknock* 1570

'little' in contrast to Fforest Fawr (q.v.).

FFOREST-FACH[2] Glam ST6395

'little forest', ***fforest, bach***

Forestvachan 1508, *Forrest Bachan* 1529, *Foresta de Vaughan* c.1534-7, *fforest vychan* 1584-5, *Forrest* 1729, *Forrest Vach* 1764, *Fforest-fach* 1832

fforest is fem. but the second el. of some of the 16cent. forms do not record the fem. ***bechan*** 'little' but a dial. var. ***bachan*** comparable with the masc. ***bychan*** which commonly throughout Wales became the pers.n. Fychan anglicized as Vaughan (which evidently influenced the c.1534-5 form). It was later replaced by ***bach***. There are several forest names in the area such as *Forrest vychan alias Forrest yssa* 1650, *Forest ycha* 1716 and *Forrest Llansamlet* 1729 (between Llansamlet and Kilvey/Cilfái three miles to the east). Most of the woodland disappeared during industrialisation.

FFOREST FAWR Brec SN8219-9619

'great forest', ***fforest, mawr***

foresta de Brechonie c.1163-74, *magne foreste Brek'* 1372, *the litle forest and great forest of Brekenok, the great forest of Brekenok* 1536-9, *Forest y Brenin* 1602

A large hunting preserve covering the whole of the Brecon Beacons. The 1602 form has ***brenin*** 'king' with reference to the forest's forfeiture to Henry VIII by the Duke of Buckingham and which remained as Crown property down to its sale in 1819.

FFOSTRASOL Card SN3747

'crowbar ditch', ***ffos, trosol***

Ffoestrasol 1811, *Ffos-drossol* 1826, *Ffôs-trasol* 1834, *Ffostrosol* 1835

The first form records the dial.var. *ffoes*. The interpretation is difficult. The 'crowbar' perhaps referred to the ditch forcing its way through marshy ground, or to the habitual need for a crowbar to extricate carts from the ditch which now provides a channel for the brook Cerdin Fach to pass under the Capel Cynon to Croes-lan road. The late forms provide inadequate support for the suggestion that the name comprises ***ffos***, ***tir*** 'land' and ***asol*** 'fallow', but the latter el. may have influenced the forms in -asol as opposed to -osol (or it may be by dissimilation of -o-/-o- to -a-/-o-). The older name, *Pentre Pensarn*, was replaced by the adoption of Ffostrasol by the post office.

FFOS-Y-FFIN Card SN4460

'ditch at the boundary', ***ffos***, ***y***, ***ffin***

Ffos y ffin 1773, *Ffoes y ffin* 1800, *Ffos-y-ffin* 1834

The ditch may have been a channel for Ceri brook which flows under Pont Ffos-y-ffin on the main Aberaeron-Llannarth road. Perhaps the brook was a farmland boundary because the present hamlet (which developed around a chapel recorded in 1780) is not close to the boundary of the parish of Henfynyw.

FFRITH Flints SJ2855

'highland pasture', ***ffridd*** var. ***ffrith***

Ffrîdh c.1700, *Ffrith* 1871

Ffrith is on the lower slopes of Hope Mountain. At one time, the area seems to have been called *Belmont* 1840 and *Bell Mount* 1852, possibly fanciful names influenced by the hamlet's inn, the Blue Bell. The form Ffrith (as opposed to Ffridd in north-west Wales) is associated mainly with north-east Wales, underlining its derivation from the OE p.n. el. ***fyrhthe*** (as in Frith in several E counties).

FFRWD-GRECH Brec SO0227

'bubbling stream', ***ffrwd***, ***crych*** fem. ***crech***

Ffroudgrech 1372, *Ffroodgreche* 1602, *Ffrwd-grech* 1814

Beside a stream which flows rapidly north down from Corn Du and Allt Ddu. With reference to streams, ***crych/crech*** has a range of possible meanings such as 'bubbling, rough, strong'.

FFWRNAIS see **FURNACE**

FFYNNON-DDRAIN Carm SN4021

'well with thorn-bushes', ***ffynnon***, ***drain***

Fonon Ddrayne 1575, *Ffynon-ddrain* 1626, *Funnon ddrain* 1657

The well appears to have been close to Llwyn-teg farm (on the north side of the hamlet) recorded as *Tythyn ffynnon ddrain* 1667 (***tyddyn***) and *Tyr finon Draine alias Lloyn Tege* 1710 (***tir***). The hamlet developed beside a small lane running north from Carmarthen and around a water-mill.

FFYNNONGROYW Flints SJ1382

'clear well', ***ffynnon***, ***croyw***

funnon Groia 1785, *Ffynnon-groyw* 1840

The water of this well in the present village was habitually clear as opposed to several wells in the area, some of which were curative chalybeate wells such as Ffynnon Goch near Mostyn (*Fynnon gôch ... a purg. water* c.1700), while others had iron traces such as Red Water Wood near Ffynnongroyw.

FFYNNON TAF/DAF see **TAFF'S WELL**

FISHGUARD, ABERGWAUN Pemb SM9537

'fish yard, yard for catching or keeping fish', 'mouth of the river Gwaun', ON ***fiskr***, ON ***garðr***, W ***aber***, r.n. ***Gwaun***

Fiscard late 12cent., *Fissigart* 1200, *Aberguemi* 1222 (1239), *Fissegard, id est, Aber gweun* 1210 (late 13cent.)

The 1222 form probably represents *Abergueun* (which reflects modern dial. pronunciation). Several p.ns on the Pemb coast have Scandinavian origins. The existence of a fish yard with a Scandinavian name suggests a settlement (not necessarily Scandinavian itself) in a W-speaking community some hundred years before the main E and Flemish settlements. The name survived partly because the Scandinavian words resembled E words in sound and meaning and were in regular use by E sailors and fishermen using the port. However, the W name Abergwaun was in parallel use. The r.n. Gwaun (*Gweun* 13cent.) is ***gwaun*** 'marsh, moor'.

FIVE ROADS, PUMP-HEWL Carm SN4905

'(junction of) five roads', E ***five***, ***roads***, W ***pump***, ***heol*** var. ***hewl***

Pump-heol 1831 *Five roads* 1875, *Five Roads* 1895, *Pum Heol* 1931

From its location at the junction of three lanes with the main Llanelli-Carmarthen road. Usage has varied over the years between ***heol*** and the dial. var. ***hewl***.

FLATHOLM, YNYS ECHNI Glam ST2267

'island of the fleet', ON ***floti***, ON ***holmr***

ynys Echni que modo Holma uocatur c.1200, *Les Holmes* 1358, *Flotholm* 1375, *the Flotholmes* 1387, *Insula Flatholm* 1478, *Fflat Holmes* 1596-1600, *the Holmes* 1567, *The Holmes being a certain island ... called the fflatholmes* 1653

The island was a base for the Scandinavian fleet but its notably flat appearance (especially in comparison with Steepholm five miles to the south) has influenced the subsequent development of the island's name. Other names for the two islands are in OE documents where they are *Bradan Relice* (918, OE ***brādan*** 'broad, wide', OIr ***relice*** 'relic, graveyard') and *Steapan Relice* (918, OE ***stēapan*** 'steep'), islands known to be occupied by a Norse fleet in 918. The apparent pl. *holmes* in some of the forms is difficult, unless it refers to associated rocks which are no longer as prominent. The meaning of W *Echni* is obscure but may refer to a saint Echnus (possibly St Éogan).

FLEMINGSTON, TREFFLEMIN Glam ST0170

'farm of Fleming', pers.n. ***Fleming***, OE ***tūn***, W ***tref***

Villa Flandr' 1254, *Fflemyngston* 13cent., *fflemyngeston'* c.1348, *Treffleming* 1536-9, *Fflymston* 1547, *Flymstone otherwise Flemingstone* 1626

Several persons called *Fleming* or *Flandrensis* occur in Glam c.1200 and it was also the name of lords of St George's in the 14cent. As with 'Bolston' for Bonvilston, Flemingston was contracted to 'Flimston' colloquially (cf. Flimstone, Pemb, *Flemingston* 1606, *Fflimston* 1609), a form now rarely heard. The W name has substituted ***tref*** (as with Trelales and Laleston).

FLINT, Y FFLINT Flints SJ2472

'hard rock', ME ***flint***, W ***y***

le Flynt 1277, *le Fflynt* 1300, *Flynt* 1368, *y flynt* 14cent., *the Flynte* 1527, *y fflynt* c.1566, *fflint* 1671, *Flint* 1795

In ME ***flint*** meant 'hard rock' rather than having today's strict geological sense. The castle at Flint was built on a stony platform jutting into the river Dee. This was 'the rock' which explains the def.art. appearing in W and F and also in the F translation (*Le Chaylou* 1277, *Le Cayllou* 1278). The river is *Avon y Fflynt* 1471. One antiquarian indulgence (which had no currency) was *Caer Cellestr* (*Caer y Gallestr* 1757, ***callestr*** 'flint'). In W it is standard practice to refer to the town as Y Fflint and to the county as Sir y Fflint (although Sir Fflint possibly has greater currency, certainly in colloquial usage).

FLINT MOUNTAIN, MYNYDD Y FFLINT Flints SJ2470

'mountain near Flint', ***mynydd***, p.n. ***Flint/Y Fflint***

mynydh Koed y Flint c.1700, *Flint mountain* 1751, *Flint Mountain* 1878

The hill south of Flint town on the Northop road was at one time quite heavily wooded (***coed*** 'trees').

FOCHRIW, Y Glam SO1005

'the bulging hill', ***y***, ***boch***, ***rhiw***

Bohrukarn c.1170, *y vougryw garn* 1584-5, *Ffoc-rhiw* 1833, *Fochrhiw* 1920

boch 'cheek' is used like ***bol*** in p.ns to mean something which bulges, here probably a reference to Mynydd (y) Fochriw. The full name, seen in earlier forms, has ***carn*** 'cairn', and must refer to one of several cairns on the mountain; the 1833 map form appears to apply to a rock.

FOEL, Y Mont SH9911

'the bare hill', ***y***, ***moel***

Voyl vellyarthe c.1546, *Tre yr voil* 1577, *Moelveliarth* 1619-20, *Moelyveliarth* 1618-19, *Moel y veliarth* c. 1679, *Moylevelyarth* 1650, *Moelfeliarth* 1795, *y Foel* 1871

The full name of the hill was Moelfeliarth (***mêl*** 'honey', ***garth***, 'ridge, wooded slope'). The village Foel developed near the bridge (*Pont Feliarth* 1836, ***pont***) over the river Twrch and on the south side of a small, round hill. Moelfeliarth is now applied to hill-slopes about two miles north of Foel.

FOEL CWMCERWYN Pemb SN0931

'(the) bare hill near Cwmcerwyn', (*y*), ***moel***, p.n. ***Cwm Cerwyn***

Coom Kerwyn hill 1602, *Cwm Kerrwn Hill* 1777, *Moel-Cwm-Cerwyn* 1860

Cwm Cerwyn (*Come Kerwyn* 1535-6) is ***cwm*** and probably ***cerwyn*** 'a vat, tub', a fancied description of the valley on its eastern side around Cwmcerwyn farm, although it has been suggested that it may be ***carw*** 'stag', suff. ***-in***. Cerwyn may have been a lost name for the small stream next to it, a tributary of Afon Wen. Cf. Cwmcerwyn (*Cumkerum* 13cent., *Cumkeron* 1538), and Ynysygerwyn, locally Ynysygerwn (*Ynys y Gerwyn* 1591, *Ynysgerwyn* 1660) Glam referring to a pool in the river Neath.

FOEL DYRCH Pemb SN1529

'(the) bare hill associated with ?boars', (*y*), ***moel***, ?***twrch*** pl. ***tyrch***

Meneth tergch 1445, *Mynethtirgh* 1461-83, *Monyth Terche, -e* 1522, *Menyth Tergh* 1535, *Moel Tirch* c.1600, *mynyth tyrch* 1602, *Moel-dyrch* 1819

An isolated, prominent hill possibly where boars were hunted. Some early documents have -y- represented by -i- and by -e-. ***moel*** and ***mynydd*** 'mountain' seem to feature in the name. An alternative explanation of ***tyrch*** is that it is the old gen. of ***twrch*** (or of a pers.n. ***Twrch***), 'hill of the boar' (or 'of Twrch') or a pl. of ***twrch*** (cf. ? Pen-tyrch). Misinterpreted as Drych on some recent maps (as if ***drych*** 'mirror').

FOEL ERYR Pemb SN0631

'(the) bare hill of the eagle', (*y*), ***moel***, ***eryr***

Moelerir c.1600, *Moel eryr* 1602, *Moel eryry* 1603-4, *Foel-gery* 1819

One of the higher summits at the western end of Mynydd Preseli. The hill is completely bare of trees and shrubs. While ***eryr*** 'eagle' is likely, cf. ***eryr*** 'ridge' in Eryri (q.v.).

FOEL FENLLI Denb/Flints SJ1660

'(the) bare hill of Benlli', (*y*), ***moel***, pers.n. ***Benlli***

Moel Venlly 1649, *Moel fenlli* 1739, *Moel Fenlli* 1810, *Y Foel Fenlli* 1838

One of a range of ***moel*** names east of the Vale of Clwyd, overlooking one of the passes into the vale. Tradition associated this, the highest of the hill-forts, with the legendary Benlli Gawr (***cawr*** 'giant') whose name was linked in battles with, amongst others, Arthur (as in the hill Moel Arthur in the range). The modern form has the lenited form Foel, suggesting that the hill was also known locally as Y Foel (but modern usage tends to omit the article).

FOEL FRAS Caern SH6968

'(the) big bare hill', (*y*), ***moel***, ***bras***

y Voel Vrâs c.1700, *Y Foel Fras* 1822, *Foel Frâs* 1838

A fairly extensive ridge in a range of ***moel*** names between Dyffryn Ogwen and Conwy.

FORDEN, FFORDUN Mont SJ2201

'settlement by a route', OE ***ford***, OE ***tūn***

Furtune 1086, *Forton* 1292, *Fordon* 1364, *fordun* c.1155-c.1195 (c.1400), *Fordyn* 1535, *Fording* 1566, *Forden* 1570, *Ffordyn* c.1630-38

OE ***ford*** in the sense 'ford' is inappropriate here since Forden church stands more than a mile from the rivers Severn, Camlad and their tributaries and there is no notable ford nearer than Montgomery on the south-western edge of the parish. OE ***ford*** here almost certainly means 'road, route' since Forden is bisected by the Roman road running from Westbury Shrops to Y Gaer at Montgomery, which has influenced the perception that Forden is W ***ffordd*** 'road' and ***hen*** 'old'. Forden (rather than *Forton*) is now regarded as the standard modern E spelling probably deriving immediately from the W form. Most historical W forms have *Ffordyn* with the usual development of OE ***tūn*** to W -tyn as with many other E p.ns in north-east Wales (such as Mostyn and Prestatyn) but here, inexplicably, the modern W form is generally given as Ffordun.

FORGE Mont SN7699

'place near a forge', E ***forge***

Forge 1813-34

The site of a small forge. Cf. Furnace Card.

FOUR CROSSES[1] Mer SJ0343

'crossroads', E ***four***, E ***crosses***

Four Crosses 1795, *Pedair Croes* 1870

The hamlet is at the crossroads of the Bala-A5 road with the Maerdy-Cynwyd road. The 1870 form may well have been simply a literary coinage.

FOUR CROSSES[2] Mont SJ2718

'crossroads', E ***four***, E ***crosses***

Four Crosses 1836

The junction of roads from Welshpool, Llanymynech, Domgae and Llandrinio near the parish church of Llandysilio.

FOUR CROSSES[3] Mont SJ0508

'crossroads', E ***four***, E ***crosses***

Four Crosses 1891

Located at the junction of roads from Llanerfyl, Welshpool, the Rhiw valley, and a small lane leading down to the Calvinistic Methodist chapel.

FOURCROSSES see **FFÔR, Y**

FOUR MILE BRIDGE, PONTRHYPONT Angl SH2878

'bridge at four miles', 'bridge at Rhyd-y-bont', E ***four***, E ***mile***, E ***bridge***, W ***pont***, ***rhyd***, (*y*)

Pont Trytbont 1536-9, *Pontrid-pont* 1680, *Pont r'ŷd pont* 1733, *4 Mile Bridge* 1805, *the Four-mile bridge* 1813, *Trepont or Four Mile Bridge* 1838, *Four Mile Bridge* 1890

Before the building of the Stanley Embankment at Valley, the major crossing between Holy Island/Ynys Cybi (q.v.) and the rest of Anglesey was by a ford at the narrowest point of the Lasinwen strait. Despite being superseded by a 16cent. bridge, the ford is known to have been in regular use (possibly to avoid later road tolls) and was referred to as Rhyd-(y)-bont 'ford of the bridge'. The construction of a subsequent, more substantial, bridge prompted the addition of the tautologous ***pont*** which can be interpreted as 'the bridge at Rhyd-(y)-bont'. Later still, the location at this point of the fourth milestone from Holyhead (c.1752) on the coach road gave rise to Four Mile Bridge. The 1838 form *Trepont* reflects the emergence of a settlement (***tref***) near the bridge. Although frequently written Pont Rhyd-bont and Pontrhyd-y-bont, local usage is Pontrhypont.

FOUR ROADS, PEDAIR-HEWL Carm SN4409

'(meeting-place of) four roads', ***pedair***, ***heol*** var. ***hewl***

Pedairheol 1811, *Pedair-heol* 1831, *Four Roads* 1875

At the junction of two small lanes with the road running from Kidwelly to the Pontyates-Carmarthen road. Usage seems to vary between ***heol*** and ***hewl***.

FRENNI FAWR, (Y) Pemb SN2035

'the big hill like the prow of a ship', (*y*), ***breni***, ***mawr***

pen e vreni vaur 13cent., *Pen y vrevi vawr* 14cent., *montem vocat' veny vaure*, (*y*) *vreny vawr* 1577, *Vrenny vawr hill* 1602, *Vrenneu Vawr Mt.* 1777

The hill is roughly oval with a flat top at its north-west end rising to a point on the opposite end, and with very steep sides, giving some perceived resemblance to the prow of a ship. Early forms also have ***pen*** 'top'. The hill is big in contrast to Frenni Fach (*Vreny vagh* c.1603, ***bach***) about a mile to the east.

FREYSTROP Pemb SM9511

'Freistr's hamlet', pers.n. ***Freistr***, OE ***throp***

Hechfreysstrop 1293, *Freystrop* 1326 (16cent.), *Nithirirfreystrop* c.1333, *Lowe freisthorp* 1451, *Freystroppe* 1376, *Frestropp* 1592

The pers.n. is not recorded elsewhere but may be an anglicized short form of some other Scandinavian name such as *Freysteinn*. The second el. could be ON ***thorp*** 'hamlet' but such forms are very rare. The *Hech-* and *Lowe* (or *Nithir-*) refer to today's High and Lower Freystrop.

FRIOG see **FAIRBOURNE**

FRON, (Y)[1] Mont SJ2203

'(the) hill', (*y*), ***bron***

Fron 1817

Named from Fron farm located on slopes above the river Severn.

FRON, (Y)[2] Radn SO0965

'(the) hill', (*y*), ***bron***

Fron 1851

Located on the western slopes of a small hill above the river Ieithon.

FRONCYSYLLTE Denb SJ2741

'the hill at Cysyllte', (*y*), ***bron***, p.n. ***Cysyllte***

Fron, Vroncysyllte, Froncysyllte, Fron 1879, *Fron Cysyllte* c.1898

The hill (*Froncysyllte* 1879) overlooks the strip of land called Cysyllte, the dial. var. of ***cysylltau*** 'junctions, links', which juts out into a loop of the river Dee. In 1391-3 there was a ferry here. On the promontory itself is the road bridge, Pont Cysyllte, which links the A5 trunk road at Froncysyllte to the northern bank of the Dee and the industrial areas to the south-west of Wrexham (such as Cefn-mawr and Rhosymedre) and also the aqueduct (built 1795-1805) carrying the Llangollen branch of the Shropshire Union Canal. Almost all historical records and certainly modern usage retain the dial. pl. var. -e for Froncysyllte and Pont Cysyllte rather than -au. However, recent research shows earlier forms for Cysyllte as *Cysylle* (*Kissille, Kyssylle* 1391-3, *Kesylley* 1572, *Kysylley* 1591, *Kysylle bridge* 1680, *Pont Kyssylhie, Pont Kysyllie* c.1700), evidence of a possible derivation from ***cyd*** 'joint, common' and ***lle*** 'place' for two of the els; however, ***syll*** 'gaze, view' as a second el. lacks conviction, as it can only be corroborated in the very late lexicographical coinages ***syllfa*** (1814) and ***syllfan*** (1848) both 'observatory, observation post'. If genuine, *Cysylle* describes the notable banks and their striking views. It was the conspicuous transport links which influenced the change to *cysyllte* (*Pont Kysyllte* 1664-5, *Pont Kyssylhtie* c.1700, *Pont Cysyllte* 1762, *Pont y Cyssyllte* 1795, *Pontcysyllte* 1829, *Pont Cysylltau* 1838) with final -lle becoming -llte (cf. Gwersyllt q.v.). Familiarly, Y Fron.

FRON-GOCH Mer SH9039

'the red slope', (*y*), ***bron***, ***coch***

y Vron Goghe 1592, *Y Vron goch* 1613-14, *Fron-goch* 1838

The hamlet is at the junction of a minor road (from Cerrigydrudion) with the main Bala-Trawsfynydd road, where Afon Mynach flows into

Afon Tryweryn. The lower slope of Y Foel to the east is characterised by reddish soil; there is a Weirglodd-goch (***gweirglodd*** 'hay-field, meadow') to the north-east.

FURNACE, FFWRNAIS

Card SN6895

'furnace', E ***furnace***

Furnace 1763, *Dovey Furnace* 1803, *Pentre'r Ffwrnes* 1841, *Furnace* 1837

The timber of Cwm Einion and river Einion powered several smelting works (of silver, lead and iron) from the mid-17cent. (such as *The Silver Mills, with 5 Furnices* 1699). The works which gave the hamlet its name was the blast furnace erected c.1755.

G

GAERWEN Angl SH4871

'(the) white fort', (*y*), ***caer***, ***gwyn*** fem. ***gwen***

I gaerwen 1294, *Gayrwen* 1352, *Y Gayrwen* 1582, *y gaerwen* 1690, *Gaerwen* 1749, *Caer Wen* 1838

Despite the persistence of the def.art. in the historical forms and the specific *Caer Wen* 1838 there is no archaeological record of a fort which would have probably been near the farm of Gaerwen-isaf (*Gaer-wen isaf* 1891). Gaerwen was adopted by the railway station and junction and by the village which developed along the Holyhead road.

GAMALLT Rad SN9570

'(the) curved wooded-slope', (*y*), ***cam***, ***allt***

Kamall c.1755, *Gamallt* 1820-1

Gamallt is a prominent curved hill above the river Wye and Afon Marteg.

GANLLWYD Mer SH7224

'(the) shaded white horse (river)', (*y*), ***can***, ***llwyd***

y ganllwyd c.1592, *Ganllwyd* 1651

In medieval W literature ***can*** is used of a white horse or white dog. Here, that meaning is extended to a lively river, particularly apt for the fairly turbulent section of the river Mawddach (which flows through Ganllwyd). ***llwyd*** 'grey, shaded' describes the narrow valley through what is today the Coed-y-brenin Forest. There is no evidence to support the suggestion that the original name was *Garn llwyd* 'grey cairn', a reference to Craig y Ganllwyd.

GARN, Y see **ROCH**

GARNANT, Y Carm SN6813

'the rough brook', *y*, ***garw***, ***nant***

y garnant 1614, *Garnant* 1660, 1895

From a r.n. rising near Blaen-garnant (*Teer blan y garnant* 1614, *Blaen-gar-nant* 1831). The name also appears in *Garnant Colliery, Cwm-gar'-nant* 1831. It is an inversion of the name found as Nantgarw (q.v.).

GARNDOLBENMAEN Caern SH4944

'(the) rock at Dolbenmaen', (*y*) ***carn***, p.n. ***Dolbenmaen***

Garn Dolbenmaen 1807, *Garn* 1809-11

The village (still referred to locally as Garn) takes its name from the mountain to the east called *Y Garn* (1838) now Craig-y-garn, north of the medieval tnshp of Dolbenmaen. It developed out of encroachment onto *the waste called Garn* (1809-11) and the grazing land of Dolbenmaen, much of it in the 18-19cent., in response to the need for accommodation for quarrymen.

GARN FAWR, Y Pemb SM8938

'the great rock', ***y*, *carn*, *fawr***

Carn Vawr 1599, *y garn fawr* 1843

A prominent hill on which stands Y Gaer Fawr (*Y Gaer m vawr*, *Y Gaer m.* c.1700), which gave its name to the district and especially the promontory of Pen Caer (*Penker* 1315, *Pen Kayr* 1318, *Pencar'* 1326 (16cent.), *Penkayr* 1318, *Penkayer* 1459, *Pencaer* 1461). Locally Pencâr.

GARREG Mer SH6141

'(the) rock', (*y*), ***carreg***

Careg 1838

An earlier form is said to be Garreg-pen-ar-Gyffin (*carreg Penne ar Keffyn* 1576, *Carreg Pen y gyffin* 1827/9), the limit (***cyffin***) of the rocky promontory in Traeth Mawr ('big strand') at Morfa Gwyllt ('wild sea-marsh') which was drained during the building of the cob at Porthmadog. However, local tradition maintains that the ***carreg*** is a substantial stone slab in the village.

GARTH[1] Brec SN9549

'ridge, hill', ***garth***

Garth 1772, *y Garth* 1778

The name is taken from Garth Bank (*Garth* 1833), a prominent, isolated hill immediately north of the village which developed in the 19cent. near a road-bridge over the river Dulas and Garth railway station.

GARTH[2] Denb SJ2542

'ridge, hill', ***garth***

y garth 1650, *Garth* 1838

The ridge overlooks the slopes to the river Dee.

GARTH[3] Glam SS8690

'ridge, hill', ***garth***

the Garth 1588, *y garth* 1630, *Garth* 1833

The name of a farm taken from Garth Hill/Y Garth and later the name of *Garth Pit* 1865 and the nearby village.

GARTHBRENGI Brec SO0433

'hill belonging to Brengi', ***garth***, pers.n. ***Brengi***

Garth bryngi brynn dewi c.1180 (14cent.), *Carthprengy* 1281, *Kardhprenghi* 1162 (1351)

The village occupies hill slopes. The pers.n. also occurs in the lost *gallt brengy* thought to be in Gwent, and is possibly the same as *Brenci* in the Bodmin Gospels c.1100. The first reference has 'Dewi's hill' (***bryn***, pers. n. ***Dewi***); Garthbrengi parish church is dedicated to David/Dewi.

GARTHELI Card SN5856

'ridge of Heli', ***garth***, pers.n. ***Heli***

Garthely 1222, *Carthely* 1326, *Gartheli* 1669

The hamlet is on a slope above Nant Meurig. The identity of Heli is obscure, but the Heli of literature (in the tale of Culhwch and Olwen) was one of Arthur's huntsmen who followed Trwyth the boar to Ceredigion.

GARTHMYL Mont SO1999

'ridge ?near a mill', ***garth***, ?ME ***mill***

Garthmuldrensll 1338, *Arthemyll* c.1546, *Garthmyll* 1556, *Garthmele* 1557, *Arthmill* 1570, *Garthmill* 1577, *Garthmyll's myll* 1637, *Garth Mill* 1836

The second el. is uncertain. It may be ME ***mill*** since there are medieval E p.ns a short distance away on the east side of the river Severn. Garthmyl has been explained as a pers.n. Gyrthmwl or Gerthmul but there is no support in any of the known forms. The 1338 form is likely to be represent *Garthmul Dreusll* with the latter referring to the nearby tnshp of Trwstllewelyn.

GATEHOLM Pemb SM7707

'goat island', ON ***geit***, ON ***holmr***

Gateholme 1480, *Insula de Getholme* 1482, *Gatholme, Gateholme Insul'* 1578

The form may have been influenced by the OE cognate ***gāt*** 'goat', but then by E ***gate*** referring to the very narrow channel between the island and Gateholm Stack on the mainland.

GAUFRON Radn SN9968

'(the) concave hill', *(y)*, ***cau***, ***bron***

Gyvrons Issa 1743, *Gyfron Issa* 1753, *Goyfron* 1769

The hamlet lies along the former main Crossgates-Rhaeadr road leading from the steep, eastern slopes of a small hill above Black Brook.

GELE, Afon see **ABERGELE**

GELL Denb SH8469

'(place near the river) Gell', r.n. ***Gell***

Gell c.1898

Afon Gell flows through a narrow valley and took its name from a hermit's cell (***cell***).

GELLI AUR see LLANFIHANGEL ABERBYTHYCH

GELLIFOR Denb SJ1262

'the big grove', (*y*), ***celli***, ***mawr***

Gettliuor 1316, *Gellifour* 1706, *Gellifor* 1838

Today the area to the north of Gellifor is called Commins ('commons') and to the south is Rhos (***rhos*** 'moor'). The original Gellifor was a farm, probably near to a large grove. In the name Gellifor, the stress shifted to the second syllable and the last syllable changed from -fawr to -for (as in ***coed-mawr*** > *Coetmor*).

GELLI-GAER, Y Glam ST1396

'the grove at the fort', *y*, ***celli***, ***caer***

Kelligaer 1254, *Kyltigayr* 1296, *Kilthigayr* 1307, *y gelli gaer* c.1566, *Kelligar* 1567, *Gelli Gare* 1739

There is a Roman auxiliary fort (1-4cent.), marked by hedge-banks, north-west of the church. The local dial. pronunciation of -gaer is as in the *Gelli Gare* 1739 form; cf. Aberdare.

GELLI GANDRYLL, Y see HAY-ON-WYE

GELLILYDAN Mer SH6840

'the wide woodland', *y*, ***celli***, ***llydan***

Y Gelli Lydan 1586-1613, *Gelli lydan* 1620, *Gelly Lydan* c.1700

There were several tracts of woodland in this parish including a few called ***celli*** (*Gelly dywyll, Gelli green, Gelly'r Gwrel*), and the general area surrounding the present village is still characterised by sporadic woodland.

GELLÏOEDD Denb SH9345

'the groves', (*y*), ***celli*** pl. ***cellïoedd***

Gelliodd 1529-36, *Celliodd* 1761, *Gellioedd* 1838

On the lower slopes above Afon Dolwen. The form *Gellioedd* has irregular lenition (C- > G-) after a def.art. stemming from the influence of the sing. ***celli*** which almost invariably appears as (Y) Gelli. Some of the historical forms have the colloquial form of the pl.

GELLISWICK Pemb SM8805

'Gelli's bay', pers.n. ***Gelly***, ME ***wick***

Gelliswyck, -wyk 1539, *Gelyeswick* 1592, *Gelliswick* 1740

The p.n. may be an ON pers.n. ***Gelli*** or the ME pers.n *Gely* 1292 and *Gelly* 1470 commonly found in this area; the Elizabethan courtier and soldier Sir Gelly Meyrick (c.1561-1601) was born here. The second el. is ON ***vík*** 'bay' in its derivative ME ***wick*** which was a common dial. name for a bay in Pemb (cf. Musselwick, *Mussellvik* 13cent., *Mussellwick* 1307, 'mussel bay').

GELLI-WEN Carm SN2723
'(the) fair grove', (*y*), ***celli***, ***gwyn*** fem. ***gwen***
y gelli wen 1582, *Gelliwen* 1744-5, *Gelli-wen* 1831
A hamlet named from a farm recorded as *y gelli wen* 1582 and *Gelliwen* 1744-5.

GERLAN Caern SH6366
'near the bank', ***ger***, ***glan***
y gerlan 1592, *Gerlan* 1789
The generally accepted view has been that Gerlan comprises ***cerdd*** and ***glan*** both having similar meanings of 'step', 'rise'. However, ***cerdd*** with this meaning is rare and seems to be limited to the 13 and 14cent. The hamlet is near the bank of Afon Caseg.

GEUFFORDD Mont SJ2114
'hollow (or enclosed) road', ***y***, ***ceuffordd***
a'r Geuffordd 1854, *Geuffordd* 1891
A reference to the narrow road running north-east from Pentre'r-beirdd towards Sarnau. The name is now applied to nearby houses on the minor road called The Street running north from Guilsfield.

GILESTON, SILSTWN Glam ST0167
'farm of Joel', pers.n. ***Joel***, OE ***tūn***,
Julestone 13cent., *Jeoleston* c.1348, *ffilstwn* (= *ssilstwn*) c.1566, *Gylston* 1567, *Siltwn* 1590-1
The surname *Joel* occurs in Glam c.1262 and it is known that *Thomas Juel* (d. 1350) and *John Joel* (c.1362) held the manor in the 14cent. and *John Gyles* hailed from *Gyles Towne* in 1530. The church is dedicated to St Giles, almost certainly inspired by the secular surname. The cymricized form can be compared to Siôn for John, Sieffre for Geoffrey.

GILFACH (FARGOED) Glam ST1598
'(the) nook', ***y***, ***cilfach***, r.n. ***Bargoed***
Gilfach Colliery 1886
The village developed near *Gilfach Colliery* from c.1900. Earlier this was the name of two farms, Gilfach Fargoed Fawr and Fach (*Tyre Kilvache vargoed* 1629, *Kilvach bargoed* 1632, *Kilvach Bargoed* 1799, ***mawr***, ***bach***). The railway station preserves the longer name Gilfach Fargoed. See Bargoed.

GILFACH-GOCH, Y Glam SS9889
'the red nook', ***y***, ***cilfach***, ***coch***
Tir y Gilvach Goch 1548, *Gilvach Goch* 1710, *Gilfach* 1833, *Gilfach-gôch* 1885
A 19cent. colliery village named from a mountain or waste ground

recorded in 1553 and a farm. ***coch*** refers to autumn ferns but the association with the colliery has given rise to the belief that it is an ancient pile of cinders.

GILFACHREDA Card SN4058

'nook of Rheda', ***cilfach***, pers.n. ***Rheda***

Kilvach Redda 1587, *Gilfachrheda* 1755-6, *Cilfachyrheda* 1756-7, *Gilfach'r-heda* 1834, *Gilfach y rheda* 1837, *Gilfach-rheda* 1891

The village is in a valley leading down towards New Quay. Possibly prompted by the obscurity of the pers.n., the def.art. was irregularly added at the beginning of some forms, and in the middle of others.

GILTAR POINT Pemb SS1298

'?Gille's tor', ?pers.n. ***Gille***, E ***tor***

Giltor poynt 1578, *a poynt or headland called Giltor* 1618, *Giltar Point* 1765

The first el. is obscure, but may possibly be a pers.n. The change from -tor to -tar is also seen in East, West Tarr (*la Torre* 1324, *the Torr* 1609, *Ester, Wester Tarr* 1670) in the same parish. This ***tor*** is a fairly small rock or hill on a narrow promontory into Caldey Sound.

GILWERN Brec SO2414

'the nook near the alder-tree marsh', (*y*), ***cil***, ***gwern***

Gilwern 1810-16, *Gilwern* 1832

An industrial town taking its name from a house Gilwern and a former railway station.

GLADESTRY, LLANFAIR LLYTHYNWG Radn SO2355

?'*Claud-'s tree', 'church of Mair in Llythynwg', ?pers.n. ****Claud***, OE ***trēow***, W ***llan***, pers.n. ***Mair***, terr.n. ***Llwyth Yfnwg***

Claudestre c.1250, *Lanfeyr Lonthonnok* 1291, *Glaudestre* 1337, *Gladestre* 1459, *Glawdestrey* 1517, *Glawstrey* 1539, *Llandeuenoge* 1566, *ll.fair llwyth ynnoc* c.1566, *Glostre* 1610

An unrecorded pers.n., possibly a formation of **Claud* or **Glaud-*, with later forms influenced by ***glade***. ***trēow*** 'tree, cross' often occurs in combination with pers.ns usually signifying meeting-places (such as Bistre q.v. and Oswestry). The W form was a terr.n. (*dir llwythofnwc* 15cent., *Comm. Loethifnuc* 1536-9) with ***llwyth*** 'tribe, clan' and a pers. n. ***Dyfnog*** or ***Yfnog***. This older, more literary, Llanfair Llwyth Yfnwg is a commonly used var.

GLAIS, Y Glam SN7000

'the stream', *y*, ***glais***

Gleys 1183-4 (1334), *Glaisse* 1650, *Clais, Glaish* 1743-4, *Clais, -e* 1764

The village adjoins the confluence of Nant Glais with the river Tawe (*Aber Gleys* 1203, ***aber***).

GLAMORGAN, MORGANNWG
'territory of Morgan', ***gwlad***, pers.n. ***Morgan***, terr.suff. ***-wg***
morcanhuc 1136-54, *morgannoc* 1191, *Glamorgan* 1315, *Glamorgan, Morganok* 1322, *Morgannok* 1403
Morgan is reputed to be the 8cent. *Morgan ab Athrwys* otherwise *Morgan Mwynfawr* ('great in riches') king of the territory previosly called Glywysing which included the present Glamorgan (although some have argued for the 10cent. *Morgan Hen*). Glamorgan, perceived as the E form, derives directly from W ***gwlad Morgan***.

GLANAMAN Carm SN6713
'bank of (the river) Aman', ***glan***, r.n. ***Aman***
Glanamon 1499-1504,
Glanamman alias Tyr y bont (in Llandeilo Fawr) 1714,
Glanamon alias Glan Amman (in Betws) 1719
A 19cent. industrial village named from its location close to farms in Betws and Llandeilo Fawr and *Penpontaman* 1791. See Ammanford.

GLAN-BAD see **UPPER BOAT**

GLANDŴR see **LANDORE**

GLANDŴR[1] Monm SO2101
'water-side', ***glan, dŵr***
Glan-y-dwr 1778, *Glan-y-dŵr* 1885, *Glan-y-dwr* 1920
A 19cent. industrial village next to the river Ebwy which developed around a Baptist meeting-house recorded as *Glan-y-dwr* which probably took its name from a farm.

GLANDŴR[2] Pemb SN1928
'water-side', ***glan, dŵr***
Glandwr 1750, 1844, *Landwr* 1800
Close to Afon Taf and Afon Gefel.

GLANDYFI Card SN6996
'bank of (the river) Dyfi', ***glan***, r.n. ***Dyfi***
Glan Dyfi 1837, *Glan Dovey* 1887
A loop of the Dyfi comes very close to the main Machynlleth-Aberystwyth road and the railway. The 1837 reference is to the medieval motte of Domen Las (built in the 1150s) north-east of the hamlet of Glandyfi, close to the river.

GLANGRWYNE, LLANGRWYNE Brec SO2416
'bank of (the river) Grwyne', ***glan***, r.n. ***Grwyne***
Llangroyne 1559, *Langroinie* 1586, *llanygrwyne* late 16cent.,

Langroney 1610, *Llangroyny* c.1814-20, *Llangrwyne* 1832, *Glan Grwyney* 1840

The generally held view is that this is one of a number of p.ns which were originally ***glan*** (from its location next to the river Grwyne [q.v.]) and where ***glan*** was lenited as *lan* (evidenced twice above) following habitual reference to ***i*** 'to' and ***o*** 'from' and then interpreted as a lenition of ***llan***. Grwyne is also the name of two hamlets distinguished by Fawr and Fach (*Gronovawr* c.1285-90, *Gronee Vaure, Gronee Vaughan* 1607-8, ***mawr, bach***).

GLAN-RHYD Pemb SN1442

'side of the ford', ***glan***, (***y***), ***rhyd***

Glanyrid 1576, *Glan y Rhyd* 1604, *Glan Rhyd* 1793

Located next to a ford which took the Nevern-Cardigan road through a small, unnamed tributary of Nant Awen, now bridged.

GLANTWYMYN see **CEMAES ROAD**

GLANYFFERI see **FERRYSIDE**

GLAN-YR-AFON[1] Mer SJ0242

'bank of the river', ***glan, yr, afon***

Glan yr afon 1698, *Glanrafon* 1781, *Glan-yr-Afon* 1795

This substantial homestead between one of the tributaries of Afon Alwen and the main A5-Bala road gave its name to the hamlet.

GLAN-YR-AFON[2] Mer SH9141

'bank of the river', ***glan, yr, afon***

Glan yr Avon c.1700, *Glan'r afon* 1763

The hamlet takes its name from a house situated between the Bala-Cerrigydrudion road and Afon Mynach.

GLASBURY, Y CLAS-AR-WY Radn SO1739

'enclosure with a monastic community', 'the monastic community on (the river) Wye', ***clas***, OE ***burh*** dat. ***byrig***, W ***y, clas, ar***, r.n. ***Gwy***

Clastbyrig 1056, *Glasburia* 1144, *Glasbir'* c.1185-90, *a'r clas* 1447-89, *Claysbury* 1460, *y klas ar wy* c.1566, *y Clas* 1760

Since no fort has been found here it is possible that the ***burh*** was simply an enclosure associated with the ***clas***. This may have been near the old church which stood on meadows close to the present village but demolished in the 1660s because of repeated flooding by the river Wye. Its successor was built on the Brec side of the river. The apparent absence of early W forms probably reflects use of L and E in documents. Most W documents refer to Glasbury simply as Y Clas.

GLASFRYN Denb SH9150
'green hill', ***glas, bryn***
Glasfryn 1880
One of the lower slopes of Mynydd Hiraethog.

GLASFYNYDD FOREST Brec SN8524
'forestry plantations near Glasfynydd', p.n. ***Glasfynydd***, E ***forest***
glas venydd 1570, *Glas Fynidd* 1776, *Glas Vynydd* 1813, *Glas fynydd* 1832
The hill Glasfynydd (***glas*** 'verdant', ***mynydd***) gave its name to the forestry plantation.

GLASGOED Denb SH9973
'saplings', ***glasgoed***
Glascoed 1652
A plantation of saplings on the borders of the Bodelwyddan and Kinmel estates and in the tnshp of Faenol (*Glascoed y Vaynol* 1658/9).

GLASGWM Radn SO1553
'green valley', ***glas, cwm***
Glascun c.1090 (c.1200), *glasgwm* c.1180 (c.1400), *Glascum* 1188, *Landou Glascom in Eluael* 1292
glas occurs several times in the area, as a derivative dim. in the r.n. Glasgwmig (*Glascwm-ig* 1833) and a stream name and farm name Glasnant (*Glasnant* c.1817). The 1292 form refers to the parish church dedicated to Dewi in the cantref of Elfael, which prompted some to interpret the first el. as ***clas*** 'monastic community' (*Klas … a small Lordship* c.1700) belonging to St David's.

GLASINFRYN Caern SH5868
'borage hill', ***glesyn, bryn***
Glas in Vryn 1585, *Glasynvryn* 1602, *Glasinfryn* 1712-3, *Glâs infryn* 1780, *Glâs-unfryn* 1838
The hill to the north-east was characterised by the common borage with its blue flowers which explains several historical forms with ***glas*** 'blue'. Locally, the village is often called Y Bont, from Pont Tŷ-gwyn which crosses Afon Cegin in the village.

GLYDER FAWR, GLYDER FACH Caern SH6457, SH6558
'(the) big/little heap', (***y***), ***cludair*** var. ***cluder, mawr, bach***
Y Glyder 1722, *Glyder Mountain* 1777, *Glyder Vawr* 1795, *The Glydars* 1809-11, *Y Glyder-fawr, Y Glyder-fach* 1839
The two mountains between Nant Ffrancon and Nant Peris are of almost identical height but Glyder Fawr is more prominent in terms of its area. The el. ***cludair, cluder*** 'heap, stack, pile' can refer to a heap of wood or stone (from ***cludo*** 'carry'). Here, it may refer to the stone-covered

summits or, perhaps more specifically, to the distinctive exposed stacks called Castell y Gwynt (***gwynt*** 'wind') on the west side of the summit of Glyder Fach. The preferred spelling for some is Gluder (on the basis of ***cluder*** and ***cludo***); however, ***clyder*** is recorded as an occasional var. of ***cluder***. (Y/The) Glyderau is frequently used as a collective pl. for the twin peaks, a form which has influenced the pronunciation. Consequently, Glyder is more usual in contemporary usage.

GLYNARTHEN Card SN3148

'valley of Arthen', ***glyn***, r.n. ***Arthen***

Glyn Harthen 1803, *Glynarthen* 1811, *Glyn-arthen* 1834, *Glyn-Arthen* 1906

The brook Arthen or Harthen, as in the nearby Aberarthen (*Aberharthen* 1606, *Aberarthen* 1685), Blaen Arthen (*Blaen Harthen* 1597), Glan Arthen and Brynarthen, flows under Pont Glynarthen in the hamlet and into Afon Dulais (or Dulas). The valley is relatively open unlike the usual meaning of ***glyn***. Tradition identifies the brook with Arthen, king of Ceredigion (killed in 807) but the r.n. is probably ***arth*** 'bear' (cf. Aber-arth) and the fem. dim.suff. ***-en***, with aspiration of the stressed syllable to -harthen.

GLYNCEIRIOG see **LLANSANFFRAID GLYNCEIRIOG**

GLYNCORRWG Glam SS8799

'valley of (the river) Corrwg', ***glyn***, r.n. ***Corrwg***

Corrok 1376, *Glyncorrog* 1519, *Glyncorroke* 1535, *Glin Corrug* 1536-9, *Glyncorog* 1542-3, *glyn korrwg* c.1566

The village lies at the confluence of the river Corrwg and Afon Corrwg Fechan (***bechan***).

GLYNDYFRDWY Mer SJ1542

'valley of (the river) Dyfrdwy', ***glyn***, r.n. ***Dyfrdwy***

Glynndyfyrdwy 1279, *Glindou(er)do* 1283, *Glyndowerdwe* 1334, *Glyndyvyrdoy* 1392, *Glyndyverdwy* 1414

The river Dyfrdwy flows through an undulating narrow valley between Llangollen and Carrog and is crossed by a bridge at the village of Glyndyfrdwy.

GLYNEBWY see **EBBW VALE**

GLYN-NEATH, GLYN-NEDD Glam SN8706

'valley of (the river) Nedd, Neath', ***glyn***, r.n. ***Nedd***

Glyn Neath c.1910

An industrial village lying near the head of Glyn Nedd/Vale of Neath (*Glynneth'* 1281, *Glyn Nedd* 15th cent., *Glynneath* 1627, *Glyne nethe* 1630).

GLYN-NEDD see **GLYN-NEATH**

GLYNOGWR Glam SS9587

'valley of (the river) Ogwr', ***glyn***, r.n. ***Ogwr***

Glynogwr o. Landavoduck 1513, *Llandyfodwg or Eglwys Glyn Ogwr* 1833

On the r.n see Ogmore-by-sea. The recently revived name for the village is taken from the lordship of Glynogwr (*Glinogor alias Glenogor* 1296, *Glynnogour* 1485) covering the parishes of Llangeinwyr and Llandyfodwg. The village of Glynogwr is actually in the valley of the river Ogwr Fach (***bach***) and is an alternative name of its parish Llandyfodwg (*Landeuodoch* c.1291, *Landyuoddok* c.1348, *ll. dyfodwc* c.1566) with the pers.n. Tyfodwg, a saint with a dedication also at Ystradyfodwg (***ystrad***).

GLYNRHEDYNOG see **FERNDALE**

GLYN-TAF Glam ST0889

'valley of the Taf', ***glyn***, r.n. ***Taf***

Glyntaff 1881, *Glyn-Taff* 1885

An industrial village taking its name directly from Glyn-taf (*Glintaf, Glyntaf* 1307, *Glyntaf* 1426, *Glyn Tâf* 1758), a historic hamlet or tnshp in Eglwysilan parish. There was an identical p.n. (*Glyntaf* 1281, *Glyntaff* 1547) in Llantwit Fardre on the opposite side of the river Taf (q.v.).

GLYN TARELL Brec SN9722

'valley of (the river) Tarell', ***glyn***, r.n. ***Tarell***

Glyntarth' 1372, *Glyntartaralth* 1454, *Glintratarell* 1635/6, *Glyn Tretarell* 1655, *Glyn* 1692, *Glyn Tarell* 1832

The r.n. is a contraction of an earlier *Tardderell* (*Tartharell* 1454, *Tartarell* 1516, *Tyrtarelle Brooke* 1536-9, *Trwtarell* 1574, *Tatharell* 1584, *Tarell* 1671), which may have the same root as ***tarddu*** 'bubble, break out, run' and ***tarddell*** 'spring, source'. The dim.suff. ***-ell*** is common in r.ns.

GLYNTREFNANT Mont SN9192

'valley with a settlement near a stream', ***glyn, tref, nant***

Glyntreuenaunt 1293, *Glyn Trefnant* 15cent., *Glyntrevnant* 1578

The name also refers to the tnshp (in Trefeglwys) around the valley and its river Trannon (q.v.), a tributary of Severn.

GLYN-Y-GROES see **VALLE CRUCIS**

GODRE'R-GRAIG Glam SN7507

'bottom of the cliff', ***godre, yr, craig***

Godre'r-graig 1884

A 19cent. industrial village near coalworks in the Swansea Valley below the steep slopes of Y Graig and Mynydd Allt-y-grug. There is insufficient evidence to judge whether it might have been ***godref*** 'homestead, small dwelling'.

GOFILON, GOVILON Monm SO2613

?'pincers', ?***gefail*** pl. ***gefeilion***

Govylon 1689, *Gavilon* 1760, *Govilon* 1760, *Goevilon* 1762, *Gofeilion* 1798, *y Gefailon* 1834, *Gofilon* 1886

This may be ***gefeilon*** an unrecorded dial. var. of ***gefeilion*** (pl. var. of ***gefail, gefel***) 'tongs, pincers' used in a topographic sense since Govilon is between steep sides at the entrance to Cwm Llanwenarth. The unstressed first syllable of **Gefeilon* became Gy- and then Go- (influenced by ***gof*** 'smith') while the diphthong -ei- was represented by E -i- (and -y-) and retained in speech as a short -i-. The area was later notable for its iron industries and furnaces.

GOGARTH see GREAT ORME

GOGINAN Card SN6881

'little ridge', ***cegin, -an***

Goginan 1680, *Ceginan* 1718, *Coginan 1747*, *Goginan* 1757, *Cegynan* 1766

Some of the forms refer to the farms Goginan-fawr and Goginan-fach from which the village tooks its name. The el. ***cegin*** 'ridge, hogback' is very rare but is found in p.ns such as Carnau Cegin and Cerrig Cegin near Llandeilo Carm and Afon Gegin Llanddeiniolen Caern. The dim. form with ***-an*** is found in Card in Goginan (*Keginan* 1605, *Kegynan* 1672, *Koginan* 1764, *Goginan* 1799) near Llanilar and in Ceginan (*Kegynan* 1564, *Ceginan* 1794) near Ffostrasol and in Denb's *He[n]dre Geginan* 1540-77. The ridge is *Cefn Coginan* 1803 (***cefn*** 'ridge'). For the change in the unstressed initial syllable from Ceg- to Cog- cf. *Bwlch-y-Gerddinen* c.1830, *Bwlch Gorddinen* 1875 Dolwyddelan Caern (with ***cerddinen*** 'rowan, mountain-ash). The lenition of initial -c- to -g- can be ascribed to the persistent use of a preceding ***i*** 'to' and ***o*** 'from' in speech. This explanation is preferable to the suggestion of ***cawgyn*** or ***cogyn*** 'little basin', which is topographically appropriate, with the addition of a further dim.suff. ***-an***. The present village appears to have developed in the 1840s when it included an inn, the *Druid*, run by a *John Sayer*, leading to the alternative 19cent. names of *Pentref y Druid als Pentre Sayer*.

GOLAN Caern SH5242

biblical chapel n.

Golen 1840, *Golan* 1953

An unusual biblical chapel name (associated with higher ground) transferred to the hamlet. The chapel (*Golen Chapel* 1891) is above Afon Dwyfor with Afon Goch flowing through the village which led to the belief that it was ***golan*** 'bank, hillock, gentle slope'.

GOLDCLIFF Monm ST3683

'gold cliff', OE ***gold***, OE ***clif***

Goldclyviæ 1072-1104, *Goldcliue* 1120,
(church of) *Sancta Marie Magdalene de Goldcliva* mid 12cent.,
Goldclif 1245-53

From the colour of the rocks according to Gerald of Wales (*Goldclive, hoc est, rupea aurea* c.1191) but can also describe areas where there were marigolds (OE ***golde***) and other yellow vegetation (cf. Guilsfield).

GOLDEN GROVE see **LLANFIHANGEL ABERBYTHYCH**

GOODWICK see **GWDIG**

GORSEDD Flints SJ1576

'tumulus', ***gorsedd***

Gorseth yr Yarles 1536, *Gorsith yr Yarlle* 1587, *Gorsedh yr Iarlh* c.1700,
Gorsedd 1734, *Gorsedd yr Iarll* 1743, *Yr Orsedd* 1840

gorsedd is commonly used in Denb and Flints for a tumulus. In this instance several tumuli are located west of Gorsedd village, the largest of which, Gorsedd yr Iarll (***yr*** 'the', ***iarll*** 'earl'), gave its name to a farm (Yr Orsedd) and to the village (after the *yr Iarll* specifier had been dropped). The *Iarll* may have been the earl of Chester. The 1536 *Yarles* is unlikely to represents a fem. form ***iarlles***.

GORSEINON Glam SS5898

'marsh of Einon', ***cors***, pers.n. ***Einon***

Corse Inon 1691, *Corsinon* 1724, *Cross Inon* 1729, 1824,
Croes-Eynon 1751, *Gorse Eynon* 1754

Einon a var. of Einion (with loss of consonantal -i- common in south Wales; cf. Llaneigon). There is no evidence to justify identifying him with Einion ab Owain, grandson of Hywel Dda. Some forms suggest confusion with ***cross***, ***croes*** and ***gorse***. The initial lenition (to G-) can be ascribed to the persistence use of ***i*** 'to' and ***o*** 'from' in speech.

GORS-LAS Carm SN5713

'the green marsh', ***y***, ***cors***, ***glas***

Gors-las 1831, *Gors Laes* 1844, *Gorslas* 1895

In an area characterised by marshes, ***cors*** also occurs in a nearby farm-name *Gors-lâs-uchaf* 1831 (***uchaf*** 'upper') and in Gors-goch (***coch*** 'red').

GOVILON see **GOFILON**

GOWER see **GOWERTON**

GOWERTON, TRE-GŴYR Glam SS5996

'town in the Gower (peninsula)', p.n. ***Gower*** , E ***-ton***, W ***tref***, ***Gŵyr***

Gowerton 1898

The c.1850 map has *Gower Road Station*, opened in 1852 as *Gower Road (Station)*, from the village's development next to the Swansea-Llanelli railway line, and changed to Gowerton in 1886. It was later translated into W as Tre-gŵyr (as opposed to the more correct 'Tre-ŵyr' or 'Tref-ŵyr'). Gower/Gŵyr (***gŵyr*** 'curved') was originally the name of an extensive commote (of which the peninsula was only a part) whose general shape was curved; others have argued that the distinctive hook-like shape of the peninsula gave its name to the commote. An earlier name was *Gwter Felen* (***gwter*** 'gutter, channel, ditch', ***melyn*** fem. ***melen*** 'yellow, discoloured'). Another alias appears to be Ffosfelen (*Foesyfelin* 1813, *Foesyvelyn* 1831), originally the name of a house at crossroads in the middle of Gowerton, with ***ffos*** 'ditch' again with what appears to be ***melen*** but the 1813 form indicates ***melin*** 'mill'.

GRAIANRHYD Denb SJ2156

'gravel ford', ***graean***, ***rhyd***

Graianrudd 1628, *Graian rhyd* 1709, *Graian-ryd* 1838, *Graianryd* 1914

The road from Rhytalog to Llanarmon-yn-Iâl forded the stream, which once took the ford's name (*Aber y Graian rhyd* 1709). The var. spelling ***graian*** is commonly found in literature for ***graean*** and is common in the historical forms and in modern usage for the p.n.

GRAIG[1] Denb SH8074

'the rock', (*y*), ***craig***

Graig 1695

A fairly prominent rocky hill south of the Bodnant estate and to the north of a hill called Brymbo ('mud-hill', ***bryn***, ***baw***).

GRAIG[2] Denb SJ0872

'the rock', (*y*), ***craig***

Graige 1586, *Graig* 1606, *Tre'r Graig* c.1700, *Y graig* 1839, *Graig* 1851

A prominent escarpment of the range of hills along which Offa's Dyke runs. *Tre'r Graig* was possibly an attempt to distinguish from the nearby Tremeirchion.

GRAIGFECHAN Denb SJ1454

'the little rock', (*y*), ***craig***, ***bychan*** fem. ***bechan***

y graige 1679-80, *Y Graig Vechan* c.1700, *Graig* 1739, *Craigfechan* 1795

An escarpment which is less prominent than the hills of the Clwydian range to the east.

GRASSHOLM, GWALES Pemb SM5909

'grass island', 'place of refuge', ON ***gras***, ON ***holmr***, W ***gwales***

Gwalas, Gwales ym Penuro 12cent., *Insula Grasholm* 15cent., *Gresse Holme* 1536-9, *Gresholme* 1584, *Walleys* 1599, *Wallis, Walleis Ilande* 1602, *the Iland Gresholme, of the neighbours [called] Walleyes* 1603, *Grasholme* 1699

The island is some 7 miles west of the most westerly promontory of Pembrokeshire. Forms with *Gres(s)-* probably reflect influence of ME var. ***gres*** 'grass'. The W name, venerated in medieval W literature and legend, has traditionally been linked with ***gwales*** 'refuge, retreat, sanctuary'.

GREATOAK Monm SO3809

'large oak', E ***great***, E ***oak***

Great Oak 1813, *Greatoak* 1920

A scattered hamlet which developed in the 19 and 20cent. near Great Oak farm.

GREAT ORME, GOGARTH Caern SH7783

'large snake headland', 'terrace', E ***great***, ON ***ormr***, W ***gogerdd***

Cogars 1283, *Gogerth* 1334, *gogarth* 1420, *Goggarth* 1428, *Gogarth* 1525; *Ormeshede insula* 15cent., *Ormeshead point* 1610, *Gt Ormes Head* 1805

The promontory north of Llandudno (q.v.), frequently called Great Orme as opposed to Little Orme (q.v.), and locally The Orme. Its strategic importance as a landmark for seafarers explains the Scandinavian name (despite the late record) which perceives the headland as a snake (see Worm's Head) although the common ON pers.n. Ormr cannot be discounted. The W name ***gogerdd*** 'ledge, step, terrace' refers to the distinctive low western ledge on which stood one of the bishop of Bangor's residences. Later forms were influenced by ***garth*** 'steep hill'. Other W names are Pen y Gogarth (***pen***), Trwyn y Gogarth (*Trwyn-y-gogarth* 1841, ***trwyn*** 'point'), and the now obsolete Cyngreawdwr Fynydd (***mynydd***) which refers to the headland's location in the tnshp of Cyngreawdwr (*villa de Kyngraydur, Gogarth Kyngreadr* 13cent., *penryn kyngrayawdre* 1420, *t[ownship] Kingrhayader* 1594, *****cyngreawdr*** 'assembly', ***penrhyn***). Cf. Little Orme.

GREDINGTON Flints SJ4438

?'gravelly farm', OE ?****grēoten***, OE ***tūn***

Gredinton 1282, 1285, *Credinton* 13cent., *Gredynton* 1356, *Gredington* 1640

It is tempting to interpret the name as an unidentified pers.n. Gred with the common OE terr.suff. ***-ingtūn*** 'farm associated with Gred', but all the early historical forms have -n- or -yn- rather than -ing-. The adjectival ****grēoten*** is consistent with the topography and similar p.ns in England except that it does not satisfactorily explain the consistent -d- rather than -t-.

GREENFIELD, MAES-GLAS Flints SJ2077

'green field', OE ***grēne***, OE ***feld***, W ***maes***, ***glas***

Folebroc 1086, *Fulbroke* 1291, *Grenefeld* 1535, *Fulbrook alias le Greenfield* 1536, *Fulbroke Al[ias] Greneffelde* 1540, *Fulbrook* 1545, *Maesglas* 1579, *Greenefield* 1639, *Maesglâs ycha, yssa* 1653, *Greenfield Brit. maes Glâs* c.1700

The stream flowing from the wells of Holywell (q.v.) (and there called Afon Gwenfrewi, *Avon gwen Vrewi* c.1700, pers.n. Gwenfrewi) passes through several former industrial sites of the Greenfield valley (now an Industrial Heritage Park). There is also evidence of medieval (and earlier) exploitation of lead and clay. This may explain why the original name of the lower reaches of the stream was *Fulbrook* (OE ***fūl*** 'foul', ***brōc*** 'brook'). Greenfield and Maes-glas referred to land adjacent to the stream and were names which, not unexpectedly, found favour.

GREGYNOG Mont SH0897

?'territory belonging to Grugun', pers.n. ***Grugun***, terr.suff. ***-og***

Tregenoch [= *Cregenoch*] 1547, *krvgvanawc* c.1550, *cregynog* 1550s, *Kregunocke or Gregunocke* 1583, (*yneuadd*) *yngrvgvnoc* before 1587, *Gregynog* c.1600, *Crygynnog* 1781

There is evidence of a pers.n. Grugun or Grugyn. Some forms appear to have been influenced by popular association with W ***crugyn***, dim. of ***crug*** 'hillock, knoll', ***grug*** 'heather' and ***cregynnog*** 'shelly, testaceous'.

GRESFFORDD see **GRESFORD**

GRESFORD, GRESFFORDD Denb SJ3554

'grass ford', OE ***græs***, OE ***ford***

Gretford 1086, *Gresford* 1273, *Gressford* 1366, *Grassford* 1399, *gressfordd* 1565-8, *Yngressffordd* 16cent., *Gresfordh* c. 1700

There was a ford here through the river Alun (probably where the Gresford Bridge is today) probably characterized by a notably grassy approach. The cymricized Gresffordd reveals the influence of W ***ffordd*** 'road, way' (related to OE ***ford***). Some documents reveal attempts to explain the name as ***croesffordd*** 'crossroads' (*y groes ffordd* c.1566, *Gresfford or Gresford perhaps in the British, Croesffordd* 1757). It has been argued that OE ***ford*** here could already have signified 'road', a grassy road (leading to the Alun ford) as opposed to a stone road.

GRIFFITHSTOWN Monm ST2999

'village of Griffiths', E ***town***, pers.n. ***Griffiths***

Griffithstown 1872

Named from Henry Griffiths (1824-1915), a stationmaster of the *Great Western Railway Co.* at *Pontypool Road* station. In 1866 Griffiths helped set up the *Pontypool Road Benefit Building Society* which built the first houses here around Coed-y-grug farm *(Coed-y-grigg ycha 1648, Coed-y-Grick 1766, Coed-y-grug* 1866) near Messrs Baldwin's ironworks.

GROES Denb SJ0064

'the crossroads', (*y*), ***croes***

Y Groes c.1700

Several minor roads converge here on the Denbigh-Bylchau road. A stone or wooden cross once marked the crossroads but was replaced by a tree (*'There was formerly a stump of a tree pitch'd on end in 4 Crossways call'd y Groes bâch'* c.1700) near A *House of Note* called *Y Groes* (c.1700). By 1839, maps recorded *Y groes-fawr* (today's Groes Fawr, the hamlet to the west of the crossroads), and *Y groes-bâch* (now the farm Groes Bach to the north-east).

GROES-FAEN, Y Glam ST0781

'the stone cross', ***y, croes, maen***

Harston 1492, *Croyse Vaen* 1570, *y groes vaen* early 17cent., *y groes faen, Croes vaen* 1630, *Groes Vane* 1636, *Grosvane* 1650, *Croes-faen* 1833

Named from a standing cross at the junction of the roads from Cardiff, Llantrisant, Peterston-super-Ely and Rhiwsaeson. The 1492 name is OE ***hār*** 'grey, lichen-encrusted' and OE ***stān*** 'stone' which, as E ***hoar-stone,*** frequently identified a boundary stone; cf. Groes-lwyd. Forms such as *Grosvane* reflect the dial. pronunciation of -oe- and of -ae-.

GROESLON, Y Caern SH4755

'the cross-road', ***y, croes, lôn***

Y Groeslon 1798, *Croes-lôn* 1838

The road from Carmel to Llandwrog crosses the major road from Caernarfon to Porthmadog.

GROES-LWYD, Y Mont SJ2111

'the grey cross', ***y, croes, llwyd***

Groes 1829, *Groes-llwyd* 1836, *Groeslwyd* 1871

Located at crossroads, it may refer to some lost wayside cross, perhaps one covered by lichen; cf. Groes-faen.

GRONANT Flints SJ0983

'shingly stream', ***gro, nant***

Gronant 1086, *Grunaunt* 1547, *Gronnant* 1550

Identification of the relevant stream is uncertain (unless it is the *'great subterranean river'* c.1700 near Gronant). The name of the low-lying area between Gronant and the sea frequently appears in documents

(*Gronantesmore* 1346-53, *Gronantes More* 1414, *Gronants Moore* 1602, *Gronantmoor* 1773, OE ***mōr*** 'marshland', 'low-lying wetland'; *Korse Ronant* c.1566, *Cors Gronant* 1611, W ***cors*** 'bog, fen' with the anglicized *Gronants Gorse* 1626 as if E ***gorse***). The persistence of spellings with -es- (such as 1346 and 1414) can probably be ascribed to W stress on the penultimate syllable, and may have led to the belief that it was 'Gronant Esmor' (as in *Gronant esmor* 1347) supposedly containing the pers.n. Esmor found in Rhosesmor or 'Gronant-is-y-môr' (*Gronant is y mor* 1396) supposedly 'Gronant below the sea' (***is, y, môr***).

GRONW, Afon — Carm SN2221

?'river of (man named) Gronw', ***afon***, ?pers.n. ***Gronw***
Afon Gronw 1891
Cf. a r.n. *Gronw* 1840 in Llangrannog Card. It appears that the river was earlier called Marlais (*the Marlais* 1586, *Marlas R.* 1695) with a farm Dyffryn Marlais a mile below Llanboidy on the banks of the river Gronw. *Gronw* probably applied specifically to the river above a point close to Llanboidy and was extended to the lower reaches of the river near a farm *Grwnw Issha* 1716 (***isaf*** 'lower') possibly to distinguish it from another Afon Marlais (q.v.).

GROSMONT, Y GRYSMWNT — Monm SO4024

'great hill', OF ***gros***, OE ***mont***, W ***y***
(*de*) *Grosso monte* 1137-8, *Grosmund* 1160-1, *Grosmunt* 1161-2, *Grosmont* 1306, *Grisesmont* 1535, *y grysmwnt* c.1566, *Grysemond* late 16cent., *Grismond* 1742
The name applies to the large mound of the castle built in the early 13cent. on the site of an earlier defensive ringwork, possibly 11 or early 12cent. OF ***mont*** had been adopted into W as ***mwnd/mwnt*** 'hill, mound, motte' (as in Mwnt Card).

GROVESEND, PENGELLI — Glam SN5900

'end of the grove', E ***grove***, E ***end***, W ***pen, y, celli***
Penygelly 1604, *Peny Gelly alias Pen y Gelly Vawr* 1724, *Grovesend* 1813-14, *Groves-end, Pen-y-gelli* 1833, *Pengelly, Grovesend* 1841
Pengelli, properly Penygelli, was from a farm Penygelli-ddrain Uchaf, 'upper head of the thorn-grove' (***draen*** var. ***drain***). There were three farms here, Penygelli (*Penygelli* 1584-5, *Pengelly* 1841) still in existence, Penygelli-ddrain Uchaf and Penygelli-ddrain Isaf (*Pengelliddrain uchaf, Pengelliddrain issaf* 1845, ***uchaf, isaf***). Grovesend, a translation of Pengelli, was adopted as the station name, as well as for the *Grovesend steam Coal Colliery* 1873, the *Grovesend Tinplate* 1886 and houses of *Grovesend Row* 1879.

GRWYNE FAWR Carm SO2720

?'large river at wet places', ?***gweryn*** pl.****gwerynau, mawr***

guerinou 12cent., *Wroneu* 1188, *Gronovawr* 13cent., *groyne* 1583, *y Groyney* 1592, *Grwyney* 1602, *Groney Vawre* 1605-6, *Groney Vaure* 1739, *Groyney vawr* 1632, *Grwyne-fawr* 1832

The r.n. probably has the same derivation as Tryweryn (q.v.) with ***gweryn***, an el. more clearly evident in the name of the source of the river *dyl[yc]atguerinou* 12cent. (***llygad*** 'source') and in *Coit Wroneu* 1188, a wood located in this general area. The area around the source on the Black Mountains was presumably habitually flooded. The subsequent development, however, suggests the influence of ***croen*** pl. ***crwyn*** unrecorded double pl. ****crwynau*** 'layer of soil, hard surface, crust' rather than ***grwyn*** pl. ***grwynau*** 'sea groyne' which is recorded only for the 20cent. and the location being many miles from the sea. Its main tributary Grwyne Fechan (*Gronee Vaughan* 1607-8, *Grwyne vychan* 1739) rises on the hill Waun Fach and joins Grwyne Fawr near Cwm Bridge.

GRYSMWNT, Y see **GROSMONT**

GUILSFIELD, CEGIDFA Mont SJ2211

'Gyldi's field', 'place of hemlock', pers.n. ***Gyldi***, OE ***feld***, W ***cegid, ma***

Kegitua 12cent., *Kegidua* 1254, *Guildesfelde* 1278, *Guldesfeld* 1286, *Gillesfeld* 1535, *kegidfa* c.1566, *Guilsfielde* 1588, *Gilsfild* 1597

The traditional explanation of Guilsfield as 'Gyldi's field' which fits well with the genitival -s has recently been challenged by the proposition that Guilsfield was a loose translation of Cegidfa rendered by the lords of Powys, noted anglophiles, in the late 13cent. on the basis of the gold colour of some members of the species umbelliferæ (OE ****gylde*** 'golden flower'). In which case it is interesting to see W ***ma*** 'place, plain, low-lying ground' being translated as ***feld*** which signified 'open country' in OE but by the 10cent. and certainly by 1278 the association was 'arable land, field'.

GUMFRESTON Pemb SN1001

'Gunfrid's farm', pers.n. ***Gunfrid***, OE ***tūn***

Villa Gunfrid 1291, *Gumfreston* 1362, *Gomfreiston* 1374, *Villa Gumfridi* 1516, *gwmffre ystown* c.1566

Almost certainly an unidentified E or Flemish settler with a Continental pers.n.

GURNOS, Y Brec SN7709

'many heaps', ***y, curn***, pl. suff. ***-os***

y Girnos 1571, *Gwernys* 1596, *Tir y Gyrnos* 1614, *the Gwernos* 1787, *Gyrnos* 1884

The suff. -*os* can signify a dim. but came to have the plural connotations of abundance. Some forms suggest it was perceived as ***gwern*** 'alder-trees' but the majority have *Gurn-*, *Girn-* (as in Gurnos Carm and Gurnos Glam and in other parts of south Wales). Because many seem to occupy elevated sites, ***curn***, ***cyrn*** 'heap, mound, cone' may indicate 'a place characterised by hillocks, heaps, mounds or small peaks'.

GWAELOD-Y-GARTH Glam ST1183

'bottom of the hill', ***gwaelod***, ***y***, ***garth***

Gwailadd-y-Garth 1827, *Gwaelod y garth* 1845

Gwaelod-y-garth is located below Y Garth (Garth Hill). Garth is also the name of the former tnshp and several farms (*ye Garth* 1729, *the Garth* 1766, *Garth Hill*, *Garth-fawr* 1833). Several maps marks the hill as *Arthor's buttes hill* (1578) where E ***butts*** refers to burial cairns on the hilltop. Similar names for cairns in Wales and England invoke Arthur; here, however, it may have been prompted by ***garth***.

GWALCHMAI Angl SH3975

'(the township of) Gwalchmai', pers.n. ***Gwalchmai***

Trefwalkemyth 1291-2, *Trefwalghmey* 1350, *Gwalghmey* 1352, *Trewalchmai* 1580, *tre walchmai* c.1566, *Gwalchmai* 1838

Gwalchmai ap Meilir (1130-80), one of the medieval court poets, is associated with a mill (*mol. Gwalghmey* 1352) and with the tnshp known as *Trewalchmai* (***tref*** 'township') which became Gwalchmai.

GWALES see **GRASSHOLM**

GWASTEDYN Rad SN9866

?'small, flat place', ?***gwastad***, ?suff. ***yn***

Gwastedin 1695, *Gwasteden* 1820-1

The hill almost certainly gives its name to Gwastedyn Fawr (*Westedin* 1544, *Gwastedyn vawr* 1614, ***mawr***) the name of former tnshp (in Nantmel parish), which it dominates, despite the hill not being particularly flat on top and rising to two points at Carn Fach and Carn Wen.

GWAUNYSGOR Flints SJ0781

'moorland by a fort', ***gwaun***, ***ysgor***

Wenescol 1086, *Guenescor* 1254, *Gwenscor* 1284, *Wenescor* 1302, *Wennscor* 1458-9, *gwayn ysgor* c.1566, *Gwayniscor* 1635, *Gwaen Yskor*, *Gwayn-Yskor* c.1700

The early documents have forms which appear to be consistently at odds with ***gwaun***. However, they do show that a form '(y) Waunysgor' (***y*** 'the') also existed. The location of the fort, encampment or defensive enclosure (***ysgor*** var. ***esgor***) has not been formally identified but the immediate area has several possible sites (including the prehistoric Gop hill). A section of the so-called Offa's Dyke (from Trelawnyd to Tre Abbot) is a third of a mile to the west (but in reality likely to be a medieval bank and with little resemblance to the Dyke proper).

GWBERT Card SN1649

?'(place associated with) Cwbert', ?pers.n.?***Cwbert***.

Gwbert 1748, *Goobert* 1839, *Gwbert-on-the-*Sea 1890, *Gwbert-on-Sea* 1990

No entirely satisfactory explanation has been offered. One plausible suggestion is the saint Cubert (Cuthbert) found in Cornwall (*Sanctus Cubertus* 1269, *Eglos Cutbert* 1402). Here, the saint's name *Cwbert* could have survived to become the location name, preceded by the def.art. (common with an apparently non-Welsh pers.n) to produce the lenited *y Gwbert*. The name also occurs in the headland *Gwbert Point* 1814, *Goobert Hd* 1838, and in the rock in the sea *Craig-y-Gwbert* 1834 (***craig*** 'rock') which preserves the def.art. and which may still prove to be the origin of the location name (but still leaves the name itself unexplained). It is not clear whether this was the same as a field name *Pant y Gilbert* 1697 (***pant*** 'hollow') with the pers.n. *Gilbert* attested locally since the 13cent. (*Philippus Gilbert* 13cent.). In 1886, the area was developed as a resort, hence the '-on (-the)-sea' additions.

GWDIG, GOODWICK, WDIG Pemb SM9437

'(place at the mouth of the river) Gwdig', r.n. ***Gwdig***

Pullgudic, Pwllgutic 1076 (late 13cent.), *Abergoodigg* 1599, *Goodig* 1602, *Goodwigg* 1622

The stream Afon Wdig (*Goodige* 1616) flows from Waun Wdig through Dyffryn Wdig (*Dyfrin Godicke* 1595, *Dyfryn Gwdyg* 1650) to *Pullgudic* (***pwll***) in Fishguard Harbour later replaced by Abergwdig (*Abergoodigg* 17cent., ***aber***) which became the Gwdig of the village name. The r.n. *Gwddig*, which appears as such in medieval W literature, became Gwdig by provection. There is an identical r.n. Gwdig Fach (*stream…Gwdig* 1571) at Pembrey Carm. It defies satisfactory explanation, but may be the Gwdd- seen in some pers.ns with the dim.suff. *-**ig***. The alternative W name Wdig derives directly from Afon Wdig. Goodwick, with anglicization under the influence of -wick common in p.ns, is now seen infrequently on signs.

GWEHELOG Monm SO3804

'mottled', ***gwehelog***

Weolok 1296, *Welok* 1314, *Gwelok* 1366, *Wehelok* 1420, *Gohellouk* 1465

In modern usage the adj. ***gwehelog*** means 'shot (of silk), motley'; a white and yellow (or brown) cow was described as 'buwch wehelog'. It is possible therefore that ***gwehelog*** was associated with some preceding fem. word such as ***coedwig*** (since most of the references are to woodland) to give *coedwig wehelog* 'diverse, variegated woodland' or ***gwaun*** (as in Gwehelog Common, *Gweyne Goheloge* 1547, *Gweyne Gwhelog* 1548). ***gwehelog*** seems to have no literary pedigree but the comparatively consistent forms for the p.n. provide evidence of its use.

GWENDDWR Brec SO0643

'(place near the river) Gwenddwr', r.n. ***Gwenddwr***

Wendor 1241, *Gwenthur* 1513, *gwen ddwr* c.1566

The r.n. Gwenddwr is ***gwyn*** fem. ***gwen***, ***dŵr***, 'white water'. ***dŵr*** is masc. but ***afon*** 'river' is fem. The river is a tributary of Cletwr (***caled***, ***dŵr*** 'rough water').

GWENDRAETH FACH, GWENDRAETH FAWR

Carm SN4312, SN4810

'great/little (river of the) white beach', ***gwyn*** fem. ***gwen***, ***traeth***, ***bach***, ***mawr***

Wendraeth, *Wendraith* c.1191, *Wandrath* 1423, *Wandreth* 1440-1, *Gwendraeth Vawr* 1532, *Vendraith Vaur*, *Guendraith Vehan*, *litle Wendraith* 1536-9, *Gwendraeth Vaughan* 1564, *River Gwendraeth Vach* 1779

The name of both rivers evidently derives from the sands of the river estuary now largely choked by sand and mud (*Gwendraeth vighian late a port* 1566). Gwendraeth Fawr rises near Gors-las and Gwendraeth Fach about three miles further north near Maesybont, both meeting in tidal water below Kidwelly. ***traeth*** is masc. but the fem. adj. ***gwen*** can be ascribed to the fact that rivers are perceived as fem. Gwendraeth Fach is generally *Gwendraeth Fechan* (***bechan***) in earlier sources.

GWENFFRWD see **WHITEBROOK**

GWENFÔ see **WENVOE**

GWENT see **CAER-WENT**

GWEPRA see **WEPRE**

GWERNAFFIELD, Y WAUN Flints SJ2064

'alder-grove of the field', 'the moorland', W ***gwern***, ***y***, ***gwaun***, OE ***feld***

Gwernaffeld 1477, *Gwernaffild* 1486, *Gwerneaffeyld* 1526, *Gwernaffield* 1598, *yrwyen* 1600, *Y Waen* c.1700, *the Wayn* 1719, *Waen* 1794

There are several ***gwern*** p.ns in the area (such as Gwernymynydd q.v.). By the 15cent. in England ***feld*** certainly carried the connotation of 'communally cultivated arable land', possibly enclosed in some way, but the use of the E word here is very puzzling. Certainly ****ffeld*** and ****ffild*** have not hitherto featured in the W lexicon. One can only conclude that it fits into that group of E agricultural terms (such as the cymricized ***acer*** and ***grofft***) which were introduced through E custom and practice (perhaps here by one of the adjoining Rhual or Gwysaney estates). A **Gwern-y-field* was then cymricized further when the stress shifted to the penultimate syllable changing the -y- into a more prominent -a-, and with the -f- written as -ff-.

GWERNESNEY see **GWERNESNI**

GWERNESNI, GWERNESNEY Monm SJ4101

'marsh of Esni', ***gwern***, pers.n. ***Esni***

Warnestny 1296, c.1348, *Warensti* 1314, *Wernesseny* 1401, *gwern esni* c.1566

Esni has been identified as an early dean of Llandaf and brother of Urban, bishop of Llandaf 1107-34. Several early forms have an excrescent -t-.

GWERNYMYNYDD Flints SJ2162

'alder-grove of the mountain', ***gwern, y, mynydd***

Gwrn y minith 1671-2, *Gwernymynnydd* 1748, *Gwernymynydd* 1815, *Gwern-y-mynydd* 1838

On the road between Mold and Rhuthun ascending to the Clwydian range.

GWERSYLLT Denb SJ3253

'Wersige's hill', pers.n. ****Wērsige***, ME ***hull***

Wersuld, Wersull, Wersullt 1315, *Wershall* 1335, *Gwersild* 1393, *Gwersyllt* 1402, *Wersyllt* 1461, *Gwershull* 1561, *Wershulte* 1620, *Gwersyllt* 1700-1

The hill is probably today's Gwersyllt Hill. It has been argued that the first el. is ***wearg*** 'felon' and that this was therefore the location of a gibbet. However, 'Wersige's-hull' (where ***hull*** is the ME dial. var. of OE ***hyll***) is the more probable derivation. Either way, the p.n. reveals late cymricization (characteristic of north-east Wales) in its change from W- > Gw-, the shift of stress (and consequent loss of the middle syllable) and the development of -l > -ll > -llt, all probably influenced by ***gwersyll*** 'camp'.

GWESBYR Flints SJ1183

'lookout fort', OE ***weard***, OE ***burh*** dat. ***byrig***

Weardbyrig 915, 939, *Waestbyrig* 1053, *Wesberie* 1086, *Westbury, Gwespur* 1332, *Westbury* 1429, *Gwesbur* 1515-16, *Gwespir* 1549, *Gwesbir* 1612, *Gwespyr* 1629, *Gwesbyr, Gwespyr (Westbury)* c.1700

The fort was a probably a strategic Mercian lookout for the Dee estuary to the north and the Gwynedd-Powys kingdom to the west and south. The development of a fortified Rhuddlan six miles south-west on the river Clwyd in 921 by Edward the Elder and then by Edward I may have reduced the importance of the lookout fort which soon came to be interpreted as the 'west fort' (OE ***west***), the westernmost fort in Mercia, perceived as offering garrisoned protection against the Welsh who had by now occupied Rhuddlan. In time, this W influence cymricized *Westbury* into *Gwesbur* and Gwesbyr through stress-shift to the penultimate syllable, loss of final syllable and introduction of a more familiar W initial consonant group.

GWNDY see **UNDY**

GWY, Afon see **WYE, River**

GWYDDELWERN Mer SJ0746

'alder marsh in the thickets', ***gwyddwal*** pl. ***gwyddeli***, ***gwern***
Gwothelwern 1198, *Gwthelwern* 1206, *Gwidelwern* 1254,
Gothelwern, *Gwydelwern* 1292-3, *ll. gwydd elwern* c.1566
The area is characterised by low-lying ground with several steep slopes and a brook on either side. A popular belief was in ***Gwyddel*** 'Irishman', based on the legend that Beuno (commemorated in the well of Gwern Beuno) restored life to an Irishman here. Another suggestion, ***gwyddel*** 'forest, grove', is not recorded elsewhere until the 18cent.

GWYDDGRUG Carm SN4635

'prominent mound, ***gŵydd***, ***crug***
Castellum Guidgruc 1145 (13cent.), *Goyd Gruc* 1331, *Gowithgrege* 1535,
Gwythegrege 1548-54, *y wyrgryg* c.1700
This was a motte-and-bailey castle and identical in meaning to Yr Wyddgrug (q.v.), traditionally interpreted as 'memorial mound' with ***gŵydd*** in the sense of 'tomb, cairn', also supposed for Yr Wyddfa (Snowdon, q.v.). However, it is more likely that the initial el. of all three is ***gŵydd*** 'prominent, conspicuous'. Both Gwyddgrug and Yr Wyddgrug, together with the lost *Gwyddgrug* at Nantcriba Mont (*Wydhercruck'* 1245, *castell yr Wydgruc* 1263 (c.1400), *Wyðegruc* 1274, *Gythe Gruc* 1281) refer to medieval castles.

GWYDIR FOREST Caern SH7555

'forest of Gwydir', E ***forest***, p.n. ***Gwydir***
Wedir 1352, *Gwedyr* 1560, *Gwydyr* c.1700
An extensive afforested area belonging to Gwydir Castle and its estate. The name is ***gwo***- 'under, low', ***tir*** 'land', a reference to the low-lying land beside the river Conwy south-west of Llanrwst. Vars are Gwydyr and Gwydr, the latter showing the influence of ***gwydr*** 'glass'.

GWYNEDD

'land of the Vēnii', Br ****Uēnedā***

Venedotis 5cent., *Venedotiam* 1194, *Gueneth* 1232-3

A kingdom and administrative county in the north-west. The name appears to be Irish, reflecting post-Roman Ir settlement in north-west Wales (cf. Llŷn) and probably similar to the Ir Féni. The 'territory of the **Vēnii*' was **Uēnedā*, latinized as *Venedotia*; a late 5cent. commemoration stone in Penmachno records a man from *Venedotis*. By the 6cent., Gwynedd was the most powerful of the kingdoms and by the 12cent. stretched from Dyfi to Dee and was divided into Gwynedd Is Conwy (***is*** 'below, beyond' the river Conwy) including most of Denb and Flints, and Gwynedd Uwch Conwy (***uwch*** 'above') corresponding broadly to Angl, Caern and Mer. The 1974 county of Gwynedd incorporated these latter three counties (although subsequent reorganisation limited it to Caern and Mer).

GWYNFE see **CAPEL GWYNFE**

GŴYR see **GOWERTON**

GWYRFAI, Afon Caern SH5555-4559

'(river of) ?curved places', ***afon, gŵyr, mai***

Gwrvai 1461-83, *Gwyrfai* 15cent., *Avon Guruay, Guirvay* 1536-9, *Gwrvay* 1590, *Gorfai* 1838

The river rises in Llyn-y-gadair near Rhyd-ddu, runs through Llyn Cwellyn, Betws Garmon and Waun-fawr and into the Menai Strait at Y Foryd. It divides the commote of Arfon into Uwch Gwyrfai (*Ughgurvey* 1303-4, *Uwch Guruei* 15cent.) and Is Gwyrfai (*Iscorvey* 1303-4, *Is Gurvei* 15cent.). The meaning is obscure although the first el. is likely to be ***gŵyr*** 'bent, curved, winding' with reference to the river's meandering course. The second el. may be ***mai*** which is possibly a pl. or oblique case of ***ma*** 'place, level terrain, open territory'.

GWYSTRE Radn SO0665

'sow farm', ***gwŷs, tref***

the Goostry 1796, *the Goosetree* 1822, *Gwystre* 1828

Comparable with many places called Mochdre (q.v.). Local people pronounce it 'Gwstri'. The early forms have ***the*** translating a lost W def. art. ***y***. The 1822 form shows the influence of E ***goosetree***.

GWYTHERIN Denb SH8761

'(the place of) Gwytherin', pers.n. ***Gwytherin***

Guythrein 1254, *Gwytherin* 13cent., *Gwytherin* 1284, *Gwytheryn* 1291, *Guytheryn* 1334

The location is at the junction of minor roads from Llanrwst, Llansannan and Llanfair Talhaearn at a crossing of Afon Cledwen. An alias was *Pennant Gwytherin* (14cent.) where ***pennant*** means 'head of a valley', a reference to the valley of Afon Cledwen. Gwytherin has been identified as a 6cent. saint Gwytherin son of Dingad ap Nudd Hael.

GYFFIN Caern SH7776

'the border land', (*y*), ***cyffin***

Geffin 1254, *Kyffyn* 1284, *Gyffyn* 1391, *Geffyn* 1422

The village of Gyffin is separated from town of Conwy by Afon Gyffin, and has the river Conwy (the boundary between the two divisions of medieval Gwynedd, Uwch Conwy and Is Conwy) to the east. Afon Gyffin (*Aberegeffyn, fluvium Geffeyn* 1199 [1232]), was the limit of the territories of Aberconwy monastery and continues to be the boundary of Aberconwy parish. It is probable that *Caer Gyffin* was the name of the fortified site before the building of the castle at Conwy. Although the def.art. ***y*** has caused the lenited Gyffin, it has not featured in later usage, but the form was perpetuated by the persistent use of ***i*** 'to' and ***o*** 'from' in speech.

GYFFYLLIOG, Y Denb SJ0557

'(the place of) pollard trees or stumps', ***y, cyffyll, -iog***

Kyffellyauc 1259-60, *Kyffylyog* 1400, *Kyffithilok* 1431, *y gyffyllioc* c.1566, *Gyffylliog* 1620, *Y Gyffylhiog, Kyffylhiog* c.1700, *Cyffylliog* 1839

The word ***cyffyll*** is used of stumps and the adj. *Cyffylliog* (recorded only in this p.n.) possibly described the location of pollard trees (perhaps willows) beside the river Clywedog. Maps have tended to use the form Cyffylliog but Y Gyffylliog is the preferred form (although usage frequently has Gyffylliog).

H

HALCHDYN see **HALGHTON**[1]

HALFWAY[1] Brec SN8232

'(place near the) Halfway', p.n. ***Halfway***

Halfway House 1819, *Halfway* 1832, *the Half-way House* 1845

The tavern was half way between Trecastell Brec and Llandovery Carm on the Brecon-Llandovery road.

HALFWAY[2] Carm SN6430

'(place near the) Halfway', p.n. ***Halfway***

Half-way 1875, *Old Halfway, Halfway (public house)* 1906

The inn (*Halfway House* 1891) was roughly midway between Llandeilo Fawr and Llansawel.

HALGHTON[1]**, HALCHDYN** Flints SJ4143

'farm on a spur between two rivers', OE ***halh***, OE ***tūn***

Halctun 1291, *Halcton* 1295, *Halghton* 1321, *Halchton* 1332, *Halton* 1427, *Halton alias Alton* 1496, *Halchdvn* c.1510, *Halchdun, Halchdyn* c.1550, *Haulghton* 1626, *Halghton Brit. Halchtyn* c.1700

Halghton is on a spur or tongue of land between two brooks. The cymricization of Halghton is seen in the retention of the aspirated OE -h- as Welsh -ch- (as in Cnicht) and the change of -ton to -tyn or -dyn (as in Sychtyn Shropshire and Sychdyn Flints q.v.); similar phonological changes are seen in Haughton Mont (*Halchton* 1503, *Halghton* 1589, *Halchdyn* late 16cent., *Haughton* 1774).

HALGHTON[2] see **HALTON**

HALKYN, HELYGAIN Flints SJ2171

'cavities', OE ***halc*** pl. ***halcen(a)***

Helchene, Alchene 1086, *Helegen* 1254, *Alkyn* 1284, *Heleng'* 1291, *Helygen* 1315, *Halkyn* 1360, *Halkin* 1508, *y lygen* c.1566, *Haulkin* 1621, *Halkyn Britan. Hylygen* c.1700

halc was commonly 'nook, corner' but here the older meaning of ***halc*** 'cavity' is more appropriate with reference to the early mining shafts on Halkyn Mountain (*Holken Mountain* 1777) and Moel-y-crio (***creuau*** 'holes')(q.v.). The E form Halkyn was probably influenced by the -yn of p.ns such as Prestatyn and Mostyn. The cymricized form was also influenced by ***helygen*** dim.sing. of ***helyg*** 'willow, osier' which is also a pers.n. Helygen in several parts of Wales. The modern spelling Helygain is an attempt to interpret it as the adj. pl. suff. -ain or as the adj. ***cain*** 'fair, beautiful'. Colloquial forms have been Lygan (as in the tnshp of

Lygan-y-wern and Lygan-y-llan) and Mynydd Helygain as *mynydh Lygan* c.1700; in these forms the unstressed first syllable has been interpreted as the def.art. *y*.

HALTON, HALGHTON
Denb SJ3039

'farm on raised ground between rivers', OE ***halh, tūn***

Hallhton 1222 (1294), *Halcton* 1295, *Halghton* 1535, *Halton* 1540

The el. ***halh*** is associated with a nook or spur of raised land sometimes between rivers or in a marsh. Halton, which is on a gradient leading up to Chirk, is bounded by the river Dee to the north-west and Afon Ceiriog to the west and south-west. The form Halghton is found in other ***halh tūn*** p.ns in England, but was in this instance probably reinforced by a cymricized form (as in Sychdyn) and under the influence of Halghton Flints.

HANMER
Flints SJ4539

'Hagena's mere', pers.n. ****Hagena***, OE ***mere***

Hengem(er)e ?1268-9, *Hangmere* 1269, *Hagnem(er)e* 1270, *Hcenemere* 1284, *Hagenemere* 13cent., *Hannemere* 13cent., *Hanymer* 1342, *Hagmer* 1387, *Hanmere* 1391, *Hanemere* 1394, *Hanmer* 1417, *hangmere* c.1566, *Hanmer otherwise Hangmere* 1588, *Hangmer* 1587-8

The identity of Hagena is unknown. The significance of -mer was eventually lost since the large lake is regularly referred to as Hanmer Mere (as in *Hanmer mere by ye village* c.1700) and in Welsh sources as Llyn Hanmer (*llyn Hanmer* 1497). A number of forms have -g- which is probably a residual -g- from Hagena, as well as -nm- > -ngm-.

HARLECH
Mer SH5831

'fine rock', ***hardd, llech***

Hardelech 1283, *Harlech* 1284, *Hardelagh* 1285, *Harlech* 14cent., *Harddlech* 1450, *Harleghe alias Hardelegh* 1608

The 13cent. castle was built on the prominent crag, possibly on the site of an earlier fortification. The -dd- (represented by -d- in some of the above forms) was lost in pronunciation but survived longer in some documents.

HAROLDSTON WEST
Pemb SM8615

'Harald's farm', pers.n. ***Harald***, OE ***tūn***

Harauldyston 1307, *Haroldeston juxta Mare* 1362 (1399), *Haroldeston West* 1519, *harstwn* c.1566

Harald and Harold are vars of an Anglo-Scand pers.n. which occurs as a family name here 1307 and 1378. The village is near the sea (L *juxta mare*) and is west by contrast with Haroldston St Issells (*Ville Ha(raldi) iuxt' Havf'* 1291, *Haroldeston* 1295, *Haroldston alias St Ismells* c.1594) near Haverfordwest with a church dedicated to St Issell (pers.n. Ismail, Isfael). The c.1566 form is a W contraction which did not survive, but the local pronunciation is 'Harasn'.

HASGUARD Pemb SM8509

'pass with a house', ON ***hús,*** ON ***skarð***

Houscard c.1290, *Huscart* c.1200 (1296), *Huscard(e)* 1291, *Hascard(e)* 1522

Hasguard lies next to the top of a small, narrow valley. An alternative suggestion for the second el. has been ON ***garðr*** 'enclosure'. The parish consists of Little Hasguard (*Parva Hascard* 14cent., *Little Hasgard* 1793) and Great Hasguard, the present Hasguard Hall (*Magna Haskart* 1522, *Great Hascard* 1580).

HATTERRALL HILL Her/Monm SO3025

?'hill shaped like the crown of the head', OF ***haterel***, E ***hill***

Haterel 1325, *Attere hille* 1536-9, *Hatterell hill* 1577, *the Atterill, the Haterelles* 1586

If the interpretation is reliable, it is not particularly descriptive. The hill possesses a steep-sided triangular summit with two wings similar to a yoke (***iau*** dial. ***iou***) half-enclosing the valley of Cwm Iou (q.v.). Another suggestion for the first el. is the ON pers.n. ***Hattr***. The W name may have been Y Cefn, 'the ridge' (***y, cefn***) if *cecin* c.740 (1136-54) can be located here, but 1536-9 has *Attere hille in walche cawlyd meneth e Cadair* (***mynydd, y, cadair*** 'seat'). Hatterrall was extended in some sources to comprise the whole or greater part of the Black Mountains (q.v.).

HAVERFORDWEST, HWLFFORDD Pemb SM9515

'western goat-ford', OE ***hæfer***, OE ***ford***, ME ***west***

Haverfordia c.1191, *Hareford* 1283, *Haverford* late 13cent., *Hereford alias Hareforde* 1385, *Heverford West* 1448, *Herefordwest* 1471; *Hawlffordd* 14cent., *Hwlffordd* 15cent.

The river (Western) Cleddau is apparently still fordable at low tide. At one time, goats may have habitually been seen near this ford. The contracted form seen in the 1283 and 1385 forms (and still heard as Harford locally) prompted the addition of the distinguishing West to avoid confusion with Hereford in England. The W form Hwlffordd is a development of the early contracted E form with -r- becoming -l- (as with ***maenor*** becoming ***maenol***) and -d becoming -dd (as in several p.ns such as Gresford and Gresffordd, Whitford and Chwitffordd and in the E word ***ford*** itself related to W ***ffordd*** 'road, way').

HAWARDEN, PENARLÂG Flints SJ3165

'high enclosure', 'headland, height rich in cattle', OE ***hēah***, OE ***worðign***, ***pennardd, alaf, -og***

Haordine 1086, *Hauardina* 1093, *Hawurdin* 1250, *Hawarden* 1439, *Harden* 1545, *Hawarden vulgo Harding* 1675, *Harden otherwise Howarden* 1839; *Pennardlaawc, pennardlaoc* 14cent., *pennarddlac* 16cent., *Pener lak* 1560-9, *pennarthlak* 1587, *Penarlâg* c.1700

The W name Penarlâg was in existence long before the E name but is not recorded until the early 14cent. The second el. ***alaf*** (***-og***), with ***alaf*** 'cattle', appears in the historical forms as *-alaog*, which resulted in the final stressed -lâg. It has been argued that it could be a pers.n. Alaog or Alaawc, one contender being described as the 6cent. *brenin penn ar laog* (1552) 'king of Penarlâg' (whose son *Karadog Alauc filius* reputedly beheaded Holywell's St Winifred). The E and W names, both secular, refer to the prominent position and strategic status of the castle and village above the Dee plain. The modern pronunciation, as Harden, is the predictable E development, while the actual spelling, as Hawarden, probably preserves what was the W pronunciation (with W stress on the middle syllable) which would have reflected some of the distinctively W districts south and west of Hawarden. Both forms, Harden and Hawarden, appear to have co-existed for some considerable time.

HAWY see **HOWEY**

HAY BLUFF Brec SO2436

'steep cliff above Hay', E ***bluff***, p.n. ***Hay***

Hay Bluff 1967

One of the highest summits of the Black Mountains with steep slopes towards Hay-on-Wye (q.v.). The name appears to be very recent, at least as a map form. Other names appear to have been *Waun Llech* 1814 (***gwaun*** 'moor', ***llech*** 'standing stone') and *Pen y Beacon* 1889 (***pen***, ***y***, E ***beacon*** 'top of the prominent peak').

HAY-ON-WYE, Y GELLI GANDRYLL Brec SO2242

'area within a fence', ?'the grove (or woodland) of many pieces', OE ***(ge)hæg***, r.n. ***Wye***, W ***y***, ***celli***, ***candryll***

Haya c.1135-47, *La Haye* 1299, *(a'r) Gelli* 1215 (c.1400), *y gelli* c.1566, *Hay, Celhŷ* c.1570, *Hay* 1578, *the hay* 1600-7, *Hay (Gelly gandrill)* c.1625, *Gelli gandrell* 1614

OE ***(ge)hæg*** 'fence' came to mean 'part of a forest fenced off for hunting' and 'area within a fence', 'enclosure' and 'garden', and the meaning of the W form Y Gelli has encouraged the suggestion that it meant 'enclosed forest' but Hay, lying just above water-meadows in a valley bottom, is an unlikely location for a hunting preserve. It is perfectly possible that the Hay was simply an enclosure for some unidentified purpose, perhaps a castle or the area later occupied by the borough of Hay. The W form has also proved contentious, partly because of its late occurrence (simply as Y Gelli) presumably reflecting the paucity of W sources. The significance of the even later qualifying ***candryll*** 'shattered, in fragments' is equally uncertain but may indicate woodland which had been cleared and divided into many plots or strips of land. Other forms, presumably documentary administrative translations, include *Castello de haia taillata* 1121, *Sepes Inscisa* 1181-93.

HAYSCASTLE, CROES CAS-LAI Pemb SM9125

'crossroads near Hayscastle', p.n. ***Hayscastle***, E ***cross***, W ***croes***, p.n. ***Cas-lai***

Cross 1841, *Hayscastle Cross* 1876

The crossroads is shown near *Penffordd* 1843 ('top of the road', ***pen***, ***ffordd***). Hayscastle is *Castrum Hey* 1293, *Castle Hay* 1325, *Heyscastel* 1326 (16cent.), *Kastell haidd* c.1566, *Castelhay* 1580, *Castell Haydd* 1743, *Castell-haidd* 1778, *Cas-lai* 1900 (ON, F, ME ***castel***, W ***castell***, pers.n. ***Hay***, ***Hey***). Some of the W forms interpret -hay as ***haidd*** 'barley' as if correcting a supposed loss of final -dd. The MnW name Cas-lai is very late having the abbreviated form ***cas-*** for ***castell*** (found several times in Pemb) referring to the castle mound, but retaining the final -l of ***castle***.

HEBRON Carm SN1827

biblical chapel n.

Hebron 1809

The Congregational chapel was erected 1805.

HELL'S MOUTH see **PORTH NEIGWL**

HELYGAIN see **HALKYN**

HENDRE Flints SJ1967

'winter dwelling', ***hendref***

Hendref Wugyl 1292, *Hendre Wgyll* 1324, *Hendrebugilt* 1364, *Hendrebugillt* 1367-8, *Hendre vigyll* 1489, *Hendrefvigill* 1540, *Hendrebigillt* 1560, *Hendrefigillt* 1612, *Hendreviggillt* 1644, *Hendre figillt* 1840, *Hendre* 1914

The hamlet beside the Mold-Denbigh road was once associated with an unidentified Bugil, the final consonant of which became -ll and then -llt (cf. Bagillt and Gwersyllt). The name still survives in Nant-figillt (*Nant Bygylht* c.1700), the narrow valley leading towards Moel y Gaer and Moel-y-crio. It was the site of much industrial development (*Hendre Lime Works, North Hendre Lead Mines* 1914) which probably explains the loss of Figillt in a more anglicized settlement.

HENDY, (YR) Carm SN5803

'(the) old house', (*yr*), ***hen, tŷ***

Hendy 1891

The name of this village is taken directly from *Hendy Tinplate* works (opened 1866) built on the lands of Hendy farm (*Hêndy* 1833). Hendy Bridge (*Hendy Bridge* 1792, *Pont-hendy* 1833, *Hendey Bridge T.G.* 1844, ***pont***) carries the Llanelli road over the stream Gwili. This may also be *Hendy alias Hendy bennalt* 1789 qualified by the name of a house Penallt (***pen, allt***), now part of the village of Fforest, about half-a-mile north of Hendy village.

HENDY-GWYN AR DAF see **WHITLAND**

HENEGLWYS Angl SH4276

'former church', ***hen, eglwys***

Henheglus 1254, *Heneglwis* 1291, *Heneglus* 1352, *heneglwys* 1441, *ll. hen eglwys* c.1566

The parish church seems, at one time, to have been associated with a (possibly Ir) saint Corbre (*Eglwys gorbre sant* 16 cent.). An alias for the church was Mynwent Corbre (*mynwent corbre* c.1250, ***mynwent*** 'grave, graveyard'). By the mid 14cent., two new saints, Faustinus and Bacellinus, were associated with the church, whose unfamiliar names probably gave rise to the substitute Llan y Saint Llwydion (*ll. y saint llwydion* 1590) ***saint*** 'saints', ***llwyd*** pl. ***llwydion*** 'blessed', a designation which prompted the contrived St Llwydion.

HENGASTELL, YR see **OLDCASTLE**

HENGOED[1], YR Glam ST1495

'the old wood', ***yr, hen, coed***

Hengoed c.1900

An industrial village which developed at the end of the 19cent. near Hengoed Colliery, Hengoed Hall (*Hengott* 1670, *Hengoed* 1775) and an early Nonconformist chapel on the slopes of Cefn Hen-goed, which is a ridge (and farm) between Nant Cylla and the river Rhymni. There are numerous p.ns and house names which suggest that there were once extensive woods in the area.

HENGOED[2], YR Radn SO2253

'the old wood', ***yr, hen, coed***

Hengoid 1649, *the Hengoid* 1760, *Hen-goed* 1833, *Hengoed* 1881

Also the name of a farm *Hengoed* 1891 with an adjoining wood. There is another Hengoed and a Burnt Hengoed (both farms) in the adjoining parish of Huntington Herefordshire.

HENIARTH Mont SJ1208

?'the old enclosure', ***(yr)***, ***hen***, ***garth***

Tre heniarthe c.1545, *Hennyarthe* c.1547, *Heyniarth* c.1565, *Heniarth* 1577, *yr hen Jarth* late 16cent., *Henniarth* 1650, *Rheniarth* 1774

The second el. (occurring almost exclusively in compounds such as ***buarth*** 'yard' and ***lluarth*** 'vegetable garden') has a range of meanings such as 'field, enclosure, fold; fort' which are appropriate to ***hen*** (which could be 'former' as well as 'old'). However, there seems to be no certain evidence of a historic enclosure. It therefore could be ***garth*** 'ridge, hill' (as in Peniarth, Broniarth, Llwydiarth) in reference to the hill dominating the tnshp and near Garth Lwyd.

HENLLAN[1] Card SN3540

'former church', ***hen***, ***llan***

henllan c.1176 (c.1300), *Henllan* 1326, *Henlandeyny* 1361, *henllan ar difi* c.1566, *Henllan Deivy* 1643, *Hen Lhan Dyvy* c.1700, *Henllan Divi* 1711, *Henllan deivy* 1768, *Henllan* 1831

The church (*long time vacant* 1514) is in a bend of Afon Teifi (the r.n. which appears in most of the historical forms for Henllan), and was supplanted by the ecclesiastical settlement Bangor Teifi (although it has been suggested that the new church was Llanfair Orllwyn).

HENLLAN[2] Denb SJ0268

'former church', ***hen***, ***llan***

Helan 1291, *Henthlan* 1311, *Henllan* 1518

Although the precise chronology is difficult to ascertain the creation of the Anglo-Norman stronghold at Denbigh with its attendant ecclesiastical significance may have reduced the importance of the former single church at Henllan. However, the large parish was supplanted by daughter churches at Bylchau and Trefnant, and this church (dedicated to Sadwrn) may have been considered ***hen***, either 'old' or 'former', in comparison to those churches.

HENLLAN AMGOED Carm SN1820

'old church in Amgoed', ***hen***, ***llan***, commote n. ***Amgoed***

Henllan Amgoid 1291, *Henllan Amgoyd* 1404, *ll. ddewi o henllan* c.1566

The commote name Amgoed (*Amgodde* 1282, *Amgoyt* 1308) is 'area around a wood' (***am***, ***coed***). The church is dedicated to Dewi.

HENLLYS Monm ST2693

'former court', ***hen***, ***llys***

Henllis 1291, *Hentles* 1349, *Henllys* 1397, *henllys* c.1566

A name transferred from Henllys to the present village. Possibly once the administrative court of the lordship of Machen.

HENRYD Caern SH7774

'old ford', ***hen, rhyd***

henerrid 1518, *yr henrhyd* 1577

The ford was through Afon Gyffin and replaced by a bridge Pont Henryd (*Pont Hen-rhŷd* 1890).

HENRY'S MOAT, CASTELLHENDRE Pemb SN0427

'Henry's castle-mound', 'Henry's castle', pers.n. ***Henri***, ME ***mote***, W ***castell***

(*Ecclesia de*) *Monte Henrici* 1291, *Henrysmote* 1325, *Harriesmote* 1488, *Kastell henri* c.1566, *Castlehenry* 1573, *Henries Moate* 1582, *Harrissmotte* 1585, *Castell henrie* 1603, *Castell Hendre* 1843

ME ***mote*** 'moat' is used here for the embankment and mount. The castle-mound is north-east of the church. A common var. of Henry was Hendri and Hendry which gave rise to ***hendref*** as the perceived second el. of the W name. However, Castellhenri is also in common use.

HEOL CLARBESTON see **CLARBESTON ROAD**

HEOL-LAS Glam SS6998

'green road', ***heol, glas***

Hoellace 1793, *Heol-las* 1832, *Heol las* 1845

The village name is taken from Heol Las, a formerly unmetalled road or one flanked by trees and hedges, which runs from Llansamlet north-east to the hill above Nant Brân. About a mile to the south-east there was a farm *Heol-ddu* 1832 ('black, dark road', ***du***) now part of Lôn-las (***lôn*** 'lane').

HEOL SENNI Brec SN9223

'road by (the river) Senni', ***heol***, r.n. ***Senni***

Heol-senni 1832, *Heol Senni* 1891

Located on the old road leading from Brecon to the Tawe valley where it crosses the river Senni.

HEOL-Y-CYW Glam SS9484

'the chick's road', ***heol, y, cyw***

Heol-y-cyw 1884

Taken from the name of the lane running through the hamlet north-south. Nearby is Gwaun-y-cyw (*gwyn y kiw* 1649, *Gwain y Que* 1680). The precise significance of ***cyw***, used of the young of animals of various kinds, is obscure. There is *Nant y que* near Mitchel Troy Monm and a *Coed-cyw-fawr* near Llannon Carm. A number of names in Glamorgan have animal or bird els (such as *Rhiwceiliog, Cockstreet, Heol y Gwydde*). Here, there may have been a connection with a local folk tale.

HEPSTE, Afon Brec SN9512

?'dry river', ***hysb*** fem. ***hesb***

hepste 1526, *Hepstey* 1536, *Hepsey flud* 1610, *Hepstey* 1626, *River Hepsteu* 1828, *Hepste* 1832

The river is periodically dry where it flows over porous limestone. Hesb is recorded in a number of other r.ns such as Hespin Denb (with dim. suff. ***-en***, ***-in***). and Hesp Alun Flints. In Hepste there has been metathesis of -sp- > -ps-. The second el. is obscure, and can be compared to the final syllable in Mellte (q.v.), the river into which Hepste flows.

HERBRANDSTON Pemb SM8707

'Herbrand's farm', pers.n. ***Herbrand***, OE ***tūn***

Herbranston c.1290, *Villa Herbrandi* 13cent., *Herbraundystone* 1307, *Herbrandeston* 1384, *harbarstwn* c.1566, *Harbarston* 1578, *Harbeston* 1613

The pers.n., probably Continental rather than Scandinavian, can possibly be identified in local sources with *Maurice Herebrand* 1242-3 and *Christine Herbrant* 1328. The pers.n. also occurs in *terram Herbrandi'* 1174-6 (c.1600) recorded with Priskilly (*Pristhili*) near Mathri. The c.1566 and 1613 forms are contracted W forms which did not survive, although the local pronunciation is still 'Harbysn'.

HERMON[1] Angl SH3868

biblical chapel n.

Hermon 1838

The Congregational chapel built in 1814 was demolished c.1995.

HERMON[2] Carm SN3630

biblical chapel n.

Hermon 1831

The Congregational chapel was erected 1825.

HERMON[3] Pemb SN2031

biblical chapel n.

Cappel Hermon 1810, *Hermon* 1841

The Baptist chapel was erected 1808.

HIGHER KINNERTON Flints SJ3261

'Cyneheard's farm', pers.n. ***Cyneheard***, OE ***tūn***, E ***higher***

Kynarton 1240, *Kynerton* 1281, *Kinyrton* 1421, *Har Kinnerton* 1553, *Cin'rtwn* 16cent., *Higher Kinnerton* 1642-3

From the 16cent., the distinction is made between Higher Kinnerton and Lower Kinnerton (just over a mile north-east in Cheshire). The cymricized *Cin'rtwn* was limited to literary usage and did not survive. Cf. Kinnerton Radn.

HIRDDYWEL Mont/Rad SO0280

'long wild (hill)', ***hir***, ***dywal***

hirddywel c.1268, *Hirthowel* 1356-7, *Herdoel, Heerthowell* 1587, *Rhydd Hywel* 1833

The name of a long hill south-west of Llanidloes. ***dywal*** also occurs, for example, in *Dywalwern* later Tafolwern (q.v.). The forms appear to have been influenced by the pers.n. Hywel.

HIRNANT Mont SJ0523

'long valley', ***hir***, ***nant***

Hyrnant 1254, *hirnant* 1377, *Hernaunt* 1559, *ll. hirnant* c.1566, *Hirnant Yr Ystrat* 1600

nant 'valley' was supplanted by ***cwm*** 'valley' of Cwm Hirnant which stretches about four miles from Blaen Hirnant to Penybontfawr in the Tanad valley, with Hirnant being applied to the stream Hirnant which flows through the valley.

HIRWAUN[1] Denb SJ1361

'long white place', ***hir***, ***gwyn***

Here Wyn 1465-6, *Hirwyn* 1513, *Hirwaun* 1750, *Hirwyn* 1838

The precise significance of ***gwyn*** 'white (place)' is unknown, which is all the more remarkable since it persisted consistently for four centuries. There is a Plas Gwyn to the west. The popular association with ***gwaun*** 'moor' is reinforced by the nearby Waen and Pen-y-waen.

HIRWAUN[2] Glam SN9505

'long moor', ***hir***, ***gwaun***

Hyrweunworgan 1203, *Hirwen Urgan* 1536-9, *Hirwain Wrgan* 1578-84 (c.1700), *Hirwaun Wrgan* 1638

Named from a large moor south-west of Hirwaun and Pen-y-waun. The pers.n. associated with the moor was Gwrgan, father of *Iestyn ap Gwrgant* (fl. 1081-93) last king of Morgannwg. The village developed near ironworks established in 1757 on part of the moor.

HÔB, YR see **HOPE**

HODGESTON Pemb SM0399

'Hodge's farm', pers.n. ***Hodge***, OE ***tūn***

Villa Hogges 1291, *Hoggeston* 1376, *Oggeston* 1396, *Hodg(e)ston alias Hogeston* 1592

The ME pers.n. ***Hogge*** and ***Hodge*** are vars (by-forms of the Continental pers.n. Roger). A *William Hogge* is recorded at Martletwy Pemb 1346. The local pronunciation is 'Hodsn'.

HOLLYBUSH, LLWYNCELYN Monm SO1603

'(place near the) Hollybush', p.n. ***Hollybush***, W ***llwyn***, ***celyn***
Hollybush, Hollybush Colliery 1885, *Holly Bush* 1903
A former mining village named from an inn recorded 1871. The village is said to have been in existence from c.1829 (but is not on the 1833 OS map). There was major development after *Hollybush Colliery* was sunk c.1860. Llwyncelyn is a recent W translation.

HOLT Denb SJ4053

'wood', OE ***holt***
Holte 1326, *le Holt* 1347, *the holt* 1535, *yr holt* c.1566
The borough is mentioned in 1285 and the castle itself (built by *John de Warenne*) before 1304. The ***holt***, beside the river Dee, was probably the area which provided timber or hunting, its purpose reinforced by the use of the def.art. in E, W and F. A further name, *Lyons*, seems to have been used regularly, emerging in the Middle Ages (*Castrum Leonis* 1316, *the castle of Leouns* 1346, *the castle of Lyons lately called the castle of le Holt,* 1347, *La ville de Lyons* 1351, *Castle Lyons* 1495, *villa leonum* 1496, *Holte alias Lyons* 1551, *Lyons alias Holt* 1638), and perceived to mean 'castle of the lion', translated into W as Llys y Llewod (*lyselawod* 1431) 'the court of the lions'. It has been argued that this medieval form may possibly be an adaptation of a *Castra Legionis* 'fort of the legion', referring to the Twentieth Legion which had its base at Chester (also known as *Castra Legionum*) and which manufactured its tiles at Holt. However, given the lack of evidence for such a survival from Roman times, it is more likely that *Lyons* was a name transferred from France (as a place-name or as a family name).

HOLYHEAD, CAERGYBI Angl SH2482

'holy headland', 'the fort of Cybi', OE ***hālig***, OE ***hēafod***, W ***caer***, pers.n. ***Cybi***
Haliheved 1315, *Holiheved* 1322, *Le Holyhede* 1394, *Holyhede* 1395, *the Holy hedde* 1536-9, *the holihed* 1565, *Holy Head* 1610;
Karkeby 1225 (1316), *Keyr'* 1254, *Castrokyby* 1291, *Castelkyby* 1310, *Chastel Keby* 1323, *Caerkeby* 1352, *kaer gybi* c.1566, *Caercubie alias Holyehead* 1577-8, *Caergiby* 1680, *Holihead called Caergyby* 1684
Holyhead is on Holy Island/Ynys Gybi (q.v.), with Holyhead Mountain (q.v.) in the north-west of the island, and its monastic settlement with the church of the 6cent. Cybi within the Roman fort in Holyhead town. Since there is no record of ***caer*** being used of a monastic enclosure as such, the name Caergybi should probably be interpreted elliptically as 'caer (o gwmpas eglwys) Cybi', 'fort (around the church) of Cybi'. Translations of ***caer*** as *castrum* and *castle* commonly occur in p.ns in legal or other documents but probably had no currency outside scribal usage.

HOLYHEAD MOUNTAIN, MYNYDD TWR Angl SH2183

'Holyhead mountain', 'mountain of the pile',
p.n. ***Holyhead***, E ***mountain***, W ***mynydd***, ***(y)***, ***twr***
Mynydd-y-Turr, ye torre by ye Holyhead, Mynydd (mons) y turr mid 16cent., *Mynydd Tŵr* 1757, *Mynydd y Tŵr* 1795, *Mynydd y Twr* 1832, *Holyhead Mountain* 1818
Generally held to be ***twr*** 'stack, heap, pile, tor' (as in ***pentwr*** 'heap'), a reference to the dramatic summit of bare rock (cf. E ***tor*** which appears in one of the forms). Other mid 16cent. references to nearby locations (*Porth y Turr, Avon y Turr*) support this, as do the early historical forms. The interpretation as ***tŵr*** 'tower' has been influenced by evidence of a Roman pharos within Caer y Tŵr (***caer*** 'fort'), believed by antiquarians to have been a watch tower. This ambiguity survives in modern usage in spelling and pronunciation, but since ***tŵr*** > ***twr*** would be unusual, the persistent survival of ***twr*** is surely dependable evidence of its seniority.

HOLY ISLAND see **YNYS GYBI**

HOLYWELL, TREFFYNNON Flints SJ1875

'holy well', 'village of the well', OE ***hālig***, OE ***wella***, W ***tref***, ***ffynnon***
Haliwel 1093, *Haliwell'* 1254, *Halywelle* 1284, *Halywall* 1320, *Holywell* 1465
Treffynnon 1329, *terfynnawn* 1375-80, *trer ffynnon* c.1566, *Holy Well (Wallice Tre ffynnon alias Gwenfrewi)* 1763, *Holywell or Treffynnion* 1813
The legend of Gwenfrewi (anglicized as Winifred) describes her as being beheaded in the 7cent. by a rejected suitor, her head rolling down a hill towards Beuno's chapel with a spring bursting forth where the head came to rest. Beuno, her uncle, restored her head, and a nunnery with Winifred as abbess (*Villa Fontis* 1284, *Llanwenfrewy* 1590) was established around St Winifred's Well (Ffynnon Wenfrewi). The well's curative waters make it a centre of pilgrimage to this day.

HONDDU[1] Brec SN994-SO0429

'pleasant river', ***hawdd***, r.n. suff. ***-ni***
Hothenei c.1100, *hodni* 1240, *hotni* 13cent., *Honddey* 1536-9, *Hodney* 1562, *Honthy* 1578
The adj. ***hawdd*** 'easy, prosperous, pleasant' may refer to the river's environs or to its flow, and occurs several times as a r.n. Since some Hondd-, Hoddn- rivers are more fast flowing, it has been argued that ***hawdd*** is either placatory or euphemistic. Later forms have metathesis of -ddn- > -ndd- , while other forms show -dd- > -d-. The dominant modern form in -ddu has probably been influenced by ***du*** 'black, dark'. See also Aberhonddu.

HONDDU[2], Afon Brec/Monm SO2434-2927

fl. Hothenei, Hodeni 1100, *hodni* c.970 (c.1136-54), *Hotheni* c.1191, *Hotheney* 1387, *Honddye* 1536-9

See Honddu[1] and Llanthony.

HOOK Pemb SM9711

'hooked spit of land', E ***hook***

West Hooke 1601, *Hook* 1748

From its location on a peninsula which projects eastwards from the village of Hook towards East Hook (*Easthooke* 1612) and the confluence of the rivers Western and Eastern Cleddau. The same el. occurs elsewhere in Pemb (as OE ***hōc***) in Welsh Hook (*Walsthor'* 1176-98 [17cent.], *Welshook* 1231 [17cent.]) .

HOPE, YR HÔB Flints SJ3058

'enclosed land in a marsh', OE ***hop***

Hope 1086, *le Hope* 1283-4, *Hopp* 1283-5, *the Hope* 1523, *Hob* 1580, *yr hob* 1565-87, *Yr Hob* 1590, *yr hope* 1628, *Yr Hôb c.* 1700

Hope is on fairly dry land beside the river Alun and the significance of the topographic feature is reinforced by the def.art. (in F, E and W). In Hope/Yr Hôb Mont (*le Hop, Hope* 1245, *Yr Hob* c.1633) and in Hope Shropshire, however, the meaning is 'small, remote valley'. The E p.n. reflects the Mercian settlement of the area but its cymricization is evidence of the otherwise overwhelming W character of the surrounding area. *Queen's Hope* (1398), *Queen Hope* (1403) and *Hope Regine* (1430) were also used to commemorate the fact that, in 1282, Edward I, after accepting the surrender of the nearby Caergwrle Castle, presented the castle and much of the parish to his wife Eleanor (*Quene hope als Kaer gorley* 1580, *Quene hope als Caergorley* 1607).

HOPKINSTOWN, TREHOPCYN Glam ST0590

'(village associated with) Hopkin', pers.n. ***Hopkin***, E ***town***, W ***tref***

Hopkin's Town, Tref Hopkin 1874, *Hopkinstown* 1875

Named from Evan Hopkin (1798-1869), owner of the Tŷ Mawr estate on which the first houses were built after opening the first shaft of *Tŷ Mawr Colliery* 1849.

HOREB[1] Card SN3942

biblical chapel n.

Horeb 1811

The Congregational chapel was erected 1784.

HOREB[2] Carm SN4905

biblical chapel n.

Eglwys Horeb 1839, *Horeb* 1851

The Particular Baptist chapel was erected 1841 in succession to an older meeting-house established c.1832 at Five Roads, near Llanelli.

HOREB[3] Carm SN5127
biblical chapel n.
Horeb 1830
The Congregational chapel was erected in 1830 near Llanegwad.

HORSEMAN'S GREEN Flints SJ4441
'pasturage near the mowing at the house', E ***house***, E ***math***, E ***green***
Horse Math's Green c.1700, *Horse Moss Green* 1775, *Horseman's Green* 1881
Green indicates one of the common pasturages in the parish. A ***math*** was a 'mowing', and almost invariably found in the phrase 'day-math', the area that could be mowed by one person in a day. The probability is that *Horse Math* was in fact an unrecorded *'House Math'*, presumably the area to be mowed near to a house. The confusion arising from an unfamiliar word ***math*** explains its later adaptation to *Moss* and then to *-man's*. However, the recent discovery of a nearby *Horsmas Howse* 1632-3, and *Husmans Croft* 1655-6 still allow the possibility of ***horseman*** or W ***hwsman, hwsmon*** 'farm-bailiff'.

HORTON Glam SS4785
'mud farm' OE ***horu***, OE ***tūn***
la Hortone 13cent., *Horton* 1319, 1650, *Hurton* 1435
The location is a hollow near the sea, and may be interpreted a 'farm on muddy land'.

HOUGHTON Pemb SM9807
'holt farm', OE ***holt***, OE ***tūn***
Holton 1541, *Houton* 1680, *Howton* 1683, *Houghton* 1708
There is another Houghton in Pemb (*Holton* 1382, *Howton* 1601) with the same meaning, located as it is on a hill-slope near what is still a copse. Both are unusual in that the regular development to *Holton* has been influenced by loss of -l- and subsequent phonological developments usually associated with OE ***hōh*** 'spur of a hill'.

HOWEY, HAWY Radn SO0558
'summer stream', ***haf***, suff. ***-wy***
Hawey 1818, *Howey* 1891
A relatively modern village named from the river Hawy or Howey which rises near a former farm Blaenhawy (*Blahenhavoe* 1297, ***blaen***). The obvious implication is of a river which was sometimes dry in summer but two water-mills are recorded in historic sources.

HUNDLETON Pemb SM9600

'farm where hounds are kept', OE ***hund*** gen.pl. ***hunden(e)***, OE ***tūn***

Hundenton, Hundyngton 1475, *Hondelton* 1573, *Huntell towne* 1661, *Hundleton* 1815

The gen. pl. ***hunden(e)*** here appears to be a ME dial. var. associated with the south-west. Substitution of -l- for -n- occurs from the mid 16cent. Pemb also has three examples of Tre-cŵn (***tref, cŵn*** 'dogs'), all probably places where hunting dogs were kennelled.

HUNDRED HOUSE Radn SO1154

'(place near the) Hundred House', E ***hundred***, E ***house***

Hundred Ho. c.1817, *Hundred House* 1833

The former meeting-place of the hundred of Colwyn. There was another Hundred House in Bleddfa Radn described as an inn 1875 and which served as a meeting place in the hundred of Maelienydd.

HWLFFORDD see **HAVERFORDWEST**

HYSSINGTON Mont SO3194

'Hussa's farm', OE pers.n. ***Hussa***, OE connective particle ***-ing-***, OE ***tūn***

Husinton 1227, *Husiton'* 1249, *Husintone* 1283, *Husendon* 1291, *Husinton under Cornedun* 13cent., *Hysyngton* 1535, *Hussington* 1542, *Hyssington* 1610, *Issattyn* 1843

The pers.n. is thought also to occur in Hussingtree Worcs. Hyssington was originally a chapel-of-ease of Churchstoke and lay at the foot of Corndon Hill. The contracted W form of 1843 (with -tyn for E -ton) may be an antiquarian coinage and did not survive.

I

IEITHON see **ITHON**

IFFTWN see **IFTON**

IFTON, IFFTWN Monm ST4688

'Ifa's farm', pers.n. ***Ifa***, OE ***tūn***

Yueton 1193-1218, *Iuetone* 1270, *Yveton* 1398, *ifftwn* c.1566

Nothing is known of Ifa. Ifton Shrop appears to be identical in meaning. Two miles north-east is Ifton Hill (*Huvetune* c.1175-1200, *Yefton* 1535, *Yfton Hyll* 1594) .

ILSTON, LLANILLTUD GŴYR Glam SS5590

'farm of Illtud', 'church of Illtud in Gower', pers.n. ***Illtud***, OE ***tūn***, W ***llan***, commote n. ***Gŵyr***

sancti Ilduti 1129 (1160-85), *Lan Ilthit* early 12cent., *Ilewitteston'* 1319, *Ilston* 1487, *Llantwid* 1576, *Llanylltyd* 1584-5

Named from the church dedicated to Illtud (*ecclesia de Sancti Iltuti de Illiston* 1490). The E form is elliptical for a 'farm near a church dedicated to Illtud' unless ***tūn*** has replaced some unrecorded el. such as OE ***stōw*** (as in Tythegston q.v.) to mean 'holy place of Illtud'. Gŵyr (q.v.) appears to be a late addition added to distinguish it from Llanilltud Fawr/Llantwit Major and Llanilltud Faerdre/Llantwit Fardre.

ISCA see **USK**

ITHON, River, IEITHON, Afon Rad SO0977

'talking river', ***iaith***, suff.-***(i)on***

yeithyon 12cent., *Yeythan* 1297, *ieithawn* late 15cent., *ython* 1580, *Ithon* 1578

iaith is 'language, speech'. Several r.ns embody babbling, noisy characteristics (such as Llafar q.v.). The river rises at Blaenieithon and joins the Wye north-west of Builth. Ieithon may also have become a pers.n. before being associated with the river. Locally pronounced as if it were Eithon (from the tendency to lose a consonantal initial i-), the r.n. is found elsewhere in Rad and particularly south Wales. The initial I- of the anglicised Ithon probably represents W Ei-.

ITTON, LLANDDINOL Monm ST4896

'settlement of ?Eoda', 'church of ?Diniol', pers.n. ?***Eoda***, OE connective particle -***ing***-, OE ***tūn***, W ***llan***, pers.n. ?***Diniol***

lann diniul 1136-54, *lann dineul* 1128, *tref din neul* 1129 (1160-85), *Editon* 1271, *Eodynton* 1311, *Itton* 1468, *ll. ddeiniol* c.1566

Eoda may be a hypocoristic form of OE Eodbald, Eoduald or OGerm Eudo. The 1311 form possibly demonstrates a short-lived W stress on the penultimate syllable. The saint has also been identified with Deiniol but there is no trace of -e- in early spellings.

J

JAMESTON
Pemb SS0599

'James's farm', pers.n. ***James***, OE ***tūn***

Sctu' Jacob' 1295, *Seint Jameston, Jameston* 1331, *Jamiston* 1363

The farm presumably once belonged to St James's church, the parish church of Manorbier, a mile to the south-east.

JEFFREYSTON
Pemb SN0806

'Geoffrey's farm', pers.n. ***Geoffrey***, OE ***tūn***

Villa Galfrid c.1214, *Uilla Galfridi* 13cent., *Geffreiston* 1362, *Jeffreston* 1411, *ssiaffre twn* c.1566

Perhaps this was the *Gaufred* father of a *Roger* recorded 1131. The pers. n. was probably the F name which became Godfrey but which was later commonly confused with Geoffrey, Jeffrey. The church's dedication to St Jeffry (and St Oswald) was probably suggested by the actual p.n. The W form c.1566 (with W *Sieffre*) does not seem to appear in other sources.

JOHNSTON
Pemb SM9310

'John's farm', pers.n. ***John***, OE ***tūn***

villa Johannis 1296, 1513, *Johanneston* 1393, *Johnyston* 1406, *Johnston* 1588

John cannot be identified. One of many similar ***tūn*** p.ns in Pemb, cf. Hodgeston, Jeffreyston, Jordanston and probably dating from the time of the E and Flemish settlement in Pemb.

JOHNSTOWN
Denb SJ3046

'John's town', pers.n. ***John***, E ***town***

Johnstown 1874

John Bury was a member of Wrexham's first Town Council and initiated the building of this planned village to the east of Rhosllannerchrugog in the parish of Ruabon, a development which was linked to the clay and coal industries.

JORDANSTON, TREFWRDAN
Pemb SM9132

'Jordan's farm', pers.n. ***Jordan***, OE ***tūn***, W ***tref***

villa Jordahi 1291, *Trefiordan* 1490, *Villa Jordani* 1513, *Jordanyston'* 1326, *Jordaneston* 1481, *Trevurdan, Treurdan Gruffin'* 1543, *Treffyordan* 1549, *tre iwrdan* c.1566, *Jordanston* 1588, *Tre Jordan* 1615, *Jurdeston* 1627, (*o*) *Drefwrdan* 1778

Jordan (OF Jourdain) is a Continental pers.n. and was fairly common in Pemb. There was a *Jordans parke* here in 1490 and *David* and *Thomas Jordan* were associated with the place in 1593; there were also West

Jordanston and East Jordeston. In this instance it was probably named after *Jordan de Hode* or *Hoda* named in connection with Cemais cantref 1241-78. The W forms shows *Iwrdan* in conjunction with ***tref***. One source has the addition of the pers.n. *Gruffin'* (Gruffudd) to distinguish from another Trewrdan or Trefwrdan (*villa Iordani* 1392, *Trefwrdan* 1486) in Pemb.

K

KEESTON, TREGETIN Pemb SM9019

'Keting's farm', pers.n. ***Keting***, OE ***tūn***, W ***tref***
villa Ketyng 1289, *Ketingeston* 1295, *Ketyngeston* c.1300, *Kettingston* 1392, *Kethingeston* 1535, *Keston* 1588, *Keeston* 1820, *Tregettyn* 1856, *Tregetin* 1859
A *Richard Ketine* occurs in Pemb c.1203-14 and there was a family called *Ketyng* here in 1456-7. The modern E form is a contraction but the W form is probably an antiquarian adaptation of Keeston.

KEMEYS COMMANDER, CEMAIS COMAWNDWR Monm SO3404

'river-bends', W ***camas*** pl. ***cemais, comander***, OF ***comandere***,
Kemmeys 1254, c.1348, *Kamoys Comaunder* 1291, *kêmais kymawndwr* c.1566, *Kemis Comawnder* 1610
From its location within a large curve in the river Usk. The church was under the patronage of the Knights Templar (*Ecclesia de Kemmeys, Templariorum* 1254) as a commandery administered by a commander. Commander distinguishes it from Kemeys Inferior, Lower Cemais or Cemais Isaf (*agrum Cemais* c.700 [c.1145], *Kemmeys* 1291, *Cammeys* 1389, *kemais* c.1566, *Kemmis Yssa* 1582, *Kemys Inferior* 1777, ***isaf***, L ***inferior***) in a similar location about nine miles further down the river (which probably gave rise to a local family name Kemeys). The W form Comawnder seems to be antiquarian (as opposed to ***comander*** elsewhere).

KENFIG, CYNFFIG Glam SS8081

'(place on the river) Cynffig', r.n. ***Cynffig***
Chenefec, Kenefec 12cent., *Kenefeic* c.1262, *Kenefeg* 1167, *Kynffyg* 1609, *Cynffig* 1839
The name of a medieval borough taken from a small river (*Kenfeg* 12cent., *Kenefeg* 13cent.) which flowed from Mynydd Margam into the sea by Kenfig Sands. The r.n. is almost certainly a pers.n. Cynffig or Cenffig (*Conficc, Cinfic* 12cent.). Alternation of Cyn-/Cen- is fairly common (as with Cencoed/Cyncoed).

KENFIG HILL, MYNYDDCYNFFIG Glam SS8483

'hill, mountain near Kenfig/Cynffig', p.n. ***Kenfig***, OE ***hyll***, W ***mynydd***, p.n. ***Cynffig***
Mynydd Kenfig 1845, *Kenfig Hill* 1851
A largely 19th and 20th cent. village which developed in the parish of Pyle and Kenfig on the western slopes of the ridge or hill of Cefn Cribwr, adjacent to the river Cynffig or Kenfig (q.v.).

KERRY, LLANFIHANGEL-YNG-NGHERI Mont SO1490

'land of Câr', pers.n. ***Câr***, terr.suff. ***-i***, ***llan***, pers.n. ***Mihangel***, ***yn***

Keri late 12cent., *Keri* c.1200-12, *Lanvihangel in commote of Kery* 1281, *Lanuhangel in Kery* 1290, *Kery* 1299, *Llanveangel in Kery* 1395, *St. Michels in Kery* 1549, *LL.V'el yngheiri* c.1562

The church dedication is recorded in 1246. The ancient commote of Ceri was once part of the lordship of Maelienydd, most of which later lay in Radn.

KIDWELLY, CYDWELI Carm SN4006

'land of Cadwal', pers.n. ***Cadwal***, terr.suff. ***-i***

Cadweli 1114, (*prouincia*) *Cetgueli* 11cent. (c.1200), *Cedgueli* c.1150, *Kedwely* c.1191, *Kydwelly* 1458, *kydweli* 1566

The identity of Cadwal is unknown. The terr. name is taken from the name of the commote of Cedweli and transferred to the borough established c.1115. The terr.suff. ***-i*** affected both vowels of Cadwal to produce Cedweli, later Cydweli anglicized as Kidwelly.

KILGETTY, CILGETI Pemb SN1207

'nook of Ceti', ***cil***, pers.n. ***Ceti***

Kylketty 1330, *Kilgetty* 1586

The name is taken from Kilgetty farm. Tthe village developed in the 19cent. next to crossroads and a rail crossing. ***cil*** is a common local el., while the same pers.n. can be seen in Sketty (q.v.).

KILLAY, CILÂ Glam SS6093

'nook of ?', ***cil***, ?

Kyllar 1554, *Kyllan* 1574, *Kellaie* 1625, *Keela* 1650, *Kyla* c.1700, *Killay* 1782

A problematic p.n. The stress falls on the second syllable in both names. The first el. is almost certainly ***cil***. On the analogy of other ***cil*** names the second el. is possibly an unidentified pers.n., or a pers.n. such as Aedd (with, contentiously on phonological and documentary grounds, -aedd > -âdd and loss of final -dd). However, the second el. could conceivably be an el. such as ***haf*** 'summer'. The 1554 form in -ar is possibly an E rendering of the W -â while the anglicized Killay represents W -â as E -ay, possibly influenced by the local surname Lay or Ley. Another suggestion is that the 1574 form in -an (rather than being a miscopy of -au) indicates a pers.n. with a final -n which was subsequently lost (cf. Penalun > Penally); if so, the 1554 in -ar could be reinterpreted as a miscopy of an earlier -an.

KILVEY, CILFÁI Glam SS6793

?'nook of Mai', ***cil***, ?pers.n. ***Mai***

Kylvey 1311, *Kylvei* 1340, *Cilfai* late 15cent.

Stress on the final syllable favours a pers.n. Mai or Mei (cf. Caer-fai Pemb, Castellmai Caern and Maes Mai Carm as well as another Cil-fai near Bridgend) although the identity of this Mai is unknown. It has been argued that the second el. may be ***mai*** var. or pl. of ***ma*** 'plain, place' (as in Myddfai Carm) but the significance of such an interpretation is unresolved.

KINGCOED, CYNCOED Monm SO4305

'wooded ridge', ***cefn***, ***coed***

Cefncoed 1813, *Kingcoed Common* 1830, *Kincoed* 1839

Sited on a ridge, still partly wooded, overlooking Nant y Wilcae and Pont-y-rhydan Brook. There is an obvious similarity to Cyncoed (Cardiff Glam, *Kevencoyte* 1449-50, *Kencoed* 1605, *Cefen-coed* 1833), Cyncoed (Llantrisant Glam, *Ken coyde* 1563, *Keven coyd* 1576) and Cencoed (Melindwr Card, *y Kevencoed* 1592, *Kencoed* 1693). The development ***cefn*** > *Cen-* is also seen in Gendros Glam *Genrose* 1735, *Gendros* 1832, with ***rhos***, and development of -nr- > -ndr-; cf. Henry's Moat. The restoration of ***cefn*** is seen in the name of a house *Cefn-y-coed* 1886.

KINMEL see **CINMEL**

KINNERTON Radn SO2463

'Cyneheard's settlement', pers.n. ***Cyneheard***, OE ***tūn***

Kynardton 1304, *Kynarton* 1343, *Keynarthe alias Keynarton* 1549, *Kinart* 1670, *Kinert* c.1700

The 1670 and c.1700 forms provide evidence of a contracted W var. Cf. Higher Kinnerton.

KNELSTON, LLAN-Y-TAIR-MAIR Glam SS4688

'farm of Knoyl', 'church of the three Marys', pers.n. ***Knoyl***, OE ***tūn***, W ***llan***, ***y***, ***tair***, pers.n. ***Mair***

Llan y Tayre Mayre 1279, *Cnoyl* 1291, *Knoylestoune* 1306, *Knoyleston in Goheria* 1367, *Knolston* 1393

A late 16cent. source claims that *Knowelston* was called after *Adam de Bien Scavoire, called after the Englishe name Adam Knowell.* However, the evidence points to a pers.n. Knoyl not *Knowell*, and although no one by this name has been specifically identified, he was probably associated with a number of individuals surnamed *Le Cnoil* and *Le Cnoyl* recorded at Swansea 1327. There are ruins of a church, reputedly once dedicated to St Taurin and later to St Maurice near the school, but the W name suggests an alternative dedication to the three sisters called Mary/Mair, traditionally daughters of St Ann. The 1367 form has a L form of Gower.

KNIGHTON, TREFYCLO Radn SO2872

'settlement of the followers', 'farm by the dyke',
OE ***cniht*** gen. pl. ***cnihta***, OE ***tūn***, W ***tref, y, clawdd***
Chenistetone 1086, *Cnicheton* 1193; *Knighton, Trebuclo* 1536-9,
Treficlaudh 1586
OE ***cniht*** (E ***knight***) had a range of meanings including 'soldier, personal follower, young man, servant, thane, freeman'. Land was probably granted to freemen in the area to form an estate held communally. The farm was adjacent to Offa's Dyke/Clawdd Offa hence Tref-y-clawdd, a fairly recent restoration as opposed to the standard form Trefyclo with regular penultimate W stress and reduction of -awdd > -aw > -o.

KNUCKLAS, CNWCLAS Radn SO2574

'green hillock', ***cnwc, glas***
Knoclas c.1220-7, *Cnoklas* 1241, *Cnuclays* 1246,
C(astell) y Cnwclas late 16cent., *Knucklas* 1670
The hillock is the mound of a castle built c.1220-5 and destroyed in 1262. The pronunciation of the anglicized forms (with initial Kn- for W Cn-) has fallen in with that of E words with initial kn-.

L

LACHARN see **LAUGHARNE**

LAMBSTON Pemb SM9016

'Lambert's farm', pers.n. ***Lambert***, OE ***tūn***

villa Lamberti late 13cent., (*Ecclesia*) *Ville Lamberti* 1291, *Lamberteston* 1321, *Lamberdiston* 1363, *Lambeston* 1392, *lamstown* c.1566, *Lamerston* 1535, *Lamston* 1602, *Lambston* 1840

Lambert may be a Flemish pers.n. (such as the latinized *Lambertus* 1131) connected with the 12cent. settlement of Flemings in Pemb.

LAMPETER, LLANBEDR PONT STEFFAN Card SN5748

'church of Pedr/Peter by Stephen's bridge', ***llan***, pers.n. ***Pedr/Peter***, ***pont***, pers.n. ***Steffan***

ecclesiam Sancti Petri de Mabonio 1146-51, *Pontem Stephani* c.1191, *Landepeter* 1255, *Lanpeder* 1284, *Lampet' Pount Steune* 1301, *Lanpedyr Talpontestephyn* 1302-3, *Lampeder Talpont* 1303-4, *Thlanbeder Talbondsteven* 1309, *Lampeder tal pont stevyn* 1407, *Lanpeder by the name of Lanpedirtalpontstephyn* 1443, *Llanbeder talpont ustephen* 1563

The W name of the church was Llanbedr (***llan***, pers.n. ***Pedr***). The E name has Peter for Pedr and anglicizes Llan- to Lan- but is intriguingly close to the local (and subsequently national) colloquial W pronunciation Llambed, with a sound change (evident throughout Wales) of -nb- > -mb- (see Brymbo and Dinbych). Stephen was probably a Norman with responsibility for maintaining the bridge, and there are many examples of a fuller name as Llanbedr Tal Pont Steffan (***tal*** 'at the end of'). The small Norman motte is mentioned 1137 and variously described between the 13-15cent. as *chastell Ystyffant, chastell Ystevyn, castello Stephani* (W ***castell***, L ***castellum***). The 1146-51 form refers to the town's location in the former cantref of Mabwynion.

LAMPETER VELVREY, LLANBEDR FELFFRE

Pemb SN1514

'church of Pedr/Peter in Efelffre', ***llan***, pers.n. ***Pedr/Peter***, terr.n. ***Efelffre***

Lampeter et Iwelfrei c.1200, *Lampeder* 1291, *Lampeter in Wylfrey* 1366, (*ecclesia parochialis*) *Sci Petri de Wilfrey* 1489, *ll. beder y selffre, ~ y velffre* c.1566, *Llampeter* c.1600

The church was in the commote of Efelffre (*Euelfre* 1136-54 [15cent.], *vfelfre* 1171 [early 14cent.], *Wylfrey* 1279, *Evelfrey* 1603) which is of uncertain meaning. One suggestion is for *Yr Efelfre* from ***yr*** 'the', ***gefel*** 'tongs, pincers' (cf. Gofilon) and ***bre*** 'hill' but the 'forked hill' or 'enclosing pass' has not been identified. Another suggestion is *Y Foelfre* (*y*, ***moel*** 'bare hill', ***bre***, with -oe- > dial. -we- seen in early forms) > Efelfre. E influence seems to have substituted E -f- and W -ff- for the original W -f- [v] to became Efelffre and Velfrey, although Efelfre also occurs in W contexts; cf. Llanddewi Velfrey.

LAMPHEY, LLANDYFÁI
Pemb SN0100

'church of Tyfái', ***llan***, pers.n. ***Tyfái***

Lantefei late 12cent., *Lantefey* 1280, *Llantfey* 1398, *Lanfey* 1535, *lamffe* c.1566, *Lamphey* 1588, *Lantphey* c.1600, *Lanfey* 1603

The saint's name also appears in Llampha Glam (*lann tiuei* 1136-54, *Lanfey* 1141, *Landefei* 12cent., *ll. ffai* c.1566, *Lamphey* 17cent.) and in Llandyfeisant Carm (*Landevaysen* 1291, *ll. dyfaysan* c.1566, with ***sant***). In Lamphey (as in Llampha) the W -f- was anglicized as -ff- and then written -ph-, while stress shifted to the first syllable with consequent reduction and loss of the second syllable. Lamphey lies in an area settled by E and Flemings in the 12cent. and forms of the p.n. taken from later W sources (such as c.1566 and 1603) suggest a direct adoption of the anglicized form. The modern W form is a very late restoration.

LANDIMORE, LLANDIMÔR
Glam SS4693

?'church of Tymór', ***llan***, ?pers.n. ***Tymór***

Landimor 13cent., *Llandymor* 1291, *Landimore* 1335, *Landymore* 1366-7, *Lanymor* 1369, *Landimore llann dimwr yngwyr* late 15cent., *Llandremor neu Landimor* 1874

A very difficult p.n. While it is almost certainly ***llan***, the precise location of the church remains uncertain. The second el. is possibly a pers.n., perhaps an OW *Timor*, whose regular development would be to W Tyfór (comprising the honorific pref. ***ty-*** and the pers.n. Môr (as in the Myfor of Merthyr Mawr); cf. Llandygái and Llandyfân. The apparent fossilization as *Llandimór* rather than the regular **Llandyfór* can be ascribed to early anglicization of the area and association with OE ***mōr*** 'fen, moor', with W ***môr*** 'sea'; E ***land*** was also a likely influence. The 1874 form shows attempts to interpret the name as ***llandref*** 'church village, small town' and ***môr*** (seen in the modern W form) partly through the proximity of Landimore to the tidal mudflats of the river Llwchwr and partly through misassociation with Llandremor near Pontarddulais Glam. The late 15cent. form refers to its location 'in Gower'.

LANDORE, GLANDŴR
Glam SS6595

'river bank', ***glan***, ***dŵr***

Tir Glandwr 1686, *Tyr Glandwr alias Tyr y bont* 1764, *Llandwr* 1771, *Landore* 1780, *Landwr* 1832

This may well be *Dourlan* 1319 with reversal of the els. Named from its location near the river Tawe. The anglicized spelling is derived from the lenited form Landŵr found after prepositions.

LANDSHIPPING Pemb SN0111

'long cow-shed', OE ***lang***, OE ***scypen***

Langshipping 1554, *Longshippinge* 1588, *Longeshippen* 1614, *Landshipping* 1683

Although the name appears late, the OE els most easily explain the forms. The p.n. was influenced by E ***land***. Compare New Shipping Pemb (*Newshippinge* 1592, *New Shippine* 1683).

LANNOG, YNYS see **PRIESTHOLM**

LANTEAGUE see **LLANTEG**

LARNOG see **LAVERNOCK**

LAUGHARNE, LACHARN Carm SN3010

?'bright rock', ?***llachar, carn***

Talacharn c.1191, *Talachar* 1223, *Tallachrn'* 1291, *Lauchern* 1288, *Telagharn alias Talagharn alias Lagharn* 1467, *Lacharn* c.1500

Talacharn (***tâl*** 'end, above') was the name of the commote and lordship, transferred at an early date to the town, and apparently replacing Abercoran (*Abercorran* c.1194, *Aber Corran* 1189 [c.1400], ***aber***, r.n.), from its location where the brook Coran reaches the estuary of Afon Taf. The first el. is probably ***tâl*** 'end' but *Lacharn* or *Acharn* remains obscure (despite attempts to link it with Coran). Suggestions include ***llachar*** 'bright, gleaming' (or a derivative pers.n.) and ***carn***, or an unidentified Ir el. The anglicized form Laugharne derives from Talacharn with loss of unstressed Ta- (possibly through confusion with F ***de***) and substitution of -gh- for -ch-. The modern E pronunciation is 'Larne'.

LAVAN SANDS, TRAETH LAFAN Caern SH7364

'sands of ?', ***traeth***, E ***sands***

Traeth ar Llevain mid 16cent., *the sandes* 1624, *ar Draeth y Lavan* 1754, *Traeth y Lavan* 1757, *Lavan Sands* 1777, *Lavan sands* 1795, *The Lavan Sands* 1841

Extensive estuary sandbanks in the Menai Strait between Caern and the south-east of Angl, one point of which, at low tide, was the location of a ferry to Beaumaris and the route to Ireland. Probably much older than the recorded forms, to judge from 18cent. forms such as *Efelafen* and *Y felafan*. It currently defies explanation, despite attempts to associate it with ***llafan*** 'laver; a type of sea-weed' and (popularly) with ***wylofain*** 'wail, lament'. It may well prove to be a pers.n.

LAVERNOCK, LARNOG Glam ST1868

'lark's hillock', OE ***lāwerce***, OE ***cnocc***

Lawernak 13cent., *Lavertok* 1306, *Lavermarke* 1401, *Lavernock* 1425-6, *Lavernoke* 1563, *Laurnock* 1584, *Larnoc* c.1678, *Larnog* c.1780, *Llarnog* early 19cent.

The first el. is also found in Laverstock Wilts and Laverton Som. The hillock may be the headland (*Lam vock poynt* 1578, *Lanveroch Point* 1610) on which the church stands. Some forms such as *Llanveroch* 1754 show attempts to identify with ***llan***. The W form Larnog probably derives directly from a contracted (oral) form of Lavernock; it has resisted a fuller cymricization to *Llarnog* (which did occur sporadically).

LAWRENNI see **LAWRENNY**

LAWRENNY, LAWRENNI Pemb SN0106

?'valley-floor of Enni', ?***llawr***, ?pers.n. ***Enni***

Lenreni 1085-1115, *Leurenni* c.1200, *Laurenny* 1291, *Lawrenny* 1326, *Lawreny* 1527, *lawr yni, lawr enni* c.1566

The p.n. may be W but the area is anglicized and no forms have been found in early W sources. The c.1566 form (which is from a W source) is probably unreliable but does appear to indicate ***llawr*** 'floor, bottom' used for the low-lying land around the Cresswell River. The second el. is equally uncertain but could be identical to that in Caer Enni Mer.

LECKWITH, LECWYDD Glam ST1574

'(place of) Helygwydd', pers.n. ***Helygwydd***

Leocwtha 1173-83, *Lecwithe* c.1179, *Lequid* 1184-5, *Lekwith* 1306-7, *Lecwyth* 1314, *Lleckwith* 1700

The pers.n. is also found in *fynnaun elicquid* 12cent. (***ffynnon*** 'well') at Mathern Monm. Unstressed *He-* must have been lost at a very early date but there are documented parallels; cf. Ely/Trelái and Leri. Popularly perceived to be W ***llechwedd*** 'slope'.

LECWYDD see **LECKWITH**

LEESWOOD, COED-LLAI Flints SJ2759

'trees by the meadow', OE ***lēah*** dat. ***lēage***, OE ***wudu***, W ***coed***, ***y***, ****llai***

Legge 1086, *Leygis Wode* 1314, *Leys Wode* 1368, *Lesewood* 1477, *Lessewood* c. 1566, *Leeswood* 1595; *Koety llai* 1337, *Coet y llai* 1397, *Koed y Llai* c.1500, *Coed Llai* 1773

Legge representes ***lēage*** the dat. of ***lēah***, with a range of meanings from 'clearing, glade' to 'meadow, pasture'; here, the reference is to a settlement near meadows beside the river Alun. The woods are west of the river. There is evidence here (and in Llai q.v.) that ***lēah*** was cymricized as ****llei*** and ****llai*** '(river) meadow' but is unattested elsewhere other than in p.ns. The regular use of the def.art. ***y*** in medieval and early modern forms point to a living el. which had topographic significance in W. Over time, ****llai*** was confused with ***llai*** 'less' (especially after the loss of the def.art.) which fortuitously reinforced the popular view that ***less*** was also the first el. in Leeswood (as in the c.1566 form).

LEIGHTON, Y LLAI, TRE'R-LLAI Mont SJ2405

'leek enclosure', OE ***lēac***, OE ***tūn***, W ***y***, ***tref***, ****llai***

Lestune 1086, *Lecton'* 1254, *Leighto*n 1399, *Y Llai* 15cent., *Llai neu Leighton* c.1700

There is evidence that ***leighton*** also became an el. in its own right meaning 'kitchen garden, herb garden, garden'; cf. Leighton Shropshire and elsewhere. ***lēac*** was confused at an early date with the common OE ***lēah*** 'meadow', a word which had already been cymricized as ****llai*** (see Llai and Coed-llai). Tre'r-llai (***tref***) is occasionally seen as an alternative for Y Llai.

LERI, Afon Card SN 6589-6191

'(the river called after) Eleri', ***afon***, pers.n. ***Eleri***

Elery 1281, *Helery* 1284, *Eleri* 1301-2, *Elery* 1303-4, *Leri* 1545-53, *Lery* 1578

Two tributaries join at Cwmere or Cymerau (*Cwmere* 1760, *Cymmerav* 1769, ***cymer*** pl. ***cymerau*** dial. var. ***cwmerau*** 'confluence') with the river flowing past Tal-y-bont across Cors Fochno and formerly into the sea at Aberleri (*Aberlerie* 1782, *Aber Lery* 1837) but now rerouted into the estuary of Afon Dyfi at Traeth Maelgwn (appearing as Maelgwyn on some maps). The identity of (the female) Eleri is unknown. The initial unstressed syllable was lost or treated as the def.art. (as in Glanleri, earlier *Glan y lery* 1602, *Glanlery* 1738-9, ***glan*** 'bank').

LETTERSTON, TRELETERT Pemb SM9329

'Letard's farm', pers.n. ***Letard***, OE ***tūn***, W ***tref***

Villa Letardi' 1176-98 (c.1600), c.1200, *Littardiston'* 1326, *Lettardston* 1332, *villa Letardi* 1363, *Letarston* 14cent., *Lettston* 1496, *Leeston* 1535, *tre letert* c.1566, *Tre Leter* 1613

Probably named from *Letard Litelking* 'an enemy of God and St David' slain by Anarawd, son of Gruffudd ap Rhys, during a campaign against the Flemings of Pemb in 1137. He is likely to have been ancestor of Yvo son of Letard who granted the church of Letterston to Slebech preceptory c.1230 and of *John Littard* who held one fee here in 1326. The pers.n. is continental. The W form is a translation.

LIBANUS Brec SN9925

biblical chapel n.

Libanus 1828, *y Libanus* 1867

A L and W form of the biblical Lebanon adopted as the name of many Nonconformist chapels in Wales, here an Independent chapel built 1823. The area and nearby house appear as *Pont-clun* 1814 and *Pont-clŷn* 1889 near a bridge over the river Clun (possibly ***clun*** 'moor, brushwood' but see Pont-y-clun Glam) a small tributary of the river Tarell.

LICSWM see **LIXWM**

LISVANE, LLYS-FAEN Glam ST1983

'stone court', ***llys, maen***

Lisfeni 1173-83, *Lysfayn* 1392, *llysvayen* 1558, *llys faen* c.1566, *Lisvane* 1693

The anglicized form has L- for Ll- and *-vane* for the dial. var. of ***maen***, comparable with Pentrebane < Pentre-baen and *Grosvane* for Groes-faen (q.v.). This may have been an important administrative centre of the commote of Cibwr which became the Norman lordship of Cardiff.

LITTLE NEWCASTLE, CASNEWYDD-BACH Pemb SM9828

'little Newcastle', OE ***niwe***, ME ***castel***, E ***little***, W ***castell, newydd, bach***

(*Ecclesia de*) *Novo Castello* c.1200 (1296), (~) *Novo Castro* 1291, *Novum castrum* 13cent., *Newcastle* 1391 *Newcastell* 1411, (*Ecclesia de*) *Castro Novo* 1517, *Castnewyth* 1518, *y kastell newydd* c.1566, *Little Newcastle* 1741, *y Castell-newydd-bach* 1778

From a small castle mound in the middle of the village. Little and -bach are late additions to distinguish it from Newcastle Emlyn/Castellnewydd Emlyn (q.v.). ***cas-*** is regularly found as a reduction of ***castell***.

LITTLE ORME, TRWYN Y FUWCH Caern SH8182

'little Orme', 'the cow point', E ***little***, p.n. ***Orme***, W ***trwyn, y, buwch***

Little Ormes Head 1805, *Trwyn y Fuwch* 1838

The headland between Penrhyn Bay (q.v.) and Llandudno Bay (or Orme's Bay) which has the Great Orme (q.v.) on the west. Earlier forms for Penrhyn Bay (*Penruyn* 1352, *Penryn* 1455, *Penrhyn* 1763) show Penrhyn to have been the original name of the Little Orme. The significance of ***buwch*** is unclear. Trwyn y Fuwch may belong to the category of animal head names, relating the shape of the headland to the perceived similarity to a cow's head as seen from a particular direction; it may record an otherwise forgotten incident or legend. The actual sea-cliffs are Creigiau Rhiwledin (***craig*** pl. ***creigiau***) where the tnshp name Rhiwledin (*Raulyn* 1284, *Rwledyn* 1349, *Rhiwleding* 1577, *Rhiw ledyn* 1676) is ***rhiw*** 'hill, slope' and ***Lledin*** possibly the name of one of the maidens (***rhianedd***) traditionally buried in Morfa Rhianedd (*morua rianed* 1298, *morva rianet maelgwn* 15cent., *Morfa Rhuanedh* c.1700, ***morfa***) between Llandudno and Conwy sands.

LIXWM, LICSWM Flints SJ1671

'agreeable, pleasant', E ***licksome***

Lixum Green 1733-4, *Licum* 1738, *Ledsom Green* 1747-8, 1785, *Luxum, Luxwm, Luxom* 1801-2, *Lixum* 1812, *Lixwm Green* 1825, *Licswm* 1838

The adj. 'likesome' in its dial. var. ***licksome*** was applied by miners from Derbyshire. The pleasant area was described by them as 'Licksome Green', and *Lixum Green* was commonly used throughout the 19cent.

At one stage this was interpreted as *Ledsom Green* in the belief that it belonged to the local Ledsham, Ledsom or Lettsome family. The older W name was *Yr Wyddfid* (*Yr rwyddfyd* 1634, *Wyddfyd o. Ledsom Green* 1747-8 and 1785) which is ***gwyddfid*** 'wood; thorn-hedged enclosure' or possibly ***gwyddfid*** 'honeysuckle'. A similarly pleasant plot of land on the outskirts of industrial Buckley was also called *Lixumgreen* 1800, *Lixwm Green* 1803-4.

LLAFAR, Afon Mer SH8833

'noisy (river)', ***afon***, ***llafar***

Lhafar, Lhavar c.1700, *Llafar* 1795

Llafar rises south-east of Arenig Fawr, flows through Cwm Llafar and under Pont Llafar (*Pont lavar* c.1700, *Pont Lafar* 1752, *Pont Llafar* 1838) into Llyn Tegid. There are several rivers called Llafar, a name evoking a babbling course (***llafar*** 'loud, vociferous, loquacious, sonorous').

LLAI[1] see **LLAY**

LLAI[2] see **LEIGHTON**

LLAN see **LLANBRYN-MAIR**

LLANABER Mer SH6017

'church at (the) estuary', ***llan***, ***aber***

Lanaber 1292-3, *Lanab'* 1308-9, *Llannaber* 1400, *ll. aber* c.1566

The parish of Llanaber bordered the estuary of Afon Mawddach, although the present village of Llanaber (with its church dedicated to Mair) is nearly two miles from Barmouth.

LLANAELHAEARN Caern SH3844

'church of Aelhaearn', ***llan***, pers.n. ***Aelhaearn***

Llanhelhayerne 1291, *Llanhayarn* 1542, *Llanaylhayarne* 1653, *Llanhaiarne* 1713, *Llanaelhayarn* 1756

The saint's name, in the forms Elhaearn, is also preserved in the tnshp (and present farm) name Eleirnion (pers.n. Elhaearn and the terr.suff. ***-ion***). The modern local pronunciation of Llanhaearn is already evident in the 1542 and 1713 forms.

LLANAFAN Card SN6872

'church of Afan', ***llan***, pers.n. ***Afan***

Llanavan 1542, *lanavan* 1548, *ll. afan or trowsgoed* c.1566, *Llanavon* 1570, *Llanafan* 1804

Afan has been identified as Afan Buellt, a saint with two churches in Brec (Llanafan Fawr and Fechan) and one in Brittany (Lanavan). This church was occasionally referred to as Llanafan Trawsgoed (from nearby Trawsgoed) in order to distinguish between the churches. The nearby Afon Ystwyth probably influenced some changes from Afan to ***afon*** 'river'.

LLANAFAN FECHAN Brec SN9750

'lesser church of Afan', ***llan***, pers.n. ***Afan***, ***bychan*** fem. ***bechan***
Llanavon vechan 1543, *Llanvethan* 1563, *Llanauan vachan* 1578, *Lanavanveghan* 1682
This Llanafan was a chapelry in Llanafan Fawr parish (*Sancti Avani quæ Britannice Lanavan* 1188, *Llanavan Vaur* c.1198-1214, *ll. afan fawr* c.1566, ***mawr*** 'great').

LLANALLGO Angl SH4985

'church of Gallgo', ***llan***, pers.n. ***Gallgo***
Llanallgo 1384, *Llan Allgo* 1536-9
Gallgo(f) was a brother of Gildas and Eugrad (commemorated in nearby Llaneugrad). A chapel in the parish was Capel Ffynnon (Allgo) (*Capel Ffynon* 1833, ***ffynnon*** 'well'). The name of the medieval secular tnshp was Y Dafarn (*Davarn* 1254) and later Tre'r Dafarn (*Tre'r Davarn* 1647, ***tafarn*** 'inn').

LLANANDRAS see **PRESTEIGNE**

LLANANNO Radn SO0974

'church of Anno', ***llan***, pers.n. ***Anno***
Thlananno 1304, *Llananno* 1392-3
Nothing reliable is known of any saint with this name.

LLANARMON Caern SH4239

'church of Garmon' ***llan***, pers.n. ***Garmon***
ll. armon c.1566, *Llanarmon* 1680
The saint is also commemorated in Betws Garmon (q.v.).

LLANARMON DYFFRYN CEIRIOG Denb SJ1532

'church of Garmon in the Ceiriog valley', ***llan***, pers.n. ***Garmon***, ***dyffryn***, r.n. ***Ceiriog***
Lanarmon 1270, *Lanerman* 1282-3, *llanarmaior in Disfrynkeyrianc* 1291, *llanarmo' in Dyffryn Keirioc* 1377, *ll.armon dyffryn Kerioc* c.1566, *Llanarmon Dyffryn Ceiriog* 1795
The village is near a bridge crossing Afon Ceiriog (q.v.). Several churches are dedicated to Garmon, necessitating a distinction according to location. Adjacent to the church is Tomen Garmon (***tomen*** 'castle mound'), a mound where Garmon is said to have preached and established a cell (in common with all churches dedicated to him).

LLANARMON-YN-IÂL Denb SJ1956

'church of Garmon in Iâl', ***llan***, p.n. ***Garmon***, ***yn***, commote n. ***Iâl***
Sancto Garmano 1254, *Lanarmavn* 1291, *Thlanharmon in Yal* 1314, *llanarmon in yale* 1658, *Llanarmon in Yale* 1748

Cf. Llanarmon Dyffryn Ceiriog. Close to the village is Tomen y Faerdre (***tomen*** 'motte', ***maerdref*** 'demesne, home farm, land adjacent to the court'), associated with Llanarmon-yn-Iâl's role as a significant administrative centre for the commote. The commote name Iâl was once believed to be 'cultivated uplands' based on the erroneous assumption that ***anial*** 'wild' is a related antonym. As with its Gaulish cognate ****-ialo-*** (seen in names such as Auteuil, Ardeuil and Brigeuil) Iâl has recently been shown to mean, in all probability, 'late-bearing land, unfruitful land'. The anglicized Yale is the form which appears as the 17cent. surname (commemorated in Yale University, Connecticut).

LLAN-ARTH Monm SO3710

'church at the ridge', ***llan***, ***garth***

Lanngarth 1136-54, *Lannarth* 1285, *Lanarch* 1291, *Lanharth* 1357, *ll. arth teilo* c.1566

Probably a reference to its location on a low hill. The church is dedicated to Teilo.

LLANARTHNE Carm SN5320

'church of ?Arthneu', ***llan***, ?pers.n. ***Arthneu***

lan hardneu 1160-85, *Lanarthneu* 1281, *Llann Arthnev* 1227 (c.1400), *LL. arthne* c.1550

If the second el. is a pers.n., it seems to have referred to a secular person. Otherwise, the church dedication to David/Dewi (recorded c.1215-29) has replaced an earlier one to an Arddneu or Arthneu.

LLANASA Flints SJ1081

'church of Asa(ff)', ***llan***, pers.n. ***Asa(ff)***

Llanassa 1254, *Lanasaph'* 1291, *ll. hasa* 1566, *Lanhassa o. Llanhassaphe* 1631-2, *Llanassa alii Lhan Asaph et Hassa* c.1700

St Asaph (q.v.) cathedral was also dedicated to this saint, as well as Pantasa (***pant***, 'hollow'), Ffynnon Asa (***ffynnon*** 'well') and Onnen Asa (***onnen*** 'ash') within the locality.

LLANBABO Angl SH3786

'church of Pabo', ***llan***, pers.n. ***Pabo***

Lanvollo 1254, *Llanbabo* 1388

Pabo Post Prydain was a saint and an important secular leader.

LLANBADARN FAWR Card SN6080

'principal church of Padarn', ***llan***, pers.n. ***Padarn***, ***mawr***

(de) Sancto Paterno 1115-47, *(ecclesiam) Sancti Paterni* 1148-76, *Lampadervaur* 1181-2, *Lanpadern maur, id est, ecclesiam Paterni magni* c.1191, *ecclesiam Llanbadarn Vawr* 1557

Padarn was founder, abbot and bishop of this church near Aberystwyth, the principal church in the area. Eight other p.ns carry dedications to him (including another Llanbadarn Fawr in Radn).

LLANBADARN FYNYDD Radn SN0977

'church of Padarn in the mountain', ***llan***, pers.n. ***Padarn***, ***mynydd***

Lanemeneth' 1291, *Llanpaderdyffeyth* 1332, *St Padern in the Desert* 1399, *Llanpadern* 1392-3, *Llanpater[n]venyth* 1431, *Llanbadarn Vynith* 1513, *Llanvynith* 1517, *ll. badarn fynydd* c.1566

The church was among hills in contrast to Llanbadarn Fawr lower down the Ieithon valley, which prompted the 1332 reference to ***diffaith*** 'desolate, wild, uninhabited', latinized as ***desertum*** and translated as *Desert* in 1399. There are several instances of a compressed form *Llanfynydd* (such as 1517).

LLANBADARN-Y-GARREG Radn SO1148

'church of Padarn at the rock', ***llan***, pers.n. ***Padarn***, ***y***, ***carreg***

Thlanbaden 1291, *Lampeter* 1401, *ll. badarn garreg* c.1566, *Llanbadarn y Garreg* 1623

There are several boulders known as Cradle Rocks on the hill south of the village but ***carreg*** may be used elliptically for 'rocky countryside'.

LLANBADOC see **LLANBADOG**

LLANBADOG, LLANBADOC Monm SO3700

'church of Padog', ***llan***, pers.n. ***Padog***

Sancti Padoci 1148-70 (1330), *Lanmadok* 1254, *Lampadok* 1291, *Lanpadoc* 1307, *Lampaddoc* c.1348, *llanbadock* 1508, *Llanbadocke Uske* 1535, *ll. badog* c.1566

The p.n. appears to be unique and nothing is known of any saint Padog. The 1254 form, *Lanvadocke* 1596 and the present church dedication, identify him with Madog, suggesting lenited alternation of Madog, Badog and Padog.

LLANBADRIG Angl SH3794

'church of Padrig', ***llan***, pers.n. ***Padrig***

Sancti Patricii 1254, *llanbadrig* 1406, *ll. badric* c.1566, *Llanpatricke* 1574, *Llanbadrig* 1762

There is no certainty whether this Padrig was the Ir patron saint (as tradition has it) or the 8cent. Padrig from Gwynedd. His name is associated with several other local features including Ynys Badrig (q.v.), Ffynnon Badrig (***ffynnon*** 'well') and Porth Padrig (***porth*** 'bay').

LLANBEDER see **LLANBEDR**[3]

LLANBEDR[1] Brec SO2420

'church of Peter', ***llan***, pers.n. ***Pedr***

inistratyu … lannpetyr 1160-85, *Lanpetr'* 1291,
St. Peter by Crughoell 1547, *ll. bedr ystrad yw* c.1566
The full name appears to have been Llanbedr Ystrad Yw (from the ancient cantref of Ystrad Yw around Llanbedr and Crickhowell) though this does not appear very often after c.1600.

LLANBEDR[2] Mer SH5826
'church of Peter, ***llan***, pers.n. ***Pedr***
Lanpeder 1292-3, *Llanpedir* c.1400, *ll. beder* c.1566, *Llambed* 1587
Originally a chapel-of-ease to Llandanwg, it is occasionally referred to as Llanbedr-ar-Artro, from the church's location on Afon Artro.

LLANBEDR[3] **(LLANBEDER)** Monm ST3890
'church of Peter', ***llan***, pers.n. ***Pedr***
Lannpetyr inhenriv 1136-54, *villam henriu cum ecclesia* 1160-80,
(de) Sco' Petro 1291, *Henru* 1307, *Llanbed* 1578, *Llanbedder* 1830
Henrhiw is 'old slope' (***hen***, ***rhiw***) and survives in the farm name Hendrew. The ancient church is said to have been on a hill north of the village but an 1830 map places *Lanbedder in Ruins* in the village.

LLANBEDR CASTELL-PAEN see **LLANBEDR PAINSCASTLE**

LLANBEDR DYFFRYN CLWYD Denb SJ1459
'church of Peter in the vale of Clwyd', ***llan***, pers.n. ***Pedr***, ***dyffryn***, ***Clwyd***
Lanpedir 1254, *Ecclia' Sci' Petri* 1291, *ll. beder* c.1566, *Llanbedr* 1795,
Llanbedr-Dyffryn-Clwyd 1851
The distinguishing location in Dyffryn Clwyd was not appended until the 19cent. possibly because there is no other Llanbedr in Denb but there are three others in north Wales.

LLANBEDR FELFFRE see **LAMPETER VELVREY**

LLANBEDR-GOCH Angl SH5180
'red church of Pedr', ***llan***, pers.n. ***Pedr***, ***coch***
Llan Peter 1582, *llan Beder* 1594, *Llanbeder* 1680, *Llanbedr goch* 1778,
Llanbedr-goch 1838
An older name (and later alias) was Llanfeistr or Llanfaestir (*llanvaystr* 1479, *llanvaistir* 1515-16, *St Peters church of llanvayst* 1557, *Llanvayster alias Llanpeder* 1620) either ***maestir*** 'open land' or a pers.n. ***Meistr***. The ***coch*** in Llanbedr-goch is a late addition probably with reference to the soil. It has been suggested that there is a possible link with Gwion Goch whose name is associated with the medieval tnshp name, Mathafarn Wion. Local pronunciation is frequently Llanbedar and Llanbedair (without -goch).

LLANBEDR GWYNLLŴG see **PETERSTONE WENTLOOGE**

LLANBEDROG Caern SH3231

'church of Pedrog', ***llan***, pers.n. ***Pedrog***

Lanredrauc 1254, *Llanpedrok* 1291, *ll. bedroc* c.1566, *llanbedrog* 1649

One of three dedications to Pedrog in Wales.

LLANBEDR PAINSCASTLE, LLANBEDR CASTELL-PAEN Radn SO1446

'church of Peter at Painscastle/Castell Paen', ***llan***, pers.n. ***Pedr***, p.n. ***Painscastle/Castell Paen***

Lampetir Pain Castle 1283, *Lanpedr'*, *Lampetr'* 1291, *llanbedr* 1447-89, *Lambed* 1559, *Lambet Castlepaine* 1620

With the exception of Lampeter (q.v.) this p.n. has most -mp-/-mb- forms of all the Llanbedr names, but unlike Lampeter they did not survive. Painscastle (q.v.) is about two miles to the east.

LLANBEDR PONTSTEFFAN see **LAMPETER**

LLANBEDRYCENNIN Caern SH7569

'church of Pedr near the leeks', ***llan***, pers.n. ***Pedr***, ***y***, ***cennin***

Wanberder 1254, *Eccl'ia Sci Peti* 1352, *llanpeder* 1453, *ll. bedyr kenin* c.1566, *llanbedr y Kenin* 1617, *Llanbedrcennyn* 1795

From the 16cent. the church may have been distinguished from other Llanbedr churches by an adjoining field of wild leeks or even daffodils (***cennin Pedr***).

LLANBEDR-Y-FRO see **PETERSTON-SUPER-ELY**

LLANBERIS Caern SH5760

'church of Peris', ***llan***, pers.n. ***Peris***

Lanperis 1283, *ll. beris* c.1566, *Llanperis* 1680, *Llanberris* 1795

The church at Nant Peris (q.v.) is dedicated to Peris, traditionally associated with two other churches in Caern. His name is also preserved in Afon Nant Peris which flows from Snowdon's Pen y Pass to Llyn Peris (q.v.). The present Llanberis, two miles north-west, is a settlement which developed rapidly during the expansion of the Dinorwig quarry (from 1788) at what was called Coed y Ddôl. The new church there was dedicated to Padarn in keeping with the lake, Llyn Padarn (q.v., earlier *Llyn Dolbadarn*), and the 13cent. Castell Dolbadarn (*Dolpadern* 1303-4). The original location was invariably referred to as Nant Peris rather than 'Llan Beris', although on at least one OS map Nant Peris is shown with an alias *Nant Peris (Old Llanberis)* 1891 and another solely as *Old Llanberis* 1898 but this has no local currency.

LLANBETHERY, LLANBYDDERI Glam ST0369

?'Bydderi brook', ?***nant***, r.n. ***Bydderi***

Landebither', *Llandebethery* 13cent., *Llanbethery* 1321-2, *Lambetherie* 1657, *Lanbyddery* mid 17cent.

Although the p.n. is reminiscent of Llanybydder Carm there is no evidence of any church (***llan***), an el. which would regularly produce 'Llanfydderi'. The lack of mutation (b > f) may be a product of E influence as in the case of p.ns such as Llanmaes and Llanmihangel but in these cases there are some recorded instances which show mutation (m > f). It is likelier that the name falls into the category of p.ns in which an earlier ***nant*** (or possibly ***glan*** 'bank') was replaced by ***llan*** (as in Llancarfan and Llanbradach). However, the stream name cannot be identified. The -d- of the 13cent. forms is probably intrusive or influenced by E ***land***.

LLANBISTER Radn SO1073

'church of ?Pister', ***llan***, pers.n. ?***Pister***

Lambister 1252, *Thlambister* 1297, *Lanbyster* 1334, *llann bisteir* 1447-89,

There is no known saint of this name and the church is dedicated to Cynllo. Some spellings have -mp-, -mb- for -nb- (cf. Lampeter Card and Llanbedr Painscastle). Located in the cantref of Maelienydd.

LLANBOIDY Carm SN2123

'cowshed brook', ***nant***, ***beudy***

Lanbedeu 1175-6, *Nambeude* 1264, *Nanthendu* c.1291, *Lanbendy* 1352, *Nantbeudy* 1361, *Nantbeudi* 1431, *llanbeydy* 1602, *Llan-Boydy* c.1700, *Llanbeudŷ* 1801

llan was confused at an early date with ***nant***; cf. Llancarfan. -boidy is the dial. var. of ***beudy***.

LLANBRADACH Glam ST1490

'(place on the) bank of Bradach', ***glan***, r.n. ***Bradach***

Lanbradagh 1597, *Lanbradach* 1726, *Llanbradach* 1616

Lan-, the lenited form of ***glan***, was interpreted as the lenited form of ***llan***. The stream name also occurs in *Blayn Bradach* 1578 (***blaen***) near its source. The modern village developed near two farms Llanbradach Fawr and Llanbradach Isaf, mainly in response to the needs of *Llanbradach Colliery* after the sinking of its first shaft in 1863.

LLANBRYN-MAIR Mont SH8902

'church at Mair's hill', ***llan***, ***bryn***, pers.n. ***Mair***

Brenmeyr 1254, *Brunmeyr* 1293, *Brynmair* 1390, *St. Mary the Virgin, Brynmair in Keveilioc* 1429, *Llambryn mayr* 1470-1, *o lanbrynmair* late 15cent. (c.1600), *ll. bryn mair* c.1566

The earlier name was simply *Bryn-mair*, almost certainly a reference to the church dedication recorded in 1429 (although instances do occur where a saint's dedication has been inspired by a secular pers.n.). The present village of Llanbryn-mair developed around the Wynnstay Arms at Pen-y-bont on the main road between Caersŵs and Machynlleth to the north of the old village which is still called Llan.

LLANBYDDERI see **LLANBETHERY**

LLANCAEO, LLANCAYO Monm SO3603

?'bank of Caeo', ?***glan***, r.n. ***Caeo***

Llan Kayo 1535, *Llankaeyo* 1539, *Llancayo* 1591

The village is about a mile from the stream in *Cwm Cayo* 1830; cf. Caeo Carm where it was a pers.n. and a commote name. Another example of the interchange of ***glan*** and ***llan.***

LLANCARFAN Glam ST0570

'(place by the) valley of Carfan', ***nant***, r.n. ***Carfan***

Lanncarvan before 1104 (13cent.), *Landcaruan* 1107, *Lancarvan* 1135-9, *Carbani Uallis, Nant Carban, Lann Caruanie, nant carban* 1136-54, *Lancarban* c.1152-83, *Nautcharvan* 12cent, *Lankarvan* c.1291, *Nantcarvan* 13cent., *ll. karfan* c.1566

This provides probably the best evidence of the interchange of ***llan*** and ***nant*** (here 'valley' rather than 'stream'). The r.n., common in Wales, is ***carfan*** 'row, ridge' probably referring to a boundary of some sort. An early 13cent. fable interpreted the p.n. as ***carw*** 'deer, hart, stag' + suff. ***-an***, 'valley of deer' (*vallis cervorum*, L ***cervus*** *'deer'*). The modern name of the river is Llancarfan Brook.

LLANCAYO see **LLANCAEO**

LLANDAF, LLANDAFF Glam ST1578

'church by (the river) Taf', ***llan***, r.n. ***Taf***

(de) landauo, (apud) landauum c.1126, *Lann tam, (ecclesie) Landauie* 1136-54, *Landaff* 1469, *Llan Daf* c.1400, *Landaph* 1536-9, *ll. daf* c.1566

The location of a cathedral overlooking the river Taf/Taff (q.v.) dedicated to Teilo (*ecclesia Sancti Teleauci* c.1191) and shrines of Teilo, Dyfrig and Euddogwy; dedications to Peter and Paul were added before 1428. The anglicized form Llandaff is the result of shift of stress to the first syllable and pronunciation of W -f- as -ff-. See also Cardiff.

LLANDAFF see **LLANDAF**

LLANDANWG Mer SH5628

'church of Tanwg', ***llan***, pers.n. ***Tanwg***

Landanwyck 1284, *Landanoc* 1292-3, *Landanok* 1325-6, *Llantanoc* 1400, *ll. danwg* c.1566

Some traditions associate Tanwg with Brittany and others (later) with Bardsey.

LLAN-DAWG see **LLANDAWKE**

LLANDAWKE, LLAN-DAWG Carm SN2811

'church of ?Tyddog', ***llan***, pers.n. ?****Tyddog***

Llandethauk 1353, *Landethauke* 1465-7, *Llandauke* 1513, *Llandawke* 1535, *ll. dawc* c.1566

The first two forms have not hitherto been identified as Llandawke but the first source records that it had a chapel *Pendyn* which is the adjoining parish of Pendine (q.v.). The pers.n. is hypothetical but may comprise the honorific pref. ***ty-*** and ***dog*** 'to take, snatch', found in the pers.n. Dogfael (as in St Dogmael's). The modern forms appear to be contractions.

LLANDDANIEL-FAB Angl SH4970

'church of Deiniolfab', ***llan***, pers.n. ***Deiniolfab***

Llandimoelwab 1254, *Llanddeynel vab* 1535, *ll. ddeiniol* c.1566, *Llanddaniel vab* 1569, *Llandeiniol-fab* 1639, *Llanddaniel* 1695-6, *Llanddaniel fab* 1730

The son of Deiniol (patron saint of the cathedral at Bangor) was called both Deiniolen (with a dim.suff. ***-en*** as in Llanddeiniolen q.v.) and Deiniolfab (***mab*** 'son'). In time, the desire to underline the link between Deiniol of Bangor and his son gave greater prominence to ***mab*** in the structure of the p.n. as in *Llanddaniel vab* 1569 and *Llanddeiniol-fab* 1639 (both demonstrating var. forms, one with biblical Daniel, the other with W development Deiniol). There was also an awareness of the significance of the el. ***mab*** in ***mabsant*** 'patron saint'. Local usage tends to be Llanddaniel.

LLANDDAROG Carm SN5016

'church of Darog', ***llan***, pers.n. ***Darog***

Landarauk 1284, *Landarok* 1333, *Llantharog* 1513, *ll. ddarog* c.1566

Nothing appears to be known of Darog. This may be *mainaur de Lantarauch* 1222 (***maenor***).

LLANDDEINIOL Card SN5672

'church of Deiniol', ***llan***, pers.n. ***Deiniol***

Karrauc c.1250, *Karrauk* 1284, *Karrank* 1290, *Carrok* 1535, *Llan thynol* 1548, *Llanthynoll alias Carrock* c.1549 (1739-61), *ll. ddeiniel* c.1566, *Llanddeiniol* 1804

The earlier name *Carrog* is taken from Afon Carrog which flows through the village, and is preserved in several local p.ns such as the archaeological site Carrog as well as Blaencarrog (***blaen*** 'source'), Felin Carrog (***melin*** 'mill') and Glancarrog (***glan*** 'bank'). The likely confusion between the r.n. and the village or church name probably precipitated the adoption of Llanddeiniol.

LLANDDEINIOLEN Caern SH5466

'church of Deiniolen', ***llan***, pers.n. ***Deiniolen***

Landeynyolen 1284, *Llandimolyn* 1384, *Llandynyollyn* 1436, *ll. ddeiniolen* c.1566, *Llanddeiniolen* 1752

Deiniol the Younger was the son of Deiniol who established the monastery at Bangor and seems to have been called Deiniolen. Another form of Deiniolen is Deiniolfab or Daniel-fab 'son of Deiniol' (or Daniel) as in Llanddaniel-fab (q.v.). The masc. dim.suff. ***-yn*** seen in some of the forms is therefore appropriate. The apparent fem. dim.suff. ***-en*** of the other forms have led some to argue that the original church was called 'Llanddeiniol' with the ***-en*** suff. in Llanddeiniolen indicating a church smaller than the cathedral of Deiniol at Bangor. The pers.n. Deiniolen (*Deiniolen* c.1553) then derived from Llanddeiniolen.

LLANDDERFEL Mer SH9837

'church of Derfael', ***llan***, pers.n. ***Derfael***

Landervael 1254, *Landerwael* 1284, *Landervayl* 1329-30, *Llandervell* 1389, *ll. derfel* c.1566, *Llandderfel* 1754

Derfael, later Derfel, is said to have shown considerable prowess as a soldier, earning him the epithet Derfel Gadarn (***cadarn*** 'mighty, firm, strong'). A var. of his name was Derwfael as if ***derw*** 'oak' (and by transference 'valiant warrior') and ***mael*** 'prince, lord'. It was this association which may have prompted the erection of a large wooden statue of Derfel in the church, which was eventually transported to London to be used in the burning of a Catholic martyr in 1538. On the hill west of the church was the well Ffynnon Dderfel (*Ffynnon Dhervel* c.1700). There was an identical p.n. in Monm (*Sti' Dervali* 1535, *Llantheruell* 1577).

LLANDDEUSANT[1] Angl SH3485

'church of the two saints', ***llan***, (***y***), ***dau***, ***sant***

Landysnant 1308-21, *Llanyddeysant* 1535, *Llanddeusant* 1557, *ll. y ddaysant* c.1566

The two saints are Marcellus and Marcellinus (possibly the 4cent. popes and martyrs).

LLANDDEUSANT[2] Carm SN7724

'church of the two saints', ***llan*** (***y***), ***dau***, ***sant***

Thlanadusant c.1282, *Thlandeuseynt* 1295, *Llannedoysant* 1506, *ll. yddey saint* c.1566, *Llanthoysant* 1576, *llanddeysaint* 1600

Dedicated to Simon and Jude.

LLAN-DDEW Brec SO0530

'church of God', ***llan***, MW ***Duyw***

Lando c.1150-75, *Landu ecclesia Dei* c.1191, *Landu* 1201-2, *Landew* 1249, *Llandou* 1281, *Llan Dduw* 1750, *Llanthew* 1804

Dwy(w) is an older form of ***Duw***; cf. Llandow/Llandŵ Glam and Llanddwy Card which is also the older name of Llandrindod Radn (q.v.). Although the association with Duw is seen in most forms, the influence of Dewi is seen in some late forms and in the addition of his dedication to that of the Holy Trinity; bishops of St David's had a palace here. The Holy Trinity also replaces dedications to Duw in Llandrindod, Llandow and Llanddwy.

LLANDDEWI Glam SS4689

'church of Dewi', ***llan***, pers.n. ***Dewi***
Landewy in Gower 1281, *Llandewy in Goheria* 1326, *Llanthewy* 1553-5, *ll. ddewi* c.1566
Occasionally distinguished as being in the cantref of Gower.

LLANDDEWIBREFI Card SN6655

'church of Dewi on (the river) Brefi', ***llan***, pers.n. ***Dewi***, r.n. ***Brefi***
Landewi Brevi, id est, ecclesiam David de Brevi c.1191, *Landewybrevy* 1281, *ll. ðewi frefi* c.1566
The town (*civitate Brevi* c.1100 [c.1200]), an important historical site (*Bremia* 8cent., the Roman fort at Llanio), is on the river Brefi which rises at Blaen Brefi (***blaen*** 'headwater') between Cwm Berwyn and Esgair Llethr and flows past Llanddewi Brefi into the river Teifi. The r.n. probably derives from ***bref*** 'bray, cry' perhaps here alluding to a wild, noisy river. Legend maintains that at the Convocation of Brefi, Dewi roared forth his accusations against heretics with a voice like a trumpet.

LLANDDEWI FELFFRE, LLANDDEWI VELFREY
Pemb SN1416

'church of Dewi in Efelffre', ***llan***, pers.n. ***Dewi***, terr.n. ***Efelffre***
Landewy & Tresendek 1291, *Llandewy Trefdentheg* 1332, *Landewy Trefendek* 1340, *Landewi in Wilfrey* 1488, *ll. ddewy y selffre*, *~ y velffre* c.1566, *Llanddewy felfrey* 1594
The church is shown in early sources as being at or near a lost location Trefendeg (*Trefdenthog* 1342, *trefeandegh* 1382, *Trefwedeg* 1412, *Trefdiawke* 1517), apparently ***tref*** and an unidentified pers.n. For Efelffre, see Lampeter Velfrey. The present village now extends northwards to the Haverfordwest-Whitland road.

LLANDDEWI NANT HODNI see **LLANTHONY**

LLANDDEWI'R-CWM Brec SO0348

'church of Dewi in the valley', ***llan***, pers.n. ***Dewi***, ***yr***, ***cwm***
Sancti David de Cum in Buelt 1176-98, *Landewycum* 1254, *ll. ddewi y kwm* c.1566
Located in the deep, narrow valley of Cwm Duhonwy in Builth (q.v.).

LLANDDEWI RHYDDERCH Monm SO3512

'church of Dewi belonging to Rhydderch', ***llan***, pers.n. ***Dewi***, pers.n. ***Rhydderch***

Landewy 1254, *Landewy Rotherath* c.1300, *Landewy Rethergh* 1369, *ll. ddewi Rydderch* c.1566

Rhydderch may have been a lay patron, perhaps Rhydderch ap Caradog, king of Ewias and Gwent Is Coed, of uncertain date, recorded in the Book of Llandaf c.1160-85.

LLANDDEWI VELFREY see **LLANDDEWI FELFFRE**

LLANDDEWI-YN-CHWITYN see **WHITTON**

LLANDDEWI YSTRADENNI Radn SO1068

'church of Dewi in the vale of Nynnid', ***llan***, pers.n. ***Dewi***, ***ystrad***, pers.n. ***Nynnid***

ystrad nynhid, ystrat nynhit 12cent. (early 14cent.), *Thlandewy* 1297, *Llandewye Stradu(n)nye* 1544, *ll. ddewi ystrad yni* c.1566, *Llanddeywy Stradyny* 1582

Nynnid is the Romano-British fem. pers.n. latinized as Nonnita; cf. Eglwys Nynnid Glam. Modern roadsigns generally omit Ystradenni which ironically seems to have been the original name, with Llanddewi being a later addition. Local pronunciation is 'Lanjŵi'.

LLANDDINGAD see **DINGESTOW**

LLANDDINOL see **ITTON**

LLANDDOGED Denb SH8063

'church of Doged', ***llan***, pers.n. ***Doged***

Landoget 1291, *ll. ddoged* c.1566, *Llandoget* 1650, *Lhan Dhoged* c.1700

The church was dedicated to a king called Doged reputedly descended from Cunedda Wledig. His name was also associated with Ffynnon Ddoged (*Ffynnon Dhoged* c.1700) a renowned healing well (***ffynnon***).

LLANDDONA Angl SH5779

'church of Dona', ***llan***, pers.n. ***Dona***

Llanddona 1535, *Seynt Dona* 1538-44, *ll. ddona* c.1566, *llan Ddona* 1613

Dona was the son of Selyf king of Powys (reputedly killed in the battle of Chester in 613). Nearby are Bryn Dona and Cadair Dona.

LLANDDOWROR Carm SN2514

'church of the water-drinkers', ***llan***, ***dyfrwr*** pl. ***dyfrwyr***

Landubrguir c.1100, *ecclesie aquilensium, lannteliau Lanndÿfrguÿr, Lannteliau lanndibrguir* 1136-54, *Landoverour* 1339, *Llandeuerour* 1398, *Landowror* 1691

The church of *Llandeilo Llanddyfrwyr* was dedicated to Teilo. ***dyfrwyr*** (here in a dial. var.) and the L *aquilensium* ('of the water-men') refer to the practice of fasting but various legends surrounding Teilo also connect him with fishermen and with saving seven sons whose father was attempting to drown them in the river Taf. There was formerly a church Llanddyfrwyr near Llangybi Fawr Monm.

LLANDDULAS Denb SH9078

'church on (the river) Dulas', ***llan***, r.n. ***Dulas***

Llanndulas 1254, *Nandulas* 1284, *Thlantheles* 1287, *Landwlas, Landuglas* 1291, *llanddulas* 1539-40, *Llanddulas* 1664-5

The church (dedicated to Cynbryd) is located beside the river Dulas (*Dulas* 1504, 'black stream, ***du***, ***glais*** var. ***glas***). The location and the fact that ***llan*** with a r.n. is fairly rare (cf. Llandaf and Llanelwy) reinforce the view that the 1284 form is evidence of the alternation of ***nant*** and ***llan***, suggesting that the original name may have been 'Nan(t) Dulas'. An occasional reference to the church as *Llangynbryd* was probably a purely literary form and does not seem to have been used as the village or parish name.

LLANDDUNWYD see **WELSH ST DONAT'S**

LLANDDYFNAN Angl SH5078

'church of Dyfnan', ***llan***, pers.n. ***Dyfnan***

Landevnan 1254, *Landeuenan* 1291-2, *Landefnan* 1352-3, *Llandyfnan* 1398, *Llanddyfnan* 1476

Dyfnan was recorded as one of the sons of Brychan Brycheiniog.

LLANDEGFAN Angl SH5673

'church of Tegfan', ***llan***, pers.n. ***Tegfan***

Llandegvan 1254, *Llandecvan* 1391, *ll. degfan* c.1566

Very little is known of the 6cent. Tegfan apart from an association with Cybi's monastery in Holyhead. Formerly it was a dispersed rural community centred on the church and a hamlet to the east, the original name of which was Bryn Minceg (*bryn-maenceg* 1822, *Bryn-minceg* 1838, *Bryn y Mintcake* 1859, *Brynminceg* 1978) from a small-holding on a slight rise (***bryn***) whose owner was, reputedly, well known for making mint-cake (***minceg***). Later the hamlet became known as Pentref and since the 1990s informally as Hen Bentref Llandegfan (*Hen Bentref Llandegfan* 1997, ***hen***, ***pentref***), to contrast with the extensive development of the present village south of the church.

LLANDEGFEDD, LLANDEGVEDD Monm ST3395

'church of Tegfedd', ***llan***, pers.n. ***Tegfedd***

Merthir Tecmed 1136-54, *Ecclesia Tegued* 1155-83, *Landegewith* 1210-22, *Landegevet* 1254, *Landegeveth* 1314, *ll. degfedd* c.1566

Tegfedd was reputedly the mother of Teilo. Earliest spellings have ***merthyr*** 'shrine' replaced by ***llan*** a characteristic of other p.ns in south Wales (such as Llanfaches). Another Tegfedd is connected with Mawddwy in Mer and with Mont.

LLANDEGLA Denb SJ1952

'church of Tegla', ***llan***, pers.n. ***Tegla***

landeglan 1277-8, *Llanddegla* 1284, *Landegla* 1291, *ll. degle* c.1566, *Lh. Degla, Llandegley* 1680, *Lhan Dekla* c.1700, *Llandegle* 1795, *Llandegla* 1838

A well (*Ffynnon Degla* c.1700, ***ffynnon***) in the village was dedicated to the female saint Tegla. Some of the later forms in -e are dial.

LLANDEGLE, LLANDEGLEY Radn SO1362

'church of Tegle', ***llan***, pers.n. ***Tegle***

Lanteglin, ecclesiam sancte Tecle early 13cent., *Landegla* 1291, *Llandegle* 1401

Possibly the same female saint as in Llandegla (q.v.). There was a well here dedicated to her. Local pronunciation is 'Landegli'.

LLANDEGLEY see **LLANDEGLE**

LLANDEGVEDD see **LLANDEGFEDD**

LLANDEILO (FAWR) Carm SN6222

'(principal) church of Teilo', ***llan***, pers.n. ***Teilo, mawr***

Lann Teliau maur 1136-54, *Lanteilawmawr'* 1222, *Lanteylavaur* 1281, *Thlanthilogh Vaur* 1294-5, *ll. deilo fawr* c.1566

mawr 'great' reflects the importance of this church, thought to be one of the earliest to be dedicated to Teilo, the 6cent. saint widely venerated in south Wales and Brittany. There is a large mound near the church described as *tumulum sancti Thilawi* 1294-5.

LLANDEILO FERWALLT see **BISHOPSTON**

LLANDEILO GRABAN Radn SO0944

'church of Teilo among corn-marigolds', ***llan***, pers.n. ***Teilo, graban***

Lann teliau 1136-54, *Llandeylar'* 1291, *Llanteylo in Elveal* 1397, *ll. deilio* c.1566, *Llandilo Graban* 1670, *Llandilo yr Graban* 1688

The qualifier may be taken from a farm Cwrtygraban (***cwrt, y, graban*** 'corn-marigold') in the adjoining parish of Llansteffan, but ***graban*** may be used of a wider area where these plants were numerous. The first form is taken from a source which places Llandeilo in Ciliau (*iciliou idifrinn machagui* 1136-54, ***cil*** pl. ***ciliau*** 'nooks') in the valley (***dyffryn***) of the river Bachawy (*machave, machavvi* 12cent., *machawy* 1447-89, *Bach Howey* on modern maps, probably a pers.n.). Llandeilo village and church lie about a mile-and-a-half north-west of Ciliau and the river and two miles from Cwrtygraban; perhaps the church (at least) was re-located at some date. It is often described as 'in Elfael, yn Elfael' from the name of its cantref. Cf. Garth Graban Glam.

LLANDEILO GRESYNNI see **LLANTILIO CROSSENNY**

LLANDEILO'R-FÂN Brec SN8934

'church of Teilo on (the stream called) Mawen', ***llan***, pers.n. ***Teilo***, ***ar***, r.n. ***Mawen***

Lann Guruaet 12cent., *Llantilio* 1503, *Llandeylo Gornagh* 1513, *ll. deilo ar faen* c.1566, *Llan Deilo ar Vawen* 1726

The stream Nant Fawen (*mauan* 1136-54, ***nant***, r.n. *Mawan* later Mawen) also occurs in *blain mauan* 1136-54, *Blaen-mawyn* 1832 (***blaen*** 'headwater') and is probably identical in meaning to Nant Mafon (*Mauhan* c.1200, and in *Maesmawan* c.1200) near Llanfabon Glam. Both r.ns may contain an el. ***maw-*** thought to be related to Breton ***mav*** 'agile, active' and a suff. ***-an***. Later sources suggest *Mawan* > Mawen through dissimilation and Fân with lenition. The significance of *Guruaet* and *Gornagh* has not been satisfactorily explained but may be a pers.n. Gurmaet.

LLANDELOY, LLANLLWY Pemb SM8526

'church of ?Tylwyf', ***llan***, pers.n. *****Tylwyf***

Landalee 1291, *Landelowe* 1307, *Llandellaw* 1326, *Llandeloe* 1491, *Landeloy* 1513, *Llantholowy* 1512, *ll. dylwyf* c.1566, *Llandyloy* 1577, *Llandelwy* 1589

The present dedication to Teilo is late and may have been based on a re-interpretation of the unrecorded and conjectural Tylwy(f). The early forms are anglicized.

LLANDIMÔR see **LANDIMORE**

LLANDINAM Mont SO0288

'church near the little fort', ***llan***, ***din***, dim.suff. ***-an***

Landinan c.1207, *Llandinan*, *Llandinam* c.1216, *Landynan* 1291, *Sclandynan Iscoyt* 1293, *Llandynan in Arwistly* 1379, *Llanddinam in Arrustly* 1424, *Llanthenam* 1542, *ll. ddinam* c.1566, *llandinam* 1597

The more usual form would be 'Llanddinam' but absence of lenition after -n- is not unknown. In several parts of Wales -dinan becomes -dinam, such as Llysdinam (*Lystynan* 1290, *Listinan* 1299, ***llys***) Brec, Dinham Monm, and Dinam Angl. No little fort has yet been found. *Nandynan* suggests an alternative first el. ***nant*** but seems to be an isolated form and there is no r.n. or valley name Dinan here.

LLANDISSILIO see **LLANDYSILIO**

LLANDOCHA FACH see **LLANDOUGH**[1]

LLANDOCHAU'R BONT-FAEN see **LLANDOUGH**[2]

LLANDOGO Monm SO5204

'church of Euddogwy', ***llan***, pers.n. ***Euddogwy***

uillam sancti Oudocei 1160-85, *lann enniaun, Lanneniaun. i. lannoudocui* 1136-54, *Landigo* 1254, *Lanthogo* 1291, *Llandogoye* 1535

Euddogwy (latinized as *Oudocui* and then as *Oudoceus*) was an early (?8cent.) bishop of Llandaf. The 1136-54 reference is a possible dedication to Einion, an early king of Glywysing (south-east Wales) who gave land here to Dyfrig, Teilo and his nephew Euddogwy. *Llaneuddogwy* became *Llanddogwy* (with loss of unstressed -eu-) and then *Llanddogwy* > *Llanddogw* > *Llanddogo*. The modern form Llandogo with -d- rather than -dd- is comparable with Llandinam. The church dedication is to Dochau.

LLANDOUGH[1]**, LLANDOCHA FACH** Glam ST1673

'(little) church of Dochan', ***llan***, pers.n. ***Dochan***, ***bach***

Landochan 1106, *Landocham* 1173-83, *Landoghe* 1254, *Landoch* 13cent., *ll. doche fach* c.1566, *llandoghe upon eley* 1573, *Llandoche juxta Cardiff* 1596

Early forms suggest loss of final -n (cf. Penally and Barry) with later substitution of -a as -e, mistakenly restored as the W pl. ending -au, -eu, and a total loss of -e in the present anglicized form. The W pronunciation was recorded as Llandocha in the late 19cent. and as recently as c.1958. This may be the location of the monastic foundation of *Docunnus* (*abbas Docguinni, Docunni, Dochou* 1136-54, which may well be latinizations), possibly the same saint as in Llandough[2]. The church is now dedicated to Dochdwy, probably arising from antiquarian confusion with Euddogwy (the saint of Llandogo q.v.). The church and village lie near the river Ely.

LLANDOUGH[2]**, LLANDOCHE, LLANDOCHAU'R BONT-FAEN** Glam SS9972

'church of Dochan (at Y Bont-faen)', ***llan***, pers.n. ***Dochan***, p.n.***Y Bont-faen***

Landoch 1254, *Landochhe* c.1262, *Landogh'* 1317, *Llandough* 1376, *Llandouhe, Landoughe* 1536-9, *ll. doche* c.1566, *Landough Juxta Cowbridge* 1762

The pers.n. may be identical to that of Llandough[1] with loss of a final -n before the forms were recorded. Local pronunciation is 'Landuff'. The addition of (Y) Bont-faen (Cowbridge) distinguishes it from Llandough[1].

LLANDOVERY, LLANYMDDYFRI Carm SN7634

'church near the waters', ***llan*, *am*, *dŵr*** pl. ****dyfri***

Llanaindewri 1163 (late 13cent.), *Lanamdeveri'* 1194, *Llandeuery* 12cent. (c.1200), *Llanamdewri* 1201, *Lanemdovri* c.1250, *Lanemdevery* 1291, *Landoveroi* 1312, *Lanymdevery* 1383, *Llanymdyfri* 1116 (c.1400), *Llandyuery* c.1545, *ll. ym ddyfri* c.1566, *Llanddyfri* 1710, *Llandovery* 1831

The town is near the confluences (*Devery* 1485) of the rivers Brân, Gwydderig, Bawddwr and Tywi. The unstressed -am- later became -em- (but seem to have co-existed for some time) and was then interpreted as -ym- (as if ***yn*** 'in'), a syllable which has been lost in the local pronunciation Llandyfri which has been anglicized to Llandovery.

LLANDOW, LLANDŴ Glam SS9473

'church dedicated to God', ***llan***, MW ***Duy(w)***

Landu c.1220, *Landou* 1254, *Landau* c.1262, *ll. duf* c.1566, *LL.Dw* before 1569

The church is now dedicated to the Holy Trinity and there are similar examples of such a change of dedication such as Llan-ddew Brec (q.v.), Llanddwy Card (*LL.ddwy* 1540-77, *Trinity Chapel* 1651) and Llandrindod Radn.

LLANDRE, LLANFIHANGEL GENAU'R-GLYN Card SN6286

'church village', 'church of Mihangel in Genau'r-glyn', ***llandref*, *llan***, pers.n. ***Mihangel***, commote n. ***Genau'r-glyn***

Lamyhangel Castel Walter 1277-8, *Castr' Walteri* 1304, *Llān Vihāgel* 1325-50, S. *Michaelis de Castello Walteri* 1440, *Llanwychangell Castell Gwalter* 1559, *ll. V'el gener glyn* c.1566, *llannihangell geneylyn* 1666-7, *llanwyhangel geneylyn o. Llanvyhangel Castell Gwalter* 1756, *Llandre* 1760, *Llandref* 1810, *Llanfihangel-geneu'r-glyn* 1837

The castle was established between 1110 and 1136 by the Norman lord *Walter le Bec* or perhaps *Walter le Saluage* both of whom are recorded in a charter referring to *Castellaria...de Penwdic* c.1158-65 (1308), from its location in the cantref of Penweddig, and *Chastel Waunter* 1317, *Castel Walter* 1361. The fortified site, today's Castell Gwallter, is a quarter of a mile west of Llanfihangel. The church was one of three in the commote of Genau'r-glyn (*Geneuyglyn* 1260, *Geneurglyn* 1352-3, *Generglyn* 1425, *Genau'r glyn* 1615, ***genau*** 'pass, entrance', ***yr*** 'the', ***glyn*** 'glen, narrow valley') through which Afon Leri flows. The later Llandre was given greater currency by the post office and the railway station east of the church.

LLANDRILLO Mer SJ0337

'church of Trillo', ***llan***, pers.n. ***Trillo***

Lantreullo 1254, *Landerillo* 1291, *Llanderychlou* 1292-3, *ll. drillo* c.1566, *Thlandrethon in Edyrnyon* 1370-1, *Llandrillo in Idernion* 1691
Trillo's brothers were Tygái (see Llandygái) and Llechid (see Llanllechid). The two churches dedicated to Trillo were Llandrillo-yn-Rhos and this Llandrillo which is occasionally still called Llandrillo-yn-Edeirnion (***yn*** 'in', commote name Rhos). Ffynnon Drillo (***ffynnon*** 'well') is north of the village.

LLANDRILLO-YN-RHOS see **RHOS-ON-SEA**

LLANDRINDOD see **LLANDRINDOD (WELLS)**

LLANDRINDOD (WELLS) Radn SO0561
'church of the Trinity at the wells', ***llan***, ***trindod***, E ***wells***
Llandynddod 1535, *Llan Yr dryndot* 1543, *Llandrindod* 1549, *Llanydrindod* 1565, *Llandrindod Wells* 1794
The original name of the parish and the old church above the town was *Llanddwy* 'church of God' (*Llandow* 1283, *Lando* 1291, ***Dwyw***). The change in dedication from God to the Trinity came later in keeping with several other churches (cf. Llandow). The modern spa town developed in the 18cent. and 19cent. near mineral springs and was initially known simply as *The Wells*.

LLANDRINIO Mont SJ2917
'church of Trinio', ***llan***, pers.n. ***Trinio***
Llantrinew 1254, *Landrimeaw* 1291, *Llandrunion in Dendour* 1309, *Landrunyawe* 1361, *Llandrunyo* 1385, *llann Drinio* late 15cent., *ll. drinio* c.1566
Nothing is known of any saint Trinio or Trunio, reputedly a grandson of Emyr Llydaw, an ancestor of a number of saints recorded in the 12cent. In 1526 Llandrinio was recorded as a place of pilgrimage.

LLANDUDNO Caern SH7881
'church of Tudno', ***llan***, pers.n. ***Tudno***
Lan Tudno 1291, *Lantudenou* 1376, *Llan Duddno* 1535, *llandidno* 1662, *Llandudno* 1838
This is the only church dedicated to this 6cent. saint of whom little is known (except that he was allegedly the son of Seithenyn who was associated with Cantre'r Gwaelod, legend's drowned kingdom in Cardigan Bay).

LLANDUDNO JUNCTION, CYFFORDD LLANDUDNO
Caern SH7978
'(place at the) Llandudno junction', p.n. ***Llandudno***, E ***junction***, W ***cyffordd***
Llandudno Junction 1891

The main Holyhead-Chester railway has branch lines at this junction to Llandudno and to Blaenau Ffestiniog. The location developed in the early 20cent. into a large village through which the A55 trunk road formerly passed.

LLANDUDOCH see **ST DOGMAELS**

LLANDUDWEN Caern SH2736
'church of Tudwen', ***llan***, pers.n. ***Tudwen***
Tutdey 1254, *ll. dydwen* c.1566, *Llandidwen* 1679, *Llandudwen* 1838
The saint Tudwen is reputed to be one of the daughters of the 7cent. Brychan. Adjacent to the church is Ffynnon Dudwen (***ffynnon*** 'well').

LLANDŴ see **LLANDOW**

LLANDWROG Caern SH4556
'church of Twrog', ***llan***, pers.n. ***Twrog***
Llam'urok 1291, *Llandwrok* 1397, *Llandwrog* 16cent.
The same 7cent. saint is associated with Maentwrog. He was reputed to have been buried in Bedd Twrog, a cairn on the north slopes of Mynydd Cilgwyn.

LLANDYBÏE Carm SN6115
'church of Tybïau', ***llan***, pers.n. ***Tybïau***
Landebyeu 1284, 1348, *Llandebye* 1535, *ll. dybie* c.1566, *Llandebea* 1607
Tybïau is though to be one of the numerous daughters of the legendary Brychan Brycheiniog. The parish possessed a well (***ffynnon***) dedicated to her, probably at Gelli Ffynnon.

LLANDYFAELOG Carm SN4111
'church of Tyfaelog', ***llan***, pers.n. ***Tyfaelog***
landivailoc 1148-66, *lann diuailauc* 1160-85, *Landevayloc* 1284, *Landyveylok* 1358, *ll. dy fayloc* c.1566, *Llandeveylogg* 1763
The saint's name also appears in Llandyfaelog Fach (q.v.).

LLANDYFAELOG FACH Brec SO0332
'lesser church of Tyfaelog', ***llan***, pers.n. ***Tyfaelog***, ***bach***
Landeuailac, *Landemayloc* 11cent. (c.1200), *Llanvayloc* 12cent. (c.1200), *Llandevaillauc* 1215-22, *Llandeveylok in Diffrin hothenhey* 1398, *Llandevaylog vach* 1794
Its location in the vale (***dyffryn***) of Hoddni and its smaller size or significance (***bach***) distinguished it from Llandyfaelog Tre'r-graig (*Laudyvayllock* [=*Landyvayllock*] 1310-11, *Llandevaylok Tref Crayg* 1535, ***tref***, ***yr***, ***craig***) on the steep bank of the river Llynfi.

LLANDYFÁI see **LAMPHEY**

LLANDYFALLE Brec SO1035

'church of ?Tyfallan', ***llan***, pers.n. ?***Tyfallan***

Landewathlan 1241, *Landewathlan* 1263, *Llanvallen* 1400, *Llandevalle* 1495, *ll. dyfalle* c.1566, *Llandefathew* 1739

The identity of the saint and correct form of the pers.n. are uncertain. Early forms suggest an unrecorded **Tyfathan* or **Tywathan* (with the honorific pref. ***ty-*** and *Bathan or Mathan) with loss of final -n and the resulting -a taken as a pl. -au dial. -e as if a pers.n. *Tyfalle*; cf. Llandough. If the early forms in -an are errors for -au it suggests a pers.n. *Tyfalleu* or *Tyfallau*. The present dedication is to Mathew, possibly a result of *Tyfalle* or *Tyfalleu* being perceived as (an unrecorded) **Tyfathew* through confusion of -ll- and -th-.

LLANDYFÂN Carm SN6417

'church of ?Tyfaen', ***llan***, ?pers.n. ***Tyfaen***

Lh.dyvân c.1700, *Llandyfaen* 1752, *Llanduvaen* 1760, *Llandyfan* 1891

The authenticity of Tyfaen is uncertain since no early forms have been found, but is probably the honorific pref. ***ty-*** and the pers.n. Maen. The pronunciation as Llandyfân is prompted by the dial. pronunciation of ***maen*** 'stone' as 'mân' and also seen in the r.n. Gwyddfaen (*Gwydhvân... at Lh. divan* c.1700) which rises nearby (although the pronunciation Llandyfán is to be heard). The church is now dedicated to Dyfan.

LLANDYFODWG see **GLYNOGWR**

LLANDYFRÏOG Card SN3341

'church of Tyfrïog', ***llan***, pers.n. ***Tyfrïog***

Lantheveyrok 1291, *Landavrak* 1299, *Landevryok* 1353, *llandevriok* 1407, *Llandevriog* 1569, *Llandyvrïog* 1739, *Llandyfriog* 1831

The saint's name Tyfrïog (*Thiuriauc* c.1000 [c.1200]) is the honorific pref. ***ty-*** and Briog (also commemorated in Saint-Brieuc, Brittany and St Breoc, Cornwall) itself generally thought to be a hypocoristic or pet form (with the suff. ***-og***) of the pers.n. Briafael (as in St Briavel's Gloucester).

LLANDYFRYDOG Angl SH4485

'church of Tyfrydog', ***llan***, pers.n. ***Tyfrydog***

ecclesia Sancti Tevredauci c.1191, *Landewredauc* 1254, *llanndyvrydoc* 1397, *ll. dyfrydog* c.1566, *Llandyfrydog* 1651-2

Tyfrydog was reputedly a saint of Bardsey. The name is also preserved in Bryn Tyfrydog, half-a-mile north-west of the village, and in a standing stone called *llidr tyfrydog* (1639-40, ***lleidr*** 'thief') a mile away.

LLANDYGÁI Caern SH5970

'church of Tygái', ***llan***, pers.n. ***Tygái***

Landegey 1254, *llandegay* 1415, *Llandygai* 15cent., *ll. ddygai* c.1566, *llandegaye* 1576, *Llandegai* 1589

Although the saint's name has long been perceived to be Tegai (as in the church dedication) the persistent stress on the final syllable of Tygái shows the pers.n. name to consist of the unstressed honorific pref. ***ty-*** and Cai.

LLANDYGWYDD Card SN2443

'church of Tygwy', ***llan***, pers.n. ***Tygwy***

Landegoe 1281, *Landogy* 1288, *Landogoy* 1290, *Landegey* 1291, *Landegwy* 1389, *llan Dygwy* 15cent., *ll. dygwy* c.1566, *Llandygwy* 1594-5, *Llanduguwydd* 1704-5, *Llandygwydd* 1752, *Llandegwy* 1819

The generally held view was that the final -dd of a pers.n. Tygwydd was lost in the local dial. (where ***newydd*** for example would regularly be 'newy' colloquially) but was then restored in the 18cent., hence the modern dedication to Tygwydd and the Nonconformist Capel Tygwydd. However, all the historical forms (until 1623) as well as the modern local pronunciation as Llandygwy are evidence of a pers.n. Tygwy with the occasional intrusion of Tegwy (*a Theguy* 12cent. [1250-75]) influenced by the saint Tegwydd (as happened with -y-/-e- alternation in Llandygái q.v.).

LLANDYRNOG Denb SJ1065

'church of Teyrnog', ***llan***, pers.n. ***Teyrnog***

Landernauc 1254, *Lant'nank, Llandurnok* 1291, *Llandyrnok* 1423, *Llandyrnog* 1654-5

The exact form of the saint's name (Teyrnog, Tyrnog) is in some doubt but it is likely that the name (but not necessarily the saint) is Irish. This is the only dedication to him in Wales.

LLANDYSILIO, LLANDISSILIO Pemb SN1221

'church of Tysilio', ***llan***, pers.n. ***Tysilio***

Landesilion 1291, *Landesilian'* 1326 (16cent.), *Lansilio* 1385, *Lan Tesulyo* 1389, *Llandissilio* 1513, *ll. dyseilio yn yfed* c.1566, *Llandissillio in Dyvett* 1603

The qualifying 'yn Nyfed', 'in Dyfed' distinguished the church from Llandysilio-yn-Iâl Denb (q.v.) and Llandysilio Mont (*Llantessilyau* 1254, *Llandisiliowe* 1385, *Llandesiliowe in Deudore* 1390, *ll. dysilio* c.1566) which lay in the division (***swydd***) of Deuddwr.

LLANDYSILIOGOGO see **LLANGRANNOG**

LLANDYSILIO-YN-IÂL Denb SJ1943

'church of Tysilio in Iâl', ***llan***, pers.n. ***Tysilio***, ***yn***, commote n. ***Iâl***

Llan Tessiliau 1234 (1295), *Sancto Tessiliao, Lantesilau* 1254, *Landesylian* 1291, *Llantissilio in Yale alias Llanekemer* 1393, *ll. dysilio* 1566, *Llandysilio* 1795

The church is situated quite close to one of the broad bends in the river

Dee into which several streams flow, hence the 1393 alias (*y* 'the', ***cymer*** 'confluence'). Although the distinguishing 'in Yale' appears only once in the historical forms, -yn-Iâl seems to have been restored in some modern usage. However, most maps prefer the form Llantysilio. On the commote name Iâl, see Llanarmon-yn-Iâl.

LLANDYSSIL see **LLANDYSUL**

LLANDYSUL[1] Card SN4140

'church of Tysul', ***llan***, pers.n. ***Tysul***

Landessul, landessel 1253, *Landussul* 1259, *Lantessul* 1272, *Lantissill* 1299, *ll. dyssyl* c.1566

Very little is known about this saint. Another church is dedicated to him in Mont and in Brittany where he was celebrated as a bishop.

LLANDYSUL[2], **LLANDYSSIL** Mont SO1995

'church of Tysul', ***llan***, pers.n. ***Tysul***

Llandeshul 1254, *Landissul* 1291, *Llandyssul in Keddewayng* 1392, *Llandissul* 1480, *LL. dysul ynghedewain* c.1562

The same saint as in Llandysul[1].

LLANEDERN, LLANEDEYRN Glam ST2282

'church of Edern', ***llan***, pers.n. ***Edern***

sancti Ederni 1173-83, *Lanedarn* 1291, *Lanedern* 13cent., *Lanyderne* 1376, *Llanedyrn* 1563, *ll. edyrn* c.1566

The pers.n., if not the same saint, is also found in Bodedern Angl and Edern Caern. Modern maps have -edeyrn, probably a var. of forms such as *Llanedyrn* and likely to have been reinforced by antiquarian confusion with pers.ns with ***teyrn*** 'king' such as Mechteyrn and Cyndeyrn (in Llangyndeyrn).

LLANEDEYRN see **LLANEDERN**

LLANEFYDD Denb SH9870

'church of Ufydd', ***llan***, pers.n. ***Ufydd***

Llanuvyth 1256, *Lanvddud* 1329, *Llanyvydd* 1511, *ll. yfydd* c.1566, *Llannefydd* 1679, *Lhan Yvydh* c.1700, *Llanefidd* 1704-5, *Llan y fydd* 1773

The perception that the saint was Nefydd rather than Ufydd is a fairly modern development; cf. the well *Fynnon Yvydh* c.1700 now Ffynnon Nefydd. Local pronunciation still favours Llanufydd. The church is dedicated to the Blessed Virgin.

LLANEGRYN Mer SH6005

'church of Egryn', ***llan***, pers.n. ***Egryn***

Llanegryn 1209 (1324), *Lanegrin* 1254, *llanegryn* 1400

The church is now dedicated to Mary the Virgin but Egryn is also commemorated in Croes Egryn, the farm Egryn Abbey and the gorge Ceunant Egryn.

LLANEGWAD Carm SN5121
'church of Egwad', ***llan***, pers.n. ***Egwad***
Lanegwade Vaur 1215-29, *Laneguadvaur* 1281, *Thlanhegodvaour* 1287, *Llanegwat* 1389, *LL.egwad vawr* c.1500, *Llanegwad* 1594
Earlier forms show that it was qualified as Fawr (***mawr*** 'the greater') to distinguish it from Llanegwad Fynydd, now Llanfynydd Carm (q.v.). Little is known of Egwad. Eisteddfa farm two miles north of the village is *Eisteddfa-egwad* 1831 (***eisteddfa*** 'seat'); cf. Eisteddfa Gurig.

LLANEIGON see **LLANIGON**

LLANEILIAN Angl SH4792
'church of Eilian', ***llan***, pers.n. ***Eilian***
Lanellen 1254, *Lanelen'* 1291, *llannelyan* 1392, *ch. of St. Hilary alias Llanelien* 1452, *St Elien, Llanelien* 1452, *in the town of Llanelien* 1470, *ll. eilian* c.1566, *Llan Elian* 1634, *Llanelian* 1795, *Llaneilian* 1838
The saint's name varies between Eilian and Elian; cf. Llanelian-yn-Rhos. The saint was also regularly confused with St Hilary of Poitiers. Here, other features also commemorate the saint, such as Ffynnon Eilian (*Ffynon Elian* 1801, ***ffynnon***), Porth Eilian (*Porth Elian* 1536-9, *Aelynus Bay* 1801, *Portheilian* 1806, *Porth Elian* 1813, ***porth***) and Trwyn Eilian (q.v.).

LLANEIRWG see **ST MELLONS**

LLANELEN, LLANELLEN Monm SO3010
'church of Elen', ***llan***, pers.n. ***Elen***
St. Helen 1100-6, *Sancta Elena* 1254, *Lan Elan* 1349, *Lanelyn* 1385, *ll. elen* c.1566
The church is now dedicated to Helen, possibly the empress St Helen (c.255-c.330) reputed to have been born in Britain.

LLANELEU, LLANELIEU Brec SO1834
'church at (a stream) Gelyw', ***llan***, ?r.n. ***Gelyw***
Langelen 1148-?55, *Langeleu* 1210, *Langelew, Langelow* c.1285-90, *Llanelewyth* 1406, *Llaneliw* 1482, *Llanelyw* 1587
Earlier forms suggest an older name of the stream flowing through the village (*Nant Elwe* 1561, *Ellyw* 1891 but now unnamed on maps) possibly an original *Gelyw, which satisfies the Llanelyw forms (with lenition) but not the earlier *Langeleu*. One suggestion is that there was early substitution of ***nant*** 'valley' for ***llan***, still surviving in some

fashion in *Nant Elwe* 1561. The later forms such as *Llaneliw* 1482, *Llan Eliw* 1541-3, *Llanelyw* 1587 may then be regarded as corrections (with lenition) under the influence of a genuine church dedication (as in *Llanelewyth* 1406) to Eiliwedd (*Eilïueth* 11cent., *Elinedd verch Vrychan* 13cent.), a daughter of the legendary Brychan Brycheiniog, and whose sister Gwen has a dedication in the adjoining parish of Talgarth. Most forms recorded after c.1400 indicate a church dedicated to an Elyw (the current church dedication).

LLANELIAN-YN-RHOS Denb SH8676

'church of Elian in Rhos', ***llan***, pers.n. ***Elian***, ***yn***, commote n. ***Rhos***
Ll. elian 1556-64, *ll. eilian* c.1566, *llanelian* 1590,
llanelian yn Rhos 1600-1, *Lhan Elian* c.1700, *Llanelian* 1840
The pers.n., a dial. var. of Eilian, is also seen in Ffynnon Elian (*Ffynnon Elian* c.1700, ***ffynnon***) and Mynydd Elian (*Mynydh Elian* c.1700, ***mynydd***). The qualifying location of Llanelian-yn-Rhos with the commote name Rhos is infrequently used in local usage.

LLANELIDAN Denb SJ1050

'church of Elidan', ***llan***, pers.n. ***Elidan***
Llanhelidan 1207, *Lanelidan* 1254, *Llanelidan* 1390
Very little is known of this saint.

LLANELIEU see **LLANELEU**

LLANELLEN see **LLANELEN**

LLANELLI[1] Brec SO2314

'church of Elli', ***llan***, pers.n. ***Elli***
Llanelly 1518-24, *Llannelly* 1540, *ll. elli* c.1566
Elli was said to be a 5cent. disciple of Cadog (of Llangadog Carm and Llangattock/Llangatwg Brec) recorded in the 12cent. Life of St Cadog. Unfamiliarity with Elli may account for the uncertainty of the church dedication given variously as Elli, Ellyw and Almeda. Llanelli was probably a chapel within the parish of Llangatwg and warranting few mentions in early historical sources,. Elli has been misidentified as a daughter of Brychan through confusion with Eiliwedd (see Llanelyw).

LLANELLI[2] Carm SN5000

'church of Elli', ***llan***, pers.n. ***Elli***
lann elli 1160-85, *Sancti Eclini* 1149-83, *monasterium Elli* c.1200,
Lanetly 1291, *Lanelthy* 1361, *ll. elli* c.1566
Probably the same saint as Llanelli[1] (q.v.). There was a well *ffynnon elli* 1604 (***ffynnon***).

LLANELLTUD Mer SH7119

'church of Elltud', ***llan***, pers.n. ***Ulltud***

Llanhuldut 1269, *llaunvlldit* 13cent., *Llanvlltud* 1415-16, *Llan Ulltyd* 1543, *ll. ylldyd* c.1566, *llenelltyd alias llanylltid* 1574

Variants of the saint's name are Ulltud, Elltud and Illtud (cf. Llantwit Major and Ilston).

LLANELWEDD Radn SO0451

'church of Elwedd', ***llan***, pers.n. ***Elwedd***

Lanelweth 1283, *Thannelwyt* 1291, *LL.elwedd* c.1560-66

Elwedd has been identified with Eiliwedd, one of the legendary twenty-five daughters of Brychan Brycheiniog (see Brecon) but this is uncertain.

LLANELWY see **ST ASAPH**

LLANENDDWYN Mer SH5723

'church of Enddwyn', ***llan***, pers.n. ***Enddwyn***

Lanendewyn 1292-3, *Lannendoyn* 1308-9, *Lanenddwyn* 1400, *Llanenddwyn alias Llanenwin* 1574

The well, Ffynnon Enddwyn (***ffynnon***), was credited with healing powers and in these legends Enddwyn is female.

LLANENGAN Caern SH2926

'church of Einion', ***llan***, pers.n. ***Einion***

Llaneign 1291, *Laneignon* 1352, *Llaneynon* 1441-50, *ll. engain frenin* c.1566, *Llaneingan* 1680, *Llanengan* 1733

The forms of the pers.n. vary between *Eingion* and *Engan* (and modern Einion) probably influenced by ***engan*** 'anvil'. The c.1566 reference is to Engain or Einion Frenin (***brenin*** 'king') a reputed grandson or great-grandson of Cunedda Wledig who ruled Llŷn and to whom the church was dedicated. Above the doorway is the early 16cent. inscription *Aeniani Rex Wallie*. Ffynnon Engan (***ffynnon***) is adjacent to the church.

LLANERFYL Mont SJ0309

'church of Eurfyl', ***llan***, pers.n. ***Eurfyl***

Llanurvyl 1254, *Lanneruel* 1271, *Thlanarvuell* 1286, *Lanurvyl* 1291, *Llannurvel* 1322, *Llanurvyll* 1406, *LL.vrfvl ynghaer Enion* c.1562, *Llanervill* 1667

This may be the female saint Urfyl (*vrvyl* 1488), reputedly a daughter of Padarn. There is a well dedicated to her (Ffynnon Erfyl) north-west of the church, and an early Christian stone in the churchyard has been associated with her.

LLANEURGAIN see **NORTHOP**

LLANFABLE see **LLANVAPLEY**

LLANFABON Glam ST1093

'church of Mabon', ***llan***, pers.n. ***Mabon***

Llanvabon 1457, *ll. fabon* c.1566, *Lanvabon* 1596-1600

The pers.n. was common enough (cf. Ruabon) and need not refer to a saint, but be a church dedication arising from a secular name. It has also been suggested that the p.n. has the name of a nearby stream Nant Mafon (see Llandeilo'r-fân).

LLANFACHES, LLANVACHES Monm ST4391

'church of Maches', ***llan***, pers.n. ***Maches***

merthirmaches 1136-54, *Lanmaueis* 1193-1218, *Lanmaes* 1254, *Lanmagheys* 1310, *ll. faches* c.1566

llan has replaced ***merthyr*** as in Llandegfedd (q.v). Maches was reputedly the daughter of Gwynllyw, after whom the cantref of Gwynllŵg (Wentloog) Monm was named.

LLANFACHRAETH Angl SH3182

'church of Machraith', ***llan***, pers.n. ***Machraith***

Lanwacreyt 1254, *Lanvachraeth* 1389, *llanvachraith* 1406, *ll. fachraith* c.1566, *Llanvachreth* 1697, *Llanfachreth* 1838, *Llanfachraeth* 1891

The saint's name Machraith has undergone two modifications. *Llanvachreth* 1697 parallels the Mer Llanfachreth (q.v.), while Llanfachraeth (commonly used locally and already anticipated in *Lanvachraeth* 1389) reflects the confusion of *-aith* and *-aeth* in pronunciation and in spelling, possibly influenced by ***traeth*** 'shore'. Cf. Cemais > Cemaes Angl.

LLANFACHRETH Mer SH7522

'church of Machraith', ***llan***, pers.n. ***Machraith***

Landacreyt 1254, *Llanvachrayth* 1400, *ll. fachraith* c.1566, *Llanvaghreth* 1695

The pers.n. Machraith has a dial. var. Machreth; cf. Llanfachraeth.

LLANFAELOG Angl SH3373

'church of Maelog', ***llan***, pers.n. ***Maelog***

Lanvalac 1254, *Llan Vaylog* 1536-9, *ll. vaelog* 1590-1, *Llanfaelog* 1763

Maelog appears in Llyn Maelog (***llyn***) and Ffynnon Faelog (***ffynnon***).

LLANFAELRHYS Caern SH2126

'church of Maelrhys', ***llan***, pers.n. ***Maelrhys***

p. valrys c.1566, *Ll. vaelrhys* 1590, *Llanvaelrhys* 1688, *Llanfaelrhys* 1765

This is the only church dedicated to Maelrhys, whose well, Ffynnon Faelrys (***ffynnon***), is in the area. Two prehistoric longstones are called

Lladron Maelrhys ('robbers of Maelrhys', ***lleidr*** pl. ***lladron***) which legend maintains to be petrified thieves who had stolen from Llanfaelrhys church.

LLAN-FAES[1] Angl SH6077

'church in open country', ***llan, maes***

Lanmaes 1199 (1332), *Lammaes* 1247 (1295), *Lanways* 1254, *Lanmaess* 1291, *lanmaes* 13cent. (14cent.), *Lammays* 1304-5, *llan vaes* 1375-80, *Llanfaes* 1763

The stress seems always to have fallen on ***maes*** (as indicated by modern orthography). One explanation is that a church in such an open location was unusual (compared to the neighbouring Llangoed). However, ***maes*** (< ***ma, -es***) was disyllabic until the 12cent. at the latest, so that *llan ma-es* would have had regular stress on the second syllable which was retained as final stress in the name Llan-faes (when ***ma-es*** became ***maes***). The name provides evidence of woodland clearing (here associated with the role of Llan-faes as a commercial centre in the 13cent.). It has been tentatively suggested that the ***maes*** could be Maes Osfeilion or Ysweilion (*maes osmeliawn* 902, *Maes Osswyliawn* 16 cent.) referring to Ysfael son of Cunedda. Such an explanation could go some way to explain the lack of lenition in the early documentary forms, by postulating a form such as *Llan Maes Osfeilion* 'the church in Maes Osfeilion'.

LLAN-FAES[2] Brec SO0328

'church in open country', ***llan, maes***

(*Gueith*) *Lannmaes* 817 (c.1000), *Landmais* c.1100, *Lameis* c.1163-74, *llann uaes* c.1180 (c.1400), *Launvays by Bregenogh* 1280, *ll. vaes dewi* c.1566, *St.David juxta Brecon* 1535

The church is dedicated to Dewi/David. The dial. pronunciation is 'Lan-veis'.

LLANFAETHLU Angl SH3186

'church of Maethlu', ***llan***, pers.n. ***Maethlu***

Lanwahllu 1254, *Llanvaythlue* 1528, *ll. faethly* c.1566, *Llanfaethlu* 1838

A former medieval chapel near Plas Ucha was also dedicated to Maethlu as is a farm Bryn Maethlu north of the village.

LLANFAGLAN Caern SH4760

'church of Baglan', ***llan***, pers.n. ***Baglan***

Bamvagan 1284, *Llanvaglan* 1306, *Llanbaglan* 1396, *Llan Vaglan* 1535, *Llanfagdalen* 1796, *Llanfaglan* 1809-11

The church is dedicated to Baglan ab Dingad (the same name, but not the same person, as Baglan Glam). The name was occasionally confused with Magdalen (as in 1796 above) but probably in literary or ecclestiastical documents only rather than in local usage.

LLAN-FAIR see **ST MARY CHURCH**

LLANFAIR Mer SH5729

'church of Mair', ***llan***, pers.n. ***Mair***

Lanmeir-in-Ardudoe c.1191, *Lanueyr* 1292-3, *Llanvayr* 1400, *ll. fair* c.1566, *Llanvayr juxta Hardlagh* 1535, *Llanvayer Ardwdye*) 1573, *llannvair yn ardudwy* 1565-87, *Llanfair-juxta-Harlech* modern

Although the modern name lacks any distinguishing qualification, earlier forms locate it as being 'in (the commote of) Ardudwy' and 'near Harlech'.

LLANFAIR-AR-Y-BRYN Carm SN7735

'church of Mair on the hill', ***llan***, pers.n. ***Mair***, ***ar***, ***y***, ***bryn***

Lanveyr 1316, *Llanvayre ar y bryn* 1546, *ll. fair y bryn* c.1566, *Llanvair ar y Brynn* 1567

Llanfair-ar-y-bryn is on a low hill overlooking Llandovery.

LLANFAIR CAEREINION Mont SJ1006

'church of Mair in Caereinion', ***llan***, pers.n. ***Mair***, cantref n. ***Caereinion***

Llanveyr 1254, *Lanveyr in Kereynon* 1281-2, *Llanvaire* 1535, *ll. fair* c.1566, *Llanvair in Krynion* 1579, *Llanvayer in Kaereinion* 1593-4

Distinguished by its location in the cantref of Caereinion (*Keiriniaun* 1263); see also Castell Caereinion.

LLANFAIR CLYDOGAU Card SN6251

'church of Mair at the Clywedog rivers', ***llan***, pers.n. ***Mair***, r.n. ***Clywedog*** pl. ***Clydogau***

Lanvair Cloydogey 1507, *Llanveirglydogey* 1517, *ll. fair gylydoge* c.1566, *Lhanvair y Clydoge*, *Lhanvair Clywedogau* c.1700, *Llanvair alias Llanfair-clydogy* 1772, *Llanfair Clydogau* 1834

Three tributaries of Nant Clywedog meet a mile to the east of the village.

LLANFAIR DYFFRYN CLWYD Denb SJ1355

'church of Mair in the vale of Clwyd', ***llan***, pers.n. ***Mair***, ***dyffryn***, r.n. ***Clwyd***

Lanweyr 1254, *Lanveyr* 1291, *Llanvair in Diffrencloyt* 1386, *ll. fair ynyfryn klwyd* c.1566, *Lhan Vair Dyffrin Cloyd* 1664, *Llanfair Dyffryn Clwyd* 1838

The original dedication was to Cynfarch (the *Sanctus Kynvarch* at one time named in one of the church windows). The re-dedication to Mair prompted the addition of the church's location in the vale of Clwyd. Dyffryn Clwyd was also the name of the hundred.

LLANFAIRFECHAN Caern SH6874

'little church of Mair', ***llan***, pers.n. ***Mair***, ***bychan*** fem. ***bechan***

Lannueyr 1254, *Lanueyr* 1284, *Llanvayr* 1291, *Llanvair Vechan* 1475, *ll. fair fechan* c.1566

This church was distinguished from the larger church of Mair at Conwy some five miles away.

LLANFAIR LLYTHYNWG see **GLADESTRY**

LLANFAIR PWLLGWYNGYLL Angl SH5371

'church of Mair in Pwllgwyngyll', ***llan***, pers.n. ***Mair***, tnshp n. ***Pwllgwyngyll***

Piwllgunyl 1254, *Llan Vair y pwll Gwinghill* 1536-9, *ll. fair ymhwll gwingill* c.1566, *Llanvayrpwllgwingill* 1653, *Llanfair-pwllgwyngyll* 1838

The church overlooks an inlet in the Menai Strait. The popularity of churches called Llanfair necessitated a defining location, in this case the tnshp of Pwllgwyngyll (*Piwllgunyl* 1254, *Pullgwingill* 1543). There is documentary evidence of white hazel (***gwyn***, ***coll*** pl. ***cyll***) in the vicinity. The internationally celebrated addition -gogerychwyrndrobwll-llantysiliogogogoch is little more than a fanciful appendage deliberately coined to ensure continued prominence for a temporary railway station and freight yard about to become redundant following completion in 1850 of the Britannia Bridge (locally Pont Llanfair). A tailor from Menai Bridge (one Thomas Hughes who died in 1890) is credited with the fabrication which is based on features in the immediate landscape. The els are ***go*** 'somewhat', ***ger*** 'near', ***y*** 'the', ***chwyrn*** 'wild', ***trobwll*** the 'whirlpool' of Pwll Ceris in the Menai Strait; *Llantysilio* is an allusion to the church of Llandysilio on Ynys Tysilio or Church Island near Menai Bridge, while the tag *-gogogoch* is partly an echo of Llandysiliogogo Card (q.v.) and partly a hint at Ynys Gorad Goch in the Strait.

LLANFAIR TALHAEARN Denb SH9270

'church of Mair (associated with) Talhaearn', ***llan***, pers.n. ***Mair***, pers.n. ***Talhaearn***

Llannber 1254, *Lanveyr'dalhaern, Lanveyr' Dalhaeyn* 1291, *Llanvair Dalhaearn* 1390, *ll. fair ddol hayarn* c.1566, *Llanvair Talhayarne* 1632, *Llanvair Dôl Hayarn* c.1700, *Llanfair Talhaiarn* 1839

The frequency of churches dedicated to Mair necessitated identification, in this case by reference to Talhaearn who was possibly a lay patron. The lenited older form *Llanfair Dalhaearn* gave rise to the occasional perception that the p.n. comprised ***dôl*** 'meadow' and ***haearn*** 'iron'.

LLANFAIR-YM-MUALLT see **BUILTH**

LLANFAIR-YNG-NGHORNWY Angl SH3290

'church of Mair in Cornwy', ***llan***, pers.n. ***Mair***, ***yn***, p.n. ***Cornwy***
Lanweyt 1254, *Lanvair* 1346-7, *Llan Vair in Kowrney* 16cent., *ll. fair ynghowrnwy* c.1566, *Lanvair y Kowrney* 1543, *Llanfair ynghornwy* 1660, *Llanfair ynghornwy* 1838
In Llanfair-yng-Nghornwy, Cornwy is possibly a tribal name (with a terr. suff. -***wy***) which also became the name of the medieval tnshp Cornwy (*Kanrywy* 1284, *Gawrnwy* 14cent., *Cowrney* 16cent., *Kowrnwy* c.1650). It has been suggested that Cornwy refers to inhabitants of the north-west corner (***corn*** 'horn, point') of Anglesey although the early forms do not seem to support ***corn***. Cf. Llanfihangel Rhos-y-corn.

LLANFAIR-YN-NEUBWLL Angl SH3076

'church of Mair in Deubwll', ***llan***, pers.n. ***Mair***, ***yn***, tnship n. ***Deubwll***
llanvayre 1399, *Lla(n)vair in nybull* 1543, *ll. fair ynebwll* c.1566, *Llanvair-yn-neubwll* 1660, *Llanfair* 1890
Deubwll (*Wlpulh* 1254) was the tnshp but also seems to have been used of the church and parish. The distinguishing location refers to Llyn Dinam and Llyn Penrhyn, now lakes (***llyn***), earlier described as two pools (***dau***, ***pwll***).

LLANFALLTEG Carm SN1519

'church of Ballteg', ***llan***, pers.n. ***Ballteg***
Landenayth'teg' 1326 (16cent.), *Llanvallteg* 1338 (c.1700), *Llanvallteg* 1499, *LLam Valdec* c.1500, *Llanbaltege* 1535
The pers.n. may be Mallteg (the present church dedication) or Ballteg indicated by the 1535 form and in Rhiw Bylltig, the name of the mound on which the church stands (with ***rhiw***, 'slope'). The 1326 form probably represents 'Landevayth'teg' which may possibly suggest the honorific ***ty-*** often prefixed to saints' names.

LLANFAREDD Radn SO0750

'church of Mareth', ***llan***, pers.n. ***Mareth***
Thlannarreyt 1291, *Llanevarreth* 1543, *ll. varaith* c.1566, *Llanverreth* 1559
Most spellings before the 18cent. suggest the form Mareth rather than Maredd; another possible var. of the saint's name was *Mariaith* (15cent.). The church is now dedicated to Mary/Mair, probably based on the similarity of Mareth/Maredd and Mary/Mair.

LLANFARIAN, PENTRE-BONT Card SN5877

'gravel stream', 'village at the bridge', ***nant***, ***marian***, ***pentref***, (***y***), ***pont***
Llanvarian 1641, *Pen y Bont Llanychaiarn* 1816, *Pentre Bont* 1819, *Pentre'r-bont* 1834, *Pentre-bont* 1890, *Llanfarian* 1895

Since Llanfarian was a tnshp and lacked a church, this seems to be one of several p.ns where ***llan*** has possibly replaced an earlier ***nant*** although there is no documentary evidence for such an assertion. Distinctive gravel banks may still be seen from the bridge. An alternative suggestion is for ***llain*** 'strip of land'. The later alias Pentre-bont refers to Pont Llanychaearn (*Pontllanychaiarn, Pont Llanchaiarn* 1803), so called since Afon Ystwyth which flows under the bridge separates the parishes of Llanbadarn and Llanychaearn.

LLANFARTHIN see **LLANMARTIN**

LLANFECHAIN Mont SJ1820

'church in Mechain', ***llan***, cantref n. ***Mechain***
Llanveccheyn 1254, *Llannetheyn* 1291, *Thlannegheyn* 1338,
llan uechann 12cent. (c.1400), *Llaunvecheyn* 1407,
ll. armon ymechain c.1566, *Llanvechen* 1577, *Llanvechan* 1585
Many forms seem to show association with ***bechan*** in its fem. form ***fechan*** 'small, little', encouraged perhaps by the shortening of the diphthong -ai-, -ei- to -a-, -e-. The church is dedicated to Garmon, with his well Ffynnon Armon 300 yards to the south-east; there is also a castle here, Twmpath Garmon 'Garmon's mound' (***twmpath***). The cantref name Mechain (*Methein* late 13cent., *Mechen, -eyn* 1278, *Comm. Meycheyn* 1536-9) is 'area or territory on (the river) Cain' (***ma*** and r.n. ***Cain*** *kein* c.1197, *Cain* 1704, *the Cain* 1783).

LLANFECHELL Angl SH3691

'church of Mechyll', ***llan***, pers.n. ***Mechyll***
Lanwechil 1254, *Lanvechyl* 1291, *llanveghyll* 1392-3, *llanvechyll* 1428,
llanveghelle 1478-9, *ll. fechell* c.1566, *llanfechell* 1640
The form of the saint's name seems to have been changed from Mechyll to Mechell (possibly for obscure antiquarian reasons). The name also appears in Mynydd Mechell to the south-west.

LLANFENDIGAID Mer SH5605

'church of the blessed', ***llan***, ***bendigaid***
Lamendyget 1292-3, *Lanuendygeyt* 1326, *llanvendiget* 1453,
llanvendigaid 1592
The significance of ***bendigaid*** is not clear. There may have been a third el. now lost (such as 'Mair' or 'Forwyn' (Virgin) or 'Drindod' (Trinity)). By 1795 it was a farmed mansion and the church is no more.

LLANFERRES Denb SJ1860

'church of Berreis', ***llan***, pers.n. ***Berreis***
Lanwerteys 1254, *Lanuerr[es]* 1283, *Lanverreys* 1291, *Llanverreys* 1310,
Llan Verreis 1557, *ll. ferrys* c.1566, *Llanverreis* 1664,
Llysickill alias Llanferres 1699, *Lhan Verres* c.1700

The identity of Berreis is unknown. Reconstructive conjecture has dedicated the church to St Britius. The 1699 alias refers to the ancient tnshp of Llys-y-cil (*llysykil* 1353, *Llisikillth* 1391, ***llys*** 'court, house', ***y*** 'the', ***cil*** 'corner, nook'). Another name for Llys-y-cil tnshp (which was almost as extensive as the parish of Llanferres itself) was Tre'r-llan (***tref***, ***yr*** 'the', ***llan*** 'church').

LLANFEUGAN see **LLANFIGAN**

LLAN FFESTINIOG see **FFESTINIOG**

LLANFFLEWIN Angl SH3589

'church of Fflewin', ***llan***, pers.n. ***Fflewin***

Lanflewin 1254, *llanflewyn* 1335, *ll. fflewyn* c.1566, *Llanfflewyn* 1689, *Llanfflewin* 1838

The pers.n. Fflewin occurs only in this p.n. He was reputedly the son of Ithel Hael who came to Wales from Brittany in the 5cent.; other sources also maintain his brothers were Tygái (see Llandygái), Trillo (see Llandrillo) and his sister Llechid (see Llanllechid). The Llanfflewyn spelling is still retained on maps.

LLAN-FFWYST see **LLANFOIST**

LLANFIGAN, LLANFEUGAN Brec SO0824

'church of Meugan', ***llan***, pers.n. ***Meugan***

St. Meugan 1251, *Sco. Moygano* 1513, *Llan Migan* 1522, *Llanvygan* 1543, *ll. feygan* c.1566, *Llanvigan* 1558

Possibly the same saint as at Capel Meugan Angl and Llanfeugan Pemb. A *Meugant ap Kyndaf* is recorded in 12cent. (16cent.).

LLANFIHANGEL ABERBYTHYCH, GOLDEN GROVE, GELLI AUR Carm SN5819

'church of Mihangel at the mouth of (the stream) Bythych', ***llan***, pers.n. ***Mihangel***, ***aber***, r.n. ***Bythych***

Aberbetthek c.1291, *Sancti Machaelis de Abvichurch* 1535, *Llanvyhangell Aberbuthick* 1555, *ll. V'el aber bythych* c.1566

The name of the house and agricultural college of Golden Grove/Gelli Aur (*Goldengroue* 1577, *Golden Grove* 1588-9, *y Gelli Aur* 1596, ***y***, ***celli***, ***aur***) is a frequent substitution locally. The r.n. Bythych is uncertain but may be related to ***byth*** 'ever, always' in the sense of a stream whose flow was continuous throughout the year. The early forms suggest *Bythig* (with the adj. suff. *-ig*) rather than Bythych.

LLANFIHANGEL-AR-ARTH Carm SN4539

'church of Mihangel on the high wooded slope', ***llan***, pers.n. ***Mihangel***, ***gor***, ***garth***

Llanvyhangel Orarth 1291, *Llanvyhangelorarth* 1395, *Llanvihangel Yerrorth* 1514, *St. Michael of Orroth* 1551, *Llanvihangell ararth* 1553, *ll. V'el Joroth* c.1566, *Llanvihangell Yeroth* 1580, *Llanfihangel ar Ararth* 1811

Forty-five p.ns in Wales have churches dedicated to Mihangel/Michael the archangel. This church was originally called *Llanfihangel Orarth* but the intensifying pref. ***gor*** was later influenced by *Iorath* and *Yorath*, vars of Iorwerth, and ultimately with ***ar*** 'on', a form which did not become established until the 19cent.

LLANFIHANGEL BRYNPABUAN Brec SN9856

'church of Mihangel at Pabuan's hill', ***llan***, pers.n. ***Mihangel***, ***bryn***, pers.n. ***Pabuan***

Laivyhangel 1299, *Llanvehangyll Brympabean* 1543, *Llanviangell bryn pabian* 1545, *ll. V'el bryn payn* c.1566, *Pryn Pabean* 1578, *Llanvihangel Brynpabean* 1585

The church is on a low hill above the river Chwefru. The unfamiliarity of the pers.n. Pabuan prompted alternative imaginative forms such as *Llanvihangel pompren Bevan* 1773 (***pompren*** 'footbridge', pers.n. ***Bevan***) and the local perception that Pabuan stood for *Pab Ieuan* 'Pope John'.

LLANFIHANGEL CRUCORNAU see **LLANVIHANGEL CRUCORNEY**

LLANFIHANGEL DYFFRYN ARWY see **MICHAELCHURCH-ON-ARROW**

LLANFIHANGEL GLYN MYFYR Denb SH9949

'church of Mihangel in the valley of Myfyr', ***llan***, pers.n. ***Mihangel***, ***glyn***, pers.n. ***Myfyr***

Llanwihagel 1254, *Lamyangel* c.1292-3, *Llanvyhangel Llenmyvyr* 1388, *ll. V'el llyn myfyr* c.1566, *Llanvihangell llyn Myver* 1614, *Llanvihangel Glyn nigfyr* 1691, *Llanvehangel Llun Myfur* 1727, *Llanfihangel-Glyn-Myfyr* 1851

The church and village are on the west bank of Afon Alwen which has a wide pool at this point, downstream of the bridge which carries several routes across the river. The pool is the original ***llyn*** found in the historical forms (*'Lhyn Myvyr is ye name only of a pool on Alwen.... just under ye churchyard wall'* c.1700). The change from ***llyn*** to ***glyn*** was prompted by the fairly narrow valley through which Afon Alwen flows providing a qualifying location because of the fairly popular dedications to Mihangel/Michael. The identity of Myfyr is unknown.

LLANFIHANGEL HELYGEN Radn SO0464

'church of Mihangel at the willow-tree', ***llan***, pers.n. ***Mihangel***, ***helygen***

Llanvehangell 1544, *Llanihangell Yelegen* 1556, *Llangyhangell Religen* 1559, *ll. V'el fach* c.1566, *Llanvihangel Helegen* 1587

helygen may be employed elliptically to describe a wet area or an area close to a stream where willow-trees grow. The church is close to Pentre Brook. The additional qualifier ***bach*** may describe either the size of the church or its status as a chapel-of-ease to Nantmel.

LLANFIHANGEL NANT BRÂN Brec SN9434

'church of Mihangel in the valley of (the stream) Brân', ***llan***, pers.n. ***Mihangel***, ***nant***, r.n. ***Brân***

Sancti Michaelis de Nantbrane 1503, *Nantbrane* 1538, *Llanihangell nant bran* c.1547, *LL. fihangel nant bran* c.1562

The r.n. (*Bran*, *-e* 1326, *Nant-bran* 1836) is also found in the name of the manor (*Braan* 1379). W ***brân*** 'crow, rook' may allude to the dark waters of the stream.

LLANFIHANGEL NANT MELAN Radn SO1858

'church of Mihangel in Nant Melan', ***llan***, pers.n. ***Mihangel***, ***nant***, r.n. ***Melan***

Sancti Michaelis de Nantmelan 1176-98, *St. Michael of Nantmelan* 1231, *St. Michael, Llanmelan* 1398, *Mychelchurche* c.1545, *ll. V'el nan melan* c.1566

Described simply as the parish of *nant melan* 1447-89, *Nantmelan* 1543. Melan also occurs in the name of the lake *Lhyn maes melan* c.1700 near Maesmelan farm and seems to be the former name of the stream Summergill Brook. The r.n. is probably ***mêl*** 'honey, sweet' and the dim.suff. ***-an***.

LLANFIHANGEL RHOS-Y-CORN Carm SN5534

'church of Mihangel at Rhos-y-corn', ***llan***, pers.n. ***Mihangel***, p.n. ***Rhos-y-corn***

Llan Viangel Roscornewe 1388, *Llanvyhangel Yscorney* 1400, *Llanvihangel Roscorne* 1540s, *Llanvihangell rosecorn* 1599, *St. Michael Roscorny o. Llanvyhangell Rhoscorny* 1632, *Llanvihangel Rhos-y-corn* 1757

The church is on a hill in a heavily wooded area, and Rhos-y-corn has the plausible meaning of 'promontory at the hill' (***rhos*** 'promontory' rather than 'moor', ***y*** 'the' and ***corn*** 'horn, cone'). However, earlier forms such as *Roscornewe* 1388, *Roscornowe* 1395 indicate that the original name was **Cornyw* or **Cornwy*, perhaps a territorial name (itself perhaps ***corn*** and the terr.suff. ***-wy***), later replaced by the sing. ***corn***. Cf. Llanfair-yng-Nghornwy and Llanvihangel Crucorney.

LLANFIHANGEL RHYDITHON, LLANFIHANGEL RHYDIEITHON Radn SO1566

'church of Mihangel near a ford on (the river) Ieithon', ***llan***, pers.n. ***Mihangel***, ***rhyd***, r.n. ***Ieithon***

Langmiclen 1291, *Thlan Mihangel Redyethan* 1304, *Llanvyangell ridythan* c.1545, *ll. V'el Rydeithion* c.1566

The church lies more than three miles from the nearest point of the river Ieithon/Ithon suggesting that Rhydieithon once applied to a much larger area or perhaps to a ford through the nearby river Cymaron (Aran on maps) or the stream Merwys in the village but on a route leading to the river Ieithon.

LLANFIHANGEL TAL-Y-LLYN[1] Brec SO1128

'church of Mihangel at the end of the lake', ***llan***, pers.n. ***Mihangel***, ***tâl***, ***y***, ***llyn***

Lan Mihangel c.1100, (*villa*) *Sancti Michael* early 12cent., *Myghhelchirche* 1403, *Sci Michaelis juxta marā* 1486, *ll. V'el tal y llyn* c.1566

The village is located about one mile from Llyn Syfaddan/Llan-gors Lake.

LLANFIHANGEL TAL-Y-LLYN[2] Mer SH7009

'church of Mihangel at Tal-y-llyn', ***llan***, pers.n. ***Mihangel***, p.n. ***Tal-y-llyn***

Llanvihangell Talyllyn 1535, *Lanviangell Talyllyn* 1545, *Llanfihangel tal y llyn* 1832

This church (actually dedicated to Mair) was at the south-east of Llyn Myngul (***myngul*** 'narrow-necked') now commonly referred to as Tal-y-llyn Lake. The whole area has regularly been called Tal-y-llyn (*Tayley llyn* 1529, *Tal y llynn* 1565-87, *Tal-y-lin* 1680, ***tâl***, ***y***, ***llyn***, 'end of the lake').

LLANFIHANGEL TRODDI see **MITCHEL TROY**

LLANFIHANGEL-UWCH-GWILI Carm SN4822

'church of Mihangel above (the river) Gwili', ***llan***, pers.n. ***Mihangel***, ***uwch***, r.n. ***Gwili***

Lanvyhangell Llez Veiler 1395, *Llanvihangle ywch gwilly* 1585, *Llanfihangel Uwch Gwili* 1811

The 1395 reference is to an unknown Llech Feilir (***llech*** 'slab', pers.n. ***Meilir***). Uwch-Gwili is a later qualifier although the village is four miles up the Tywi valley from the confluence of the rivers Tywi and Gwili.

LLANFIHANGEL-Y-CREUDDYN Card SN6676

'church of Mihangel in Creuddyn', ***llan***, pers.n. ***Mihangel***, ***y***, commote n. ***Creuddyn***

Thlanvyhangel in Cruthyn, Thlanmyhangel en Crythuyn 1295,

ll. V'el y kreyddyn c.1566, *Llanvyhangell Croythin* 1578, *Llanfihangel-y-Creiddyn* 1834
The commote is Creuddyn (*Crewdin* 1279, *Creudyn* 1281) which is ***crau*** 'defence' and ***dynn*** 'enclosure'. Some forms record the dial. var. Crouddyn. One alias for the church and village, Llanfihangel Gelynrod (*Llann Vihagel Gelynrot* 1254 [c.1400], *Llanvyhaellkelynrode* 1390, *Llanvihangell Gelynred* 1535, *Llan-Fihangel y Croythin alias Gelindrode* 1763) referred to the tnshp Celynrod (*Kelenroyth* 1298-1300, *Kellonrod* 1361, ***celyn*** and ***rhod*** 'circle of holly trees').

LLANFIHANGEL-YNG-NGHERI see **KERRY**

LLANFIHANGEL-YNG-NGWYNFA Mont SJ0816
'church of Mihangel in Gwynfa', ***llan***, pers.n. ***Mihangel***, ***yn***, terr.n. ***Gwynfa***
Llanvihangel 1254, *Lamvyhangell in Gwunva* 1375, *Llanvehangel Ygonva* 1393, *Llanehangell Ywynfa* 1545, *Lanyhangell in Gounvae* 1547, *ll. V'el yngwynfa* c.1566
Gwynfa, probably 'fair (or blessed) land' (***gwyn***, ***-ma***), covered an area extending as far as the mill Melin Wynfa on Nant Llwydiarth (*Guinna, Guynna, Methelyn* [= *Melyn*] *Guynna* 1309, *melin wonva, Melin gwnva* 1588, *Melin-wnfa* 1836). There are also references in medieval poetry to *Dreic Wynua* (c.1155-87, ***draig*** 'dragon').

LLANFIHANGEL-YN-NHYWYN Angl SH3176
'church of Mihangel in Tywyn', ***llan***, pers.n. ***Mihangel***, ***yn***, area n. ***Tywyn***
Llanvihangell in Towyn 1535, *Llanvihangel* 1543, *ll. V'el yn howyn* c.1566, *Llanfihangel-yn-Howyn* 1851
The area was known as Tywyn or Tywyn Trewan (*Towyn Trewan* c.1700, *Towyn Trewan* 1795, *Tywyn tre wan* 1838) from its sandy character (***tywyn*** 'sand-dune') and probably ***tref*** and the pers.n. Owain. A common var. is the spelling *Towyn*. One alias *Llan Vihegel yn y traethe* 1536-9, was perhaps influenced by Llanfihangel-y-traethau (q.v.) with ***traeth*** pl. ***traethau*** but there is no other evidence for such an alternative.

LLANFIHANGEL YNYS AFAN see **CWMAFAN**

LLANFIHANGEL-Y-PENNANT[1] Caern SH5244
'church of Mihangel in Pennant', ***llan***, ***Mihangel***, ***y***, tnshp n. ***Pennant***
Ippēnant 1291, *Llanvihangell Y Pennaunt* 1535, *ll. V'el y pēnant* c.1566, *Llanvihangel y Pennant* 1685-6, *Llanfihangel-y-Pennant* 1795
(Y) Pennant was the name of a tnshp in the long valley known as Cwm Pennant (***pennant*** 'head of a valley').

LLANFIHANGEL-Y-PENNANT[2] Mer SH6709
'church of Mihangel in Pennant', ***llan***, pers.n. ***Mihangel***, ***y***, tnshp n. ***Pennant***
Beati Michaelis 1254, *Llamyhangel* 1292-3, *Llanvihangel* 1327-8, *ll. V'el y pēnant* 1566, *Llanvihengel y Pennant* 1662
Llanfihangel-y-Pennant is distinguished by its location in the tnshp of Pennant which probably took its name from Mynydd Pennant at the head (***pennant***) of the Dysynni valley.

LLANFIHANGEL YSTRAD see **YSTRADAERON**

LLANFIHANGEL-Y-TRAETHAU Mer SH5935
'church of Mihangel at the beaches', ***llan***, pers.n. ***Mihangel***, ***y***, ***traeth*** pl. ***traethau***
Nanmyhangeletrayth 1284, *Lamyhangel apud Traythe* 1292-3, *Lanmihangel* 1325-6, *Llanvyhangell y Traythe* 1455, *Llanvihangel y traethe* 1695, *Llanfihangel-y-traethau* 1838
Distinguished by its location near the sandy estuaries of Glaslyn and Dwyryd before the Cob was built at Porthmadog. The references may even have been to the two major beaches (Traeth Bach and Traeth Mawr) on either side of Penrhyndeudraeth (q.v.). Occasionally it is referred to as Llanfihangel-y-traeth (the adjacent Traeth Bach), and some of the forms cited above could be the dial. var. ***traethe*** for ***traethau***. The 1284 form may record the occasional alternation of ***nant*** and ***llan***.

LLANFILO Brec SO1033
'church of Bilio', ***llan***, pers.n. ***Bilio***
Lanbilio c.1203-14, *Lanbylien* 1291, *Lamvilio* 1399, *ll. fillo* c.1566
Bilio (or Beilo) may be Belyau, one of the many daughters of the legendary Brychan Brycheiniog recorded as saints. The parish has a Ffynnon Filo (***ffynnon***) and Allt Filo (***allt***). The reference to this village as (a place called) *Millewe* 1503 probably derives from a misinterpretation of the mutated form -filo since -f- is a lenition of both -b- and -m-. This may also explain the misattribution of the church dedication to Milburga, eldest daughter of Merewalh, king of Mercia.

LLANFOIST, LLAN-FFWYST Monm SO2813
'church of Ffoist', ***llan***, pers.n. ***Ffoist***
Lanfoist 1254, 1335, *Lanfoyst* 1348, *ll. ffwyst* c.1566, *llann ffwyst* late 16cent.
The pers.n. Ffoist, possibly an unrecorded saint, later developed regularly as Ffwyst.

LLANFOR Mer SH9336

'big church', ***llan***, ***mawr***

Lanvaur 1291, *Llanvaur* 1390, *ll. fawr ymhenllyn* c.1566, *llanfor o. Llanvawr* 1571, *Llanfawr* 1789, *Llanfor* 1838

This large church (dedicated to Deiniol) is prominently situated overlooking the low-lying land east of Bala through which the river Dee flows (from Llyn Tegid). The original *Llan-fawr* underwent stress shift to the first syllable leaving an unstressed -for. Significantly, however, -fawr persisted for some time side-by-side with -for, because of the visual reinforcement of the church's size, the extent of the parish, and the strategic importance of the village as a commercial centre. The additional distinguishing *ymhenllyn* in c.1566 refers to its location in the hundred of Penllyn (***pen*** 'head', ***llyn*** the lake of Llyn Tegid). See also Llanuwchllyn.

LLANFRECHFA Monm ST3193

'church at Brechfa', ***llan***, p.n. ***Brechfa***

Llanvrechva 1452, *Lanvrechva* 1535, *Lanvreychva* 1539, *ll. frechfa* c.1566

Brechfa is probably ***brych*** fem. ***brech***, ***-ma*** 'speckled field' rather than a pers.n.; cf. Brechfa Carm.

LLANFROTHEN Mer SH6241

'church of Brothen', ***llan***, pers.n. ***Brothen***

Lanfrothin 1292-3, *Lanvrothen* 1325-6, *Llanvrothen* 1393, *Llanfrothen* 1688, *Llanfrothan* 1771

This is the only church dedicated to Brothen. Tradition holds him to be a son of Helig ap Glannog (*Helic m. Glannawc* 12cent.[13cent.]) whose lands were swallowed by the sea. The 1771 form records the dial. var. commonly heard today.

LLANFRYNACH Brec SO0725

'church of Brynach', ***llan***, pers.n. ***Brynach***

Lanbernach 1291, *Lambernach* 1310, *Sci Bernaci juxta Brechon* 1408-9, *ll. frynach* c.1566

Identical to Llanfrynach Glam and Llanfyrnach (q.v.) which have similar historical forms.

LLANFWROG[1] Angl SH3084

'church of Mwrog', ***llan***, pers.n. ***Mwrog***

Lanmutauc 1254, *Llannvorok* 1389, *ll. fwrog* c.1566, *Llanfwrog* 1758

Traditionally, there was also a chapel dedicated to Mwrog in a field named Mynwent Mwrog (in Cefnglas farm).

LLANFWROG[2] Denb SJ1157

'church of Mwrog', ***llan***, pers.n. ***Mwrog***

Lanwrauc 1254, *Llanmurrok* 1291, *llanvorok* 1559, *ll. vwrog* c.1566, *Llanvoorog* 1684, *Llanfwrog* 1838

The church was rededicated to the Blessed Virgin. The tnshp (*Murrok* 1330, *Murrock* 1378) and church are west of Rhuthun.

LLANFYLLIN Mont SJ1419

'church of Myllin(g)', ***llan***, pers.n. ***Myllin(g)***

Llanvelig 1254, *Lanvyllyn* 1291, *Lanvethlyng* 1309

Myllin has been identified with the 7cent. Ir saint Moling (with vars Moling, Mullin and Mulling) but it is not known if he visited Wales.

LLANFYNYDD[1] Carm SN5527

'church on a mountain', ***llan, mynydd***

Laneguadveniz 1281, *Lanvenyth* 1276 (13cent.), *Llanvenyth* 1391, *ll. fynydd* c.1566

The church is located on the slopes of a hill. An earlier name was Llanegwad Fynydd recording the church's dedication to Egwad with ***mynydd*** distinguishing it from Llanegwad (q.v.).

LLANFYNYDD[2] Flints SJ2756

'church on a mountain', ***llan, mynydd***

Llanfynydd 1871

Between 1843 and 1845 a church was built (as a focal point for a new parish) on the boundary between the tnshps of Uwchmynydd Ucha and Uwchmynydd Isa. Previously the hamlet appears to have been known as Penuel (*Penuel* 1840) after the Congregational chapel there.

LLANFYRNACH Pemb SN2231

'church of Brynach', ***llan***, pers.n. ***Brynach***

ecclesiam Sancti Brenachi de Bleintaf 1176-98 (17cent.), *Ecclesia S[an]cti Bernaci sup[er] Taff* 1291, *Llan vernagh super Tafe* 1490, *Llanvernach ar tave* 1507, *Llanvrenache* 1543, *Llanvernachardave* 1551, *ll. frynach ar daf* c.1566

Brynach seems to have had vars Bernach or Byrnach; cf. Llanfrynach. The church stands next to the River Taf near its headwaters (***blaen)*** in the manor of Dyffryn Taf (*Diffrin tave* 13cent,. *Diffrin Tafe* c.1419).

LLANGADFAN Mont SJ0110

'church of Cadfan', ***llan***, pers.n. ***Cadfan***

Llankadvan 1254, *Llangadeuan* 1286, *Langadvan* 1291, *Thlangadeuen* 1295, *LL.gadvan kaer einion* c.1550-62, *ll. gadfan* c.1566

Cadfan is also reputed to have founded the church at Tywyn Mer.

LLANGADOG Carm SN7028

'church of Cadog', ***llan***, pers.n. ***Cadog***

lanncadauc 1160-85, *Lancadauc* 1281, *Lankadoc* 1284,
Ll. Cadog Fawr 1590

Some late forms have ***mawr*** 'great' to distinguish it from identical p.ns. Cadog is thought to be a 5cent. saint and has a large number of churches dedicated to him in Wales, Cornwall, Brittany and Scotland. Cf. Llangattock.

LLANGADWALADR[1] Angl SH3869

'church of Cadwaladr', ***llan***, pers.n. ***Cadwaladr***

Llankydwaladr 1508, *ll. Gydwaladr* c.1566, *Llangadwalider* 1573,
Llangadwalader alias Eglwysale 1695, *Eglwysal alias Llangadwalader* 1761,
Llangadwaladr 1838

Cadwaladr was one of the princes of Gwynedd, whose court was at nearby Aberffraw, and is reputed to have been canonised in 689 twenty-five years after his death. The church had previously been commonly referred to as Eglwys Ail (*Eglusheyl* 1254, *Eglusell* 1569), a reference either to the method of constructing the church itself or to the protective boundary (***ail*** 'building of wattle and daub'); an alternative explanation is ***ael*** 'brow' from its location above the Ffraw estuary. The vill of *Eglussell* was held *'de sancto Cadwaladre rege'* 1352. In the church is the 7cent. inscription to *Catamanus*, the Cadfan who was Cadwaladr's grandfather.

LLANGADWALADR[2] Denb SJ1830

'church of Cadwaladr' ***llan***, pers.n. ***Cadwaladr***

Bettws Badwalardyr 1291, *Llangydwaladr* 1547, *ll. gydwaladr* c.1566,
Llangadwaladr 1795

The church is located in a fairly remote mountainous area of Llansilin which may well explain the earliest designation as a ***betws*** 'prayer-house' or 'chapel-of-ease'. Cadwaladr is associated with the royal lineage of Gwynedd; see Llangadwaladr[1].

LLANGADWALADR[3] see **BISHTON**

LLANGAFFO Angl SH4468

'church of Caffo', ***llan***, pers.n. ***Caffo***

Llangaffo 1254

The older name was Merthyr Caffo (*Merthir-Caffo* c.1200, ***merthyr*** 'shrine'). A well, Crochan Caffo (*Crochan Caffo* 1710, ***crochan*** 'cauldron'), is also associated with the saint, and is still retained as a farm name north of Llangaffo.

LLAN-GAIN Carm SN3816

'church of Cain', ***llan***, pers.n. ***Cain***

St. Keyn 1174-6, *Egluyskeyn* 1180-4, *Mainergein* 1288, *Langau* 1291, *Maynorgeyn* 1395, *ll. gain* c.1566, *Llangainge* 1598
Generally described as *Eglwys Cain* before c.1250 (***eglwys***) and *Maenorgain* down to the 16cent. (***maenor*** 'estate', probably for 'estate at Eglwys Cain' as in Maenordeilo at Llandeilo Carm). Cain was reputedly one of the 24 daughters of the legendary Brychan and may also have been called Ceinwen and Ceinwyry (cf. Llangeinor).

LLANGAMARCH, LLANGAMARCH WELLS Brec SN9347
'church by (the river) Camarch', ***llan***, r.n. ***Camarch***
Langamarch 1249, *llann gamarch* 12cent. (c.1400),
Llangamarch in Buelthe 1547, *Llangamarch ym myellt* c.1592,
Llangammarch 1833
The r.n. (*aber kammarch* 13cent. [c.1400], *Camarch flu:* 1578) prompted a church dedication to a saint Camarch or Cadfarch; the original (at least 12cent.) dedication was probably to Tysilio. Some qualifiers locate the church in the cantref of Buellt/Builth (q.v.). Wells referred to the mineral wells at the Lake Hotel, allegedly discovered in the early 19cent.

LLAN-GAN Glam SS9577
'church of Canna', ***llan***, pers.n. ***Canna***
Landegenne 1254, *Lamgan* 1291, *Langan* c.1348, *Langanne* 1431,
ll. gain c.1566, *Llanganne* 1769
Dedicated to Canna, reputed wife of Sadwrn and mother of Crallo; there is a Canna's Well at Henllanfallteg Pemb. Some authorities still refer to Llanganna. The final unstressed -a was lost although it may survive in some of the forms as a residual -e, which, in later forms, could represent an attempt to convey the long vowel in -gan. It has been suggested that the same name may be found in the Cardiff suburb Canton (*Canetun* c.1230) and the bridge Pontcanna (*bridge of Canne* 1559, *Pontganne* 1690).

LLANGATHEN Carm SN5822
'church of Cathen', ***llan***, pers.n. ***Cathen***
Langattkek 1291, *Langathen* 1318, *ll. gathen* c.1566, *Llangathen* 1596
The pers.n. Cathen or Cathan also occurs in Catheiniog or Cetheiniog (*Ketheinneauc* 1261, *Ketheynoc* c.1287, *Cathenock* 1532, with terr.suff. ***-iog***), the commote which includes Llangathen. Possibly identifiable with a *Kathen ap Gwlyddien* in Dyfed.

LLANGATTOCK, LLANGATWG Brec SO 2117
'church of Cadog', ***llan***, pers.n. ***Cadog***
llangadawc c.1180, *Lancadok* 1291, *Llangattok* 1412, *Ploeth Caduk* 1503,
ll. gattwc c.1566, *Llangatwg-cerrig-Howell* 1767
Catwg is a var. of Cadog, dedications to whom are concentrated in south-east Wales (apart from Llangadog Carm q.v.). His father is reputed to

have been Gwynllyw (St Woolo's at Newport Monm) and his mother Gwladus, according to tradition, was a daughter of Brychan Brycheiniog. The 1503 form has ***plwyf*** 'parish' in the dial. var. ***plwydd***.

LLANGATTOCK LINGOED, LLANGATWG LINGOED Monm SO3620

'church of Cadog at ?Celyngoed', ***llan***, pers.n. ***Cadog***, p.n. ?***Celyngoed***
Lancadok 1254, *Lankaddok Kellenny* 1291, *Lancadok Lyncoyd* 1348, *Lankadok Ekelleni* 1349, *ll. gattwg klēnic* c.1566
Llangatwg. Lingoed (*Linchoit* 1146, *Lyncoyd* 1348, 1434, *Lynquad* 1388, *llingoed* 1600-7) is used in reference to woodland (*Parkellingoed* 1611, *parke llyngoed* 1615) which suggests ***coed*** but there is no obvious lake (***llyn***) here so that may derive from a *Celyngoed* 'holly wood' (***celyn, coed***). Other forms such as *Kellenny* c.1291, c.1348, *Kyllenny* 1397, *Genelyge* 1556, *celenyg* 1578 and *Lann celinni* 1160-85 (which may be located here) suggest a var. qualifier ***celynnig*** 'abounding in holly'.

LLANGATTOCK NIGH USK, LLANGATWG DYFFRYN WYSG Monm SO3309

'church of Cadog near the (river) Usk', 'Llangatwg in the valley of (the river) Usk/Wysg', pers.n. ***Cadog***, E ***nigh***, W ***llan***, ***dyffryn***, r.n. ***Usk/Wysg***
Lancadou iuxta Usk 1254, *Lancadoc Defrenusk* 1273, *ll. gattwg dyffryn wysk* c.1566, *Llangattock-nigh-Usk* 1885-6
On Catwg see Llangatwg. The addition *nigh Usk* appears to have been adopted in the 19cent., probably a deliberate translation of the medieval L ***iuxta*** 'near'.

LLANGATWG see **LLANGATTOCK**

LLANGATWG DYFFRYN WYSG see **LLANGATTOCK NIGH USK**

LLANGATWG LINGOED see **LLANGATTOCK LINGOED**

LLANGATWG NEDD see **CADOXTON-JUXTA-NEATH**

LLANGEDWYN Denb SJ1824

'church of Cedwyn', ***llan***, pers.n. ***Cedwyn***
Wangedwyn 1291, *Langetwin* 1354, *llann gedwyn* 16cent., *Llangedwyn* c.1700
Little is known of Cedwyn, thought to be the son of Gwgon Gwron and Madrun ferch Gwrtheyrn Gwrthenau (12cent. [13cent.]). There is also a dedication in Brec.

LLANGEFNI Angl SH4675

'church on (the river) Cefni', ***llan***, r.n. ***Cefni***
Llangevni 1254, *llangeffny* 1456, *ll. gefni* c.1566, *Llangefni* 1707

The church is adjacent to the river Cefni but is dedicated to Cyngar (*Sti Kyngar in Meney* 1481, *llangyngar* 1509, *St. Kengar de Llangefny* 1534). The r.n. Cefni (*Avon Kefni, avon vawr* 1536-9, *Cefni Fluvius* 1573, *Avon Keveney, Afon Fawr* 1629) is ***cafn*** 'dip, hollow, trough' and the r.n. suff. ***-i***, probably referring to the narrow gorge (*Nant y Diluw* 1816-23, ***dilyw*** 'torrent, flood, deluge'), now Nant y Pandy (***pandy*** 'fulling mill') or The Dingle, on the outskirts of Llangefni. The obsolete alternative name *Afon Fawr* (***mawr*** 'big') refers to its canalised realigned course from the Malltraeth (q.v.) estuary to Llangefni; maps have Hen Afon Cefni (***hen*** 'former') for the meandering section of its original tidal course.

LLANGEINOR, LLANGEINWYR Glam SS9287

'church of Ceinwyr', ***llan***, pers.n. ***Ceinwyr***

Egluskeynor 1139-49, *Sancte Kehinwehir* 1180-1208, *Egleskeinwir* late 12cent., *Egliskeynor* 1335-6, *Llanginwire* 1536-9, *Langeynor* 1546, *ll. igain wyr* c.1566, *llann gainwyry* c.1600

Earlier prefixed with ***eglwys*** 'church'. Ceinwyr has the same el. as Cain and Ceinwen (see Llan-gain and Llangeinwen Angl) with the qualifier ***gwyryf*** 'virgin', and is also found in Llwyncynhwyra, a former chapel of Talyllychau Carm.

LLANGEITHO Card SN6159

'church of Ceitho', ***llan***, pers.n. ***Ceitho***

Lankethau 1284, *Langeytho* 1290

Ceitho is probably an Ir form of the W pers.n. Ceidio found in p.ns., such as Rhodogeidio in Angl and Ceidio in Caern and in the r.n. Ceidio or Ceidiog in Mer. Ceitho was one of the five saints to whom Llanpumsaint (q.v.) is dedicated.

LLANGELER Carm SN3739

'church of Celer', ***llan***, pers.n. ***Celer***

Martir Keler' 1291, *Merthirkeler* 1326, 1418, *Llangeler in Emblyn* 1532, *llangeler* 1648

Most forms before c.1500 are prefixed with ***merthyr*** 'shrine'. The parish, in the cantref of Emlyn, also has a Ffynnongeler (***ffynnon***), Rhosgeler (***rhos***) and Plasgeler (***plas***).

LLANGELYNNIN Mer SH5707

'church of Celynnin', ***llan***, pers.n. ***Celynnin***

Lankellnin 1254, *Llangelynyn* 1543, *ll. gylynin* c.1566, *llanglynin* 1632, *Llangelynin* 1837

All that is known of Celynnin is the tradition that he was another son of Helig ap Glannog (see Llanfrothen). Another church, in the cantref of Arllechwedd (Caern), is dedicated to him, but he is probably a different Celynnin to the saint who was one of the five commemorated in Llanpumsaint (q.v.).

LLANGENAU, LLANGENEU see **LLANGENNY**

LLANGENDEIRNE see **LLANGYNDEYRN**

LLANGENNECH Carm SN5601

'church of Cennych ', ***llan***, pers.n. ***Cennych***

L. geniz ynglann LLychwr c.1500, *Llangenech* 1545, *ll. genych* c.1566, *Llangynych* 1627

Cennych or Cennech may be the Ir saint Cainnech, reputedly a disciple of Cadog in Llancarfan. The c.1500 form refers to its location on the bank (***glan***) of the river Llwchwr.

LLANGENNITH, LLANGYNYDD Glam SS4291

'church of Cynydd', ***llan***, pers.n. ***Cynydd***

lann Cinith 1160-85, *Langenith* 1284, *Langenyth* 1300, *ll. gynydd* c.1566

The saint, who had close connections with Brittany, also appears in the (lost) name of the promontory *Seynt Kenyth' is hedde* 1472 west of the village, a former hermitage *St Kenyth atte Holmes* 1398 on Burry Holms, and the priory recorded here in 1135. Llangennith lies in the Gower peninsula and the former commote of Gŵyr. The Llangenith/Llangynydd vars reflect the regular dial. alternation of -y- and -e- (cf. Kenfig/Cynffig); Llangennith is an anglicized form.

LLANGENNY, LLANGENEU Brec SO2418

'church of Ceneu', ***llan***, pers.n. ***Ceneu***

ll. gene c.1566, *Llangeney* 1554, *Llangenny* 1547-51

The saint Ceneu is named as a son of the legendary Coel Godebog in medieval pedigrees. Early references to the p.n. are lacking probably because Llangeneu was a chapel within the parish of Llangattock Brec.

LLANGERNYW Denb SH8767

'church of Cernyw', ***llan***, pers.n. ***Cernyw***

Llangernyw 1261, *Nangernew* 1284, *Langernyw* 1291, *Llann Gernyw* 16cent.

The church was associated with Cystennin Gorneu ('Cystennin of Cernyw/Cornwall') who also founded Llangystennin Caern. His son, Digain, is thought to have established this church early in the 5cent. The *Nangernew* form is another example of the alternation of ***llan*** and ***nant***, but here the probablity is that the p.n. is an original ***llan*** name.

LLANGÏAN Caern SH2928

'church of Cian', ***llan***, pers.n. ***Cian***

Lanekiant 1254, *Llangyan* 1291, *Langean* 1352, *ll. gian* c.1566, *Llangian* 1664

The saint is usually referred to as ***Cian*** (with two syllables) while the village is Llangïan (with -ï- indicating the penultimate stress).

LLANGIBBY see **LLANGYBI**

LLAN-GIWG Glam SS7205
'church of Ciwg', ***llan***, pers.n. ***Ciwg***
Langyuk, Lan Cyok in Gower 1284, *Langwych* 1291, *Langyock* 1299, *Langyouk* 1343, *Llann Giwc* 1217 (c.1400), *ll. giwg* c.1566, *Llangiwick* 1617, *Languicke* 1650
Little is known of this saint. Llan-giwg matches local W pronunciation but it is also pronounced as in the 1617 form by E-speakers.

LLANGLYDWEN Carm SN1826
'church of Clydwyn', ***llan***, pers.n. ***Clydwyn***
Langledewen 1291, *Llancledewen* 1398, *Llanglodwyn* 1435, *ll. glydwen ar daf* c.1566
Probably Clydwyn ap Nyfed (*Gloitguin map Nimet* 10cent.) or Clydwyn, a son of the legendary Brychan (see Brecon). According to later sources the church was dedicated to All Saints.

LLANGOED Angl SH6079
'church near the wood', ***llan***, ***coed***
Langoet 1254, *llangoyt* 1335, *llangoyd* 1443, *ll. goed neu gowrda* 1590, *Llan Gowrda als Llangoed* 1586-1613, *Llangoed* 1790
The most extensive late medieval wood in Angl was the Coedcadw (or Llan-faes) wood near Beaumaris, and so 'in a wooded landscape' would perhaps be appropriate. The church was dedicated to Cawrdaf whose name is commemorated in the occasionally used alternative name of Llangawrdaf.

LLANGOEDMOR Card SN2045
'church in Coedmor', ***llan***, tnshp n. ***Coedmor***
Lancoynmaur 1268, *Lancoytmaur* c.1258-71 (1324), *Langoydmaur* 1291, *Lancoydmour* 1302-3, *Lancoidmor, -maur* 1320, *Lancoydmaur* 1293, *Llangoydmore* 1472, *ll. goedmor* c.1566, *Llangoedmor* 1642-3
The tnshp Coedmor (***coed***, ***mawr*** 'extensive forest', *Coydmor* 1301-2, *Koydmour* 1302-3) was in the commote of Iscoed Mortimer (***is*** 'lower, this side', *Oscoid Mortemer* 1586, *Yskoed Mortimer alias Koydmawr* 1630, where Mortimer is *John Mortimer of Koidmore* 1584-5). The southern part of the parish near the river Teifi is still heavily wooded.

LLANGOLLEN Denb SJ2141
'church of Collen', ***llan***, pers.n. ***Collen***
Lancollien 1234 (1295), *Sancti Colyenni, Llancallen* 1254, *Thlangothlan* 1284, *Langollen* 1291, *Llangollenn* 1391-3, *ll. gollen* c.1566
Little is known of this 7cent. saint. There is some doubt whether this is the same saint for whom dedications occur in Brittany and in Cornwall (*Sanctus Culanus* 1201, *Sien Colan* 1302).

LLANGOLMAN Pemb SN1227

'church of Colman', ***llan***, pers.n. ***Colman***

Llangolman 1394, 1575, *ll. golmon* c.1566, *Penvay Llangolman* 1487, *Llangolman Penyvaie* 1646

Probably named from an Ir saint Colmán Eala (died 555) who is also commemorated at Lann Eala or Lynally, co. Meath, where he established a church, and at Capel Colman (*Langol* 1292, *Llangolman* 1394, 1513, *Llangolman Penbedw* 1591, *Capel colman* 1578, *Ecclesia colman pen[rit]h* c.1600) a former free chapel (***capel***) near Penbedw and Penrhydd. The 1487 and 1646 forms have *Pen-y-fai* probably 'end of the open lands' (***pen***, ***y***, ***ma*** pl. ***mai***).

LLAN-GORS Brec SO1327

'church at the marsh', ***llan***, ***cors***

Lann Cors 1136-54, *Sancti Paulini de Lancors* 1147-76, *Mara* c.1210-12, *La Mare* 1331, *Llangors* 1543, *ll. gors peylyn sant* c.1566, *Mara...otherwise Llangorse* 1739

The location is the marshy area around Llyn Syfaddan (Llan-gors Lake q.v.). The lake gives the village an older, obsolete name *Mara*, a latinized form of OE ***mere*** 'lake, pool'. The anglicized form Llangorse, influenced by E ***gorse***, is still encountered occasionally. The church is dedicated to Peulin, L Paulinus.

LLAN-GORS LAKE, LLYN SYFADDAN Brec SO1327

'lake near Llan-gors', 'lake of ?Syfaddan', p.n. ***Llan-gors***, E ***lake***, W ***llyn***, ?pers.n. ***Syfaddan***

Brecenan Mere 916 (= 919), *linn Syuadon* 1143-54, *Mara* 12cent., *Lake of Brekeniauc* c.1200, *la Mare* 1327, *llŷn syuadon* late 15cent., *Breknoc Mere … in Walche Llin Seuathan* 1536-9, *Mara langors* 1689, *Savaddan or Langors Pool* 1777, *Llyn Savaddon* 1798

The largest lake in Brec, immediately south of Llan-gors (q.v.). L and F sources with *Mara* (L ***mara*** 'swamp') and F *la Mare* correspond to OE, ME ***mere***. Another putative name was *Clamosus* (c.1191) seemingly L ***clamosus*** 'full of clamour' but probably in error for L ***calamosus*** 'reedy' which is the ***cors*** 'reeds' of Llan-gors. The W form has not been satisfactorily explained, but is probably a pers.n., possibly a divine personification.

LLANGORWEN Card SN6083

'church at the sanctuary stone', ***llan***, ***côr***, ***maen***

Llan Gorwen 1732, *Llangorwen* 1734, *Llangarwen* 1760, *Llangorwen* 1889

The very late documentary evidence makes for an uncertain etymology. However, if -corwen is the same as Corwen Mer (q.v.) it suggests either a church with a distinctive sanctuary or altar stone, or that the former church, traditionally built on the site of an even older church, was located around the only trace of the older church namely a prominent sanctuary stone. Another etymology proposed is Cyrwen the name of Padarn's staff, a suggestion which satisfies some spellings (*Pont Llangwrwen* 1803, *Pont Llangurwen* 1804) but then influenced by Corwen (q.v.). The present church was built in 1841 and all the pre-1841 references are to the bridge (over Afon Clarach) and the nearby houses.

LLANGOVAN, LLANGOFEN Monm SO4505
'church of ?Cofian', ***llan***, pers.n. ?***Cofian***
Lancomen 1254, *Lanconyan* 1291, *lanchouian* 13cent, *Llangeven* 1465, *Langoveyn* 1463
Forms vary considerably and many with -u- and -n- are probably errors for -v-. If it is a pers.n., it appears to be Cofian, later Cofan, Cofen. The church, however, is dedicated to Mihangel/Michael (*Launvihangel* 1234-62 [1307]).

LLANGRALLO see **COYCHURCH**

LLANGRANNOG Card SN3154
'church of Crannog', ***llan***, pers.n. ***C(a)rannog***
p. krānoc c.1566, *Llanrannock* 1578, *llan krānoc* 1590-1, *Llangrannog* 1595
The older name of the church was Gogof (*Gogof* 1284, *Gogoffe* 1291, *Gogo, Gogoff* 1535) a reference to Ogof Crannog (***gogof*** 'cave') still preserved in the name of the adjacent parish Llandysiliogogo (*Llandissilior Gogof* 1338, *Llandisslio & Gogof* 1535, *Llandissiliogogo* 1643). Carannog, believed to be the son of Ceredig ap Cunedda, also has a dedication at Crantock Cornwall (*Sanctus Carentoch* 1086).

LLANGRISTIOLUS Angl SH4373
'church of Cristiolus', ***llan***, pers.n. ***Cristiolus***
Llan Cristiolis 1535, *Llan christioles* 1543, *ll. gristiolys* c.1566, *Llangristiolus* 1674
Cristiolus is referred to in *Cristiolus yn Lledwigan* (12cent. [c.1510], ***yn*** 'in' the tnshp of Lledwigan, Anglesey), described as the son of Hywel Fychan ap Hywel ap Emyr Llydaw.

LLANGRWYNE see **GLANGRWYNE**

LLANGUA, LLANGIWA Monm SO3825
'church of Ciwan', ***llan***, pers.n. ***Ciwan***
Lonkywen 1067-71, *Lanquian* 1148-83, *Lagywan* 1254, *Langkywan* 1270, *Langywan, Languwan* 1291, *Llangua* 1330
Little is known of the fem. saint whose name was probably Ciwan although the forms tend towards Cywan. From the 14cent. there was loss of final -n.

LLANGUNNOR see **LLANGYNNWR**

LLANGURIG Mont SN9079
'church of Curig', ***llan***, pers.n. ***Curig***
Lankiric 1254, *Langerig* 1310, (*i*) *lann giric* late 15cent., *Llangeryk* 1535, *Llanguric* 1578 *Llanguric, Llankyryk, Langerik* 1578, *langericke* 1597
Curig, reputedly bishop of Llanbadarn Fawr c.700, also has a dedication at Capel Curig (q.v.) and at Eglwys Fair a Churig Carm, and is recorded in Eisteddfa Gurig on the western edge of the parish. As with Capel Curig, some forms seem to show confusion with ***cerrig*** 'stones'.

LLANGWATHAN Pemb SN1315
'Gwaiddan's grove', ***llwyn***, pers.n. ***Gwaiddan***
Lann teliau luin guaidan 1136-54, *Lanwaythan* 1330, *Lanwaithan* 1413, *Lloynwathen* 1543, *Llanwathan alias Lloyngwaythell* 1581
The earliest form represents 'church of Teilo in Llwyngwaiddan'. Many later forms, including the modern form, show the more familiar ***llan*** substituted for ***llwyn*** 'grove'. The pers.n. also appears in Robeston Wathen (q.v.).

LLANGWM[1] Denb SH9644
'church in the valley', ***llan***, ***cwm***
Langun 1254, *Langvm* 1291, *Llanigomdynmael* 1391, *Llangwm Dymmel* 1397, *ll. gwm dinmel* c.1566, *Llangwm* 1668, *Llangumdimell* 1763
The church is in a valley formed by Afon Medrad which flows into Afon Geirw at Ystrad Fawr (***ystrad*** 'valley bottom, river meadow'). The fuller name incorporates the commote name Dinmael.

LLANGWM[2] Pemb SM9909
'church in the valley', ***llan***, ***cwm***
Landegoin 1291, *Landegumme* 1303, *Landecombe* 1376, *Llangome* 1539, *Langwm* 1595
The early forms with -d- are paralleled in other ***llan***- p.ns (cf. Llangwm), possibly under the influence of E ***land***. Llangwm occupies the bottom of a short, deep valley next to the river Cleddau.

LLAN-GWM Monm SO4200
'church in the valley', ***llan***, ***cwm***
lann Cum, lanncúm 1136-54, *Lancum superior* 1254, *Landcom* 1291, *Lambcumbe* 1307, *ll. gwm ychaf* c.1566, *Langwm Ucha* 1621
Llan-gwm is used of two distinct places in the same valley (through which flows a tributary of the Olway stream) only half-a-mile apart. Llan-gwm Uchaf (***uchaf*** 'upper') is certainly the place referred to in the forms for 1254, c.1566 and 1621 (and probably other references) while

Llan-gwm Isaf (*ll. gwm isaf* c.1566, *llangome isha* 1555, ***isaf*** 'lower') is also known in later sources as Gwarthacwm (*Warkecom* 1291, *Warthecomb* 1296, 'uppermost part of the valley', ***gwarthaf***, ***cwm***, a name also borne by that of the manor) and as Gwarthacwm Bach (*Gurre de Bache* 1595, *Langome yssa alias (gwr)da baigh* early 17cent., ***bach*** 'little'). E land is seen in 1291. Cf. Llangwm².

LLANGWNNADL Caern SH2032

'brook of Gwynhoedl', ***nant***, pers.n. ***Gwynhoedl***

llangenenel 1335, *Nangwnadyll* 1522, *Llangwnadle* 1553-5, *Nangwynedyle* 1557, *nan gwnadl* c.1566, *Nangwnadle* 1614-15, *Llangwnadle* 1673, *Llangwnadl* 1840

The river now known as Afon Fawr (***mawr***) appears to have been originally associated with Gwynhoedl (traditionally reputed to be a son of Seithenyn, king of Cantre'r Gwaelod) whose name is possibly preserved as *Vendesetli* on a 6cent. inscribed stone in nearby Llannor. As occasionally occurred, ***nant*** when followed by a pers.n. became confused with ***llan***, although in this instance, somewhat perversely, the first recorded instance is ***llan***.

LLANGWYFAN Denb SJ1166

'church of Cwyfen', ***llan***, pers.n. ***Cwyfen***

Langrifin 1254, *Llan Goyffen* 1535, *ll. gwyfen* c.1566, *Llangoyven* 1612, *Llangwyfen* 1732, *Llangwyfan* 1795, *Llangwyfen* 1838

Cwyfen was reputedly of Ir extraction, and his name also appears in its later form of Cwyfan, in Llangwyfan Angl (*Nangoewan* 1254, *Llan gowyen* 1535).

LLANGWYLLOG Angl SH4379

'church of Cwyllog', ***llan***, pers.n. ***C(y)wyllog***

llangwillok 1522, *ll. gwyllog* c.1566, *Llangwyllog* 1838

The only dedication to this saint (*Kywyllawg* 1514, *Kuyllog* 16cent.), believed to be a son of Caw (or daughter, according to some sources). Some maintain that the original dedication was to Gwrddelw and that Cwyllog is merely a fictitious name derived from Llangwyllog perceived to be a dedication to 'the hooded one' (***cowyllog*** 'hidden', 'cowled').

LLANGWYRYFON Card SN5970

'church of (the) maidens', ***llan***, (***y***), ***gwyryf*** pl. ***gwyryfon***

Llanygroddon 1543, *llanygorython* 1564, *ll. y gwyryddon* c.1566, *Llangorothen* 1594-5, *llanygorython* 1599, *Llanygrwddon* 1697-8, *Llanygrwyddon* 1757, *Llangwyryfon* 1831, *Llangrwyddon or Llanygwyryfon* 1851

The church was dedicated to the eleven thousand virgins traditionally martyred with Ursula in the 4cent. The var. pl. ***gwyryddon*** (with dial.

alternation of -f- and -dd-), more common in literary texts, is dominant in the historical forms above, and is still heard in the modern dial. var. Llangwrddon.

LLANGYBI[1] Caern SH4241

'church of Cybi', ***llan***, pers.n. ***Cybi***

(villam de') Geibi 1325 [?], *Langiby* 1361, *Llan Gyby* 1535, *ll. gybi* c.1566, *Llangybi* 1838

There is a Ffynnon Cybi (*Ffynnon Gybi* 1892-3, ***ffynnon***) nearby and a rock on a hillside called Cadair Gybi (***cadair*** 'chair, seat').

LLANGYBI[2] Card SN6053

'church of Cybi', ***llan***, pers.n. ***Cybi***

Lankeby 1284, *Lankelby* 1299, *Llangeby* 1535, *Llangybby* 1532

There are other churches dedicated to the 6cent. saint Cybi, in Caern, in Monm and in Cornwall, in addition to the monastery he founded in Caergybi (q.v.) where he was abbot.

LLANGYBI[3] Monm ST3796

'church of Cybi', ***llan***, pers.n. ***Cybi***

Lancubi, sancti Cubi 1155-83, *Lankepi* c.1200, *Llanguby* 1499, *ll. gybi* c.1566

Cybi was also the name of the river (*Keby* 1397). Occasionally described as Tre-grug (*Tregurc* 1155-83, *Tregruk* 1262, *Treygrug* c.1291, *Trergryke* 1539, *Trey Grig in Llangibby* 1547-51) with ***tref***, ***y***, ***crug*** probably referring to the castle mound (rather than ***grug*** 'heather').

LLANGYNDEYRN Carm SN4514

'church of Cyndeyrn', ***llan***, pers.n. ***Cyndeyrn***

Lankederne 1358, *L. gynn dauyrn* c.1500, *ll. gyndeyrn* c.1566, *Llangendeirne* 1579, *Llangyndeirn* 1600

Cyndeyrn was probably a saint, possibly the same as St Kentigern or Mungo (died c.612), the founder of the church in Glasgow and possibly identical to the Cyndeyrn ap Cyngar described as a great grandson of the 5cent. Cunedda of Strathclyde. However, Cyndeyrn is a fairly common early W pers.n.

LLANGYNFELYN Card SN6492

'church of Cynfelyn', ***llan***, pers.n. ***Cynfelyn***

Llangynvelyn 1543, *ll. gynfelyn* c.1566, *Llangynvelyn* 1559, *Llangynfelyn* 1798, *Llancynfelin* 1808, *Llancynfelyn* 1837

This saint is reputed to be Cynfelen ab Meirion ab Tybion ab Cunedda. There is also an Ynys Cynfelyn on the edge of the adjacent Cors Fochno, which may have influenced the local change from Llangynfelyn to Llancynfelyn, a form which also appears on several maps.

LLANGYNHAFAL Denb SJ1263

'church of Cynhafal', ***llan***, pers.n. ***Cynhafal***

Langenhaval 1254, *Lankynaval, Llanganhavall'* 1291, *ll. gynhafal* c.1566

Little is known of Cynhafal, although a 16cent. poet attributes the death of the legendary 5cent. giant Benlli Gawr to the saint's miraculous powers (elsewhere ascribed to Garmon).

LLANGYNIDR Brec SO1519

'church of Cynidr', ***llan***, pers.n. ***Cynidr***

Llankgenedire, Llangenedre 1398, *(de) Sco' Kenedro* 1513,
Llangeneder 1535, *Llangenyder Eglosyell* 1561,
llangenider egloys Yayle 1600-7

Eglwys Iail (*Egglesseil* 1263, *Egluseyll* 1291, *Egloisieyle* 1517) 'church by the (stream) Iail' (*Nant Yail* 1832) has been considered an earlier name for Llangynidr, or as the name of a separate church in close proximity. However, there is a similar name Eglwys Ail in Angl as an alias for Llangadwaladr[2] (q.v.) suggesting in both instances ***ail*** 'building of wattle and daub'. The parish churches of Kenderchurch Herefordshire, Aberysgyr and Cantref Brec and Glasbury Radn also have dedications to Cynidr.

LLANGYNIN Carm SN2519

'church of Cynin', ***llan***, pers.n. ***Cynin***

Lankenyn 1325, *St. Kennyns* 1446, *ll. gynin* c.1566, *Llangynon* 1600,
Llangynning 1752

The church is dedicated to Cynin, probably a Br pers.n., recalled in an inscription in Eglwysgynyn church. The village is a mile-and-a-half to the north of the church.

LLANGYNLLO, LLANGUNLLO Radn SO2171

'church of Cynllo', ***llan***, pers.n. ***Cynllo***

Llangetlau 1323, *Llankenllowe* 1395, *llann gynllo* 15cent.

Little is known of Cynllo but he was the leading saint of Maelienydd and Gwrtheyrnion (the northern part of Radn) where his churches include Nantmel, Llanbister and formerly Rhaeadr, as well as Llangoedmor and Llangynllo Card (*Lankenlan* c.1291, *Llangynllawe* 1399, *ll. gynllo* c.1566).

LLANGYNNWR, LLANGUNNOR Carm SN4320

'church of Cynfor', ***llan***, pers.n. ***Cynfor***

Lanconor alias Langonefor 1283, *Langonour* 1394, *ll. gwnwr* c.1566,
Llangynnor 1831

This may also be *villam de Kelnur* 1222. Cynfor or Cynfwr also has a dedication at Capel Cynnor (*Lancumnour* 1358), a former chapel of Pembrey Carm.

LLANGYNOG Mont SJ0526

'church of Cynog', ***llan***, pers.n. ***Cynog***

Lankenauc 1254, *Langenauk* 1291, *llangenoc* 1377, *ll. gynog* c.1566, *Llangunog* 1578, *llangynocke* 1597

Probably the same Cynog son of Brychan found in Merthyr Cynog (q.v.) and Llangynog (*ll. gynog* c.1566) Brec, Llangynog Monm (*henlenic cinauc* 1136-54, *Llankanynoke* 1488) and Llangunnock Herefordshire. The church in nearby Llanrhaeadr-ym-Mochant is dedicated to Doewan, another son of Brychan.

LLANGYNWYD Glam SS8588

'church of Cynwyd', ***llan***, pers.n. ***Cynwyd***

Sancti Cunioth' de Leueni 1173-83, *Langenuth* late 12cent., *Landgenud* 1254, *Langenoith* 1400, *ll. gynwyd fawr* c.1566

Nothing certain is known of Cynwyd who is also found in Cynwyd Mer. *Leueni* refers to its location near the river Llynfi.

LLANGYNYDD see **LLANGENNITH**

LLANGYWER, LLANGOWER Mer SH9032

'church of Cywair', ***llan***, pers.n. ***Cywair***

Nanngeweyr 1284, *Langewoyr* 1291, *Llan Gowair* 14cent., *ll. gywair* c.1566, *Llangower* 1681

Nothing is known about Cywair (generally held to be female). The 1284 form probably reflects the occasional alternation of ***llan*** and ***nant*** 'valley'. The narrow valley (***glyn***) south-east of Llangywer is Glyn Gywer leading to Nant Rhyd-wen (***rhyd***, ***gwyn***); it is arguable that this was the original *Nant Gywer*. Llangywer would therefore be a later development of *Nant Gywer*. If so, the second el. could have been the adj. ***cywair*** 'arranged, well-made' referring to the ***nant***. The saint ***Cywair*** would then be antiquarian fiction. There is a legend that failure to replace the cover on the nearby Ffynnon Gywer (***ffynnon***) created Llyn Tegid.

LLANHAMLACH Brec SO0926

'church of Anlach', ***llan***, pers.n. ***Anlach***

Lanhamelach 1188, *Lanhameloch* c.1203-14, *Lanhamelak* 1230-40, *Lanhankelok* 1373, *Llanhamlagh* 1378, *Llanamolch* 1545, *ll. hamwlch* c.1566

The p.n. defies a totally satisfactory explanation. There was an Anlach (*Anlac, Anlach* post 1130 [c.1200]) described as the father of Brychan Brycheiniog (see Brecon) reputedly buried in front of the porch of Llansbyddyd church 5 miles east. If he is a genuine person, he is unlikely to have been a saint. In this instance, the stressed medial syllable produced an unusual intrusive -h- (possibly as in Llanharan and Llanharry) and was evidently influenced by ***am*** and later occasionally by *llwch* (cf. Amlwch Angl.), possibly with reference to a pool in the nearby river Usk. The church was dedicated (at least in 1486) to Peter, and now to Peter and Illtud (whose hermitage was recorded here c.1191).

LLANHARAN Glam ST0083

'church of ?Haran', ***llan***, pers.n. ?***Haran***

Lanharan 1173-83, *ll. haran* c.1566

The church is dedicated to saints Julius and Aaron, allegedly martyred at Caerleon, perhaps mid 3cent., but the latter may well have been prompted by an earlier one to Haran. There is a Lanharan (Tréguier) in Brittany. It has also been strongly argued that the saint was Aran or Aron with an intrusive -h- in the stressed medial syllable (as in Llanhamlach and possibly Llanharry).

LLANHARRY, LLANHARI Glam ST0080

'church of ?Hari', ***llan***, pers.n. ?***Hari***

Landhary 12cent., *Lanhary* c.1262, *Llanharry* 1538-44, *ll. hari* c.1566

The pers.n. Hari is otherwise unattested although a similar name appears in the adjoining parish Llanharan It is possible that the name was an otherwise unattested Ari with an intrusive -h- in the stressed medial syllable (as in Llanhamlach and possibly Llanharan). The church is dedicated to Illtud.

LLANHENNOCK, LLANHENWG Monm ST3592

'church of ?Henog', ***llan***, pers.n.?***Henog***

Lanhenoke 1535, *Lanenoch, -ock* 1539, *Lanhenoge* 1565, *ll. hynwg* c.1566, *Llanhenog* 1707

This may also be *Landenag* 1291. There is no other evidence of any saint with this name. The modern W form (perhaps anticipated by *ll.hynwg* c.1566) has probably been influenced by pers.ns in -wg (such as Tyswg and Corrwg), while the -og/-wg alternation is seen in Llangattock/Llangatwg.

LLANHOWEL, LLANHYWEL Pemb SM8127

'church of Hywel', ***llan***, pers.n. ***Hywel***

Lanhowel 1291, *Lannowell* 1302, *Llanhowell* 1491, *ll. howel* c.1566

Nothing is known of any saint Hywel, and so the name may refer to a secular sponsor, popularly believed to be one of Arthur's knights. He has been misidentified with Llanllywel Monm (q.v.).

LLANHUADAIN see **LLAWHADEN**

LLANIDLOES Mont SN9584

'church of Idloes', ***llan***, pers.n. ***Idloes***

Lanidloes 1254, *Thlanidloys* 1280, *Lanydlos* 1478, *Llanidloes* 1582

This is the only church dedicated to a saint of whom very little is known. He has been identified with a reputed saint Idloes son of Gwydnabi.

LLANIESTYN Caern SH2633

'church of Iestyn', ***llan***, pers.n. ***Iestyn***

Lanyustin 1254, *Lanyestyn* 1291, *Llan Yestin* 1543, *Llan Estyn* 1551, *ll. iestin* c.1566, *Llaniestyn* 1765

The church was dedicated to the 6cent. saint Iestyn. The 1551 form was possibly influenced by ***estyn*** 'reach' perceived as spiritual consolation.

LLANIGON, LLANEIGON Brec SO2140

'church of Eigon', ***llan***, pers.n. ***Eigon***

Sancto Egynon 1148-c.1155, *Sancti Eggiani* c.1150-75, *Sancti Egyon* 1222, *Llaneygan* 1291, *ll. eigion* c.1566

Eigon was said to have been born in Bronllys c.1100 and is described as son of Gwynllyw and brother of Cynidr and Cadog (see Llangynidr and Llangattock Brec). Llanigon has -ei- > common dial. -i- while Llaneigon shows the south W characteristic of loss of -i- unlike the north W var. Eigion; cf. Gorseinon.

LLANILAR Card SN6275

'church of Ilar', ***llan***, pers.n. ***Ilar***

Lanhinar 1277-80, *Lanelar* 1298-1300, *Lanhillar* 1304, *Lanelar* 1361, *Llanyler* 1498, *Llanylar* 1535, *ll. ilar* c.1566, *Lhan Hilar* late 16cent., *Llan Ilar* 1834

The W Ilar does seem to derive from Hilary and the occasional -h- in the stressed middle syllable reflects the deliberate attempt to introduce continental saints into the W church, here Hilary of Poitiers (died c.367). Cf. St Hilary (q.v.) with cymricized forms *Sant (H)ylari* stressed on the second syllable. Another candidate is Ilar ab Nudd or Ilar Bysgotwr (***pysgotwr***, 'fisherman').

LLANILID Glam SS9781

'church of Ilid', ***llan***, pers.n. ***Ilid***

sancta Ilith 1173-83, *Sancta Julita* late 12cent., (*de*) *Sancto Ilith* 1208, *Sancte Iulite* 1254, *Lhanyllid* c. 1545, *ll. ilid a chirig* c.1566, *Llanylyd* 1578

Nothing certain is known of Ilid though she may well be commemorated at Lanillis (Léon) in Brittany. Several forms indicate attempts to identify her with St Julitta and associate her son Cyricus with Curig, both legendary Roman martyrs.

LLANILLTERN see **CAPEL LLANILLTERN**

LLANILLTUD FAERDREF see **LLANTWIT FARDRE**

LLANILLTUD FAWR see **LLANTWIT MAJOR**

LLANILLTUD GŴYR see **ILSTON**

LLANISHEN see **LLANISIEN**[1, 2]

LLANISIEN[1]**, LLANISHEN** Glam ST1781
'church of Nisien', ***llan***, pers.n. ***Nisien***
Sancti nisien 1128 (1160-80), *Sancti Dionisii de Kibur* 1173-83, *Landyneys* 1317, *St. Denis in Kybour* 1400, *Lanysan in Kybour* 1440, *Llan Isen* 1536-9, *ll.issen* c.1566
The saint's name appears to be Nisien or Isien, possibly Isanus summoned by Illtud to his monastery at Llantwit Major. He has also been identified (probably in error) in some sources with Dionysius (St Denis) of Paris (died c.258). Llanisien had a Ffynnon Denis (or Llandennis) (***ffynnon***) near a house recorded as *Capel Denis* 1833 (but called *Dyffryn* in 1886) which may have been a medieval chapel.

LLANISIEN[2]**, LLANISHEN**
'church of Nisien', ***llan***, pers.n. ***Nisien*** Monm SO4703
lann nissien 1136-54, *Sancti Dionisii*, *Lanissan* 1223, *Lannissen* 1254, *Landinessen* 1296, *ll. issen*, *ll. Jssen* c.1566
As Llanisien[1].

LLANLLAWDDOG Carm SN4529
'church of ?Llywoddog', ***llan***, pers.n. ?***Llywoddog***
Llanllawothog 1395, *Llanllawddok* 1535, *ll. llawddog* c.1566
The correct form of the pers.n. is uncertain. He has been identified with a saint recorded in connection with the church of *Sancti Leodoci* c.1191 (c.1214), *Sancti Ludoci* 1221-9 at Cenarth Carm but this appears to be a different saint, possibly Llwydog. Llanllawddog had a Ffynnon Llawddog (*Ffynnon Lawdhog* c.1700, ***ffynnon***) and a feast-day Dygwyl Llawddog (*Dygwyl Lawdhog* c.1700, ***dygwyl*** 'feast-day').

LLANLLECHID Caern SH6268
'church of Llechid', ***llan***, pers.n. ***Llechid***
Lanleghyt 1254, *Llanlechyc*, *Llanllechith* 1291, *Llanllechet* 1400, *Llanlleched* 1408-17, *llan llechyd* 1515, *ll. llechid* c.1566, *Llanllechid* 1763
Llechid was the daughter of the 6cent. Ithel Hael of Brittany and sister to Tygái (of Llandygái). Associated with her is the nearby Ffynnon Llechid (***ffynnon***).

LLANLLEONFEL, LLANLLYWENFEL Brec SN9349
'church of Llywenfel', ***llan***, pers.n. ***Llywenfel***
Lanloeluayl 1280, *Llanllewenvoyl* 1360-7, *ll. llywen fel* c.1566, *Llanlloenwell* 1671
A 15cent. oath *myn Llawenfel* ('by Llawenfel') supports an otherwise unattested saint's name. The present form Llanlleonfel is a very late development possibly influenced by antiquarians who misinterpreted Llanllywenfel as *lleon* and the Roman road here, properly Sarn Helen, as

Sarn Lleon, perceived to be the *lleon* supposedly derived from *legionis* 'of the legion' (see Holt).

LLANLLOWELL see **LLANLLYWEL**

LLANLLUGAN Mont SJ0502
'church of Llugan', ***llan***, pers.n. ***Llugan***
Llanlugan 1239, *Lanlugan* c.1291, *Llanlligan* 1536-9, *Llanllugan* 1562
The church is dedicated to an otherwise unattested Llugan. Despite the consistent forms with *-an* several attempts have been made to identify Llanllugan with a pers.n. Llugyrn, identified with Llorcan Wyddel alias Gwyddelan, an Ir saint with dedications at Gwyddelwern Mer and Llanwyddelan Mont (q.v.). There was a Cistercian nunnery here.

LLAN-LLWCH Carm SN3818
'church by a pool', ***llan***, ***llwch***
Lanlok 1298-1300, *Lanlogh* 1302, *Llanllogh* 1395, *Llanloz* 1397, *ll. llwch* c.1566, *Landlothe* 1230 (16cent.), *Llanllwch* 1750
There is a large marshy area extending for about two miles west of the village, described in 1811 as *Morass,* formerly a lake, visible in parts only.

LLANLLWCHAEARN Card SN3857
'church of Llwchaearn', ***llan***, pers.n. ***Llwchaearn***
Lanluchaern 1284, *Llanlloghaeron* 1389, *ll. llwch hayarn* c.1566, *Llanllwchaiarn* 1834
The forms of the saint's name reveal the occasional influence of (the river) Aeron and ***haearn*** 'iron'. There is an identical p.n. Llanllwchaiarn in Mont.

LLANLLWNI Carm SN4741
'church of ?Lleweni', ***llan***, pers.n. ***?Lleweni***
Lanthleweny 1329, *Llanllewony* 1395, *Llanlloyny* 1560, *ll. llwni* c.1566
There is no record of a saint Llywynni or Llewenni although the early forms resemble the Denb Lleweni (pers.n. ***Llawen*** and the terr.suff. ***-i***). The name seems to have undergone perplexing modification including loss of the unaccented first syllable of the pers.n. It has been transferred to a 19cent. village on the Carmarthen-Llanybydder road about two miles south-east of the parish church at Maesycrugiau.

LLANLLYFNI Caern SH4751
'church beside (the river) Llyfni', ***llan***, r.n. ***Llyfni***
Thlauthleueny 1352, *Llanllyfne* 1432, *ll. llyfni* c.1566, *Llanllyfni* 1657
The river Llyfni (*Leueny* 1303-4, *Thlyfny* 1342-3, *llyfni* 1518, ***llyfn*** 'smooth', r.n. suff. ***-i***) flows from Llyn Nantlle through Tal-y-sarn and Llanllyfni

to enter the sea at Pontllyfni. The church (dedicated to Rhedyw as in Ffynnon Rhedyw, ***ffynnon***) is on a slight rise beside the river.

LLANLLŶR see **LLANYRE**

LLANLLYWEL, LLANLLOWELL Monm ST3998

'church of Llywel', ***llan***, pers.n. ***Llywel***

Lanluuayl 1155-83, *Landlovel* 1254, *Lanlouel* c.1348, *Llanlloell* 1563, *ll. howel* c.1566, *llann llwel yngwent* late 16cent.

Llywel also has a dedication at Llywel Brec (q.v.). The c.1566 form is an attempt to identify the p.n. with the pers.n. Hywel as in Llanhowel Pemb (q.v.).

LLANLLYWENFEL see **LLANLLEONFEL**

LLAN-LWY see **LLANDELOY**

LLANMADOG, LLANMADOC Glam SS4493

'church of Madog', ***llan***, pers.n. ***Madog***

Landmadoch 1249, *Lanmadok* 1284, *Lammadok in Gouer* 1312, *Llanvadog* 1513, *Llanvadoc* 1534, *Lanvadocke* 1626, *Llanvadog* c.1700

The forms record the existence of the more regular lenited *Llanfadog*. Llanmadog is probably due to E influence; cf. Llanmaes and Llanmihangel.

LLANMAES, LLAN-FAES Glam SS9869

'church in the open countryside', ***llan***, ***maes***

Lanmays 1238-40, *Lanmaes, Landmais* 1254, *Lammays* 1291, *Llanvays* 1535, *ll. faes* c.1566

In open countryside in contrast perhaps to the nearby church of Llantwit Major/Llanilltud Fawr. Identical in meaning to Llan-faes[1] and Llan-faes[2]. Here, Llan-faes is the regular W form, while Llanmaes is probably due to E influence; cf. Llanmadog and Llanmihangel. Cf. similar forms for Llanmaes St Fagans (*lanvase* 1675, *Lammace* 1708, *Lanmace* 1755, *Lammas* 1766). The forms also show the dial. -ae- > -a- and then to the narrowed sound represented by the anglicized -ay- , -ai- spellings.

LLANMARTIN, LLANFARTHIN Monm ST3989

'church of Martin', ***llan***, pers.n. ***Martin***

aecclae st. Martini 1086, *lann marthin* 1160-85, *Lanmartin* 1254, *Lanmartyn* c.1348, *ll. fartin* c.1566, *Lanmarthen* 1620

Martin or Marthin is probably St Martin of Tours (d. 397). Llanfarthin is the regular W form (identical to Llanfarthin, the W name of St Martins Shropshire and Marstow Herefordshire) while Llanmartin is probably due to E influence; cf. Llanmadog.

LLANMORLAIS Glam SS5352

'bank of (the river) Morlais', ***glan***, r.n. ***Morlais***

Glanmorleis 1617, *Lanmorlais* 1650, *Glanmorlais* 1715, *Llanmorlais* 1764

glan has been confused with ***llan***; cf. Llanbradach. The r.n. is *Morlais* 1522 (***mawr, glais*** 'stream').

LLANNARTH Card SN4257

'church of the ridge', ***llan, garth***

Llann Arth fl. 1170, *Lanarth* 1284, *Lannarth* 1291, *llan arth* c.1566

The church is on a hill. The second el. has popularly been associated with ***arth*** 'bear' particularly as a pers.n. Arth and with the r.n. Arth (as in Aber-arth some five miles away). An early dedication was to Meilig, but is now to Dewi/David.

LLANNARTH see **LLAN-ARTH**

LLANNERCH BANNA see **PENLEY**

LLANNERCH-Y-MEDD Angl SH4184

'glade of mead', ***llannerch, y, medd***

llann'meth 1445-6, (*i*) *Lannerch y medd* 15cent.,

Llan Vair yn Llanerchymedd 1536-9, *llannerch y medd* c.1566

One possible explanation is that bees frequented the glade and that their honey was used in the production of mead (*Hydromelis Vicus vulgo Llanerchymedd* 1710). However, it is equally possible that the glade was habitually the location of convivial gatherings.

LLANNEWYDD see **NEWCHURCH**[2]

LLAN-NON[1] Card SN5167

'church of Non', ***llan***, pers.n. ***Non***

Lannon 12cent. (c.1700), *lannon* 1215-29, *Llannon* 1326, *llanon* 1598

It has been argued that the second el. could have been simply ***onn*** 'ash-tree' but was transformed into Non the mother of Dewi/David in order to strengthen Dewi's association with Ceredigion.

LLAN-NON[2] Carm SN5308

'church of Non', ***llan***, pers.n. ***Non***

LLann Onn c.1500, *Llanon* 1543, *ll. onn* c.1566

Identical in meaning to Llan-non[1]. The absence of early spellings is likely to be due to Llan-non's status as a former chapel-of-ease to Llanelli.

LLANNOR Caern SH3537

'big church', ***llan, mawr***

Lanvaur 1254, *Llanvawr* 1291, *Lannawr* 1350-1, *Llano[u]r* 1543,

llannor 1565-87, *Llannor* 1687, *Llanor alias Llanfawr* 1763

The church itself cannot be described as distinctively large, but the parish was extensive and divided into three parishes in the middle of the 19cent. It was occasionally distinguished by its location in Llŷn (*ll. vawr yn lloyn* 1590). The phonological development was from Llan-fawr to Llanfor to Llannor, with stress shift, although Llanfawr appears to have survived fairly late (at least in documents).

LLANOFER see **LLANOVER**

LLANORONWY see **ROCKFIELD**

LLANOVER, LLANOFER Monm SO3109
'church of Myfor', ***llan***, pers.n. ***Myfor***
(de) Sancto Menoro 1254, *Lammovor* 1285, *Llanimor* 1291, *Lanmovor* 1349-53, *Lannovor* 1357, *Llan Over* 1559, *ll. ofor* c.1566
The pers.n. is the honorific pref. my- and the pers.n. Môr (seen also in Merthyr Mawr Glam). Original **Llanfyfor* appears to have developed to *Llanofor* and then to Llanofer influenced, at least in spelling, by E ***over*** and W ***ofer*** 'wasteful, vain'. Local pronunciation of the E form tends to stress the first syllable. The church is now dedicated to St Bartholomew.

LLANPUMSAINT Carm SN4129
'church of five saints', ***llan***, (*y*), ***pump***, ***sant*** var. ***saint***
Lanipymseynt c.1258-71, *Llanypymseint* 1331-2, *Llanpemsaunt* 1547, *ll. y pymsaint* c.1566
The church is traditionally dedicated to Gwyn, Gwynno, Gwynoro, Celynnin and Ceitho. The stream here is *nant y pumsant* c.1700 (***nant***).

LLANRHAEADR-YM-MOCHNANT Denb SJ1226
'church of the waterfall in Mochnant', ***llan***, ***rhaeadr***, ***yn***, commote n. ***Mochnant***
Llanracarder 1254, *Thlanrather in Meuhenhand* 1284, *Lanraiader en Mochnant* 1344-57, *llanrraydr* 1377, *Llanraeader* 1465, *ll. Rayadr ymochnant* c.1566, *Llanrhaiader in Moughnant* 1606, *Llanrhaiadr* 1795
The church at Llanrhaeadr-ym-Mochnant is dedicated to Doewan, commemorated in Cwm Doefon and Ffynnon Ddoefon. The church and town have popularly been associated with the impressive waterfall of Pistyll Rhaeadr (***pistyll*** 'waterfall, cataract') which is four miles north-west and gave its name to Afon Rhaeadr, the river on which Llanrhaeadr stands and which divided the commote into Mochnant Is Rhaeadr (Denb) (*Mochnant* 1278, ***is*** 'lower') and Mochnant Uwch Rhaeadr (Mont) (*Mochnant uch Raeadir* 1263, ***uwch*** 'upper'). Mochnant is either ***moch*** 'pigs' or the adj. ***moch*** 'quick, rapid', and possibly ***nant*** 'valley' although the significance of the first el. favours ***nant*** 'stream, river' which would make Mochnant an even earlier name of Afon Rhaeadr before Mochnant became the commote name.

LLANRHAEADR-YNG-NGHINMEIRCH Denb SJ0863

'church near the rushing stream in Cinmeirch', ***llan***, ***rhaeadr***, ***yn***, commote n. ***Cinmeirch***

Lanrayadyr 1254, *llannraeadur* 1349, *Llanreyadur in Kymmerth* 1455, *ll. ddyfnoc* c.1566, *llanrhayader in Kinmerch* 1661-2, *Llanrhaiadr* 1795

The church at Llanrhaeadr-yng-Nghinmeirch is dedicated to Dyfnog whose name is preserved in the healing spring Ffynnon Ddyfnog (*ffynnon dhyfnog* c.1700). However, if the name *Llanddyfnog* ever existed (as recorded in one, probably antiquarian, form) it appears to have been superseded by its association with the turbulent forceful spring which emerges here after a subterranean course through limestone from the direction of Prion. The village is referred to simply as Llanrhaeadr and the later industrial ***pentref*** less than half-a-mile away is Pentre Llanrhaeadr. Cinmeirch or Ceinmeirch (*Kunnerch* c.1253, *Keinmeirch* 1334) is ***cain*** 'ridge', ***march*** 'horse' pl. ***meirch***.

LLANRHEITHAN Pemb SM8628

'church of Rheithan', ***llan***, pers.n. ***Rheithan***

Lanrethan 1259 (14cent.), *Lanreythan'* 1326 (16cent.), *Llanrithan* 1513, *Llanrythan* 1543, *ll. Reithon* c.1566, *llanrithon* c.1600

The pers.n. is otherwise unattested.

LLANRHIAN Pemb SM8131

'church of Rhian', ***llan***, pers.n. ***Rhian***

Lanrian late 12cent., *Laurian* 1291, *Lanrian'* 1326 (16cent.), (*ecclesie*) *Sancti Riani* 1486, *ll. Riaian* c.1566

This is not the fem. pers.n. Rhiain or Rhian (***rhiain*** 'maiden') but a masc. pers.n. Rhian (probably ***rhi*** 'king' and the dim.suff. ***-an***). Nearby is *Kader Rhian* 1669 where ***cadair*** 'seat' is frequently associated with pers.ns and often incorporates the name of the patron saint of the parish.

LLANRHIDIAN Glam SS4992

'church of Rhidian', ***llan***, pers.n. ***Rhidian***

Landridian 1185 (13cent.), *Lanrydyan* 1291, *Lanridyan* 1319, *ll. Riden* c.1566, *Llanrhidian* 1679

The saint Rhidian is otherwise unattested. The occasional form *Land-* is probably a development from -nr- (cf. Cyn(w)rig > Cyndrig and Henry/Hendry), but does appear in other ***llan*** names.

LLAN-RHOS Caern SH7980

'church in Rhos', ***llan***, p.n. ***Rhos***

Llanrhos 1680

An alternative name for Llan-rhos appears to have been Eglwys-Rhos (*Egluysros* 1254, *Egluwys Ros* 1291, *Eglwys Rhos* 1659) from its location in the hundred of Rhos (see Llandrillo-yn-Rhos). Within the parish of Eglwys-rhos, Llan-rhos or Llan Rhos was probably the settlement or home tnshp around the church.

LLANRHUDDLAD Angl SH3389

'church of Rhuddlad', ***llan***, pers.n. ***Rhuddlad***

Lanruthalat 1254, *llann ruddlad* 1497, *ll. Ryddlad* c.1566, *llanriddlad* 1682, *Llanruddlad* 1758, *Llanrhuddlad* 1838

The saint is reputed to have been the daughter of an Ir king of Leinster. The occasional form Llanrhyddlad is possibly influenced by ***rhydd*** 'free' or by ***rhyddhad*** 'relief'. The name is also found in Moel Rhyddlad.

LLANRHYSTUD Card SN5369

'church of Rhystud', ***llan***, pers.n. ***Rhystud***

Llan Rystut 1149 (c.1400), *Llan Ristut* 1151 (late 13cent.), *Lanrustud* 1229, *Llanrustud* 1229, *ll. Rystyd* c.1566

Rhystud is believed to be the brother of Cristiolus (see Llangristiolus). The church is on the boundary between two commotes so that the adjacent civil parishes, originally two parts of one ecclesiastical parish, were called Llanrhystud Anhuniog and Llanrhystud Mefenydd.

LLANRUG Caern SH5363

'church in the heather', ***llan***, ***grug***

Lanruk 1284, *Llanrucke* 1517, *Llan Ruge* 1535, *ll. V'el yn Ruc* c.1566, *llan Ruge, llanvihengle in Rug* 1614, *Llanrug* 1763

Although it has been customary to give the meaning as 'church in (the tnshp of) Rug', the historical forms show that the original name of the church was evidentally *Llanrug* with ***grug*** 'heather'. A later extended var. for the church, Llanfihangel-yn-Rug, referred to its saint Mihangel and qualified it by its location in what had by then become the tnshp of Rug. The tnshp name Rug (*Ruke* 1475, *Rug* 1541-58, *Ruk* c.1553) was taken directly from the church name Llanrug; cf. Pont Rug (and Rug near Corwen Mer). Later still, Llanrug was used of the village, a form long established by usage resisting the more regular Llan-rug.

LLANRWST Denb SH8061

'church of Gwrwst', ***llan***, pers.n. ***Gwrwst***

Lhannruste, Llannvrewist 1254, *Lañwrvst* 1291, *Llanroust* 1386, *Llanwrwst* 1398, *Llanrwst* 1453

This is the only church dedicated to this little-known saint (whose fuller name was Gwrwst Ledlwm ap Ceneu Godebog).

LLANSADURNEN see **LLANSADYRNIN**

LLANSADWRN[1] Angl SH5676

'church of Sadwrn', ***llan***, pers.n. ***Sadwrn***

Lansadorn 1308, *Llansadwrn* 14cent., *Llansadorn* 1443, *ll. sadwrn* c.1566

The saint's name derives from the L pers.n. Saturnus. In the church, an early 6cent. stone commemorates *Satvrninvs* which is probably a distinct pers.n. Sadyrnin (cf. Llansadyrnin) but could conceivably denote a follower of Sadwrn.

LLANSADWRN[2] Carm SN6931
'church of Sadwrn', ***llan***, pers.n. ***Sadwrn***
Laisadurn 1229, *Lansadurn* 1244-71 (?1258-71), *Lensadorn* 1284-7, *Lansadorn* 1308, *ll. sadwrn* c.1566
The saint is also called Sadwrn Farchog (***marchog*** 'rider, knight').

LLANSADYRNIN, LLANSADURNEN Carm SN2811
'church of Sadyrnin', ***llan***, pers.n. ***Sadyrnin***
Launcedurni 1328, *Lasedurny* 1307, *ll. sadyrnyn* c.1566, *Llansadornen* 1661
The saint's name derives from the L pers.n. Saturninus, but may indicate 'a follower of Sadwrn' cf. Llansadwrn.

LLAN SAIN SIÔR see **ST GEORGE**

LLAN-SAINT Carm SN3808
'church of (the) saints', ***llan***, (*y*), ***saint***
Ecclesiam Omnium Sanctorum 12cent., *Halwencherche* 1280, *Halthenchirche* 1319, *llann y saint* c.1500, *Halgenchirch* 1505, *Alhalonchurch* 1525, *Llan-saint* 1831
The church is dedicated to All Saints or All Hallows (a designation which may be seen in the forms for 1280 and 1525). The E form *Halkenchurch* (which did not survive) presents a particular difficulty. A survival from OE ***hālga*** 'saint' pl. ***hālgena*** cannot be parallelled elsewhere. The presence of two early medieval inscribed stones built into the outer wall of the church and a tradition of a third stone in the churchyard has given rise to the suggestion that these are associated with the saints.

LLANSAMLET Glam SS6897
'church of Samled', ***llan***, pers.n. ***Samled***
Lansamle 1153-84 (1334), *Lansambled* 1535, *ll. siamled* c.1566, *Llansamlete* 1575
The single reliable reference to a saint Samled is in a 15cent. poem.

LLANSANFFRAID[1]**, LLANSANTFFRAED** Brec SO1223
'church of saint Ffraid', ***llan***, ***sant***, pers.n. ***Ffraid***
Lansefred c.1100, *Lan San Fraid* 1140-50, *Lanseffrei, -ey* 1148-c.1155, *Llansanffreit* 1215-22 (1231-2), *Sancta Brigida* 1254, *Brydecherch* 1310-11, *St. Mary de Sancto Brigida* 1476, *ll. san ffred* c.1566
Ffraid and Ffrêd are W versions (usually northern and southern respectively, but not exclusively so) of the Ir Brigid (L Brigida) found also as Bride and the cymricized Brid. Several different saints bear this name. Dedications are very common in Ireland and Scotland with some 17 dedications in Wales and 30 in Brittany. Loss of final -t was common when W ***sant*** was prefixed to a pers.n. Cf. St Brides Major/Saint-y-brid.

LLANSANFFRAID[2] Card SN5167

'church of saint Ffraid', ***llan, sant***, pers.n. ***Ffraid***

Lansafrei 1158-65 (1308), *Lansanfreit* 1215-22 (1231-2), *Lansanfred* 1284, *Llansenfreyd* 1291, *Llansanfride* 1536-9, *Llanseynt Frede* 1535, *ll. san ffraid* c.1566

See Llansanffraid[1]. The church dedication to *St. Bridget the Virgin* is recorded in 1433. In Ceredigion one other church (Llanffraid) and one chapel (Capel Ffraid in Llandysul) are also dedicated to her. An occasional alias was Llansanffraid yn y Morfa Mawr (*Llansanfrayd by Morva Mawer* 1394) from its location on the extensive coastal plain (***morfa***) south of Llanrhystud.

LLANSANFFRAID CWMTEUDDWR, LLANSANFFRAED CWMDAUDDWR Radn SN9667

'church of saint Ffraid in the commote of Deuddwr', ***llan, sant***, pers.n. ***Ffraid, cwmwd***, commote n. ***Deuddwr***

Launsanfret by Raeyrdyr 1368, *Llansanfrid in Comytoyther* 1536-9

See Llansanffraid[1]. The commote is *Comot Deudor* 12cent., *Cwmtoythur* 1406, *k. dayddwr* c.1566), the two waters (***dau, dŵr***) of the rivers Elan and Wye. W ***cwmwd*** has been confused with ***cwm***. Two of the forms refer to the adjoining town of Rhaeadr.

LLANSANFFRAID GLAN CONWY Denb SH8075

'church of saint Ffraid beside (the river) Conwy', ***llan, sant***, pers.n. ***Ffraid, glan***, r.n. ***Conwy***

Dissech 1254, *Dyserth sanfreyt* 1291, *Disserth al. Llansanfraid* 1535, *ll. san ffraid* c.1566, *Lhan St Ffraid c.*1700, *Llan Sanfraed Glan Conwy* 1713

See Llansanffraid[1]. The earlier names *Dyserth* (***diserth*** 'hermit's cell') now a tnshp name and *Dyserth Sanffraid* were eventually replaced by a parish name Llansanffraid which was in regular use until Llansanffraid Glan Conwy emerged. Today, there is a tendency to refer to the village simply as Glan Conwy.

LLANSANFFRAID GLYNCEIRIOG Denb SJ2038

'church of saint Ffraid in the valley of (the river) Ceiriog', ***llan, sant***, pers.n. ***Ffraid , glyn***, r.n. ***Ceiriog***

Lansanfreit 1291, *Llansanffraid ynglyn* 1538, *llansanffraid y glyn* 1560, *ll. sain ffred glyn kerioc* c.1566, *Llansantfraid Glyn Keiriog* 1691, *Lansantffraid Glynn Ceiriog* 1795

See Llansanffraid[1]. The locational qualification refers to the narrow valley (***glyn***) through which the river Ceiriog runs and which also gave its name to a terr. division (*Glynn* 1391-3, *Y Glyn* 1778). The village is now more commonly referred to as Glynceiriog. Occasionally, the church is called Llansanffraid y Glyn.

LLANSANFFRAID GLYNDYFRDWY see **CARROG**

LLANSANFFRAID GWYNLLŴG see **ST BRIDES WENTLOOGE**

LLANSANFFRAID-YM-MECHAIN Mont SJ2220
'church of saint Ffraid in Mechain', ***llan***, pers.n. ***Ffraid***, terr.n. ***Mechain***
Llansanfret 1254, *Lansanfreit* 1291, *Llansanfred* 1284,
Llannsanfrayd in Mechayn 1390,
(church of) *St. Bride (Brigide) in Mechein* 1425,
llan.sanffraid y mechain c.1600, *Llansanffraid in Deythor* 1600
The church was in the cantref of Mechain (see Llanfechain) and the commote of Deuddwr (see Llansanffraid Cwmteuddwr). This is also likely to be the place of pilgrimage called *llansaynte frayde* 1526.

LLANSANFFRAID-YN-ELFAEL, LLANSANTFFRAED-IN-ELWEL Radn SO0954
'church of saint Ffraid in Elfael', ***llan***, pers.n. ***Ffraid***, cantref n. ***Elfael***
Lansanfret in Elevain c.1200, *Lannsanffered* 1276, *Bridechurch* 1291,
St. Bridget in Elwael Uchmynydd 1434
The cantref Elfael (*Elwael* c.1100-3, *Eluen* 1142, *Elevein* 1198, *Eluail, elmail* 1136-54, probably a pers.n. Elfael) was anciently divided into two commotes Uwch Mynydd (*Eluael uch Mynyth* 1276) and Is Mynydd (*Elvellismenyth* c.1277), 'above ~, below the mountain' (***uwch***, ***is***, ***mynydd***).

LLANSANNAN Denb SH9365
'church of Sannan', ***llan***, pers.n. ***Sannan***
Llannsannan 1254, *Lansaman* 1291, *Llansannan* 1458
Sannan is said to be an Ir saint who founded churches in Cornwall and Brittany and was buried in Gwytherin. There is a dedication to him in Bedwellte. Sannan, Gwnnadl (see Llangwnnadl) and Tudno (see Llandudno) were said to be sons of Seithenyn, of Maes Gwyddno in the mythical Cantre'r Gwaelod. One suggestion is that the pers.n. Sannan could be a derivative of ***sant*** (***san***, dim.suff. ***-an***).

LLANSANTFFRAED see **LLANSANFFRAID**[1]

LLANSANTFFRAED-IN-ELWEL see **LLANSANFFRAID-YN-ELFAEL**

LLANSAWEL[1] Carm SN6136
'church of Sawyl', ***llan***, pers.n. ***Sawyl***
Lansawyl 1265, *Lansawel* 1301
The pers.n. Sawyl, Sawl derives from the L pers.n. Samuelis, and is believed to be the son of Pabo Post Prydain (see Llanbabo). Local pronunciation is frequently Llansewyl.

LLANSAWEL[2] see **BRITON FERRY**

LLANSBYDDYD see **LLANSPYDDID**

LLANSILIN Denb SJ2028

'church of Silin', ***llan***, pers.n. ***Silin***

ecclesie silin c.1191, *Llansilyn* 1254, *Lansylyn* 1291, *Ecclesia Si Egidii de Kynlleith* 1296, *Llansilin* 1419, *ll. silyn yng hynllaith* c.1566

The reference to St Egidius stems from a (probably mistaken) belief that Silin corresponds to Giles, of which Egidius is a latinized var. The parish is in the commote of Cynllaith which also appears in two of the historical forms. Cynllaith is probably a pers.n.; cf. Machynlleth.

LLAN-SOE, LLANSOY Monm SO4402

'church of Tysoe', ***llan***, pers.n. ***Tysoe***

Lann Tyssoi, podum sancti Tisoi 1136-54, *Landesoy* 1254, 1451-8, *lansoy* 1464, *ll. soe* c.1566

The unstressed honorific pref. ***ty-*** had been lost by the 15cent. Tysoe was reputedly a disciple of Dyfrig.

LLANSOY see **LLAN-SOE**

LLANSPYDDID, LLANSBYDDYD Brec SO0128

'church of ?Ysbyddyd', ***llan***, pers.n. ?***Ysbyddyd***

Lannspitit 1100, *Lanespetit* 11cent. (c.1200), *Lamdespidic* 1127 (1374-7), *ll. ysbyddaid* c.1566

The occasional early forms with -de- may represent the honorific pref. ***ty-*** though no such pers.n. is recorded and the church is dedicated to Cadog. Alternatively, the pers.n. name may be a by-form of the pers. n. Ysbyddaden; a giant of that name appears in the medieval tale of Culhwch and Olwen.

LLANSTADWEL, LLANSTADWELL Pemb SM9404

'church of ?Tudwal', ***llan***, pers.n. ?***Tudwal***

Lanstadhewal late 12cent., *Lanstowel* 1291, *Llanstadwell* 1517, c.1600, *ll. ystydwal* c.1566, *Llanystadwel* 1591

A difficult p.n. for which no satisfactory explanation has been offered. The church's dedication to Tudwal supports the suggestion that it might be a contracted form of an original 'Llan Sant Tudwal' (cf. Llansanffraid). However, the forms consistently indicate -a- rather than -u-. Another suggestion is a contraction of 'Llan Ynys Tudwal', 'church of Tudwal's island' (***ynys***) and connected with Neyland (q.v.) about a mile to the east. P.ns such as Sketty (Ynys Ceti) and Skewen (?Ynys Cuen) Glam show the effect of such a contraction, but the problem of -a- remains. A further suggestion is a rare feminine pers.n. *Stradweul* or *Ystradfael* but the forms have no -r-.

LLANSTADWELL see **LLANSTADWEL**

LLANSTEFFAN[1] Carm SN3510

'church of Steffan', ***llan***, pers.n. ***Steffan***

(*ecclesiam*) *Sancti Stephani de Landestephan* 1176-98 (17cent.), *Landestephan* c.1191, *Landestefan'* 1228, *Nanstephan* 1484, *ll. ystyfann* c.1500

Probably not the biblical martyr but a native W saint from Powys, traditionally a friend of Teilo (see Llandeilo). Some of the earlier forms, however, suggest a pers.n. Ysteffan (*Ystyphan* 13cent., and the 15cent. form *Llanystyffan* for Llansteffan[2] [q.v.]) which may then explain the persistence of *Land-* with its intrusive -d- before the vowel in early spellings especially under E influence. Alternatively, the -d- may be lenition of -t- in the honorific pref. *ty-*, and point to an otherwise unattested Tysteffan. The modern form follows the commonly known Steffan.

LLANSTEFFAN[2] see **LLANSTEPHAN**

LLANSTEPHAN, LLANSTEFFAN Radn SO1242

'church of Stephen', ***llan***, pers.n. ***Steffan***

Llanystyffan wen 15cent., *Llanstyffan* 1513, *Llanstephyn in Elwell* 1504, *Seint Stevyns parisshe* 1553-5

Cf. Llansteffan[1]. Located in the cantref of Elfael; cf. Llansanffrid-yn-Elfael. The fem. adj. ***gwen*** 'white' of the 15cent. form probably refers to the church building.

LLANTARNAM Monm ST3093

'valley of (the stream) Teyrnon', ***nant***, r.n. ***Teyrnon***

Nant Thirnon 1179 (14cent.), *Lanternen* 1252, *St. Mary Lanternan* 1383, *Lantarnam* 1476

nant has been replaced by ***llan*** (cf. Llancarfan Glam). The village is now usually called Llantarnam but some sources (including some modern documents) call it Llanfihangel Llantarnam from the church's dedication to Michael/Mihangel (*Sancti Michaelis* 1479, *St. Michaell's next Lanternam* 1582, ***llan***, ***Mihangel***) near the Cistercian abbey of Llantarnam established in c.1175 at *Emsanternon* (possibly representing *Enisanternon* with ***ynys*** 'river-meadow'). The original abbey may have been located at Pentre-bach (*y penntref bach* late 15cent.), about two miles west of the later abbey, next to an unnamed stream, possibly the lost Nant Teyrnon. The village has also been described as Llanfihangel Ton-y-groes (*Lanvyhangell Tonygroes* 1566, ***ton*** 'unploughed land', ***y***, ***croes***

probably referring not to a religious cross but to crossroads at Croes-y-mwyalch, ***mwyalch*** 'blackbird'), and as Llanfihangel y Fynachlog (***mynachlog*** 'monastery'). The development from 'Llan Teyrnon' to Llantarnam was probably influenced by the Cistercian decision in 1272-3 to use the latinized (and symbolic) *Lanterna* of the abbey.

LLAN-TEG, LANTEAGUE Pemb SN1810

'fair stream', ***nant, teg***

Lanteg 1324, *Nanteg'* 1329, *Nantege* 1376, *Llanteage* 1569

nant is very probably replaced by ***llan*** (cf. Llanbradach and Llancarfan). There is a small stream to the south-east which enters Carmarthen Bay near Amroth Castle.

LLANTHONY, LLANDDEWI NANT HODNI Monm SO2827

'church of Dewi in the vale of Hoddni', ***llan***, pers.n. ***Dewi, nant,*** r.n. ***Hoddni***

Lanthoni 1125-7, *Lantony* 1160-80, *Lanthotheni*, *Landewi Nanthodeni* c.1191, *Landewi Nanthotheni* 13cent., *Lanthonddye* 1536-9, *Lhan-Dhewi yn Nant Hodeni* 1722

The river Honddu (q.v.) rises on Hay Bluff and flows through the Vale of Ewyas past Llanthony and into the river Monnow at Allt-yr-ynys. In Llanddewi Nant Hoddni ***nant*** was probably supplanted by ***llan*** as 'Llanthoddni' but retained the residual -t of ***nant*** to become Llanthowni (with -oddn- > -own-) and later Llanthoni, now pronounced 'Lantoni'.

LLANTILIO CROSSENNY, LLANDEILO GRESYNNI Monm SO3914

'church of Teilo at Cresynych', ***llan***, pers.n. ***Teilo***, ?terr.n. ***Cresynych***

Lentiliau 1162-3, *sancti teilaui de crisinic* 1160-85, *llanteylo cresseny* 1193-1218, *Lentilio Crosenwik* 1223, *Llandylo Crosseney* 1559, *ll. deilo groes ynyr* c.1566, *llantillio Gressenny* 1604

Llanteilo (as opposed to the regular W version Llandeilo) can probably be ascribed to anglicization (cf. Llanmadog and Llan-maes). Cresynych has not been satisfactorily explained. The first el. is possibly ***croes*** 'cross' (which appears sporadically with E ***cross***) which was then reduced to Cres- in the initial unaccented syllable from the earliest records. The second el. may be a pers.n. (changed to ***Ynyr*** in the c.1566 form) but the 1160-85 form points to a location. The final -ch was also reduced (cf. Solfach/Solva).

LLANTRIDDYD see **LLANTRITHYD**

LLANTRISANT[1] Angl SH3683

'church of (the) three saints', ***llan***, (*y*), ***tri***, ***sant*** pl. ***saint***

Clansann' 1254, *Llantrissent* 1408-1417, *llanyt'ssaynt* 1419, *Llantrissaint* 1452, *ll. y trisaint* c.1566, *Llantrisainte* 1647, *Llantrissant* 1763, *Llantrisaint* 1838

The three saints are Sannan, Afan and Ieuan. The early forms provide evidence of the def.art., subsequently lost. Most of the historical forms also have the pl. ***saint*** after the numeral ***tri***, a common enough occurrence in MW and a spelling retained by some writers, but today's preference is for Llantrisant in keeping with the MnW convention of a singular following a numeral (and probably influenced by Llantrisant Glam).

LLANTRISANT[2] Glam ST0483

'church of three saints', ***llan***, ***tri***, ***sant*** pl. ***saint***

Llantrissen 1247, *Landtrissen* 1246, *Lantrisan* 1254, *Thlanatrissent* 1297, *Lantrissan in Meskyn* 1386, *Lantrissain* 1535, *ll. y trissaint ymisgyn* c.1566

The three saints of Llantrisant are Tyfodwg, Gwynno and Illtud; see also Llantrisant[1]. Llantrisant lay in the commote of Meisgyn (q.v.), distinguishing it from Llantrisant[3].

LLANTRISANT[3] Monm ST3996

'church of three saints', ***llan***, ***tri***, ***sant*** pl. ***saint***

ecclesia sancti Petri de Lantrissen 1155-83, *Lantrissan* 1220-1, *Lantrissen super Usk"* 1296, *Lantrissen Parva* 1307, *Parva Lantrissan* 1327, *y trisaint* c.1566, *Lantrissen* 1630

The three saints are Dyfrig, Teilo and Euddogwy; see also Llantrisant[1,2]. Some modern sources, perplexingly, call it Llantrisaint Fawr 'great, larger Llantrisaint' (***mawr***); older sources call it Llantrisaint Parva, 'little' (L ***parva***), probably in contrast to Llantrisant[2] in the same diocese.

LLANTRITHYD, LLANTRIDDYD Glam ST0472

'stream called Rhirid', ***nant***, r.n. ***Rhirid***

Landrirede c.1126, *Lanririth* 1254, *Lanririd* c.1262, *Lanryryd* c.1348, *Llantrithid* 1533-8, *Nantririd* c.1545, *Nant Triryd* 1550-1600, *Nant Ririd* 1569, *ll. triddid* c.1566, *Lloyntrithed* 1596, *Llwyn Ridit* 1657-60

Despite the dominance of forms with *Lan-* in early (predominantly E) sources, the original was almost certainly ***nant***, because forms such as *Nant Ririd* are drawn from W sources and because the medial -t- in Llantrithyd (as -d- in *Landrirede* c.1126) is probably a trace of ***nant***. The stream, with pers.n. Rhirid, is now Nant Llantriddyd. The assimilation of -rhirid > -rhiddyd (possibly influenced by ***rhyddid*** 'freedom') is found in other p.ns. such as Llwynriddyd (in Pendeulwyn). The unfamiliar name prompted some antiquarians to postulate the church's name as Llan Treuddyd founded by a fictitious Treiddyd Sant. The 1596 and

1657-60 forms show the influence of ***llwyn*** 'bush, grove', another el. which occasionally interchanged with ***llan***.

LLANTWIT FARDRE, LLANILLTUD FAERDREF
Glam ST0886

'church of Illtud at the demesne', ***llan***, pers.n. ***Illtud***, (*y*), ***maerdref***
Lantwyt 1536, *Llanylltuyt Verdre* 1545, *Llanilltyd Fairdre* 1547-51, *Lantwit vayrdre* 1556, *ll. ylldyd or faerdref* c.1566, *Lantwit Fardre* 1762, *Llanilltyd-faerdref* 1856, *Llanilltyd Fardre* 1892
There was a well of Illtud (*fonte Sancti Ylthuti* late 12cent.) supposedly at Dihewyd about a mile south of the church. In both E and W usage, Faerdre and Fardre appear to be the regular forms with the latter displaying the widespread reduction in south Wales of -ae- to -a-. Faerdref is uncommon and may be a literary restoration. See Llantwit Major.

LLANTWIT MAJOR, LLANILLTUD FAWR Glam SS9768

'principal church of Illtud', ***llan***, pers.n. ***Illtud***, ***mawr***, L ***major***
Llan Iltut c.1100, *Landiltuit* 1106, *Landhiltwit* 1184-5, *Lannyltwyt* 1291, *Lan Iltut* 1295-6, *Llanntwyt* 1316, *Llanulltut* 1378-86, *Lantwytt* 1431, *Lantwyt* 1480, *Lantwyd* 1536, *ll. ylldyd fawr* c.1566, *Lantwit Major* 1580
Illtud reputedly established a monastery here and became abbot in the 6cent. A var. Illtwyd, seen in many of the forms, is thought to be from a Goidelic or Ir genitival derivative *Illtuaith* and gave rise to the contracted Llantwit (cf. Llantwit Fardre), later perceived to be the E form partly because of the addition of ***major*** to correspond to W ***mawr***. Three other churches dedicated to Illtud in Glam were Llantwit-juxta-Neath or Llanilltud Nedd or Llanilltud Fach (*Laniltavit* 1289 [1468], *Saint Illtyde, Llantwytt* 1535, *Saint Iltyde* 1546), Llantwit Fardre or Llanilltud Faerdref (q.v.), and Llanilltud Gŵyr or Ilston (q.v.). The var. Illtwyd is seen in Llantwyd Pemb (*Langetot* 1291, *Lantote* 1370, *Lantwyd* 1535, *Lantood* 1549). Another var. was Elltud (see Llanelltud Mer).

LLANUWCHLLYN Mer SH8730

'church above the lake', ***llan***, ***uwch***, ***llyn***
Thlanhughelyn 1283, *Lanvthllyn* 1291, *Lanughlyn* 1390, *ll. ywch y llyn* c.1566, *Llanuwchllyn* 1695
The church at the south-west end of Llyn Tegid is dedicated to Deiniol but there is no evidence to support the belief that the church was once called 'Llanddeiniol-uwch-y-llyn' (and that Llanfor was 'Llanddeiniol-is-y-llyn'). ***uwch*** can also carry the connotation 'the far side' (from Bala) as opposed to ***is*** 'this side'.

LLANVACHES see **LLANFACHES**

LLANVAPLEY, LLANFABLE Monm SO3614

'church of Mable', ***llan***, pers.n. ***Mable***

ecclesiam Mable 1136-54, *Eglouismapel* 1254, *Lanvappele* 1361, *ll. vablle* c.1566

llan has replaced an earlier ***eglwys*** 'church'. Here, the W pers.n. Mable (with two syllables) is probably a version of E Mable a var. of Mabel rather than the W var. Mabli (cf. Cefn Mabli Glam). The modern anglicized form Llanvapley, however, argues for the later influence of Mabli. There is no record of any Mable here.

LLANVETHERINE, LLANWYTHERIN Monm SO3617

'church of Gwytherin', ***llan***, pers.n. ***Gwytherin***

Ecclesia guethirin 1136-54, *Linwerthin* 1254, *Lanwytheryn* c.1348, *Lanvetherin* 1348, *ll. y ffyryn* c.1566, *Llanvetherynge* 1576-77, *Llanaferyng* 1577, *ll. fetherin* 1590-1, *Llanffyrin* 1695, *llanveryn* 1763

Probably the same saint as in Gwytherin Denb which has probably influenced the modern W form. Llanvetherine illustrates the variation of -f- and -w- . There is also evidence of a contracted, probably colloquial, *Llanferyn*, *Llanfyryn* and *Llanffyryn*.

LLANVIHANGEL CRUCORNEY, LLANFIHANGEL CRUCORNAU Monm SO3220

'church of Mihangel at Crucornau', ***llan***, pers.n. ***Mihangel***, terr.n. ***Crucornau***

lann Mihacguel cruc cornou 1136-54, *Sancti Michaelis de Crukorn* 1254, *Sti' Mich'is Kilcornu* 1291, *ll. f'el gil kornel* c.1566

Crucornau is ***crug*** 'mound' and a pers.n. ***Cornau*** (OW or early MW Cornou) perhaps a var. of (modern) Cornwy, Cernyw. Many forms for Crucornau (such as *Kilcornu* c.1291, *Kylcorneu* 1350, *Kylkorny* 1407) show confusion of ***crug*** with ***cil*** in an unstressed syllable.

LLANWARW see **WONASTOW**

LLANWDDYN Mont SJ0219

'church of Gwyddyn', ***llan***, pers.n. ***Gwyddyn***

Llanwothin 1205, *Llanothyn* 1547, *ll. wyddyn* c.1566, *Llanwothyn* 1585-6, *LLanwddyn* c.1600, *Llanwoothyn* 1612

The pers.n., of an otherwise unattested saint, also occurs in Llwybr Wddyn (***llwybr*** 'path, track') referring to part of the road leading to Pennant Melangell. *Gwely Wddyn* 1838 was the name of a smooth mound; ***gwely*** 'bed' was sometimes used to describe a house, a family holding, or a topographical feature associated with a named person. The dedication of the old church appears to have been changed to John the Baptist, probably in consequence of a part of the parish being granted to the Knights Commandery of John of Jerusalem at Halston Shrophsire. The present village of Llanwddyn is new. Both the old church and former village now lie about two miles away under the waters of the Llyn Efyrnwy (Lake Vyrnwy) reservoir (constructed by Liverpool Corporation in the 1880s) and known to some W speakers as Llyn Llanwddyn.

LLANWENOG Card SN4945

'church of Gwenog', ***llan***, pers.n. ***Gwenog***

Lanwenauk 1284, *Llanwennok* 1389, *Llanwenog* 1540, *ll. wenoc* c.1566

Gwenog (also a man's name) was taken as a fem. saint, also commemorated in Ffair Wenog (***ffair*** 'fair') and a well (*ffuñon wenog* c.1700, ***ffynnon***).

LLAN-WERN Monm ST3688

'church at the alder-grove', ***llan***, ***gwern***

lann guern tiuauc, lannguern timauc 1136-54, *Lanwarin* 1254, *Lanwaryn* 1321-2, *Llanwaern* 1535, *ll. wern* c.1566

The village is located where a small valley opens out onto the Levels. Early forms suggest 'Llan-wern Dyfog' with the additional qualifier of the saint's name Tyfog, to distinguish from the 'Llan-wern Gynog' of Llangunnock Herefordshire (*lannguern cinuc* 1160-85, *Lannguern Cynuc* 1160-80, pers.n. Cynog), and from Llanwarne Herefordshire (*Lann Gvern* 1136-54, *Lann guern teliau ha dibric* 1160-85, dedicated to Teilo and Dyfrig).

LLANWINIO Carm SN2626

'church of Gwynio', ***llan***, pers.n. ***Gwynio***

Sancto Wynnoco 1260, *Lanwynnean* 1291, *Lanweneaw* 1378, *ll. wnio* c.1566, *Llanwinio* 1671

Gwynio is a familiar form of Gwyn. Gwynio was reputed to have been killed by the Ir and his well Ffynnon Gwynio (*Fynon Gwnio* c.1527, ***ffynnon***) marks the place where his head fell. The 1260 (latinized) form has been misidentified with Llanwenog (q.v.).

LLANWNDA[1] Caern SH4758

'church of Gwndaf', ***llan***, pers.n. ***Gwndaf***

Llanwnda 1199, *Lanwndaph* 1203, *Lanwndaf* 1237-67, *Llanwnda* 13cent.(14cent.), *Llanonda* 1291, *ll. wnda* c.1566, *Llanwnda* 1819

The saint's name Gwndaf was a var. of Gwyndaf, found also (in addition to Llanwnda[2]) in Capel Gwnda (*Capel-gwnda* 1834) Card and in a 12cent. reference to Gwyndaf Hen of Brittany (see Llangadfan).

LLANWNDA[2] Pemb SM9339

'church of Gwndaf', ***llan***, pers.n. ***Gwndaf***

Lanwadaph c.1200, *Lanwndaph* 1202, *Lanuda* 1291, *Llanunda* 1513, *ll. wnda* c.1566, *parish of gunda* 1568

Possibly the same saint as in Llanwnda[1].

LLANWNNEN Card SN5347

'church of Gwynnen', ***llan***, pers.n. ***Gwynnen***

Lanwynnan 1361, *Lanwynen* 1363, *Llanuuonnen* 1535, *ll. wnen* c.1566, *Llanwnnen* 1612

On -wy- > -w-, cf. Llanwnnog. While early calendars show Gwynnen to be male, here the saint appears to be female. The church was eventually rededicated to Lucy of Syracuse (who shared the same feast-day) and to Gwynin in 1843.

LLANWNNOG, LLANWNOG Mont SO0293

'church of Gwynnog', ***llan***, pers.n. ***Gwynnog***

Lanwinnauch 1195-6, *Lan Wynnauc* 1207, *Llanwennauc* c.1216, (*i*) *lan wnoc* early 15cent., *Llanwynnoge* 1545, *llanwnnawg* c.1550, *Llanwonnocke* 1559, *ll. wnoc* c.1566

On -wy- > -w- (cf. Llanwnnen, Llanwnda[1,2] and Llanwddyn). The church dedication to Gwynnog is also found at nearby Aberhafesb and possibly in Llanwonog Herefordshire.

LLANWNOG see **LLANWNNOG**

LLANWONNO see **LLANWYNNO**

LLANWRDA Carm SN7131

'church of Gwrdaf', ***llan***, pers.n. ***Gwrdaf***

Lanurdan 1244-71 (=?*Lanurdav*), *Launwrdaf* 1282, *Llanwrdaf* 1302-3, *Llanurda* 1537-9, *ll. wrda* c.1566

An otherwise unattested saint. On the loss of final -f, cf. Llanwnda.

LLANWRIN Mont SH7803

'church of Gwrin', ***llan***, pers.n. ***Gwrin***

Llannwrin 12cent., *Lanwryn* 1291, *Llanoryn* 1318, *Lannoryn* 1382, *LL.wrin* c.1562, *p.wirn* c.1566, *Llanworing* 1578, *llanwryn* 1597, *Llanwooryn* 1617

Gwrin may be the name of a saint but in the 12cent. Ust and Dyfnig are recorded as saints in *Llannwrin yNghyfeilioc* (the cantref of Cyfeiliog). The same pers.n. occurs in Gwrinydd (later appearing in confused spelling as Gorfynydd), the name of a cantref, and Llyswyrny (***llys***) both in Glam; these have the suff. ***-ydd*** in the loose sense of 'territory associated with'.

LLANWRTHWL Brec SN9763

'church of Gwthwl', ***llan***, pers.n. ***Gwthwl***

Lannochul 1280, *Llanwthwl* 1283, *Lanuchul* 1291, *Llanuthull* 15643, *LL.wrthwl* c.1550-62

Gwthwl is an otherwise unattested pers.n. Attempts have been made to identify the name with Gwrthmwl (MnW Gwrthfwl) and Gyrthmwl/ Gwerthmwl Wledig recorded c.900 (13cent.) and which may have influenced forms with -r- . The 1280 and 1291 forms almost certainly have -c- in error for -t-.

LLANWRTUD (WELLS) Brec SN8746

'wells near Llanwrtyd', p.n. ***Llanwrtyd***, E ***well***

Llanwortid Wells 1740, *Llanwrtyd Well* c.1778

The name of the town is taken from Llanwrtud (*Llanworted* 1543, *Llanwrtid* 1553, *ll. wrtyd* c.1566, ***llan***, pers.n. Gwrtud) a little over a mile further up the Irfon valley. The spa town developed after the discovery of a mineral well, traditionally by Rev. Theophilus Evans of Llangamarch in 1732, at a place called *Pont Rhydferan* c.1700, *Pont Rheed Vere* 1754, *Pont-rhyd-y-feri* 1833, possibly 'bridge at the ford of the short share-land', ***pont***, ***rhyd***, ***berran*** (as in Ystalyfera). There is uncertainty as to whether the pers.n. was Gwrtud or Gwrtyd a fact which is reflected in usage varying between Llanwrtud and Llanwrtyd.

LLANWYDDELAN Mont SJ0801

'church of Gwyddelan', ***llan***, pers.n. ***Gwyddelan***

Llanoedelan 1254, *Lanuydelan*, *Lanwydelay* 1263, *St. Ewddelan* 1363, *St. Gwithelan de Llanwythelan in Kedewen* 1431, *ll. wyddelan* c.1566, *llanwythelan* 1597

The church is dedicated to Gwyddelan, probably found also in Dolwyddelan (q.v.); it also gave rise to a surname. Located in Cedewain (see Betws Cedewain).

LLANWYNNELL see **WOLVESNEWTON**

LLANWYNNO, LLANWONNO Glam ST0395

'church of Gwynno', ***llan***, pers.n. ***Gwynno***

Lanwonno 1449-50, 1603, *ll. wno* c.1566, *Llanwynno* 1670

There are dedications to Gwynno at Vaynor/Y Faenor (formerly Maenorwynno) Brec, Llantrisant Glam (q.v.) and at Llanpumsaint (q.v.). The absence of early forms may be because Llanwynno, as a daughter church of Llantrisant did not warrant separate mention in many historical sources.

LLANWYTHERIN see **LLANVETHERINE**

LLAN-Y-BRI Carm SN3312

'church of ?Morbri', ***llan***, ?pers.n. ***Morbri***

Moraburia 1419, *ll. fair y byri* c.1566,
Morbichurche, otherwise Morbulchurch 1567, *Marblechurche* 1598,
Morbill churche 1611, *Llanbrea* 1675,
Marble Church otherwise Llanibree 1716, *Llan y Bri* 1753

The name is obscure. Also said to be called *Llanddewi Forbri* and later *Llanforbri*. Evidence for the existence of *Llanforbri* is later interpretation, such as the c.1566 form as 'Llanfair y byri' (as if ***Mair***, ***y***, and a possible E ***bury***), and as ***bri*** 'fame, honour', as well as the 1598 *Marble-*. The dedication to Mair is possibly the result of such confusion rather than its cause; the dedication is now to the Holy Trinity.

LLANYBYDDER Carm SN5244

'church of the ?deaf ones', ***llan***, ***y***, ?***byddar*** pl. ***byddair***

Thlanebetheir 1319, *Llan y Byddair* late 15cent., *Llanybydder* 1535,
ll. y byddar c.1566, *Llanybyther* 1671

An unusual name, possibly a reference to deaf saints, but no such tradition seems to have survived.

LLAN-Y-CEFN Pemb SN0923

'church at Cefn', ***llan***, ***y***, p.n. ***Cefn***

Ecclesia de Kevyn 1287, *Kevyn'* 1326 (16cent.), *Llannekevyn* 1499,
ll. y kefyn c.1566

The church stands on a prominent ridge (***cefn***) called Cefn extending southwards from near Maenclochog to Glancleddau.

LLANYCHAER see **LLANYCHÂR**

LLANYCHÂR Pemb SM9835

'glade of ?bondsmen', ***llannerch***, ?***caeth*** pl. ***caith***

ecclesiam Sancti David de Lanavch'uer 1221-9 (14cent.),
Launerwayth 1291, *Landirkayth* 1325, *Llanerchaeth* 1408,
Llan Yghaer 1512, *ll. a chaer* c.1566, *Llanachaier* 1578,
llannerch kaeth c.1600, *Llanerchaith* 1612

The stressed second el. may be ***caeth*** pl. ***caith***, 'bondsman, serf' (cf. Cricieth) or a pers.n. Aedd. There are other examples of changes of -th and -dd to -r in Pemb, here probably influenced by ***caer*** 'fort'; subsequently, ***llannerch*** was interpreted as ***llan y***. Llanychâr shows regular dial. change of -ae- to -â-; Llanychaer is a common modern var. The church is dedicated to David/Dewi.

LLANYCIL Mer SH9134

'church of the nook', ***llan***, ***y***, ***cil***

Lanekyl 1291, *Lanekil* 1292, *Llanyckyl* 1292-3, *Llaynykill* 1392, *ll. y kil* c.1566, *Llanyckill* 1670, *Llan-y-cil* 1838
The church dedicated to Beuno (*Llan Veuno* 1284) is located in a nook beside Llyn Tegid, between the lake and the main Bala-Dolgellau road. From very early on, the stress seems to have fallen on the penultimate syllable despite it being the def.art. This in turn results in the alternation of -y- and -e- seen above; cf. Penegoes, Penyberth (Caern), Bodygroes/Bodegroes (Caern) and Bachygraig/Bachegraig (Flints).

LLAN-Y-CRWYS Carm SN6445
'church of the crosses', ***llan***, ***y***, ***croes*** pl. ***crwys***
Llanndewi y Crwys late 12cent. (13cent.), *Lanecros* 1291, *Landewi Crus* 1324, *Llandewy Cruys* 1495, *Llanecroys*, *Rodechurche* 1535, *ll. y krwys* c.1566, *Llanycroise* 1671
The early Llanddewi y Crwys (with Dewi). Probably a reference to standing crosses, also recorded in the farm name Esgair-crŵys (*Tir Esceir y Krwys* 1633) on a hill above the village. Several stones are recorded on the county boundary with Card, two of which may be recorded c.850. The 1535 form has E ***rood*** 'cross, crucifix', probably a learned translation, taking ***crwys*** as 'rood cross, crucifix'.

LLANYMAWDDWY Mer SH9019
'church in Mawddwy', ***llan***, ***yn***, commote n. ***Mawddwy***
Llanemaudoe 1254, *Lanemadwe* 1291, *Llan Ymoddwy* 1382, *ll. y mowddwy* c.1566, *Llan-y-mowthwy* 1566, *Lhan ym Mowdhwy* 1600, *Llan-y-Mawddwy* 1836
The patron saint Tydecho has never featured in the church's name and there is no evidence for a 'Llandydecho ym Mawddwy', although he is commemorated in Capel Tydecho and Ffynnon Tydecho (***ffynnon***) and in the churches of Mallwyd and Garthbeibio. As the above forms show, 'ym Mawddwy' has long been perceived as Y Mawddwy '(of) the Mawddwy'.

LLANYMDDYFRI see **LLANDOVERY**

LLANYMYNECH Mont SJ2620
'church of the monks', ***llan***, ***y***, ***mynach*** pl. ***meneich***
Llanemeneych 1254, *Tlanimenach* c.1277, *Lan meneyth* 1291, *ll'ameneich* 1377, *Lannemynagh* 1396, *Llanemeneyth* 1422, *ll. y menych* mid 16cent.
Possibly the location of a former monastic cell or oratory. Llanymynech now straddles the national and the county boundary (with Shropshire). The modern form in -mynech probably reflects the dial. pronunciation of a standardized pl. ***mynaich***.

LLANYNGHENEDL Angl SH3881

'church of Enghenedl', ***llan***, pers.n. ***Enghenedl***

Llan Enghenell 1534, *ll. ynghenill* c.1566, *ll. ynghenell* 1590, *Llanynghenedle* 1697, *Llanynghenedl* 1798

The name may have been Enghenedl, Ynghenedl or Enghenel, or, according to some, Anghenell, daughter of Elise ap Gwylog (*Anghenell verch Elissav* 12cent.[13cent.]). Later forms were influenced by ***cenedl*** 'nation'.

LLANYNYS Denb SJ1062

'church on an island', ***llan***, ***ynys***

Lanenys 1254, *Llanenys* 1260, *Llanynnys* 1291, *Llanynys* 1386

The church (dedicated to Saeran) and village are located on the valley bottom between the rivers Clwyd and Clywedog (which are no more than a mile apart at this point), and are surrounded by a number of rivulets and drainage channels (*upon great flouds it becomes an island* c.1700). A number of related meanings are similarly ascribed to E ***island***: 'area of raised ground in wet country'; 'well-watered land'. In this instance 'land between rivers' is also appropriate.

LLAN-Y-PWLL Denb SJ3751

'bank of the pool', ***glan***, ***y***, ***pwll***

Llanypwll 1819, *Glan-y-pwll* 1838, *Llanypwll* 1848

The pool or pit is no longer in evidence, but the nature of the terrain is indicated by the adjoining Sandy Lane, the industrial sandpit, the house called Clays and the stream flowing south-east (to Afon Clywedog). The road from Gresford joins the Wrexham-Holt road on the bank (***glan***) of the erstwhile pool or pit. This is another example of ***glan*** being supplanted by ***llan***; the 1838 form may be an isolated attempt at restoration in the light of what was perhaps local knowledge.

LLANYRE, LLANLLŶR-YN-RHOS Radn SO0462

'church of ?Llŷr in the moor', ***llan***, ?pers.n. ***Llŷr***, ***yn***, ***y***, ***rhos***

Thloynyare 1291, *Thlanhur* 1304, *Llanner* 1554, *ll. llyr yn Ros* c.1566, *Llanyere* 1566, *Llanyr yn rose* 1575-6, *Llaniryrhos* 1610, *Llaneere* 1753, *Llanyereŷrhos* 1797, *Llanyre Rhos* 1833

The first el. is ***llan*** but the remainder is uncertain. The standard W form is generally given as Llanllŷr with the pers.n. Llŷr despite the lack of supporting forms and the church dedication to Llŷr not being recorded until c.1700; it was possibly influenced by Llanllŷr Card. Loss of -ll- after ***llan*** is rare but may occur, for example, in Llanychaiarn Card. An occasional form shows the influence of ***ieir*** (pl. of ***iâr***) 'hens, game-birds' (possibly even ***ieir-y-rhos*** 'grouse'). The ***rhos*** was alongside the river Ieithon, but several forms (including the modern Llanllŷr-yn-Rhos) interpret it as a terr. location, Rhos.

LLANYSTUMDWY Caern SH4738

'church at the bend in (the river) Dwy', ***llan***, ***ystum***, r.n. ***Dwy***

Llanystwmdwy 1324, *Llanstyndwy* 1562

Dwy 'holy one' was the original name of two broadly parallel rivers just over a mile apart, distinguished from each other as *Dwy-fawr* (***mawr*** 'great') and *Dwy-fech* (***bech*** 'little'), today's rivers Dwyfor (q.v.) and Dwyfach (q.v.) (*dwyvor a dwyfech* 1495). The church (of St John the Baptist) and the later hamlet lie on the northern bank of a wide bend (***ystum***) of Afon Dwyfor where several roads converge. The hamlet's name developed while the river Dwyfor was still known as *Dwy*. Llanystumdwy lies half-a-mile east of the confluence of Dwyfor and Dwyfach to form Afon Dwyfor which flows into the sea west of Cricieth. The tnshp between (***rhwng***) the two rivers was *Rhwng Dwyfor a Dwyfech* (*Ronddowaraddowegh* 1352, *Rongdoyvor and doyvech* 1484, *Rhwng dwyvor a dwyvegh* 1567, *Rhwng Dwyfor a Dwyfech* 1631). The popular belief is that the ***ystum*** is the area between the two rivers just before their confluence and that ***dwy*** refers to the two rivers (*Llan-ystum-dwy: fanum in flexu duorum fluviorum* 1721). Colloquially, Llanstumdwy and Llanstundwy.

LLAN-Y-TAIR-MAIR see **KNELSTON**

LLAWHADEN Pemb SN0717

'church of Huadain', ***llan***, pers.n. ****Huadain***

Egluyss Hwadeyn 12cent., *Lanwhadein*, *Lanwadein* 1197,
Lanwadyn, *Lawadyn* 1288, *Lawadeyn* c.1148-76 (1308), *Lawhaden* 1326,
llan y hadein 14cent., *Llanhuadain* 1447-89, *Llawhaden* 1527,
llan y haden c.1566

llan has replaced ***eglwys*** 'church'. The church, now dedicated to Aidan, was dedicated to Hugh in the 14cent. (*ecclesia sancti Hugonis* 1334), both pers.ns being attempts at making sense of, and replacing, a W pers. n. which appears to be a hypothetical Huadain, otherwise unattested. E influence may account for loss of -n in Llan- before an aspirated hw- from the 13cent.; others have argued it could be a trace of a perceived F ***la***. However, forms with -n seem to have survived for some time. Several forms seem to interpret the medial syllable as the definite article ***y***, which probably accounts for the colloquial Llanihaden and Llaniaden heard today.

LLAWR-Y-GLYN Mont SN9391

'floor of the valley', ***llawr***, ***y***, ***glyn***

Llawr-y-Glyn 1836, *Lawr-y-glyn* 1891

From its location in the wooded dingle (*Llawr y Glyn* 1891) of the river Trannon. The hamlet developed around a Calvinistic Methodist chapel established in 1809.

LLAY, LLAI Denb SJ3355

'river meadow', ***llai**

Lhay 1385, *y llay* 1405, *Y Llai* 1470, *y llai* 1550-62, *llay* 1620, *Llai* 1639

The location of Llai beside Afon Alun is evidence of a settlement in a well-watered meadow. Other p.ns in the area (such as Coed-llai q.v.) prove that W ***llai** 'river meadow, pasture' is a hitherto unrecognised cymricized el. derived from OE ***lēah*** (with similar meaning) and preserved only in p.ns. The use of the def.art. *y* is evidence of its currency as a common noun.

LLECHGYNFARWY Angl SH3881

'stone of Cynfarwy', ***llech***, pers.n. ***Cynfarwy***

Leccanwey 1254, *Leghgynwarwy* 1352, *Lechgynvarwy* 1359, *Leghkynvarwy* 1422, *Llechgwen farwy* 1643, *Llechcyn farwy'* 1838

South-west of the church (dedicated to the saint Cynfarwy) was a substantial nine-foot ***maen-hir*** beside the old Post Road to Holyhead, recorded as *Longstone* on a 1675 map and was in existence in 1843 but then removed and broken up to build a wall. Occasionally spelt *Llechcynfarwydd*. The church has also been called Llangynfarwy.

LLECHRYD Card SN2143

'stone ford', ***llech***, ***rhyd***

Lechred 1288, *Thlaghred* 1302, *Llechred* 1340, *Llechryd* 1557 (1739-61), *Leghrid* 1603, *Llecherid alias Leghred* 1603-25

There is evidence of a ford of stepping stones and a weir across Afon Teifi which was later replaced by a bridge (*Pont Lechryd* 1798). All the early forms consistently record *-red* (not the expected *-rit*, *-ryt* or *-ryd*), as does another Llechryd (*Leghred* 1334, *Llechryd* 1683) in Llanefydd Denb. The name also appears in *Llechryd* 1693 (Mont) and *Llechryd* 1856 (Monm).

LLECHRYDAU Denb SJ2334

'stone fords', ***llech***, ***rhyd*** pl. ***rhydau***

llechryddey c.1610, *Llychryde* c.1700, *Llechrhydau* 1838

The minor road between Glyn Ceiriog and Oswestry crosses two tributaries of Afon Morda. The original route was facilitated by fords which were either naturally stoney, or man-made perhaps with slabs or flags; today a (disused) quarry can be seen very close to Llechrydau. The earlier forms show the dial. var. Llechryde.

LLEDROD Card SN6470

'semicircular defensive enclosure', ***lled***, ***rhod***

Ledrod 1284, *Ledred'* 1291, *Lledrod* 1302-3, *Lledrwd* c.1700

The meaning of ***lled*** is 'half, semi-', while ***rhod*** can mean 'wheel' but was also used of 'shield'; there may even be an unrecorded el. ***lledrod**. The implication is a semicircular defensive enclosure which was perhaps the mound half-a-mile south-east of the church of Llanfihangel Lledrod (*ll. V'el lledrod* c.1566, *Llanvihangel yn Lledrod* 1586-1613, *Llanfihangel Lledrod* 1834).

LLEYN see LLŶN

LLITHFAEN Caern SH3543

'lodestone', ***llithfaen***

Llythvaen 1281, *Lathvaent* 1352, *llythvayn* 1552, *Llithfaen* 1785

Although the name is now associated with the village, the earlier references seem to be to a hill. The traditional belief is that the rocky cliffs of Yr Eifl have the power to affect a mariner's compass taking the first el. to be ***llith*** 'lure, decoy' (recorded since 1160), and that ***llithfaen*** means 'lodestone'. Perplexingly, ***llithfaen*** is not independently recorded until 1858. In view of the evidence for an Ir presence along the coast of Llŷn (as seen in Porthdinllaen and Aberdesach) the Ir adj. ***liath*** 'grey' could possibly have been part of a name-phrase describing the grey granite of hills above Nant Gwrtheyrn (which is also called Nant y Llithfaen *Nant Arthlythuaen* 1281, *Nantyllithvaen* 1612). A futher complication is that ***ithfaen*** is 'granite' which was widely quarried in the area; however ***ithfaen*** is not recorded until 1850.

LLIW, Afon Glam SS5999

'bright river', ***afon, lliw***

Lyv 1176-98, *lliv* mid 13cent., *Liv* early 13cent. (1332), *Llyw* 1478, *Thlu* 1578, *Llyew* 1590-6, *Lhu* 1612

Afon Lliw was used of two rivers but above their confluence the name is now applied only to the northern river (*Norther Lyu* 1306, *Llugh ye greater* 1584-5, *Luw ycha* 1697, ***uchaf*** 'upper'). The southern river, now Afon Llan, was formerly Lliw Eithaf or Lliw Issa (*Llugh ye lesser* c.1584-5 [c.1700] , *Luw issa* 1697, ***eithaf*** dial. ***itha*** 'furthest', ***isaf*** 'lower'), but also recalled in Llewitha Bridge (*Pont liw Eitha* 1720, *Pont llewydde* 1833) about two miles above the point where the rivers meet. Lliw rises near Mynydd y Gwair. The forms with -gh are perplexing but may have been influenced by the river Lougher/Llwchwr (q.v.) into which Lliw flows south of the town of Lougher. See also Pont-lliw.

LLOC Flints SJ1476

'pound', ***lloc***

Llok 1479, *Y Llocke* 1517, *Y Lhock* 1683, c.1700, *Llock* 1693, *Lloc* 1743

The pen was probably a pound for straying animals. An adjacent house (dated 1683) and called *Y Lhock* became the Post Office, a community role which probably explains the adoption of Lloc as the name of the hamlet.

LLONG Flints SJ2662

'swamp', ***llong***

y Lhong c.1700, *Llong* 1838

llong is a noun which developed out of the fem. adj. ***llong*** (masc. ***llwng*** 'swampy, engulfing'; cf. Trallwng). The land between Llong hamlet (alongside the Mold road) and Afon Alun is prone to flooding. The bridge across the river is Llong Bridge and nearby was a mill (*Melin y Lhong* c.1700). By a convenient linguistic coincidence, an entirely separate word ***llong*** means 'ship', and so a roadside inn here (1775-1875) adopted the name The Ship (with an appropriate inn-sign painted by Richard Wilson). It has been argued that the area could be identified with the unidentified Domesday Book *Wiselei* (1086) which is probably OE ***wisc*** 'marshy meadow' and OE ***lēah*** 'meadow pasture'.

LLOWES Radn SO1941

'(church of) Llywes', pers.n. ***Llowes***

podum liuhess in eluail 1136-54, *Locheis* late 12cent., *Lewas* 1291

The church was evidently dedicated to Llywes who was joined here by Meilig or Maelog (*Lann meilic halyguess* 1136-54). Forms of the p.n. seem to fall into two groups. One group is *Locheis, Lockwas, Llochaes* 1517, and *Lloghas* 1535 which probably stands for ***lloches, llochwes*** 'refuge, place of safety', corresponding to L ***podum*** (of the first form) 'religious settlement'. The other group is *liuhess, Lewas* 1291, *Llowis* 1513 and *llowes* 1570, forms of the saint's name.

LLUGWY, Afon Caern SH7059

'bright river', ***afon, llug,*** suff. ***-wy***

Llugwy 1485, *Lhygwy* c.1700, *Afon Llugwy* 1841

Llugwy occurs several times as a r.n. This river rises in Ffynnon Llugwy (*Ffynnon Lygwy* c.1700, ***ffynnon*** 'well, spring') and flows past Capel Curig, through the valley formerly known as Glyn Llugwy (*Glinthlulguth* 1283, *ynglyn Llugwy* 16cent., *Glyn Llugwy* 1650, *Glyn Lugwy* 1809-11) and into the river Conwy near Betws-y-coed.

LLUNDAIN-FACH Card SN5556

'little London', p.n. ***Llundain, bach***

Lyndon vach 1749-50, *Llundain fach* 1814, *London-fach* 1834, *London-fâch* 1891, *Llundain-fach* 1904

Probably a jocular name for a comparatively insignificant place (similar to Little London in Mont) but on a busy, especially drovers', route. There are several London p.ns in Card such as another Llundain-fach (*London-fach* 1891) near Llandysul, Temple Bar some two miles away, Bow Street and Chancery. Names of towns and cities are treated as fem.

LLWCHWR, Afon see **LOUGHOR**

LLWYDIARTH see PONTLLOGAIL

LLWYNCELYN Card SN4459

'holly grove', ***llwyn***, ***celyn***
Llwyn-celyn 1891
An earlier name seems to have been *Penylone* 1811, *Pen-lôn* 1834 (***pen***, ***lôn***), from its location at the junction of a minor road with the main Aberaeron-Llannarth road.

LLWYNCELYN see HOLLYBUSH

LLWYNDAFYDD Card SN3755

'Dafydd's grove', ***llwyn***, pers.n. ***Dafydd***
Llwyn Dd' c.1485, *Llwyn David* 1488, *llwyn Davydd* pre 1569, *Llwyn David*, 1586-1613, *Llwyn Dafydd* 1758, *Llwyn Davydd* 1833, *Llwyn Dafydd* 1834
The village developed near a farm which was the residence of a *Davydd ab Ieuan*. The name was also associated with a motte-and-bailey Castell Llwyn Dafydd, earlier Caerwedros (which became the name of a nearby village and of a commote).

LLWYNDYRYS Caern SH3741

'dense grove', ***llwyn***, ***dyrys***
lloynederies 1572, *y llwyn dyrys* 1565-87, *llwyn dyrys* 1636, *Llwyn-dyrys* 1838
Several meanings are possible for ***dyrys*** in relation to a copse or grove, such as 'dense, tangled (with undergrowth), thorny'. The same features appear in the name of the nearby Trallwyn (*Trallwyn* 1795, ***tra*** 'exceedingly, considerable', or 'beyond').

LLWYNELIDDON see ST LYTHAN'S

LLWYNGWRIL Mer SH5909

'grove of Gwril', ***llwyn***, pers.n. ***Gwril***
Longoril 1292-3, *Lloyngwryl* 1454, *Lloyngoryll* 1593, *Llwyngwril* 1689, *Llwyn Gwril* 1796
The identity of Gwril is not known. His or her name also appears in Afon Gwril which passes under the Arthog-Tywyn road at the village.

LLWYN-MAWR Denb SJ2237

'big grove', ***llwyn***, ***mawr***
llwyn mawre 1572, *Y llwyn mawr* 1681, *Llwyn Mawr* 1795, *Llwyn-mawr* 1838
There are several p.ns in the vicinity with ***llwyn***.

LLWYN-Y-GROES Card SN5956

'grove at the crossroads', ***llwyn, y, croes***

Llwyngroes 1815, *Llwyn-y-grôs* 1824, *Llwyn-y-groes* 1834

The village is at a road junction. It has also been alleged that the village can be associated with routes followed by the monks of Strata Florida (q.v.), and that ***croes*** could be interpreted in that context despite its late appearance. It is more likely that the cross, if there was one as such, was simply a wayside cross for travellers.

LLYFNI, Afon see **LLANLLYFNI**

LLŶN Caern SH 4335-3737-1325

'the *Lageni', tribal n.****Lageni***

Lhein c.1191, *Lein* 1195-6 (15cent.), *Leyn* 1263 (15cent.), *Thleen* 1283, *llyyn* 14cent., *Llëyn* 15cent., *Llyyn* 15cent., *Lhŷn* 1722

The south-western part of the north-west peninsula of Wales. The tribal or family name is Ir (cf. Leinster and Porthdin-llaen q.v.) as are several p.ns in Llŷn. The older Lleyn has been preserved in some literary and antiquarian contexts but has come to be perceived as the E form at least in spelling. The pronunciation in both languages tends to be Llŷn. The development of -ey- was to -yy- followed by a contraction to -ŷ-.

LLYN BERWYN Card SN7456

'lake (near river called) Berwyn', ***llyn***, r.n. ***Berwyn***

Llyn Verwyn 1578, *Llyn Berwyn* 1803, *Llyn Berwin* 1834, *Berwyn Pool* 1832

The r.n. Berwyn (*Berwin* 1750, *Berwin R.* 1760, *Berwyn* 1808, *Afon Berwyn* 1834) is ***berw*** 'bubbling, boiling, seething', suff. ***-yn*** or ***-in*** or ***gwyn*** 'white'. The river does not appear today to have a direct connection with the waters of the lake, but the tributaries all rise west of the lake in Cwm Berwyn (*Komberwin* 1611). There is a tendency to refer to the river and the lake simply as Berwyn. It is possible that Berwyn is a lost mountain name (cf. Berwyn with a different meaning) or a pers.n.

LLYN BRIANNE Card/Carm/Brec SN8049

'lake (on river called) Brianne', ***llyn***, r.n. ***Brianne***

A reservoir constructed 1971-2 on the course of Afon Brianne or Briannau (*Nant Brianne* 1891) probably ***breuant*** 'throat' pl. ***breuannau*** to signify a series of narrow gorges or defiles. The development was probably colloquial medial -eu- > -ei- > -i- and final -au > -e. However, it has been suggested that it is ***breuan*** pl. ***breuanau*** 'quern, millstone'.

LLYN CELYN Mer SH8540

'lake (on the river) Celyn', ***llyn***, r.n. ***Celyn***

Kelin 1232, *Kelyn* 1645, *Celyn* 1838

The r.n. is ***celyn*** 'holly', an abundance of which must have grown on its banks. The river, Afon Gelyn (*Afon Gelyn* 1891) rises in Blaen Celyn on Arennig Fechan and flows into Afon Tryweryn below Capel Celyn (*Capel Celyn* 1874). Controversially, in 1965 the valley of Tryweryn and village of Capel Celyn were drowned to create the reservoir of Llyn Celyn.

LLYN CLAERWEN Brec/Card/Rad SN8465

'reservoir (on river called) Claerwen', ***afon***, r.n. ***Claerwen***

The river Claerwen (*Claerwen* 1426, *Calarwenn* 1184 (1285), *Clarwen* 1536-9, *Clayrwen'* 1548, *Clarwen flud.* 1645, *Afon Claerwen* 1833) is 'clear (or bright) white river' (***claerwyn***, modified to fem. ***gwen***) and is also the name of a farm (*Claerwen* 1833). It is in contrast with a second stream Claerddu (*Clarduy, Clardue, that is to say Blak Clare* c.1536-9, *Clarthie* 1586, *Clarwy* 1612, ***du*** 'black') which it meets just above the reservoir. The reservoir was built 1952-8, one of the last to be built by Birmingham Corporation as part of the Elan Valley Reservoirs.

LLYN CLYWEDOG see **CLYWEDOG[2], Afon**

LLYN CORON Angl SH3770

'lake of ?Coran', ***llyn***, ?pers.n. ***Coran***

llyn coron 13cent. (14cent.), *Llyn Coran* mid 16cent., *Llyn Corran* 1610, *Llyn Coran* 1645, *Llyn Carran* 1772, *Llyn y Goron* 1795, *Llyn Coron* 1818

The lake was once part of an inlet and separated from the sea by dunes. The river Ffraw flows from it (*the greatest lake in the ysle and the Fraus cymmyth owt of this poole* 1536-9). While the meaning is uncertain, most of the early forms favour an otherwise unrecorded pers.n. Coran rather than ***coron*** 'crown' which appears in later forms, a perception which was influenced by association with the court of the princes of Gwynedd at Aberffraw.

LLYN COWLYD Caern SH7262

'lake at Cawlyd', ***llyn***, p.n. ***Cawlyd***

cawlwyd 13cent. (14cent.), *Llinne Colluid* 1536-9, *llyn cowloyt* 1584, *Llyn Cowlid* 1795, *Llyn Cawlyd* 1810, *Llyn Cowlyd* 1838, *Llyn Cwlyd* 1841

A lake, now a reservoir, in Cwm Cowlyd (*Cum Kawlwyt* 13cent. [14cent.], *Llyn Cwm Cawlyd* 1818) whose derivation is obscure but is possibly a pers.n. ***Caw*** and ***llwyd*** 'holy'.

LLYN CRAFNANT Caern SH7561

'lake at Crafnant', ***llyn***, p.n. ***Crafnant***

Linne Cravenant 1536-9, *Llyn Crafnant* 1795

The lake, now a reservoir, between Capel Curig and Trefriw from which Afon Crafnant (*Cravenant* 1602, *Crafnant* 1655) flows into Afon Conwy. ***craf*** is 'wild garlic' but it is not clear whether ***nant*** is 'valley' or 'stream'.

LLYN CWELLYN Caern SH5555

'fish-trap lake', ***cawell, llyn***

Cywellyn 1795, *Quellyn Pool* 1810, *Cawellyn* 1810, *Llyn Cwellyn* 1816

Probably a reference to creels, baskets or fish-traps which may have characterised the lake (although it has been argued that perhaps the lake itself was deemed to act like a fish-trap) or that the bowl-like location is reminiscent of a basket. Cwellyn seems also to have been the name of one of the lake's principal tributaries (*rivulum Cwellyn* 1513-4). An older name for the lake and the tributary was Tarddennin (*Darddennin Auon* 1375-80, *llyn Tarddenin* 1500, *Llinne Tarthennyne* 1536-9, *Llyn Tarddenin* 16cent., *Llyn Tarddynni or Cawellyn* 1818) 'abounding in small springs' (***tardden*** 'small spring', adj. suff. ***-in***).

LLYN EFYRNWY, LAKE VYRNWY see **EFYRNWY**

LLYNFI, Afon Brec SO1331

'smooth river', ***llyfn, -i***

Lyfni 12cent., *Leveni* late 12cent., *Leveny* 1331, *Lhynvi, Lhyfni* c.1500, *Llyfny* 17cent., *Lhyfni* c.1700

The river flows into the Wye about a mile west of the village of Aberllynfi (q.v.). Several r.ns have metathesis of -fn-; cf. Llyfni Caern, Glam and Denb.

LLYN LLYDAW Caern SH6354

'lake of ?furies', ***llyn***, ?***llid*** pl. ***llidiau*** var. ****llidau***

Llinn Lleddau 1536-9, *Lhyn Lhydaw* 1722, *Llyn Llydaw* 1819

An obscure name for a lake enclosed by three of Snowdon's ridges. Suggestions include ***lled*** pl. ***lledau*** 'breadth, width' and ***llaid*** 'mud'. The pl. ****llidau***, although unrecorded, meets most of the problems, and could describe unrelenting, ferocious, conditions in certain weather. Whatever its origin, the subsequent development has been influenced by Llydaw 'Brittany', an association which prompted some to venture a similar derivation signifying 'lake-dwelling'. The river Glaslyn flows from Llyn Glaslyn through Llyn Llydaw and Cwm Dyli (*chwmdelif* 13cent. [14cent.], *Connduly* 1508, *Cwm Dylu* 1756, *Cwm Dyli* 1810, ***dylif*** 'torrent, deluge') with its hydro-electric scheme.

LLYN NANTLLE see **DYFFRYN NANTLLE**

LLYNNAU MYMBYR Caern SH7057

'lakes at Mymbyr', ***llyn*** pl. ***llynnau***, pers.n. ***Membyr, Mymbyr***
aqu(a)e member 13cent. (14cent.), *Llynmumber* 1645,
Llyniau'n capel cerrig 1795, *Llyniau Mymbr* 1804, *Llyniau Mymbyr* 1818
Twin lakes in an area associated, somewhat obscurely, with an unidentified pers.n. preserved in the r.n. Mymbyr (*fluvius member sicut torrens* 13cent. [14cent.], *broke of mymber* 1565, *mymber* 1589, now Nant y Gwryd) and in Dyffryn Mymbyr (*dyffryn mymbyr* 1341, *diffryn mymber* 1499-50, ***dyffryn*** 'valley'). The lakes west of Capel Curig are separated by a neck of land called Baladeulyn (***bala*** 'strip of land affording a route', ***dau*** 'two', ***llyn***). The more usual pl. of ***llyn*** is ***llynnoedd***, whereas the slightly more archaic and literary ***llynnau*** is retained for several pairs or groups of lakes in Caern.

LLYN PADARN Caern SH5661

'lake at Dolbadarn', ***llyn***, p.n. ***Dolbadarn***
Llyn Dolpadarne 1518-9, *llyn Dolbadarne* 1526,
Llinne Dolbaterne, Dolbatern Poole, Lynne Dolebaderne 1536-9,
Llyn Dôl Badarn 1818, *Llanberis Lake* 1805, *Llyn Padarn* 1816
Dolbadarn (*Dolpadern* 1303-4, *Dolbadern* 1352, *Dolbadarn* 1544) is the meadowland (***dôl***) at the north-west end of Llyn Peris (q.v.), the neck of land separating the two lakes Padarn and Peris and called Glan Bala (earlier Baladeulyn, *Baladeuclyn* 1284, ***bala, dau, llyn***) above which is Castell Dolbadarn (*Castedolbadern* 1578, *Castell Dolbadern* 1795). The modern name Llyn Padarn is a contraction of *Llyn Dôl Badarn* probably influenced by the single name in the adjacent lake Llyn Peris (q.v.); cf. *Llyn Padarn and Llyn Peris or the Llanberis Lakes* 1816. Padarn, to whom the modern church in Llanberis is dedicated, may or may not have been the saint whose name is commemorated in several large churches in Wales. The ***dôl*** may have been associated with the Coed y Ddôl in which the later Llanberis (q.v.) developed.

LLYN PERIS Caern SH5959

'lake of Peris', ***llyn***, pers.n. ***Peris***
Linne Peris alias Nant Monach (Vallis monachis) 1536-9,
Poole of Peris 1588-9, *Llyn Perys* 1601, *Llyn Llanberis* 1645,
Lhyn Peris 1695, *Llyn Peris* 1818
The lake is at the lower end of the narrow valley (***nant***) of Nant Peris, near the village of Nantperis (q.v.). There are several valleys in Wales described as *Nant (y) Mynach* or *Manach* (***manach, mynach*** 'monk'). The reference to *Llyn Llanberis* is clear evidence of the location of the ***llan*** 'church' here, associated with the saint Peris, but intriguingly before the development of the modern Llanberis (q.v.).

LLYN SYFADDAN see LLAN-GORS LAKE

LLYN TEGID, BALA LAKE Mer SH9032

'lake of Tegid', ***llyn***, pers.n. ***Tegid***, E ***lake***, p.n. ***Bala***
Thlintegid 1154, *Pemmelsmere* 1194, *Thlintegit: Pemblemere* 1285, *Pimbilmere* 1387, *Llyn Teget* 1523, *Llyn Tegyd, Lake Tegid* 1559, *Pymblemere, Llyn Tegyd* 1592, *Llyn Tegid in English Pimble mere* 1645, *Llyn Tegidd alis Pemble meer* 1698, *Llyn Tegid* 1796, *Llyn Tegid or Bala Lake* 1838
The lake south-west of Bala (q.v.). The obsolete E name is believed to be ME ****pimble*** an otherwise unrecorded nasalized var. of ME ***pibel***, E ***pebble*** 'stone', referring to the bed and the shores of the lake (ME ***mere***). Cf. Pymbylu Moors (*Papelmore, Paplimor* 13cent., *Pipelmore* 1492) with gravelly deposits in Dinas Powys Glam. The identity of Tegid is unknown. In addition to the fairly common name Bala Lake, another name, mainly in medieval literature, was *Llyn Aerfen* (*lynn aerfen* 15cent.) from the pers.n. Aerfen the goddess of war associated with the river Dee which flows from Llyn Tegid.

LLYN TEIFI see TEIFI, Afon

LLYN Y FAN FACH Carm SN8021

'little lake (near) the peak', ***llyn***, ***y***, ***ban***, ***bach***
Llynyfan fach 1814, *Llyn-y-fan-fach* 1831
Beneath Bannau Sir Gaer; slightly smaller than Llyn y Fan Fawr (q.v.).

LLYN Y FAN FAWR Carm SN8321

'great lake (near) the peak', ***llyn***, ***y***, ***ban***, ***mawr***
Llynyfan fawr 1814, *Llyn Fawr* 1819, *Llyn-y-fan-fawr* 1832
Great in contrast to Llyn y Fan Fach (q.v.) about two miles westward; a small lake located in a col beneath (Y) Fan Brycheiniog.

LLYSBEDYDD see BETTISFIELD

LLYSFAEN Denb SH8877

'stone court', ***llys***, ***maen***
Lleswaen 1254, *Lisnaen* 1291, *Lessemeyr* 1316, *Lesmaen* 1334, *llysvayn* 1544, *Llys Vaen* c.1700, *Llysfaen* 1737
The term ***llys*** may have been used to signify an imposing stone building in a strategic location or even to designate it as a royal court (as tradition asserts). Its stone construction would have been an unusual and significant feature, the availability of limestone being evident in the extensive modern quarries close by. The church was dedicated to Cynfran, and Llangynfran appears as an alias (*ll. gynfran ne llysvaen* 1545-53, *Llysvaen in Llangenvrayn* 1559, *ll. gynfarn* c.1566, *ll. gynfran* 1590).

LLYS-FAEN see **LISVANE**

LLYS-WEN Brec SO1338

'white court', ***llys***, ***gwyn*** fem. ***gwen***

Lisewan c.1127, *Liswen* 13cent., *y llyswen* c.1566

In MnW ***llys*** is treated as masc. but was formerly fem.; see Llysfaen. The significance of the adj. is not altogether clear but ***gwyn***, normally 'white', may be used in similar fashion to L *candida casa* and *album monasterium*, NF *blancmoustier* and E ***white*** for stone or white-washed buildings often referring to churches; cf. Whitland. It may also refer to something 'splendid, excellent, fair'; local traditions describe it as 'the gorgeous palace of the Princes of South Wales' and locate it in the *Warren Field near Dderw.*

LLYSWORNEY see **LLYSWYRNY**

LLYSWYRNY, LLYSWORNEY Glam SS9674

'court of Gwrinydd', ***llys***, terr.n. ***Gwrinydd***

Liswini 1173-84, *Liswrony* 12cent., *Liswrini* c.1262, *Leswryny* 1314, *Liswerny* 1349, *Lesworney* 1466, *Lyswronnyth* 1474, *Llysworney* 1495

Probably the administrative centre of the cantref of Gwrinydd (*Gurunid* c.1100 [c.1200], *Wrenid* c.1170, *Grunuhd* 1180-1208) and thought to be the pers.n. ***Gwrin*** (as in Llanwrin Mont) with the terr.suff. ***-ydd***. Late spellings such as *Grouneth* 1443 and *Goruenith* 1536-9 produced Groneath, the name of the deanery, and Gorfynydd (influenced by ***mynydd***), the later name of the cantref.

LLYS-Y-FRÂN Pemb SN0424

'court of Brân', ***llys***, ***y***, pers.n. ***Brân***

Lysurane 1326 (16cent.), *Lysfrane* 1402, *Llysvrane* 1535, *Lesfrayne* 1563, *Lisyfraen* 1594, *Llysyvran* c.1600

Early forms favour the pers.n. Brân. Names of animals and birds, frequently associated with fanciful names for ruined houses and castles (such as Llys-y-dryw 'the wren's court' and Frog Hall), prompted the intrusive def.art. ***y*** in later forms as the state of the site deteriorated and became the haunt of the raven (***brân***); cf. Dinas Brân, Llangollen Denb. The earthwork north of the church is believed to be the remains of the ***llys***. The valley to the north is now the Llys-y-frân Reservoir.

LLYWEL Brec SN8730

'(church of) Llywel', pers.n. ***Llywel***

Luhil 12cent., *Luel* c.1200, *llan yn llywel* c.1180 (c.1400), *lliwuel* late 15cent.

Described as 'church of the three saints' in 1239, including Dewi, Teilo and Llywel (reputed to have been a disciple of the 6cent. Dyfrig and

Teilo). There is also a dedication at Llanllywel (q.v.) and probably Lanlouel in Brittany. The p.n. falls into a small category of p.ns which consist of a pers.n. with no prefixed generic such as ***merthyr***, ***llan*** or ***eglwys***; cf. Gwytherin and Margam.

LOGGERHEADS Denb SJ1962

'(place near the) Loggerheads', E ***loggerheads***

We three Loggerheads ?1782, *The Loggerheads* 1800

The name of an inn which gave its name to the hamlet on the Denb/Flints border. Nearby is the county boundary stone set in 1763 to resolve disputes over mineral rights between Mold (Flints) and Llanferres (Denb), a lengthy legal impasse which, it appears, set landowners 'at loggerheads'. However, the artist Richard Wilson, who frequented the inn, painted an inn-sign (reputedly in 1782, the year of his death) giving the name an additional interpretation (of blockhead, drunkard) by depicting two heads looking in opposite directions with the inscription *We three Loggerheads* inviting the observer to identify himself as the third, a feature of several inn-signs in England.

LOGIN Carm SN1623

'little polluted (river)', ***halog***, dim. ***-yn***

Loggin 1684, *Llogin* 1782, *Login* 1843

Ha- has been confused with the def.art. ***y***. Several brooks or rivers are described in this way, such as Logyn (*Y Logyn* 1564) near Llandysul Card, and in Brec, Radn and Glam, and *Logyn-dwr* 1831 near Llangynnor Carm.

LOUGHOR, CASLLWCHWR Glam SS5798

'castle on (the river) Llwchwr', ***castell***, r.n. ***Llwchwr***

Locher c.1191, *Logherne* 1203, *Lochor* 1207-8, *gastell llychwr* 1375-80, *Castellwchwr* 1539, *Castell Logher* 1543, *Caslougher* 1691, *Câs Lychür*, 1719

The river (*Luchur*, *lychur* 1136-54, *Lochor* c.1191 [c.1214], *Llwchwr* 1778) gave its name to the Roman fort *Leucaro*, *Leucarum* c.300, *Leuca* c.700, although there is some uncertainty as to the precise Brythonic form which gave rise to both L *Leuca* and L *Leucaro*, but the meaning seems to be 'bright, shining' (as in the r.n. Llugwy in Angl, Caern and Mer). The older W form Llychwr is also found in ***llychwr*** 'daylight'; Llwchwr is a later development (cf. ***cymwd*** > ***cwmwd***). AN and E settlers employed the r.n. for their castle and borough at the estuary of the river (*Aber Llychwr* 1151 (c.1400) with ***aber***), and influenced the modern form Lougher. The W name (with ***cas***, a contracted form of ***castell***, found in a number of south Wales p.ns such as Casnewydd and Cas-gwent q.v.) was used specifically of the castle and extended to the borough.

LUDCHURCH, YR EGLWYS LWYD Pemb SN1410

'church of Hlūd', pers.n. ***Hlūd***, OE ***cirice***, W ***yr***, ***eglwys***

Ecclesia de Loudes 1324, *Loudeschirch(e)* 1353, *Loudechirche* 1381, *Loudeschourch* 1390, *Lowdescherche* 1440, *Ludcherche* 1450, *yr eglwys lwyd* c.1566

It has been argued that the original pers.n. was W ***Llwyd*** anglicized as Loud, but the usual anglicization of Llwyd was Lloyd or Loyd. The forms do not favour that explanation but rather support the converse, that the name was the OE pers.n. ***Hlūd***, ME Loud and Lowde (cf. Lydstep). After *Loudes-* lost the genitival -s, *Loud-* was cymricized to ***llwyd*** 'grey', 'holy'; the church then became Yr Eglwys Lwyd 'the holy church'. The church was dedicated to Elidyr.

LYDSTEP Pemb SS0898

'Hlūd's bay', pers.n. ***Hlūd***, ON ***hóp***

Loudeshope 1362, *Ludsoppe* 14cent., *Lludeshope* 1576, *Leadstep* 1798

The pers.n. is also found in Ludchurch Pemb (q.v.). The ON ***hóp*** 'inlet, bay' is Lydstep Haven (*Ludsop haven* 1393) occurring in two other p.ns in Pemb, Goultrop Roads (*Goldhap* 1422, *Goltop* 1578) and Santop Bay. The modern form shows the influence of ***step***. The village lies on steep slopes descending to Lydstep Haven.

M

MACHEN Monm ST2189

'plain of Cein', ***ma***, pers.n. ***Cein***

Mahhayn 1102, *Machein* 1236, *Macheyn* 1317, *Machen* 1403, *machain* c.1566

The name is now applied to the industrial settlement in a narrow part of the Rhymni valley but the parish church and older village, now Lower Machen, lie in a wider part of the valley. The identity of Cein or Cain is unknown.

MACHNO, Afon see **PENMACHNO**

MACHYNLLETH Mont SH7400

'plain of Cynllaith', ***ma***, pers.n. ***Cynllaith***

Machenthleith 1201-13, *Machenloyd* 1254, *Maghenthleyth* 1291, *Mathkenlleyth* 1318, *Machynllaith* 1385, *Machenlleth* 1545, *bachynlleth* c.1566

Occupying a flat, open area close to the river Dyfi. The pers.n. may also occur in a r.n. Cynllaith Denb. Local dial. accounts for the change of -llaith to -lleth. The p.n. has long been identified quite incorrectly with the Roman fort *Maglona* which has no etymological connection with Machynlleth. There was also a notion that the Dyfi was once called Llaeth or Cynllaeth, presumably through some perceived association with ***llaeth*** 'milk'. The c.1566 form represents a common enough confusion of ma- as ba-; cf. Mathafarn > Bathafarn Denb.

MAELIENYDD Radn SO1371

'land of Maelien', pers.n. ***Maelien***, terr.suff. ***-ydd***

Mailenith c.1191, *Melienydh* 1722, *Melenydd* 1833, *Moelynaidd* 1891

The name applies to moors between the rivers Ithon and Aran near Llanbister, located in the ancient cantref of Maelienydd ([*y*] *Uaelenyd*, *Maelenyd* 1109 (c.1400), *maelenyt* c.1160 (early 14cent.), (*o*) *uaelyenyt* c.1190 (early 14cent.), *Melenith* c.1200, *Maelienid* 1273-4, *Cantref Melenyd, -ith* 1536-90), the cantref which included the greater part of the north of Radn.

MAENADDWYN Angl SH4584

'stone of Addwyn', ***maen***, pers.n. ***Addwyn***

y mayn ddwyn 1549, *Maenaddwyn* 1733-4, *Maen-addwyn* 1890

The original stone has long since been removed, but another ten foot stone half-a-mile south of the village is popularly identified as Maen Addwyn.

MAENCLOCHOG Pemb SN0827

'rocks sounding like a bell', ***maen*** pl. ***mein, clochog***

Meinclothog c.1291, *Maynclochanc* 1303,

Maenclochawc 1257 (late 13cent.), *y maen kloch(og)* c.1599

Apparently named from two large stones (recorded c.1700) near the church, which could be struck to produce a sound like a bell. There are similar names elsewhere, such as Clochfaen Mer and Mont.

MAENDY[1]**, Y** Glam ST0176

'the stone house', ***y, maen, tŷ***

Y Maendy 1612, *Maendy* 1799, *Maendu* 1811-14

A very common p.n.; there are identical p.ns in Pendoylan (*Maindy, Mayndy* 1670), Peterston-super-Ely (*Maendy* 1833), Cardiff (*Maindy* 1739), Llantrisant (*Maenduy* 1669) and Gelligaer (*Maynduy* 1693) Glam. Rather than being a house built entirely of stone, it may have been a house with a roof of slate or stone tiles.

MAENDY[2]**, Y** see **MAINDEE**

MAENORBŶR see **MANORBIER**

MAENORDEILO, MANORDEILO Carm SN6726

'estate of Teilo', ***maenor***, pers.n. ***Teilo***

Meynaur Teylau 1257, *Meynerdelow* 1287, *Maynordeylou* 1309,

Manerdylo 1588-9

This may also be *lann teliau mainaur* 1160-80 (unless it is an error for Llandeilo Fawr about three miles south-west). Cf. a similar name Maenorfabon (*Mainoruaban* 1316-7, *Maynor Vabon* 1652-3, Manorafon or Manoravon on later maps). Mabon was possibly a saint (see Llanfabon). ***maenor*** later developed the sense 'manor' and as such was a very common el. in Carm.

MAENTWROG Mer SH6640

'rock of Twrog', ***maen***, pers.n. ***Twrog***

Maynturroc 1292-3, *Maenturok* 1444, *men twroc* c.1566, *Maentwrog* 1695

The church was dedicated to the 6cent. Twrog. Some late medieval sources make Twrog a sister of Tygái (Llandygái q.v.) and Trillo (Llandrillo q.v.), children of Ithel Hael of Brittany. The stone at the south-west corner of the church is traditionally said to mark the saint's grave having been thrown there by the saint from the top of Moelwyn or, in another version, by a giant called Twrog.

MAEN Y BUGAIL, WEST MOUSE Angl SH3094

'shepherd's rock', 'west little island', ***maen***, ***y***, ***bugail***, E ***west***, E ***mouse***

le mouse prope le Fouleforland 1478,

*le mouse island in the north isle of Anglesey, insula vocata Mewysisland*15cent., *Maen Bigail* mid 16cent., *W. Mouse* 1777,

West Mouse or maen Bigel 1795, *West Mouse or Maen Bigel* 1801,

Maen bugail or West Mouse 1838, *West Mouse/Maen y Bugael* 20cent.

Cf. Middle Mouse and East Mouse. ***mouse*** is used figuratively to denote a small island (suggested by the def.art. of *le Mouse*), an explanation which is preferable to this island, or all three, being mouse-infested. The *Fouleforland* is the Carmel Head (q.v.). In the W name, the island was perceived as shepherding smaller rocks in the area, or, given its location east of the navigationally important Skerries (q.v.), guiding ships. Vars of Bugail are *Bugael* and *Bigel*, forms which have been influenced by the tradition that on the island was a hermitage for the saint Bugail commemorated in *Llanfugail* now variously spelt Llanfigael and Llanfigel (the local pronunciation and the more usual form). There is also a *Maen Bigel or Bugail* 1816, *Maen Bugael* 1890 north of Bardsey. Cf. the lost *Merthir buceil* 12cent. near Merthyr Mawr Glam.

MAERDY[1] Carm SN6220

'dairy-farm', ***maerdy***

Maerdy-bach 1831, *Maerdy*, *Maerdy-bâch* 1891

See Maerdy[2,3]. The name is probably taken from a farm Maerdy-bach adjoining the village. This is small (***bach***) perhaps in contrast to a lost *Maerdy-mawr* (***mawr***) in the same area.

MAERDY[2] Denb SJ0144

'demesne farm', ***maerdy***

Y Maerdy, *Maerdy*, *maerdu* c.1700, *Maerdy* 1761, *Maerdy* 1838

The origin and earlier meaning of ***maerdy*** was 'steward's house' (***maer***, ***tŷ***) which then developed a number of secondary meanings particularly 'summer dwelling for the tending of cattle, dairy farm' and 'home farm'. There is evidence here that the farm could have been the dwelling of the ***maer*** or steward to the lords of Dinmael. By c.1700 the farm had become *a small pentre of 4 houses*. Although the definite article ***y*** appears occasionally and is the form recommended by some, modern colloquial usage tends to omit it.

MAERDY[3]**, Y** Glam SS9798

'dairy-farm', ***maerdy***

Mardy 1813, *Meardy* 1833, *Mairdy* 1845

See Maerdy[1,2]. A name found regularly in valley bottoms, such as Maerdy Newydd at Welsh St Donat's Glam (*Mardu Newydd* 1764); there are other examples in Mountain Ash and Merthyr Tudful. This village developed near a pit here c.1880 which gave access to the Abergorky coal vein of 1876. On the 1813 form and local pronunciation see Maerdy[4].

MAERDY[4], MARDY Monm SJ3015

'dairy-farm', ***maerdy***

Merdiu 1256-7, *Maerdy* 1832

See Maerdy[2,3] Denb. The Mardy form, reflecting local pronunciation, is the dial. -ae- > long -a-; cf. Llantwit Fardre. Located in former pastures adjoining the river Gafenni.

MAERUN see **MARSHFIELD**

MAES-GLAS see **GREENFIELD**

MAES-GLAS Monm ST3086

'green field', ***maes, glas***

Maisglase 1536-9, *y maes glas* c.1550, *Greinfelde* 1570-1, *Maes Glas* 1833

Maes-glas probably gave rise to the name of the manor of Greenfield alias Ebboth (= Ebwydd). The castle in Maes-glas called Castell Glas (*Grenefeld cast.* 1577, ***castell, glas***) and lies in an open, flat area near the river Ebbw/Ebwy.

MAES-GWYN Carm SN2023

'fair field', ***maes, gwyn***

Maynor y maesgwyn 1591-2, *Place y Maesgwynne* 1689-90, *Maesgwyn* 1730-40, *Maesgwynne* 1843

gwyn here may also be 'white' of vegetation. *Maesgwynne* has perhaps been influenced by the anglicized surname Gwynne. The first form has ***maenor***, a very common el. in Carm p.ns and often applied to manors or subdivisions of parishes or commotes. *Maenor y Maes-gwyn* was a subdivision of Traean March (***traean*** 'third' of the barony of St Clears).

MAESGWYNNE see **MAES-GWYN**

MAESHAFN Denb SJ2060

'open land by the gorge', ***maes, hafn***

Maeshavan 1795, *Maes-y-safn* 1878, *Maeshafn* 1914

The open land is on the lower slopes of Moel Findeg to the east of a narrow pass or gorge leading down to Afon Alun near Llanferres. The area has been associated with quarrying which explains the late appearance of the name, although the 1795 form (with an intrusive -a-) seems fancifully to associate the area with ***hafan*** 'haven' and 1878 with ***safn*** 'jaws'. Convention requires Maes-hafn (to conform with final stress) but usage favours Maeshafn.

MAES-LLYN Card SN3644

'field by the pool', ***maes, llyn***

Maesllyn 1773, *Maes llyn* 1839, *Maes-y-llyn* 1891

Several springs and a brook (Afon Cwerchyr) flow through a fairly narrow valley. The mill there was dependent upon a mill pool.

MAESMYNYS Brec SO0147

'open country of Mynys', ***maes***, pers.n. ***Mynys***

Maisminuth 1280, *Maesmenus* 1291, *Maysmenys in Buelt* 1491, *ll. ddewi maes mynys* c.1566

Nothing is known of Mynys. The church is dedicated to Dewi and the formal name of the church appears to have been Llanddewi Maesmynys but, apart from the c.1566 form, there is very little evidence to suggest that it was ever in common use.

MAESTEG Glam SS8591

'fair field', ***maes, teg***

maes tege issa 1543, *Maesteg ycha* 1647, *Maesteg genol, ~ Isha* 1740, *Maes-têg* 1884

An industrial town centred on the former farm Maes-teg Uchaf (*Maesteg uchaf* 1813) which grew up near the *Maesteg Ironworks* established 1826. There were two other nearby farms Maes-teg Genol (***canol***, 'middle') and Isaf (***isaf*** 'lower'). Its proximity to another farm Y Llwyni (*Llwyney* 1773, 'the bushes', ***llwyn*** pl. ***llwyni***) has given rise to the suggestion that the area was once called by that name. Maesteg appears as a fixed name for the town from 1858 when it formed a separate Local Board of Health. Standardized orthography requires Maes-teg (to reflect final stress) but in established usage Maesteg has long prevailed.

MAESYCRUGIAU Carm SN4741

'field of the mounds', ***maes, y, crug*** pl. ***crugiau***

Maes-y-crugiau 1831, 1891

A relatively modern hamlet around the ancient parish church of Llanllwni. The name is taken from a nearby house on a small, wooded hill.

MAESYCWMER Monm ST1594

'field at the footbridge', ***maes, y, cwmwr*** var. ***cwmer***

Maesycwmer 1828, *Maesycwmwr* 1841, *Maes-y-cwmmer* 1885, *Maescwmwr* 1903

The name probably derives from the name of the house (built in 1826) of a local Baptist minister, approached by a footbridge over a small stream flowing into the river Rhymni. Mainly a Glam word (but also Cwmwr Du Carm), ***cwmwr, cwmer*** is usually a narrow wooden bridge. ***cymer*** 'confluence' may have influenced some forms.

MAESYFED see **NEW RADNOR**

MAGOR see **MAGWYR**

MAGWYR, MAGOR Monm ST4287

'fortification', ***maguwyr***

Magor 1153-76, *Magour* 1495, *maguwyr* c.1566, *Magur* 1685

It may refer to one of the important walls adjoining Whitewall Common and Whitewall Reen (extending south-eastwards from the village) associated with drainage works on the former marshland of Caldicot Levels. Alternatively it might indicate 'ruin' or 'enclosure with walls', possibly referring to a Roman villa.

MAIDEN WELLS Pemb SR9799

'maiden's well', OE ***mægden***, OE ***wælle***

Mayden Welle 1336, *Mayden Wells* 1583, *Maiden Wells* 1818

mægden is a common el. in E p.ns sometimes associated with the Virgin Mary, or simply with social gatherings; cf. Maidenwell Cornwall (*Medenawille* 1347) and Maidenwell Lincs (*Maidenwell* 1212).

MAINDEE, MAENDY, Y Monm ST3388

'the stone house', (*y*), ***maen, tŷ***

The Maendy 1615, *Mayndee House* 1675, *yr maine dee* 1678

A common name in Glam and Mon. Named from two former farms Y Maendy Bach and Y Maendy Fawr (***bach, mawr***). Cf. Maendy[1].

MALLTRAETH Angl SH4068

'unwholesome strand', ***mall, traeth***

Maltraeth 1304-5, *Maltraith, Maltraeth* 1346, *Malldraeth* 15cent., *Malltraeth* 1600-1, *Malldraeth* 1777

Although tidal to Llangefni (q.v.), the course of the slow-moving shallow Afon Cefni (q.v.) from Llangefni was through the mud-flats and marshes of Cors Ddyga (q.v.) to its estuary in Malltraeth Sands (*the estuary of Maltraheth* 1536-9, *the bay of Malltrayth and the crick in the myddest of the said bay* 16cent., *Malldraeth Sands and Bar* 1805), with shores that were dank and fetid. Between 1788 and 1859 some three thousand acres were reclaimed mainly with the building of Cob Malltraeth. The village now known as Malltraeth was once called *Rhyd y Maen Du* (1787, 'ford of the black stone' ***rhyd, y, maen, du***) from one of the several fords across Afon Cefni. Much later, it was the base for workers on the Cob and the railway bridge. In 1860, a small coalfield was opened to provide coal for the Mynydd Parys copper mines, and Malltraeth Yard or Yr Iard ('the yard') became a small port and shipbuilding yard.

MALLTRAETH MARSH see **CORS DDYGA**

MALLWYD Mer SH8612

'place ?in shadow', ***ma, llwyd***

Malluet 1254, *Mallwyt* c.1291, *mallwyd* c.1566

The significance of ***llwyd*** here is uncertain. The current location of the church may loosely be described as ***llwyd*** 'grey' or 'in shadow', or the meeting of the waters of Afon Dugoed and Afon Dyfi here could be 'muddy'. However, there is a tradition that the original church was in the hills behind Aberangell, which may have prompted the association with 'holy' or 'blessed', but such a meaning is found almost exclusively in poetic contexts (once, coincidentally, in the 15cent., with reference to Tydecho, the patron saint of Mallwyd). Some distance to the south-west is Nant Mynach and Abermynach (***mynach*** 'monk') which may or may not be relevant. The pers.n. Llwyd cannot be ruled out.

MALPAS Monm ST3090

'bad passage', OF ***mal***, OF ***pas***

Maupass 1184-5, (*de*) *Malo Passu* 1239, *Le Maupas* 1291, *Malpas* 1392, *y malpas* c.1566

A difficult route through a marshy area adjoining the church and a bridge over Malpas Brook, and thought to be on the line of a Roman road. There are identical p.ns in Cheshire and Cornwall.

MANAFON Mont SJ1102

'plain associated with Anafon' ***ma-***, pers.n. ***Anafon***

Manauon 1254, *Mannavon* 1338, *Mynafon* mid 14cent., *Manavan* 1390, *Manavon* 1393-4, *manafon* c.1566

The pers.n. Anafon probably also occurs in Afon Anafon near Abergwyngregyn Caern. *Nafon has also been proposed (on the analogy of pers.ns Nefydd and Neifion with ***naf*** 'lord') but it is not otherwise attested. Manafon parish had three townships, Manafon-gaenog (*Mananougynok* 1291, ***caenog*** 'lichen-encrusted'), Manafon-llan (*Mananoulan* 1291, ***llan***, the tnshp in which the church stands) and Manafon-llys (*Mananoueles* 1291, ***llys*** 'court, hall' probably Henllys).

MANCOT Flints SJ3266

'Mana's shelter', pers.n. ***Mana***, OE ***cot***

Mancote 1282-3, *Manecote* 1284, *Manicote* 1324, *Mancot* 1450

The shelter might have been a hut for herdsmen. A distinction was made between the westerly Big Mancot (*Great Mancot* 1553, *Mancoat Magna* 1666, *Big Mancot* 1764) and the easterly Little Mancot (*Lyttyll Mancott* 1550, *Parva Mancot* 1594), and, later still, Mancot Royal (occasionally Mancot Regis) an estate built in 1917 to house workers in the Royal Ordnance Factory.

MAN-MOEL Monm ST1703

?'(place associated with) the son of Moel', ***mab***, pers.n. ***Moel***

Massmoil 1101-7, *Mapmoil* 1102 (1330), *ecclesia Mac moilo* c.1200, *Melyn Vam Hoell* 1570, *Mamm Howell* 1630, *Mamhole* 1653, 1804, *Cefn Manmoel* 1833

Uncertain. If it is a pers.n., Moel is probably a nickname (***moel*** 'bald'). The Ir *Macmoil* is recorded c.1100 as the name of a disciple of Cadog, with *Mab Moel* (***mab*** 'son of') being a W adaptation of *Macmoil*. Later forms reveal the influence of the pers.n. Hywel, ***man*** 'place' and ***mam*** 'mother'.

MANORBIER, MAENORBŶR Pemb SS0697

'estate of Pŷr' , pers.n. ***Pŷr*** , W ***maenor***, E ***manor***

Mainaur pir 1136-54, *Manerbire* 1331, *manor bir* c.1566

Very little is known about Pir or Pŷr. The same name (and probably the same person) is found in Ynys Bŷr (q.v.) a few miles west. Although modern Manorbier is a village, it was originally a division of a commote and even described as the commote itself (*kymwt Maenawrbir* c.1400, ***cwmwd***), suggesting that it was an old and important centre. The p.n. became anglicized by the 14cent.

MANORDEILO see **MAENORDEILO**

MANOROWEN Pemb SM9336

'estate of Gnawan', ***maenor***, pers.n. ***Gnawan***

Maynernawen 1369, *Maynornawan* 1326 (16cent.), *maner nawan* c.1566, *Mannernawen* 1596

The same pers.n. is found in Cilnawan in Llanboidy Carm. Later forms appear to have been influenced by AF ***manor*** and the pers.n. Owen, Owain.

MARCHWIEL Denb SJ3547

'large saplings' ***marchwia(i)l***

Marchocil 1254, *Marchwoel* 1284, *Marthwyel* 1291, *Marchwyaill* 1488, *y marchwiel* c.1566, *Marchwiail*, *Marchwial* c.1700, *Marchwiail* 1795, *Marchwiel* 1838

The saplings, large twigs or strong shoots were possibly cultivated specifically as a source for rods to strengthen hedges or for withies for tying bundles (or even for charcoal burning). The dial. var. ***marchwiel*** has long established itself in spelling, but whereas it was once a three-syllable name, the anglicized pronunciation (as if E -ie-) has become the regular form when speaking W or E.

MARCROES see **MARCROSS**

MARCROSS, MARCROES Glam SS9269

?'boundary cross', ?OE ***(ge)mǣre***, OE ***cros***

Marcros 1148-66, c.1262, *Marcrosse* 1545, *markroes* c.1566, *Marcroes* 1578

Marcross church lies only 100 yards from a stream marking the boundary of Marcross and Monknash parishes. Marcroes is a W adaptation, substituting ***croes*** 'cross'. However, it has also been explained as an anglicization of W ***march, rhos*** (cf. Marros) but the forms provide no evidence of -ch-.

MARDY see **MAERDY**[3, 4]

MARFORD Denb SJ3656

'boundary ford', OE ***(ge)mǣre***, OE ***ford***

Merford 1315, *Merffordd* 1393, *Merford, merfordh* c.1700

The ford west of the village (now a footbridge) is through the river Alun which is the Denb/Flints boundary here. The 1393 and c.1700 forms record a cymricized form influenced by W ***ffordd*** 'road, way' (cf. nearby Gresford) but which did not survive. In England, several p.ns with initial ***(ge)mǣre*** have modern forms in Mer- and Mar-.

MARGAM Glam SS7887

obscure

marcan 1136-54, *Margan* 12cent., 1291, *Morgan* 1208, *margam* c.1566

The name has generally been understood as 'church dedicated to Margan', one of a number of p.ns consisting of a saint's name without any prefixed generic such as ***llan, merthyr*** and ***eglwys***; cf. Gwytherin and Llywel. The name, however, is recorded as a 12cent. *provincia* in the terr. division of Glywysing covering Margam and some of the adjoining parishes. Some forms show confusion with the pers.n. Morgan, plainly under the influence of Morgannwg, the ancient lordship and kingdom in which it is later recorded. The village was originally centred on its church near Port Talbot railway station. The replacement of -n with -m is common; cf. Mawdlam.

MARIAN-GLAS Angl SH5084

'verdant rock-strewn land', ***marian, glas***

Marrian Glas 1774, *Marian-glâs* 1838

Grass covered much of the otherwise rocky ground. Marian-mawr is to the south.

MARLAIS, Afon Pemb SN1415

'stagnant stream', ***afon, marw, glais***

Marleys 1331-2, *Marleis Broke* 1536-9, *Marles* 1633, *Marles R.* 1760, *Marlais* 1814

The river rises near Narberth and joins Afon Taf near Whitland after a series of undulations and oxbows. There are several streams so called in the vicinity (including a former name of Afon Gronw (q.v.) which joins Taf about a mile further downstream) and elsewhere in south Wales.

MARLOES Pemb SM7908

'bare promontory', ***moel, rhos***

Malros 1234-42, *Marlas* 1529, *Marlas, Marlos* 1543, *Marlasse* c.1600, *Marlos* c.1602, *Marloes* 1748

The first el. is more properly a residual form of the Br ***mail*** (which became ***moel*** in W) as in the Scottish Melrose and in Malvern, Shropshire (with ***bryn***). The village is located on a headland, the earlier meaning of ***rhos***. From the 16cent., a further sound change was -lr- > -rl-. The forms in -as may be influenced by ***glas*** and this is still a local var. pronunciation. The modern written form in -oes results from a hypercorrection, through association with well recorded dial. development of -oe- > -o-; cf. Marros q.v. (with its var. *marchroes* c.1566) and Bargoed.

MARROS Carm SN2008

'horse moor', ***march, rhos***

Marcros, Mairos 1307, *Marros* 1531, *marchroes* c.1566

Some spellings are reminiscent of Marcross Glam (q.v.). The village occupies the exposed moorland of Marros Mountain on which, presumably, wild horses were to be seen regularly.

MARSHFIELD, MAERUN Monm ST2682

'marshy land', ?'land associated with Meuryn', ?OE ***mersc***, OE ***feld***, ?W pers.n. ***Meuryn***

Maervn 1136-54, *Meresfeld* 1230, 1401, *Marshefeld* 1531, *Mairin* 1536-9, *meyryn* c.1566, *Meiryn or Marshfield* 1779

The E name is possibly from the village's location adjoining the former marshes of Wentllooge Levels. However, the first el. could also represent OE ***mere*** 'pool, wetland' in the possessive ***meres*** (as in Maresfield Sussex), or OE ***(ge)mǣre*** 'boundary' (as in Marshfield Gloucester). It has been suggested that either of the OE first els could have given rise to the first el. in the W name; however, that seems to be the pers.n. Meuryn or Maerun. The interpretation of marshy land is supported by *sarne vayrin* 1630 (***sarn*** 'causeway').

MARTEG, Afon Radn SN9975

'very fair (river)', ***march, teg***

Marcdac 1200, *(Blaen) marchdeg* late 15cent., *Marteigry* 1688, *Afon Marteg* 1833

march occurs several times in the sense 'great, large' (cf. Marchwiel) and in the case of a r.n. an extended meaning of that could be 'strong, vigorous'. Since this r.n. has an adj. ***teg*** perhaps ***march*** has the reinforcing sense of 'very'. The lenited -deg is in keeping with the fem. river, whereas the restored -teg reflects other p.ns where lenition does not occur. One of the tributaries of Marteg is Marcheini which can similarly be explained as 'very vigorous' (***heini*** 'lively'). Cf. Varteg and Cwm Farteg Glam, Varteg Hill Monm.

MARTLETWY Pemb SN0310

'burial-place of ?Tywai', ***merthyr***, pers.n. ***Tywai***

Martletwye c.1230, *Marthletroi* 1231-2, *Martheltwy* 1273, *Martiltwy* 1291, *Marthe tywi* c.1566, *ecclesia Sancte Twye de Martletwie* c.1600

Anglicization may account for some of the radical changes. The fairly common development of final -r to -l (here *Merthyr* to *Marthel-*, *Martl-*) is paralleled in some 14cent. forms of Merthyr Dyfan (*Martheldeuan* c.1348) and 13cent. forms of Merthyr Mawr Glam (q.v.). Tywai may be a by-form of Tyfái, the name of the saint with a dedication at Lamphey (q.v.), and referred to elsewhere as *Tyfei martir* 1136-54.

MATHRI Pemb SM8731

?'place of woe', ?***marth***, ?***tru***

Marthru, *mathru* 1136-54, *Martru* 1197, *Marthre* 1403, *Marthery* 1554, *Marthri* c.1566, *Mathri* 1633

An obscure name despite the fairly consistent evidence, with two rare, mainly literary, words, certainly not occurring elsewhere in p.ns. ***marth*** signifies 'sorrow, shame' while ***tru*** means 'miserable, pitiful'. That this was a shrine of some sort was certainly enhanced by the legend of the seven saints of Mathri (*seith seint mathru* 1136-54) and by later references to the parish (***plwyf***) as *Plwyf Merthyri* (1613) which shows the influence of ***merthyr*** pl. ***merthyri*** either in the usual sense of ***merthyr*** 'shrine' or possibly, since it seems to be a plural, simply 'martyrs' or the seven saints themselves. However, the early forms have no evidence of merth- as the basis of *Marthru*. Some have argued for an OIr ***martra*** 'relics' with the final syllable again influenced by W ***merthyri***. The loss of -r- in the modern form could be ascribed to the influence of names such as Mathafarn Ang and Mathrafal Mont but is more likely to be the reduced E -r- (as in the standard E pronunciation of Martha).

MAWDDACH, Afon Mer SH7629-6416

'little Mawdd', r.n. ***Mawdd***, dim.suff. ***-ach***

Mauach, *Mawhech* 13cent., *Mautheche* 1592, *Mouthegh* 1695, *Afon y Bermo* c.1700, *river Mawddach o.c.Barmouth River* 1770, *Mawddach* 1838

There is considerable confusion arising from the names and identity of two closely related rivers, one of which is a tributary of the other. *Mawdd* (which may well have been a pers.n. originally) features in the names of both rivers. The larger of the two was simply *Mawdd* (*Maviae* 13cent., *Maw Ryver* 1536-9, *Auon uaue* 1578, *Avon vawr* 1717, where ***mawr*** has influenced later forms) with loss of final -dd from a very early period. It rises in Waun y Griafolen west of Llanuwchlyn and flows into the sea at *Abermawdd*/Barmouth (q.v.). Later it seems to have became known as *Mawddu* and then *Mawddwy* (*Maudhu 1209*, *Mawddv* 1356, *Mothuaye* 1610) with ***du*** 'black' but then changing to the suff. ***-wy*** common in r.ns. Mawddwy was also associated with a wider area and was the name of the commote (*Mautho* 1232, *Maudoe* 1254, *Mauthov* 1319, *Mowthewau* 1502, *Mowthoy* 1583-4) with the terr.suff. ***-wy***, denoting either the territory around the river *Mawdd* or belonging to an individual called *Mawdd*. Cf. Dinas Mawddwy and Llanymawddwy. Consequently, because of this ambiguity (of river and territory), the major river adopted the name of its tributary Mawddach, while the original *Mawddach* was renamed Wnion (q.v.), a river which flows from near Rhyd-y-main, through Dolgellau to join (the newly-named) Mawddach at Cymer (***cymer*** 'confluence', q.v.).

MEIDRIM Carm SN2820

'middle ridge', ***mei-***, ***trum***

Meitrym late 12cent. (13cent.), *Meydrym* 1291, *meidrim* c.1566, *Mydrim* 1749

The village lies at the eastern end of a long slope above Afon Dewi Fawr. Cf. Meifod Mont.

MEIFOD Mont SJ1512

'middle dwelling', ***mei-***, ***bod***

Meiuot 12cent. (13cent.), *Meyvod* 1254, *Meynot* 1278, *Meyfote* 1287, *Meivot* 1346, *Ymeiuot* c.1155-95 (c.1400), *Meyvotte within Powys Lande* 1443, *Myvod* c.1520, *Meifod ymhowys* c.1560-90

Meifod lies in the Efyrnwy valley, roughly midway between Mathrafal (with its medieval court) and Llansanffraid-ym-Mechain.

MEINCIAU Carm SN4610

'banks, hillocks', ***mainc*** pl. ***meinciau***

Mancha 1760, *Min Key* 1765, *Maingieu* 1831, *y Meincau* 1839, *Minkau* 1851, *Meinciau* 1920

mainc generally meaning 'bench' is used topographically here for an area of low hills, ridges and terraces.

MEIRIONNYDD
'territory of Meirion', pers.n. ***Meirion***, terr.suff. ***-ydd***
Merionyth c.1191, *Meirionyth* 1279, *Meirionnydd* 1450-1500
Meirion mab Dybion fab Cunedda is reputed to have lived in the 5cent. The county name was originally that of a cantref (comprising the commotes of Tal-y-bont and Ystumanner). Merionethshire still survives as an anglicized form; Merioneth is obsolescent.

MEISGYN see **MISKIN**

MELIDEN, ALLT MELYD Flints SJ0680
'hill of Melydn', ***allt***, pers.n. ***Melydn***
Estradmelened 1241, *Altimeliden* 1256, *Aldmelyden, Altmoledynn* 1291, *Alltmelydyn* 1346-53, *Moledyne alias Allthmeldyn* 1413, *Altemeleden* 1465, *Gallt Melydon* 1586-1613, *Galht Meliden* c.1700
The hill on the north of Graig Fawr was associated with an unidentified saint Melydn. His name survived in the E form Meliden but was eventually truncated in W through loss of the final -en. Recently, Gallt Melyd has been given some prominence (possibly based on some of the historical forms), ***gallt*** being a later development of ***allt***. The first form relates to the lower land (***ystrad***) to the north.

MELIN IFAN DDU see **BLACKMILL**

MELIN-Y-COED Denb SH8160
'mill by the trees', ***melin, y, coed***
Melyn y coed 1605, *melin y Koed* c.1700, *Melin y coed* 1830
The mill (*Corn mill* 1915) was located on Afon Cyffdy. Then, as now, the area had several tracts of woods (appearing in names such as *Avon y Koed* and *Pont melin y Koed* c.1700).

MELIN-Y-DDÔL Mont SJ0907
'mill at the water-meadow', ***melin, y, dôl***
Melin-y-ddol 1832, *Mellynddol* 1858-9
On the river Banw. There was still a corn mill here in 1891.

MELIN-Y-WIG Mer SJ0348
'mill of the clearing', ***melin, y, gwig***
mellyn y wyke 1570, *Melin y weeg* 1612, *Melin y Wŷg* c.1700
This was a mill erected at an appropriate location on Afon Clwyd in a clearing near the junction of minor roads from Betws Gwerful Goch and Clawdd Newydd. It became a hamlet (*Melin y Wyg is a village of six or 7 houses* c.1700) and gradually became the centre of a scattered community.

MELLTE, Afon see **YSTRADFELLTE**

MENAI BRIDGE, PORTHAETHWY Angl SH5572

'(the town near the) Menai bridge', 'ferry of Daethwy', r.n. ***Menai***, E ***bridge***, W ***porth***, pers.n. ***Daethwy***

Porthaethay' 1190-99, *Porthatheu* 1291, *Porthaethwy* 1316, *Porthaithwe* 1551, *Menai Bridge (or Y Borth)* 1859

There were several ferries across the Menai Strait (q.v.). The shortest route from the mainland was the ferry called Porth Ddaethwy, subsequently Porthaethwy, the area in Angl belonging to the Daethwy tribe, whose ***din*** 'fort, stronghold' was Dindaethwy (*Dynndaethwy* 1284, *dyndaetho* 1304-5). Several documents evidently have the ferry in mind rather than a place of any significance, such as *Porthaethwy alias Bangor Ferry* (1742-3). Porthaethwy, or its local var. Y Borth (*Borth* 1839), later became the name of the town. When Thomas Telford built the suspension bridge in 1826 the bridge was called Pont y Borth (***pont*** 'bridge') and Menai Bridge. In time, Menai Bridge was also taken to refer to the town. A later derivative of Porthaethwy was Aethwy, taken as a pers.n. and the name of a former administrative district.

MENAI STRAIT, Y FENAI Angl/Caern SH4462-6378

'strait called Menai', 'the ?flowing one', E ***strait***, W ***y***, ?****men-***

Mene c.800 (11cent.), *Menei* 13cent., *Onguleyarsund* 13cent., *Meney* 1304-5, *Freto Meneviaco* ?14cent., *Menai* 1455-85, *Meney Salte Arme* 1536-9, *Str. of Menai* 1777, *Menai Strait* 1805

The name of the strait separating Angl and Caern whose precise origin and meaning are obscure. Menai is the name of several rivers of varying size and location in Wales, and therefore no link should be established with the name Môn (q.v.). It may possibly be based on an el. ****men-***, comparable with ***myn-*** as is in ***myned*** 'go', and signify 'a flow, a current'. *Ǫngulseyjarsund* is ON, the 'sound, strait' (ON ***sund***) of *Ǫngulsey* 'Anglesey' (q.v.), recorded in a Norse text, further evidence of Scandinavian coastal routes. *Freto Meneviaco* is a Latin documentary form (L ***fretum*** 'strait'). Although it is a strait, W usage commonly refers to it as Afon Menai (***afon*** 'river') and Y Fenai. The narrow south-west mouth (***aber***) of the Strait is Abermenai (*aber menai* 13cent., *Abermeney* 1297-8, *aber menei* 1300, *Aber Menei* 1378-80, *Aber Menai* 1648, *Aber Menai Point* 1890-1) with a distinctive curved spit of land, sand bar and breakwater the significance of which as a major access point was reduced in the early 14cent. when sand and sea began submerging inland routes. An alternative name for the spit, now defunct, was *Southcrook* 1400, *South Croke* 1536-9, which is ME ***crok*** 'crook' but might be ON ***krokr*** 'bend' given the Scandinavian name for the Menai Strait and Angl. See also Menai Bridge.

MERLIN'S BRIDGE, PONT MYRDDIN Pemb SM9414
'bridge near (the chapel of) Magdalen', pers.n. ***Magdalen***, E ***bridge***, W ***pont***
Mawdlyns brydge 1564, *Maudlin Bridge* 1697, *Merlins Bri.* 1798, *Mawdlens Bridge* 1824
Named from a nearby former chapel dedicated to Mary Magdalen (*domus Sanctæ Mariæ Magdalenæ* 1472, *the Mawdlens, le Mawdlyns* 1535); some modern sources refer to it as Pont Fadlen. Cf. Mawdlam Glam (*Mawdlen* 1596-1600) which has a church dedicated to the same saint. Locally, *the Marlan's bridge*. The p.n. has been influenced by antiquarian association with the legendary Merlin and since Merlin is an E version of Myrddin (see Caerfyrddin), recent W forms record Pont Myrddin.

MERTHYR Carm SN3520
'shrine consecrated with a saint's bones', ***merthyr***
Merthier in Derthles 1399, *Merther, Merthir* 1535, *merthyr* c.1566, *Merthir Elved* 1600
In the former commote Derllys; later sources place it in Elfed hundred. The saint does not appear to have been identified.

MERTHYR CYNOG Brec SN9837
'shrine of Cynog', ***merthyr***, pers.n. ***Cynog***
Kynauc in Merthyr Kynauc 13cent., *Merthir* c.1291, *Marteconot* 1127 (14cent.), *Merthyrkynock* 1558
Cynog is another of the numerous progeny of the legendary Brychan Brycheiniog (see Brecon) with dedications at Battle, Defynnog, Llangynog, Ystradgynlais, all in Brec, and at Boughrood Radn, Llansteffan Carm as well as Plogonnec in Brittany. Llangynog (q.v.) may commemorate a different saint. Cynog was held in high respect and Merthyr Cynog was a place of pilgrimage because the church preserved his torque or collar.

MERTHYR MAWR Glam SS8877
'shrine of Myfor', ***merthyr***, pers.n. ***Myfor***
Matthelemaur 1146, *merthirmimor, merthir Miuor* 1136-54, *merthir myuor* 1160-80, *Merthur Maur* c.1262, *Marthelmaur* 1317, *merthyr mawr* c.1566
The pers.n. Myfor is also found in Llanofer Monm and was confused at an early date with ***mawr*** 'great, big'. The church is now dedicated to Teilo. Some medieval forms show dissimilation of -r- to -l-; cf. Martletwy Pemb.

MERTHYR TUDFUL, MERTHYR TYDFIL Glam SO0506
'shrine of Tudful', ***merthyr***, pers.n. ***Tudful***
Merthir 1254, *Merthyr Tutuil* 13cent.

Interpretation of ***merthyr*** as 'martyr' has produced a fanciful tale of the martyrdom of Tudful, one of the many daughters of legendary Brychan Brycheiniog (see Brecon). Tudful may actually be a masc. name. The name is spelt Tydfil on some maps and by the local authority.

MERTHYR TYDFIL see **MERTHYR TUDFUL**

MERTHYR VALE, DYFFRYN TAF Glam SS0799

'valley near Merthyr', 'valley of the Taf', p.n. ***Merthyr***, E ***vale***, W ***dyffryn***, r.n. ***Taf***

Tir Duffrin Tâf alias Tir Ynis Owen 1750,
Tyr Dyffrin Taf or Tyr Ynis Owen 1797

Dyffryn Taf was the name of a farm (otherwise Ynysowen), a name replaced by the translation Merthyr Vale which became the name of the village and railway station which developed next to *Merthyr Vale Colliery* sunk by the colliery proprietor John Nixon between 1869 and 1875 at Ynysowen (*Ynys Owen* 1769, *Ynysowen* 1813, *Ynys-Owen* 1884 'river-meadow of Owen', ***ynys***, pers.n. ***Owen***). Ynysowen is now regarded as a separate part of the village.

MICHAELCHURCH-ON-ARROW, LLANFIHANGEL DYFFRYN ARWY Radn SO2450

'church of Michael on (the river) Arrow', 'church of Mihangel in the valley of (the river) Arwy', pers.n. ***Michael***, ***Mihangel***, OE ***cirice***, E ***on***, W ***llan***, ***dyffryn***, r.n. ***Arwy***

Michaeleschirche c.1257, *Seint Michel* c.1270,
Mihelescruch alias Mihellescherch 1309, *ll. V'el dyffryn arw* c.1566

The river Arwy is *Arewe*, *Arue* 1256, *Hareye* 1272, *arwy* 1447-89, *Arroy* 1592-3 and anglicized as Arrow. It is possible that Arwy is ****arwy*** 'the bright, silvery river'. However, a much older reference to the river as *Erge* 958 in an OE source suggests an ON ***erg*** 'hill pasture, sheiling' or its Middle Ir derivative ***airge*** (as in Arrowe Cheshire, *arwe* 1240, *arwey* 1311, *Arowe* 1397), which was then cymricized as Arwy.

MICHAELSTON-LE-PIT, LLANFIHANGEL-Y-PWLL Glam ST1573

'church of Michael in the hollow', pers.n. ***Michael***, ***Mihangel***, OE ***stōw***, OE ***pytt***, ME ***le***, W ***llan***, ***y***, ***pwll***

Sancti Michaelis de Renny 1254, *Michelstowe* 1291,
Landmihangel 13cent., *Myhelstowe* 1463, *Michelstow* 1488,
ll. fihangel or pwll c.1566, *Michelston* 1559, *Mighelston in le pitt* 1567,
ll. V'el y pwll 1590-1, *Michellston the Pitt* 1596, *Michelston le Pytte* 1603,
Mychelston-ye-pitt 1661, *Llanvihangel y Pwll* 1799

OE ***stōw*** had a range of meanings such as 'place' and 'location of an assembly' but in association with saints' names signified 'holy assembly', 'holy place', 'church'. The later forms show that -stow was replaced by the more common -ton. The late appearance of what purports to be the Fr. def.art. ***le*** confirms that, as in other instances, it was a conventional, formulaic insertion in some English medieval p.ns to signify 'in, at, near'. The hollow (of the synonymous ***pytt*** and ***pwll***) describes the location of the church and the village around a tributary of the Cadoxton River. In the 13-14cent. the area was held by the de Reigny family.

MICHAELSTON-Y-FEDW, LLANFIHANGEL-Y-FEDW

Monm ST2484

'church of Michael near the birch-grove', pers.n. ***Michael, Mihangel,*** OE ***tūn***, W ***llan, y, bedw***

Lanmihangel, (de) Sancto Michaele 1254, *Sci' Michis'* 1291, *Lanuhangel in Wentlok* 1319, *Migheleston* 1392, *Mychelston super Rompney* 1546, *llanvihangell ye Vedowe* 1600-7, *Michaelstone y vedowe* 1652

Distinguished successively by its location in the cantref of Gwynllŵg, by its proximity to the river Rhymni and as an 'area characterised by birch-trees' (***bedw***). Part of the parish was called Llanfedw (*Landivedon* 1281, *Lanvedue* 1296, *Lanvedu* 1307, *Lanvedu in Sengh'* 1401, *Llanbedow* 1476) west of the river in the cantref of Senghennydd Glam, and is probably a contraction of Llanfihangel-y-fedw.

MIDDLE MILL, FELINGANOL

Pemb SM8025

'(the) middle mill', E ***middle***, E ***mill***, W ***y, melin, canol***

Midle Mill 1632, *the Bishopps mill or Middle Mill* 1650, *Velin Ganol* 1811, *y Felinganol* 1839

A mill which belonged to the bishops of St David's midway between Felin Ban and Caerforiog Mill.

MIDDLE MOUSE see YNYS BADRIG

MIDDLETOWN, TREBERFEDD

Mont SJ3012

'middle settlement', OE ***middel***, OE ***tūn***, W ***tref, perfedd***

Trefperuet 1265, *Trefberveth under Breydin* 1290, *Tre Berveth* 1577, *Mydelton'* 1245, *Middelton* 1322, *Middletowne* 1634, *Middleton alias Treberaseth* 1677

Both names are identical in meaning. The later forms with -town are unusual since many neighbouring p.ns (such as Buttington) do not show the same development. Middletown lies close to the mountain Breiddin (*under Breydin* 1290).

MIGNEINT, Y

Caern/Denb/Mer SH7642

'(the) swamp brooks',(*y*), ***mign, nant*** pl. ***naint***

Mycknant 1592, *Mikneint* 1695, *Mikneint, Micknint* c.1700, *Migneint* 1838

Uplands west of Ffestiniog characterised by pools, bog and streams.

MILFORD HAVEN, ABERDAUGLEDDAU Pemb SM9005

'harbour of the fjord by the sand-bank', 'the estuary of the two (rivers called) Cleddau', ON ***melr***, ON ***fjǫrðr***, OE ***hæfen***, W ***aber***, ***dau***, r.n. ***Cleddau***

(de) Milverdico portu c.1191, *Mellferth* 1207, *Milford* 1219, *Milford Haven* 1394, (port of) *Melford* c.1402-3, *Milford Havyn* 1453, *Aberclethif*, *Aber-Deu-gledyf* late 13cent., *Aber Dau Gleddau* 15cent., *Aber milffort* c.1588, *Aberdoygledde that is the mouth…of both Cleddies* 1603

Both p.ns (and the 1197 *portu)* refer to the river estuary, with ***melr*** probably referring to sand-banks along the fjord. When the significance of ***melr*** and ***fjǫrðr*** was lost the subsequent development of the name was probably influenced by the common E p.n. Milford 'mill ford' to which ***haven*** was then added. Milford was the name given to the new town established in 1790 on the north side of the haven, and Haven was formally added when the railway terminus was built c.1868. *Milford Haven* was in use in 1851-56 for the railway terminus at Neyland Pemb. The W name describes the estuary of Daugleddau or Deugleddau, the confluence of the rivers Western Cleddau (or Cleddy) or Cleddau Ddu (*Cleddey ddŷ* 1603, ***du*** 'black, dark'), and Eastern Cleddau (or Cleddy) or Cleddau Wen (*Cledeu* c.1191, *Cledyf* 14cen.t, *(ar) Gleddau Wen* 1460-8, ***gwyn*** fem. ***gwen*** 'white, fair') where ***cleddyf*** 'sword' is used for a deeply-incised river. The masc. ***dau*** refers to ***cleddyf***, whereas Cleddau Wen and Cleddau Ddu have the fem. adj. (***gwen***) and fem. lenition (Wen, Ddu) with reference to the perceived gender of a river.

MILTON Pemb SN0403

'mill farm', OE ***myln***, OE ***tūn***

Milton 1362, *Mylton* 1544

There was a fulling mill next to a small tributary of Milford Haven flowing through Carew Cheriton.

MILWR Flints SJ1974

'(belonging to) Meilwr', pers.n. ***Meilwr***

Meilwr 1796, *Milwr* 1878

One of the extensive lead mines between Milwr, Holywell and Brynford seems to have been owned or worked by an unidentified Meilwr. In time, the pers.n. was taken to be ***milwr*** 'soldier'.

MINERA, MWYNGLAWDD Denb SJ2751

'mine', L ***minera***, W ***mwynglawdd***

Minera 1343, *La Minere* 1351, *Moynglawth* 1549, *Minera* 1581, *Minêra Brit. mwyn glawdd* c.1700

The lead mines were south of Afon Clywedog with further evidence of mining on Minera Mountain/Mynydd Mwynglawdd and Esclusham Mountain. It has been suggested that the Latin name was due to association with the chapel-of-ease here. Some have proposed that it was introduced by Anglo-French miners (as in the 1351 form) and recorded in its Latin form on leases. It is almost certainly a description which would have been found on manorial records and its use by manorial officials (and on later maps) transferred to local mining usage.

MINFFORDD[1] Mer SH7311

'roadside', ***min, ffordd***

Mînffordd 1795, *Minffordd* 1837

This hamlet is at the junction of the road from Tal-y-llyn with the road from Corris before it starts its long climb up the pass of Bwlch Llyn Bach.

MINFFORDD[2] Mer SH5938

'roadside', ***min, ffordd***

Minffordd 1795

A road-side hamlet which has developed between Porthmadog and Penrhyndeudraeth (before the Cob was built), because of the nearby granite quarry and the junction of the Cambrian railway (which built a station here in 1873) and the Ffestiniog railway (to export slate).

MINLLYN Mer SH8514

'lakeside', ***min, llyn***

Minllan 1787, *Minllyn* 1795, *Min-llyn* 1836

Minllyn seems to have been the name of the stream (Nant Minllyn) which rises beside the lake at Foel Dinas and joins Afon Dyfi at Pont Minllyn. The 1787 form, if a genuine ***llan*** and not an error for ***llyn,*** appears to refer to a 'church', 'parish', and the fact that the bridge here, Pont Minllyn, was also known as Pont-y-ffinnant ('bridge of the boundary stream', ***ffin, nant***) may suggest a parish boundary. The quarry here lasted from 1870 until 1916 to be replaced by a woollen mill. The quarry and the mill may have resulted in a workers' hamlet beside the Dinas Mawddwy-Mallwyd road which crosses Afon Dyfi via Pont Minllyn.

MINWEAR, MYNWAR Pemb SN0413

?'edge of the alder-marsh', ?***min, gwern***

Mynwere c.1175-6 (c.1600), *Minuer* 13cent., *Minewer* 1338, *mynwar* c.1566

The meaning is obscure. If it is W, loss of final -n seems to have occurred before any documentation (as in Crunwear/Cronwern q.v.). If it is E, it has been suggested that the second el. is OE ***wer*** 'weir, dam' and that the first el. is a r.n. comparable with the lost r.n. *Mine* Devon (meaning 'smooth') but there seems to be no evidence of a weir or that Minwear Brook was ever *Min(e)*. A further suggestion is of a saint's name.

MISKIN, MEISGYN Glam ST0480

'field of ?Cyn(n)', ***maes***, ?pers.n. ***Cyn(n)***

Meyskin 1242-62, *Meyskyn* 1268, *Meskyn* 1296, *Kymwt Meisgyn* c.1400

A name of uncertain origin. The pers.n. ***Cyn(n)*** is not attested elsewhere and is inferred from *Meis-*, a form of ***maes*** produced by vowel affection. The forms refer to the ancient commote (***cwmwd***) of Meisgyn, also recorded in the moor Gwaun Feisgyn (*Waun Vyskin* 1588, *Waen Miskin* 1799, ***gwaun***) and then transferred to Miskin House (built c.1660), later (19cent.) known as Miskin Manor; in fact, the manor house of the lordship was Llantrisant Castle. The village of Miskin developed around Melin Newydd from the 18cent. The name was also transferred c.1850 to an industrial village near Aberdare Glam in the same commote.

MITCHEL TROY, LLANFIHANGEL TRODDI Monm SO4910

?'big Troddi', 'church of Mihangel by (the river) Troddi', ME ***michel***, W ***llan***, pers.n. ***Mihangel***, r.n. ***Troddi***

Troi 1148-83, *Troie* 1254, *Troy* 1291, *Sancti Michis' super Troye* 1324-5, *Michell Troy* 1545, *Mychell Troie* 1551, *ll. V'el troddi* c.1566, *St. Mitchell Troy* 1757

Named from the r.n. Troddi (q.v.) contracted by E speakers to Troy. Mitchel, although seemingly Michael, may be a late dial. adoption of ME ***michel*** 'big' which distinguished the village and parish from the adjoining manor of *Troy Parva* (1314, *Lytletroye bridge* 1549, L ***parva***); cf. Mitcheldean Gloucester. The absence of any comparative qualifer such as Lat ***magna*** in early sources is not necessarily significant (cf. Monmouth and Monmouth Parva or Little Monmouth, *Monemuth Parva* 1362). The alternative explanation is that Mitchel stands for the pers.n. Mitchel(l) (in common use in the medieval period) derived from the pers.n. Michael and that this refers to the church dedication to Michael and then to the Mihangel of the W name.

MOCHDRE[1] Denb SH8278

'pig farm', ***moch***, ***tref***

Moghedreue 1334, *Mochtre* 1549, *Mochdref* 1795

The name of several villages or hamlets in Wales, referring to farms which kept pigs. However, the perception that this was a disparaging name encouraged camouflaging the name to *Bochdre* 1685, *Boughetre* 1695 and *Boughtre* 1701 (cf. Mathafarn/Bathafarn Denb, and see Machynlleth), but these gentrified forms did not survive. Several Mochdre locations have been associated with the taking of Pryderi's pigs in the Fourth Branch of the Mabinogi.

MOCHDRE[2] Mont SO0788

'pig farm', ***moch***, ***tref***

Mochdref 1200, *Mochtref* 13cent., *Moghtre* 1497,
Mochdre yngheiri c.1562, *Moughtrey* 1618, *Moughtre* 1836, *Moghtrellan*, *Mochdre Vechan* 1542, *Moughtreyllan* 1685

See Mochdre[1]. Mochdre possessed two townships, a larger one, Mochdre-llan, containing the parish church (***llan***) and a lesser one, Mochdre-fechan (***bechan***). The parish lay in the commote of Ceri (*yng Ngheri*).

MOEL EILIO Caern SH5557

'bare hill of Eilio', ***moel***, pers.n. ***Eilio***

moyleilio 1538-9, *Moel Eilio* 1810

The extensive highland between valleys at Llanberis and Betws Garmon. The identity of Eilio is unknown. Local usage, over many years, has been Moel Eilian (as if pers.n. Eilian).

MOEL FAMA(U) Denb/Flints SJ1662

'bare hill of Mama', ***moel***, pers.n. ***Mama***

Moelvamma 1391, *Moyle vamma* 1597, *Moel Vamma* c.1700,
Moel-fama 1737, *Moel Fammau* 1795, *Moel famma* 1810,
Moel Famau 1983

This is the most prominent of a series of ***moel*** hills in the Clwydian range. The regional pronunciation continues to be Fama which is the preferred spelling. The modern var. Famau has been prompted by the antiquarian perception that it was the pl. ***mamau*** 'mothers' (sing. ***mam***), in this case mother-goddesses, but there is no documentary evidence of a pl. Another suggestion is Br ****mamma*** 'breast' for a 'breast-shaped hill' which, although topographically appropriate, is phonologically unacceptable since the W development of Br ****mamma*** would be ****mam*** (cf. Mam Tor, Derbyshire) and any pl. of that word is again unsupported by the historical forms and topography. An unidentified pers.n. Mama is the least problematic explanation.

MOELFRE Angl SH5186

'bare hill', ***moel***, ***bre***

Moylvry 1399, *Moylvre* 1528-9, *Moylfra* 1774, *Moelfre* 1838

Many hills in Wales are described as ***moel*** and there are at least seven places called Moelfre.

MOEL HEBOG Caern SH5646

'bare hill of flight', ***moel***, ***ehed***, adj. suff. ***-og***

Morlehedauc 1269, *Moel Ehedog* 1737, *Moel Happock* 1781,
Moel Hedog 1810, *Moel Hebog* 1816

A peak west of Aberglaslyn. The meaning of the rare ***ehedog*** is 'flying, able to fly' and is recorded from 18cent. only, whereas ***ehed*** is used of 'flight' from 13cent. Common to these words is a description of a peak frequently characterised by soaring birds. The unstressed initial syllable of *Ehedog* was lost and the subsequent *Hedog* later influenced by ***hebog*** 'hawk'.

MOEL HIRADDUG

Flints SJ0678

'bare hill at Hiraddug', ***moel***, p.n. ***Hiraddug***
Moilye Riathig 1551-2, *Moel Huriathicke* 1589, *Moelriaddig* 1602, *Y Voel sev voel yriadhig, moel Iriadhig* c.1700, *Moel Hiraddug* 1810
A steep, long, limestone hill overlooking Dyserth (q.v.), on which stands a hill-fort. A battle of 1034 was fought at the place called Hiraddug (?*Raduch* 1086, *Yradoc* 1093, *Hiraduc* 1340, *Hyraduk* 1378, *Hirathik* 1440, *Huraduk* 1442-3) which is ***hir*** 'long' and ***addug*** of uncertain meaning, but probably 'feat, attack' here in the sense of 'stronghold'. The hill's ridge was fairly long, almost three-quarters-of-a-mile before quarrying, with the southern end called Y Foel (as in the c.1700 form).

MOELRHONIAID, YNYS(OEDD) Y see SKERRIES

MOEL SIABOD

Caern SH7054

'?scabbed bare hill', ***moel***, ?E ***shabbed***
Mollesshabbowe 1552, *Moel Siabot* c.1700, *Moel Siabod* 1719, *Moel Shiabod* 1795
A ridge and summit (*Carnedd Moel-siabod* 1891) between Capel Curig and Dolwyddelan. Interpretation is uncertain. The E ***shabbed*** 'scabbed' may refer to predominantly scabby rocks, perhaps lichen-encrusted; cf. Foel Grach (***crach*** 'scabby'). The final syllable has been influenced by ***bod***. However, ***shabbed*** as an E dial. var. of ***scabbed*** and its presence here defies explanation, unless it be in the form of an unrecorded pers. n.; cf. Cnicht six miles south-west. However, the significance of the crucial 1552 form and its relationship with later forms are also unclear, since the c.1700 form seems to render -ow as if a F -ot, leading to the suggestion that it was the E derivative ***jabot*** 'frill'.

MOEL SYCH

Denb/Mer/Mont SJ066318

'dry bare hill', ***moel, sych***
Moel-sych 1838, *Moel Sych* 1890-1
It is a steep hill from which rainwater clears rapidly.

MOELWYN, Y

Caern SH6544

'the white bare hill', ***y, moel, gwyn***
y moelwyn bychan a mawr c.1700, *Moelwyn* 1722, *Moel Wyn, Moel Wyn Bach* 1818, *Moelwyn Mawr* 1832, *Moelwyn-bach* 1838
The collective name of two adjoining mountains, Moelwyn Mawr and Moelwyn Bach, between Cwm Croesor and Blaenau Ffestiniog. ***moel*** is

customarily fem. which would result in *moelwen* but here the form has been influenced by the adj. ***moelwyn*** 'bare and white'. Moelwyn is also a pers.n. from at least the 13cent.

MOEL-Y-CRIO Flints SJ1969

'bare hill of the holes', ***moel, y, crau*** pl. ***creuau***

Moel y Kreie c.1700, *Moel y Crio* 1778, *Moel y Creiau* 1795

creuau 'apertures/holes' refers to natural clefts and industrial shafts in limestone crags. The perceived resemblance of ***creuau*** to ***crio*** 'to weep' (through colloquial forms of ***creuau*** such as ***crïa***) has led to the modern form and to consequent local legends. Cf. Rhyd-y-creuau near Betws-y-coed.

MOEL Y GAER Denb SJ1461

'bare hill of the fort', ***moel, y, caer***

Moil y gair 1550, *Moel Gaer* 1737, *Moel y Gaer* 1810, *Moel-y-gaer* 1838

One of the range of ***moel*** hills east of the Vale of Clwyd, featuring a hill-fort, on a spur of Moel Fama (q.v.).

MOLD, YR WYDDGRUG Flints SJ236

'high hill', 'the prominent mound', NF ***mont***, NF ***hault***,
W ***yr, gŵydd, crug***

(*de*) *Montealto* 1151-81, *Moaldis* 1220, *Muhaud, Muhaut* 1241, *Mohault* 1277, *Montem Altum* 1278, *Moald* 1284, *Mohaut* 1297, *Molde* 1341, *Mohaut otherwise Molde* 1595, *yr Wyddgrug* 15cent., *yr wydd gryc* c.1566, *yr Wyrgric* 1565-87, *Wythgric* 1612

The 'mound, hill' (***crug***) is the Bailey Hill, near the centre of Mold, on which the Normans built a castle (*kastell yr wydgruc* 14cent.), a dominant feature of the town's landscape. In the past, ***gŵydd*** has generally been explained as 'tomb, cairn' similar in meaning to ***crug*** (also applied to a 'cairn' or 'tumulus'). However, it is far more likely that ***gŵydd*** here signifies 'prominent' (an interpretation also relevant to Gwyddgrug, Carm and Mont) and bringing it closer in meaning to the name Mold as clearly illustrated in the early L references (L ***mons, montis*** 'hill, mound', ***altus*** 'high'). Two strands can be detected in the later phonological development of Mold. One is shown in the more formal F usage of *Mont-haut* and *Mohault, Mohaut* which eventually became obsolete. The other is the local colloquial var. *Muhaud* and *Moald* which survived as Mold. There is a possibility that the original name was transferred from France, where there are several places called Monthaut (as happened with Montgomery q.v.). A recent suggestion is that *Montalt, Monhault* was transferred as the name of the Fitz Norman family from Moffat, Scotland with close links to land in Chester, Hawarden and Mold. In either case, there is a fortuitous parallel between the meaning of the NF and the W names.

MONINGTON, EGLWYS WYTHWR Pemb SN1343

'(place called after) Monington', 'church of Gwythwr', p.n. ***Monington, eglwys***, pers.n. ***Gwythwr***

Monington 1272-1307, *Manyngton* 1326, *Manetu'* 13cent. (16cent.), *Eglois Goithir* 1222, *Egloiswither* 1578

A p.n. transferred from Monington-on-Wye Herefordshire which was also held by the D'Audley family in the 14cent. Monington is 'farm of Man(n)a's people' (pers.n., OE ***-ing-***, ***tūn***). No saint Gwythwr is recorded but the pers.n. is attested in early sources and survives as a surname Gwyther found mainly in south-west Wales. Popularly interpreted as 'church of the eight men' (with ***wyth*** and ***gŵr***).

MONKNASH, YR AS FAWR Glam SS9270

'(place) at the ash-tree of the monks', 'the great ash', OE ***atten***, OE ***æsc***, E ***monk***, W ***yr***, ***mawr***

Aissa c.1140, *Essam* 1173-83, *Asse* 1291, *Nashe magna* 1578, *Monken Ashe alias Magna Aish* 1607, *Race vawor* 1670, *Monkston or Rase Vawr* 1782

In E the location by the distinctive tree was described as *atten ash* 'at the ash' > Nash, and in W as the cymricized *yr ash* 'the ash' > Yr As. The qualifying ***monk*** (referring to a grange held by Neath abbey), ***magna*** and ***mawr*** were added to distinguish it from Nash/Yr As Fach or Nash Parva or Little Nash or Osmund's Ash in Llysworney parish three miles north-east (*Ess* 1173-83, *Aissa* 1208, *Fraxino* 13cent., *le Nasshe* 1431, *Parva Fraxino alias Lytell Nash* 1499 [L ***fraxinus*** 'ash-tree'], *Osmond is asshe* 1528 [an unidentified *Osmund*], *yras fach* c.1566, *Nash alias Osmond Ashe* 1686, *Race or Little Nash* 1764-5).

MONKSTONE POINT Pemb SS1403

'monk's rock (point)', E ***monk***, E ***stone***, E ***point***

Munkeston rock 1578, *Monks Stone* 1748, *Monkstone* 1839, *Monkstone Point* 1891

Monkstone is a an area of rocks projecting eastwards into Saundersfoot Bay. There seems to be no recorded link with any monks or monasteries but there were two medieval hospitals in nearby Tenby.

MONKSWOOD, CAPEL COED-Y-MYNACH Monm SO3402

'wood belonging to monks', 'chapel at monks' wood', E ***monk***, E ***wood***, W ***capel***, ***coed***, ***y***, ***mynach*** pl. ***meneich***

Koed y Menaich 1550-1600, *Monkeswood* 1588-9, *Monckes woodde* 1602

The land was owned by Tintern abbey. The 16cent. W version treats the first el. as if a pl. possessive (in a var. pl. ***meneich***) but the modern form as if singular (***mynach***). In earlier (and some later sources) called Pellenni (*Pethllenny* 1148-70 [1330], *Pochlenny* 1223, *Pethelenny* 1246 [1307], *Pelhenny* 1307, *Pellenny* 1692) with reference to a wood and a farm (see Penperllenni). The meaning is uncertain, but is probably ***perllan*** 'orchard' pl. ***perllenni*** although the topography and forms tend to favour ***pellen*** pl. ***pellenni*** 'round mass' (of a hill) possibly influenced occasionally by ***perth*** 'hedge'.

MONMOUTH, TREFYNWY Monm SO5012
'mouth of (the river) Mynwy', 'town by (river) Mynwy',
r.n. ***Monnow/Mynwy***, OE ***mūtha***, W ***tref***
Monemue c.1075-83, *Monemude* 1086, *Munuwi muđa* 11cent., *Monemuta* 1186, *Munemuth* 1243, (*castellum de*) *mingui* 1160-85, *tre fynwe* c.1566, *Tref vynwy* 1609
From its location where the river Mynwy (anglicized as Monnow) (*mingui, myngui* 1136-54, *mynvy* c.1100, *Monuwe* 1432-4, *Monwy* 1722) meets the river Wye. Monmouth may be a translation of an older name of the town *Abermynwy* (*aper myngui, aper Mynuy* 1136-54, *Aber Mynwy* c.1400, ***aber***) where the church was already in existence in 1086. The r.n. may mean 'fast-flowing' like Menai (q.v.). The Roman town and fort here *Blestium* (*Blestio* 3cent.) is probably a pers.n. *Blestus*.

MONNOW see **MONMOUTH**

MONTGOMERY, TREFALDWYN Mont SO2296
'(place named after) Montgomery', 'town of Baldwin',
p.n. ***Montgomery***, ***tref***, pers.n. ***Baldwyn***
Muntgumeri, Montgomeri 1086, *Monte Gomeri* 1166, *Montis Gomeri* 1304-5, *Trefaldwyn* 1440, *Montgomerike, in Walche Treualdwine* 1536-9
Montgomery was first applied to the motte-and-bailey castle Hen Domen ('old mound', ***hen***, ***tomen***) near the river Severn, named after Sainte-Foy-de-Montgommery or Saint-Germain-de-Montgommery (Calvados) in Normandy. The p.n. was transferred to the new castle constructed 1223-4. The first W name was evidently Castell Baldwyn 'Baldwin's castle' (***castell***) referring directly to the castle. Trefaldwyn is a late medieval adoption used of the settlement that emerged near the castle. Both p.ns refer either to *Baldwin de Bollers* (early 13cent.) or more likely *Baldwin* son of William of Hodnet who first occurs 'in the service of the lord king at the new castle ... outside Mungumeri' 1223. *gaer ... valdwyn* c.1400 (***caer***) applies either to the castle or the hillfort Ffridd Faldwyn (*Cairaovalduine* 1536-9, ***ffridd***).

MORFA BYCHAN Caern SH5437
'little sea marsh', ***morfa***, ***bychan***
morua bychan 1303-4, *Morfa Bychan* 1801, *Morfa Bychan* 1838

The sea-marsh may have been compared to the much more extensive Morfa Harlech or to the lengthy inland tracts of the estuary of Afon Glaslyn (then known as Traeth Mawr 'the great strand' before the Cob was built at Porthmadog, and later as Dyffryn Madog). In recent years, tourism development has reclaimed much of the marshland, and the beach south-east of the prominent outcrop of Craig Ddu (***craig*** 'rock', ***du*** 'black' locally Y Greigddu) is popularly known as Black Rock Sands.

MORFA NEFYN Caern SH284

'sea marsh of Nefyn', ***morfa***, p.n. ***Nefyn***

Morva 1230-4 (late 15cent.), *Morfa Nevin* 1838

The village of Morfa Nefyn is just over a mile west of Nefyn.

MORFIL, MORVIL Pemb SN0330

'(place named after) Morville', p.n. ***Morville***

Morvin 1291, *Moruile* 1397, *Morvill* 1488, *y morfil* c.1566

Possibly a transferred p.n. taken from one of several Morville places in France and Normandy. The c.1566 form interprets it as W ***y morfil*** 'the whale'.

MORGANNWG see **GLAMORGAN**

MORGANSTOWN, PENTRE-POETH Glam ST1281

'settlement of Morgan', 'settlement cleared by burning', pers.n. ***Morgan***, E ***town***, W ***pentref***, ***poeth***

Pentre 1845, *Pentre-poeth* 1850, *Treforgan* 1857, *Morgan's Town* 1865, *Morganstown (otherwise Pentrepoeth)* 1878

A village which developed in the early 19cent. near ironworks in neighbouring Pen-tyrch with a tram road linking them with tinplate works about a mile further down the river Taf at Melin Griffith, in Whitchurch. The identity of the Morgan in question is uncertain. There have been several suggestions including Morgan Williams (d. 1852) of Tynberllan farm (on which most of the village and Bethel Calvinistic Methodist chapel, constructed in 1842 were built), or Evan Morgan (d. 1886?), one of Williams's main tenants here in 1841, described in 1861 as a blacksmith and in 1865 as a grocer. The village is earlier recorded as *Pentre* 'village', and *Pentre-poeth* (***poeth*** 'hot') probably in the sense of one built on land cleared by burning or in an area notable for industrial activity such as the ironworks and local lime-burning. *Pentre-poeth* was the dominant form among W-speakers down to the late 19th cent. and still retains considerable currency. The form Treforgan is also very common.

MÔR HAFREN see **BRISTOL CHANNEL**

MORRISTON, TREFORYS Glam SS6698

'town of Morris', pers.n. ***Morris***, E ***-ton***, W ***tref***

Morriston 1780, 1840, *Morristown* 1792, *Treforris* 1870

Named from Robert Morris (1700-68) or more likely his son Sir John Morris (1745-1819) of Clasemont who started an industrial company including copperworks in 1768 with housing for employees, initially at Morris Castle on Graig Trewyddfa.

MORVIL see **MORFIL**

MOSS Denb SJ3053

'bog', E ***moss***

The Moss 1837, *Moss* 1879

The name was given by industrial workers from north-west England where it is common as a term for a bog. Local usage still refers to it as The Moss. The whole area from Bersham and New Broughton up to Brymbo, Moss and Bryn-mali had extensive coal and iron works. There is ample evidence of atrocious conditions underfoot for the transport of coal, and Brymbo (***bryn, baw*** 'mud or dirt hill') itself shows a long-standing characteristic. There is no record of a W name for the village, suggesting the designation reflects wholesale import of workers from England similar to Pentre Saeson (***Saeson*** 'Englishmen') between Brymbo and Bwlch-gwyn.

MOSTYN Flints SJ1580

'bog farm', OE ***mos***, OE ***tūn***

Mostone 1086, *Muston* 1272, *Moston* 1285, 1610, *Mostun* 1316, *Mostyn* 1567

Low-lying land on the Dee estuary. The later cymricization of -ton to -tyn is a characteristic of north-east Wales.

MOT, Y see **NEW MOAT**

MOUNTAIN ASH, ABERPENNAR Glam ST0499

'(place named after the) Mountain Ash', 'mouth of (the stream) Pennar', E ***mountain ash***, W ***aber***, r.n. ***Pennar***

Aber Pennarthe 1570 *Aberpennarth* 17cent., *Aberpennar alias Dyffryn* 1691, *Mountain Ash* 1814

Mountain Ash is named from a public house in Commercial Street recorded 1814. The name was reputed (in 1875) to have been given to the inn by the wife of John Bruce Pryce of Dyffryn 1809, a prominent local landowner, from the presence of rowan or mountain ash trees; conclusive proof, however, seems to be lacking. The name was later transferred to the industrial town which developed in the mid 19cent. and was used by both E and W speakers and historians down to the early 20cent. Aberpennar seems to appear as the W name of the town in 1905 (when the National Eisteddfod visited the town) and originally applied specifically to the area where the rivers Pennar and Cynon meet, later the site of the mansion called Dyffryn, just above the town, and was applied, possibly consciously, as a W name for the town. The river name Pennar, earlier *Pennardd*, (***pennardd***, 'top of the ridge') has its source on Cefn Pennar (seen in two farms *Keven Penare yssa, ~ ycha* 1582, *Keven Penarth* 1638, ***cefn***, ***uchaf***, ***isaf***).

MOYLGROVE, TREWYDDEL Pemb SN1144

'Matilda's grove', 'grove farm', pers.n. ***Matilda***, OE ***grǣfe***, W ***tref***, ***gwyddwal***

Trefgoithel 1222, (*de*) *gr'n Matild'* 1291, *Molde Grove* 1325, (*de*) *Grava Matildis* 1513-17, *Trewethell* 1543, *tre wyddel* c.1566, *Moylgrove* 1598

Possibly named from Matilda, wife of Robert Fitzmartin, lord of Cemais, c.1115-1159. The pers.n. has a variety of forms including Mathild and Mauld. The W name ***gwyddwal*** in its var. ***gwyddel*** refers to the same thicket or grove, but has been popularly interpreted as ***Gwyddel*** 'Irishman'.

MUMBLES, MWMBWLS, Y Glam SS6188

?'mumbling rocks', ME ***momele***, W ***y***

Mummess 1536-9, *Mommulls* 1549, *Mombles* 1580, *Mommells* 1583, *y Mwmlws* 1609, *Mumbles* 1650

An obscure name. The Mumbles consist of two small islands and adjoining rocks off Mumbles Head (*Mumbles poynt* 1578, *Mumbles Cliff, ~ Hill* 1764). If it is indeed ME ***momele*** 'to mumble', it describes the perpetual mumbling of the sea near the rocks. Other suggestions are L ***mamillae*** 'breasts' and ON ***múli*** 'snout, promontory'. Y Mwmbwls (with the def.art.) is a W adaptation.

MUMBLES HEAD see **MUMBLES**

MWMBWLS, Y see **MUMBLES**

MWYNGLAWDD see **MINERA**

MYDDFAI Carm SN7730

?'bowl-shaped land', ?W ***mydd***, ?***mai***

Meduey 1284, *Medevey alias Methevey* 1316, *Methvey* 1535, *ll. V'el y myddfai* c.1566, *Mothvey* 1685

The meaning is obscure. Since -e- and -y- do occasionally alternate in medieval documents (cf. Llandybïe, Llandyfaelog and Llandyfalle) the early forms can be accommodated to a derivation from ***mydd*** 'tub, dish'. A pers.n. ***Mai*** has also been proposed for the second el. The c.1566 form stands for Llanfihangel 'church of Mihangel'.

MYDROILYN Card SN4555

'(the confluence of the river) Mydr and (the brook) Eilin', r.n. ***Mydr***, r.n. ***Eilin***

Mydreilin 1565, *Mydur Oilin* 1760, *Medroylin* 1764-5, *Mydroylin* 1779, *Mydroylyn* 1803

A name which currently challenges a satisfactory explanation. The village is at the confluence of Afon Mydr (a part of the hamlet is Bro Mydyr) and Nant Eilin. Mydr may be ***mudwr*** 'wanderer' in reference to the course of the river; Eilin is possibly ***eilun*** (***berllys***) 'hedge parsley' which has a dial. var. ***oilin***.

MYNACHLOG-DDU Pemb SN1430

'dark, bleak monastic grange', ***mynachlog, du***

Capella de Nigra Grangia 1291, *Manoghloke Duy* 1535, *Y fynachlog ddy* c.1566, *Capell St. Sylin; Nigra grangia alias…capella Scti Egidii, Monachloggduy* c.1600

Not ***mynachlog*** in its usual sense of 'monastery' but a grange (L ***grangia***) of St Dogmael's abbey set in bleak surroundings on the foothills of Mynydd Preseli. The chapel was dedicated to Silin (cf. Llansilin Denb), sometimes confused with Giles (L ***Egidius***).

MYNWAR see **MINWEAR**

MYNWY see **MONMOUTH**

MYNYDD-BACH Monm ST4894

'little mountain', ***mynydd, bach***

Myniddbache, mynidd bach 1630, *Mynydd-bach* 1830

From a low hill on the south side of the village.

MYNYDD BODAFON Angl SH4684

'mountain in Bodafon', ***mynydd***, p.n. ***Bodafon***

mynyth bodavon, montem de Bodavon 1549, *mynydd Bodavon* 1713

The tnshp of Bodafon (*Bodaon* 1352, *Bodavon* 1505) is ***bod*** 'abode' and pers.n. ***A(e)ddon*** believed to be a medieval chieftain. The lake or tarn nestling in the hilltop has been variously called Llyn Bodafon, Llyn Mynydd Bodafon, *Llyn Archaeddon* (18cent., ?***arch*** 'daughter' a var. of ***merch***) and *Gors Fawr* (1887, ***cors*** 'bog', ***mawr***). All the documentary sources reveal the influence of ***afon*** 'river' with regular interchange of -dd- and -f-.

MYNYDD BWLCH-Y-GROES Brec SN8533

'mountain at the cross-road pass', ***mynydd, bwlch, y, croes***

Mynydd Bwlch y Groes 1819, *Mynydd Bwlch-y-Groes* 1832

The mountain is a broad ridge on the crest of which is an ancient ridgeway leading north from Llywel towards Mynydd Epynt (q.v.)

crossing over a gated road at Clwyd Bwlch-y-groes (*Mountain Gate* 1734, ***clwyd*** 'gate') between Llandeilo'r-fân and Llandovery. Bwlch-y-groes is a fairly common name for such a location.

MYNYDDCYNFFIG see KENFIG HILL

MYNYDD DU see BLACK MOUNTAINS

MYNYDD EPYNT Brec SN9140

'mountain crossed by a horse-path', ***mynydd, eb-, hynt***
ipynt 12cent., *Epyn* 1241, *Epynt* late 12cent (c.1400), *Epint* 13cent., *Eppint* c.1700, *Mynydd Epynt* 1832
There are several ancient roads, later used by drovers, crossing these mountains, notably that extending north-eastwards from Llandeilo'r-fân past Tafarn-y-mynydd, Ffynnon David Bevan, Drover's Arms, and Pen-y-gefn-ffordd to Llangynog. This route may have also have been called Y Gefnffordd (*Y Genffordd ar Eppint* 1623, *Y Gevenffordd* 1632, 'the ridgeway', ***y, cefnffordd***). The mountain range has long been called Epynt with ***mynydd*** being a late addition.

MYNYDD HIRAETHOG Denb SH9155

'long gorse-land mountain', ***mynydd, hir, aith***, adj. suff. ***-awg/-og***
Hiraythok 1200, *Hir'hadock* 1291, *Hirraythok, hiraethauc* 13cent., *hiraethawc* 1400, *Hiraethawc* 1500, *Hiraethog* 1501-2, *Mynydh Hiraethog* c.1700
The extensive highlands north of Cerrigydrudion and Pentrefoelas were called Hiraethog, moorland characterised by ***aith*** 'gorse, furze' (a pl., the sing. being ***eithin***). The addition of ***mynydd*** is late. The territory was once the property of Aberconwy (later Maenan) Abbey, as recorded in some alternative names such as *terr yr abbod* 1540, *Tir r Abbott o. Hiraethog* 1664, *Hiraethog als Tyr yr Abbott* 1684, *Hiraethog o. Tir Abbot* 1841, 'the abbot's land' (***tir, yr, abad***). The forms (and popular perception) have long been influenced by ***hiraeth*** 'longing'. Familiarly referred to as the Denbigh Moors.

MYNYDDISA Flints SJ2564

'lower mountain', ***mynydd, isaf***
mynydh isaf c.1700, *Mynydd-isa* 1914
The lower of two hills between Buckley and Mold. The higher hill is Buckley Mountain (*Mynydh Bwkley, Buckley mountain* c.1700).

MYNYDD LLWYDIARTH Angl SH5479

'hill at Llwydiarth', ***mynydd***, p.n. ***Llwydiarth***
mvnyth llwdiart 1636, *munydd Llwydiart* 1667, *Mynydd Llwydiarth* 1817
Llwydiarth ('grey hill', ***llwyd, garth***) was the name of the medieval tnshp, which took its name from the extensive highland between

Pentraeth, Llanddona and Red Wharf Bay. -iarth is probably the result of residual lenition of ***garth***, but its persistence here (and, for example, in Peniarth, Mer) has led some to argue that ***garth*** and ****iarth*** may be separate elements.

MYNYDD MALLAEN Carms SN7244

'mountain in Mallaen', ***mynydd***, p.n. ***Mallaen***

Mynidd Mallaen 1554, *Mallaen mountain* 1649

Located in the former commote of Mallaen (*Machayn* 1257, *Methlaen* 1282, *Mathlaen* c.1287, *Mallaen* c.1400) which is 'plain of Llaen' (***ma-***, pers.n. ***Llaen***; cf. Porth Dinllaen). Mallaen, formerly trisyllabic with medial stress, is now disyllabic with final stress.

MYNYDD MARCHYWEL Glam SN7602

?'mountain of Marchywel', ***mynydd***, pers.n. ***Marchywel***

March Howel 1584-5, *Marchhowell* 1601, *March Howell* 1666, *Mynydd March Howel* 1832

The first two forms refer to the (unidentified) Marchywel associated with the mountain. The origin of the pers.n. is ***march*** 'powerful, strong' and pers.n. Hywel, and some of the forms show the name as separate els, or perhaps assume it was ***march*** 'horse'. Historical forms have *Howel(l)*, the var. of Hywel. Mynydd is a late addition.

MYNYDD MAWR Caern SH5354

'big mountain', ***mynydd, mawr***

Mynydd Mawr 1810

An extensive upland area between Llyn Cwellyn and Llyn Nantlle. Colloquially, Mynydd yr Eliffant (***eliffant*** 'elephant') from its distinctive profile from north and west.

MYNYDD PARYS, PARYS MOUNTAIN Angl SH4390

'Parys mountain', ***mynydd***, pers.n. ***Parys***

Parry's mountain, Paris Mountain 1818, *Parys Mountain* 20cent.

The hill south of Amlwch which was the site of extensive copper mining from pre-historic and Roman times and particularly during the 18cent. (when the Parys mines were the world's largest). The name Parys is associated with the 15cent. Parys family, burgesses and constables of Caernarfon Castle, probably *Robert (de) Parys* known to be linked with Anglesey in 1406. An older name was Mynydd Trysglwyn (*Trysclwyn* 1352, *Mynydd y Trysclwyn* c.1798, ***trwsg*** 'coarse, dense', ***llwyn*** 'grove, bush') with Trysglwyn-fawr, Trysglwyn-isaf still the names of two farms south of the hill. Cf. several hills called Y Drysgol and Drosgol.

MYNYDD PEN-Y-FÂL see **SUGAR LOAF**

MYNYDD PRESELI Pemb SN0832

'mountain of Preseli', ***mynydd***, p.n. ***Preseli***

montium de Presseleu, Presseli c.1191, (*y*) *bresselev* 14cent., *Pressely* 1303, *Briscely Mt.* 1777, *Perselli -Top* 1795

Originally, Preseli was presumably a specific location. The name is ***prys*** var. ***pres*** 'thicket', pers.n. ***Selyf, Selef*** (derived from the biblical L ***Salomon***) becoming Presely (a common var. with loss of final -f) and Preseli, the dominant local form. The pers.n. var. ***Seleu***, and the modern derivative Preselau, were probably archaic and perceived to represent the pl. -au, because of the association with the range of hills. Commonly referred to as Y Preseli or Y Preselau (*y* 'the').

MYNYDD RHIWSAESON Mont SH9006

'mountain of Rhiwsaeson', ***mynydd***, p.n. ***Rhiwsaeson***

Rhiwsaeson 1795, *Rhiw-saeson* 1890-1

Rhiwsaeson refers directly to the mountain (a later pref.) rather than the actual tnshp of Rhiwsaeson (in Llanbryn-mair parish) which was *Rywsaisson* 1586, *Rhusayson* 1598, *Rhusaisson* 1623-4, (*o*) *Riw Saeson* 1627, 'Englishmen's slope' (***rhiw***, ***Saeson***). ***Saeson*** and the sing. ***Sais*** occur several times not only to denote someone who was from England but someone who spoke English well, or who was perceived to be anglicized in some way.

MYNYDD TWR see **HOLYHEAD MOUNTAIN**

MYNYDD Y FFLINT see **FLINT MOUNTAIN**

MYNYTHO Caern SH2931

'(place by the) mountain' ***mynydd***, suff. ***-o***

Mynytho 1581

The village is at the foot of Foel Gron and Mynytho Common (*Mynyth Myniffo* 1549, *Mynydd Mynythaw* 1615) surrounded by several hills. The suff ***-o*** (earlier ***-aw***) designates the feature of an area, but the change from -ddo to -tho has not been satisfactorily explained unless the suff. was, for some reason here, ***-ho***. Another suggestion is that there was a second el. ***hawdd*** 'pleasant' so that *Mynyth-hawdd* became *Mynythaw* with loss of final -dd and then Mynytho.

N

NANHORON Caern SH2831

'valley of (the river) Oron', ***nant***, r.n. ***Oron***

Nanhoron 1352, *Nanhoronne* 1598, *Nan'horon* 1838

The development of (the undocumented) *Nant Oron* into Nanhoron (with -nt- > -nh-) gave rise to the perception that the valley and river name was Horon (as in the modern Afon Horon). The name Oron is probably ***ôr*** 'boundary' and the noun suff. ***-on***, indicating its role as the boundary between the commotes of Cymydmaen and Cafflogion. A similarly named mountain, Yr Oron, separates Mer and Mont.

NANHYFER see **NEVERN**

NANMOR Caern SH6046

'great valley', ***nant, mawr***

Nantmawr 1284, *Nanmor, Nanmore* 1508, *Nant-y-môr* 1838, *Nantmor* 1891

That this is the masc. ***nant*** 'valley' (rather than the fem. ***nant*** 'stream') is indicated by the masc. ***mawr***. The brook in the valley rises in Llyn yr Adar north of Cnicht and over steep cliffs into Llyn Llagi then flowing past Blaen Nanmor, before entering Afon Glaslyn north of the upper reaches of the Glaslyn estuary at Deudraeth (*Nanmaur deudrayth* 1292-3). The brook itself is quite wide and prominent nearest the hamlet of Nanmor (although still a mile away). The form Nanmor (and the colloquial Namor) with loss of -t has long been the recognised usage, despite attempts to restore the -t in some sources and current maps. The 1838 form is a fanciful interpretation of -mor as ***môr*** 'sea', a reference to its link with the Glaslyn estuary.

NANNERCH Flints SJ1669

'dappled stream', ***nant, erch***

Nannerch 1254, *Nanherch* 1284, *Nannergh* 1423-4

Nannerch was originally the name of the stream which flows down a valley (*Kwm Nannerch* c.1700) from Blaen-y-cwm past the mill (*Velin y Kwm* c.1700) to Afon Chwiler. As the ***nant*** el. lost its recognisable significance the stream was also referred to as *Avon Kwm Nannerch*; it is now Nant-y-cwm. The el. ***erch*** appears in several r.ns (such as Abererch).

NANTCLWYD Denb SJ1151

'valley of (the river) Clwyd', ***nant***, r.n. ***Clwyd***

Nancloid 1481-2, *Tre Nancloide* 1576, *Nantecloyd* 1627, *Nanclwyd* 17cent.

A considerable estate stretches from Nantclwyd Hall (built in c.1430) past Nantclwyd Uchaf (*Nancloid ucha* 1587) to Nantclwyd-isaf (*Nancloid issa* 1587), along part of Dyffryn Clwyd itself. The historical form is *Nanclwyd* but probably due to the influence of the estate name, Nantclwyd seems to be in general use today.

NANT CONWY Caern/Denb SH8062-7878

'valley of (the river) Conwy', ***nant***, r.n. ***Conwy***

Nanconewey 1301-2, *Nanconwy* 1303-4, *Nanntconewey* 1317, *Nanconwy* 1330, *Nanconwey* 1535, *Nant Conwey* 1536-9

The name of the valley through which the river Conwy flows from Betws-y-coed to the town of Conwy (q.v.) and Aberconwy. Forms with -t- are scarce reflecting the regular assimilation of -nt- > -n-, but Nant Conwy is the modern usage. As the name of the valley, Nant Conwy has largely been supplanted by Dyffryn Conwy (*Dyffryn Conwy* 16cent., ***dyffryn*** 'valley'), but was retained as the name of an administrative district.

NANT-DDU Brec SO0014

'black stream', ***nant, du***

Cappel Nantee 1548, *Capel Nantye* 1578, *Nantdu* c.1670, *y Nant dy* 1702

From a stream which rises on the south side of the mountain ridge Craig Fan-ddu. There was a chapel-of-ease (***capel***) here, demolished in 1998. Some forms appear to show confusion with ***nant*** and ***tŷ***.

NANTERNIS Card SN3756

'valley of Ernis', ***nant***, pers.n. ***Ernis***

Nant Ernis 1806, *Nant-ernis* 1834

The river is Afon Soden, spanned by Pont Nanternis, so that ***nant*** here refers to the narrow valley in which Nanternis Farm is situated.

NANT FFRANCON Caern SH6363

'valley of spears', ***nant***, ****ffranc*** pl. ****ffrancon***

Nant frankon 1415, *Nantfrancon* 1488, *Nanfrancon* 1488, *Nantffrangkon* 1505, *Nant Franco Valley* 1536-9, *Nant Ffrancon* 1810, *Nant Francon* 1841

This was considered to be ***ffranc*** 'mercenary, foreigner, Frenchman' pl. ***ffrancon***, on the basis of its occurrence in W poetry, but now believed to be OE ***franca*** 'spear, lance, javelin' adopted into W as ****ffranc*** with a pl. ****ffrancon***, an interpretation which is appropriate in at least one literary context. It is otherwise unattested in W, but the topographical significance of spears here is the precipitous streams feeding into the river Ogwen in Nant Ffrancon.

NANTGAREDIG Carm SN4921

?'gentle brook', ***nant, caredig***

Nant-garedig 1808-9, 1831, *Nantgaredig* 1875

The forms are very late and it is possible that ***nant*** is used here in its earlier sense of 'valley' since there is no stream of any consequence here. The second el. might also be a pers.n. Ceredig as in Ceredigion (q.v.).

NANTGARW Glam ST1285

'rough valley (or stream)', ***nant, garw***

Nant Garro 1729, *Nantgarw* 1742, *Nant Garw* 1833

The name is probably taken from the valley defined by steep slopes particularly by those of the hill Craig-yr-allt on its south side. It might also be taken from the small stream (*Nant Garw* 1885) in the valley next to the main road leading to Caerphilly but ***nant*** 'stream' is fem. leading, usually but not exclusively, to 'Nant arw'. The village was once mistakenly described (on the basis of a mapping error) as *Portobello* (1799) but this was a shortlived alternative name for Taff's Well (q.v.) a mile to the south, a name taken from a public house near the wells. On the r.n. see Abergarw.

NANT-GLAS Radn SN9965

'blue stream', ***nant, glas***

Nant-glas 1833

A small stream (*Nant Glas* 1891) flows through the hamlet southwards towards Nant Treflyn.

NANTGLYN Denb SJ0062

'stream in the valley', ***nant, glyn***

Nantlym 1254, *Nanclyn* 1291, *nanklyn* 1566, *Nantglyn* 1636

Several streams in this vicinity flow from Mynydd Hiraethog towards Afon Clwyd. This ***nant*** flows through a fairly narrow valley (***glyn***), stretching from Nantglyn to Segrwyd, to become Afon Ystrad as it emerges from the glen. There is evidence of the form without the -t- in the forms, and in *a Place caullid corruptely Nanclin for Nantglin by Astrat-brooke* (1536-9). A bridge across the stream was called Pont Rhyd y Saint, since, allegedly, *divers Sainctes were auncient Tyme buried* (1536-9) at the old Capel Mordeyrn. The parish was divided into Nantglyn Canon (*Nanthyn Canon* 1334, *Nantclyn Canonicorum* 1542) and Nantglyn Sanctorum (*Nanthyn Sanctorum* 1334, *Nantclyn y saint* 1523). The stress falls regularly on the first syllable, with occasional local pronunciation without the -t- (as in 1291 and 1566).

NANT GWRTHEYRN Caern SH3545

'valley of Gwrtheyrn', ***nant***, pers.n. ***Gwrtheyrn***

Nant Gortheyrn' 1281, *Vortigens Valley,*
rok Guortheren i.e. Vallis Vortegerni 1536-9, *Nantgwtherin* 1798,
Nant Gwrtheyrn 1838

Associated in legend with the 5cent. Gwrtheyrn (Vortigern) and possibly influenced by the hill-forts of Tre'r Ceiri (***ceiri*** 'giants'), the valley (frequently referred to as Y Nant as in the bay Porth y Nant) appears also to have been called Nant ar Lithfaen or Nant y Llithfaen (*Nant Arlithuaen* 1281, *Nantyllithvaen* 1612, *Nantarllithvaen* 1614, *Nant y llythfaen* 1838) from the rocky hillside above Nant Gwrtheyrn; see Llithfaen. Gwrtheyrn also appears in the name of the nearby tumulus Bedd Gwrtheyrn and the hill fort Castell Gwrtheyrn or Caer Wrtheyrn (*Caer Guortigern* 1586).

NANT GWYNANT Caern SH6250

'valley of lively streams', ***nant, hoyw, nant*** pl. ***naint***
nanhoenein 13cent., *nanhoeunin* 15cent., *Nantwhinan* 1508,
Nanhwynen 1524-5, *Nanhoynen* 1559, *Nantgwynyn* 1569,
Nanthwynen 1651, *Nanwhinen* 1680, *Nant Hwynant* 1804,
Nant Gwynan 1810, *Nant Gwynant* 1838, *Nanthwynant* 1851
The name has ***nant*** 'valley' and ***nant*** pl. ***naint*** 'stream'. Numerous vigorous brooks (***naint***) flow into Afon Glaslyn from the steep hillsides on either side of the valley (***nant***) of Nant Gwynant. The older forms show not only the el. ***hoyw*** as well as the disappearance of the final -t in both ***nant*** and ***naint***. Later forms show, not only ***Nant*** 'valley' but the influence of ***gwyn*** 'white' and restoration of the -t in -nant (substituted for ***naint*** 'streams'), hence the perception that the name means 'valley of the white stream'. An alternative etymology formerly proposed was that of a pers.n. Gwynein, Gwynain or Gwynan but early forms make this unlikely.

NANTLLE Caern SH5053

'valley of lakes', ***nant, llyn*** pl. ***llynnau***
Nanthlyne 1291, *Nantllew* 1300-25, *Nantlley* 1529, *Nanlley* 1658,
Nantlle 1795
The *-thlyne* in the 1291 form can reasonably be interpreted as ***llynnau***, a reference to two lakes which were once on either side of Baladeulyn (*Baladeulyn* 1283, ***bala*** 'neck of land', ***dau*** 'two', ***llyn***) near the village of Nantlle (see Llyn Nantlle). The original ***nant*** was probably the narrow valley from Drws-y-coed (*Druscoyt* 1370-1, *Drws y coed* 1640, ***drws*** 'pass', ***y, coed***) to the lakes at Nantlle; today Dyffryn Nantlle (q.v.) also includes the wider valley down to Pen-y-groes. Many documents record the colloquial pronunciation *Nanlle* or *Nanlla* (with loss of -t). However, in popular perception and literary tradition, the name has long been interpreted as 'Nant Lleu', associating the valley with Lleu, the central character of the Fourth Branch of the Mabinogi; cf. the interpretation of Dinas Dinlle. The 1300-25 form perceives the name as ***llew*** 'lion', while *Nant-y-llef* (map 1838) interprets the name as ***llef*** 'cry'.

NANTMEL Radn SO0366

'Mael's valley', ***nant***, pers.n. ***Mael***

Nantmayl 1259, *Nan Mayl* 1304, *Nantmel* 1513

The valley is that of the river Dulas. The pers.n. Mael is also found in the names of the cantref Elfael and cantref Maelienydd Radn.

NANTMOR see **NANMOR**

NANTPERIS Caern SH6058

'valley of Peris', ***nant***, pers.n. ***Peris***

Nant Peris 1891

The hamlet in the narrow valley of Nant Peris, associated with the saint Peris, with Llyn Peris (q.v.) and with the transferred name Llanberis (q.v.). The valley is commonly referred to as Llanberis Pass, at the head of which is Gorffwysfa ('resting place', ***gorffwys***, ***-ma***) which seems to be recorded in *sedem peris* 13cent.(14cent.) rendering an unrecorded W 'Gorffwysfa Peris'. Other names for the summit of the pass are Pen y Pass and Pen-y-gwryd formerly *gwryt Kei* 13cent. (14cent.) (***gwryd*** 'fathom', pers.n. ***Cai***), the width of the pass measured in terms of the outstretched arms of the medieval knight Cai or Kay. Pen-y-gwryd is popularly preserved in the cartographic acronym Pyg, the name of a route up Snowdon (q.v.) which starts at Pen y Pass.

NANT-Y-CAWS Carm SN4518

'river of the cheese', ***nant***, ***y***, ***caws***

Nant y Cause 1609, *Nant-y-caws* 1831

Similar names such Nant Llefrith (***nant***, ***llefrith*** 'milk') and Afon Llaethnant (***llaeth*** 'milk, cream') are fairly common r.ns usually alluding, as here, to rich pasture capable of supporting dairy cattle. Occasionally it could refer to a stream's cloudy waters.

NANTYDERI, NANT-Y-DERRY Monm SO3306

'stream with oak-trees', ***nant***, ***y***, ***deri***

Nantydery station 1871, *Nant-y-derry* 1886

Located on a small unnamed stream joining the river Usk on the south side of Nant-y-derry House.

NANT-Y-DERRY see **NANTYDERI**

NANTYFFYLLON Glam SS8592

'farthing stream', ***nant***, ***y***, ***ffyrling*** var. ***ffyrlling***

Nant firlling 1570, *forest Nant Firlloige* 1588, *nant ffyrllinge* 1630, *Nant ffirlling* c.1700, *Nant Fyrling* 1736, *Nant Furling* 1740, *Nant-y-ffyllon* 1884

ffyrlling, the south Wales var. of ***ffyrling*** 'farthing' (which does appear in some of the forms), is not used in a monetary sense but figuratively for a 'small, puny' or 'insignificant' stream (as a tributary of the river Llynfi). The modern form retains the -ll- but with loss of the preceding -r- and with an intrusive def.art. possibly influenced by ***ellyllon*** pl. of ***ellyll*** 'ghost, bogey, fiend'. The village itself is named directly from a farm bought by the *Cambrian Iron Company* in the 1830s.

NANT-Y-GLO Monm SO1910

'valley of the coal', ***nant, y, glo***

Nantygloe 1752, *Nant y Glo Works* 1798, *Nant-y-glo* 1832

The name is quite common for a valley with a stream associated with charcoal burning but there were also exposed coal-seams here. The village developed near ironworks (*Nant y glo iron works* 1810). Coalbrookvale (q.v.) is an adjacent area in these upper reaches of the Ebbw/Ebwy Fach.

NANT-Y-MOCH Reservoir Card SN7687

'the pigs' stream', ***nant, y, moch***

Nant-y-moch Reservoir 1966

The name is taken from a small stream recorded as *Nant Moch* 1946 in the valley of Nant Moch (*Nant y Moch* 1747). The reservoir was completed in 1964. ***moch*** may refer to actual pigs or figuratively to a burrowing or fast stream (cf. Llanrhaeadr-ym-Mochnant).

NANT-Y-MOEL Glam SS9392

'valley of the bare hill', ***nant, y, moel***

nant moel 1585-5, *Nantmoel* 1703, *Nant-y-moel* 1833, *Nant-moel* 1884

The valley is now called Cwm Nant-y-moel where ***nant*** has now been taken to refer to the stream Nant y Moel at the north end of the village. The north side of the valley is now afforested. The def.art. *y* is probably intrusive (cf. Nantyffyllon) but it has given rise to the suggestion for Y Moel, 'the bald man'.

NANTYR Denb SJ1537

'stream by the plot of land', ***nant, erw***

Nanterow 1277-8, *Nanter* 1568, *Nantir* 1625, *Nantyr* 1838

The meanings of ***erw*** include 'acre' (its commonest meaning) as well as 'enclosed field' and 'plot of land'. The final unaccented syllable (consonantal -w-) was lost resulting in stress shift to the penultimate syllable; cf. Bryncir. The stream flows by land possibly the location of today's Plas Nantyr (*Plâs Nantir* 1795, *Plâs Nantyr* 1838) which was distinctive in some way, probably by being cultivated and enclosed. The stream's name, however, survived independently of Nantyr and in its three-syllable form but developed into 'Nant Teirw', today's Afon Teirw (*Tierw* 1665-6, *Teirw* 1795) as if ***teirw*** 'bulls'. It is unlikely that the 1277-8 form does in fact represent 'Nant Teirw' in the first place.

NANT-YR-EIRA Mont SH9605

'valley of the snow', ***nant, yr, eira*** var. ***eiry***

Na(n)t ereyre, Na(n)t er ere 1185, *Nantereyre* 1226, *Nant yr ira* 1588, *Nant eiry* 1650, *Nant yr Eira* 1836

Early forms (and certainly 1650) probably have the obsolete var. ***eiry*** (apparently monosyllabic) which was later replaced by the more common ***eira***. Records refer to the valley and the stream near Llanerfyl as one of the boundaries of the abbey of Strata Marcella. However, ***nant*** is probably 'stream', denoting very cold waters (such as the common Oernant, Nant Oer and Oerddwr); cf. especially Odnant Mont (***ôd*** 'snow') and Iaen Glam and Mont (***iâ*** 'ice').

NARBERTH, ARBERTH Pemb SN1014

'near Arberth', ***yn***, p.n. ***Arberth***

Nerberd 1197, *Neyrberd* 1246, *Nerberth* 1283, *Nerberth* 1291, *Arberth* 1300-25, 1116 (14cent.), *la Nerbert* 1331, *Narberth* 1337, *Ar berth* c.1566

Arberth seems to have been a district name for an area opposite or adjacent to (***ar***) part of the formerly extensive wooded area of Narberth Forest (an earlier sense of ***perth***). This was before any castle (*castellum Arberth* 1116 [14cent.]) was built; the later Narberth Castle is no earlier than the 13cent. Narberth, perceived to be the form used in E, developed from the phrase *yn Arbeth* 'in Arberth' > *y Narberth*. For the same process occurring with an E el. ***atten*** see Nash.

NASH, TREFONNEN Monm ST3483

'at the ash-tree', 'ash-tree farm', OE ***atten***, OE ***æsc***, W ***tref, onnen***

(de) Fraxino 1154-8 (1290), *Frenne* 1290, *Assh* 1322, *Nasse* 1348, *trer onnen* c.1566, *y nais* 1606

The -n of ***atten*** has become attached to ***æsc***. The tree also appears as the dative of L ***fraxinus*** and F ***fre(s)ne*** 'ash-tree'. The W form is properly Tre'ronnen 'settlement of the ash' as in c.1566 (***tref, yr, onnen***) but has been standardized as modern Trefonnen 'ash settlement' (***tref, onnen***); the cymricized *y nais* (cf. Nottage) did not survive.

NEATH, CASTELL-NEDD Glam SS7597

'castle on (the river) Nedd/Neath', ***castell***, r.n. ***Nedd***

Nethe c.1129, *Ned* 1136-54, *Neeth* c.1140-80, *Need* 12cent., *kastell ned* 14cent., *Castle Neth* 1486, *Neath* 1578

First recorded as *Nido* 3cent. referring to the Roman fort which took its name from the river as did the medieval castle (Castell Nedd), town (Castell-nedd) and abbey (recorded 1129-30). The meaning of the river is uncertain but 'shining' and simply 'river' have been suggested; it is almost certainly related to the r.n. Nidd NYorks. Neath is an anglicized form.

NEBO Denb SH8356

biblical chapel n.

Nebo 1832

The name of the chapel (built in 1832), appropriate to its location on elevated ground, was taken as the hamlet name.

NEDD see **NEATH**

NEFYN Caern SH3040

'(associated with the person called) Nefyn', pers.n. ***Nefyn***

Nevin 1194-1200 (15cent.), *Newin* 1254, *Nevyn* 1282, *Newyn* 1284, *Nefyn* 1291, *Nevyn* 1303-4

Appears to have been named after an unidentified person (who may be Ir). Occasionally, Nefyn's reputation as a fishing port features in an alias *Nefyn y Pysgod* 1756 (***pysgod*** 'fish').

NELSON Glam ST1195

'(place near the) Nelson', p.n. ***Nelson***

Nelson 1833, *Nelson Village* 1840, *the Nelson, Nelson's Arms* 1845

From a public house reputedly named after a visit by Lord Nelson 1803 (two years before the battle of Trafalgar).

NERCWYS Flints SJ2361

'at the dark furrow', ***yn, erch, cwys***

Nerchgwys 1291, *Nerthgoys* 1397-8, *Nerchgoys* 1398-9, *Nerchois* 1477, *Nerth Gwys* 1490, *Nercwys, Nerthkwys* 1492, *Nerquis als Nerthkwys* 1634, *Nerkwys, Ner-cwys* c.1700, *Nerquis* 1878

*Erchgwys was the conjectural name of one of the tributaries of Afon Terrig from Nercwys Mountain, or possibly the stretch of Afon Terrig which is very close to Plas Nercwys. The furrow describes the stream's course or possibly Afon Terrig's fairly narrow stretch at this point. The el. ***erch*** 'dappled, dark' is also seen in Nannerch and Aber-erch. *Erchgwys possibly became the name of a place. To this name was added the preposition ***yn*** 'in', 'in Erchgwys' (possible vestiges of which may be seen in *Enercwys* 1685), with 'yn Erchgwys' becoming *Nerchgwys* and then Nercwys (cf. Narberth). Difficulties in discerning recognizable els explain the later intrusion of such els as ***nêr*** 'lord', ***nerth*** 'strength' and ***gwŷs*** 'sow, pig' (to describe a burrowing river).

NEVERN, NANHYFER Pemb SN0840

'valley of (the river) Nyfer', r.n. ***Nyfer, nant***

Nan-, Llanhever, Lanever c.1191, *Nanhyfer* 13cent,

Nevern 1315, 13cent.(16cent.), *Neuer* 1325, *Nevarn, Nantnyver* 1546

The original name was probably *Nant Nyfer* which is also found as an early *Llanyfer* (with an interchange of ***nant*** and ***llan***). The castle is *Castell Niuer*

1191 (late 13cent.) (***castell***). The r.n. Nefer or Nyfer (*flumen Neuer* c.1200, *Nant nimer, Nant Niver* late 13cent.) is obscure, but is possibly ***hyf*** 'bold, valiant' in the sense of a strong, lively river. On the development of -n after final -r in the later var. *Nefern/Nevern* cf. Trefelgarn Pemb (*Trefelgar'* 1326 [16cent.], *Treavelgarne* 1641). Nyfer has also been used as the W name but Nanhyfer has become established usage in recent years.

NEWBOROUGH, NIWBWRCH — Angl SH4265

'new borough', OE ***nīwe***, OE ***burh***

Villa de Nouo Burgo 1304-5, *Novus Burgus* 1305, *Neuburgh* 1304-5, *Newborough* 1379, *Nuburche* 1496-7, *Nuburch* 1536-9

In 1294, Edward I built his castle and town of Beaumaris a mile from Llan-faes (q.v.). To appease the burgesses of Llan-faes, he established a 'new borough' for them in the commote of Rhosyr twelve miles to the west. Early cymricization ensured that the -gh (which in the E speech of the time would have been pronounced as the W -ch) was retained as W -ch. The commote name Rhosyr (*Rossuir* 1254, *Rosfeyr* 1318, probably 'moor of the seas' from ***môr*** pl. ***mŷr*** rather than 'the moor of Mary' ***Mair***) was recognized as an alternative in some sources (*Y Rosur alias Nuburch* 1536-9).

NEWBRIDGE[1] — Denb SJ2841

'new bridge', E ***new***, E ***bridge***

New Bridge 1746

This bridge (built c.1825) replaced another stone bridge (whose foundations are still evident) and provided an additional Dee crossing, linking the south of the river with the industrial areas around Cefn-mawr (q.v.). A series of bridges (from 1392) had previously taken advantage of this site which was called *Cefn gerllaw'r Bontnewydd* 1867, ('ridge adjacent to the new bridge') and Cefn Bychan in comparison with the higher ridge of Cefn-mawr, the name until superseded by Newbridge. A house *Pen-y-bont* (1819, ***pen, y, pont***) was on the south side of the bridge. *Bontnewydd* 1828 (***pont, newydd***) is a W translation used of a Baptist chapel there which either did not survive as a name of the location or was restricted to the chapel.

NEWBRIDGE[2], TRECELYN — Monm ST2197

'new bridge', 'holly settlement', E ***new***, E ***bridge***, W ***tref, celyn***

Newbridge 1566, *y bont newyth* 1630, *y bont newidd* 1718, *New Bridge* c. 1790, *y Bontnewydd* 1839, *Trecelyn* 1880

This was a new bridge over the river Ebwy/Ebbw in the parish of Mynyddislwyn. The W description *Y Bontnewydd* ('the new bridge' ***y, pont, newydd***) appears to have been replaced with Trecelyn which was once an area within Newbridge.

NEWBRIDGE-ON-WYE, Y BONTNEWYDD AR WY

Radn SO0158

'(the) new bridge on (the river) Wye', r.n. ***Gwy/Wye***, E ***new***, E ***bridge***, E ***on***, W ***y***, ***pont***, ***newydd***, ***ar***

Pont Newydd 1679, *New bridge uppon Wye*, *Pont newidd ar Wye* 1682, *New-Bridge* 1750

W and E names duplicate each other, referring to a bridge over the river Gwy/Wye probably near the modern bridge. Despite being described as 'new' in 1679, the bridge was evidentally much older since it is *antient* in 1679. This or a predecessor may be the one shown on a 1610 map and perhaps was the timber bridge recorded 1536-9. The village itself probably developed around the Baptist chapel erected 1760, recorded as *Pentref-newydd* 1778 (***pentref*** 'village', ***newydd*** 'new') which was new in contrast to an older meeting-house *Pentref*, but this name did not survive.

NEWCASTLE, CASTELL-NEWYDD

Monm SO4417

'new castle', E ***new***, E ***castle***, W ***castell***, ***newydd***

(de) Castro Novo 1186, *Noef Chastel* 1361, *Newcastell* 1539

New was perhaps in contrast to Oldcastle Monm or Skenfrith (q.v.) about ten miles north-west. This appears to have replaced a castle in this area near St Maughan's called *castell merych* 1136-54 ('castle of horses', ***castell***, ***march*** pl. ***meirch***) near St Maughan's. The E form seems to occur first in 1477 possibly replacing an earlier *Noef Chastel* (NF ***noef***, ***chastel***) referring to a small medieval motte.

NEWCASTLE EMLYN, CASTELLNEWYDD EMLYN

Carm SN3040

'new castle in Emlyn', cantref n. ***Emlyn***, OE ***nīwe***, OE ***castel***, W ***castell***, ***newydd***

Novum Castrum de Emlyn c.1240, *Emlyn with New Castle* 1257, *Newcastle Emlyn* 1295, *Castell neuweydd in Emlyn* 1541

The new castle, built c.1240, replaced the older castle at Cilgerran eight miles away, which may be *Castelhan Emelin* 1176-98 and *Castellan* 1231. The cantref (later a lordship) Emlyn (*Emelinn* 1130, *Emelin* 1236, *Emlyn* 1257) is '(area) around the valley', ***am***, ***glyn***) of the river Cuch. Regularly heard locally as 'Castellnewy' with the common loss of final -dd.

NEWCHAPEL, CAPEL NEWYDD

Pemb SN2239

'new chapel', E ***new***, E ***chapel***, W ***capel***, ***newydd***

New Chapel Meeting House 1803, *New Chapel* 1814, *Cappel Newydd* 1830

The Calvinistic Methodist chapel was erected in 1763.

NEWCHURCH[1], YR EGLWYS NEWYDD AR Y CEFN Monm ST4597

'new church', 'the new church on the ridge', E ***new***, E ***church***, W ***yr***, ***eglwys***, ***newydd***, ***ar***, ***y***, ***cefn***

Newchurch 1509, *Newchurche* 1535, *yr eglwys newydd ar y kefen* c.1566

Probably a late medieval church despite the traditional explanation that it was built by monks of Tintern abbey. This may be the ***betws*** recorded in *Monyth y bettus* 1613 (***mynydd***) and *Hewle y Bettus* 1664 (***heol***) in this area.

NEWCHURCH[2], LLANNEWYDD Radn SO2150

'new church',E ***new***, E ***church***, W ***llan***, ***newydd***

Newchurch in Elwell 1497, *ll. newydd* c.1566

There seems to be no record of the church being established but its dedication to Mary may favour the 13 or 14cent. when many churches acquired a dedication to her. The parish lay in the cantref of Elfael.

NEW CROSS Card SN6377

'new crossroads', E ***new***, E ***cross***

New Cross 1834, *New-cross*, *New-cross Inn* 1891

Located at the meeting point of the Trawscoed to Aberystwyth road and two lanes.

NEWGALE, NIWGWL Pemb SM8422

?'new lane', ?OE ***nīwe***, ON ***geil*** 'ravine, narrow lane'

(*sabulum de*) *Nivegal* 1197, *Niwegal*, *Neugol* c.1191, *Neugyll* 1291, *Newgall* 1568, *Newgull* 1590, *Newgol Haven* 1602, *Newgal Sands* 1824

An obscure name. Possibly of Ir origin and probably identical to (Porth) Neigwl Caern (*Neugyll* 1291, *Newgwl* 1352. *Porthnegoll* 1561-2). Both places lie next to sandy beaches (L ***sabulum***). A recent suggestion is that the second el. is ON ***geil*** 'ravine, narrow lane', a reference to access to the bay. The modern W form is a cymricization.

NEW HEDGES Pemb SN1202

'(place enclosed by) new hedges', E ***new***, E ***hedges***

New Hedges c.1773

Probably referring to land enclosure.

NEW INN Carm SN4736

'(place near the) New Inn', p.n. ***New Inn***

New Inn 1773, *the New Inn* 1804

References to fairs here in 1818 and 1831 occur in W language sources, showing the adoption of inn names into local usage (whatever the language of the speaker). Located on the road between Carmarthen and

Llanybydder, the inn is also said to be have been known as *The Traveller's Rest*, reputedly built c.1711. There is another New Inn (*ye New Inn* 1744, *New Inn* 1831, near Llandeilo Carm.

NEW MILLS[1] Monm SO5107

'(place near) new mills', E ***new***, E ***mills***

New mills 1871, *Newmills* 1896

Located beside White Brook, a tributary of the r. Wye. In 1886 there was a corn mill here and a disused paper mill, and there were others at Fernside Mills downstream. An earlier map shows the site as *Twldu* (1819), possibly ***twll***, ***du***, a reference to the dark, narrow hollow.

NEW MILLS[2]**, FELIN NEWYDD** Mont SJ0901

'new mills', '(the) new mill', E ***new***, E ***mill***, W (*y*), ***melin***, ***newydd***

New Mills 1817

The location of several mills on the river Rhiw. The local W name is Felin Newydd, appearing in some literary works but not recorded in official sources; it may therefore precede New Mills or be a later, loose, translation.

NEW MOAT, Y MOT Pemb SN0625

'new mound', OE ***nīwe***, OF ***mote***

Nova Mota c.1200 (1296), *La Mote* 1297, *Newemote* 1535,
Y mod, y Mot, y Newmot c.1566, *Plwyv mod* 1599, *Newemotte* 1600,
Newmoat 1602, *Newmoate* 1752

The L ***nova***, ***mota*** refers to a Norman castle mound or motte on the north-east side of the church. Traces of an older motte lie south-west of the church. The use of the def.art. ***y*** in the forms for c.1566 may indicate that W speakers cymricized the name recognising its topographical application to the castle mound but such a word is not recorded elsewhere in literature. Later E forms show the influence of ***moat***.

NEWPORT[1]**, CASNEWYDD (AR-WYSG)** Monm ST3188

'new town', 'the new castle (on the river Usk)', OE ***nīwe***, OE ***port***,
W ***castell***, ***newydd***, ***ar***, r.n. ***Wysg***

Novi Burgi 1072-1104, *Novus Burgus* 1138, (*de*) *Nouo burgo* 1156,
Nova Villa mid 13cent., *Neuburc* 1262, *Neweporte* 1265, *Neuborh'* 1291,
Neuport 1316, *Newport on Husk* 1439, *Castell Newyd ar Wysc* 14cent.,
y castell newyd ar Wysc c.1400, *y kastell newydd ar uwysc* c.1566

Most sources before c.1300 describe it as 'new borough' (L ***burgus***, OE ***burh***) and occasionally 'new town' (L ***nova***, ***villa***) possibly in contrast to an older settlement on Stow Hill or perhaps Caerleon. Stow Hill may also have been the location of the old castle which preceded the new castle of Casnewydd constructed by the Normans c.1090 in the borough next to the river Usk. ***port*** was often used of a town or borough which had been granted market rights. ***castell*** was commonly abbreviated to ***cas*** (as in Cas-gwent q.v.) in later usage.

NEWPORT[2], TREFDRAETH Pemb SN0539

'new town', 'town near the shore', E ***new***, ME ***port***, W ***tref***, ***traeth***

(de) Novo burgo 1231, *Nuport* 1282, *Newburgh* 1296, *Novus Burgus* 1316, *castell Treftraeth* 1215 (c.1400), *castell Trefdraeth* 1215 (14cent.), *Tredraith* 1536-9, *tref draeth* c.1566

On ***port*** 'town' and L ***burgus***, OE ***burh*** 'borough' see Newport[1]. Newport was a late 12cent. planted borough with a new castle and may have been new in contrast to an earlier settlement around an older castle nearer the sea and destroyed in 1195. Trefdraeth may also have applied to the older site and been transferred as a name for the new borough. The W name refers to its location on the south side of Newport Sands (*Traeth Edrywy* 18cent.) near the estuary of Afon Nyfer. Local pronunciation 'Tredraeth' is evidenced as *Tredraith* 1536-9, and later pronunciation is commonly 'Tidrath'.

NEWQUAY, CEINEWYDD Card SN3859

'new quay', E ***new***, E ***quay***, W ***cei***, ***newydd***,

New Key 1700, *Newkey* 1748, *Cai newydd* 1762, *New Quay* 1798, *Cei Newydd* 1831

The fishing-port expanded with the building of the harbour and later the pier (1820) to facilitate coastal trading, making New Quay Card's major shipbuilding centre in the 19cent. Locally the village is referred to as (Y) Cei.

NEW RADNOR, MAESYFED Radn SO2160

'new Radnor', 'open-field of Hyfaidd', OE ***nīwe***, p.n. ***Radnor***, W ***maes***, pers.n. ***Hyfaidd***

maes hewed c.991 (1286), *Radnoure Nova* 1277, *Maes Hyueyd* c.1400, *New Radnor* 1487, *Radnor, in Welsh Maesyuet* 1584

Maesyfed appears to be a name of considerable antiquity referring to the vale of Radnor (*vro hyueid*, c.1258 [c.1400]), 'territory (or lowland) of Hyfaidd', but nothing certain is known of him. The modern form with -yfed reflects association with ***yfed*** 'to drink'. Radnor was probably taken directly from the medieval lordship (*Radenovere* 1231, *Radenore, de Valle de Radenoure* 1293). Old Radnor/Pen-craig, less than three miles away, is *Raddrenove* 1086, *Radenouram* 1188, *Old Radenouere* 1253, *Pen Craig* 1447-89, *pen Kraic* c.1566 ('red ridge', OE ***readan***, ***ofer***, and 'top (of the) rock', ***pen***, ***craig***), both referring to the prominent, isolated hill immediately behind the village. The castle of New Radnor is probably late 11cent. but there was no need to distinguish between Old and New

Radnor until the establishment of a new borough, in the late 12 or early 13cent. The county of Radnorshire, Sir Faesyfed, was established 1536-42.

NEWTON[1] Glam SS6088

'new farm', E ***new***, E ***-ton***

Newton 1626

-ton is a common p.n. el. in Gower. The same parish (Oystermouth) also has Norton (*Norton* 1574) north of Oystermouth castle.

NEWTON[2] Pemb SM9000

'new farm', E ***new***, E ***-ton***

Neuton 1375, *Newton* 1522, *Newton West* 1545

New perhaps in contrast to Wogaston about a mile away. There are a number of other ***-ton*** p.ns in the immediate area. Newton East was in Hayscastle.

NEWTON NOTTAGE, DRENEWYDD YN NOTAIS Glam SS8377

'new farm near Nottage', p.n. ***Nottage***, OE ***nīwe***, OE ***tūn***, W ***y***, ***tref***, ***newydd***, ***yn***

Nova Villa 1147-83, *Neweton* 13cent., *Neuton by Nottashe* 1315, *Newton Notage* 1535, *y dre newydd ynottais* c.1566, *y dre newydd ynotes* 1613

The parish church was in Newton while an adjacent manor to the west was Nottage (q.v.) but both units came to be regarded as one (*Nova Villa et Nottasse* 1272, *Newton at Notesche* 1452) and eventually becoming the name of the parish. The W form appears to be a late translation of Newton, ***yn*** 'in' and a cymricization of Nottage. There is some evidence of a var. *Trenewydd*, recorded in a field name (*Caetrenewydd* 1862, ***cae***) and hill (*Mynydd Trenowydd* c.1700, ***mynydd***) referring to Newton Down (about a mile north of the village).

NEWTOWN, Y DRENEWYDD Mont SO1191

'new town', OE ***nīwe***, OE ***tūn***, W ***y***, ***tref***, ***newydd***

Llanweyr 1254, *Thlanveir in Kedewey* 1279, *Nova Villa* 1295, *the Newtown* 1350, *Neueton* 1365, *Drenewyth alias Llanvayr in Kedewen* 1395, *the Newe town of Kedewen* 1478, *y dre newydd* c.1566

Duplicated by early forms with L ***nova***, ***villa***. Newtown probably earned its name as a new borough, established with markets and fairs in 1280 and centred on Broad Street. The older settlement *Llanfair* (in the cantref of Cedewain) probably lay around the old church or chapel of St Mary, was ruinous in the 19cent. and now destroyed by the river Severn.

NEW TREDEGAR, TREDEGAR NEWYDD Monm SO1403

'new Tredegar', E ***new***, p.n. ***Tredegar***

New Tredegar 1859

A settlement which grew around the *New Tredegar Colliery* held by J. Powell & Son 1859 and located near Aberysibwr and Cwmysibwr. It was new in contrast to the older industrial settlement of Tredegar (q.v.). The area is reputed to have been earlier called *White Rose*, probably from the *Whiterose Colliery* opened in 1857.

NEYLAND Pemb SM9605

'at the low-lying marsh land', OE ***atten***, OE ***ēg-land***

the Neyland House 1508, *Nailand* 1596, *Nayland* 1773

Although the first recorded form is late for an OE derivation the location on low-lying land close to the estuary of Milford Haven points to a much older name. For similar metanalysis involving ***atten*** see Nash.

NICHOLASTON Glam SS5188

'settlement of Nicholas', pers.n. ***Nicholas***, OE ***tūn***

Nicholastoune 1306, *Niclaston'* 1435, *Nicholaston'* 1459,
niklas down c.1566

The church dedication to St Nicholas is recorded 1435 but it may have originated with the name of some secular lord of the manor. No distinct W name has been recorded. The c.1566 form is simply an attempt at presenting a W form by replacing *-ton* with *-town* and then applying lenition to ***down***. There is a St Nicholas/Tremarchog in Pemb.

NIWBWRCH see **NEWBOROUGH**

NIWGWL see **NEWGALE**

NOLTON Pemb SM8618

'(at the) old settlement', OE ***atten***, OE ***ald***, OE ***tūn***

Veteri villa 1291, *ecclesiam de St. Madoci de Vetervilla* 1296,
Noldeton in Ros 1317, *Nolton* 1403, *Nowlton* 1592

The dedication of the church to the W saint Madog may suggest that the church and village preceded the E and Flemish settlement of Pemb in the 12cent. On metanalysis involving ***atten***, see Nash and compare Neyland.

NORTH CORNELLY see **CORNELI**

NORTHOP, LLANEURGAIN Flints SJ2468

'dry land to the north', 'church of Eurgain', OE ***norð***, OE ***hop***, W ***llan***, fem. pers.n. ***Eurgain***

Lhanensgeyn 1254, *Northoppe* 1283, *Northope* 1284, *Lanewrgayn'* 1291, *Llaneurgern* 1315, *ll. eirgain* c.1566, *Llan-eurgain* 1612, *Northope al' dict Llanergen* 1458-9

Eurgain was reputedly a 6cent. saint of princely descent, the daughter of Maelgwn Gwynedd and the wife of Elidir Mwynfawr. The village is flanked by two brooks and so could be perceived to be 'dry land in the middle of marsh land' as was Hope Flints. Northop was north of Hope and of Mold. An adjoining hamlet is Northophall, which developed near a hall, now a farm, called *Northop Hall* 1698 (*y Plâs yn Lhan Eyrgen...y penna'n plwy yr awrhon* ['the mansion in Llaneurgain...the principal one in the parish at the moment'] c.1700), *Northop Hall* 1750. At the eastern end of Northophall is another farm called Pentre Moch (*Pentre mock* 1682, *Pentre'r Môch* 1698, ***pentref*** 'village', ***moch*** 'pigs') which has frequently been used as a W name for Northophall.

NORTHOPHALL see **NORTHOP**

NORTH STACK, YNYS ARW Angl SH2183

'north stack', 'rough island', E ***north***, E ***stack***, W ***ynys***, ***garw***

Nth. Stack 1777, *The north Stack or Ynys Arw* 1818

An island a mile north-west of South Stack (q.v.). Stack could feasibly be ON ***stakkr*** in keeping with other Scandinavian coastal names. However, Stack does not seem to be recorded elsewhere on the north Wales coast, and the late recording of North and South Stack here makes it more likely to be a generic name for a coastal feature (perhaps given by seafarers) although its precise significance here is unclear. The island is not a particularly precipitous or column-like rock, the usual meaning of stack, so it may describe an island in very close proximity to the steep or sheer cliffs as seen from the sea, certainly the most dramatic cliffs in Anglesey. In Ynys Arw, 'rough' probably refers to turbulent seas rather than the island.

NORTON, NORTYN Radn SO3067

'north farm', OE ***norð***, OE ***tūn***

Nortune 1086, *Norton'* 1192, *Nordton'* 1193, *Norton* 1291, *nortyn* c.1566

'North' perhaps in contrast to the lost *Clatretune* (probably OE ***clater*** 'noise') perhaps Whitewall Farm near Presteigne Radn. The W substitution of -tyn for -ton also occurs in north-east Wales (see Prestatyn), Mont, Shropshire and Herefordshire.

NORTYN see **NORTON**

NOTAIS see **NOTTAGE**

NOTTAGE, NOTAIS Glam SO8178

'pollard ash-tree', OE ***hnott***, OE ***æsc***

Nottasse 1272, *le Nothasse* 1329, *Notasche* 1351, *Nottesassh* 1376, *Notage* 1557

Located a mile-and-a-half from the village (and in the parish) of Newton Nottage/Y Drefnewydd yn Notais. Also the name of a farm called Nottage in Oystermouth Glam.

NYFER see **NEVERN**

O

OAKDALE Monm ST1899

'oak dale', E ***oak***, E ***dale***

A model village built by the *Tredegar Iron & Steel Co.* 1910-11 to house workers of its subsidiary *Oakdale Navigation Colliery* opened in 1907 near Penrhiwsirdavy (*Penrhiwsirdavy* 1833, possibly ***pen***, ***rhiw*** 'slope, hill', ***syr*** 'sir' and pers.n. ***Dafydd***). The pers.n is seen in a farm (*Rhiw-Sir-David* 1871), a road (*heol Sir David* 1546, *hewle Sir David ap Hoell* 1565, ***heol***) and a bridge (*Pont Sir Davy* 1813, *Pont Syr Dafydd* 1886). Given that there is a Cwm Gelli nearby (***celli*** 'grove') Oakdale may have been a translation of an unrecorded *Cwm Deri* (***deri*** 'oak').

OAKFORD, DERWEN-GAM Card SN4558

'oak ford', 'crooked oak', E ***oak***, E ***ford***, W ***derwen***, ***cam***

Derwen-gam 19cent., *Oakford* 1891

The E name was apparently coined by a local magistrate Morgan Evans on the basis of the ford (through Afon Dryw) and a distinctive oak tree in the village (which had been the source of the W name for the village). Morgan Evans lived in a nearby house called Rhydygwinllanau (*Rhyd-y-gwinllanau* 1834, ***rhyd*** 'ford', ***y*** 'the', ***gwinllannau*** 'vineyards') taken from what seems to have been the original name of the ford.

OFFA'S DYKE, CLAWDD OFFA

Denb/Flints/Mont/Rad/Monm SJ2951, 2855, ST5493, 5593

'Offa's dyke', OE ***dīc***, W ***clawdd***, pers.n. ***Offa***

Offedich 1184, (*ad*) *fossam offe* late 12cent., *Klawt Offa* c.1215 (c.1300), *Offediche* 1378, *Clawth offa* 1454, (*fossa*) *Offas diche* 1567, *'fossa' Clawdd offa* 1585, *Klawdd Offa* 1605, *the Offa diche* 1614, *Clawdh Offa viz Offa's Ditch* 1684, *Clawdd Offa* 1827

Constructed in the reign of the Mercian king Offa (757-796) as a linear earthwork to mark the boundary of the Mercian territory. It corresponds to the modern Wales/England border in only short sections, but in W parlance 'tu draw i Glawdd Offa' ('beyond Clawdd Offa') is still used figuratively for 'in England'. Although it was alleged (c.900) to be 'from sea to sea', broadly from Dee to Severn estuaries, archaeological and historical confusion with other dykes have made the precise route a matter of continuing research. It was some six feet in height by approximately 30 feet in width (including the dyke and the westerly ditch). The el. ***dīc*** became modern E ***ditch*** but the prevailing term for a boundary earthwork is ***dyke*** or ***dike*** (from ON ***dík***). The forms cited refer to various county sections of the dyke but serve to illustrate the continuity and unity of the name as a political and administrative statement in E and W.

OGMORE-BY-SEA, ABEROGWR Glam SS8876

?'(place next to the river) Ogmore by the sea', r.n. ***Ogwr/Ogmore***, E ***by***, E ***sea***

Hoggemora 1148, *Uggemor* 1139-49, *Wuggemore* 1173-83, *Ogemor* 1281

A difficult name. The name is taken from the early 12cent. castle (*Ogmore Castrum super Mare* 1479, *kastell ogwr* c.1566) next to the river Ogwr/Ogmore (*Ocmur* 1136-54, *Ogmor* c.1200, *Ogur* 13cent. (16cent.), *Ogmorewater* 1479, *Aber Ogwr* 1609) a mile-and-a-half from the sea and from the village of Ogmore-by-sea. The first el. of the r.n. may contain ***og***- 'sharp, keen, fast' or ***og***- 'burrow, rut' (as in the r.n. Ogwen q.v.); the early forms may have the el. in an Ir form. The second el. is obscure. The early forms (and later E pronunciation) suggest ***môr*** which is appropriate to its location but poses problems with the W form Ogwr. The most acceptable explanation is an obscure el. ****-mur*** (> W *-fwr* > *-wr* and E *-more*) but of unknown significance. The r.n. is also found in Blaenogwr (*Blayne ogur* 1576, *Blaen-Ogwr* 1766, ***blaen***), Glynogwr (q.v.) and Cwmogwr (q.v.). Whatever its precise origin, Ogmore, perceived as being the E name, is in fact a fossilized form of the OW *Ocmur* (cf. Pembroke) while the W form is the regular phonological development; cf. Pembroke.

OGMORE VALE, CWM OGWR Glam SS9390

'valley of (the river) Ogwr', r.n. ***Ogmore/Ogwr***, E ***vale***, W ***cwm***

Ogmore Vale 1884

On the r.n. see Ogmore-by-sea. A late 19cent p.n. The older name was that of a farm Ty-newydd (*Tŷnewudd farm* 1767, *Tenewith* 1799, *Ty-newydd* 1833, 1884, 'new house', ***tŷ***, ***newydd***) which survives in Tynewydd Terrace and a ward.

OGWEN, Afon, Dyffryn, Llyn Caern SH6069, SH9560,

'lively piglet river', ***afon***, ***dyffryn***, ***llyn***, ***og***, ***banw***

ogwanw ?15cent., *ogwayne* 1499-50, *Ogweyne* 1536-9, *Ogwen* 1590-1

The river rises on Carnedd Dafydd and flows into Llyn Ogwen (*Llinne Ogweyne* 1536-9, *Llyn Ogwen* 1795) through Dyffryn Ogwen to enter the Menai Strait at Aberogwen. Several rivers in Wales have the el. ***banw*** (such as Aman and Banw). The first el. is probably OW ***og*** 'fast, lively' (although it has been suggested that it may be Ir ***óg*** 'young'). The phonological development was *Ogfanw* > *Ogfan* (with loss of final -w- and stress shift to the initial syllable) > *Ogwan* which is still the local pronunciation (preserved in some publications) which was then influenced by the perception that -wan was the non-standard colloquial pronunciation of ***gwen*** fem. of ***gwyn*** 'white'.

OGWR see **OGMORE-BY-SEA**

OLDCASTLE, YR HENGASTELL Monm SO3224

'old castle', OE ***ald***, NF ***castel***, W ***yr***, ***hen***, ***castell***

(de) Veteri Castro 1279, *old Castelle* 1501, *Oldecastle* 1537, *Ouldecastelle* 1602

There was an ancient castle earthwork believed to be under the Court, although it has been suggested that it was contrasted with the castle at Walterstone Herefordshire about a mile away.

OLD CASTLE HEAD Pemb SS0796

'headland next to the old fort', E ***old***, E ***castle***, E ***head***

Old Castle Hd. 1798, *Old Castle Head* 1839

The castle was recorded in 1773 as a defensive enclosure, possibly medieval, and as a *Camp* 1839.

OLD RADNOR see **RADNOR**

ONLLWYN, YR Glam SN8310

'the ash grove', ***yr***, ***onn***, ***llwyn***

The Onllwyn 1838, *Oerllwyn* 1832, *Onllwyn* 1851

This is probably a deliberate inversion of the more usual Llwyn-onn. The industrial village appeared after the opening of anthracite coal mines in the mid 19cent. The map form *Oerllwyn* seems to treat it as if ***oer*** 'cold'.

ORIELTON Pemb SR9599

'Oriel's hill', pers.n. ***Oriel***, OE ***dūn***

Orieldon 1335, *Orieldoune* 1353, *Orleton* 1381, *Orielton* 1480

The family name *Oriel* occurs in several of the E parts of Pembs, in this instance probably the forebears of the later *Stephen Oriell* (1480) of Castlemartin. Now a field centre, Orielton lies on the north side of a small hill but its association with the settlement of a named family influenced its development as -ton.

ORME see **GREAT ORME**

ORSEDD, YR see **ROSSETT**

OVERTON, OWRTYN Denb SJ3741

'settlement on the bank', OE ***ōfer***, OE ***tūn***

Ouerton' 1195 (1331), *Overtone* 1201, *Oureton* 1309, *Owrtun* 13cent., *Awrtun* 14cent., *Wrtun* 15cent., *owrtyn* 1527, *Orton* 1551, *Ortyn* 1566

Although it can be contended that the first el. is ***ofer*** 'flat topped ridge with a convex shoulder' on which Overton stands, what gives this location greater distinctiveness is the large ox-bow (***ōfer***) in the river Dee. Cymricized forms of Overton and of *Orton* with -tyn have had considerable currency in literary (and probably colloquial) usage.

OWRTYN see **OVERTON**

OXWICH Glam SS4986

'ox farm', OE ***oxa***, OE ***wīc***

Oxenwiche 1176-98, *Oxenwych* 1230, *Oxewyche* 1306, *Oxinwich* 1352, *Oxewiche* 1409, *Oxmoche* 1517, *ogsmids* c.1566, *Oxmuch* 1583, *Oxewyche alias Oxemyche alias Oxmyche* 1543, *Oxmugh* 1584-5, *Oxenwich* 1609, *Oxwich* 1670

This was a farm specializing in rearing oxen; there are similar p.ns in England for other animals such as sheep (Shapwick Somerset) and goats (Gatwick Shropshire). The modern form derives from an earlier form with *Oxen-* but both forms coexisted to the end of the 16cent. A number of 16cent. forms (which did not survive) show confusion of -n- with -m- and loss of -w- which may have been the basis for the c.1566 cymricized form (with -ds to represent E final -ch).

P

PADESWOOD

Flints SJ2762

'Padda's wood', pers.n. ***Padda***, OE ***wudu***

Patdeswde, Pateswode 1198, *Paddeswode* 1477, *Padeswood* 1518-29, *Paddyswood* 1536

The identity of Padda or Patta is unknown.

PAINSCASTLE, CASTELL-PAEN

Radn SO1646

'Pain's castle', pers.n. ***Pain***, ME ***castel***, W ***castell***,

Matildis castrum 1195, *castellum Paen* 1198, *Castle Maude* 1298, *kastell paen yn eluael* 1196 (14cent.), *Castell Payne* 1535

Reputedly named from *Pain fitz John* (died 1137) who may also have given his name to Painswick Gloucester. His wife *Maud de St. Valéry* gave the castle its alternative name (in 1195 in a documentary L Matilda). The 1196 (14cent.) form refers to Painscastle's location in the cantref of Elfael. The pers.n. is cymricized as Paen (which has led, possibly, to the fanciful association with ***paun*** 'peacock'). Cf. Pentrebane Glam (< *Cefn-tre-bane* c.1485-1515, *Pentrebaen* 1564, *Pentrepayne* 1567) from ***cefn*** 'ridge', ***pentref***, and the NF pers.n. Payn(e).

PALE

Mer SH9836

'park', ***pâl*** pl. ***palau*** dial. var. ***pale***

y Paley 1652, *Pale* c.1700, *y Palau* 1889

This mansion in Dyffryn Penllyn, rebuilt 1869-1871, was surrounded by a distinctive boundary of stakes or pale. The E ***pale*** was adopted into W as ***pâl*** from at least the 16cent. and, as in E, referred to the area enclosed by the pale, synonymous with park (as in Penrhiw-pâl Carm and other examples in Wales). However, in W, although it was used in the singular for a row of stakes, it also developed a pl. ***palau*** 'stakes'. Fortuitously, the spelling of the W dial. var. pl. ***pale*** was identical with E ***pale***, thus both pronunciations, W disyllabic Pale and E monosyllabic Pale, can be heard locally.

PANDY[1]

Denb SJ1935

'fulling-mill', ***pandy***

Pandy 1872-4

The mill is situated on Afon Teirw's confluence with Afon Ceiriog. There were several fulling-mills here as well as quarries and clay-pits linked to Chirk by the (now defunct) *Glyn Valley Tramway*. The site is described as *Factory* on an 1830 map.

PANDY[2] Mer SH6203

'fulling-mill', ***pandy***

y Pandy 1592, *y Pandû* 1633, *Pandy* 1795

The first two references are to a croft associated with the mill (*Tyddyn y Pandy* 1592, *Tythyn y Pandû* 1633, ***tyddyn***) which was located on Afon Cwm-pandy. A 1901 map has *Flannel Factory* here.

PANDY[3] Monm SO3322

'fulling-mill', ***pandy***

Pandy 1814

The village developed around and on the south side of a toll-gate (*Pandy T. Gate* 1814) and inn (*Pandy Inn* 1871) close to the river Honddu but no fulling-mill is marked on 19cent. maps. A weir on the river supplied water to a former corn mill at Allt-yr-ynys about half-a-mile below the village.

PANDYTUDUR Denb SH8564

'dirty fulling-mill', ***pandy, budr***

Pandv bvdvr 1589, *Y Pandy budur* 1670, *Pandy Bidir* 1795, *Pandy-budr* 1839, *Pandy Tudyr* c.1880

This fulling-mill was on Afon Derfyn, but seems to have been habitually contaminated by water from peat-bogs, a reputation which tempted the Victorians to make the probably conscious change to the more gentrified pers.n. Tudur for the emerging hamlet.

PANT-GLAS Caern SH4747

'verdant hollow', ***pant, glas***

Pant Glas 1696, *Pant-glâs* 1838

The low-lying land adjacent to Afon Dwyfach and the main Caernarfon-Porthmadog road, between Bwlchderwin and Foel to the west and the foothills of Mynydd Craig-goch on the east. An older name for the area was Nancall (*Nankall* pre 1240, *Namcall, Nancall* 1291, *Nancall* 1554, *Nanccall or Pant-Glas* 1696), from ***nant*** and the stream name Call (*Kall* pre 1240), preserved in several modern farm names such as Hendre Nantcall (variously spelt Nantcyll, taking the stream name to be ***cyll*** 'hazel trees').

PANTLASAU Glam SN6500

'hollow of streams, ***pant, glais*** pl. *****glasau***

ye Causey, Pantloose 1702, *Pant Lasse* 1783, *Pant-lâsau* 1832

The second el. is probably an unrecorded pl. ***glasau*** of the common ***glais*** var. ***glas***. The rivulets or watercourses accord well with the wet terrain of Nant y Gors and Gors-wen which necessitated the causeway (seen in the 1702 form and in *alias Cawsey* 1764, E ***causey***).

PANTPASTYNOG Denb SJ0461

'hollow for cudgels', ***pant***, ***pastwn*** pl. ***pastynod***

Pantpystynog 1509-47, *Pant-pastynog* c.1879

The hollow is between Moel Prion and Ffridd Fawr, where, it seems, cudgels could be cut (despite the lack of actual documentary forms). The change from ***pastynod*** to Pastynog was probably influenced by Llewesog, Clywedog and Cyffylliog in the vicinity and possibly Pantperthog Denb.

PANTPERTHOG Mer SH7404

'bushy hollow', ***pant***, ***perthog***

Pantperthog 1598, *y Pantperthog* 1650

This part of the narrow valley between Machynlleth and Corris was characterised by a proliferation of bushes, possibly thorn bushes.

PANT-Y-DŴR Radn SN9874

'hollow of the water', ***pant***, ***y***, ***dŵr***

Panty Dŵr c.1755, *Pant-y-dŵr* 1833

A scatter of houses in a hollow between the river Marteg and stream Nant Tawelan.

PANT-Y-FFRIDD Mont SJ1502

'hollow near the upland pasture', ***pant***, ***y***, ***ffridd***

Pantyffrieth 1764, *Pantyfreeth* 1784, *Pant-y-ffridd* 1817

Named from two farms, one now called simply Pant. The ***ffridd*** is on the hill *Ffridd Penthryn* (1889) between *Little Ffrîdd* (1889) and Bank Farm to the north and east, with a *Pont y ffreeth* 1716/17 nearby.

PANTYFFYNNON Carm SN6210

'hollow of the well', ***pant***, ***y***, ***ffynnon***

Pant y ffynnon 1751, *Pantyffynnon* 1839

Originally a farm name, it was also applied to a railway junction.

PARC SEYMOUR Monm ST4091

'park belonging to Seymour family', ***parc***, pers.n. ***Seymour***

Park Seymor 1567, *Park Seymour* 1830, *Parc Seymour* 1886

A largely modern village west of a former park belonging to the Seymour family of Penhow Monm.

PARKHOUSE Monm SO4902

'house near a park', E ***park***, E ***house***

Parkhurst 1813, *Parkhouse* 1851, *Parcas* 1886

Located about a mile north of Old Park farm (*the Old Parke* 1581) and Wain-y-parc farm (*Wern-y-parc* 1886, ***gwaun*** 'moor' or ***gwern*** 'marsh', ***y***, ***parc***).

PARKMILL Glam SS5489

'mill near the park', ***park, mill***

Parke mill 1583, *the Parke mills* 1650, *Park Mill* 1832

Probably from Parc le Breos (*parcum de Breoz* 1306, *Park brewes* 1547), a reference to the *de Breos* family, lords of Gower (1203-1326), a mile to the west, and whose park extended to the stream Pennard Pill at Parkmill. Alternatively, a reference to a park at Mor Park (*the ould parke Ditche of the Marshe by the mill* 1650). Two mills are recorded in the 17cent.

PARLWR DU see **POINT OF AYR**

PARROG Pemb SN0439

'flat land along the shore', ***parrog***

Parrog 1793, *the parrog* 1796

Possibly also *the parcke* 1592. This and other examples such as Y Parrog, the name for the sea-shore between Fishguard and Goodwick Pemb, and *the perroge* 1592 (E ***parrock***) at Swansea Glam, refer to flat land along the sea-shore, possibly for unloading boats or a fishery. The same el., however, also had the sense of 'a fence enclosing a piece of ground' and (by extension) 'a small enclosure, a paddock' and this is clearly the meaning with a number of minor p.ns in Pemb and Glam.

PARYS MOUNTAIN see **MYNYDD PARYS**

PEDAIR-HEWL see **FOUR ROADS**

PELCAM see **PELCOMB BRIDGE**

PELCOMB BRIDGE, PELCAM Pemb SM9317

'bridge near Pelcomb', E ***bridge***, p.n. ***Pelcomb***

Pelkam Br. 1798, *Pelcomb Bridge* 1824

(East) Pelcomb itself is *Pelkam* 1282, *Pelcam* 1325, *Estpelcam* 1564, *Easter Pelcam* 1581, *East Pelcomb* 1865 and West Pelcomb is *Westirpelcan* 1324, *West Pelcam* 1564, *Wester Pelcam* 1581; there is also a Pelcomb Cross. Possibly named from Pelcomb Brook but the meaning is obscure; an OE pers.n. Pēol (as in Pelsall WMidlands and Pelton Durham) has been suggested, with later forms showing association with E ***coomb***. W ***pêl*** 'ball' does occur elsewhere in a topographical sense and ***cam*** 'crooked' is certainly possible for the second el. but absence of lenition (to **Pelgam*) deter such a derivation.

PEMBREY, PEN-BRE Carm SN4201

'top of the hill', ***pen, bre***

Penbray 1141, *pennbre* 1160-85, *Penbrey* 1361, *Pembeyre* 1417, (*o*) *bennbref* c.1500, *penbre* c.1566, *Pembray* 1577

Pem- with -m- replacing -n- before -b- is found in both W and E p.ns. Here, *Pembrey* 1831 occurs in a W document, suggesting the widespread use of what is now perceived to be the E form.

PEMBROKE, PENFRO Pemb SM9801

'land's end', Br ***penno**, Br ***bro(g)**

Pembroke c.1100, *pennbro* 1136-54, *Pembroch* c.1191, *Pembrok* 1283, *Penbrocia* 1231, *Penbrok* 1245

Comparable with other directional p.ns such as Land's End and Finistère since the name was used specifically for the peninsula extending from Amroth to Gateholm roughly corresponding to the medieval lordship of Pembroke. The change -n- to -m- before -b- in Pembroke and similar forms is common (cf. Lampeter Card). The final -broke is especially interesting because Br ***brog** became W **bro** before c.800 and because -b- is properly lenited to -f- (in the standard MnW form Penfro). It is possible that forms such as *Pembroke, Pembroch* preserve fossilized written features which had disappeared in speech but then reintroduced themselves as the spoken form Pembroke. Cf. Ogmore.

PEMBROKE DOCK, DOC PENFRO Pemb SM9603

'dock near Pembroke', p.n. ***Pembroke/Penfro***, E ***dock***, W ***doc***

Pembroke Dock, ~ Dockyard 1817, *Dock Yard and Town* 1840

The town developed around the royal dockyard established in 1814 on the site of the house called *Pater* (*Pater, henceforward called Pembroke Dock* 1818, *Dock or Pater* 1865) three miles from Pembroke; the dock is still known locally as Pater Dock. Very little is known of the original Paterchurch (*Patrecheryche* 1289, *Patrichurch* 1594, *Patrick chyrch* 1597, *Paterchurch* 1603) 'church of Patrick'. In recent years, Doc Penfro has established itself in W contexts.

PENALLY, PENALUN Pemb SS1199

'Alun's headland', ***pen***, r.n. ***Alun***

Penn Alun, (princeps) aluni capitis 1136-54, *Pennally* 1301, *Pennalun* 9cent. (14cent.), *pēnal* c.1566, *Pen ale* 1590-1

Near a promontory reaching to Giltar Point. The main reason for identifying with a r.n. is that Alun (q.v.) is well documented as a r.n. in Flints and elsewhere in Pemb. However, there is no evidence of a river with this name here unless it was an alternative name for the river Ritec (locally The Pill), a name restored to it on the strength of references to a river *ritec* 1136-54 known to have been near Penally. There is no record of a pers.n. Alun here but the 1136-54 form could be interpreted as a pers.n.

PENALUN see **PENALLY**

PENARLÂG see **HAWARDEN**

PENARTH Glam ST1871

'top of the headland', ***pen***, ***garth***

Penarth 1254, *Penardd* 1291

Named from its location on Penarth Head. Persistent stress on the second syllable is ample evidence of ***garth*** 'hill, headland'.

PEN-BONT RHYDYBEDDAU Card SN6783

'bridge-end at the ford of the graves', ***pen***, (***y***), ***pont***, ***rhyd***, ***y***, ***bedd*** pl. ***beddau***

Y Bont 1747, *Penbontrhydyubeðau* 1777, *Pennbont Rhydybeðau 1800*, *Pen-y-bont-rhyd-y-beddau* 1891

The reference is allegedly to a place of execution. Cf. Beddau. Rhydybeddau was probably the original name of the village, a reference to one of two fords through Afon Seilo at the eastern end of the village, near Pen-bont House. The village had three fords which were replaced by bridges. The extensive 19cent. lead mining gave rise to the development of the village.

PEN-BOYR Carm SN3636

'hill of (the river) Beyr', ***pen***, ?r.n. ***Beyr***

Penbeyr 1222 (1239), *Penbeher* 1291, *Penbeir* 1535, *Penbeyr* 1543, *pen boyr* 1590-1, *Pemboir* c.1631, *Penbeyre* 1788

The location is a semicircular terrace marked by the deep narrow valleys of Nant Bargod and an unnamed stream. That the second el. should be a r.n. is entirely conjectural but is suggested by *Rhydvoyr in Pemboyr* 1754, ***rhyd*** 'ford') and by the valley called Nant Bargod (*r. bargod* 1553) (***bargod*** 'border, limit') on its east side marking the parish boundary between Penboyr and Llangeler. The meaning of *Beyr* has tentatively been proposed as ***pau*** 'district' and ***hir*** 'long' reinforcing the association with a boundary (although a pers.n. *Beyr* has been proposed).

PEN-BRE see **PEMBREY**

PENBRYN Card SN2952

'hill-top', ***pen***, ***bryn***

Penbrin 1180-97 (1424), *Penbryn* 1291, *Pembryn* 1631

The village is on a hill above Traeth Penbryn. Some late references (*Pen Brynn, or, Llanfihangel Pen y Brynn* 1811) seem to suggest the parish may also have been known as Llanfihangel Penbryn or Llanfihangel Pen-y-bryn. The church (*ecclesia sancti Michaelis de Penbrin* 1216-29, ~ *Penbryn* 1331) is dedicated to Michael/Mihangel.

PENCADER Carm SN4436

'top of the mound', ***pen***, ***cadair*** dial. var. ***cader***

Pencadeir 1039 (late 13cent.), c.1191, *Pencader-Capel* 1680, *Pencader* 1754

cadair 'seat' is regularly used of a hill top and in the names of mountains (such as Cadair Idris q.v.) Occasionally, it referred to a fort or defensive settlement in that location, here on slopes above the confluence of three streams. The c.1191 *Pencadeir* has a L gloss of *cathedrae caput*, probably referring to a castle built on a mound in 1145.

PEN-CAER see **STRUMBLE HEAD**

PENCARNISIOG Angl SH3573

'above Conysiog', ***pen***, p.n. ***Conysiog***

Pen-y-carnisiog 1839, *Pencaernisiog* 1879

A village taking its name from a farm on slightly elevated ground within the tnshp of Conysiog or Conisiog (*Commissauc* 1254, *Conyssiok* 1335). The first el. of the medieval tnshp name is the pers.n. *Conws* or *Cwnws*, derived from an Ir pers.n. latinized as *Cunugusus* (commemorated on a stone in the area as *Cvnvgvsi hic iacit*). The second el. is the terr.suff. *-**iog***. The earlier form of the name would probably have been *Penconisiog*, but later forms show the influence of ***caer*** and then ***carn*** (both influenced by the existence of a burial chamber to the north-west). Colloquial local pronunciation is frequently Gnisiog.

PENCARREG Carm SN5345

'stone headland', ***pen***, ***carreg***

Penkarreck 1291, *Pencarrik* 1331, *Pencarrek* 1424, *p. kareg* c.1566

The village lies on the slopes of a low hill. Blaencarreg is about a mile east near the source (***blaen***) of a small stream.

PENCELLI Brec SO0925

'end of a grove', ***pen***, ***celli***

Penkelly, *Penkelli* 1233 (late 13cent.), *Penkethly* 1310-11

The name of a castle (*kastell peñ kelli* 1215 [c.1400]), which also became the name of a lordship (to which some of the forms may refer), in the commote of Tir Ralff (*Tyraph* 1292, *Tyrrauf* 1294, 'land belonging to Ralff', ***tir***, pers.n. Ralff) and of several manors including English Pencelli and Welsh Pencelli (*P(enkelly) Anglican*, ~ *Wallens* 1521-22, *Penkellye Wallenses alias ye Welche Penkelly* 1651).

PEN CEMAIS see **CEMAIS HEAD**

PEN-CLAWDD[1] Glam SS5495

'end of the ditch', ***pen***, ***clawdd***

Penyclawdd 1650, *Penclauth or Kevenbuchan* 1688, *Penclawdd* 1729

This may also be the *Penclau* in the name of *Nicholas de Penclau* (1199) with early loss of final -dd. It may refer to the ditches of the Iron Age fort Pen-y-gaer. Cefnbychan (*Cefn Bychan* 1719, ***cefn***, ***bychan***) refers to a long ridge south of Pen-clawdd.

PEN-CLAWDD[2] see **PEN-Y-CLAWDD**

PENCOED Glam ST9581

'top of the wood', ***pen, coed***

Pencoyt 1149-83, *Pencoyd* 1415, *Pencoit* 1536-9

A largely modern village which developed in the 19cent. along the Bridgend-Llantrisant road. ***coed*** is a very common el. in the area, and the village stands in Coety (q.v.) near the south-eastern slopes of the hill Cefn Hirgoed (***cefn, hir, coed***) and north-east of several farms Coedymwstwr Ganol, Isaf and Uchaf and Torcoed. Convention requires Pen-coed but usage favours Pencoed.

PENCRAIG see **OLD RADNOR**

PENDERYN Brec SN9409

'bird's head', ***pen, aderyn*** var. ***ederyn***

Spemederm 1281, *Pennyderyn* 1291, *Penederyn* 1372

The name probably refers to some apparently bird-like topographical feature such as the hill Foel Penderyn. It was once believed (but now not widely accepted) that such an allusion may have had some totemic significance such as placing an animal's head on a pole to mark a place of assembly (cf. Pentyrch Glam).

PENDINE, PENTYWYN Carm SN2208

'headland by a fort', 'headland above the sea-shore', ***pen, din, tywyn***

(*terra*) *Pentewy* 1125-48, *Lann teliau penntÿuinn* 1136-54, *penntiwin* 1126, *Pendyn* 1307, *Pendyne* 1544, *pendyn* c.1566, *Pendine* 1672, *Pendein* 1710, *Pendain* 1814

From its location extending down a slope to the sea. Although the two names have long been regarded as alternatives somehow related phonologically, it has been argued that the names refer to distinct topographical features, the sea-shore (***tywyn***) and a fort (***din***) although there is no record of a fortress here. The modern pronunciation Pendine or Pen-dein (seen in the late historical forms, and represented in some by E -y-) is an E re-interpretation of *-din* and is adopted by W and E speakers. Cf. Pen-llin. Pentywyn may well be an antiquarian revival since there is no documentary evidence of *Pentywyn* after the 13cent. when forms in W sources tend to favour *Pen-din* or *Pen-dein* (which could easily be much earlier than 13cent.). The church is dedicated to Teilo (as in the 1136-54 form).

PENEGOES Mont SH7701

'top of the leg', ***pen, y, coes***

Pennegoys early 13cent., *Penegees* 1254, *Penegos* 1291, *Penegoes* 1293, *Pennegos* c.1575, *Pennegois* 1578-9

coes 'leg' is sometimes used to mean 'long, narrow land with a slight bend like a leg'. Here, the village lies on a terrace between a hill and Afon Crewi. Shift of final stress to the penultimate stress of Penygoes has caused -y- > -e-; cf. Bach-y-graig > Bachegraig Flints. Antiquarians gave Penegoes a fictitious, alternative name Llangadfarch, from the church dedication to Cadfarch, while others allege a bogus Egoes.

PEN-FFORDD Pemb SN0722
'top of the road', ***pen***, (*y*), ***ffordd***
Park pen y ffordd c.1773, *Penfurth* 1805, *Penffordd* 1814
On a low hill at the junction of four lanes. The first form may refer to a farm Parc-y-drain near the south side of the village.

PENFFORDD-LAS see **STAYLITTLE**

PENFRO see **PEMBROKE**

PENGAM Monm ST1597
'crooked head', ***pen***, ***cam***
Pengam 1859, *Pengam, or Pontaberpengam* 1860
The 'crooked head' could describe a large stone or more likely the twisting course of a stream and valley since Pengam takes its name directly from a former farm near a large bend in the river Rhymni, and is common in house names and field names in Glam and Monm. It is a large industrial village which developed on both sides of a bridge Pont Aber Pengam or Pont Pengam (*Pont y manpengam* 1704, *Pont a Pengam* 1716, *Pontar Pengam* c.1790, *Tir Pont Pengam, Pont Aber Pengam* 1813, *Pont pengam* 1815, *Pontmaenpengam* 1851) over the river Rhymni. Forms vary so much that the bridge may be named either from its location near an unidentified stone (***maen***) as in the 1704 and 1851 forms or from its proximity to the ***aber*** of the river Rhymni and an unidentified stream (perhaps the later named Nant Cascade) just below the bridge or a very small stream, now culverted, in the middle of the village. This is probably *Nant Pengam* 1873 but this name may be drawn directly from that of the village. Earlier forms with *a* (1716) and *ar* (c.1700) could be reduced forms of *-aber-*.

PENGENFFORDD Brec SO1730
'end of the ridgeway', ***pen***, (*y*), ***cefnffordd***
Pen-y-genffordd 1832
This may also be *Geuffordd* 1760 if *-u-* represents *-n-*. Near Genffordd (*Genffordd* 1801) and two farms *Genffordd uchaf* 1819 and *Genffordd-isaf* 1832. The ridgeway is the old road running south-east from Talgarth up a steep ridge to the pass at Pengenffordd. ***cefn*** is sometimes found as cen- or cyn- (cf. Gendros Glam with ***rhos*** and Cyncoed Monm with ***coed***).

PENGELLI see **GROVESEND**

PENGORFFWYSFA Angl SH4692

'top of the resting-place', ***pen, gorffwysfa***

Pengorphwysfa 1818, *Pen gorphwysfa* 1838

The highest point on the road from Pen-y-sarn to Llaneilian on the side of Mynydd Eilian.

PENGWERN Flints SJ0176

'marsh-end', ***pen, gwern***

Pengnernen 1291, *Penguern* 1439, *Pengwern* 1450

The modern Pengwern Hall and Farm are on slightly higher ground in low-lying land between Bodelwyddan and the confluence of the rivers Elwy and Clwyd south of Rhuddlan. The 1291 description of the location as *Insula Pengnernen* suggests a possible ***gwernen*** 'alder-tree', perhaps a grove of alders within a marsh or swamp; the nearby Sarn Wood (***sarn*** 'causeway') may help explain the terrain.

PENHOW, PEN-HW Monm ST4290

'(place at the) ridge', W ***pen***, OE ***hōh***

Penhou 1130-9, *Penho* 1254, *Penhow* 1306, 1712, *Penhoo* 1363, *pen hw* c.1566

The first el. probably refers to a small, steep-sided hill on the south side of the village. The second el. is probably OE ***hōh*** 'projecting ridge' but in its dat. form ***hō*** 'place at the ridge' (cf. Hoe Hampshire, Norfolk). It seems likely that the castle built 'at the ridge' was described as 'Hoe' and the W inhabitants added the tautologous 'Pen'.

PEN-HW see **PENHOW**

PENIEL Denb SJ0363

biblical chapel n.

Peniel 1837

The chapel was built in 1837.

PENISA'R-WAUN Caern SH5563

'lower end of the moor' ***pen, isaf, yr, gwaun***

Penisarwain 1851

The old name of the area to the east of the present village was *Waen Wineu* (1808), *Waun Wynau* (1816) with ***gwinau*** 'reddish brown, dark brown', while to the north was *Waun fawr* (1816) with ***mawr***. The village is also at the lower end of Gwaun Gynfi (in terms of altitude). See Deiniolen.

PENLEY, LLANNERCH BANNA Flints SJ4139

'clearing of Penda', pers.n. ***Penda***, OE ***lēah***, W ***llannerch***

Pendele 1300, *Pendelegh* 1314, *Pendley* 1333, *Pendelei* 1347, *Penley* 1492; *Lannerpanna* 1270, *Llannerghpanna* 1381, *Llannerchpanna* 1383, *Llanerchbanna* 1430

Panna is a W development of Penda (probably via a form *Pantha*) and may have been consciously substituted for Penda, as ***llannerch*** was for ***lēah***. Both ***lannerch*** and ***lēah*** imply 'clearing' but both also evolved to mean 'pasture'. Penda's identity is unknown, but he is popularly believed to be the 7cent. king Penda of Mercia. Panna also appears as a r.n. in the area (*Panna* 1347).

PENLLECH Caern SH2234

'capstone', ***penllech***

Penllec 1254, *Penllegh* 1381, *penllech* 1490-1, *Penllech* 1636

The Cefn Amwlch cromlech (occasionally called Coetan Arthur) near Coed y Gromlech has a large rectangular capstone, and is over half-a-mile nearer the sea than Penllech village between Cefn Amwlch and Traeth Penllech near Plas-ym-Mhenllech. Although ***penllech*** has not hitherto been treated as a separate el., its existence here and at Benllech Angl seem to justify an el. independent of ***pen*** 'head' and ***llech*** 'stone'.

PENLLE'R-GAER Glam SS6198

'end of the site of the fort', ***pen, lle, y, caer***

Penllergeer 1608, *Penller gâr* 1650, *Pen lle yr gaer* 1665, *Penllargare* 1694, *Penllergare* 1729

A late 19cent. industrial village on the site of *The Camp* 1884 next to Gorseinon Common. Originally a house name, it is one of several similar names in Glam such as Penlle'r-castell, Penlle'r-bebyll (***pebyll***), Penlle'r-fedwen (***bedwen***) and Penlle'r-neuadd (***neuadd***); but Penlle'r-brain Swansea is ***pen, tyle*** 'hill', ***y, brain*** 'crows'. On the 1694 and 1729 forms and the modern pronunciation cf. Gelli-gaer and Aberdare.

PEN-LLIN, PENLLINE Glam SS9776

'flax headland', ***pen, llin***

Pendelino 1208, *Penthlin* c.1262, 1401, *Penllin* 1403, *pen llin* c.1566

Frequently spelt *Penlline* from 16cent. probably to represent the long -i-, but may also have led to the modern anglicized pronunciation as if E ***line***. W language sources generally have Pen-llin, Penllin. There has been confusion with ***llyn*** 'lake', supposed to be a feature in the valley of the nearby river Ddawan, and modern maps have adopted the erroneous spelling Penllyn. The 'headland' is probably the promontory on which the castle stands.

PENLLINE see **PEN-LLIN**

PENMACHNO Caern SH7950

'uplands of Machno', ***pennant***, pers.n. ***Machno***

Pennan 1247, *Pennanmachno* 1254, *Pennant Machno* 1301-2, *Penanmaghno* 1335, *Penmaghno* 1514, *Pennamachno* 1527-8, *Penmachno* 1650

The uplands associated with the unidentified Machno were probably at Cwm Penmachno (near the source of the river Machno at Blaen-y-cwm) some three miles from the village of Penmachno. The original name of the uplands, Pennant Machno, was eventually shortened to Penmachno (through the phonological stages evidenced in the historical forms) reinforcing the transfer of Machno from a pers.n. to the r.n. Afon Machno (*Machno* 1662).

PENMAEN DEWI see **ST DAVID'S HEAD**

PENMAENMAWR Caern SH7176

'great stone headland', ***penmaen, mawr***

Penmayne mawre 1473-4, *Penmain Vaure, Penmayne Maur* 1536-9, *Penman-maure* 1698, *Penmaen mawr* 1795, *Penmaen-mawr* 1838

The prominent headland became the focus for much granite quarrying and the associated growth of the village. The considerably lower mountain nearer Conwy was Penmaen-bach (*penmen byghan* 1499, *Penmaen Bach* 1795) with ***bychan*** and ***bach***. Standardized orthography requires Penmaen-mawr (to conform with final stress) but prevailing usage favours Penmaenmawr.

PENMAEN-PŴL Mer SH6918

'pool at Penmaen', p.n. ***Penmaen***, E ***pool***

Penmaen Pool 1838

The pool is a wide section of Afon Mawddach with its low-lying land bounded by two roads and a linking toll road. To the south is a prominent outcrop (***penmaen***) which was the location of *Penmaen*, now Craig y Castell. The W name of the pool was Llyn y Penmaen (*Llyn y penmaen* 1796, *Llynypenmaen* 1860). The ascendancy of E ***pool*** is ascribed to the station and the popularity of the area for tourism, particularly Fairbourne and Barmouth. Commonly also Penmaenpool.

PEN-MARC, PENMARK Glam ST0568

'stallion's headland', ***pen, march***

Penmarc 1173-83, *Penmark* 1254, *Penmarc* c.1262, *pen mark* c.1566

If it is ***march***, the absence of spellings with -ch (except a solitary and doubtful *Penmarch* 13cent.) suggests an early replacement by -c/-k under

E influence. Its location is on a bluff (overlooking the river Waycock) probably with some topographical association with a stallion's head. A ritual or ceremonial meaning has been suggested for a stallion head, to mark a meeting place. There is a Penmarch in Pemb and a Penmarc'h in Brittany.

PENMARK see **PEN-MARC**

PENMON Angl SH6380

'tip of Môn', ***pen, Môn***

Penmo(n)n 1237 (1295), *Penmon* 1238 (1295), *Penmôn* 1795, *Pen-mon* 1838

The promontory at the north-east corner of Angl (Môn) was known for the Augustinian priory there (and the associated settlement on Ynys Seiriol or Priestholm). A nearby farm is named Pentir (***pentir*** 'headland') and there are several rocky headlands (***trwyn***), such as Trwyn Dinmor and Trwyn Du (popularly called Trwyn Penmon).

PENMORFA Caern SH5440

'end of the sea-marsh', ***pen, morfa***

Penmorva 1505, *Penmorfa* 1685-6

The estuary of Afon Glaslyn was extensive sea-marsh (Traeth Mawr), one branch of which extended west through Glan-y-morfa to Penmorfa. The whole area was later reclaimed after the building of the Cob at Porthmadog.

PENMYNYDD Angl SH5074

'mountain top', ***pen, mynydd***

Penniminit 1254, *Penmynyth* 1383, *Penmynydd* 1685-6

This was the highest point on the route between Menai Bridge and Llangefni (and which became the old coach road). The 1254 form (in a reference to the church dedicated to Gredifael) probably included ***y*** 'the', 'top of the mountain'.

PENNAL Mer SH7000

'moor headland', ***pen, hâl***

Penhal 1254, *Penhale* 1292-3, *Pennall* 1543, *Pennal* 1771

The headland is the high ground north-east of Pennal overlooking the meandering Afon Dyfi and its wide flats. Another el. ***hâl*** 'salt' has been suggested, since, despite now being a half mile from the estuary of Afon Dyfi, high tides did reach Afon Pennal (as the 1871 map shows) and Roman ships are believed to have had trade access up Afon Dyfi south of Pennal village.

PENNANT[1] Card SN5163

'the head of the valley', (*y*), ***pennant***

y-pennant 1640, *y pennant, Pennant* 1652, *Pen-'nant* 1836

The village is located in the upper reaches or uplands of Afon Arth and probably evolved around the mill (*Tir-y-velin alias Tir-y-pennant* 1640, *Melyn y pennant* 1652, *Tyr y velin o. Tyr y pennant* 1755, *Felin Cwm* 20cent.) with ***tir*** and ***melin***.

PENNANT[2] Denb SH8759

'head of the valley', ***pennant***

Pennant Gwytherin 14cent., *Pennanth lugeyn* 1334, *Pennant Llygvy* 1574, *Pennant* 1734-5

In common with several ***pennant*** names, the second defining el. has disappeared, here the parish name Gwytherin (q.v.) and the stream Llugwy (q.v.).

PENNANT MELANGELL Mont SJ0226

'head of the valley of Melangell', ***pennant***, pers.n. ***Melangell***

Pennant c.1160, *Penant Mellagel* 1291, *Pennant' Monachorum* 1293, *Pennant Malankith* 1482, *Pennant Melanghelth* 1559, *pênant mallangell* c.1566

The 5cent. Melangell was reputedly a daughter of Cyfwlch and a contemporary of Brochwel Ysgithrog. The latinized *Monacella* probably accounts for the 1293 *Monachorum* 'of the monks'. However, Pennant Melangell was certainly a place of pilgrimage in 1526 and a shrine of *St Monacella* was recorded in 1778-81.

PENPARCAU Cards SN5880

'top of the fields', ***pen***, (*y*), ***parc*** pl. ***parc(i)au***

Pen y Parkiau 1756, *Penyparcau* 1811, *Penparke* 1813, *Penparkey* 1816, *Pen Parciau* 1834, *Pen-y-parcau* 1890, *Pen-y-parciau* 1890

The area which overlooked fields between Afon Rheidol and the major road south of Aberystwyth, now extensively developed for housing. Several forms record the dial. pl. ***parc(i)e*** while the anglicized 1816 form can still be heard.

PENPERLLENNI Monm SO3204

?'hill at Pellenni', ***pen***, p.n ***Pellenni***

Pen-pwllenni 1833

The first el. is almost certainly ***pen*** in the sense 'hill' since it lies on a low hill. The second el. refers to the manor and wood of Pellenni which includue the parish of Goetre in which Penperlleni lies and perhaps parts of Monkswood (q.v.) about two miles to the south-east. Pellenni (*Pethllenny* 1148-70 [1330], *Pethelenny* 1307, *Pellenny* 1349) may be ***pellen*** pl. ***pellenni*** 'round mass, globe' used of an area of round hills.

The current Penperllenni had been influenced by ***perllan***, pl. ***perllenni*** 'orchard'.

PEN-PONT Brec SN9728

'bridge end', ***pen, pont***

Penpont 1223-5, *Penponte* 1536

The bridge spans the river Usk. It was the location of a former chapel-of-ease Capel Betws (*Chapelle of Bettus* 1547, *Capelbettus* 1578, ***capel, betws***).

PENRHERBER Carm SN2939

'above the arbour', ***pen, yr, herber***

Penrherber 1811, *Pen'r-herber* 1831

The third el. is almost certainly ***herber*** 'garden, herb-garden, arbour, orchard, shelter' which occurs in this immediate area as *Yr Herber 1785*, and a house recorded as *Dan-yr-herber* 1831 (but also called *Danyrhelig* 1811, *Dan-yr-helyg* 1891, ***helyg*** 'willows') a little further down the slope below (***dan***) Penrherber towards Newcastle Emlyn. Elsewhere ***herber*** occurs in Park yr Herber (in nearby Llandyfrïog Carm), Pen-y-herber (near Castell Caereinion Mont) and Rherber (Llanwenog Card) where it is probably a shelter for animals. Also referred to as Penyrherber.

PENRHIW-CEIBR Glam ST0597

'hilltop by the beamed branches', ***pen, rhiw, ceibr***

Rhiw'r Kibier 1748, *Rhyw Kibyr* 1771-81, *Penrhiwceibyr* 1784, *Penrhiw'rceibir* 1788

ceibr 'beams' is probably used to indicate a thick arched covering of branches reputedly the avenue of trees on the Llanwynno-Glyn Cynon road which looked like the joists of a house. ***ceibr*** is also recorded in Llandybïe in 1732 to describe rafters or *Kibers* used in constructing the church porch, and it has been argued that Penrhiw-ceibr was a suitable location for cutting joists or beams. Several forms retained the def.art. which was ultimately lost in the modern form.

PENRHIW-GOCH Carm SN5518

'top of the red hill', ***pen, (y), rhiw, coch***

Penyrhiwgoch 1813, *Pen-rhiw-goch* 1831, *Penrhiwgoch* 1839

On a low watershed between two slopes and two streams above the valley of the river Tywi, in contrast to Troed-rhiw-goch (*Troed-y-rhiw-goch* 1831, *Troedrhiwgoch* 1895, ***troed*** 'foot').

PENRHIW-LLAN Card SN3641

'church hilltop', ***pen, rhiw, llan***

Penrhiwllan 1815, *Penrhiw-llan* 1831

The church (of Mair) is at Llanfair Orllwyn less than a mile to the south. The hill adjoins Troedrhiw-llan (***troed*** 'foot').

PENRHIWPÂL Card SN3445

'hilltop at the pale', ***pen, rhiw, pâl***

Penrhiwpal 1811, *Penrhiw-pale* 1819, *Penrhiw-pâl* 1834, *Pen-rhiw-pal* 1891

A pale (a row of stakes or posts) marking a boundary of a hunting park (*Park y Pâl* 1787).

PENRHOS[1] Angl SH2781

'moor headland', ***penrhos***

Penros Bradwen 1522, *Penrhos Bradwen alias Penrhos Isa* 1629, *Penrhos brydwen* 1795, *Penrhos brodwen* 1838

The older meaning of ***rhos*** (and its cognates in Breton, Cornish and Ir) seems to have been 'headland, promontory, spur', with later developments referring more specifically to the vegetation to mean 'moor' (the modern meaning of ***rhos*** in W). There are several examples of Penrhos in Angl minor names in headland locations, pointing to ***rhos*** 'headland'. With the semantic shift from 'headland' to 'moor' the addition of ***pen*** reinforced the original meaning of 'headland'. On this evidence, ***penrhos*** 'moor headland' qualifies as a p.n. el. in its own right. The identity of Bradwen is unknown. The 1629 *Isa* (***isaf*** 'lower') probably distinguishes it from *Penrhose ucha alias Penrhosyfeilw* (1695, ***uchaf*** 'upper'), today's Penrhosfeilw west of Holyhead.

PENRHOS[2] Caern SH3434

'moor headland', ***penrhos***

Penros 1335, *Penrhos* 1763

See Penrhos[1].The moorland was west of Pwllheli, with several streams on either side of Penrhos. Afon Penrhos flows into the sea at Pwllheli.

PEN-RHOS[1] Brec SN7911

'end of the moor', ***pen, rhos***

Pen-rhôs 1891

Named from a farm (*Penrhose* 1729, 1829) on moorland on the west slopes adjacent Mynydd y Drum.

PEN-RHOS[2] Monm SO4111

'end of the moor headland', ***pen, rhos***

Panrox 1186, *Penros* 1196, *Ecclesia beati Caddoci de penros* 1193-99, *Lancaddoc Penros* c.1348, *Penrhos* 1588

The village stands at the end of a short ridge. Although the form *Penrhos* (with final stress) might have been expected (as in Penrhos[1,2] q.v.), ***rhos*** 'moor' has been the predominant influence on its later development. Forms for 1285 and c.1348 have the pers.n. Cadog but *Llangadog* did not establish itself as the name of the parish.

PENRHOSLLUGWY Angl SH4886

'moor headland at Llugwy', ***penrhos***, r.n. ***Llugwy***

Penros 1291-2, *Penros* 1352, *Penrhôs* 1795, *Penrhos-lligwy* 1838

On the meaning of ***penrhos*** see Penrhos[1]. The moor extended from the lower slopes of Mynydd Bodafon towards the Moelfre promontory and the bay of Traeth Llugwy. The river Llugwy (commonly Lligwy) flowed through the moor (*Rhos Lligwy*) which has also been used of the village.

PENRHYN BAY Denb SH8281

'promontory', ***penrhyn***, E ***bay***

Penruyn 1352, *Penryn* 1455, *Penrhyn* 1763, *Penrhyn Bay* c.1900

Penrhyn was the name of the promontory east of Llandudno Bay, now Little Orme (q.v.). Penrhyn is now the name of the bay and associated modern development to the east of the promontory. The adjacent area is Penrhyn-side (q.v.).

PENRHYN-COCH Card SN6484

'red headland', ***penrhyn***, ***coch***

Penrhyn Coch 1760, *Penrhyn-coch* 1837

The village is situated on a ridge between two rivers (Afon Stewy and Nant Seilo). At the eastern end of the village is Garth ('ridge'). ***coch*** may refer to bracken but can also signify land which is exposed to the sun and dries out quickly.

PENRHYNDEUDRAETH Mer SH6139

'promontory between two beaches', ***penrhyn***, ***dau***, ***traeth***

Penrindeudrait 1292-3, *Penryn Devdraeth* 1457, *penryn deydraith* 1570, *Penrhyndeudraeth* 1699

The two strands are Traeth Mawr (*Traitmaur* 1194, ***mawr***) and Traeth Bach (*Traitbochan* 1191, ***bach***) where the two rivers Glaslyn and Dwyryd flow on either side of Penrhyndeudraeth and into the Dwyryd estuary (formerly within the parish of Llanfihangel-y-traethau, pl. ***traethau***). The enclosure of Traeth Mawr and the building of the embankment to create the port of Porthmadog greatly altered the extent of the estuary.

PENRHYN GŴYR see **WORM'S HEAD**

PENRHYN-SIDE Caern SH8181

'land beside the promontory', ***penrhyn***, E ***side***

Penrhyn-side 1891

The modern Penrhyn-side, to the east of Penrhyn Bay (q.v.), developed in association with tourism and the popularity of the resorts at Llandudno and Llandrillo. The addition of ***-side*** is also seen in the nearby Craigside (probably referring to Craig-y-don, ***craig*** 'rock', ***ton*** 'wave'). Sometimes in W as Yr Ochr, or Ochr y Penrhyn (***ochr*** 'side').

PEN-RHYS see **PENRICE**

PENRICE, PEN-RHYS Glam SS4987

'hill of ?Rhys', ***pen***, ?pers.n. ***Rhys***

Penres 1282, *Penrys* 1347, *Pen Rys* c.1566, *Penrice* 1670

Two other places with identical names are Penrhys near Port Talbot and Penrhys in Rhondda (*Penryce* 1535). In all three cases, ***pen*** seems to refer to hills (despite fanciful tales of lost heads and battles), but there has been no reliable identification of Rhys or a satisfactory alternative explanation of -rhys (despite efforts to identify with an OW el. meaning 'glory, power' in the sense of a prominent hill). Penrice stands on a small hill overlooking Oxwich Bay. Another suggestion is that the word is somehow related to ***rhysfa*** 'sheepwalk'.

PEN-SARN[1] Angl SH4690

'end of the causeway', ***pen***, ***(y)***, ***sarn***

Pensarn 1812, *Penysarn* 1820, *Pen-sarn* 1838, *Pensarn* 1891, *Penysarn* 1997

The causeway, probably near the centre of the present village, was formerly known as Sarn yr Offeiriad Du (*Sarn y Feiriad Dy* 1612) 'causeway of the black priest', perhaps a reference to the priory at Llaneilian. The first houses were located on Rhos Sarn yr Offeiriad Du (*Rhos sarn Offeiriad du* 1839). The full name was probably 'Pen-sarn-yr-offeiriad-du'. While colloquial usage favours Pen-sarn, forms with the def.art. ***y*** are common.

PEN-SARN[2] Denb SH9578

'end of the causeway', ***pen***, (***y***), ***sarn***

pen y Sarn c.1700, *Pen-y-sarn* 1840, *Pen-sarn* c.1880

Crossing the marsh of Morfa Rhuddlan was facilitated by a causeway close to the sea. This route was later flanked by the holiday development of Towyn and Kinmel Bay.

PEN-SARN[3] Mer SH5828

'end of the causeway', ***pen***, (***y***), ***sarn***

Pen y sarn hir 1636, *Penysarnhîr* 1795, *Pen-y-sarn* 1838

The road from Harlech to Llanbedr passes through several tracts of low-lying sandy ground. One was the stretch of road known as Sarn Hir (*the causey called Y Sarn-hir* 1761, *Sarn Hir, Sarn-hir* 1765, ***hir*** 'long') adjacent to Morfa Mawr (***morfa*** 'sea-marsh', ***mawr***). Pen-sarn is at the northerly end of Sarn Hir.

PENTIR Caern SH5766

'headland', ***pentir***

Pentyr 1306-7, *Pentere* 1484, *Pentir* 1544

The village stands at what was the furthest southerly extent (from

Bangor) of the bishop of Bangor's lands (with his ***maenol*** 'demesne' seen in the name of the Faenol estate). Pentir is also used of the parish whose church was Llangedol (*Pentire alias Llangedol* 1763) dedicated to Cedol.

PENTRAETH Angl SH5278

'end of the beach', ***pen, traeth***

Pentrayth 1254, *Pentreth* 1352, *Pentraeth* 1639

Pentraeth is at the head of the narrow valley through which the river Nodwydd (***nodwydd*** 'needle') flows into the sea at Traeth Coch (q.v.). During the Middle Ages the area was also called *Betws Geraint* and *Llanfair Betws Geraint* (allegedly associated with a 13cent. Geraint).

PENTRE[1] Denb SJ2840

'village', ***pentref***

Pentre 1838

An industrial settlement developed in association with the *Black Park* coalpits and later with the *Pen-y-bont Brick and Tile Works* nearby and with the industries across the river Dee (via Newbridge) in Cefn-mawr.

PENTRE[2] Mont SO0686

'top of the township', ***pen, tref***

Pentref 1817, *Pentre* 1891

pentref 'village' is inappropriate for such a small settlement. The hamlet of Pentre lies at the southern, hilly part of the parish of Mochdre Mont (q.v.) above the parish church and village of Mochdre.

PENTRE-BACH[1] Card SN5547

'little village', ***pentref, bach***

Pentre Shon 1803, *Pentre bach* 1811, *Pentre-bach* 1834

A hamlet on the road between Lampeter and Llanwnnen. The identity of Shon is unknown. Pentre-bach may have developed in connection with the quarries between Pentre-bach and Llanwnnen.

PENTRE-BACH[2] Glam SN6005

'little village', ***pentref, bach***

Pentrebach 1814, *Pentre-bach* 1832

It was small perhaps in contrast to Pontarddulais.

PENTREBERW Angl SH4772

'village in Berw', ***pentref***, tnshp n. ***Berw***

y Plas y merw 1565-87, *Pentre Berŵ* 1795, *Pentre Berw* 1838, *Pentre-berw* 1891

A village which developed at the junction of the Newborough-Ceint and the Menai Bridge-Holyhead roads in the medieval tnshp of Berw (*berwe* 1319, *Berrow* 1612, ***berwr*** 'cress' or ***berw*** 'waterfall'). An inn at the crossroads bore the arms of the Holland family of Plas Berw (built in 1615 by Sir Thomas Holland on the site of an earlier house built by Ithel ap Howell of Berw c.1480). The inn name Holland Arms is frequently used as a local alias for Pentreberw but the name has no official status.

PENTRE-BONT see **LLANFARIAN**

PENTRECELYN Denb SJ1453

'Cuhelyn's farm', ***pentref***, pers.n. ***Cuhelyn***

pentre kvhelvn 1550-1600, *pentre kyhelyn* 1556-64,
Pentre Kaie Heilin 1657, *Pentre Kae Heylyn…an Kyhelyn?* c.1700,
Pentrecaehelyn 1811, *Pentre-celyn* 1838

Although Cuhelyn was once a fairly common pers.n. it seems to have been replaced in people's perceptions by ***cae*** and the pers.n. ***Heilyn*** (although the c.1700 record does doubt its authenticity). It was further supplanted by association with ***celyn*** 'holly'.

PENTRE-CHWYTH Glam SS6695

'windy village', ***pentref, chwyth***

Pentrechwith 1818, *Pentre* 1884, *Pentrechwyth* 1908, *Pentre-chwyth* 1920

From its exposed location on the lower slopes of Kilvey Hill; cf. Cold Blow Pemb (q.v.). At one time, it also appears to have borne the alternative name *Grenfell Town* after its builder Pascoe Grenfell. However, it has been suggested that the el. is ***chwith*** 'left' in the sense 'dark, forbidding, sinister'; cf. Gwernllwynchwith Llansamlet Glam (*Gwern llwyn whith* late 18cent., *Wernllynwith* 1792, ***gwern*** 'alder-grove', ***llwyn*** 'brake, thicket').

PENTRECLWYDAU Glam SN8405

'village near streams called Clwyd', ***pentref***, r.n. ***Clwyd***

Pentreclwyd 1814, *Pentre-clwyda* 1833, *Pentre-clwydau* 1884

-clwydau is probably pl. referring to two streams both called Clwyd. The name survives in Nant Clwyd (*Clwyd vawre* 1657), the stream which rises at *Blaenclwyd* 1814 (***blaen***) above Craig Clwyd and passes through the hamlet to the river Nedd at Aberclwyd (*Aber Clwyd* 1675), and in Clwyd Fechan (*Clwyd vechan* 1657, now Rheola Brook) which rises near Craig Clwyd Fechan and flows into Nedd about half-a-mile below Aberclwyd. The r.ns Clwyd may be identical to the r.n. Clwyd in Denb and Flints, signifying a river named after a ford protected by a hurdle (***clwyd***).

PENTRE-CWRT Carm SN3838

'village near the court', ***pentref, cwrt***

Pentrecwrt 1875, *Pentre-cwrt* 1891

A village which developed near Cwrt mill (*Cwrt Mill* 1811), the farm Waun-cwrt (*Waun* 1811, ***gwaun*** 'moor') and the house Cwrt (*Cwrt* 1811, *Cwrt-manfor-wylon* 1831) otherwise Maenor Forion (*Maynoruorion* 1309,

Manervorian 1535, *Courtmanarborion* 1562, ***maenor***, pers.n. ?***Borion***) a grange of Whitland abbey.

PENTREDŴR[1] Denb SJ1946

'water village', ***pentref, dŵr***

Pentre-dwfr 1838, *Pentre-dŵr* 1884

Located where a stream from Oernant runs into Afon Eglwyseg, the village probably developed in association with several quarries nearby. To the north is Bryn yr Odyn ('hill of the kiln', ***odyn***).

PENTREDŴR[2] Glam SS6996

'water village', ***pentref, dŵr***

Pentredwr 1799, *Pentre-dwr* 1832

Near Crymlyn Bog.

PENTREFELIN[1] Denb SH1524

'the mill village', ***pentref, yr, melin***

Pentre yr felin 1740, *Pentre Felin* 1819, *Pentre-felin* 1838, *Pentrefelin* 2000

The mill was on Afon Lleiriog which passes under the Llanrhaeadr-ym-Mochnant road. The def.art. is no longer used.

PENTREFELIN[2] Denb SH8074

'the mill village', ***pentref, yr, melin***

Pentre-felin 1838, *Pentrer-felin* 1879

The village appears to be associated with a mill at the confluence of two streams. In fact, two mills are recorded later (*Felin-uchaf* and *Felin-isaf* 1871, ***uchaf*** 'upper', ***isaf*** 'lower'). The 1879 form seems to refer specifically to one of them (***yr*** 'the') but the def.art. is no longer used.

PENTREFELIN[3] Caern SH5239

'the mill village', ***pentref, yr, melin***

Pentre felin 1891, *Pentre-felin* 1898, *Pentre'r-felin* 1947

The first mill built in 1680 was called Melin Aberdowarch (***tywarch*** 'sod, turf') or Felin y Tywysog (***tywysog*** 'prince', indicating a crown mill) erected at Garreg y Felin, and was demolished in 1820 (with its ruins below the road) to enable the building of a new mill (*Y Felin newydd* 1816) half-a-mile downstream (originally Afon Melin Gest now Afon Cedron). The def.art. is no longer used.

PENTREFOELAS Denb SH8751

'village near Foelas', ***pentref***, p.n. ***Foelas***

Pentre vidog chappel 1680, *Pentre vidog* 1740, *Capel Voelas* 1801, *Capel Voelas* 1819, *Pentre Voelas* 1838

The original ***pentref*** took its name from the chapel-of-ease called *vidog* *chappel* (from ***bid*** 'quickset hedge' and the adjectival ***-og***). Later, it was named after the mansion Foelas or Hen Voelas (*Voelas* 1838, *Foelas Hall* 1838) which is at the foot of Foel Las (*Voelas* 1199 [1332], *Voylas* 1680), the verdant (***glas***) hill on the bare top (***moel***) of which stands a motte (Yr Hen Foel).

PENTREGALAR Pemb SN1831
'miserable village', ***pentref, galar***
Pentre Galar 1860, *Pentregalar* 1891
In the absence of evidence of a specific social or industrial tragedy, W ***galar*** 'grief, sorrow, mourning' is perhaps used here for a village in an exposed, poor site on east-facing hill-slopes. Also called *Union Inn* 1865 but no inn appears in 1891.

PENTREGÂT Card SN3551
'gate village', ***pentref, gât***
Pentre-gât 1891
The name of the village is recorded as *Capel-gwndwn* in 1834, from the Baptist chapel there (built in 1830), which in turn took its name from the nearby farm Gwndwn (***gwndwn*** 'lay-land, open space'). Eventually, for travellers, the dominant features was the turnpike gate constructed before 1787 (*T.G.* 1834) and the inn (*Gate New Inn* 1843, *New Gate Inn* 1904) although Capel Ffynnon (a Calvinistic Methodist chapel built in 1849) referring to the well (***ffynnon***) in the village has also been used of the village.

PENTREGWENLAIS Carm SN6016
'village near (the stream) Gwenlais', ***pentref***, r.n. ***Gwenlais***
Pentregwenlais 1760, *Pentre Gevenles* 1765, *Pentregwenlas* 1831
Gwenlais 'white stream' (***gwyn*** fem. ***gwen, glais***) is a common r.n.

PENTRE HALKYN, PENTRE HELYGAIN Flints SJ2072
'Halkyn's hamlet', ***pentref***, p.n. ***Halkyn, Helygain***
Pentre Halkin 1805
The established village Halkyn (q.v.) gave its name to a satellite industrial hamlet Pentre Halkyn over a mile away. Possibly workers from Halkyn village found it convenient to establish temporary accommodation nearer to lead mines and quarries on Halkyn Mountain. It may also have housed immigrant workers since a row of cottages built c.1725 is said to have been specifically for miners brought in particularly from Derbyshire. The W form Pentre Helygain is a fairly recent usage for this hamlet.

PENTRE HELYGAIN see **PENTRE HALKYN**

PENTRE-ISAF Denb SH8768
'lower village', ***pentref, isaf***
Pentre 1819, *Pentre-isaf* c.1880
The village is lower down the valley (of Afon Gallen) from Llangernyw.

PENTRE LLANRHAEADR Denb SJ0862
'village near Llanrhaeadr' ***pentref***, p.n. ***Llanrhaeadr***
Pentre 1795, *Pentre Llanrhaeadr* 2000
There are at least two other ***pentref*** names in the vicinity, which probably necessitated the recent differentiation, although Pentre continues to be the local name. This village is less than half-a-mile from Llanrhaeadr.

PENTRE LLWYN-LLWYD Brec SN9654
'village near the grey grove', ***pentref, llwyn, llwyd***
Llwynllwyd 1742, *Pentre-llwyn-llwyd* 1833
Near a farm Brynllwyd (*Bryn-llwyd* 1833, ***bryn***). ***llwyd*** can also refer to a shaded location.

PENTRE-LLYN Card SN6175
'pool village', ***pentref, llyn***
Pentre-llyn 1891
The village is less than half-a-mile from several deep pools in Afon Ystwyth (with two weirs nearby) which is crossed by a bridge (Pen-y-banc Bridge) to the village. The quarry to the south may have been the reason for the village's existence. A house here called Tanllyn (*Dan-llyn* 1834, ***tan*** 'below') refers to its position downstream of the pool which is now a bog.

PENTRELLYNCYMER Denb SH9752
'village of the lake at the confluence', ***pentref, llyn, (y), cymer***
Pentre llyn Cymmer 1812, *Pentre Llyn y cymmer* 1824
The village is located by Llyn y Cymer (*llyn kemer* 13cent. [14cent.], *Llyn y Kymmer* 1506, *llyn y Kymer* 1582, *Llyn y Cymmer* 1670) near the confluence of Afon Alwen and Afon Brenig.

PENTRE MOCH see **NORTHOPHALL**

PENTRE-POETH[1] Monm ST2686
'burnt village', ***pentref, poeth***
Pentre-poeth 1833, 1920
The settlement was either burnt and then rebuilt, or, as is more likely, was on land that had been cleared by burning There are a number of places with this name, several in Glam such as in Llanfedw (*Pentrepoeth* 1721, *Pentref Poth* 1767, *Pentra Poeth* 1795) three miles away, in Llangyfelach (*Pentre- poeth* 1832) and as the W name of Morganstown Glam.

PENTRE-POETH[2] see **MORGANSTOWN**

PENTRE'R EGLWYS see **CHURCH VILLAGE**

PENTRE'R-FELIN Brec SN9230
'the mill village', ***pentref, yr, melin***
Pentreyr Velin 1754, *Pentre-felin* 1832
The site of a mill on the river Cileni.

PENTRE TAFARNYFEDW Denb SH8162
'village near Tafarn-y-fedw', ***pentref***, p.n. ***Tafarn-y-fedw***
Pentre-tafarn-y-fedw c.1880
The tavern Tafarn-y-fedw (*Tavarn y vedw* 1654, *Tavarn y fedw* 1669), identified by the birch tree (***bedw***), is on the main road, where several roads converge just over half-a-mile from Llanrwst. Local tradition maintains that the present chapel stands on the site of the original tavern.

PEN-TWYN Monm ST5209
'top of the hillock', ***pen, twyn***
Pantgwyn 1812, *Pen-twyn* 1831, *Pentwyn* 1871
The village is on a hill overlooking the river Wye. A very common minor p.n. in Monm and Glam. The 1812 form misinterprets the name as ***pant, gwyn***.

PENTRE TŶ-GWYN Carm SN8135
'village near Tŷ-gwyn', ***pentref***, p.n. ***Tŷ-gwyn***
Pentre-ty-gwyn 1832
The village developed near the Calvinistic Methodist chapel built in 1749 near a house called Tŷ Gwyn (***tŷ, gwyn***).

PEN-TYRCH Glam ST1081
'boar's head' or 'hill of boars', ***pen, twrch*** gen. or pl. ***tyrch***
penn tyrch, pentirch 1129 (1160-85), *Pentirech* c.1262, *Pentirch'* c.1348, *Pentyrgh* 1535
The hill may be the actual site of the village, or the hill which extends to Garth Wood or Garth Hill. The latter is particularly steep-sided with some fancied likeness to the shape of a boar's head (***tyrch*** gen. sing.). There may have been associations with boars (***tyrch*** pl.), wild or domesticated, or some other unknown significance.

PENTYWYN see **PENDINE**

PEN-UWCH Card SN5962
'higher end', ***pen, uwch***
Penywch, Penuwch 1678, *Pen Ywch* 1755, *Penuwch* 1834
The higher end of several summits on Mynydd Bach where squatter

settlements encroached on the commons in the early 19cent. It was also the highest end of a detached part of Llanbadarn Odyn.

PEN-Y-BANC Carm SN6124
'top of the bank', ***pen, y, banc***
Penybank 1724, *Penbank* 1753, *Pen-y-banc* 1831
From its location on a lane running east-west over a low bank.

PEN-Y-BONT Radn SO1164
'end of the bridge', ***pen, y, pont***
Pen y Bont 1720, *Penpont Rhyd y cleifion* 1778
The village lies at the east end of a bridge over the river Ieithon, and superseded a *Ponthrydycleifion* c.1757 and *Penpont Rhyd y cleifion* ('ford of the sick people or lepers', ***rhyd, y, cleifion***). On the west side of the river is Dolau Jenkin (*Dole Jenkyn alias lloyn y Clyvyon* 1603 and *Lloyn y Clyvyon* 1714 (with ***llwyn***); ***cleifion*** is also found in two field-names here.

PEN-Y-BONT AR OGWR see **BRIDGEND**

PEN-Y-BONT-FAWR Mont SJ0824
'end of the big bridge', ***pen, y, pont, mawr***
(*o*) *benn y bont* c.1641, *Penybontvaur* 1794, *Pen-y-bont, Pont-fawr* 1838
The bridge is over the river Tanat.

PEN-Y-CAE[1] Brec SN8413
'end of the field', ***pen, y, cae***
Pen-y-cae 1819
Named from a house which preceded the growth of the village in the 19cent.

PEN-Y-CAE[2] Denb SJ2845
'top of the field', ***pen, y, cae***
Pen-y-cae 1838
An industrially associated village south-west of Rhosllannerchrugog.

PEN-Y-CAE-MAWR Monm ST4195
'end of the big field', ***pen, y, cae, mawr***
Pencamawr 1813, *Pen-y-cae-mawr, Cae Mawr Gate* 1830
Cae-mawr is a short distance to the north of the hamlet.

PEN-Y-CLAWDD Monm SO4507
'end of the dyke', ***pen, y, clawdd***
Penetlan (= *Peneclau*) 1254, *Penclau* 1288, *Penclaud* 1314, *Penclauth* 1348, *pen y klawdd* c.1566, *Pen-y-clawdd* 1831
y appears in later forms. The church stands at the end of a ditch. Cf. another Pen-clawdd Glam.

PENYCOEDCAE Glam ST0687

'hill near the hedged field', ***pen, y, coetgae***

Pencoedca 1799, *Pen y Coed-cae* 1833

pen here probably has the sense of 'hill' since the village stands on a hill above a farm Coedcae-du (***du*** 'black, dark'). The var. ***coedcae***, frequently found in various parts of Wales, is evidence of enclosure, a field (***cae***) enclosed by trees (***coed***) or a hedge.

PEN-Y-FFORDD Flints SJ3061

'end of the road', ***pen, y, ffordd***

Pen y ffordh newydh c.1700, *Pen y ford, Penyffordd, Pen y fford* 1797, *Pen-y-ffordd* 1838

The Chester-Bala road was crossed here by the Wrexham-Hawarden route which was no more than a cart track in the 17cent., but with an increase in transport, was improved as *y ffordh newydh* c.1700 ('the new road'). In time ***newydd*** became redundant.

PEN-Y-GARN Carm SN5731

'top of the cairn', ***pen, y, carn***

Pen-y-garn 1831

The name may be taken either directly from some local cairn since a small stream Nant y Garn (*Nant-y-garn* 1811) flows from its west side at Blaen Nant-y-garn to Afon Cothi. The el. ***carn*** is also found in *Y Garn* (1831), the name of a small, pointed hill about a mile south-west of Pen-y-garn.

PENYGARNEDD Mont SJ1023

'top of the mound', ***pen, y, carnedd***

Penygarnedd 1829, *Pen-y-garnedd* 1838

The mound may be the hill between the village and the farm (*Tan-isaf-garnedd* 1838, ***tan*** 'below', ***isaf*** 'lower'). There is currently no evidence of a cairn or a ***carnedd***.

PENYGARREG Reservoir Rad SN8967

'top of the rock', ***pen, y, carreg***, E ***reservoir***

Named from a small farm Penygarreg (*Pen-y-garreg* 1833, *Pen-y-gareg* 1890) just above the north side of the reservoir which was constructed by Birmingham Corporation as part of its Elan valley reservoirs 1892-1903. The rock may refer to a cairn Crugyn Gwyddel (***crugyn*** 'hillock', ***Gwyddel*** 'Irishman', pers.n. ***Gwyddel***, or ***gwyddel*** 'grove, brushwood') on the top of the hill Esgair-pen-y-garreg (***esgair*** 'ridge').

PEN-Y-GRAIG Glam SS9991

'top of the rock', ***pen, y, craig***

Penygraig c.1814, *Pen y graig* 1833, *Pen-y-graig* 1885

A farm name transferred to a colliery (sunk 1858) and to the village.

PEN-Y-GROES[1] Caern SH4653

'top of the crossroads', ***pen, y, croes***

Penygroes 1802, *Pen y Groes* 1816, *Pen-y-groes* 1891

Roads from Carmel, Rhyd-ddu and Pontllyfni cross the main Caernarfon-Porthmadog road at Pen-y-groes.

PEN-Y-GROES[2] Carm SN5813

'top of the crossroads', ***pen, y, croes***

Penagroes 1680, *Pen-y-groes* 1831

At the crossing of the road between Llandybïe and Gors-las road and between Capel Hendre and Castell-y-rhingyll.

PEN-YR-HEOL Monm SO4311

'top of the road', ***pen, yr, heol***

Penyrheol 1895, *Pen-yr-heol* 1920

It lies at the head of four lanes. The one which leads east is *The Waste Road* 1831, the waste possibly being the ***gwaun*** recorded in a farm or cottage *Twyn-y-waun* 1831 (***twyn*** 'mound') near Pen-yr-heol.

PEN-Y-SARN see **PEN-SARN**[1]

PEN-Y-STRYT Denb SJ1951

'end of the street', ***pen, y, stryd*** dial. var. ***stryt***

Pen ŷ Street 1809, *Pen-y-street* 1838, *Pen-y-stryt* 1879

The minor road from Llandegla village crosses the main Bala-Chester road with several houses along it. The dial. var. ***stryt*** is represented in two of the above forms as if it were E ***street***.

PETERSTONE WENTLOOGE, LLANBEDR GWYNLLŴG
Monm ST2680

'village of Peter in Wentlooge', 'church of Pedr in Gwynllŵg',
pers.n. ***Peter, Pedr***, OE ***tūn***, W ***llan***, terr. n. ***Gwynllŵg***

monasterium sancti Petri de Mora 1147-57, *Petriston, (de) Sco' Petro* 1291, *Petresmor* 1295, *St. Peter de la More* 1401, *Petruston* 1470, *Petirston'* 1448, *St. Peter's in the moor* 1533, *Peterstone in the Marshes* 1763, *Peterstone Wentllwg* 1851, *Lampader…in Low-Wenllugh* 1536-9, *ll. beder gwayn llwc* c.1566, *Llanbad or Peterston* 1833

Peterstone is 'settlement near church dedicated to Peter'. The late additional W Gwynllŵg, E Wentlooge, refers to its location in the cantref of Gwynllŵg (*Wenloch* c.1191, *(o) winllyuc* c.1000 (13cent), *Guinnligiauc, gwynllywc* 13cent., *Wenthelehuc* c.1236, *Wentlok alias Wentlouk* 1296, *Wenllok'* 1432, pers.n. Gwynllyw, terr.suff. ***-wg***) the anglicized form of which was probably influenced by Gwent and the E substitution of -tl- for -ll-. Most earlier historic forms describe its position in the moors (OE ***mōr***) and marshes of the low-lying Wentlooge Levels, topography which has introduced ***gwaun*** 'moor' into some forms of Gwynllŵg. The local W form *Llanbad* is shown in 1833 (cf. Peterston-super-Montem).

PETERSTON-SUPER-ELY, LLANBEDR-Y-FRO Glam ST0876
'farm of Peter on (the river) Ely', 'church of Pedr in the Vale',
pers.n. ***Peter, Pedr***, OE ***tūn***, L ***super***, r.n. ***Ely***, W ***llan, y, bro***
Peterston 1291, *Petreston* 1376, *Petriston* c.1376, *Llanpeder* 1536-9,
Peterston upon Elley 1567, *Peterston super Elye* 1595,
Llanbeder y uro 1578, *Llanbedr-ar-y-fro* 1778, *Llanbedrfro* 1818,
Peterston-supr.-Ely or Llanbad arfro 1833
Peterston is 'settlement near the church dedicated to Peter'. The ecclesiastical identity is reinforced by ***llan*** suggesting that the W name (despite its late appearance in historical sources) may well be the original from which Peterston is derived since it lies in an area occupied by E settlers in the Middle Ages. Located near the river Ely (q.v.) and in the Vale of Glamorgan/Bro Morgannwg (frequently referred to simply as Y Fro). Cf. Llanbedr-ar-fynydd/Peterstone-super-montem (*llambet ar Menedd, in English Lambete upon the hill* 1596-1600, *Lanbeder ar vynidd* 1637, *Petrston Chap Super Montem* 1799).

PÎL, Y see **PYLE**

PILLETH, PYLLALAI Radn SO2568
'slope by the pools', OE ***pyll*** oblique ***pylla***, OE ***hlið***
Pelelei 1086, *Pulele* 1142, *Pullelit* c.1270, *Pululith* 1297, (*o*) *bilale* c.1566,
Pilleth (in Bryttysh Pylale) 1573
A difficult name. The first el. seems to be the OE ***pyll*** which is used of a pool in a river, here used in an oblique form such as ***pylla***. Most forms (leading to Pilleth) show the second el. as OE ***hlið*** 'slope' whereas others suggest an alternative form with OE ***lēah*** (an el. cymricized as ***llai*** in several W p.ns in north-east Wales such as Llai and Coed-llai q.v.). This may also be the source of the W name whose modern form is uncertain, with forms indicating Pylallai (with W -ll-) or Pylalai with medial stress, while Pyllalai (again with W -ll-) has been influenced by W ***pwll*** 'pool' pl. ***pyllau***.

PISTYLL Caern SH3242
'spring', ***pistyll***
Pistibus 1254, *Y pistylh* 1352, *Pistill* 1535, *Pystyll* 1763, *Pistyll* 1838
The spring is to be seen between Pistyll Farm and the bay of Porth Pistyll. Beside the church (dedicated to Beuno), the water channel is quite vigorous after heavy rain. It has also been associated with a resting place on the pilgrim route to Bardsey. The 1254 form probably represents L ***pistillus*** from which W ***pistyll*** derived.

PISTYLL RHAEADR Denb/Mont SJ0729

'waterfall on the river Rhaeadr', ***pistyll***, r.n. ***Rhaeadr***

Pistill Rhaiadr, Pestill Rhaider 1781, *Pistyll Rhaiadr* 1795

The dramatic waterfall gave its name to the river Rhaeadr (***rhaeadr*** 'waterfall, cataract, torrent') and the village of Llanrhaeadr-ym-Mochnant (q.v.). In turn, the waterfall itself was distinguished by another word ***pistyll***.

PLWMP Card SN3652

'pump', ***pwmp*** var. ***plwmp***

Plwmp 1891, *Plump* 1953

The el. ***plwmp*** as a var. of ***pwmp*** (as indeed E ***plump*** was a var. of E ***pump***) occurs several times in W p.ns. Originally, Plwmp was the name of a farm on the road-side west of the crossroads, and whose pump provided a convenient source of water for the travellers and animals on the turnpike road. The house was earlier called *Maes-y-crugiau* 1891, a name which also appears as an alias for the village.

PLYNLIMON see **PUMLUMON**

POINT LYNAS, TRWYN EILIAN Angl SH4893

'headland of Eilian', E ***point***, W ***trwyn***, pers.n. ***Eilian***

la baye sancte Elene 1297, *the Creek of St Hillary* 16cent.,
Porth Elian alias Saint Hylarys bay mid 16cent., *Hyllary Point* 1573,
C[ape] Hylary 1646, *Hillary pt* 1693, *Aelianus Point* 1748,
Point Linas 1781, *Aelynys or Hillery Point* 1801, *Point Elianus* 1802,
point Lines 1812, *Point Ælianus* 1818, *Linus Point* 1814,
Point Lynas 1898, *Trwyn Eilian* 20cent.

The headland, and more specifically the name of the lighthouse, near Llaneilian (q.v., especially for the confusion of Eilian and St Hilary), with some of the above forms referring to the associated bay. Eilian was latinized (possibly by cartographers) as *Aelianus* which in maritime usage was contracted to Lynas. Older names were Penrhyn (*Penryn* 1352), Penrhyn y Balog (*Penryn y balok* 1445, ***penrhyn***, ***balog*** 'priest') and Trwyn y Balog (*Trwyn y baloc* 1513, ***trwyn***).

POINT OF AYR, Y PARLWR DU Flints SH1384

'gravel headland', 'the black parlour', E ***point***, E ***of***, ON ***eyrr***, W ***y***, ***parlwr***, ***du***

Point of Eyre 1558, *Poynt of Ayre* 1656, *Point of Aire* 1689,
Pont of Aer c.1700, *Air Point* 1777, *Point of Air* 1796;
Parlwr Du or the Black Parlour 1793, *Parlwr Dee* 1834, *Parlur Dee* 1835,
Parlor Dee 1840

The north tip of Flintshire, at the Dee estuary, now largely sand-dunes and marsh. The ON ***eyrr*** 'gravel or sand bank' (with a similar p.n. in the Isle of Man) points to the headland's function as a Scandinavian navigational landmark despite its comparatively late documentation; it must have survived in maritime usage. Cf. *Point of Ayr lighthouse* 1834. Y Parlwr Du was the name of the colliery there with extensive sub-marine workings under the river Dee and also known as the Point of Ayr Colliery. ***parlwr*** is probably used ironically, in an industrial context, of a small, select, private room, an inner chamber or the best room. Several forms interpret ***du*** as Dee.

PONT ABER Carm SN7322

'bridge at the confluence', ***pont***, ***aber***

Pont-Aber 1891

The confluence is *Aber-ddwyafon* 1831, the two (***dau***, ***dwy***) streams (***afon***) being Sawdde Fechan and Clydach.

PONT ABRAHAM Carm SN5707

'Abraham's bridge', ***pont***, pers.n. ***Abraham***

Pont Abraham 1995

The actual bridge over Afon Gwili is *Gwili Bridge* 1891, *Pont Gwili* 1921, probably constructed for the road between Fforest (Llanedi) and Cross Hands in the late 18cent. Now the name of a motorway service station, almost universally called Pont Abram.

PONTAMAN Carm SN6412

'bridge over (the river) Aman', ***pont***, r.n. ***Aman***

Amman Bridge 1811, *Pontamman* 1831

The road to Dre-fach crosses Afon Aman (see Ammanford for the r.n.) here. Several maps have Pontamman.

PONTANTWN Carm SN4413

'Anthony's bridge', ***pont***, pers.n. ***Anton***

Pont Anton 1760, *Pont-anton* 1831, (*o*) *Bontantwn* 1839

A bridge over the river Gwendraeth Fach. Anton has not been identified. The pers.n. also occurs in *tir Res Anton'* 1561 (***tir***, pers.n. *Rhys*) in Llangyndeyrn (Carm). Antwn is a cymricized form.

PONTARDAWE Glam SN7204

'bridge on (the river) Tawe', ***pont***, ***ar***, r.n. ***Tawe***

Tir penybont ardawe 1584, *Ty pen y bont ar y Tawe* 1675,
Pont ar Dawen 1682, *Ty pen y bont ar tawey* 1706, *Pontardawey* 1710-11,
Pont ar Dawye 1760

The original el. is probably ***tir*** 'land' which became called ***tŷ*** referring to land and a house (*Pontardowey* 1707) at the end of a bridge over the river Tawe (*Ar Dawy* 1584-5 [c.1700]). Local pronunciation of the r.n. includes Tawy but most older forms favour Tawe or occasionally Tawa (*Pont Ardawa* 1707). See also Abertawe.

PONTARDDULAIS Glam SN5803

'bridge on (the river) Dulais', ***pont, ar***, r.n. ***Dulais***

Pen y bont aber Duleis, Brige end 1550, *Pontartheleys* 1557, *Penybont ar ddylays* 1584-5 (c.1700), *Pontardulais, Pontardilash* 1740

Most of the modern village lies in Glam adjoining the river Dulais but earlier sources and several later ones (*Arthelas bridge over Logor* 1586) show that the bridge is the old bridge (still standing) which crosses the river Loughor and that the older village (now Hendy) lay west of the river in Llanedi Carm. The earlier form would seem to be 'Pen-y-bont Aber Dulais', which referred to a broader area at the mouth (***aber***) of the (river) Dulais. The modern form is a syncopated form of 'Pont Aber Dulais' (cf. Pontyberem) and understood, at an early date, to represent 'Pont ar Dulais'. Hence, later forms have both the unlenited *-dulais* and the lenited *-ddulais* (after ***ar***). The river Dulais (*dubleis* 1136-54) is 'black stream' (***du, glais***).

PONTARFYNACH see **DEVIL'S BRIDGE**

PONT-AR-SAIS Carm SN4428

'the Englishman's bridge', ***pont, y, Sais***

Pontarsais 1744, *Pont-yr-Sais* 1831, *Pantarsais* 1875

The original name was probably 'Pont y Sais' subsequently influenced by the familiar 'pont ar' (as Pontardawe and Pontarddulais). The Englishman has not been identified. The bridge crosses Afon Gwili.

PONTBLYDDYN Flints SJ2760

'Bleiddyn's bridge', ***pont***, pers.n. ***Bleiddyn***

Pont Blethin 1612, *Pont Blythin* 1675, *Pont bleddyn, Pont-Blethin* 1668, *Pontblyddyn* 1692, *Pont Bleydhyn, Pont Bledhyn* c.1700, *Pont Blethin* 1720, *Pont Bleuddin* 1795, *Pont Bleiddyn* 1838

Although the forms record the pers.n. as Bleddyn and Bleiddyn it is the latter which explains the emergence of an E spelling in -y- to represent the W -ei-. Today, Pontblyddyn has become the standard spelling. The E (and local W) pronunciation is still -ai- or -ei- which retains, fairly closely, the original Pontbleiddyn. The more general W pronunciation, however, now treats -y- as the W -y- (as in ***tyddyn***). Cf. nearby Treuddyn with occasional historical forms as *Tryddyn*.

PONTERWYD Card SN7480

'?Erwyd's bridge', ***pont***, ?pers.n. ***Erwyd***

Pen Bont Erwyd 1622, *Pen Pont Erwyd* 1660, *pont erwyd* 1671, *Pont Erwyd* 1744, *Pontherwid* 1798

The identity of Erwyd is not known. An 1876 description of the bridge as *pont dros afon Rheidol...o brennau hirion* ('a bridge across Rheidol river... of long pieces of timber') prompted the suggestion that the second el. is

erwydd 'rails, poles, wattling rods'. The old road bridge, Hen Bont, across Afon Rheidol is slightly north of the present trunk road bridge.

PONTFADOG Denb SJ2338

'Madog's bridge', ***pont***, pers.n. ***Madog***

Pont Vadog, Bont Badog c.1700, *Pont fadock* 1703, *Pont Fadog* 1838

The bridge crosses Afon Ceiriog into the village (*Pentre Pont Fadog* 1795). The unknown Madog was probably the builder of the bridge or one whose house was close by.

PONT-FAEN[1] Brec SN9934

'stone bridge', ***pont, maen***

Pontfaen 1819, *Pont-faen* 1832

Named from the bridge over Afon Ysgir (***ysgwr*** pl. ***ysgyr*** 'splinters, smithereens') at the confluence of Ysgir Fechan and Ysgir Fawr in the village.

PONT-FAEN[2]**, Y BONT-FAEN** Pemb SN0234

'the stone bridge', ***y, pont, maen***

Pons Lapideus, Pontvaen 13cent., *Pontvayn* 1325, *y bont faen* c.1566, *Pontvane* 1794

Over the river Gwaun. The c.1566 form is the only one found with *y* 'the' and the subsequent lenition of -p- to -b-, but modern usage in W contexts favours (Y) Bont-faen possibly by analogy with Y Bont-faen/ Cowbridge.

PONTGARREG Card SN3354

'stone bridge', ***pont, carreg***

Pontgerrig 1811, *Pont-gareg* 1834

The bridge built in 1865 spans Nant Hawen, replacing a bridge the earliest record of which appears to have been the pl. ***cerrig***.

PONT-HENRI Carm SN4709

'Henry's bridge', ***pont***, pers.n. ***Henry***

Pont Henry c. 1627, *Ponthenry* 1697, *Pont Hendry* 1760

Named from a bridge over the river Gwendraeth Fawr. Henry seems to be unidentified. The spelling Henri is frequently preferred in W contexts but Pont Henry is also in common use. The 1760 *Hendry* is a common var.

PONT-HIR Monm ST3292

'long bridge', ***pont, hir***

Pontheere 1605, (~) *Pont heer* 1677, *y Bont-hir* 1778

The original bridge over the river Llwyd was superseded by the present bridge in 1800. The village developed near 18cent. ironworks.

PONT-HIRWAUN Card SN2645
'bridge on (the river) Hirwaun', ***pont***, r.n. ***Hirwaun***
Penbont Hirwain 1766-7, *Pont Hirwen* 1803, *Pont Hirwern* 1812, *Pont Hirwaun* 1826
The bridge spans the river Hirwaun, earlier *Hirwern* (*Blaenhirewern* 1241, *Hirwin Brook* 1760, *Afon Hirwaun* 1891) 'long alder marsh' (***hir***, ***gwern***), which divided the two parts of the commote of Is Coed.

PONT-IETS see **PONTYATES**

PONTLLAN-FRAITH Monm ST1896
'bridge by the speckled pool', ***pont***, ***llyn***, ***brith*** fem. ***braith***
tre penybont llynvraith 1492, *tre penbont* 1502, *Pontllynfraith* 1713, *Pontlanfraith* 1782, *Pont-llan-fraith* 1886
Named from a farm (***tref***) near a bridge over a pool in the river Sirhywi. ***llan*** later replaced the unaccented ***llyn*** giving rise to the belief that there was a saint Braith perceived to be a form of Ffraid.

PONT-LLIW Glam SN6101
'bridge on (the river) Lliw', ***pont***, r.n. ***Lliw***
Pont-llew 1698, *Llue br.* 1729, *Llew Bridge* 1792, *Pont-lliw* 1832
The village developed around the bridge over the river Lliw (q.v.), a flour mill and along the Swansea-Pontarddulais road in the 19cent. and expanded with the construction of housing estates after 1950.

PONTLLOGAIL Mont SJ0315
'bridge with wattled sides', ***pont***, ***llogail*** var. ***llogel***
llogell in Meghen 1588, *Pont y llogel* 1636, *Pont Llogell* 1710, *Pont-llogel* 1836
Possibly a description of a bridge here over the river Efyrnwy. The precise significance of ***llogel*** is obscure. Perhaps the bridge had wattle-sides or was a bridge composed of beams. Some of the forms show ***llogell*** 'small place; dwelling' as if referring to a small hovel at one end of the bridge; cf. possibly Cefn Llogell Monm (*Cefn-llogell* 1833). The modern form has a standard form ***llogail*** but Pontllogel is in common usage.

PONTLLYFNI Caern SH4352
'bridge on (the river) Llyfni', ***pont***, (***ar***), r.n. ***Llyfni***
Pont ar Lyfni 1800, *Pontlyfni* 1803
The bridge (dated 1777) carries the main Caernarfon-Pwllheli road over Afon Llyfni (see Llanllyfni) which enters the sea here. In recent years, the more grammatically correct Pontlyfni, regularly used in some literary contexts, has been superseded in local and national usage by Pontllyfni.

PONTLOTYN Glam SO1106

'wide bridge', ***pont, llydan***

Pont Lydan 1729, *Pont lydan* 1754, *Pont lottyn* 1813, *Pont Lottin* 1824, *Pont-y-lotyn* 1833, *Pont Lothine, ~ Lottin* 1845

The original name appears to have referred to a wide bridge over the Rhymni after the narrower stretch from Blaen Rhymni. Cf. *Pont Lludan* c.1700 Aberdare and *Pont llydan* c.1700 Llantwit Major. However, dial. unvoicing of -d- > -t- (cf. *Bryn Llutan* 1776 Llantwit Fardre) gave rise to the perception of it being ***tlotyn*** 'pauper' (sufficient to prompt the further change from *-lytan* to *-lotyn*) and the local tradition of a poor man who lived in a thatched cottage near the bridge. When the Bute iron works were established here the houses west of the bridge over the river Rhymni were called *Gomorah* (1857) and those on the north side towards the ironworks were called *Sodom*. The names may reflect the alleged immorality of the inhabitants but reinforced, it was said, by the similarity between Pontlotyn and the biblical Lot.

PONT MYRDDIN see **MERLIN'S BRIDGE**

PONTNEATHVAUGHAN see **PONTNEDDFECHAN**

PONTNEDDFECHAN, PONTNEATHVAUGHAN Brec SN9007

'bridge on (the river) Nedd Fechan', ***pont***, r.n. ***Nedd, bechan***

Pont Neath Vechan 1617, *Pont Neath vychan* 1666,
Pontneath Vaughan Farm 1798, *Pont-nedd-fechan* 1832

The bridge was over the river Nedd Fechan (*Nethe vaghan* 1502, *Neath Vychan* 1596-1600), the 'lesser Nedd', a tributary of Nedd or Nedd Fawr (see Neath). Rivers are habitually regarded as fem. which explains the fem. ***bechan*** (lenited as ***fechan***). However, some forms have the masc. adj. ***bychan*** (lenited as ***fychan*** in the historical forms *vychan* and *Vaughan*) possibly because the fem. adj. ***bechan*** was unfamiliar or under the influence of the pers.n. Fychan (anglicized as Vaughan).

PONTNEWYDD Monm ST2996

'new bridge', ***pont, newydd***

Newbridge, Pont-newith 1634, *Pontnewydd* 1638

The village developed near a bridge over Afon Llwyd (*Auon* 1307, *Avon lwyd* 1677, *Avon lloyd* 1739, *Avon Lwyd* 1801), Pontnewydd House and tin-plate works established in 1802.

PONTNEWYNYDD Monm SO2701

'bridge on (the river) Newynydd', ***pont***, r.n. ***Newynydd***

Ponte y Thywonith 1602, *Pont-y-duwinydd* early 17cent.,
Pont y newenith 1720, *Pont Newydd* 1833, *Pont-newynydd* 1886

Named from the bridge called Pont Newynydd. The def.art. *y* of the earlier forms refers to the stream Dywynydd which may be identical to a r.n. in Brec (*nant y ddiwneth* 1515, *ddywydd* 1627, *Ddwynith, Ddiwinidd* 1819, *Blaen Newynydd* 1840) both of which are of uncertain meaning, but is possibly based on a fem. pers.n. Dywynydd or Dywenydd (possibly related to ***dywynnig*** 'shining, bright, prominent'). Other forms show the influence of ***duwinydd*** 'theologian, divine', ***newyn*** 'famine' and ***newydd*** 'new'.

PONTRHYDFENDIGAID Card SN7366

'bridge of the blessed ford', ***pont, rhyd, bendigaid***

Pont Rhydvendigaeth 1673, *(Pen)pontrhydvendigaid* 1738, *Ponthrydvendiged* 1746, *Pont Rhyd Vendigaid* 1807, *Pont Rhyd-fendigaid* 1834

The original ford (*Ryt Wendigait* 1184 [1285], *Ryd Bendigeyt* 1202 [1336], *Rydvendygheyt* pre 1282 [1425], *(de) Vado B'nd'o* c.1291, *Rid Vendiget* 1426, *Rhydfendigaid* 1804) through Afon Teifi was blessed and used by the monks of Strata Florida just over a mile east. The c.1291 form has the L ***vadum*** 'ford', ***benedictus*** 'blessed'. A second bridge was built c.1780.

PONT-RHYD-Y-CYFF Glam SS8689

'bridge at the ford near the stump', ***pont, rhyd, y, cyff***

Pontrhydycyff 1813, *Pont-rhydd-y-cyff* 1833, *Pont Rhyd-y-cyff* 1884

A bridge over the river Llynfi replacing a ford which was apparently known for its location near a prominent tree stump.

PONT-RHYD-Y-FEN Glam SS7994

'bridge at the ford of the wagon', ***pont, rhyd, y, men***

Ryd y venn 1460-80, *Ponte Retheuenne, the forde of the Waine* 1536-9, *Rydyfen* 1584-5 (c.1700), *Pont Rhyd y ven* 1714

A ford, known for its habitual use by wagons, was replaced by a bridge. The village developed near ironworks from 1825.

PONT-RHYD-Y-GROES Card SN7372

'bridge at the ford of the cross', ***pont, rhyd, y, croes***

Pont Rheed y Groes 1760, *Pont Rhyd-y-Groes* 1815, *Pont-rhyd-y-groes* 1891

The ford which crosses Afon Ystwyth was superseded by a stone bridge (the latest built 1893). The village itself developed in response to the opening of at least six lead mines within three miles and (later) extensive afforestation. The cross probably marked the site of the ford and the route taken by monks of Strata Florida; there was also monastic land at nearby Lledwenau.

PONTRHYPONT see **FOUR MILE BRIDGE**

PONTROBERT Mont SJ1012
'Robert's bridge', ***pont***, pers.n. ***Robert***
Pont Robert ap Oliver alias Pont y ddole feiniog 1669,
Pont Robert ab Oliver 1743, *Pont Robert* 1794
Several sources state that the bridge was built in stone in 1669 by a *Robert ap Oliver* to replace an earlier bridge destroyed by a storm in 1622 which took its name from Dôl-feiniog 'stony meadow' (***dôl***, ***meiniog***). The bridge here was still described as new in 1819.

PONTSENNI see **SENNYBRIDGE**

PONTSIÂN Card SN4346
'Siân's bridge', ***pont***, pers.n. ***Siân***
(i) Bont Shân c.1830, *Pontshaen* 1874, *Pont-Shân* 1891, *Pont Sian* 1899
Earlier names of the hamlet were *Penpont newydd* 1791, *Penybont newydd* 1798, *Penybont* 1811, from its location near the end (***pen***) of a new (***newydd***) bridge over Afon Cletwr. The name of the bridge and the village point to a pers.n. Shân or Siân. The 1874 form shows the influence of ***tsiaen*** 'chain'.

PONTSTICYLL Reservoir Brec SO0512
'reservoir near Pontsticill', E ***reservoir***, p.n. ***Pontsticill***
A reservoir completed in 1927 by the Taf Fechan Water Supply Board and generally known as Taf Fechan Reservoir from its location on the river Taf Fechan. Pontsticill (*Pont Stucketh* 1698, *Pont Stickel* 1729, *Pontystickill* 1748, *Pont-y-stickyll* 1807, *Pontsticell* 1814) is 'bridge near a stile' (***pont***, ***sticil*** var. ***sticill***).

PONT-TYWELI Carm SN4140
'bridge on (the river) Tyweli', ***pont***, r.n. ***Tyweli***
Twelly Bridge 1811, *Pont-Tyweli* 1891
The river is *Dywely* c.1700, *Tyweli* 1891, and occurs in *Tir glan deweli* 1563, *Glandewely* 1698, *Glandiwely* 18cent., a r.n. which is probably ***dywal*** 'fierce, brave, cruel' referring to its wild course, but may also be a pers.n. ***Dywel*** or ***Dyfel***, with the suff. ***-i***, commonly found with r.ns.

PONTWALBY Glam SN8906
'Walby's bridge', ***pont***, pers.n. ***Walby***
pontwhalby 1814, *Pont Walby* 1833, *Pont Whalby* 1884
The surname *Walby, Walbeof* occurs from the Middle Ages in Glam and Brec. He may have been *John Waldboeuf*, receiver of Hay and Huntington lordships 1499-1501 and steward and receiver of the lordship of Brecon 1503.

PONTYATES, PONT-IETS Carm SN4608

'Yates's bridge', ***pont***, pers.n. ***Yates***

Pont Yates 1760, *Pontyetts* 1764, *Pontyjet* 1765-6, *Pont Yeats* 1813, *Pontyeats* 1844

The bridge was over the river Gwendraeth Fawr. A *Walter Yates* is recorded in nearby Llangyndeyrn in 1642 and 1665, and the surname appears in the local *Tŷ-iets* 1739, *Tir Yates* and *Ynys Yates* 1790. Local tradition has long associated the name with the dial. ***iet*** 'gate' (here interpreted as 'tollgate') which has influenced the modern W spelling and pronunciation.

PONTYBEREM Carm SN5011

'bridge at the mouth of (the river) Beran', ***pont***, ***aber***, r.n. ***Beran***

Pont y Beran 1609, *Pont Beram* 1760, *Pont y berem* 1798, *Pont-y-berem* 1831

A bridge over the river Gwendraeth Fawr just below its confluence with Nant Berem. It is believed that the original p.n. probably lost ***aber*** through contraction (of ***aber*** and ***Beran***) and the interpretation of the -a- of ***aber*** as the def.art. ***y*** (*Pontaberberan* > *Pontaberan* > *Pontyberan*). The final -m may have been influenced by ***berem*** a var. of ***burum*** 'yeast'.

PONTYBODKIN Flints SJ2759

'bridge at the bodkin', ***pont***, ***y***, E ***bodkin***

Ponty Bodkin 1841, *Pont y Bodkin* 1844, *Pont-y-bodkin* 1871

The Bala-Hawarden and the Mold-Wrexham roads originally crossed Black Brook by means of a ford (*Rhyd Osber* 1611, *Rhydosper* 1840, ***rhyd***, pers.n. Osber), which was then replaced by the bridge. The comparison with a ***bodkin*** boring a hole was prompted by the 19cent. industrial developments (collieries and an oil works) in a narrow valley with two rivers, two major routes, four minor roads and a railway. The use of the E word ***bodkin*** (as opposed to the W word ***botgyn***) can be ascribed to immigrant workers, but was evidently also adopted by W speakers.

PONT-Y-CLUN Glam ST0381

'bridge on (the river) Clun', ***pont***, ***y***, r.n. ***Clun***

Pont Clun 1833

Named from a bridge over the river Clun, earlier Clown, next to a former farm (called *Pont Clun* 1811). This farm and bridge have sometimes been confused with a second bridge (*Pont Gloun* 1536-9, *Pont y Clown* c.1700, *Pont Clown* 1720, *Clun Bridge* 1811), a mile to the east on the same river near a former farm Pont-y-parc. Clown also appears in early records as the name of a manor of Clown (*Cloune* 1281, *Clune* c.1405, *Cloon(e)*

1578-84, *Clwnn* 1600-25) centred on Llantrisant and two former parks (next to the river). The r.n. is probably related to several rivers Colne and Clowne in England and Clun (W Colunwy) Shropshire, all of unknown meaning. The local pronunciation seems to have been close to Clown but it was later confused, in spelling at least, with W ***clun*** 'meadow; moor'. The river was also recorded as Dowlais (*Dowlais als. Clou* 1588; cf. Dowlais) but the name Nant Dowlais is now confined to a headwater of one of Clun's tributaries Nant Myddlyn.

PONTYCYMER Glam SS9091
'bridge at the confluence', ***pont, y, cymer***
Pont y Cymmer 1719, *Pont-y-cymmer* 1884
The bridge is about a mile north of the confluence of the rivers Garw and Garw Fechan; a farm between them is Braichycymer (*Braich-y-cymmer* 1833, ***braich*** 'arm'). An identical name occurs at the confluence of the rivers Rhondda Fawr and Rhondda Fechan (*P(ont) y Cummar* c.1700, *Pont-y-cymmer* 1833).

PONT-Y-GWAITH Glam ST0194
'bridge near the works', ***pont, y, gwaith***
Pont y Gwaith 1760, *Pontgwaith* 1833, *Pont-y-Gwaith* 1885
Named from coal-works. An identical p.n. (*Pont y gwaith* c.1700, *Pont y Gwaith* 1754) took its name from a bridge over the river Taf and a former ironworks near Quakers Yard.

PONTYPOOL see **PONT-Y-PŴL**

PONT-Y-PŴL, PONTYPOOL Monm SO2800
'bridge of the pool', ***pont, y,*** E ***pool***
Pont y poole 1614, *Pontpoole* 1681, *Pontipool* 1682, *Pontypool* 1718, *Pontypwl* 1834
The bridge is over Afon Llwyd (***afon, llwyd*** 'grey, dark') near a river pool. The use of E ***pool*** and its cymricized pŵl (rather than W ***pwll***) suggests that it was used in some specialist sense, perhaps connected with industrial works such as the iron forges recorded from the late 16cent. The town itself developed with the growth of heavy industry in the 18 and 19cent. near the parish church Trevethin.

PONTYPRIDD Glam ST0789
'bridge of the earthen house', ***pont, y, tŷ, pridd***
Newbridge 1701, *Pont y Ty Pridd, Pont y Pridd c.* 1700, *Pont y Tŷ Pridd* 1764, *Pont y prîdd or the new bridge* 1781, *New Bridge or Pont yprydd* 1813
Early forms show that it was the house with distinctive earthen walls which gave the bridge (over river Taf) its name. Spellings such as those

for 1781 and the modern form give the impression that the second syllable is the def.art. ***y*** but current colloquial references to the town as Ponty (pronounced 'Pontee') tend to indicate loss of ***y*** and retention of ***tŷ*** (in its south W pronunciation 'tee'). In addition to *Pont y Tŷ Pridd*, two other bridges Pont Lledan (*Pont Ludan* c.1700, ***llydan*** 'wide' fem. ***lledan***) and Pont Newydd or New Bridge (*Pont Newith* 1536-9, ***newydd*** 'new') are recorded here, both on the river Rhondda. Pont Newydd gave rise to the alternative name Newbridge, popularly associated with the new bridge constructed by William Edwards over the river Taf 1773-77 and adopted for the *Taff Vale Railway* station 1840 but was dropped in favour of Pontypridd to avoid confusion with Newbridge Monm.

POOL QUAY Mont ST1511

'river-quay of Welshpool', E ***pool***, E ***quay***

New Quay 1608, *New-key* 1698, *the quay of Welsh Poole* 1774, *Pool Quay* 1784

This was the head of navigation for barges on the river Severn near Welshpool (q.v.)(*Pool* 1774).

PORT EYNON, PORTHEINON Glam SS4685

'Einon's cove', ***porth***, pers.n. ***Einon***

Portheniaun early 13cent., *Portheinon* c.1250, *Porteynon* 1347, *Porthynon* 1433

porth (which can mean 'harbour, landing-place, bay') is replaced in E sources with ***port***. This Einon, more commonly Einion in north Wales p.ns, has not been identified.

PORTFIELD GATE Pemb SM9215

'gate near Portfield', E ***gate***, p.n. ***Portfield***

A gate which marked an entrance to Portfield (*Portefelde* late 13cent., *le Portefeld* 1452, *the commons of portefyld* 1554, *Portfilld* 1592, *Porfeild* 1652, *Portfield otherwise Poorfield* 1837-8, OE ***port*** 'town', OE ***feld***), which was a common field (enclosed 1837-8) of the town of Haverfordwest and the site of horse races.

PORTH, Y Glam ST0291

'gateway', ***porth***

porte Kemes [= ~ *Kemer*] 1596-1600, *Porth* 1789, *Porthycumma* 1813, *Porth Pont-y-cymmer* 1833

At the entrance to the valleys of the rivers Rhondda Fawr and Rhondda Fechan near their confluence (***cymer***) at Cymer (*Kemmer* 1314, *kymer dwy rhoddne* c.1624, *Cummer Day Rondda* 1787, *the Cymmer* 1789, ***dwy*** 'two').

PORTHAETHWY see **MENAI BRIDGE**

PORTH-CAWL Glam SS8277

'sea-kale harbour', ***porth, cawl***

Portcall 1632, *Pwll Cawl o(r) Porth Cawl* 1825

cawl is used of 'cabbage' and of the broth or soup made of vegetables. The sea-kale (ME ***cole***), often found in historical sources as 'sea-cole', must have grown abundantly or even been collected here for food or cultivation. The 1632 form with *-call* reflects the pronunciation heard in an E context. The 1825 form appears to give an alias W ***pwll*** 'pool'. The town developed after the completion of the tramway to the coalfields and ironworks around Maesteg 1826-7 and the construction of a harbour (earlier *a station or haven for shippes* 1536-9).

PORTHCERI see **PORTHKERRY**

PORTHDIN-LLAEN Caern SH2741

'harbour of Dinllaen' ***porth***, commote n. ***Dinllaen***

Portdinllain 1263 (15cent.), *Porthdynllayn* 1561-2, *Portynllayn* 1591, *Portinllain* 1639-40, *Porthyllaine alias Portinllaine* 1729, *Porth dynlleyn* 1805, *Porth-dinlleyn* 1839

The harbour and sheltered bay served the commote of Dinllaen (*Dynthlen* c.1295-1303 [15cent.], *Dynllayn* 1303-4) a name which refers to the hill fort (***din***) located on the narrow promontory of Trwyn Porth Dinllaen and the pers.n. Llaen. See Llŷn. It was always a busy harbour and boatyard; as recently as the 19cent. it was considered as a possible harbour for Ir mail-boats. Common usage (as seen in the above forms) refers to the harbour as Portin-llaen.

PORTHEINON see **PORT EYNON**

PORTH-GAIN Pemb SM8132

'fair bay', ***porth, cain***

Porth Gaen 1785, *Porthgain* 1815

Cain (with the same meaning as ***cain*** 'fair') does occur as a r.n. in several parts of Wales but there is no evidence to support the view that here Cain was a lost name for the small river entering the bay. The epithet is far more likely to refer to the bay.

PORTHKERRY, PORTHCERI Glam ST0866

'harbour of ?Ceri', ***porth***, ?pers.n. ***Ceri***

Porciri 1254, *Porthkery, Porthkire* 13cent., *Porthkyry* c.1348, *Portkerry* 1558, *porth kiric* c.1566, *Porthkerry* 1595-6, *Porthcurig* 1742

There has been much speculation on the second el. The well-attested pers.n. Ceri seems to be the least contentious despite the dominance of the earlier forms with *-ciri* and *-kyry* and (possibly deliberate) attempts to associate the place with the pers.n. ***Curig*** (cf. Capel Curig). Other suggestions are the ON ***geiri*** 'triangular piece of land' and the ON pers.n. ***Kári***.

PORTHMADOG Caern SH5638

'port of Madocks', E ***port***, pers.n. ***Madocks***

Portmadoc 1838

Between 1800 and his death in 1828 William Alexander Madocks (the Member of Parliament for Boston, Lincolnshire) was responsible for enclosing a large area of the marsh and shore called Traeth Mawr (*Trait mawr* 1194 'the great strand'). He developed the village of Tremadoc (q.v.) (*Tre-madoc* 1810, ***tref*** 'settlement, town'), constructed an embankment (the Cob in 1821), and by 1824 had built a *Harbour at a place extending from Garth Penclogwyn to Ynys Towyn* (1821) to export slate from the Blaenau Ffestiniog quarries. The larger village of Portmadoc (*the new town at Towyn* 1828) accompanied the harbour. The two names which commemorate Madocks, Tremadoc and Portmadoc, later adopted W versions as Tremadog and Porthmadog (with W ***porth*** 'landing place, bay' replacing E ***port***) probably influenced by the W pers.n. Madog (notably the adventurer who, legend has it, discovered America and returned to be buried here). Although Portmadoc has been supplanted by Porthmadog, the town in colloquial local usage is still frequently referred to as Port.

PORTH MAWR see **WHITESANDS BAY**

PORTH NEIGWL, HELL'S MOUTH Caern SH2426

'bay of Neigwl', ***porth***, p.n. ***Neigwl***, E ***hell***, E ***mouth***

The bay of Nygull 16cent., *Porthnegoll* 1561-2, *porth Nigwl* 1629, *Neigwi or Hells Mouth* 1805, *Porth Neigwl or Hells Mouth* 1816

Neigwl (*Neugyll* 1291, *Newgwl* 1352) was the centre of the commote of Cymydmaen, for which Porth Neigwl would have provided important sea access. The origin of Neigwl is obscure but was probably a pers.n. perhaps Ir or ON. Newgale (q.v.) may feasibly be of similar origin. The late E name is found elsewhere for exposed bays.

PORTHSGIWED see **PORTSKEWETT**

PORTH SWTAN, CHURCH BAY Angl SH2989

'bay of the whiting-pout', 'church bay', ***porth***, ***swtan***, E ***church***, E ***bay***

Porth Swttan mid 16cent., *Church Bay* c.1816, *Swtan or Church Bay* 1818, *Porth Swtan* 1830, *Porth-swtan* 1838

A bay noted for the whiting-pout or 'miller's thumb', despite antiquarian attempts to identify the bay as the landing-place of Suetonius Paulinus in AD 61. A brook, Afon Swtan (*Avon Suttan…a little rille* 1536-9), flows into the bay. The E name is first recorded in navigation charts, with reference to the landmark of the nearby Llanrhuddlad church steeple.

PORTH TYWYN see **BURRY PORT**

PORTH-Y-RHYD[1] Carm SN5215
'gateway of the ford', ***porth, y, rhyd***
Porth-y-rhyd 1831, *Portyrhyd* 1895
The village developed around a toll-gate (*Porth-y-rhyd Gate* 1813) near a house called *Porth-y-rhyd* (1813). Located close to a ford which has been superseded by a bridge over Gwendraeth Fach.

PORTH-Y-RHYD[2] Carm SN7137
'gateway of the ford', ***porth, y, rhyd***
Tyr Porth y Rhyd 1716, *porth y Rhyd* 1727, *Porth Rhyd* 1819, *Porthrhyd* 1831, *Porthyrhyd* 1844
A gate leading to a ford through Afon Mynys.

PORTIN-LLAEN see **PORTH DINLLAEN**

PORTSKEWETT, PORTHSGIWED Monm ST4988
'harbour of ?Ysgewin', ***porth***, ?pers.n. ***Ysgewin***
Poteschiuet 1086, *Portascihð* 1065 (c.1100), *Porth is ceuin* 1128, *Porth iscewin* 1160-85, *Porth scuwet* 1190, *Portscuet* 1307, *Porteskewin* 1536-9
An alternative, if archaic, name is Porth Ysgewin where Ysgewin may be a pers.n. or it could be related to ***ysgawen*** 'elder-tree' to indicate a cove, port or harbour characterised by elder-trees. The relationship (if there is one) between -sgewett/-sgiwed and -ysgewin is as obscure as its meaning. The harbour is now a marshy area at the mouth of Nedern Brook and Caldicot Pill.

PORT TALBOT Glam SS7589
'Talbot's port', E ***port***, pers.n. ***Talbot***
The Port Talbot 1840, *Port Talbot Station* c.1850, *Port Talbot* 1884
Named from CRM Talbot of Penrice Castle, builder of Margam Castle. In 1835, the development of a new harbour at Aberafan was begun by the *Aberavon Harbour Co.* later renamed the *Port Talbot Co.* in recognition of Talbot's co-operation.

PORT TENNANT Glam SS5579
'Tennant's port', E ***port***, pers.n. ***Tennant***
Port Tennant 1824
Named from George Tennant (1765-1832), builder of a canal completed in 1824 linking the river Tawe and Swansea docks to the Glan-y-wern Canal and completing the link with the Neath Canal.

POST MAWR see **SYNOD INN**

POWYS

'inhabitants of the country district', L ***pagēnses***

regionem Poýuis 822 (c.1100), *Powys* c.1130-80, *Powis* 1158-9

Apparently an adoption of L ***pagēnses*** through late Br ***pōuēses*** and OW ***powes*** to W Powys. Although the precise nature of Romano-British administrative units is still unclear, it seems that *pagēnses* 'country dwellers', from ***pagus*** 'territory, district, hinterland, province' (cf. W ***pau***, F ***pays***), may have referred to people who did not inhabit the towns. In this case, Powys was used of extensive parts of mid Wales, probably extending between Chester and Shrewsbury (near which was the medieval W court of Pengwern) and possibly Wroxeter. The same term appears in Dinas Powys (q.v.) west of Cardiff. In the early medieval period, Powys was divided into Powys Fadog (pers.n. Madog) and Powys Wenwynwyn (pers.n. Gwenwynwyn). The 1974 administrative county includes (broadly) the historical counties of Mont, Rad and Brec.

PREN-GWYN Card SN4244

'white tree', ***pren***, ***gwyn***

Prengwyn 1831, *Pren-gwyn* 1891

The earlier hamlet is situated at the junction of five roads which seems to have been characterized by a white tree or a wooden post, but there is also a belief that a cross here marked a pilgrim route.

PREN-TEG Caern SH5841

'fine tree', ***pren***, ***teg***

y prenteg 1741, *Prenteg* 1767, *Pren-têg* 1838

The hamlet is on a hillside in the midst of extensive woodland, possibly a place which provided superior timber for the boatyards of Aberglaslyn and later Porthmadog.

PRESELI see MYNYDD PRESELI

PRESTATYN Flints SJ0682

'farm of the priests', OE ***prēosta***, OE ***tūn***

Prestetone 1086, *Prestattune* 1257, *Prestatton* 1301, *Prystatun* 1325, *Prystaton* 1420, *Prestatyn* 1536, *Prestatton* 1733

Farms supporting, or run by, priests were fairly common, and in England such a p.n. usually became Preston. In Flints, however, the name took on a distinctively W character. The medial syllable survived by adopting the regular W stress as the penultimate syllable, and the final syllable followed the W sound system to become -tyn as in several ***tūn*** names in Flints (such as Mostyn, Mertyn and Golftyn).

PRESTEIGNE, LLANANDRAS Radn SO3164

'border meadow of the priests', 'church of Andreas', OE ***prēosta,*** OE ***hemm,*** OE ***mǣd,*** W ***llan,*** pers.n. ***Andreas***

Prestehemed 1137-9, *Prestmede* 1249, *Presthemed* 1291, *Prestende* 1378-9, *Presteyne* 1545, *Llanondras* 1262 (c.1286), *Llanandrewe* 1536-9, *ll. andras* c.1566

The p.n. must refer to a flat area near the river Lugg/Llugwy. 'Priest' distinguished it from Upper and Lower Kinsham (*Kingesmede* 1210-12, *Kingshemed* 1216) 'king's border meadow' (OE ***cyning***) about three miles to the east in Herefordshire held by the kings of England. The priests presumably served at the parish church of St Andreas (Andrew as he appears in one form). Later development of the name involved reduction to two syllables (occurring several times in border p.ns), confusion of -emd- with -ende- and subsequent loss of -d.

PRIESTHOLM, PUFFIN ISLAND, YNYS LANNOG, YNYS SEIRIOL Angl SH6582

'priest island', 'puffin island', 'Glannog's island', 'Seiriol's island', ON ***prestr,*** ON ***holmr,*** E ***puffin,*** E ***island,*** W ***ynys,*** pers.n. ***Glannog,*** pers.n. ***Seiriol***

Enislannach id est Insula ecclesiastica c.1191, *Insula Glannauch* 1220, *Onyslannauc* 1258, *Prestholme alias Evys Llannoc* 1468, *Prest-holm* 1478, *Prestholme, Ynys Seiriol, Porth seiriol, alias Insula ecclesiastica* mid 16cent., *Prestholm…abounding with Rabbits and Puffins* 1684, *Priestholme Island or Ynys Seiriol* 1795, *Puffin island or Priest holm* 1797, *Priestholm or Ynys Seiriol* 1838

The church on Ynys Seiriol was traditionally founded in the 6cent. for Seiriol by his brother Cynlas, and extended to include a monastic settlement on the island and at Penmon (q.v.) later an Augustinian priory. The ON name, although it is recorded late, falls into the category of Scandinavian coastal names (such as Bardsey and Anglesey itself) probably owing their survival to maritime usage. Helig ap Glannog is, somewhat obscurely, associated with the island, and Ynys Lannog, at least on current evidence, appears to have been the oldest name. Puffin Island is recent but has attained considerable popularity.

PRINCES GATE Pemb SN1312

'Prince's gate', E ***gate,*** pers.n. ***Prince***

Princes Gate 1792, *Princess Gate* 1833

The name of a former toll-gate, probably named after a person.

PRION Denb SJ0562

'territory of Pereu', pers.n. ***Pereu,*** terr.suff. ***-ion***

Pereyon 1334, *Prion* 1501, *Pryon* 1624-5, *(Tre)Breyon, (Moel) Breyan* c.1700

The early forms provide clear evidence of an unidentified Pereu. The popular belief is that Prion is a biblical name (as Peniel and Pentre Saron in the vicinity), prompting the chapel's adoption of the name as Capel Prion in 1792; there was also a classical Prion in Carthage.

PRYSOR, Afon Mer SH7639

'(the river) abounding in thickets', ***afon***, ***prysg*** var. ***prys***, coll.suff. ***-or***

Pressor 1284, *prissor* 13cent., *Prysor* 1838

The river rises east of Foel Cynfal, and flows through Cwm Prysor (*Cwmprysor* 1493-4, *Cwm Prysor* 1796) past Castell Prysor (*Castelh Prysor* 1695) into Llyn Trawsfynydd.

PUFFIN ISLAND see **PRIESTHOLM**

PUMLUMON (PLYNLIMON) Card/Mont SN7886

'five stacks', ***pump*** vars ***pum***, ***pym***, ***llumon***

pumlumon 12cent., *Pimplumman* 1187 (15cent.), *Pymlumon* 1278/9, *Plimlvmon* 1478, *Penlinmon* 1536-9, *Plymllymon hill* 1578, *Plinlimon* 1596, *Plymlimmon* 1604, *Pumlumon* 1824

The name of a group of peaks north of Eisteddfa Gurig, the highest of which is denoted Pumlumon Fawr or Pen Pumlumon Fawr (*Pen-Plinlimon-fawr* 1891, ***pen*** 'top, peak', ***mawr*** 'big') on some maps. The rivers Severn, Wye, Rheidol and a tributary of Ystwyth have their sources here. The el. ***llumon*** has caused some discussion since its principal meaning seems to be 'chimney (stack)'. Plynlimon, a form commonly heard in W and E, has the intrusive -l- after -p- as well as the var. ***pym*** and dissimilation of -ml- > -nl-. The 1536-9 form perceives it to be ***pen*** 'top'.

PUMP-HEWL see **FIVE ROADS**

PUMSAINT Carm SN6540

'five saints', ***pump***, ***sant*** var. ***saint***

Pymsaint 1704, *Pymsant* 1798, *Pumsaint* 1831

Earlier Llandeilo Pumsaint Caergaeo; a former chapel in the parish and hundred of Caeo dedicated to the same five saints as Llanpumsaint Carm (q.v.). An old stone here was said to bear the footprints of the saints.

PUNCHESTON, CAS-MAEL Pemb SN0029

'(place named after) Pontchardon', 'Mael's castle', p.n. ***Pontchardon***, ***castell***, pers.n. ***Mael***

Pounchardon 1291, *Ponchardon* 1325, *Punchariston* 1488, *Poncherdiston* 1523, *Castellmale* 1559, *kastell mal* c.1566, *Castle Male* 1578, *Casmâl* 1827, *Castellmael* 1839

The name may have been transferred to Pemb from Pontchardon

Normandy by a Norman settler, and then reformed (on the assumption that it contains a pers.n. *Ponchard*) with E genitival -es and -ton under the influence of similar p.ns. elsewhere in Pemb (such as Robeston and Cosheston). The W name has ***cas-***, the reduced form of ***castell*** found widely in south Wales (see Newport[1]); Mael became Mâl in local dialect.

PWLL Carm SN4801

'pool', ***pwll***

Pool 1726, *Pwll* 1831

This may refer to one of the coastal pools. Parts of the area were drained after the construction of the Llanelli-Carmarthen railway.

PWLLCROCHAN Pemb SM9202

?'bay near (the river) Crachan', ***porth***, ?r.n. ***Crachan***

Porttrahan (= *Portcrahan*?), *Portcrachan* 1291, *Porthcrachan* 1348, *Poullecrochon* 1535, *pwll krochan* c.1566, *Pwllcrochan* 1571

porth has been replaced by ***pwll*** 'pool, bay, pit' from c.1500. The pool is in the estuary of Milford Haven immediately north of the village. The second el. may be an unrecorded r.n., perhaps Crachan (***crach*** 'scabs, scabby eruption' and ***-an***), replaced by ***crochan*** 'cauldron, pot' from some fancied likeness. However, it has been argued that ***crochan*** was the original form since there are three other identical names in Pemb.

PWLL-DU HEAD Glam SS5786

'headland near Pwll-du', p.n. ***Pwll-du***, E ***head***

Pool dy Point 1807, *Powldy Point* 1831, *Pwll dû head* 1832

Pwlldu (*Puldie* 1650, *Pwlldy* 1675, *Pwll-du* 1832), 'dark pool or pit' (***pwll***, ***du***) applies to some houses and a hotel (Beaufort Arms) immediately north of the headland adjoining Pwlldu Bay. There is a house just above Pwlldu recorded as *The Pit* 1883. E ***pit*** does occur elsewhere in the area, but ***pwll*** in the sense 'pool' is also used of very small coves in Pemb. The stream in the valley is recorded as *Puldie River* 1650.

PWLL-GLAS Denb SJ1154

'verdant pool' ***pwll***, ***glas***

Pwll-glâs 1872-3

The hamlet, alongside the main Rhuthun-Bala road, has a stream running through it. A pool in this stream was characterised by the foliage surrounding it.

PWLLHELI Caern SH3735

'brine pool', ***pwll***, ***heli***

pwllhely 1292-3, *Purthely* 1303-4, *Porthelli*, *Porthelly* 1350, *Pulthely* c.1402-3, *Pullelly* 1501, *Pullhelye* 1565-6, *Pwlleli* 1612, *Pwllheli* 1795

By the 13cent. a tidal pool had been created by the formation of the sand-bar to form the harbour (the 1350 ***porth***).

PWLLMEURIG see **PWLLMEYRICK**

PWLLMEYRICK, PWLLMEURIG Monm ST5192

?'pit near (the river) Meurig', ***pwll***, r.n. ***Meurig***

Putei mouric 11cent., *pull mouric* 1136-54, *Pelmeurich* 1193-1218, *Polmeurik* 1310

Pwll- has been interpreted as 'pool' and identified as a salt-water pool in the river Severn but Pwllmeurig is nearly two miles from the river. However, the earliest form with L ***puteus*** suggests ***pwll*** 'pit' probably referring to some such feature near the stream Meurig (*mouric* 1136-54, *Polmericysbroke* 1458) later Mounton Brook. Meurig is also a pers.n.

PWLL-TRAP Carm SN2616

'trap pool', ***pwll, trap***

Pwlltrapp 1682, *Pwll Trap Mill* 1688, *Pwll trap* 1786, *Pwltrap* 1875

Possibly a reference to a mill-pool (in the sense of waters which have been trapped and contained) or perhaps a fish-trap but the village is located along the St Clears-Whitland road on a low hill about a mile from the rivers Cynin and Taf. No suitable water-mill has been identified and there seems to be no evidence of a pool or pit close to the village. The occurrence of ***trap*** in inn names (see Trap) may be relevant here.

PYLE, Y PÎL Glam SS8282

'tidal stream', E ***pill***, W ***y, pil***

Pyll 1420, *The Pile* 1536, *Pylle* 1545, *y pil* c.1566, *The Pille* 1602

E ***pill*** is associated with the Bristol Channel and the Severn estuary as a word for a tidal creek, or a pool in a creek or in the confluence of a stream with a larger river. That word and its derivative W ***pil*** occur along the coast of Glam and Monm. Here, it might apply to the mouth of the river Kenfig/Cynffig, currently tidal for less than a mile from the sea which is two and a half miles from Pyle (although spreading sand dunes may have been a factor here). Both E ***pill*** and W ***pil***, however, have a short vowel and in order to account for Pyle and Y Pîl, we have to suppose a W var. with a long vowel (cf. *pîl* 1803) which in turn produced the diphthong -ai- heard today in the E pronunciation. It is worth noting, however, that in E usage in England a var. recorded spelling is ***pile***, which has persuaded some to suggest the influence of ***pile***, 'stake', possibly a boundary marker, but Pyle, Isle of Wight is the only known example of such an el. There is another Pyle near Bishopston Glam.

PYLLALAI see **PILLETH**

Q

QUEENSFERRY Flints SJ3168

'queen's ferry', E ***queen***, E ***ferry***

Queensferry 1837

There were several ferries across the river Dee before and after it was canalized in 1737. One of them, at this location, was *Lower Ferry* (1726) as opposed to the Higher Ferry at Saltney. Eventually, the name of the *Lower Ferry* was changed to the *Lower King's Ferry* (1826) or simply *King's Ferry* (1828) in honour of George IV's accession in 1820. At the coronation of Queen Victoria in 1837 the name was further changed to Queensferry.

R

RACHUB Caern SH6268

'the holding', *yr*, ***achub***

Achib 1781, *yr Achub* 1790, *Rachub* 1838, *Yr Achub* 1840

The traditional view is that this was land 'occupied' or 'held' (***achub***) as a method of effecting ownership in accordance with the 13cent. Welsh Laws (*lle ny bo tydyn y neb nac achub kyn no hynny*, 'where no one had a tyddyn or achub previously'). The remarkable survival of such a term centuries later can only be ascribed to an unrecorded, oral use. However, the emergence of the first record of the name in the late 18cent. with the building in 1793 of the actual Nonconformist chapel (*yr Achyb-uchaf* 1793, *Capel yr achub* 1801) has prompted the suggestion that in 1781 this had been a mission hall (***achub*** 'to save'), although the existence of such a cause at that date poses many problems. The ***r*** of the definite article ***yr*** has been transferred in usage to Rachub (cf. Rhewl and Rhyl).

RADNOR see **NEW RADNOR**

RADNOR FOREST, CLUD Rad SO2064

'hunting preserve in (lordship of) Radnor', 'pile, heap', p.n. ***Radnor***, E ***forest***, W ***clud***

Clud which is called the chace of Radenore 1304, *Radenore Forest* 1383-4, *Forrest Cluid* 1536-9, *forest of Radnor, otherwise fforest Gledey* 1550, *y fforest Gluid* 1588

A large area of former hunting forest close to New Radnor (q.v.). The forest is on a considerable hill, and the el. ***clud*** also appears in Gludre farm (probably the *Glut* in poetry c.1215, with ***bre*** 'hill') at the foot of Llethr Du on the north side of the Forest, and in the epithet of Einion Clud (*Eniald' Cluth* 1183-4, *Eynaun Clut* 1170), a ruler of Maelienydd [q.v.], killed in 1177. Fforest-fach (*y fforest vach* c.1700, ***fforest***, ***bach***) is probably in contrast to the much larger Radnor Forest. Cf. Glyder.

RADUR Glam ST1280

'oratory', ****aradur***

Arad[ur] c.1100 (c.1200), *Radur* 1254, *Aradur* 1506, *Aradyr* 1533-8, *Errader* c.1545, *Aradier, the Radyr* 1554, *Y Radur, yr adyr* c.1566, *Yradur* c.1569, *y Radir* 1734

W ****aradur*** is a development from L ***oratorium*** 'house of prayer, chapel'. Many forms show interpretation of the unaccented first syllable *Ar-* as the def.art. ***y***, ***yr***, which gave rise to anglicized forms with ***the***. The modern village developed around what was Upper Radur or Radur Uchaf (*Radyr ycha* 1671, *Upper Radyr farm* 1766) a farm about a mile north of the parish church (now absorbed into a housing estate). The older village became known as Lower Radur (*Radyr isha* early 17cent.). Cf. Radyr Monm (*Radour* 1556-8, *Radyr* 1833), a spelling frequently used for the Glam Radur.

RAGLAN, RHAGLAN Monm SO4107

'rampart', ****rhaglan***

Ragalan 1172, *Ragthan* 1174, *Raglam* c.1100 (c.1200), *Ragelan* 1234, *Raghelan* 1254

Although ***rhaglan*** is not independently evidenced, its existence seems probable since ***rhag*** 'front, fore' has the sense 'projecting' and ***glan*** can mean 'bank'; cf. ***rhagfur*** (with ***mur*** 'wall') 'bulwark, rampart'. An 11cent. motte-and-bailey castle is believed to lie under the 15cent. castle palace.

RAM Carm SN5946

'(place at the) Ram', p.n. ***Ram***

Ram, Ram Inn 1875

The name of a public house (named after the animal) at a road junction, whose architecture suggests a date c.1800.

RAMSEY, YNYS DEWI Pemb SM6923

'Hrafn's island', 'Dewi's island', pers.n. ***Hrafn***, ON ***ey***, W ***ynys***, pers.n. ***Dewi***

(*insula de*) *Ramesey* 1293, *Ramsey (Iland)* 1385, *Ramesey (Isle)* 1536-9, *Ynis Devanog* 1722, *Ramsey alias Ynys Tevannogge* 1728, *Ynis yr hyrdhod* 1722, *Ynys yr Hyrddod or Ramsey Island* 1748, *Ynys Dewi* 1825

As with several examples of p.n. in Ram- in Essex, Kent, Yorkshire and Staffordshire, alternative interpretations fit the forms. The preference for the ON pers.n. Hrafn is influenced by at least two other islands (Anglesey and Bardsey q.v.) having an ON pers.n. in combination with ON ***ey***. It may still be 'garlic island' (ON ***hramsa***, ***ey***); there is evidence of wild garlic on the island and headland called Trwyn Garlic (***trwyn*** 'point'). Several late names emerge with varying status and usage. The W name Ynys yr Hyrddod is a translation based on interpreting Ramsey as 'rams' (***hwrdd*** pl. ***hyrddod***) while Ynys Hwrddod is also the name of a small rock, and one cove is Aber Myharan (***myharen*** 'ram') but these lack historical forms. Ynys Dyfannog commemorates an obscure person Tyfannog; there was a chapel (*Capel Divanog* c.1600) dedicated to the saint on the island. The modern name Ynys Dewi associates the island with Tyddewi/St David's (q.v.). Ramsey Sound/Swnd Dewi (*The Sound* 1593, E ***sound***, W ***swnd***, ***swnt***) separates the island from the mainland near St David's. There appears to have been an even older name, *Lymen* c.150, *insula Lemeneia* 14cent. (1516), which may be Br ***līm-*** the antecedent of W ***llif*** 'stream, flood' but the evidence is inconclusive.

RASAU, RASA Monm (formerly Brec) SO1512

'races', ***ras*** pl. ***rasau***

Rhas-y-Mwyn 1697, *Rhasau'r mwyn* 1778, *the Race mine works* 1810, *Racey* 1830, *Rassa* 1840

Earlier forms show that this was Rhasau'r Mwyn, 'watercourses at the mine' (***y, mwyn***) possibly in contrast to nearby Rhasau'r Glo Aberystruth (***glo*** 'coal'). Here, the specific sense was of 'scourings, a rush', a technique of damming watercourses and releasing water to expose and wash minerals.

REDBERTH Pemb SN0804

?'ford by the bush', ?***rhyd, y, perth***

Ridebard 1361, *Ridbert* 1543, *Redbarte* 1548-58, *Redberte* 1541, *Redberth* 1602

The early forms with -bard, -bart, -bert are similar to those for Narberth (q.v.). The ford is probably Norchard Ford in Carew River immediately north of the village.

RED ROSES, RHOS-GOCH Carm SN2011

'red moor', E ***red***, W ***rhos, coch***

Rosgoch 1307, *Great Rosegough* 1653, *Y Rhosgoch* 1775, *Rhosgoch-fach, ~ -fawr* 1819, *Red Roses* 1843, *Red Roses, Rhosgochfawr* 1875

The E name translated ***coch*** but misinterpreted ***rhos*** as E ***rose***. The emergence of a pl. *Roses* may be ascribed to the existence of the two farms (***great, mawr, bach***). However, it has to be noted that there the W pl. word ***rhos*** 'roses, rose bushes, representation of roses, esp. as a heraldic device' may have encouraged the association with roses; cf. both Rhos^2 and Rhos^3 as *Rose*. That perception was reinforced by the adoption of The Red Roses as the name of the tavern here.

RED WHARF BAY, TRAETH COCH Angl SH5481

'red strand (bay)', E ***red***, E ***warth***, E ***bay***, W (***y***), ***traeth, coch***

The bay of the Reyde Warth 16cent., *Ytrath Coch (redde)* mid 16cent., *Traeth Koch* 1562, *the red Warthe* 1566, *Y Traeth Koch* 1617, *Red Warth* 1617, *Red Wharfe* 1730, *Red Warf Bay & Harbour* 1777, *Red Wharf or Traeth Coch* 1795

The extensive mud and sand flats are clayey. The E form has the west of England word ***warth*** 'shore, strand, stretch of coast' which was eventually adapted to E ***wharf*** 'quayside area' probably because of the major medieval and early modern harbour there. ***warth*** and ***wharf*** frequently alternate along the Monm side of the Bristol Channel. An older name for the location was *Porth y llong duy* 1470, *Porth Llongau* 1536-9, *Porth longdi* 1541, *Porth Longdy* 1732 (***porth*** 'cove', ***llong*** 'swamp', ***tŷ*** 'house') referring to the mud flats; cf. Llong.

REDWICK Monm ST4184

'reed farm', OE ***hrēod***, OE ***wīc***

Redewic 1153-76 (1290), *Radewyk(e)*1317, *Redewyk* 1387-8, *yr Redwic* c.1566

The village's location in the marshy Caldicot Levels adds support to it being a house or village where reeds were abundant or which harvested reeds.

RESOLFEN Glam SN8202

'?stubble moor', ***rhos***, ?***soflyn***

Rossaulin c.1193-9, *Roshowelin* c.1203-c.1208, *Rossaulyn* 1245-53, *Rossoulyn* 1261, *Resowlen* 1535, *Resolwen* 1651, *Resolven* 1667

A difficult name. The pl. ***sofl*** 'stubble' occasionally appears in p.ns in the masc. dim. ***soflyn*** which is possibly in the early forms. There is reason to believe that there was a fem. var. ***soflen*** probably influenced by the term ***sofl wen*** 'white stubble' and ***adsol*** (from ***adsofl*** 'untilled stubble' as in Adsofl-wen Pemb and Adsol-wen Card); this emerges in the later forms. It appears that -fl- became -wl- in some early forms but that alternative forms with -fl- suffered metathesis of -fl- to -lf- . The unstressed first syllable ***rhos*** became Rhes-. The name applied earlier to a former medieval chapel near Tyn-y-cwm on higher ground (now afforested). It is not quite clear how a moor could be associated with stubble, unless ***rhos*** was used in the sense of 'upland' or the 'outcrop, promontory' of Mynydd Resolfen.

REYNALTON Pemb SN0908

'Reginald's farm', pers.n. ***Reynold***, OE ***tūn***

Reynaldeston 1394, *Reynalton* 1409, *Reynoldon*, *Renalton* 1535

The pers.n. is derived from OF Reinauld, Reynaud and probably referred to an E or Flemish settler. The genitive -s seems to have been dropped early.

REYNOLDSTON Glam SS4890

'Regenweard's farm', pers.n. ***Regenweard***, OE ***tūn***

Renewardestoune 1306, *Reynewardeston'* 1396, *Reynoldeston* 1465

The pers.n. was replaced with the more familiar Reynold.

RHAEADR EWYNNOL see **SWALLOW FALLS**

RHAEADR (GWY) see **RHAYADER**

RHAGLAN see **RAGLAN**

RHANDIR-MWYN Carm SN7843

'portion of land with a mine', ***rhandir, mwyn***

Rhandir y Mwyn 1814, *Rhandirmwyn* 1822

mwyn is 'ore' and later 'mine'. The stream in the village is *Nant-y-mwyn* 1831. ***rhandir***, literally 'share-land', can also encompass meanings such as 'region, piece of land'. Here it probably refers to that share of the parish of Llanfair-ar-y-bryn which was divided into Rhandir Abad (*Rhandir Abad, or Abbots hamlet* 1710) belonging to the abbot of Strata Florida, and Rhandirganol (*Rhandir ganol, or middle hamlet* 1710), Rhandirisaf (*Rhandir Isha Hamlett* 1671, *Rhandir issa, or lowest hamlet* 1710) and Rhandiruchaf (*Rhandir Ycha* 1671, *Rhandir ucha, or highest hamlet* 1710), distinguished as 'middle' (***canol***), 'lower' (***isaf***) and 'upper' (***uchaf***). During the 18cent. up to 400 workers were employed in the lead mines. The def.art. of the first form (and in *Nant-y-mwyn* stream) is clear evidence of the noun ***mwyn*** 'mine' (cf. Rhyd-y-mwyn Flints) rather than the adj. ***mwyn*** 'fair, pleasant' which is the popular perception.

RHATH, Y see **ROATH**

RHAYADER, RHAEADR (GWY) Radn SN9768

'waterfall (on the river Gwy)', ***rhaeadr***, r.n. ***Gwy***

Rayadyr Gwy 1177, *Raidergoe* c.1191, *Rayader* 1295, *Raiadergwy* 1543, *Rayadr* 1709

Once a spectacular waterfall, but now only rapids in the Wye/Gwy, the result of cutting a water-channel in the river during the erection of a bridge 1780.

RHEIDOL, Afon Card SN7987-6380

'swift (river)', ***afon, rheidiol*** var. ***rheidol***

Retiaul 1120, *Ridol* 1301-2, *Rheidiol* 1613, *R. Ridal* 1646, *Ridol R.* 1760, *Rheidol R.* 1834

The river (as Nant-y-llyn) flows from Llyn Llygad Rheidol (***llygad*** 'eye; source of river or well') and then, as Rheidol, through the present Nant-y-moch reservoir into the sea at Aberystwyth. Near Devil's Bridge (q.v.) the river is particularly rapid, with several waterfalls. In some of the anglicized forms, the -i- of the first syllable probably represents -ai- or -ei-. There is evidence of some local use of *Rhediol* as late as 1892.

RHES-Y-CAE Flints SJ1870

'row next to the field', ***rhes, y, cae***

Rese y cae 1744, *Rhesycae* 1779, *Rhes y Cae* 1807, *Rhês-y-cae* 1839, *Rhes-y-Cae* 1840, *Rhes-y-cae* 1878

The 1744 document refers to two messuages, which later became a row of houses (probably for the quarrymen on Halkyn Mountain) adjacent to the road between Moel-y-crio and Lixwm and to the mountain road itself.

RHEWL[1] Denb SJ1060

'the road', ***yr*, *heol*** var. ***hewl***

Rhewl 1872-3

Several minor roads converge on this hamlet where the main Ruthin-Denbigh road crosses Afon Clywedog (formerly via a ford, Rhyd-y-cilgwyn). The modern route takes the road across a bridge less than a hundred yards downstream.

RHEWL[2] Denb SJ1844

'the road', ***yr*, *heol*** var. ***hewl***

Rhewl 1819

The name of the hamlet at the junction of the road north of the river Dee with a mountain road which leads from the foothills of Mynydd Llandysilio (probably from a quarry there). It was this quarry (and others in the vicinity) which possibly account for the growth of the hamlet.

RHIGOS, Y Glam SN9205

'the heath', ***y*, *grugos***

Rugois 1281, *Rugoys* 1314, (*o*) *Regoes* 16cent., *Rhygos* 1793

Despite the *-ois/-oys* of the early forms this is probably ***grugos*** (which appears almost exclusively in a few p.ns), here lenited after the def.art. to *Y Rugos* and later modified to Rhigos in the supposition that it was a mutation of rh-. The common local pronunciation among W speakers is (Y) Ricos. *Y* is not used by E speakers.

RHINOG FAWR, RHINOG FACH Mer SH6629, 6627

'great, little ?threshold', ***rhiniog*** var. ***rhinog*, *hinog*, *mawr*, *bach***

Yr Hinog Fawr, Yr Hinog Fach 1795, *Rhinog Fawr, Rhinog Fach* 1819

Two prominent hills flanking (Bwlch) Drws Ardudwy (*Drws Ardydwy* 1597, *Drwsardudwy* 1604, *Bwlch Drŵs Ardidwy* 1795, *Bwlch drws Ardudwy* 1813, ***bwlch*** 'pass', ***drws*** 'gap, pass'), a route into Dyffryn Ardudwy (q.v.). Collectively, they are known as Y Rhinogau (pl. ***-au***). The derivation of ***rhin(i)og*** is ***yr*** 'the' and the rare ***hin*** 'side, edge' (as in Rhuthun q.v.). The word ***rhin(i)og*** can mean 'door-frame' leading some to argue that it refers figuratively to the door-frame provided by the two hills on either side of the ***drws*** 'door'. However, the very late appearance of Rhinog suggests the more common meaning of the 'threshold' of the ***drws***.

RHISGA see **RISCA**

RHIW, Afon, River see **BERRIEW**

RHIW Caern SH2228

'hill', ***rhiw***

Riu 1254, *Rew* 1352, *Riw* 1553, *Rhiw* 1619

The roads from Aberdaron and from Rhoshirwaun lead up to the hamlet which has Mynydd y Graig and Mynydd Rhiw on either side. The church is dedicated to Y Ddelw Fyw 'the Living Image' but is said by some to have commemorated an otherwise undocumented Aelrhyw, whose well, Ffynnon Aelrhiw, is half-a-mile north-east. Such a pers.n. is probably an adaptation of Y Ddelw Fyw influenced by ***ael*** 'brow' and ***rhiw***.

RHIWABON see **RUABON**

RHIWBRYFDIR Mer SH6946
'hill of the land of the hunted animal', ***rhiw***, ***pryf***, ***tir***
Riwe Brythdir 1508, *Riw bryvdir* 1532, *Rhywbryfdyr* 1632
A p.n. which defies satisfactory explanation. The common alternation of -f- and -dd- in the first two forms make identifying the original el. uncertain. The middle el. could be ***brith*** 'variegated', but runs counter to other examples of Brithdir which show no evidence of a change from -i- to -y- (which is found consistently from the beginning). If the middle el. is ***pryf*** in reference to a wild animal which is hunted, possibly a fox, it is easier to explain the change in the character of the vowel. The historical forms point clearly to a place described as *Pryfdir*, which would be land noted for its hunting. The ***rhiw*** is the hill on the north-easterly slopes of Craig Nyth-y-gigfran, bordering the Oakley Quarry.

RHIWLAS[1] Caern SH5765
'verdant hill', ***rhiw***, ***glas***
Rhiwlas 1808, *Rhiw-las* 1838
The hill leads up the lower slopes of Moelyci and Moel Rhiwen.

RHIWLAS[2] Denb SJ1932
'verdant hill', ***rhiw***, ***glas***
Riwlas 1329, *Rhywlas* 1580, *Rhiwlas* 1659
The hamlet is south of Foel Rhiwlas whose verdant southern slopes were in contrast to the bare (***moel***) summit.

RHIWLAS[3] Mer SH9237
'verdant hill', ***rhiw***, ***glas***
y Rhiwlas 1592-3, *Rhiwlas* 1613-14
The hamlet took its name from the house with wooded slopes and parkland north of Bala.

RHONDDA Glam SS9796
'noisy (river)', ***rhodd***, noun suff. ***-ni***
Rotheni late 12cent., *Rotheny* 1297, *Rodney* 1600
Rhondda consists of a series of industrial villages which developed from the mid 19cent. in the valleys of the river Rhondda and its upper reaches Rhondda Fawr (*Rotheni maur* 1203, ***mawr*** 'big, bigger') and Rhondda

Fechan (*Rotheney Vehan* 1536-9, ***bechan*** 'small, lesser'). The valley and commote are *Glenrotheny* 1268, *Glynrotheni* 1307, *Glynrotheney* 1415, *glyn Roddne* c.1566, *Glynronthie* 1559 'valley of (river) Rhoddni'. The r.n. developed by metathesis from *Rhoddni* into Rhondda by the 18cent. probably by way of an intermediate form *Rhonddi* suggested by spellings such as *Rhonddyvechan* 1711. The r.n. probably has the sense of 'noisy (river)' containing ***rhawdd*** (as in ***adrodd*** 'to relate, to report') and the noun suff. ***-ni*** found in several r.ns. However, a case has been made for considering that there are two groups of forms, one in -i the other in -eu/-ey, and that this second group suggests that the original second el. was OW ****gneu*** 'beget' rather than ***-ni***. Forms supporting this el. seem to be somewhat later that the -i < -ni forms. Whatever the el., the vars *Rhoddni, Rhoddneu, Rhoddnei* and *Rhoddne* have been interpreted as vars of the pl. ending -au, taken to refer to the two valleys, then becoming -a. The p.n. did not become fixed until 1897 when Ystradyfodwg UDC adopted the name.

RHONDDA FACH, FAWR see **RHONDDA**

RHOOSE, Y RHWS Glam ST0666

'(the) moorland', ***y, rhos***

Rhos 1533-8, *Rouse* 1538-44, *Rowse* 1587, *Roouse* 1596, *Rows* 1610-30, *Rooss* mid 17cent., *y Rwss* 1540-77, *Rws* c.1569, *Roose* 1595-6

The village is on formerly extensive heathland. ***rhos*** usually remains as Rhos or Ross, which has led some to argue that this Rhws/Roose should be ascribed to a var., an otherwise unrecorded OW ****rōs*** (seen also in Rhos[2], Roose Pemb and Roose Cornwall and Lancashire). However, the late appearance of the name here (as *Rhos*) suggests that its development was analogical with the instances of over-rounding of -ō- > -ū- seen in medieval records. A similar characteristic is seen elsewhere in a few examples of forms for Rhos[2] Glam. In local E speech, the initial consonant is R- rather than Rh-.

RHOS[1] Carm SN3835

'moorland', ***rhos***

Rhos-Geler 1891, *Rhosgeler* 1906, *Rhos* 1947

A late name referring to its location in the moorland part of Llangeler parish and taken directly from an adjoining farm Rhosgeler described in 1899 as a piece of the former common.

RHOS[2]**, Y** Glam SN7303

'the moorland', ***y, rhos***

le Rose 1529-30, *Roos* 1610

A late 19cent. village established on moorland above the Tawe valley. On *Roos* see Rhoose, and on *Rose* see Red Roses.

RHOS[3], THE Pemb SN0114

'the moor', ***rhos***

Rowse 1554, *Rhose* 1772, *Ross* 1615, *Rhos* 1818, *Lower, Upper Rose* 1847

Since the location is in a wedge of land between the Eastern Cleddau and Millin Brook near Rose Castle Point, it is possible that the sense of 'promontory, headland' is appropriate and that the name applied to a much wider area.

RHOSCOLYN Angl SH2675

'Colyn's headland', ***rhos***, pers.n. ***Colyn***

Roscolyn 1254, *Rhosgolyn* c.1329, *Rosgolyn* 1393,
Llanwenvayn alias Roskolyn 1583, *Rhoscolyn* 1695,
Rhoscolyn Llanwenfaen 1990

The identity of Colyn is unknown. ***rhos*** probably signified 'headland' (see Penrhos), located as it is on a promontory culminating in Rhoscolyn Head. The church was dedicated to Gwenfaen whose well is nearby, and Llanwenfaen (*Llanwe(n)vayn* 1543) is documented for the church and the area.

RHOSCROWDDER see RHOSCROWTHER

RHOSCROWTHER, RHOSCROWDDER Pemb SM9002

'crowder's moor', ***rhos***, W ***crythor***

Rostruther 1291, *Roscrouthur* 1324, *Rosecrowther* 1488,
Rosgrothor 1545

The W ***crythor***, ***crythwr*** 'crowder, ffidler' (from W ***crwth*** 'crowd, fiddle') is the more likely origin but its derivative E occupational surname ***Crowther*** (drawn directly from ME ***crouth*** 'fiddle') have certainly influenced the later development. The secular p.n. may have replaced Eglwys Ddegeman or Llanddegyman (*Eglwys Degemman* late 12cent., *Llan Degeman, Eglwys Degemman* 13cent.,) since the church is dedicated to Decumanus or Degyman (Degman). Cf. Llanddegyman (*Llandegeman* 1816-7) Brec and St Decuman's Somerset.

RHOSESMOR Flints SJ2168

'Esmor's moor', ***rhos***, pers.n. ***Esmor***

Rosesmor 1533, *yrros* 1577, *Rhos Essmor* 1615, *y Rhos* 1628,
Rhos Esmore 1664, *Rose Esmor* 1683, *Rhose* 1740, *Rhosesmor* 1742,
Rhos Esmor 1838

Esmor has not been identified. The moor is on the south-east of Moel-y-gaer but there is no evidence to support the popular belief that it is 'rhos's moor' or that -esmor is 'east moor'.

RHOSFARCED see ROSEMARKET

RHOS-FAWR Caern SH3839

'big moor', ***rhos, mawr***

Rhosvawre 1656-7, *Rhos-fawr* 1838

The hamlet is west of the village of Y Ffôr and ***rhos*** appears in several farm names nearby.

RHOSGADFAN Caern SH5057

'Cadfan's moor' ***rhos***, pers.n. ***Cadfan***

Rhos y Gadfan 1827, *Rhos-gadfan* 1838

The unidentified Cadfan's name was interpreted in the 1827 form as ***y gadfan*** 'the battlefield'.

RHOS-GOCH[1] Angl SH4089

'red moor', ***rhos, coch***

y Ros goch 1549, *y Rhose goch* 1707, *Rhôs-gôch* 1838

The actual soil and water channels of the moor are to be associated with the mineral deposits of what came to be called Mynydd Parys a mile-and-a-half to the east. Extensive copper mines and subsequent pollution was a feature of the 18cent. and 19cent., seen also in an Afon Goch on the north-west of Mynydd Parys.

RHOS-GOCH[2] Radn SO1847

'red moor', ***rhos, coch***

Rose goch 1666, *Rhosgoch* 1791

Perhaps the colour of autumnal ferns and bracken on Rhos-goch Common (*Rhos Goch* c.1817).

RHOS-GOCH[3] see **RED ROSES**

RHOS-HILL, RHOS-HYL Pemb SN1940

'moorland hill', W ***rhos***, E ***hill***

Rhos 1544, *Rhos-hill* 1891

An unusual hybrid in a W-speaking area with ***hill*** as a late addition to a modern hamlet, possibly under the influence of nearby *Windy Hill* 1891; ***rhos*** is found in Tŷ-rhos and Rhosygilwen in the close vicinity. The cymricized -hyl does appear occasionally elsewhere; cf. Rhyl.

RHOSHIRWAUN Caern SH1929

'long white moor', ***rhos, hir, gwyn*** fem. ***gwen***

Rhose herwenn 1597, *Rhosehirwen* 1640-1, *Rhos hirwen* 1776, *Rhôshirwaun* 1795, *Rhos hirwaun* 1802

The moor stretches alongside the Aberdaron road as evidenced in the scattered farms Hirwaun and Cefn Hirwaun. The white of the moor was possibly a reference to cotton grass which is a feature of unploughed wetlands during the summer. Further deterioration of the land account for the perception that the final el. was ***gwaun*** 'moor' rather than ***gwen***. Today the land is in agricultural use.

RHOS-HYL see **RHOS-HILL**

RHOSILI Glam SS4188
'Sulien's moorland promontory', ***rhos***, pers.n. ***Sulien***
rosulgen 1136-54, *Rossili* 1230, *Ros ssili* c.1566, *Rhosily* 1583
Rhosili lies on the exposed north slopes of a promontory. The unstressed ending *-en* is lost; cf. Barry. Frequently spelt Rhossili, probably a residual form of Rhos-Sili.

RHOS-LAN Caern SH4840
'bank moor', ***rhos***, ***glan***
ros y lan 1562, *rose y llan* 1577, *Rhos y Llan* 1838, *Rhoslan* 1947
The 1562 and the modern form suggest an association with ***glan*** 'bank' since Rhos-lan is midway between Afon Dwyfach and Afon Dwyfor and is a mile-and-a-half from Glan Dwyfach. The other two forms show popular association with ***llan*** 'church' (rather like Rhos-y-llan, Tudweiliog) although there is no church in the immediate vicinity, Llanystumdwy being the nearest.

RHOSLEFAIN Mer SH5705
'flat moor', ***rhos***, ***llyfn*** fem ***llefn***
y roes leaven 1592-3, *Rhôsleven* 1731, *Rhos Leven* 1796, *Rhosllefen* 1840
The moor is a fairly level stretch with hills on either side. The adj. has maintained the dial. two-syllable form ***llefen*** (with an intrusive vowel as opposed to the more usual ***llefn***), which has allowed the modern form to be influenced by ***llefain*** 'cry', readily associated with a battle ascribed to this location.

RHOSLLANNERCHRUGOG Denb SJ2946
'moor of the heather glade', ***rhos***, ***llannerch***, ***grugog***
Rose lane aghregog 1544-5, *Rhos Llannerch Rirgog* 1546, *Rowse* 1698, *Rhos Llanerchrugog* 1838
The moor was between Ponciau (***ponciau*** 'hillocks') and Afon Eitha, where a large village developed here in response to industrial exploitation in the 19cent. Frequently called Rhos.

RHOS-MAEN Carm SN6424
'moor of the stone', ***rhos***, (***y***), ***maen***
Rosmayne 1532, *Rosemayne* c.1580, *Rhos y Maen* 1760, *Rosemaen* 1804
On the slopes of a low hill above the river Tywi. The location of the stone is unknown but a nearby house is *Cil-maen* (1891).

RHOS-MEIRCH Angl SH4677

'moor of (the) stallions', ***rhos***, (*y*), ***march*** pl. ***meirch***

Rhos-y-meirch 1710, *Rhos-meirch* 1838

The moor appears to have been the range of wild horses.

RHOSNEIGR Angl SH3173

'Neigr's moor', ***rhos***, pers.n. ***Neigr***

Rhos Neigr 1582, *Rhosneigr* 1747, *Rhose Neigir* 1768

Neigr has been traditionally identified with the Yneigr who reputedly fought in the battle of Cerrig-y-Gwyddyl in 450 to oust the Irish from Angl and who may also be commemorated in Gorsedd Neigr (*Gorsadd yneigr* 1760) near Llaneilian.

RHOSNESNI Denb SJ3450

'Nesni's moor' ***rhos***, pers.n. ***Nesni***

Rhosenesnie 1593, *Rhos nessa, Nissa, Nyssa* 1620, *Rhôs nesney* c.1700, *Rhosnesney* 1738

Rhosnesni seems to have been part of one of the most extensive of the moors on the outskirts of Wrexham, namely Acton Moor (*alias Gwayn y Tervyn* 1561, *y Werne Acton* 1569, ***gwaun*** 'moorland, heath, ***y*** 'the', ***terfyn*** 'boundary, edge', ***gwern*** 'alder-marsh'). The identity of Nesni is unknown but the association with a pers.n. can be compared to Rhosrobin in the north-west of Wrexham. The form of his name also seems to have been unfamiliar, because a 1620 map offers ***nesa(f)*** 'closest, next' and one 18cent. writer registered it as *Rhos-nessa-i-ni* 'the moor closest to us' (***i*** 'to', ***ni*** 'us').

RHOS-ON-SEA, LLANDRILLO-YN-RHOS Denb SH8381

'Rhos by the sea', 'church of Trillo in Rhos', cantref n. ***Rhos***, E ***on***, E ***sea***, W ***llan***, pers.n. ***Trillo***, ***yn***

Lantreullo 1254, *Llandrillo* 1538, *llann drillo yn Ros* 1565-87, *Llandrillo in Rhose* 1691, *Llandrillo-yn-Rhos* 1742-3, *Llandriloo yn Rhos (Rhos-on-Sea)* 1898

Rhos was the medieval administrative cantref. Rhos-on-Sea is recent, having been coined in the 19cent. to highlight the area's attraction as a resort (cf. nearby Colwyn Bay). By now, a perceived distinction exists between the village of Llandrillo-yn-Rhos and the resort of Rhos-on-Sea. A secular name was Dinerth or Dineirth (*Dynerth'* 1291, *Dynardh, Dinard* 1270) seen in the modern Dinarth Hall probably ***din***, ***arth*** pl. ***eirth***, possibly a reference to fearless warriors.

RHOSTRYFAN Caern SH4957

'moor of Tryfan', ***rhos***, p.n. ***Tryfan***

Rhos y Tryfan 1816, *Rhos Tryfan* 1827

The hill south-east of Rhostryfan is Moel Tryfan (*Moel Tryfan* 1827,

Moel-y-Tryfan 1838, ***moel*** 'bare hill'). The ***rhos*** and the ***moel*** take their name from a house called Tryfan (*Tryfan* 1625-49, *Tryvan* 1646-7, *o'r Tryfan* 1689), now Tryfan Mawr and Tryfan Bach, although the reason for the house name itself is unclear, since the adjacent Moel Tryfan is more of a ***moel*** than a ***tryfan*** 'distinctive summit, sharp peak' (cf. Tryfan).

RHOSTYLLEN Denb SJ3148

'moor on a ledge', ***rhos, ystyllen***

Rhos Stellan 1546, *Rhôs ystylhen c.* 1700, *Rostyllan* 1752, *Rhosdyllen* 1793, *Rhos-estyllen* 1838

The usual meaning of ***ystyllen***, var. ***astell*** or ***astyllen*** was 'plank, board, lath', but here it is used figuratively of a ledge (a common meaning for ***astell***) of rock, above the meadows beside the river Clywedog.

RHOS-Y-BOL Angl SH4288

'hillocky moor', ***rhos, y, bol***

ros y bol 1549, *Rhos y bol* 1609-10, *Rhos-y-bol* 1891

The usual meaning of ***bol*** is 'belly, paunch' probably a reference to landscape around Rhos-y-bol characterised by hummocks and hollows, as in the commote's name Talybolion 'end of the hillocks' (***bol*** pl. ***bolion***).

RHOSYGWALIAU Mer SH9434

'moor at the walls', ***rhos, y, gwaliau***

Rose y Gwallie 1592, *Rhos y Gwalie* 1722, *Rhos-y-gwaliau* 1838

The moor was near the walls of Plas Rhiwaedog. The early forms display the dial. var. ***gwalie***. It has also been argued that the walls were attempts to enclose moorland.

RHUALLT Flints SJ0775

'extreme hill', ***rhy-, allt***

Ryallt 1585, *Rhuallt* 1658-9, *Rhyalht als (ut creditur) Rhiw yr Alht* c.1700

The steep hill leads from the Clwyd range down to the flatlands of the Clwyd and Elwy rivers. The intensive pref. ***rhy-*** was replaced in spelling by Rhu- probably by analogy with Rhuddlan and Rhuthun, and even interpreted as ***rhiw*** 'hill' (c.1700).

RHUDDLAN Flints SJ0278

'red bank', ***rhudd, glan***

brudglann 10cent. (late 13cent.), *Roelend* 1086, *Ruthelan* c.1191, *Rothelan* c.1253, *Rundlan* 1254, *Rodlan* 1291, *Rhuttlan* 1320, *Rothelan* 1381, *Rudlan* 14cent., *Ruthlan* 1437, *Rhuddlan* 1577-8, *Rutland* 1582, *Ruthland* 1623, *Rhyddlan* 1795

The banks of the river Clwyd are distinctively red at this point. The early records occur in the context of E and NF settlements with several forms showing the influence of the E ***land***. The 14cent. form *Rudlan* reflects an anglicized pronunciation which is still heard today, possibly influenced by E ***ruddy***. It has been associated with references to *Cledemutha* 921 (probably r.n. Clwyd, OE ***mūða*** 'mouth, estuary').

RHUTHUN see RUTHIN

RHYD

Mer SH6342

'ford', ***rhyd***

Rhyd y Gyrffinie c. 1700, *Rhyd cyffinia* 1792-1800, *Rhyd-y-gyffiniau* 1838, *Rhyd* 1898, *Rhŷd* 1901

The hamlet is near a ford which crosses the stream now called Afon Rhyd, the boundary (***y, cyffin*** pl. ***cyffiniau***) of the parishes of Llanfrothen and Ffestiniog. Rhyd-cyffiniau is still the name of a house here.

RHYDAMAN see AMMANFORD

RHYDARGAEAU

Carm SN4326

'ford at the weirs', ***rhyd, argae*** pl. ***argaeau***

Rhyd ar Gaye 1747, *Rhyd yr caie* 1798, *Rhyd-y-caeau* 1831, *Rhydargaeau* 1839

On a stream Nant Brechfa. The forms show ***argaeau*** being interpreted as ***ar*** 'on' and ***cae*** pl. ***caeau*** 'fields'.

RHYDCYMERAU

Carm SN5738

'ford at the confluences', ***rhyd***, (***y***), ***cymer*** pl. ***cymerau***

Rheed y Cumere 1760, *Rhydcymere* 1851

A small settlement around a chapel (*Capel* 1831) at the confluence of two tributaries of Afon Melinddwr.

RHYD-DDU

Caern SH5652

'dark ford', ***rhyd, du***

Rhyd-ddu 1891, *Rhyd-ddû* 1920

The main Caernarfon-Beddgelert road and the minor Drws-y-coed road cross Afon Gwyrfai through a ford which was in the shadows of adjacent hills. The village at the junction of the two roads grew in response to several quarries, particularly Glan yr Afon quarry.

RHYDFELEN, RHYDYFELIN

Glam ST0988

'yellow ford', ***rhyd, melyn*** fem. ***melen***

y Ryd velen 1522, *ryd velen* 1570, *rhyd velen* 1630, *Rhydfelen* 1839, *Rhyd felen* 1856, *Rhyd-y-felin* 1885

The yellow-brown water was probably the result of frequent passage by carts through a muddy ford (through the river Taf). Very late forms and widespread usage give some currency to the name as Rhydyfelin, 'the mill ford' (*y*, ***melin***) despite the absence of any mill.

RHYDLEWIS Card SN3447

'Lewis's ford', ***rhyd***, pers.n. ***Lewis***

Rhydlewis 1791, *Rhyd Lewis* 1803, *Rhyd-Lewis* 1891

The identity of Lewis is unknown. The bridge, Pont Rhydlewis, which superseded the ford, spans Nant Coll.

RHYDLIOS Caern SH1830

'ford of many', ***rhyd***, ***lliaws*** var. ***llios***

Rhyd llios 1656-7, *rhydlios* 1682, *Ridlios* 1727-8, *Rhyd-y-lluaws* 1840

A var. of ***lliaws*** 'multitude, abundant' is the ***llios*** preserved in this p.n. and in two other places of the same name (in Llanasa Flints and in Llansilin Denb). However the significance of ***llios*** has not been satisfactorily explained. Perhaps the ford (through Afon Cyllyfelin) was characterised by the many people who either lived close by or gathered there (for whatever reason). Some have assumed them to be pilgrims on the way to Bardsey, but since the ford was at the junction of three parishes (Aberdaron, Bryncroes and Bodferin) it may have been a convenient meeting place. It has also been plausibly argued that the practice of beating parish bounds may have some bearing on the name.

RHYDLYDAN Denb SH8950

'broad ford', ***rhyd***, ***llydan***

y Rhyd llydan 1602, *Rhyd llydan* 1673, *Rhydlydan* 1787

Several minor roads from mountainous areas converge here to cross the river Merddwr where ***merddwr*** 'stagnant water' suggests a slow-moving river which could accommodate a wide ford. The ford has been superseded by a bridge. Two of the documents cited above also offer an alias which has not survived, *monte Rendesvous* 1673, *monte Rendevous* 1787, which seems to apply to the convergence of the mountain routes.

RHYDODYN see **EDWINSFORD**

RHYDOWEN Card SN4445

'Owain's ford', ***rhyd***, pers.n. ***Owain***

Rit Iweyn 1235-65 (1324), *Ryt Yweyn* 1244/71 (1324), *Ryt Ywein* after 1271 (1331), *Ryde Owen* 1568, *Rhyd Owen* 1580, *Rhydowen* 1742

The ford through Afon Cletwr was superseded by Pont Rhydowen to the west of the village. In the medieval period the name was also identified with a farm held by Talley abbey.

RHYDRI, Y see **RUDRY**

RHYD-SBENS see **RHYDSPENCE**

RHYDSPENCE, RHYD-SBENS Radn SO2447
?'ford near the spence', ***rhyd***, ?***sbens***
Rhydspence 1817, *Rhydspence* 1875
The second el. may be ***sbens*** (attested in W from the 15cent.) which has a number of meanings including 'buttery, pantry', less commonly 'place in which drink is kept', or, given the more anglicized area in the 19cent., directly from the modern E ***spence*** with similar meaning (and from which W ***sbens*** is a borrowing). The significance of ***spence*** here is not known.

RHYDTALOG see **RHYTALOG**

RHYDUCHAF Mer SH9038
'higher ford', ***rhyd***, ***uchaf***
Rhyd Ucha 1739, *Rhyd-uchaf* 1838
The ford has now been replaced by a bridge (*a Bridge called Rhyducha* 1801, *Rhyducha Bridge* 1802, *Pont Rhyd-uchaf* modern) for the minor Bala-Llidiardau road to cross a stream called Nant Aberduldog which flows into Afon Trywervn. Where that stream is crossed by another minor road from Ty'n-ddôl was presumably the lower ford. The name Tal-y-bont is occasionally used.

RHYD-WYN Angl SH3188
'Gwyn's ford', ***rhyd***, pers.n. ***Gwyn***
Rhydwyn 1818, *Rhyd-wen* 1838
The ford carried the road between Llanfaethlu and Llanfair-yng-Nghornwy through Afon Rhyd Wyn. The ford was probably associated with an unidentified Gwyn or Wyn possibly also found in the farm name Bodwyn (*bodwyn* 1561, *Bodwyn* 1678) half-a-mile to the south-east of Rhyd-wyn. The fact that ***rhyd*** is fem. led at one stage to *Rhyd-wen* 'white-ford' (as with some twenty Rhyd-wen or Rhydwen p.ns in Wales). However, the original Rhyd-wyn survived.

RHYDYCLAFDY Caern SH3234
'lazar-house ford', ***rhyd***, ***y***, ***clafrdy***
Rhyd y claverdu 1662-3, *Rhydclaverdy* 1729, *Rhydyclafdy* 1775, *Rhyd y clafrdu Rhyd-y-clawrdu* 1838
The 1775 and modern forms show the association with (the related) ***claf*** 'sick' while the 1838 form is a var. usually identified with south Wales. A mile-and-a-half to the south-west is Tyddyn-yr-haint (***tyddyn***, ***yr***, ***haint*** 'pestilence, plague, disease').

RHYDYCROESAU Denb SJ2430

'ford of the crosses', ***rhyd, y, croesau***

Rhyd y Croyse 1568-9, *Rhŷd y Kreosae* c.1700, *Rhyd-y-croesau* 1838

Several roads join the Llansilin-Oswestry road here which crosses a river (*Avon Rhyd y Kroesae* c.1700) which is the boundary between Denb and Shropshire and between Wales and England. The crosses denoted the road junctions and were also possibly boundary markers.

RHYDYFELIN[1] Card SN5979

'the mill ford', ***rhyd, y, melin***

Ritheuelin 1165-82, *Rithenelin* ?1181-2 (1285), *Rhyd y Velin* 1645, *Ridavlin* 1798, *Rhyd-y-Felin* 1834

The ford through Nant Paith was superseded by a bridge carrying the main road south of Aberystwyth. The medieval mill (*Moledino de Llech'* 1301 'mill of Llechweddllwyfen' grange, ***llechwedd*** 'slope', ***llwyfen*** 'elm tree') was adjacent to the ford.

RHYDYFELIN[2] see **RHYDFELEN**

RHYD-Y-FOEL Denb SH9176

'ford of the bald hill', ***rhyd, y, moel***

rydvoel c.1700, *Rhyd y Voel* 1867

The village is at the foot of Pen-y-corddyn-mawr, site of a large hill fortress and settlement. A minor road skirting the hill crosses Afon Dulas.

RHYD-Y-FRO Glam SN7105

'ford in the ?vale', ***rhyd, y, ?bro***

Redevro 1504, *Reed Evro* 1558, *Rhyd y Vro* 1615, *Rhydyfro* 1767

Named from a ford over the river Clydach Uchaf at *Gweyn Redvro* 1504, *Gweyne Reed Evro* 1558 (***gwaun***), immediately above that river's junction with the river Egel where the valley widens.

RHYD-Y-MAIN Mer SH8022

'ford of the stones', ***rhyd, y, maen*** pl. ***main***

Rhydymain 1746, *Rhyd-y-main* 1890

Replaced by a bridge (*Pont Rhydymain* 1746) which carried the main Bala-Dolgellau road over Afon Eiddon. The original ford may have had several large stone slabs as a track through the river or which were marker stones.

RHYD-Y-MEIRCH Monm SO3107

'ford of the horses', ***rhyd, y, meirch***, pl. of ***march***

Ryde Mirghe 1559, *rhyd y mairch yn LLanofer* late 16cent., *Rhyd-y-meirch* 1832

At the bridge carrying the Pontypool-Abergavenny road over a tributary of the river Usk. The horses were presumably seen regularly at the ford.

RHYD-Y-MWYN Flints SJ2066

'ford of the ore', ***rhyd, y, mwyn***

Rydymwyn 1554, *Rhyd y Mwyn* 1569, *rryd y mwyn* 1580, *rhyd y mwyn* 1725, *Rhyd-y-mwyn* 1838

The lane flanked by various mines between Rhyd-y-mwyn and Pant-y-mwyn crosses the river Alun (*'a foard on Alyn'* c.1700) by a ford which saw regular transport of minerals.

RHYDYRONNEN Mer SH6102

'the ash-tree ford', ***rhyd, yr, onnen***

Rhyd yr Onnen 1633, *Rhyd-yr-onnen* 1837

The minor road south-east from Bryn-crug crossed Nant Braich-y-rhiw through the ford which was once marked by a prominent ash-tree.

RHYD-Y-WRACH Carm SN1619

'the witch's ford', ***rhyd, y, gwrach***

Rhyd-wrach 1810, *Rhydywrach* 1906

Located on a lane which crosses a small unnamed tributary (now bridged) of Afon Taf. Named from some long-forgotten witch or a fanciful description for a treacherous ford.

RHYL Flints SJ0181

'the hill', W ***yr***, OE ***hyll***

Hulle 1292, *Hul 1296*, *Ryhull* 1301, *Hyll* 1506, *the hill*, *Yrhill* 1578, *Rhyll* 1660, *Rhil* 1706, *Rhyl* 1840

The early forms show this hybrid p.n. to be E ***hill*** preceded by W ***yr*** 'the'. Several documents refer specifically to a house (*Hillous, Hullhouse* 1351, *Ty yn Rhill alias Rhill* 1779). The exact significance of the original hill is more problematic since there is now no feature currently of even modest altitude. It may have been slightly raised dry ground in the marshland of *corse y rhul* 1454 (***cors*** 'marsh') and the use of the definite article in W, E and F (*Gronou del Hull* 1303) does suggest a visible feature, perhaps a man-made English garrisoned motte, an outpost of Rhuddlan castle, guarding the Clwyd estuary, and referred to by E and W speakers alike as 'the hill', 'yr hill'. The later absence of an identifiable hill probably explains why the spelling did not settle as 'Rhill' (despite some examples above).

RHYMNEY see **RHYMNI**

RHYMNI, RHYMNEY Monm SO1107

'(place by the river) Rhymni', r.n. ***Rhymni***

Rymni 1828, *Rumney Works* 1831, *Rhymney* 1832

Named from Rhymney ironworks established by the *Union Iron Works Co.* in 1801 and amalgamated with the Bute ironworks (established 1825) in 1837 to form the *Rhymney Iron Co*. The r.n. Rhymni is *Ru(m)nia, Ru(m)ni* 1147-57, *Remni* 1101-20, *Renni* c.1191, *Rymni* early 13cent. *Rempny* 13cent., *Rompney* 1314, a name which is cognate with ***rhwmp*** 'auger, gimlet' and ***-ni***, 'river which bores like an auger or a gimlet'.

RHYTALOG
Flints SJ2354

'dirty ford', ***rhyd, halog***

Ride Taloc 1391, *Redalok* 1448, *rryd talog* 1580-1, *Rhŷd Halawg* c.1700, *Rhydtalog* 1879

The medial consonantal cluster of -dh- has caused provection to -t-. The Hawarden-Bala road and the Rhuthun-Wrexham road both cross Afon Terrig (***terrig*** 'muddy') at this point reinforcing the significance of ***halog***. There are several examples of Rhydtalog and Rhytalog in Wales.

RIDLEYWOOD
Denb SJ4051

'wood at the cleared glade', OE ***(ge)ryd(d)***, OE ***lēah***, OE ***wudu***

Rid(e)ley Wood(e) 1391, *Rideley* 1397, *Ryddeley* 1472, *Ridley Wode* 16cent.

The wooded areas south of the E stronghold of Holt were extensively cleared for pasture, especially along the water-meadows close to the river Dee.

RISCA, RHISGA
Monm ST2490

'bark', ***rhisgl*** var. ***rhisg*** pl. ***rhisgau***

Risca 1146, *Ryscha* 1535, *Risgaf* c.1566, *Riskay* 1584, *Risga* 1623, *Rhisga* 1778

The name is probably the pl. ***rhisgau*** (with dial. -a for -au), a var. of ***rhisglau***. However, the actual significance of 'barks' is unclear. One tentative suggestion is of a house built of logs with the bark still on them or of bark being used as shingles on the walls. Another, possibly to be favoured, is that Risca was a place where trees were regularly stripped of bark, for whatever purpose. The same el. recurs in Nant Risca (*Riska* 1564), a former name of Nant yr Aber, near Caerphilly, four miles to the west, and in the lost r.n. Rhisga (*Risga* 1623) probably located in Cwmrisca (*Cwmyrisca* 1813 *Cwm-risca* 1884) near Bridgend Glam. It also occurs in Hafodrhisg (Denb and Caern), and in *Tir Rhisgog* 1688 in Pennardd Card and *Bwlch Rhisgog* c.1700 near Llangollen Denb.

ROATH, Y RHATH
Glam ST1977

'fortification', ***y, rhath***

Raz 1107, *Rath* 1149-83, *Raath* early 13cent., *Roth* 1296, *Rooth* 1375, *y Raff* c.1566

W ***rhath*** 'mound' (probably a borrowing from Ir ***ráth*** 'fort') and although no fort has been found it may refer to a former ditched area containing a mound (*Mote* 1584-5 [c.1700]) thought to have been located at Roath

Court. It occurs frequently as an el. in Pemb (as in Amroth q.v.). E influence may explain -a-/-ā- > -o-/-ō > -ou-/-oa- . It was once believed that the name is derived from Nant y Rhath or Roath brook, possibly ***rhath-*** as in ***rhathu*** 'scratch, file' describing a river which erodes its banks or scours its bed, but there are currently no forms earlier than the 17cent.; the brook's name was Nant Fawr or Nant Mawr, and became Roath brook simply because it flowed through Roath. A number of spellings with -ff(e) illustrate the confusion of -th- and -ff- sometimes found in W.

ROBESTON CROSS Pemb SM8809

'crossroads near Robeston', p.n. ***Robeston***, E ***cross***

Robeston Cross 1827, *Robeston cross* 1875

At a crossroads near Robeston West (q.v.).

ROBESTON WATHEN Pemb SN0815

'Robert's farm', pers.n. ***Robert***, OE ***tūn***, pers.n. ***Wathen***

Villa Roberti 1282, *Roberdeston* 1357, *Robeston* 1376, *Roberston Waytham* 1435, *Robertson Wathen* 1545, *Robestown* c.1566, *Robestonwathan* 1600

Wathen is an anglicization of Gwaiddan found in the unidentified *Rosewaithan* 1499 (***rhos***) at Vaynor a mile-and-a-half north-east of the village and in Llangwathan (q.v.) three miles to the east.

ROBESTON WEST Pemb SM 8809

'Robert's farm to the west', p.n. ***Robert***, OE ***tūn***, E ***west***

Villa Roberti 1343, *Robertyston* 1392, *Roberston in Rowse* 1554, *Robertston alias Robeston in Rowse* 1592, *Robestwn* c.1566, *Robeston west* 1603

In the cantref of Rhos, the settlement is west of Robeston Wathen (q.v.).

ROCH, Y GARN Pemb SM8721

'rock', OF ***roche***, W ***y***, ***carn***

(de) Rupe 1259, 1535, *la Roche* 1271, *Roch* 1403, *Roeds* c.1566, *Y Garn* 1602

The p.n. may also occur in the name of *William de Roche* who lived in Pemb some time between 1176 and 1198. The name was applied to the castle built on a prominent rock. The 1259 form with L ***rupa*** 'rock' was probably a documentary L description. The castle later appears as *Kastell Roach* 1591, *K[astell] y Garn* 1613, *Roche Castle* 1616. The W form seems to be late but could well have been in existence far earlier in local usage.

ROCKFIELD Monm SO4814

'(place named after) Rocheville', p.n. ***Rocheville***

Rochevilla c.1069, *Rokevilla* 1181, *Rochevill* 1230-40, *Rokfylde* 1545, *Rocfeylde* 1560, *Rokefeld* c.1610, *Rockfield* 1639

This was probably a transferred name from Rocheville (Manche, Normandy) since the tenant in the late 11cent. was *Ralph de Rocheville*. Anglicized as Rockfield through association with E ***rock*** and ***field***.

ROGERSTONE, TŶ-DU Monm ST2787

'Roger's settlement', 'black house', pers.n. ***Roger***, E ***-ton***, W ***tŷ***, ***du***

Trevewillym 1476, *Rogerstone* 1506, *Rogerston* 1570, *Treguyllym* 1576-7, *Rogerston...in Welsh Tre-Gwillim* 1657-60, *Rogeston Castle in Welsh Tre Gwillim, or William's House* 1801

Roger has been identified with *Roger de Berkerolles* who held land and probably the castle here in 1169 but the historical p.n. forms are too late to confirm this. The W name for the castle is Trefwilym or Tregwilym and was the name of two former farms (*Tregwilym* 1813 and *Tre-Gwilym-fach* 1887) a short distance to the north. The identity of Gwilym or William is also unknown and he cannot be confidently linked with Roger's father William recorded before 1146. The standard form would normally be 'Trewilym' but non-mutated p.ns are well documented in Monm (such as Llanmartin Monm). Before c.1920 Rogerstone applied solely to the eastern part of the modern village near the castle and ironworks but was extended to the industrial village of Tŷ-du (*Tydee* 1871) which developed half-a-mile to the west on the north side of Tŷ-du tinworks (*Tydu Tin Mill* c.1813, *Tydee Works* 1859) and this is now regarded as the W name for the whole of modern Rogerstone.

ROGIET Monm ST4687

?'passage for roe-deer', OE ***rā***, OE ***geat***

Rogiet 1193-1218, *Rogiate* 1270, *Roggate* 1276, *Roygereth* c.1291, *Rogerate* c.1348, *Roggeyate* 1419

Probably similar to Rogate Sussex (*Ragata* 12cent., *Rogate* 1203) but with the OE var. that gave rise to Havyatt Somerset and Symond's Yat Herefordshire as well as south W ***iet***; here, unusually, the initial g- has been retained. The hills to the north are still heavily wooded. Rogiet is also used as a later qualifier for the adjoining village Llanfihangel Rogiet (*Lann mihacgel maur* 1136-54, *Lanmihangel* 1254, *Llanvihangell Roggiet* 1597, *Lañihangel y Rogied* 1657-60). Some forms appear to show the influence of the pers.n. ***Roger*** although the pronunciation is the Roggiet occasionally used in some publications.

ROSEMARKET Pemb SM9508

'market in Rhos', cantref n. ***Rhos***, ME ***market***

Rosmarche c.1230, *Rosm'che* 12cent. (16cent.), *Rosmarkett* 1338, *Rosemarket* 1418, *Ros marked* c.1566, *Rhosmarket* 1867

A market probably established by the Knights Hospitallers in the 12cent. near *the church of St. Leonard of the castle of Ros* (1115-48) in Rhos cantref (although the present dedication is to St Ishmael). An earlier reference to the church itself may have been *ecclesia ville Theob'i* (1291) but no settlement associated with Theobold has as yet been identified.

ROSSETT, YR ORSEDD Denb SJ3657

'the (red) mound', ***yr***, ***gorsedd***, (***coch***)

le Orseth Goch 1473, *yr orsedd goch* 1530, *Rossett Goch* 1554, *orsedd goch* 1572, *Orseth goch* 16cent., *yr orsedh gôch*, *Rhossedh* c.1700

Rossett seems to have replaced the Domesday Book p.n. *Radenoure* (1086, OE ***readan*** 'red', ***ōra*** 'bank'). Three centuries later that edge of the sandstone and gravel escarpment north of Marford Hill was called *yr allt goch* (1391, ***gallt*** 'hill', ***coch*** 'red'). The actual mound of Yr Orsedd Goch may have been more specifically the part of the hill behind the Trevor Arms at Marford on which the motte of Roft Castle was built inside an Iron Age fort. It was the form Yr Orsedd which became Rhosedd, and then anglicized to Rossett, probably influenced by the association of 'red hill' with 'russett'. Rossett village is just under a mile from the motte, *the green called Rorseth goch* (1607) referring to the dominant feature of Yr Orsedd as seen from the water-meadows at Rossett. Several examples of Gorsedd and Yr Orsedd used of a hill are to be found in Wales, a number in Flints and Denb and some associated with a tumulus (as in Bryn Rossett north of Hanmer).

RO-WEN Caern SH7571

'the white gravel', ***y***, ***gro***, ***gwyn*** fem. ***gwen***

Y Roe 1729, *Yro* 1795, *Y Ro* 1838

The name of the village was formerly *Y Ro* (*Y Pentre a elwir y Rô* c.1700 'the village called y Rô') from the gravel bank and bed of the river at this point. The def.art. ***y*** points to a distinctive feature of the landscape. The river which flows through the village was formerly called Afon Gastell (*Avon Gastelh* c.1700) from its stretch between Castell near Llanbedrycennin and the Roman fort of *Canovium* (see Conwy). Its upper reaches (from Bwlch y Ddeufaen) are now Afon Tafolog and its lower reaches (from Ro-wen down to Afon Conwy) are now Afon Ro (or Roe). Associating the name Y Ro with the river rather than with the village resulted in the village becoming known as Y Ro-wen or, more generally, simply Ro-wen.

RUABON, RHIWABON Denb SJ3043

'Mabon's hill', ***rhiw***, pers.n. ***Mabon***

Rywnabon 1291, *Riwuabon* 1362, *Riwvabon* 1394, *Riwabon* 1397, *Ruabon* 1462, *Rhiw vabon* c.1566

The identity of Mabon is unknown but his name did remain a distinct feature of the p.n. for some time (in the lenited form -fabon).

RUDBAXTON Pemb SM9620

'Rudepac's farm', pers.n. ***Rudepac***, OE ***tūn***

Rudepagastona 1176-98 (c.1700), *villa de Rudepac* ?12cent. (c.1600), *Rudpakeston* 1391, *Rudbaxton* 1554

Possibly named from the 12cent. *Alexander Rudepac* was associated with the church of Slebech in the 12cent. The church is recorded as *ecclesia Sancti Maidoci* in the ?12cent reference above, possibly the W saint Madog; now dedicated to Michael.

RUDRY, RHYDRI, Y Glam ST1986

obscure

Rutheri 1254, *Rethery* 1281, *Rudri* 1307, *Riddrie* 1583, *Ruddry* 1707, *y Rydri* c.1566, *Rudry* 1833

Obscure in origin and development. Early spellings favour ***rhuthr*** 'a rush, torrent' with the suff. ***-i*** commonly found with streams and rivers, but there is no evidence of it being a stream name. The persistence of forms in -dd- could suggest ***rhydd*** 'unrestricted' or ***rhudd*** 'red' (cf. Ruthin). The subsequent change of -dr- is difficult to account for unless it be the influence of ***rhyd*** 'ford'.

RUMNEY, TREDELERCH Glam (formerly Monm) ST2179

'(place by the river) Rhymni', 'farm of Telerch', r.n. ***Rhymni***, ***tref***, pers.n. ***Telerch***

Ru(m)nia, *Ru(m)ni* 1147-57, *Renni* c.1191 (c.1214), *Remeny* 1295, *Rempny* c.1348, *Tredelerch* 1536-9, *tref delerch* c.1566

Telerch (or Tylerch) is composed of the honorific pref. ***ty-*** (often found with pers.ns) and a pers.n. Elerch, earlier Eleirch, a form which led some antiquarians and historians to claim that Elerch was an alternative name of the river Rhymni (q.v.) and misinterpreting Tredelerch as 'abode of the swans' with ***eleirch***, ***elyrch*** pl. of ***alarch*** 'swan'.

RUTHIN, RHUTHUN Denb SJ1258

'red edge', ***rhudd***, ***hin***

Ruthin 1211, *Ruthi(n)* 1225 (1316), *Ruthun* 1253, *Ruthyn* 1324, *Ruthin* 1795

Traditionally, the second el. was believed to be ***din*** 'fort', a reference to the red sandstone in the ruins of the 13cent. castle *Y Castell Coch yng* *gwernfor* 1545-53 (***y*** 'the', ***castell*** 'castle', ***coch*** 'red', ***yn*** 'in'); Gwernfor (***gwern*** 'marsh', ***fawr*** 'great') was the extensive marsh. However, such a derivation should have resulted in 'Ruddin' whereas the historical forms consistently have -th-; cf. Ruthin Glam (*Ruthun* after 1131 [c.1200], *Ruthyn* 1281). The ***hin*** is the 'border, edge' of the river Clwyd or of the sandstone rock of the castle. Although -in is historically more appropriate, the almost exclusive spelling in a W context has always been -un (probably influenced by the -u- of the preceding syllable); the occasional spelling -yn was probably influenced by Flints -tyn p.ns (cf. Prestatyn).

S

SAGESTON Pemb SN0503

?'Sager's farm', E pers.n. ***Sager***, OE ***tūn***

Sagerston 1362, *Sagiston* 1372, *Sageston* 1541

From an unidentified E settler with the pers.n. or surname *Sager, Sagar*. There are a considerable number of p.ns in the surrounding area composed of pers.n. and -ton.

SAIN DUNWYD see **ST DONAT'S**

SAIN FFAGAN see **ST FAGANS**

SAIN NICOLAS see **ST NICHOLAS**

SAIN PETROG see **ST PETROX**

SAIN SIORYS see **ST GEORGE'S**

SAIN TATHAN see **ST ATHAN**

SAINT HARMON Radn SN9872

'(church of) St Garmon', W ***san(t)***, E ***saint***, pers.n. ***Harmon***

Sancti Germani c.1191, *(de) Sancto Germano* 1291,
Sanharmon late 15cent., *Saynt Hermand* 1542, *ll.harmon* 1545-64,
saint harmon c.1566, *Sayntharmon* 1565, *Sanarmon* 1740

There are many example of *Germanus* in early L sources. From the 15cent. the name is regularly *Harmon*. It is possible that here was a conscious substitution of one name and saint for another. However, on the analogy of dedications to Garmon in several examples of Llanarmon (q.v.) it is possible to postulate a development such as *Saint Garmon* > *Sangarmon* > *Sanarmon/?Llanarmon* > *Sanharmon* > Saint Harmon (with intrusive H- before the stressed syllable).

SAINT HILARI see **ST HILARY**

SAINT-Y-BRID see **ST BRIDES**

ST ANN'S HEAD Pemb SM8002

'headland near St Ann's chapel', E ***saint***, pers.n. ***Ann***, E ***head***

Sct. Annes head 1595, *St. Anns Point* 1729

Named from a former chapel (*Sct. Ans Chap* 1578, *Sct. Annes Chappell* 1594).

ST ARVAN'S, Monm ST5196

'(church of) St ?Arwyn', E ***saint***, pers.n. ***Arwyn***

(de) sancto Aruino 1193-1218, *St. Arvyn* 1307, *(de) sancto Aruyno* c.1348, *Seynt Aruane* 1434

Many early spellings suggest a pers.n. Arwyn, later replaced by Arvan and Arfan of whom nothing is known. The W name may have been *Llanarfan* but its authenticity is uncertain since it is recorded only in late sources (such as *Lhan Arvan* c.1700).

ST ASAPH, LLANELWY Denb SJ0374

'(church of) St Asaph', 'the church on (the river) Elwy', E ***saint***, pers.n. ***Asaph***, W ***llan***, r.n. ***Elwy***

Lanelvensis Ecclesiae 1143, *Lanelvensis ecclesiam* c.1191, *Assavensi ecclesia* 1284, *Ecclesia Cathedralis de Sancto Asaph* 1291, *Lanhelewey* 1345, *Lanelwy* 1365, *Llan Elwy alias S. Asaphe* 1536

The cathedral is said to have been established by Cyndeyrn (*Eglwys Gyndeyrn* 1657) but was dedicated to his disciple, the 6cent. bishop and saint Asaph or Asaff (a name also preserved in Flints Llanasa and Pantasa). The W name refers to the location of the cathedral beside the river Elwy (q.v.).

ST ATHAN, SAIN TATHAN Glam ST0168

'(church of) St Tathan', E ***saint***, W ***sain***, pers.n. ***Tathan***

Sancte Thathane 1254, *Sancta Tathana* 13cent., *Seint Athan* 1349, *Seintanthan* 1427, *Saint tathan* 1582

The E form has developed from misdivision of St Tathan as St Athan, possibly influenced through association with saints Athanasius of Alexandria and Athanasius the Anchorite. Comparatively little is known of Tathan; he may once have had a church dedication at Caer-went.

ST BRIDES BAY Pemb SM8416

'bay next to St Bride's', p.n. ***St Bride's***, E ***bay***

Bridebay 1566, *St. Briedes Bay* 1695, *St. Bride's Bay* 1777

On the south side of this extensive bay is the church of St Bride's (*Sancta Brigida* 1242-6, *Ecclesia de Sancta Brigid'* 1291, *Bridechurche* 1311, *Ecclesia Sancte Brigitte* 1535, *Sent Brids* 1550, *Seynt Bryde* 1547-53, *St. Brides* 1594), and which probably had a W name (*Abbas Llan Sanfrigt* 9cent. [16cent.]) identical to Llansanffraid[1, 2] (q.v.) and St Brides Major (q.v.).

ST BRIDES MAJOR, SAINT-Y-BRID Glam SS8974

'greater (church of) St Brigid', pers.n. ***Bride/Brid***, E ***saint***, W ***saint***, ***y***, L ***major***

Ste. Brigide virginis 1138, *Sancta Brigida superiori* 1247, *Sancte Brigide majoris* 13cent., *saint y brid* c.1566, *Sct. Brides maior* 1578, *Sant Bryd* 1839

Major distinguishes it from St Brides Minor (W Llansanffraid-ar-Ogwr) (*Sancte Brigide Parve* 1254, *Sancte Brigide Minoris* 13cent., *ll. sanffred or ogwr* c.1566) and from St Brides-super-Ely (W Llansanffraid-ar-Elái) (*Lann sant breit* 1136-54, *Lann Sanbregit* 1160-85, *St Brides the Moore* 1586), all dedicated to Brigid of Ireland. Saint-y-brid is a late adoption by W speakers based on the E name. There is no evidence St Brides Major was ever 'Llansanffraid' in contrast to St Brides Wentloog/Llansanffraid Gwynllŵg (q.v.).

ST BRIDES WENTLOOGE, LLANSANFFRAID GWYNLLŴG Monm ST2982

'(church of) St Bride in Gwynllŵg', pers.n. ***Bride/Ffraid***, E ***saint***, W ***san(t)***, ***llan***, terr. n. ***Gwynllŵg***
Sancta Brigida 1296, *Seynt Bride* (in *Wenllouk*) 1476, *ll. sain ffred* c.1566, *St. Brides in the Marshes* 1769
St Brides lies in the marshy Wentlooge Levels. Wentlooge is an anglicized form of Gwynllŵg (see Peterston Wentlooge).

ST CLEARS, SANCLÊR Carm SN2716

'(church of) St Clear', pers.n. ***Clear/Clêr***, E ***saint***, W ***san(t)***
Seint Cler 1189 (c.1400), (*de*) *Sancto Claro* 1283, (*de*) *Sancto Claro* 1291, *Seint Cler* 1316, *Sencler* c.1386-7, *Saint clers* 1544, *castell sain kler* c.1566
Identified with a 9cent. saint, who also has a dedication at St Cleer Cornwall but whose main cult was at St Clair Normandy. The dedication may have been introduced about the time of the foundation of the 12cent. Cluniac priory of Mary Magdalene. Locally pronounced *Singclêr or Sangclêr* c.1700, sometimes with Sh-.

ST DAVID'S, TYDDEWI Pemb SM7525

'(church of) St David', 'house of Dewi', pers.n. ***David/Dewi***, E ***saint***, W ***tŷ***
(*de*) *Sancto David* 1113-5, (*episcopus*) *Sancti David de Gualis* 1121, (*episcopus*) *sancti Deui* 1119 (1160-80), (*yn*) *Hy Ddewi* 15cent., *Tŷ Dewi* 1586
tŷ is used here in the biblical sense of 'house (of the Lord), church' (as in some Ir p.ns. with ***teach***. ***Dewi*** is derived from L ***David(us)*** by way of *Dewidd* with loss of final -dd. An alternative E form may have been *Dewstow* (OE ***stōw***) on the basis of evidence such as *John Doustow* late 13cent., *John de Sancto David* 1325, *Thomas de Dowystawe* 1331, *Thomas de Sancto David* 1330; cf. the identical Dewstow in Monm (*Sanctum Dewin* 1086, *sancti Dauid* 1186-91, *Dewystowe* 1219-75, *Deustowe* 1290, *Llandewy* 1539). An earlier name was Mynyw (*Miniu* 810 late 13cent., *Mineu* 9cent., *Mynyw* 810 [c.1400]) latinized as *Menevia* 1078 (late

13cent.) and *ecclesia Menevensis* (before 1223), with ***mynyw*** 'brake', a cognate of Ir ***muine*** 'thicket'; Ir sources refer to St David's as *Cille Muine* (before 588)) with ***cill*** 'cell, church'.

ST DAVID'S HEAD, PENMAEN DEWI Pemb SM7227
'headland near St David's', 'stony headland of Dewi', p.n. ***St David's***, E ***head***, W ***penmaen***, pers.n. ***Dewi***
Saynt Davys Head 15cent., *Pendewi [or] S. David Hedde* 1536-9, *Sct Davids Hedd* 1595, *Penmaen* 1840, *Pen-maen-dewi* 1843
The rocky headland north-east of St David's/Tyddewi (q.v.). A very early name appears to have been *Octapitarum Promontorium* (2cent.) of uncertain significance, but may refer to the headland as being near the Bishops and Clerks rocks (q.v.).

ST DOGMAELS, LLANDUDOCH Pemb (later Card) SN1646
'(church of) St Dogfael', 'church of Tydoch', E ***saint***, pers.n. ***Dogfael***, W ***llan***, pers.n. ***Tydoch***
Llan Dethoch 988 (late 13cent.), *(ecclesia) sancti Dogmaelis* 1100-35, *Landodog* 1115-47, *Seynte Documele* 1296-7, *llan dydoch* c.1400, *St. Dogmaels alias Llandudock* 1544, *ll. dydoch* c.1566
The site of an abbey called Cemais (*Cameis* 1116-20, *ecclesie Sancte Marie abbatie de Camays* 1120-48) in early sources from its location in the cantref of Cemais (cf. Cemais[1, 2]). Dogfael may have been anglicized as Dogmael but it could be argued that Dogmael may derive directly from the latinized form, or be a fossilised form of OW *Docmail*. The p.n. seems to have borne the additional name of Tyddoch or Tydoch which developed from Tyddog with the honorary pref. ***ty-*** and the ***dog-*** derived from Dogfael (cf. Llandawke), perhaps under Ir influence. However, the relationship between the names is complex and obscure.

ST DONAT'S, SAIN DUNWYD Glam SS9368
'(church of) St Dunwyd', E ***saint***, W ***sain***, pers.n. ***Dunwyd***
sancti Donati 1173-83, *Sancto Donato* c.1262, *Seint Donats* 1307, *Sanctus Donatus* 1314, *sain dondwyd* 1540-77, *saint dunwyd* c.1566
The E form derives from Donatus a latinized form of Dunwyd, probably through misassociation with the Ir saint Donatus of Fiesole (died c.876). The W form imitates the E name. Contrast with Welsh St. Donat's/ Llanddunwyd.

ST FAGANS, SAIN FFAGAN Glam ST1277
'(church of) St Fagan', E ***saint***, W ***sain***, pers.n. ***Fagan***
sancto Fagano 1173-83, *Sanctus Faganus* 1307, *Seint Fagan* 1402, *Saint Fagans* 1547, *Sain ffagan* c.1566
Reputedly one of the four missionaries sent to Wales by Pope Eleutherius c.180. The name is Ir.

ST FLORENCE Pemb SN0801

'(church of) St Florence', E ***saint***, pers.n. ***Florence***

Sanctus Florencius 1248, (*ecclesia de*) *Sancto Florenco* 1291, *St. Florentius* 1295, *St. Florence* 1341, *sain fflwrens* c.1566

Probably St Florent commemorated in Anjou, the area in France with which the *de Valence* earls of Pembroke had connections.

ST GEORGE, LLAN SAIN SIÔR Denb SH9775

'(church of) St George',E ***saint***, W ***llan***, ***san(t)***, pers.n. ***Siôr***, ***George***

Lan S. George 1536-9, *ll. sain sior* 1566, *St. George al's Llansansior* 1607, *Lhan St. Shôr, als Kegidog, Lh. San Shôr, St George's als kegidog* c.1700, *Kedidock alias St. George* 1763, *Llan St Georges* 1795

The name of the secular tnshp (now no longer in general use) was Cegidog (*Kegidauc* 1254, *Kekydoc* 1392, *Kekydogg* 1522), usually taken to be ***cegidog*** 'abounding in hemlock', since ***cegid*** and ***cegidog*** do appear in a few p.ns, but equally possible is another ***cegid*** 'green woodpecker, jay' followed by the adj. suff. ***-og***. The church in the tnshp was dedicated to Siôr or George which was then adopted as the tnshp name. Usage varies between Llansan-siôr, Llansansiôr and Llan Sain Siôr (with ***sain*** for W ***saint***).

ST GEORGE'S, SAIN SIORYS Glam ST1076

'(church of) St George', E ***saint***, W ***sain***, pers.n. ***George***, ***Siorys***

Sancti Georgii 1254, *Sco' Georg', St Georges* 1291, *Seynt Georgis* 1542, *sain siorys* c.1566, *Sant Jorys* 1609

This was George the 3-4cent. martyr and patron saint of England, one of a number of AN and continental saints with dedications in the Vale of Glamorgan. Siorys may be explained as a var. of Siôr or Siôrs with colloquial intrusive -y-, or as a cymricized adoption of St George's. Some documents refer to St George-super-Ely.

ST GOVAN'S HEAD Pemb SR9792

'headland near St Govan's', p.n. ***St Govan's***, E ***head***

Sct. Gouens poynt 1578, *St. Govens pointe* 1603, *St. Gowans Pt.* 1777, *St. Gowens Head* 1839

Named from St Govan's Chapel (*Sct. Gouen* 1578, *St. Govens, Govens chapell* 1602, *St. Goven* 1610).

ST HILARY, SAINT HILARI Glam ST0178

'(church of) St Hilary', E ***saint***, W ***saint***, pers.n. ***Hilary***

sancti Hilarii 1160-85, *Sancti Ylarii* 1160-80, *Sancto Hilario* 1185-91, *Saynt Hilary* 1545, *Saint y lari* c.1566, *sain tilari* 1540-77

Dedicated to St Hilary of Poitiers (died c.367) or St Hilary of Arles (died 449), both F saints.

ST MARY CHURCH, LLAN-FAIR Glam ST0071
'church of St Mary', E *saint*, pers.n. *Mary*, *Mair*, W *llan*
Sayntemariechurche 1314, *Seynt Merychurche* 1440, *Seintmarichurch* 1508, *Llanvayre* c.1545, *ll. fair or Bewpyr* c.1566, *Llan-fair* late 19cent.
A former chapel-of-ease to St Hilary (q.v.). Its relatively minor status probably explains the paucity of early forms. The form for c.1566 refers to its location near Beaupre/Y Bewpyr (*Bewerpere* 1376, *Y Bewper* 1485-1515, *the Bewper* 1526) 'pleasant retreat' (F ***beau***, ***repaire*** confused with ***pré*** 'meadow').

ST MARY HILL, EGLWYS FAIR Y MYNYDD Glam SS9579
'(church of) St Mary on the hill', 'church of Mair on the mountain', E *saint*, E *hill*, W *eglwys*, *y*, pers.n. *Mary*, *Mair*, *y*, *mynydd*
Beate Marie super Montem 1254, *St. Mary's super montem* 1288, *Sce' Marie juxta Kyltikarn* 1291, *St. Mary on the Hill* 1386, *ll. fair or mynydd* c.1566, *Eglwys Fair y Mynydd* 1612
Named from the location of the church on a hill, though the village itself is on its south slopes adjoining the area Gelli-garn (*Kilticar* 1208, *Kilthekarn* 1254, *Kyltikarn* 1291, *Kellegarne* 1538-44, ***celli***, ***carn*** 'woodland at a cairn').

ST MELLONS, LLANEIRWG Glam (formerly Monm) ST2281
'(church of) St Melan', 'church of ?Eirwg', E *saint*, pers.n. *Melan*, W *llan*, ?pers.n. *Eirwg*
Sancto Melano 1254, 1320, *Sanctus Melanus* 1399, *Seynt Melen* 1476, *LL. leiruc* 1550, *ll. lirwg* c.1566, (*o*) *Lan Leirwg* late 16cent.
Melan may be St Melanius or Melaine, the 6cent. bishop of Rennes, associated with Brittany and Cornwall (St Mellion and Mullion). The apparent absence of early medieval forms for the W name is unexplained as is the unidentified second el. whether it be Eirwg or Lleirwg or whether it is necessarily a pers.n. Some modern usage favours Llaneurwg.

ST NICHOLAS, SAIN NICOLAS Glam SS0974
'(church of) St Nicholas', E *saint*, W *sain*, pers.n. *Nicholas/Nicolas*
Sto Nicholao 1153-83, *Sanctum Nicholaum* 1248, *St. Nicholas Malefaunte* 1540, *Saint Niclas* 1556, *sain nikolas* c.1566
Probably St Nicholas, 4cent. bishop of Myra, another imported continental dedication which also occurs in St Nicholas Pemb (*Saynt Nycolas* 1554, *St. Nicholas* 1592) with the W form Tremarchog (*Villa Camerarii* 1287, *Tremarchoc* 1551, L ***villa***, ***camerarius*** 'chamberlain' or 'knight', ***tref***, ***marchog*** 'knight'). The 1540 form recalls the *Malefant* family of St George's and St Nicholas.

ST PETROX, SAIN PEDROG Pemb SR9797
'(church of) St Petroc', E *saint*, W *sain*, pers.n. *Petroc/Pedrog*

(*de*) *Sancto Petroco* 1291, *Saincte Petrok* 1539, *Saynt Petrocks* c.1545, *sain pedrog* c.1566, *St. Petrox* 1594, *St. Petrocks* 1603
Apparently dedicated to the same saint as Llanbedrog (q.v.) and in Padstow Cornwall (*Sancte Petroces stow* 981, *Petrocys stow* c.995, with OE ***stōw*** 'holy place'). The W form follows the standard development from Petroc to Pedrog while the E form retains Petroc's, written Petrox.

ST TUDWAL'S ISLAND see **YNYS TUDWAL**

SALEM Carm SN6226
biblical chapel n.
Salem 1814
From an Independent chapel. Described as *Heol-galed* 1831, 'hard (stone-surfaced?) road' (***heol***, ***caled***) referring to the road running through the village from Llandeilo.

SALTNEY Flints SJ3764
'salty marshland', OE ***saltan***, OE ***ēg***
Salteney c.1230, *Salteneye*, *Saltneye* 1284-5, *Saltney* 1379
If there was a settlement here it would have been on an island of dry land in marshland (one of the meanings of ***ēg***). However, in later names, ***ēg*** could simply refer to the well-watered land itself (*Salteney Marshe* 1249, *Mariscus de Salteneya* 1250, *Morva Kaer Lleon* 14cent., ***morfa*** 'sea-marsh', *Caerlleon* being Chester). The river Dee was tidal up to Chester until the gradual silting resulted in the river changing its course, leaving *a 'great pasture called Salteney'* (1639) and *Saltney moore* (1652). Canalization in 1737 placed the village of Saltney on the banks of the Dee.

SANCLÊR see **ST CLEARS**

SANDYCROFT Flints SJ3366
'sandy croft', E ***sandy***, E ***croft***
Sandycroft 1840
The original *Sandy croft* (1688-9) gave its name to an industrial location on Buckley Common (*Sandicrofte Coalworks* 1760, *Sandycroft ... colliery and ironstone work* 1768). The owner Sir John Glynne (of Hawarden Castle) built the Old Canal specifically for transport across Saltney Marsh, and a quay on the river Dee (upstream of Queensferry) called *Sandycroft Quay* 1840 which later became the village of Sandycroft.

SARDIS Pemb SM9708
biblical chapel n.
Sardis 1825
From a Baptist chapel erected 1822.

SARN Mont SO2090

'causeway', ***sarn***

Sarn 1816

Possibly applying to the road which passes from Churchstoke to Ceri over a flat, somewhat marshy area between Sarn village and Gwern-y-go.

SARNAU[1] Card SN3150

'causeways', ***sarn*** pl. ***sarnau***

Sarnau 1808, *Sarne* 1809

The main Aberystwyth-Cardigan road was facilitated by several causeways through an area which featured a bog and many springs. The forms in *Sarne* are dial. vars.

SARNAU[2] Carm SN3318

'causeways', ***sarn*** pl. ***sarnau***

Sarnau 1811

At the junction of the former main road between Carmarthen and St Clears and a lane. There is another *Sarnau* recorded 1757 at Meidrim.

SARNAU[3] Mer SH9739

'causeways', ***sarn*** pl. ***sarnau***

Sarnau 1795

The main road north-east of Bala passes through the marshy ground called Cors y Sarnau (***cors*** 'marsh') which had at one time necessitated several stretches of paved track or causeways. Two such stretches are referred to in the p.n. Cefnddwysarn (***cefn*** 'ridge', ***dau*** fem. ***dwy*** 'two').

SARNAU[4] Mont SJ2315

'causeways', ***sarn*** pl. ***sarnau***

Sarnau 1829, *y Sarnau* 1871, *Sarney* 1891

There are several roads here crossing a marshy area around Sarnau Brook and Holywell Brook and tributaries.

SARN HELEN

'paved road of Elen', ***sarn***, pers.n. ***Elen***

surne Ellen 1627 [Mont], *Sarn Elen* c.1700 [Carm],

Sarn Elen ar vynydh y dhol yng Horwen c.1700 [Mer],

Sarn Helen 1808 [Mer], *Sarn Helen* [Caern] 1810,

Sarn Helen 1832 [Glam, Brec]

sarn has a variety of meanings, including 'causeway, stepping stones', but because it also characterised a paved stone surface it has traditionally been take as evidence of a Roman road. In several instances ***sarn*** can actually be identified with sections of Roman roads, a link reinforced by antiquarian association with Elen or Helen, princess of Segontium (see Caernarfon), wife of Magnus Maximus, the Roman governor of Britain and later emperor (d.388). Medieval W literature features *Sarn (H)elen* routes, 'the roads of Elen', from one stronghold to another across Britain. It is possible that some native Elen has been confused with her. Some examples of Sarn Helen show confusion with ***halen*** 'salt' with reference to salt routes.

SARN MELLTEYRN Caern SH2332

'causeway at Mellteyrn', ***sarn***, pers n. ***Mellteyrn***

Sarne Meillteyne 1701, *Sarne* 1795, *Sarn Meyllteyrn* 1840

The causeway brought the Botwnnog-Tudweiliog road across Afon Soch, south of the hamlet and church of Mellteyrn (*Melteren* 1352). A var. Meyllteyrn is commonly used in Sarn Meyllteyrn, a fairly recent settlement name. Pont y Sarn now supersedes the original ***sarn***.

SARON Denb SJ0260

biblical chapel n.

Pentre Saron 1872, *Saron* 2000

The chapel, *Saron Chapel (Calvinistic)* 1872, was erected in 1826. While it is common for the chapel name to become the village name (as in the nearby Peniel), it is less common for the village name to be prefixed with Capel (but cf. Capel Seion etc.), and rare for it to be prefixed with Pentre, which probably explains the modern drift towards simply Saron.

SAUNDERSFOOT Pemb SN1304

'Saunders' foot-hill', pers.n. ***Saunders***, E ***foot***

Saunders foot 1602, *Saundersfoot* 1726

Walter Elisaundr held a mill in this area 1330-1 and Saunders, Sanders are still local family names. The village lies near the bottom of hill-slopes next to Carmarthen Bay, and local pronunciation stresses -foot .

SCETHROG see **SGETHROG**

SCLEDDAU Pemb SM9434

?'court near (the river) Cleddau', ?***llys***, r.n. ***Cleddau***

Lysclethe 1326 (16cent.), *Isklethy* 1632, *Ishcledde* 1673

The name of a village and several farms near the headwaters of the Western Cleddau. The first form suggests that the initial el. is ***llys***. Is Cleddau or Is Cleddy (***is*** 'below') has clearly influenced the p.n. Cf. Sketty/Sgeti Glam from *ynys Ceti*.

SCOLTON Pemb SM9922

?'farm with a temporary hut', ON ***skáli***, OE ***tūn***

Scaneton 1326 (16cent.), *Skolden, Skaldon* c.1604, *Scolton* 1575

The scarcity of reliable early spellings make this a difficult p.n. A similar name may well be the neighbouring Scollock (*Scolhok* 14cent., *Skolloke* 1463, with ***hōc*** 'spur of land'). The first el. is unusual in that it is a feature of north-west England, where it is probably derived directly from ON ***skáli***, but is also possible in Pemb. Another possibility, perhaps more likely, is the surname ***Scall*** found in Pemb (*Richard Scall* 1483, *Henry Scalle* 1575).

SEALAND Flints SJ3568

'sea land', E ***sea***, E ***land***

Sealand 1726

The gradual silting of the river Dee and its canalization in 1737 resulted in major reclamation of land in the former tidal basin of the Dee, the pastures of Saltney and (to the north of the river) Sealand. The existence of the name before the completion of canalization indicates the extent of the silting.

SEBASTOPOL Monm ST2898

'(place named after) Sebastopol', p.n. ***Sebastopol***

Sebastopol 1859

A name given to the village adjoining the Monmouthshire Canal developed in 1855-56 by George Steedman and especially John Nicholas, after the siege of Sebastopol in the Crimea (1854-55).

SENGHENNYDD Glam ST1190

'territory of Sangan', pers.n. ***Sangan***, terr.suff. ***-ydd***

Seinhenit c.1179, *Seingeniht* c.1262, *Seynhenyz* 1268, *Saing henydd* c.1566

Senghennydd was an ancient cantref extending from the north of Cardiff between the rivers Taf and Rhymni to Merthyr Tudful and the name was revived c.1893 for the village built after the *Universal Colliery* was sunk 1891-93 and for the railway station (*Senghenith Sta.* 1894). The identity of Sangan is unknown and the name is not otherwise attested which probably prompted the popular misinterpretation as 'Sain Cenydd' (***sain*** 'saint'), with a new name Trecenydd (***tref***) introduced for a housing estate in Caerphilly in the 1950s.

SENNI, Afon Brec SN9222

'(river named after) Senni', pers.n. ***Senni***

Senney 1540-50, *Senny* 1549-60, *Senny R.* 1754

A river which rises in Blaen Senni and flows past Abersenni into the Usk at Sennybridge (q.v.). Also found in *Dolysene* 1295 (***dôl***), *Sennye Mill* 1651 and *Abersenny* 1773 (***aber***). The pers.n. probably occurs in Tresenni Monm (***tref***). A related pers.n. is ***Sannan*** in the r.n. Sannan Carm and in Llansannan (q.v.).

SENNYBRIDGE, PONTSENNI Brec SN9228

'bridge over (the river) Senni', r.n. ***Senni***, E ***bridge***, W ***pont***

Senny Bridge 1829, *Senni Bridge* 1833, *Senny-Bridge (Pont-Senni)* 1891

The village developed around a bridge constructed c.1819 for the new mailcoach road over the river Senni (q.v.) and particularly after the construction of the *Neath & Brecon Railway* 1872.

SEVEN SISTERS, BLAENDULAIS Glam SN8109

'seven sisters', 'headwaters of (the river) Dulais', E ***seven***, E ***sisters***, W ***blaen***, r.n. ***Dulais***

Seven Sisters 1882, *blayth Tulleys* 1296, *Blaen dilas* 1631

The colliery, sunk in 1872, is said to commemorate the seven sisters of Evan Evans Bevan son of Evans Evans of Neath, partner with David Bevan in various colliery undertakings. The p.n. was officially recognised 1882 but it is locally called Y Sefn. Although established in the general headwaters of Blaendulais (see Dulais[1]) there is evidence to suggest that the village developed in an area known specifically as Cwmdulais (***cwm***) said to have been an earlier name for Bryndulais farm. Bryndulais is also recorded as the area around Soar chapel 1885.

SGETHROG, SCETHROG Brec SO1025

?'rocky (settlement)', ***sgathrog***

Skadroc 1215-22 (c.1710), *Skathrok* early 13cent., *Scatheroc* 1254, *Skatherok* 1373, *Skatherock* 1434-5, *skatherogg* 1583. *Skethrog* 1578

sgathrog dial. var. ***sgethrog*** are reduced vars of ***ysgathrog***, ***ysgethrog*** and ***ysgithrog*** and refer to land which is rough, rugged or craggy, or is regularly wind-swept.

SGETI see **SKETTY**

SGIWEN see **SKEWEN**

SHIRENEWTON, DRENEWYDD GELLI-FARCH

Monm ST4793

'sheriff's new farm', 'new farm at stallion's grove', OE ***scīr-(ge)rēfa***, OE ***nīwe***, OE ***tūn***, W ***y***, ***tref***, ***newydd***, ***celli***, ***march***

(Ne)wetuna 1090, *Noua uilla* 1222-9, *Sherrevesneuton* 1287, *Shirenewt'* 1291, *Le Neuton* 1299, *y dre newydd gelli farch* c.1566

This has been identified with a manor reputedly granted to the sheriff of Gloucester in 1090, but 'sheriff' is not certainly evidenced before 1287. The el. probably distinguishes it from Wolvesnewton (q.v.). There is no indication why it should have been regarded as new. Another Gelli-march appears near Cilfrew Glam, both referring to the habitual location of a stallion. The area is still notable for its woodland.

SHOTTON Flints SJ3068

'settlement on a hill' OE ***scēot***, OE ***tūn***

Schottone 1281-2, *Schotton* 1283-5, *Shotton* 1452, *Shotten* 1576

The original settlement was atop a hill in what is now called Higher Shotton. The name Shotton has been more readily linked with the area of industrial expansion, particularly steelworks, within Lower Shotton beside the river Dee.

SIGINSTON, TRESIGIN Glam SS9771

'Sigin's farm', pers.n. ***Sigin***, OE ***tūn***, W ***tref***

Sigineston c.1260, *Siginstone* 1576, *Tresigan* 1764,
Treshigin or Sigginstone 1791

Named after *Hugo Sigin de Siginstone*. The pers.n. occurs elsewhere in the Vale of Glamorgan such as *Sygyns londs* 1488, *Sygenslandes* 1543, *Tir Sygyn Ycha* 1569 (OE ***land***, W ***tir***, ***uchaf***) at Lampha (St Brides Major). Frequently Siginstone, Sigingstone.

SILI see **SULLY**

SILIAN Card SN5751

'(church of) Sulian', pers.n. ***Sulian***

Sullen 1284, *silian* c.1566, *Sylian*, *Siliane* 1598-9, *Sullyeñ* 1482,
Sillien 1632, *Silian* 1804

Both Sulien and Sulian appear as vars for this saint. This is another example of a church named after the saint without the addition of ***llan***. An inscription in the church records *Silbandus* but the connection with Sulian is problematic, unless it was an attempt to render the saint's name as a L Silvanus.

SILSTWN see **GILESTON**

SIMPSON CROSS Pemb SM8919

'crossroads near Simpson', E ***cross***, p.n. ***Simpson***

Simpson Cross 1967

A 20cent. development near a smithy and a farm (*Keep Hill* 1891). Simpson is 'Symond's farm' (*Symondiston* 1383, *Symondeston* c.1419, *Symeston* 1444, *Simston* 1580, pers.n. ***Symond***, OE ***tūn***). A *Water Symond* lived in nearby Druidston in 1393.

SINGRUG see **EISINGRUG**

SKENFRITH, YNYSGYNWRAIDD Monm ST4520

'water-meadow of Cynwraidd', ***ynys***, pers.n. ***Cynwraidd***

Scenefrid 1162-3, *Schenevrit* 12cent., *Skenefrith* 1225,
Ynys Gynwreid 1215 (c.1400), *ysgynfraith* c.1566

W ***ynys*** generally means 'island', hence the antiquarian translation as *Ile of Kynvryk* 1559, but it properly reflects the location of the village next to the river Monnow. Loss of reduced unstressed syllables probably explains an original *Ynys Gynwraidd* (reflected in the form recorded c.1400) developing to (an undocumented) *(Yny)sgynwraidd* and *Sgynfraidd* and then Skenfrith. Cf. Sketty and Skewen.

SKERRIES, (THE), YNYS(OEDD) Y MOELRHONIAID

Angl SH2694

'the rocks', 'island(s) of the seals', (ON ***sker***), E ***skerry***, E ***the***, W ***ynys*** pl. ***ynysoedd***, ***y***, ***moelrhon*** pl. ***moelrhoniaid***

enys y moelrhonyeit 13cent., *Insula focarum walic' ynys y moelronyed* 1492, *le Skerrys* 15cent., *Ennys moilronyn* c.1500, *Ynis Moel Rhoniad* 1586, *the Skerres* 16cent., *Scerries* 1761, *Skerry I.* 1805, *The Skerries* 1818, *The Skerries or Ynysoedd-moelroniaid* 1838

The island consists of a series of interconnecting reefs or low crags which explains the pl. in E, and the W use of both ***ynys*** and ***ynysoedd***. The E name, in common with other coastal names of Scandinavian origin, has traditionally been ascribed to its landmark position on the sea routes from Ireland (a role still maintained by the lighthouse). However, there is no record of the rocks being called 'Sker', the singular form regularly seen in Pemb and Glam, such as Sger (*Bla(c)kescerre* 1153-83, *Skarre* 1536, *Scerr* c.1700) and Tusker Rock (q.v.) and in England (such as Skerton Lancashire) leading to the conclusion that the late appearance of Skerries is heavily influenced by E ***skerry*** (itself derived from ON ***sker***) 'rugged sea-rock, stretch of rocks, reef' (but preceding any record of ***skerry*** elsewhere in Britain). The island was the property of the bishops of Bangor (as in *seynt Danyels Isle* c.1500 with the occasional references to *Ynys Deiniol* and *St Daniel's Isle*) who had fishing rights there, with at least three recorded instances of the poaching of seals (L ***phoca***) in the 14 and 15cent.

SKETTY, SGETI

Glam SS6292

'water-meadow of Ceti', ***ynys***, pers.n. ***Ceti***

Enesketi 1319, *le Skette* 1400, *Skety* 17cent., *Eskelthee* 1698, *Yscetty* 1867

The original *Ynys Ceti, Ynysgeti* seems to have been re-interpreted as *Ysceti* and *Sceti* through loss of unstressed syllables. The AF ***le*** of 1400 is a probably conventional documentary insertion as in Michaelston-le-pit (rather than a replication of any residual *Y-* being interpreted as the def.art. ***y***). Ceti's identity is unknown, but the same pers.n. probably occurs in Kilgetty/Cilgeti Pemb and Maen Ceti (an alternative name for the prehistoric burial chamber of Maen Arthur or Arthur's Stone about eight miles west of Sketty on the hill Cefn Bryn). Cf. Skenfrith and Skewen.

SKEWEN, SGIWEN Glam SS7297

?'water-meadow of ?Cuen', ?*ynys*, pers.n. ?***Cuen***

Skuen 1680-97, *'r Skuen* c.1700, *Skuan* 18cent., *Scuan* 1784, *y Scuen* 1785, *Skewen* 1851, *i'r Sciwen* 1908

On the analogy of Skenfrith and Sketty, it is possible that *Skuen* is a re-interpretation of an earlier (undocumented) *Ynys Cuen* with loss of reduced unstressed syllables. However, unlike Skenfrith and Sketty, there seems to be some evidence in the forms (and in the colloquial Y Sciwan) of a residual *y* interpreted as the def.art. *y, yr*. The pers.n. could be Cuen (with later dial. -an for -en) but cf. Cuan in Esguan (Tywyn) Mer. Later forms seem to be influenced by the pers.n. Ciwen, Ciwan which is closer to the modern form and especially the colloquial Y Sciwan used by W-speakers. The first reference is to a rivulet (a tributary of the river Neath/Nedd) rising on the hill Mynydd y Drumau, and so Cuen might have been the name of the stream (taken from the pers.n. Cuen). Cf. Skenfrith and Sketty.

SKOKHOLM Pemb SM7305

'island of the sound', ON ***stokkr***, ON ***holmr***

Scogholm 1219-31, *Stokholm* 1275, *Scugholm* 1276, *Scokholm* 1324, *Stokeholme* 1376, *Stokeholme alias Scolcam* 1592, *Scockholme* 1599, *Scokum* 1761, *Scowkom* 1714, *Skokum* 1777

Probably derived from an original *Stok-holm* which became *Scok-holm* by assimilation and by analogy with the nearby Skomer Island (q.v.). ON ***stokkr*** 'a stock, a trunk' was also used of a 'sound' probably referring to Broad Sound (*Broad Sound* 1748) between Skomer and Stokholm.

SKOMER Pemb SM7209

'cleft island', ON ***skálm***, ON ***ey***

Skalmey(e) 1324, *Schalmey* 1325, *Scalmey* 1387, *Skalme* 1536-9, *Skalemey* 1592, *Scomer* 1761, *Skomar I* 1777

North Haven and South Haven almost separate the eastern peninsula, The Neck (*The Kneck* 1837, *The Neck* 1843), from the rest of the island. The modern form Skomer is probably the result of loss of -l- before -m-, subsequent rounding of -a- > -o- and the reduction of the final unstressed syllable to a neutral vowel.

SLEBECH Pemb SN0214

'muddy stream', OE ****slǣpe***, OE ***bece***

Slebyche c.1175-6 (c.1600), *Slebache* 1176-98 (17cent.), *Slebech* c.1148-76 (1308), *Slebech* 1270, *Slebache* 1353, *Slebets* late 15cent., *slebaids* c.1566, *slebiche* 1586

The old church and site of the hospital of the Knights of St John of Jerusalem lie in an angle between the Eastern Cleddau and an unnamed stream which was probably the 'muddy stream'. The noun ***slǣp*** is usually 'a slippery, muddy place, marsh' . The modern village and church have developed on the Haverfordwest-Narberth road.

SNOWDON, YR WYDDFA

Caern SH6054

'snow hill', 'the prominent place', OE ***snāw***, OE ***dūn***, W ***yr***, ***gwyddfa***
Snawdune 1095, *Snaudune* c.1191, *Snaudon* 1284, *Snowdon* 1341;
Weddua vaur 1284, *wedua vaur* 13cent.(14cent.), *Moel y Wyddfa* c.1450,
the Withvay or Snoyden Hill 1533

Both names characterise the mountain as being visible from considerable distances and likely to be snow-covered. The form *capud wedua vaur* 13cent. (14cent.) is probably a L rendering of 'Pen y Wyddfa Fawr'. ***gwyddfa*** here is 'height, eminence, promontory' (from ***gŵydd*** 'presence, sight' and thus 'prominent', ***-ma*** 'place'), probably the same el. as in Yr Wyddgrug (q.v.). It occurs in several hill names, leading to this, the highest mountain in Wales, being described occasionally as Yr Wyddfa Fawr (***mawr*** 'big'). The els ***gŵydd*** and ***gwyddfa*** also developed the meaning 'burial mound, memorial cairn, tumulus' (probably from the location of such cairns on prominent hills) and this meaning has been attributed to Yr Wyddfa, with popular association with a legendary giant R(h)ita Gawr (***cawr*** 'giant') reputedly buried under the large cairn at the summit. The var. Y Wyddfa results from -ŵy- > -wŷ- colloquially from an early period.

SNOWDONIA, ERYRI

'the area around Snowdon', 'highland', L ***Snowdonia***, W ***eryri***
Ereri 1191, *Snoudonia…terram Snaudoniae* 1284, *Eryri* 15cent.,
Eryri Hilles 1536-9, *Snowdone hilles, called Eryri* 1559

eryr is 'ridge', probably related to ***âr*** 'ridge' (see Aran Benllyn). The collective var. ***eryri*** refers to the highland comprising the hills and mountains surrounding Snowdon (q.v.). It is popularly believed to be 'place of the eagle' (***eryr*** 'eagle' and the terr.suff. ***-i***); ***eryr*** 'eagle' is probably cognate with ***eryr*** 'ridge' in the sense of 'rise, mount'. The 1284 *Snowdonia* was a conventional latinization, but there is no evidence that it survived in continuous vernacular or literary usage until it re-emerged in the 19cent. in antiquarian association with travel and tourism.

SOLFACH see SOLVA

SOLVA, SOLFACH

Pemb SM8024

'(place by the river) Solfach', r.n. ***Solfach***
Saleuuach before 1223, *Saluach* 1326 (16cent.), *Solvach* 1385,
Salvagh 1599, *Solvagh* 1603, *Solfach* 1801, *Upper ~* , *Lower Solva* 1843

The r.n. has an el. related to ***salw*** 'poor, mean' and the suff. ***-ach*** frequently occurring in r.ns. Cf. r.ns such as Salwach (Carm) and Porth Solfach (on Bardsey Caern), although the precise significance of 'poor, mean,' is obscure; 'insignificant', 'discoloured', 'pale' and 'unhealthy' are possible connotations. A cognate OE ***salu*** 'discoloured, sallow, dark' may have featured in the early development (cf. Salwarpe Worcestershire). The modern loss of -ch in pronunciation and spelling are the result of E influence as in Denbigh and Tenby (q.v.).

SOUGHTON see **SYCHDYN**

SOUTH CORNELLY see **CORNELLY**

SOUTHERNDOWN Glam SS8873

'southern hill', OE ***sūðer***, OE ***dūn***

Southdoune 1361, *Southerdoune* 1501, *Southerndown* 1605

Despite the 1361 spelling, the great majority of (later) spellings favour ***sūðer***- (gradually replaced by ***southern***) rather than ***sūð*** 'south'. Probably 'south' in contrast to Norton (*Northdowne* 1631).

SOUTHGATE Glam SS5588

'south court', OE ***sūð***, ME ***court***

Southcourte 1399, *Southcott* 1640, *Southgate* 1729

'South' in contrast to Norton or perhaps Courthouse Farm near Ilston. Later developments of the unstressed final syllable show the influence of ***cot*** 'cottage' and ***gate***.

SOUTH STACK, YNYS LAWD Angl SH2982

'south stack', 'agitated island', E ***south***, E ***stack***, W ***ynys***, ***llawd***

Ennes llawde 1555-6, *Inys laud* 1640, *yr ynys Lawd* 1738,
South Stack 1805, *The south Stack (The light house)* 1818,
The South Stack or Ynys blaw 1838

An island a mile south-west of North Stack (q.v. for the meaning of ***stack***). The W ***llawd*** is not independently recorded before 1604 (and then to mean 'in heat') but its occurrence in compounds well before then and in this p.n. suggests 'heat, agitation, tumult' probably a reference to the turbulent sea in the narrow passage between the island and the steep cliffs.

SPITTAL Pemb SM9723

'hospice', ME ***spitel***

(*de*) *Ospitali* 1259, (*de*) *Hospit'* 1290, *Spital* 1319, *Spyttell* 1393,
Spyttell otherwise manerium de Hospitali 1531, *Spittell* 1535,
Ysbitwal c.1566

A former hospital of St David's cathedral church, of which nothing remains. The c.1566 form is an (otherwise unattested) W rendering as ***ysbyty*** and ***gwâl*** 'den; litter, couch, bed'. This location has also been identified with Frowling church (*Frowlynchirch* 1326 [16cent.]) of uncertain meaning.

STACKPOLE ELIDOR see **CHERITON**[2]

STACKPOLE HEAD Pemb SR9994

'headland near Stackpole', p.n. ***Stackpole***, E ***head***

Stackpoole orde 1578, *Stackpole Hd.* 1777

For Stackpole see Cheriton (Stackpole Elidor). The 1578 form also has ME ***orde*** 'point, spit of land', found in the adjacent Mowing Word and in earlier forms for Dale Point (q.v.).

STAR Pemb SN2435

'(place near the) Star', p.n. ***Star***

the Starr, Starr 1734, *Star Inn* 1823

From an inn at crossroads on the once-important road between Cynwyl Elfed, Boncath and Cardigan. The name occurs elsewhere.

STAYLITTLE, PENFFORDD-LAS Mont SN8892

'stay only a little while', 'top of the green road', E ***stay***, E ***little***, W ***pen***, ***ffordd***, ***glas***

Staylittle 1827, *Stay a little* 1833, *Stay-a-little* 1836, *Staylittle* 1839, *Penfforddlas* 1839

Reputedly named after the *Staylittle* inn near a meeting-house established in 1805 at Esgair-goch near Gardd y Crynwyr or Quaker's Garden (recorded in 1716). It suggests a remote unattractive place for travellers. Popular tradition maintains that two blacksmith brothers here worked so rapidly that travellers need only 'stay a little'. Penffordd-las may refer to its location at the head of the lane (partly unsurfaced in 1891) leading up to the village from Trefeglwys but it is poorly-evidenced and many local people refer to it as Y Stae or Y Stay.

STEPASIDE Pemb SN1307

'step aside', E ***step***, E ***aside***

Stepaside 1694, *Stepaside Meadow* 1743, *Stoppa-side* 1813

The name of an inn on the road running between Kilgetty and Ludchurch. There is another Stepaside (*Step a side* 1657, *Stepaside* 1746) at New Moat Pemb and at least three Pemb inns called Step-in (*Step Inn*, *Stepin* 1797, 1814, 1844-52).

STRATA FLORIDA, YSTRAD-FFLUR Card SN7465

'vale of (the river) Fflur', L ***strata***, L ***florida***, W ***ystrad***, r.n. ***Fflur***

Stratflur, *Strad Flur* 1163-62 (1285), *Estatflur* c.1191, *Strata Florida* 1284, *Ystrad Flur* c.1400, *ystraed flur als Strata Florida* 1760

The name of the monastery founded in 1164 at Henfynachlog (***hen*** 'old',

mynachlog 'monastery'), later the Old Abbey Farm three miles south-west near Afon Fflur, before being moved to the present site in 1201. The river, rising below Carn Fflur, is a tributary of the Teifi. The r.n. Fflur (*Flur* 1163, *Fflyr* 16cent.) is a pers.n. thought to be an adaptation of L ***flora*** (but later perceived to mean 'beautiful, fair'). The latinized Strata Florida evidently interpreted it as a description of a flowery valley.

STRUMBLE HEAD, PEN-CAER Pemb SM9041

?'storm bill promontory', ?E ***storm*** var. ***strom***, E ***bill***, E ***head***

Strumble heade 1578, *Stumble Head* 1761, *Strumble Head* 1777

The E name is obscure. The first el. may well be ***strom***, an obsolete and rare var. of ***storm***. Local usage refers to the headland simply as Strumble which reinforces the possibility that the original name was *Strom Bill*, with Head being a later addition. The modern W name is Pen-caer (***pen*** 'promontory', ***caer*** 'fort'), a name taken from the fort on Garn Fawr (q.v.) and also applied to a much larger area of the promontory and to at least one farm. The local W name for this particular headland was Trwyn-câr (***trwyn*** 'point', ***câr*** dial. var. of ***caer***).

STRYT-YR-HWCH Denb SJ3346

'the sow's street' ***stryd*** dial. var. ***stryt***, ***yr***, ***hwch***

Streete yr hwch 1620, *Street yr hwch* 18cent.

The street was probably the road between Sontley and Plas Eyton with Stryt-yr-hwch Farm (*Street yr Hwch Hall* c.1700) adjacent. Stryt-yr-hwch is now the name of the area around the minor road, modern Bwgan-ddu Lane (***bwgan*** 'ghost, hobgoblin'). It is not now known whether the road led to a pig-farm, or whether this was a derogatory name. The historical forms show the dial. var. W ***stryt*** as E **street**.

SUDBROOK Monm ST5087

'south brook', OE ***sūð***, OE ***brōc***

Suthebroc, Suthebroch 1193-1218, *Suthebrok* 1254, *Sutbroc* 1333, *Sudebrok* c.1348, *Sutbroke, Sutbroche* 1539, *Southbrook or Sudbrook* 1830

The village lies next to the site of an Iron Age promontory fort on the Severn estuary (near the mouth of the Severn railway tunnel) at what was probably a crossing point. There is a small stream to the west. Several p.ns in England show ***sūð*** as Sud- when followed by an el. with initial b- (such as Sudbrooke, Sudborough, Sudbury, Sudbourne).

SUGAR LOAF, MYNYDD PEN-Y-FÂL Brec/Mon SO2718

'(the hill shaped like a) loaf of sugar', 'mountain at the top of the peak', E ***sugar loaf***, W ***mynydd***, ***pen***, ***y***, ***bâl***

Pennauel hill 1577, *Pen y vale Hill* 1695, *the Vale, Pen y val* c.1700, *Pen y Vale Mount* 1777, *Sugar Loaf* 1787, *the Pen y Vale hills* 1801, *the Sugar Loaf Mountain* 1824, *Mynydd Pen-y-fal* 1832

In several forms, *Vale* represents *Vâl* an anglicized spelling of Fâl. The hill seems to have been known simply as Y Fâl (*the Vale being sharp on the tope & at a distance shaped like a sugar loaf* c.1700) with the summit (and eventually the whole hill) called Pen y Fâl. ***mynydd*** is a late addition. Map drawings of 1813 show *Sugar Loaf* and *Penfoel* as distinct names applying to the same hill, where *Fâl* was interpreted as *foel*, ***moel***, a confusion possibly exacerbated by the hill's location in open common land known as Fforest Moel (*Fforest Moyle* 1627, *forest moyle* 1685, *fforest Moel* c.1700). Cf. another Sugar Loaf in Carm.

SULLY, SILI Glam ST1568

(place associated with de) Sully', pers.n. ***Sully***

Sulie 1193-8, *Sully* 1205, *Sulye* 1254, *Silly* 1376, *Scilley* 1536-9, *sili* c.1566

The family name de Sully (*de Suli* c.1180-90, *de Sulia* 1200, *de sulie* 1200/31) was also associated with lands in Gloucester and Devon. It has also been suggested that Sully was possibly a name transferred directly from Sully or Silly in Normandy. The family held the manor from the 12cent. The name was transferred to the nearby Sully Island (*Sylye Insul.* 1578, *Sulye Island* 1646) some forms for which (*Scilly I[sland]* 1754, *The Isle of Scilly* 1807) reveal imitation of the Scilly Isles. The W name Sili is a cymricization; cf. *dyffryn Syli* 1584, *Afon Sily* 1780, *Abersili* c.1805-10.

SUMMERLEAZE Monm ST4285

'summer pasture', OE ***sumor***, OE ***lǣs***

Somerlees 14cent., *Summerleaze Common* 1830

The village lies on low summer pastures on the Caldicot Levels. There are other summer names in the area relating to routes either used particularly for tending animals in summer or which were passable only in summer, such as *Sumerwei* 1153-76 in Goldcliff, *Somerwey* 1466 at St Brides Wentlooge, and *Somerwayebusches* 1480 probably at St Brides Netherwent.

SWALLOW FALLS, RHAEADR EWYNNOL Caern SH7657

'swallow(-tailed) falls', E ***swallow***, E ***falls***, W ***rhaeadr***, ***y***, ***gwennol***

Rhaiadr y wenol or the Waterfall of the Swallow 1773, *Rhaidr-y-wennel* 1777, *Rhaiadr y wenol* 1797-1805, *Rhaidr y Wenol* 1810, *Rhaidr y wennol* 1830, *Rhaiadr-y-wennol* 1838, *The Falls of the Swallow* 1860, *Swallow Falls* 1883

A waterfall (*a noted cascade* 1773) on Afon Llugwy between Capel Curig and Betws-y-coed. The ***gwennol*** is the distinctive swallow tail formed by two sheets of water divided by a prominent rock. There is no documentary evidence for the recent, probably learned, supposed restoration to a form ***ewynnol*** 'foaming' (itself an idiosyncratic coinage first recorded 1795), possibly prompted by a desire to demonstrate W linguistic ownership of a popular tourist attraction and a concern that *Rhaeadr y Wennol* would be perceived as a deferential translation of what came to be the better known name Swallow Falls.

SWANSEA, ABERTAWE Glam SS6494

'island of Sveinn', 'mouth of (the river) Tawe', pers.n. ***Sveinn***, ON ***ey***, W ***aber***, r.n. ***Tawe***

Swensi c.1140, *Sweynesse* 1153-84 (14cent.), *Sueinesia* 1187, *Sweinesei* 1209-10, *Sweineshea* 1210, *Swense* 1235, *Swe(y)neseye* 1277, *Swannesey* 1505, *Swanzey* 1598-1600, *Swansea* 1530, *Abertawe* c.1191, *Abertawi* 1192 (c.1286), *Aber Tawy* c.1300

ey occurs elsewhere around the W coast in the names of islands in combination with ON pers.ns (such as Ramsey, Bardsey and Anglesey) but here the spelling has been influenced by ***sea*** (and by ***swan***). The ON names can be ascribed to Scandinavian forays from Ireland between the 9 and 11cent., but the existence of coins marked *Swensi* minted at Swansea c.1140 suggest at least a trading post of some kind. The island may have been a bank at the mouth of the river Tawe (q.v.) (removed during construction of docks in 19cent.) described as *Ilond* 1400, *Iselond'* 1432 and *The Island* 1641, or perhaps an area of raised ground in marshes.

SWYDDFFYNNON Card SN6966

'district of the well', ***swydd***, ***(y)***, ***ffynnon***

Suidd y fynon-oer 1635-6, *Swydd-y-ffynnon-oer alias Mynachty-hen* 1721-2, *Swydd y ffynnon* 1738, *Swydd-y-Ffynnon* 1834, *Swyddffynnon* 1851

The abbey of Strata Florida held land at Ffynnon Oer (*Fenaunoyr* 1181-2, *Ffynnaun Oyr* 1202, *de Fonte Frigido* 1291) and later deeds link two smallholdings, *Managhtie Heane* 1616-17, *Mynachty-hen* 1635-6 (***mynachty*** 'monastery', ***hen*** 'old') and *Ffinnon Oyre* (1616-17, *Suidd-y-fynon-oer* 1635-6, ***oer*** 'cold'). A farm south of the village is still called Swydd. The precise location of the well (allegedly dedicated to St Ffraid) is not known but was probably at the west end of the village (whose inn is called Fountain Inn).

SYCHDYN, SOUGHTON Flints SJ2466

'bog farm', OE *****sōg***, OE ***tūn***

Sutone 1086, *Sychtun*, *Sychton* 1271, *Sotton* 1283, *Sutton* 1284, *Scychton* 1317, *Soughton* 1363, *Sughton* 1446-7, *Sychtyn* 1512, *Sychton*, *Syghtyn* 1539, *Sowghton* 1604, *Sychdyn* c.1700

The bog was probably what is today called Fawnog (***mawnog*** 'peaty'), or the several patches of wet ground between Sychdyn and Soughton Hall (such as the *lhyn ... a elwir pwlh y Gasseg*, 'the lake ... known as Pwll y Gaseg' c.1700) belonging to the Conway family of Soughton Hall. Sychdyn has long been explained as ***sūð-tūn*** 'the south farm', an explanation supported by being to the south of Northop and of the probable location of *Castretone* 1086 which has Aston to the east of it. The later *Sutton* forms (and innumerable Sutton p.ns in England) support the 'south-ton' etymology. However, the phonology (of the forms in -cht- and in -ought-) presents difficulties which are more easily explained by OE ****sōg*** later ME ***sogh*** or ***sough*** 'bog' (as in the case with Sychtyn Shropshire). The preservation of ME -gh- as Welsh -ch- is common as is the cymricized -tyn (for -ton) in the north-east, but there is no doubt that later development was influenced by W ***sych*** 'dry' reinforcing the perception that the village itself was on slightly raised dry ground in a wet area. Today, Soughton tends to be used mainly of the Hall and farm.

SYLEN — Carm SN5107

'(place near) Sylen', p.n. ***Sylen***
Mount Selen 1800, *Capel-sulen* 1833, *Capel Sylen* 1875, *Sylen* 1889
The name is taken from the nearby hill Mynydd Sylen (*Mynidd Sylen* 1609, *Mynydh Syle* c.1700). Sylen may have been the name of the stream immediately south of the village which flowed through *Glyn-sulen* 1833, *Glyn Sylen* 1875 but it could also be a pers.n., a var. of Silin (cf. Llansilin). The 1800 form seems to have been the name of the Baptist chapel.

SYNOD INN, POST MAWR — Card SN4054

'synod inn', 'main post', E ***synod***, E ***inn***, W ***post***, ***mawr***
Synodd 1760, *Synod* 1798, *Post* 1834, *Post-mawr*, *Synod Inn* 1891
Associated with the crossroads and a house called *Synodd* 1760 which later included a public house *Synod House (part Public House)* 1837 earlier *Black Cock* 1803, and the hill *Black Cock-pit-hill* 1813. The name is also preserved in three farms, Synod Uchaf (*Ssinod ycha* 1728-9, ***uchaf***), Synod Ganol (*Synod ganol* 1771, ***canol***), Synod Isaf (*Synod isaf* 1771, ***isaf***) and Synod Mill, all on the banks of Afon Soden; another farm is called Bryn-synod. Synod Ganol has been identified with *Synod* 1189-95 (1214), *Sinod* 1447, *Synodd* 1760, *Sinod ganol* 1781, *Synod* 1795, *Synnad, Synod ganol* 1837 which suggests continuity with an unknown ecclesiastical synod or convocation. No such synod is recorded for the area, but there are several ecclesiastical associations within a mile in Tir-esgob ('bishop's land', ***tir***, ***esgob***) and the medieval site Ffynnon Ddewi (*Synod Ffynon Dewi, or St. David's well* 1807). Whitland abbey reputedly had lands here. The el. ***synod*** also occurs in Lletysynod (*Tythyn-llety-synod* 1571, ***llety*** 'lodging') and Banc Lletysynod a mile-and-a-half north-west of Pont-rhyd-y-groes. There is evidence in England of ***synod*** being used of an assembly of any kind (usually flippantly) which reinforces its perpetuation here in connection with the inn. The W name Post Mawr refers to a posting-house for travellers.

T

TAF see **TAFF**

TAFARNYGELYN Denb SJ1861

'holly tavern', ***tafarn, y, celyn***

Dafarn gelin 1680-1, *Tafarn y Celin Gate* 1795, *Tafarn-gelyn* 1838, *Tafarn-y-Gelyn* 1983

The tavern was located at the junction of roads from Cilcain and from Moch Farm with the Rhuthun-Mold road. The holly was traditionally used as a tavern-sign but the erection of a turnpike gate here influenced the 1795 form by introducing the definite article '*y*', (as if 'the inn at the Celyn Gate'). In time ***y celyn*** 'the holly' changed into ***y gelyn*** 'the enemy' (probably in response to antagonism to the turnpikes). Both forms have survived in local usage.

TAFF, River, TAF, Afon Brec, Glam SO9921, ST1874

'?flowing one', Br ****tam-***

Taf 1102, *Tamii fluminis* c.1140, *Tam, Taf maur, taf bechan* 12cent., *Taam, Taaph* c.1200, *Taffe vawr* 1461, *Taue uaure, ~ uachan flu:* 1578

Its two main headwaters are Taf Fawr and Taf Fechan (***mawr*** 'big', ***bychan*** fem. ***bechan*** 'small'). The root is Br ****tam-*** once thought to mean 'dark' but now generally understood to be 'to flow'. A form such as **Tamo-* > Taf and a genitival **Tami-* > Tyf as in Cardiff (q.v.). As such, Taf is comparable with other r.ns such as Taf Carm (*Tam, taf* 1136-54, *Taph* c.1191) and, outside Wales, Team, Tame, Tamar, Thame and Thames (W Tafwys), as well as similar Continental names; see also Tawe.

TAFF'S WELL, FFYNNON TAF/DAF Glam ST1283

'well near (the river) Taf', r.n. ***Taff/Taf***, E ***well***, W ***ffynnon***

Ffunnon Tave 1802, *Ffunnon Taf or Taffs Well* 1803, *Tâf Well* 1811, *Ffynhon Daf* 1814, *Taffs Well* 1825, *Fynnon Tâf, or 'the well of Tâf'* 1840, *Taff's Well* 1875

Most sources favour Ffynnon Taf but regular 19cent. local usage was Ffynnon Daf with lenition and is still the form favoured by older inhabitants. Named from a medicinal well (*Hot-well* 1729, Ffynon Daf, called by some *Ffynhon Dwym, ot the Tepid Well* 1811, *the tepid well* 1843) supposed to cure rheumatism, an area called *Portobello* from an inn recorded in 1799 (after the Colombian seaport). The south part was occasionally described as *Walnut Tree Bridge* (1860) from the former railway station.

TAFOLWERN Mont SH8902

'frightening marsh', ***dywal, gwern***

Dwalwern 1185, *Dewalguern* c.1191, *Duwalwern* 1200,

de Walwern 1168 (c.1286), *Walwern* 1293,
Dywalwern 1173-1220 (15cent.), c.1215(c.1400), *Tafolwern* 1577,
Tavolwerne 1586, *Frith Dovelwerne al's Dolweren* 1664
The marsh presumably posed a danger to travellers. The p.n. *Dewalwern* was interpreted by AF and L copyists as *de walwern*, 'of Walwern', leading to the form *Walwern*. Later development of -w- to -f- were influenced by ***dyfal*** 'diligent' (cf. Waun Ddyfal, the W name of Little Heath, Cardiff, *Waynddy fall* 1578-84, *Y-wayn-ddyval* 1650, with ***gwaun***), and by ***tafol*** 'dock (-leaves)' (cf. Tafolog Mont). This was the location of an important medieval castle in the cantref of Cyfeiliog (*kastell walwern yn kyueilyawc* 1162 [14cent.], *castell Dafalwern* 1162 [c.1400]).

TAI-BACH Glam SS7788
'little houses', ***tŷ*** pl. ***tai***, ***bach***
Taybach 1773, *Tai-bach* 1833
The village developed during the construction of copperworks in 1770-74 taking its name from four cottages at Y Groes-wen, anglicized as Crosswen, which stood at the foot of St Alban's Terrace.

TALACHDDU Brec SO0833
?'end of (the stream) Achddu', ***tâl***, r.n. ***Achddu***
Talachtu 1263, *Talaugh'duy* 1400, *talachddy* c.1566
The village lies immediately south of a stream Nant Achddu, a tributary of the river Dulas, but forms are late (*Achddu* 1889); cf. the stream Achddu (*achduy* 1499, *Achddy* 1587) in Brec. The medial el. could feasibly be ***ach*** 'line, lineage' but its significance is obscure unless it is used in a topographical sense of 'scar'; cf. *Cwm yr Ach* 1744 Glam. The pl. ***achau*** is possibly seen in the r.n. Achau or Ache a tributary of Honddu Brec at Cwmache (*Cwm Achey, Blaen Achey* 1812, *Cwm-achau, Blaen-achau* 1832). The final el. is probably ***du*** 'dark, black' or an abbreviated form of Dulas if Talachddu can be identified with *Tuchlarduveleys, Tuchlar Duueleys* 1241 (the nearby river Dulas).

TALACRE Flints SJ1284
'end of the acres', ***tâl***, ***acr*** pl. ***acrau*** dial. ***acre***
Tallacre 1381-2, *Taleacrey* 1569, *Taleacre* 1596, *Talaccrey* 1602,
Tallacre 1621, *Talachre* c.1700, *Talacre* 1840
acre is the dial. var. of the W pl. ***acrau*** and is not the E ***acre***. Cf. Acre-fair. The acres were the extensive pasture land of the Point of Ayr.

TALBENNI see **TALBENNY**

TALBENNY, TALBENNI Pemb SM8311
'end of the ?crests', ***tâl***, ?***ban*** pl.****benni***
Talbenny 1291, *Talebenni* 1292, *Talebenny* 1306, *Talbeni* 1587
The pl. of ***ban*** 'peak, mountain' is usually ***bannau*** (as in Bannau Brycheiniog). However, an unrecorded ****benni*** is also found in *Garthbenni*

1136-54 (identified with Welsh Bicknor Herefordshire) located next to high, prominent ridges jutting into the course of the river Wye, and in Y Fenni-fach Brec (*Benni* c.1143-54, *Benny* 1454, *le Venne inferior* 1373). Talbenny lies close to the sea on an elevated, rolling plateau, and ***benni*** may here refer to the smaller promontories extending westwards from Borough Head.

TALBOT GREEN, TONYSGUBORIAU Glam ST0482
'green near the Talbot', 'sward of the barns', E ***green***, p.n. ***Talbot***, W ***ton***, ***ysgubor*** pl. ***ysgubor(i)au***
Tonisca Borra 1754, *Ton Ysguborau* 1833, *Talbot Arms (P.H.)*, *Talbot Row* 1885
The 1754 spelling is an attempt at representing the local pronunciation Ysgubora. The E name originated with the tavern *Talbot Arms* (named after the Talbot family of Hensol Castle) around which the village developed. The railway station took the name *Talbot Road*. Both station and village later became Talbot Green.

TALERDDIG Mont SH9300
'end of the little hill', ***tâl***, ***ardd***, dim.suff. ***-ig***
Talerdic 1185, *Talherthic* 1187, *Talherdyk* 1291, *Tallerddik* 1535, *Talertheg* 1545, *Talerthicke* 1608-9, *Talerthuge* 1627
Talerddig lies at the foot of several gradients. (Erddig Denb has an entirely different origin, OE ***hierde***, OE ***cot*** 'shepherd's hut').

TALGARREG Card SN4251
'rock end', ***tâl***, (*y*), ***carreg***
tal y garreg 1587, *Tall y Garreg* 1630, *Talygarreg* 1788, *Tal-gareg* 1834
The village stands on a short ridge above Afon Cletwr extending south from Graig (***craig*** 'rock'). A nearby farm is called Esger (***esgair*** 'ridge').

TALGARTH[1] Brec SO1533
'ridge end', ***tâl***, ***garth***
Talgart 1121, *Talgar* c.1163-75, *Talgard* post 1130 (c.1200), *Talgarth* 1203-8, *talgarth* c.1566
The ridge is either the low promontory which extends north from Penywyrlod or that extending west from Rhos-fach towards the town.

TALGARTH[2] Mont SN9690
'ridge end', ***tâl***, ***garth***
talgarth 12cent. (13cent.), *Talgar*, *Talgarth* 1293, *Talgarthe* 1595-6
The hamlet is located on slopes above Afon Tarannon on either side of a stream Nant y Bachws. The ridge may be that on the north side of the stream extending eastwards from the hill Fforest or that on the south side extending northwards from an unnamed hill near Dolgwden.

TALLARN GREEN Flints SJ4444

'open space', ***talwrn***, E ***green***

Tallarne Owen commonly called Tallorne Greene 1657, *Talwrn, The Talyrn Green* c.1700, *Tallarn Green* 1881

Talwrn was used of one of the *Houses of Note … but there's at present no house* (c.1700), while *The Talyrn Green* referred to the commons in the sense of common pasturage. ***green*** was perceived as being very close in meaning to ***talwrn*** (as in a similar *Talwrn green* 1792, Hope Flints). The anglicized pronunciation can be seen in *Talyrn* and the modern Tallarn. The Owen of 1657 is unknown but could, however, represent ***ywen*** 'yew-tree'.

TALLEY see **TALYLLYCHAU**

TALOG Carm SN3325

'dirty ford', ***rhyd, halog***

Talog 1811, *Rhyd talog Mill now called Havod Halog* 1816, *Talog* 1831

Talog Mill 1891 is located on the east side of Afon Cywyn close to a footbridge over the river, and probably the location of the ford. The forms are very late but it is likely that the muddy condition of the ford prompted the epithet ***halog***, with *Rhyd Halog* becoming *Rhytalog* with -dh- > -t-. See also Rhytalog Flints and cf. Rhydhalog (*Rheed Talog* 1729) near Barry Glam. *Talog* resulted from loss of the unstressd *Rhy-*. Cf. other instances where the reduced form Talog or Talwg was taken to be the name of the river (such as Talog Pencader Carm and Nant Talwg Barry Glam). In the alternative name of the mill, *Havod Halog* (***hafod*** 'summer-dwelling'), *Halog* was probably a conscious restoration of the original el. with reference to the ford rather than the *Hafod*.

TAL-SARN Card SN5456

'causeway end', ***tâl, sarn***

Talsarne 1397, *Talsarn* 1413-22, *Tal y Sarne* 1541, *Talaserne* 1578, *Talsarn* 1798

The causeway is across low-lying ground through which Afon Aeron flows. The river is spanned by Pont Tal-sarn (*Bridge of Timber over Ayron* c.1700). The location seems to have attracted several fairs to the central green prompting the name Tal-y-sarn Green (E ***green*** 'common pasture', 'grassy spot') which was in regular use at one period (*Talesarne Greene* 1539, *Tal y sarn grin* c.1566, *Tallaserne Greene* 1631). The def.art. ***y*** (variously represented by -y-, -a- and -e-) featured in many of the forms but has disappeared since the 19cent. Another name was Maenor Silian (*Maynor Sullen* 1301/2, *Manorsulyn otherwise Tallasarne or Syllyan* 1552) from its status as a ***maenor*** 'district manor' (with pers.n Silian).

TALSARNAU Mer SH6135

'end of (the) causeways', ***tâl***, (*y*), ***sarnau***

Tal y sarne 1455, *Tal y sarney* 1576, *Talysarney* 1674, *Tal-y-sarnau* 1838

The road north-east of Harlech skirts the sea-marsh of Morfa Harlech following several stretches of causeway some of which crossed Afon Dwyryd. The sea at one time reached the village of Talsarnau which had causeways on either side of it.

TALWRN[1] Angl SH4977

'threshing-floor', ***talwrn***

Talwrne mawr 1655, *Talwrn mawr* 1713, *Talwrn* 1888

In 1655 the reference was to a farm called *Talwrne mawr* (***mawr*** 'big') which led to the reasonable assumption that the farm's 'threshing floor' is the most appropriate of several meanings of ***talwrn***, and that ***mawr*** was added to indicate the farm's prominence. However, several 18cent. diary entries for the Bulkeley family (of Dronwy and Brynddu) refer to cockfighting at *Talwrn Mawr* which may indicate that the place was also well-known as the location of a ***talwrn*** 'cockpit'. By 1812, *Talwrn mawr* was listed as one of several tracts of common land which suggests that ***talwrn*** 'open ground, grassland' had given its name to the farm, with ***mawr*** referring to an extensive area. The three meanings, 'threshing-floor', 'cockpit' and 'open ground', must therefore be considered feasible. Significantly, perhaps, there is no evidence of a 'Talwrn-bach'. Either way, ***mawr*** became redundant in the name of the village.

TALWRN[2] Denb SJ2947

'open space', ***talwrn***

Talwrn y tarw 1386-7, *Talwrn* 1838

The original *Talwrn y tarw* (*y* 'the', ***tarw*** 'bull') lay in what are now meadows adjoining Pentrebychan Brook. The name also survives in *Ty'n y talwrn* (19cent., ***ty'n*** 'small-holding') now Talwrn Farm.

TAL-Y-BONT[1] Caern SH6070

'the bridge end', ***tâl***, *y*, ***pont***

Talybont 1275, *tal y bont* 1622, *Talybont* 1781, *Tal-y-bont* 1838

The village is fairly close to the bridge which carries the old road (from Chester and from Bethesda) across Afon Ogwen. A wooden bridge (a hundred yards upstream) was replaced by a stone bridge rebuilt in 1881.

TAL-Y-BONT[2] Caern SH7668

'the bridge end', ***tâl***, *y*, ***pont***

Talybont 1535, *tale y bont* 1661, *Tal-y-bont* 1838

The village is adjacent to the bridge (*Pont tâl y bont* c.1700) which carries the Conwy-Dolgarrog road across Afon Dulyn (formerly Afon Tal-y-bont, *Avon Tal y bont* c.1700).

TAL-Y-BONT[3] Card SN6589

'the bridge end', ***tâl***, ***y***, ***pont***

Talebont 1301, *Talybont* 1654

The village of Tal-y-bont is at the northern end of the bridge over the river Leri.

TAL-Y-BONT[4] Mer SH5821

'the bridge end', ***tâl***, ***y***, ***pont***

Talypont in Meyryonyd late 13cent., *Talepont* 1545, *Talpont* 1582, *Talybont* 1658, *Tal-y-bont* 1838

The road between Harlech and Barmouth crosses Afon Ysgethin at Tal-y-bont.

TAL-Y-BONT[5] see **BUTTINGTON**

TAL-Y-BONT ON USK, TAL-Y-BONT AR WYSG Brec SO1122

'end of the bridge on (the river) Usk/Wysg', ***tâl***, ***y***, ***pont***, r.n. ***Usk/Wysg***

Talpont 14cent., *Talybont* 1560

The additions 'on Usk' and 'ar Wysg' occurring from c.1960 are misleading since the bridge is that over the stream Caerfanell. The Usk/Wysg is about half-a-mile away.

TAL-Y-CAFN Denb SH7871

'ferry-boat end', ***tâl***, ***y***, ***cafn***

Taley Caven 1518, *Tal y Kafn Gronant* 1554, *Tal y Cavn* 1617, *Tal y Kavn* c.1700, *Talycafn ferry* 1789, *Tal-y-cafn* 1838

This is one of the lowest crossing points on Afon Conwy, reputedly used by the Romans. The ferry was known as Cafn Gronant (*Kavn Gronant* c.1700), Gronant being a tnshp of the western bank. The eastern end of the ferry ('*where the ferie man dwelte by*' 1617) was Tal-y-cafn. The word ***cafn*** originally referred to a small dug-out boat, and came to be used of a ferry-boat and then of the ferry itself. Cf. Gabalfa (***ceubal*** 'ferry' from ***ceubal*** 'skiff, wherry' and ***ma*** 'place') occurring in Cardiff, Swansea, Radn and Brec.

TAL-Y-FAN Caern SH7372

'top of the peak', ***tâl***, ***y***, ***ban***

Talyfan 1810, *Tal-y-fan* 1838

One of the most easterly peaks in the range of mountains from Dyffryn Ogwen to Conwy. ***tâl***, found extensively in p.ns, also means 'end, highest or furthest' so the significance here could be its location towards the furthest point in the range, or the highest of a series of hills in the proximity. As with many other p.ns where ***tâl*** is the unstressed first el. of a name phrase, it is customarily written and pronounced Tal-.

TALYLLYCHAU, TALLEY Carm SN6332

'end of the stone slabs', ***tâl, y, llech*** pl. ***llechau***

Thalelech 1222, *Telelechu* 1239, *Tal y Llecheu* 1271 (c.1400), *Taleleze* 1291, *Talleghu* 1343, *Talilazhau* c.1348, *Tallagh, Talley* 1382, *Tallay* 1395, *tal y lleche* c.1566, *Tal y llychau* 1710, *Talau* 1740

The name has long been taken as ***llwch*** pl. ***llychau*** 'pool, lake' with reference to two large fishponds immediately north of the Premonstratensian abbey established c.1184-9. Certainly ***llychau*** has influenced the modern form. However, the historical forms provide clear evidence of ***llech*** pl. ***llechau***, 'slate, rock, stone slab' although the topographical significance is as yet unexplained. It may refer to the site of a former chapel Capel Crist (*Mynwent Capel Crist* 1891) on the east side of the village or perhaps an antiquity suggested by the *Old Wall* stretching part way across the lower pool shown on an 1891 map but the age of both is uncertain. It could feasibly refer to a causeway once providing access to the abbey, possibly between the two fishponds. Many early spellings such as *Talcleulau* 1284-7 and *Tilachlargy* 1307 show the difficulty which non-Welsh clerks had with this p.n. Talley may therefore have its origins in a purely clerical abbreviation or, simply, a colloquial contraction.

TAL-Y-SARN Caern SH4853

'the causeway end', ***tâl, y, sarn***

Tal y Sarn 1525, *Talysarn* 1661, *Talsarn* 1783, *Tal-y-sarn* 1838

The causeway carried the route from Rhyd-ddu, Baladeulyn (q.v.) and Llyn Nantlle to Tal-y-sarn across the wetlands on the north side of the slow-moving river Llyfni (***llyfn*** 'smooth'), the area of the drained lower lake. The present village developed largely between 1850 and 1870 in response to the expansion of the slate quarries. Colloquially Tal-sarn, and frequently referred to as Y Nant.

TANAT, Afon Mont/Denb SJ 0226-1624

'bright one', ***afon, tân,*** suff. ***-ad***

Tauad c.1215 (c.1300), *Tanat* 1324, *Tanad* 15cent., *Tanat* 1548, *Tannatt* 1627, *Tanad* 1838

The river rises on the Berwyn range, flows through Dyffryn Tanat (***dyffryn*** 'valley') and joins the Efyrnwy river at Abertanat (*Abertannat* 1299, *Abertanad* 1455-85, *Aber Tanad* 1535-80). The first el. is ***tân*** 'fire', which suggests waters that are either turbulent or, more likely, bright or gleaming. A reference to a 6cent. fem. pers.n. *Tannat* and to several males called *Tanet* in the Middle Ages leaves open the possibility that the river name has been transferred from a pers.n. In some Welsh contexts the preferred form is Tanad but general usage tends towards Tanat.

TAN-Y-BWLCH Mer SH6540

'under the pass', ***tan, y, bwlch***

Tan y Bwlch 1613, *Tan y bwlch* c.1700

Originally the name of a mansion situated beneath the narrow heavily wooded pass leading from Dyffryn Ffestiniog to Rhyd. Another older name for the pass was Bwlch Coed Dyffryn (*bulgh coet dyffryn* 1438, *Bulgh coetdyffryn* 1437), referring to Dyffryn Ffestiniog (***dyffryn*** 'vale', see Ffestiniog) while the house was *y te gwyn dan volch koyd dyffryn* 1509 'the white house below Bwlch Coed Dyffryn'.

TAN-Y-FRON Denb SH9564

'below the hillside', ***tan, y, bron***

Tan-y-fron 1880

The hamlet is at the junction of several minor roads in a fairly narrow valley (Nant y Fleiddiast) with hills on either side.

TANYGRISIAU Mer SH6845

'below the steps', ***tan, y, gris*** pl. ***grisiau***

Tenygrisa 1771, *Tan-y-grisiau* 1838

Slate was quarried here by cutting galleries, levels or terraces. The hamlet for quarrymen and their families came to be known from its location below these terraces, although contemporary records recall huge steps leading up to Cwmorthin and Dolrhedyn.

TAN-Y-GROES Card SN2849

'below the crossroads', ***tan, y, croes***

Tan-y-groes 1891

The name seems to have been used initially for the chapel built 1849-50 and preceded by *Llain y Groes* 1787 and *Bwlchygroes* 1818. The hamlet is beside the main road adjacent to the minor road from the direction of (now disused) quarries which may have given rise to the settlement.

TAVERNSPITE Pemb SN1812

'(place near) Tafarn Spite', p.n. ***Tafarn Spite***

Tavern Spite 1767, *Tavern Spit* 1794, *Tavern-y-Spite* 1797

The first el. is ***tafarn*** 'tavern'. The second el. is probably W ***sbeit*** although the spelling frequently adopts the E form ***spite***. Both els occur elsewhere in Wales apparently meaning a house or place which had been set up in contentious circumstances, a 'tavern set up in spite'. In an E context, ***spite*** is also known to have had a broader derogatory sense for something unpleasant, perhaps unproductive agricultural land or land difficult to plough as in the frequent use of it in field-names in England. Tavernspite could therefore possibly indicate an 'unpleasant, unsavoury tavern'. The frequency of ***spite*** and ***sbeit*** in inn names coupled with the use of the def.arts. ***the*** and ***y***, has led to the suggestion that they may be distinct words derived from L ***hospitium*** with the sense of 'lodging' (as with Ysbyty q.v.); their consistently late appearance in the 18 and 19cent. make this most unlikely. The def.art. ***y*** can also be explained as the W var. ***ysbeit*** being interpreted as ***y sbeit***.

TAWE, River Brec, Glam SN8322-SS662

'?flowing one', Br *****tam-***, W ***-wy***

taui c.1126, *Thavy* c.1129, *Tauuy* 1136-54, *Tavue* 12cent., *Thawi* 1208, *Tawy* 1449, *Tawe* 1536-9, *Tauy flu:* 1578

The river rises on the slopes of the Black Mountain and flows through Cwm Tawe to the sea at Abertawe (q.v.). The r.n. has the same root as Taf (q.v.) with the suff. ***-wy***, hence **Tafwy* > *Tawy* > dial. Tawe. Cf. Pontardawe.

TEIFI, Afon Card SN6150

?'flowing one', Br *****tam-***, r.n. suff. ***-i***

Tuerobios, Tuegobios c.150, *Teibi* c.830 (11cent.), *Theiui* 1115-47, *Teywy* 1184 (1285), *Teivi* 1317, *Teifi* 15cent., *river Tyvi* 1559

The river rises in Llyn Teifi (*Llin Tyue* 1536-9, *Llyn Teyvy* 1603, *Llyn Teifi* 1834) east of Strata Florida and flows through Dyffryn Teifi (*Difrin Teiui* c.1150) to the sea at Aberteifi (q.v.) and is frequently the boundary between Card, Carm and Pemb. The second transliteration given above (c.150) of Ptolemy's Greek could have resulted in Teifi, but is still obscure. The suggestion has been made that Ptolemy's form, although geographically accurate (*Tuerobis Fluvii Ostia*), has been corrupted beyond restoration, and that it is more profitable to trace Teifi back to a var. of the **Tam-* 'to flow' seen in the *Tyf* of Cardiff (q.v.) and Tawe (q.v.).

TEMPLE BAR Card SN5354

'(place named after) Temple Bar', p.n. ***Temple Bar***

Temple Bar 1821, *Temple-bar* 1834, *Temple Bar* 1891

There are identical names in Card, such as *Temple Bar* 1787 between Tan-y-groes and Sarnau, *Temple Bar* 1844 Llanfair Clydogau, *Temple Barr* 1760 Penbryn as well as a Temple Bar near Newport Pemb, a *Temple Bar* 1831 near Llandeilo Carm and a *Templebar* 1817 in Clatter Mont. All refer to turnpike gates and belong to a group of places named after London streets and landmarks (such as Chancery (q.v), Bow Street (q.v.) and *Piccadilly* 1834). In this instance, the name seems to have supplanted a *Cross Inn* 1819 and is said to have been given by Lord Carrington who had bought the lordship of Cellan in 1809. There is further evidence of a house recorded as *Temple Barr* 1728, probably identical to *Templebar Cottage* 1891 Carm, but in this case there is no evidence of a turnpike gate and the *bar* here may be an elliptical allusion to the adjoining village Crug-y-bar.

TEMPLETON, TREDEML Pemb SN1111

'Templars' farm', OE ***tempel***, OE ***tūn***, W ***tref, teml***
Villa Templarii 1282, *Villa Templariorum Campestris* 1283,
Tempiltun late 13cent, *Templeton* 1338, *Tredeml* 1867
Probably named from a former hospice of the Knights Templars (established in the late 12cent., suppressed in 1312) of Slebech Commandery; cf. Templeton, Berkshire and Devon. Ruins of a chapel are recorded in 1811. The significance of L ***campestris*** (gen. of ***campester***) 'of the field', is uncertain. It may indicate a settlement in open land as distinct from Slebech Commandery located on a small promontory next to the river Eastern Cleddau. The W form is a translation.

TENBY, DINBYCH-Y-PYSGOD, Pemb SN1300

'little fort of the fish', ***din, bych(an), y, pysgod***
dinbych 1150 (14cent.),*Tynebeh* 1208-10, *Dinbych* c.1275,
Tynebegh 1292, *Tyneby* 1324, *Deneby* 1386, *Tenby* 1482,
dinbych y pysgod c.1566, *Tenby y piscoid* 1586,
Tenby…in Welshe Dynbigh y Pysgod mid 16cent., *Tenby* c.1700
Cf. Denbigh. The fort probably lies under the medieval castle on the headland. The addition of ***y pysgod*** indicated its importance as a fishing port. Provection of D- > T- is also found in Tintern (< Dindeyrn)(q.v.). Anglicization accounts for -bych > -bigh (as in Denbigh) but here the -by spelling is probably influenced by ON p.ns in Pembs (as Colby and Derby) and in England.

THREE COCKS, ABERLLYNFI Brec SO1737

'(place near the) Three Cocks', 'mouth of the river Llynfi', E ***three***, E ***cocks***, W ***aber***, r.n. ***Llynfi***
Abberlenevy 1234, *Aberleueni, -leweny* 1251, *Aberlhyfni* c.1700,
Three Cocks c.1755, *Aberllynfi* 1778
The Three Cocks inn, located in Aberllynfi, is named from the arms of the Williams family of Gwernyfed. Aberllynfi is named from the river Llynfi (q.v.) whose confluence (***aber***) with the river Wye is about a mile from the village.

THREE CROSSES, Y CRWYS Glam SS5794

'three crosses', 'the cross', E ***three***, E ***crosses***, W ***y, crwys***
Y Crooyse 1594, *the Three Crosses* 1642, *'r Croes or Three Crosses* 1832,
y Crwys 1867
On the significance of the name see Fourcrosses. Here, there is a junction of three roads forming a triangle on the west side of the village. ***crwys*** was earlier sing. and the 1594 form probably has this sing. use with

reference to the crossroads; cf. *'r Croes* 1832 'the cross' ***croes***. However, ***cruwys*** later came to be seen as a pl. of ***croes***, and *y Crwys* 1867 probably has this pl. connotation favouring (unidentified) standing wayside or boundary crosses.

TIERS CROSS
Pemb SM9010

'crossroads near Tierson', E ***cross***, p.n. ***Tiers***

Tears Cross 1729, *Tiers Cross* 1798, *Tier's Cross* 1824

The forms are late and so it is likely to be an analogous re-formation on the basis of Tierson a mile to the south of the crossroads (*Terreston* 1283, *Teriston* 1392, *Terston* 1577) which is the AN pers.n. *Ter(r)i, Terrey* with OE ***tūn***.

TINTERN, TYNDYRN
Monm SO5200

'fort of Dwrn', ***din***, pers.n. ***Dwrn***

Tinterna 1131, *din dirn, Dindyrn, tindirn* 1136-54, *Tyntern* 1267, *Tynterne* 1314

The final -dyrn is probably a gen. form of ***Dwrn***, a pers.n. derived from ***dwrn*** 'fist'. The popular explanation has long been ***teyrn*** 'king, prince'. The hill-fort was probably at 'upper Tintern' (*dintarn ychaf* c. 1566, ***uchaf***) as distinct from nearby 'lower Tintern' (*dintarn isaf* c.1566, ***isaf***) or Tintern Parva (*Tinterna Parva* 1307, *Parva Tynterne* 1322, *Little Tintern* 1787, L ***parva***). Provection caused initial Din- > Tin- (cf.Tenby).

TIRABAD
Brec SO8741

'abbot's land', ***tir***, ***abad***

Tyr yr abate 1619, *Mickeland or tir yr Rubat* 1623, *Newchurch Tyr Abbott* 1821

Land formerly in the possession of the monastery of Strata Florida Card. The 1623 form must be in error for *Munckeland*. *Newchurch* refers to the church built on a new site in 1716.

TIR-PHIL
Glam SO1303

'?overgrown land', ***tir***, ***?ffyll***

Tir Phil 1841, *Tir-phil Station* 1873, *Tyr Phil* 1875

Probably W ***tir*** but the second el. is uncertain and problematic. It has tentatively been suggested that it may be ***ffyll*** 'wild, overgrown', but that is a word of doubtful origin (appearing first in 1707), possibly found in Nantyffyllon Mont. Equally problematic is ***ffull***, ***ffill*** 'bud, blade'. The greatest difficulty with both suggestions is that there is no evidence of forms which might represent the W -ll; anglicization of W -ll- > E -l- would have to have occurred locally before the first record. There was a (highly unlikely) popular belief that the land formerly belonged to a certain *Phil* but identifying 'Phil' as an independent name or abbreviation has proved impossible; cf. *Tir Phillipp Gwillim* 1536. Equally unacceptable is any connection with Phillipstown immediately across the river Rhymni in Monm named after a local colliery manager Nehemiah Phillips (1845-1929). ***fill*** 'backfill, tip' is also possible.

TON-DU Glam SS8984

'black lay-land', ***ton***, ***du***

Tondu 1525, 1833, *Y Toune Dy* 1631, *Tonduy* 1719

The name was originally that of a house, now Ton-du House. ***ton*** regularly appears in the p.ns of Monm, south Brec and particularly Glam for unploughed grassland, lay-land, sward.

TONGWYNLAIS Glam ST1382

'lay-land by (the stream) Gwynlais', ***ton***, r.n. ***Gwynlais***

Tonn Gwenglais 1591, *Ton Gwinlas* 1733, *Tongwynlais* 1776-87

The r.n. Gwynlais (later *Forest Brook* 1885, now Nant y Fforest, named from the woodland Fforest Fawr) is 'white stream' (***gwyn***, ***glais***), and appears in *aper gungleis* 1136-54, a lost p.n. at the confluence (***aber***) of the stream and the river Taf. *Pont Gwenlas* 1729 (***pont***) and *Pantgwynlais* 1790 (***pant***) may refer to the same place or to distinct names referring to a bridge and a hollow respectively in or near the village. The river rises near Blaengwynlais (*Blaen-gwynlais* 1885, ***blaen*** 'headwaters, source').

TONNA Glam SS7799

'lay-lands', ***ton*** pl. ***tonnau***

Tonna 1700-1, 1841, *Tonna alias Ynis Neath* 1737

Tonna has the dial. var. pl. -a for -au. The 1737 alias refers to Ynys Nedd 'river-meadow (***ynys***) by the (river) Nedd/Neath'.

TON-TEG Glam ST0986

'fair lay-land', ***ton***, ***teg***

Ton-teg 1856, *Tonteg* 1861, *Ton-têg* 1874

A village which developed around a small farm above the Taf valley. There is an identical p.n. at Cadoxton-juxta-Neath (*Tonteg* 1688).

TONYPANDY Glam SS9992

'lay-land of the fulling mill', ***ton***, ***y***, ***pandy***

Tonypandy 1875, *Ton-y-pandy* 1885

The fulling-mill is *Pandy'r Ystrad 1740*, *Pandy yr Ystrad Tavodog* 1764 (with the parish name Ystradyfodwg) and *Pandy* 1799.

TONYREFAIL Glam ST0188

'lay-land of the smithy', ***ton***, ***yr***, ***gefail***

Tonyrevel 1732, *Ton y refail* 1811-14, *Ton-yr-efail* 1833

The smithy lay near the modern post office. The village developed rapidly with the arrival of the railway in 1860 and the opening of Collenna, Glyn and Cilely (or Cilelái, ***cil***, r.n. ***Elái***) collieries in the 1870s. Familiarly known as Y Ton.

TONYSGUBORIAU see **TALBOT GREEN**

TOWYN, TYWYN Denb SH9779
'sea-shore', ***tywyn*** var. ***towyn***
Towyn 1283, *Towyn Abergelley* 1633, *Towyn Abergeley* 1649,
y Towyn 1693, *Tywyn* c.1700, *Towyn* 1758, *Towyn Abergelau* 1795
The sandy shore is a characteristic of this area between Rhyl and Abergele. The addition of Abergele was to distinguish it from Tywyn (Towyn) in Meir. The spelling variation between Tywyn and Towyn continues to be contentious but usage tends to favour Towyn.

TRAETH COCH see **RED WHARF BAY**

TRAETH DULAS, DULAS BAY Angl SH4988
'shore (or estuary), and bay, of Dulas', W ***traeth***, E ***bay***, r.n. ***Dulas***
Traeth Dulas 1563-9, *The Crik of Dulas* 16cent., *Dulas Bay* 1777,
Dulas Bay and Harbour 1805
The extensive shore-line formed by the estuary of the river Dulas (q.v.).

TRAETH LAFAN see **LAVAN SANDS**

TRALLONG Brec SN9629
'very muddy area', ***trallwng***
Tralan 1210-12, *Trallan* 1281, *Trallwng* 1283,
(*a*) *thrallwng kynuyn* c.1180 (c.1300), *Trathelan* 1361, *Trathllong* 1502,
Trallonge 1513
Cf. Trallwng Mont. The full name appears to have been *Trallwng Cynfyn* with the pers.n. Cynfyn, possibly a saint, though the church is now dedicated to David/Dewi. The village lies very close to the point where the road from Aber-brân crosses the stream Nant Sefin. Later forms have ***llong*** (see Llong Flints) but ***llong*** 'bog, swamp' may have been the origin of this name.

TRALLWNG, Y see **WELSHPOOL**

TRANNON, Afon Mont SN9590
'?great wanderer' or 'river likely to flood' or '(river of goddess of the way called) Sentona', Br intensive pref. ****tri-***, Br ****santōn-***
Tarrannon 1572, *flu. Tarannon* 1578-9, *Tranon* 1595-6, *Trannon* 1603,
Tarannon flud 1610, *Taranon* 1632
The r.n. is much older than the recorded forms but is believed to be identical in origin to the r.n. Tarrant Devon (*Terrente* 1016 [12cent.], *Tarente* 1253, Trent (*Trisantonam* 2cent., *Treente* c.730) and an earlier name of the river Arun Sussex (*Trisantonis* 2cent., *Tarente* c.725). However, this r.n.'s earlier recorded forms seem also to have been influenced by ***taran*** 'thunder'.

TRAP Carm SN6519

'trap', E ***trap***

Tuy Watkin or Velin alias Tafarn Trap 1720, *Tavern y Trap* 1765, *Trap* 1831

Uncertain. The first reference is to a mansion house (***tŷ***) while the mill (***melin***) (later *Carreg Cennen Mill* 1891) is in the middle of the village near the bridge Pont y Trap. The trap may possibly refer either to the mill-dam or leat or perhaps to a fish-trap in the adjoining river Cennen. It has also been explained as a refuge for thieves, a belief no doubt encouraged by its location in Cwm Lladron 'robbers' valley' (***cwm, lleidr*** pl. ***lladron***). However the occurrence of Tafarn (y) Trap names elsewhere (*Tavern y Trap* 1774 Berriew Mont, *Tavarn Trap* 1763 Hay Brec, *Trap* 1875, *The Trap (P.H.)* 1891, *Tavern Trap* 1895 Kingsbridge, Gorseinon Glam and Mer) suggests 'a place which attracts and detains'.

TRAWSFYNYDD Mer SH7035

'across the mountain', ***traws, mynydd***

Trausuenith 1292-3, *trausvenyth* 1420-1, *Trawsfynydd* 1838

The village is central to several mountain routes, the more obvious today being those to Bala, Ffestiniog and Dolgellau. The extensive Roman settlement at Tomen-y-mur near the roadside a few miles to the north points to a long-established strategic route. At one time, it also appears to have been called *Trawsbryn* or *Trawsybryn* (*Trausbrin o. Trausvenithe* 1562, *Trawsvynith o. Trawsybryn* 1636, ***bryn*** 'hill'.

TRAWSGOED Card SN6773

'opposite (the) wood', ***traws, coed***

Trausgoed 1547, *Y Trowscoyd* 1624, *y trowscoed* 1640, *Trouskoed* 1652

The exact significance of ***traws*** is unclear in several p.ns. It may well mean 'across' or 'slanting' or even 'strong'. Both sides of Afon Ystwyth are still heavily wooded. The p.n. seems to have originated as the name of Trawsgoed Mansion (*The place at Trowsgoed* 1547) later translated as Crosswood (*Crosswood Park* 1798, *Crosswood, or, Traws Coed* 1811) and was subsequently used almost exclusively of the mansion and the adjacent estate developments.

TREAMLOD see **AMBLESTON**

TREARDDUR Angl SH2579

'settlement of Iarddur', ***tref***, pers.n. ***Iarddur***

Treffyarddr 1409, *Tre Iarthur* 1609, *Trefarthur* 1633, *Treyarddur* 1691, *Trearddur* 1749, *Tref Arthur* 1838

Iarddur was a notable medieval figure, and his settlement was one of the largest in north-west Angl. The advent of the railway and tourism ensured the rapid growth of the hamlet, and its seaside location was further publicized by its designation as Trearddur Bay and by attempts to link the name with the legendary Arthur. The actual bay was originally *Porth y Capel* 1838 (a chapel dedicated to the saint Ffraid), while the dunes were called *Towyn y Capel* 1781, *Twyn-capel* 1838.

TREBEFERED see **BOVERTON**

TREBERFEDD see **MIDDLETOWN**

TRECASTELL, TRECASTLE Brec SN8829
'settlement by the castle', ***tref***, ?***(y)***, ***castell***
Trecastle 1298, *Trecastel Toune* 1536-9, *Trerecastell* 1569, *Trecastell yn llywel* 1600
Refers to a small, probably Norman, motte-and-bailey castle. The absence of lenition (c > g) after ***tref*** may be explained by the def.art. ***y***, ***yr*** or perhaps by the dominant use of E ***castle*** rather than W ***castell***.

TRECASTLE see **TRECASTELL**

TRECELYN see **NEWBRIDGE**[2]

TRECŴN Pemb SM9632
'dogs' farm', ***tref***, ***ci*** pl. ***cŵn***
Trefcone 1524, *Trekone* 1542, *Trecoone* 1575
Presumably places where dogs or hounds were kept, perhaps for breeding. Identical names are Tre-cŵn (*Trecwn* 1739) Llantwyd Pemb and Tre-cŵn (*Trecwn* 1596, *Trecoon* 1739) St Dogmael's Pemb.

TRECYNON Glam SO9903
'town by (the river) Cynon', ***tref***, r.n. ***Cynon***
Trefcynon 1850-60
The name was chosen in an eisteddfod competition in the 1850s for the growing industrial settlement near the river Cynon probably on the analogy of Abercynon (which explains the irregular lack of mutation (c > g); contrast Tregynon Mont. An earlier name was Heolyfelin (*Heol y felin* 1751, *Heol-y-felin* 1833) 'the mill road' (***heol***, ***y***, ***melin***) referring to Llwydcoed mill.

TREDEGAR Monm SO1409
'village near Tredegar (works)', ***pentref***, p.n. ***Tredegar***
gwaith haiarn Tredegar 1806, *Tredegar Iron Works* 1832, *Tredegar* 1839
A village which developed near the *Tredegar Iron Works* established in 1800 on land 15 miles to the south near Newport Monm belonging to the Morgan family of Tredegar (*Tredegyr* 14cent., *Dre-Degyr* c.1460, *Tredeger* 1536-9, *tredegyr* c.1550, *Tredegare* 1569) with the pers.n. Tegyr (cf. Botegyr Denb with ***bod***). See also New Tredegar.

TREDEGAR NEWYDD see **NEW TREDEGAR**

TREDELERCH see **RUMNEY**

TREDEML see **TEMPLETON**

TREDREYR see **TROED-YR-AUR**

TREDUNNOCK, TREDYNOG Monm ST3894
'ferny farm', ***tref***, ***rhedynog***
Tref redinauc i.e. uilla filicis 12cent., *Tredenauc* 1254, *Tredenauch* 1327, *tre Rydynog* c.1566
The unstressed initial and second syllables (tre-re-) were assimilated. The 12cent. gloss is L ***filix***, gen. ***filicis*** 'fern'.

TREDYNOG see **TREDUNNOCK**

TREFALDWYN see **MONTGOMERY**

TREFALUN, ALLINGTON Denb SJ3856
'farm on (the river) Alun', ***tref***, r.n. ***Alun***, OE ***tūn***
Alentune 1086, *Alynton* 1315, *Alunton* 1374, *Allington* 1391, *Trefalyn* 1383, *Trevallin* 1561, *Trevalyn* c.1700, *Trevallen otherwise Allington* 1653
The ***tūn***, located on the bank of the river Alun (q.v.), was part of the anglicized area between the river Dee and Wrexham. In time, its form (as *Alunton*) fell in with E p.n. suff. in ***-ington*** as if 'estate associated with Alun'. Although the W form appears somewhat later, the fact that W ***tref*** is used for OE ***tūn*** suggests that both forms were used side by side considerably before 1383 but that early documents recorded the E form rather than the W form. Both are current today, although the tendency is to use Trefalun.

TREFASSER Pemb SM8937
'Asser's settlement', ***tref***, pers.n. ***Asser***
Treffasser 1326 (16cent.), *Asheston alias Trevasser* 1632, *Trevasser* c.1640
Traditionally associated with Asser (d.909) bishop of St David's. The 1632 form is otherwise unattested and is probably a literary, antiquarian translation without any currency.

TREFDDYN see **TREVETHIN**

TREFDRAETH Angl SH4070
'shore farm', ***tref***, ***traeth***
Trefdraeth 1199 (1332), *Tredieyt* 1254, *Trefdraes* 1294, *trefdraeth* 13cent. (14cent.), *Treffdrayth* 1519-20, *Trefdraeth* 1536-9
Prior to the building of the Cob at Malltraeth (q.v.), Afon Cefni was tidal east of Trefdraeth (evidenced in several other settlement and farm names with ***traeth***).

TREFDRAETH see **NEWPORT**[2]

TREFECA Brec SO1432

'Becca's settlement', ***tref***, pers.n. ***Becca***

Traneck [=Traveck] 1309, *Trevek* 1398, *Treveckke* 1409, *Trevecta* 1574, *Trevecka* 1595, *Tre Vecca* c.1590-1610

As a biblical name Rebecca and Be(c)ca regularly appear as W and E pers.ns but in this case Becca may be an OE pers.n. (cf. Beckbury Shropshire, Beckham Norfolk). Tradition explains the p.n. as named from a *Rebecca Prosser*. Cf. Trefeca Pemb. Also commonly written Trefecca.

TREFEGLWYS Mont SN9790

'settlement with a church', ***tref***, ***eglwys***

Trefeglus 1143-51, *Treveglus* 1143-5, *Treuegleys* 1293, *Treff Eglwys* c.1291, *LL.drefeglwys* c.1562, *Trevegluys* 1597

Trefeglwys may the 'settlement containing the church' in contrast to the nearby Tregymer (*Trefgemer* c.1157, *Trefkemer* c.1200, *Maes tregymer* 1577) 'settlement at the confluence' (***cymer***) of the rivers Gleinant and Trannon.

TREFELEN see **BLETHERSTON**

TREFESGOB see **BISHTON**

TREFFLEMIN see **FLEMINGSTON**

TREFFOREST Glam ST0888

'forest settlement', ***tref***, ***fforest***

Trefforest 1833, *Tre forest* 1842, *Treforest* 1845

A settlement which developed near tinplate works from 1792. The former *Lower Forest Ironworks* here took its name from a farm Fforest Isaf (*Forrest Issa* 1729, ***isaf*** 'lower'). Several p.ns with ***fforest*** occur on both sides of the river Taf below Pontypridd.

TREFFYNNON see **HOLYWELL**

TREFFYNNON Pemb SM8428

'settlement by a well', ***tref***, ***ffynnon***

Treffonnon 1584, *Treffunnon* 1678, *Treffynnon* 1813

Springs are recorded on the east side of the village and the west side next to Afon Solfach in 1891.

TREFGARN Pemb SM9523

'farm by a rock', ***tref***, ***carn***

Traveger 1259-60 (14cent.), *Trefgarn* 1368, *Trawger*, *Trauger* 1404, *Trefgare* 1513, *Treffgarne Owen* 1539

Evidence for the derivation is clearer in the nearby Little (or Eastern)

Trefgarn (*Trefgarn* 1410, *Trefecarn* 1174-6, *Trefgarn* 1579), located near Little Trefgarn Mountain. A var. Trowgarn seems to have established itself for (Great) Trefgarn, arising from interchange of -f- and -w- (although no example is known with ***tref***), and is still the local pronunciation. In the form *Trawger, Trauger*, loss of -n- may have been influenced by ***caer***. Little Trefgarn shows none of these vars. *Owen* may refer to Llywelyn ap Owen (d. 1309) whose wife Ellen inherited the manor. A common local alternative, under E influence, is Treffgarn(e) with W -f- pronounced and written as E -ff-.

TREFIL Monm (formerly Brec) SO1212

'farm of the ?lesser celandine', ***tref***, ?***mil***

Trevill 1600-7, *y Truvill* 1704-7, *Trevill* 1766-9, *Treville* 1795, *Trevil Du, Trevil Glas* 1828, *Trefil* 1832

There is no evidence of a settlement of note before industrialization in the 19cent. The name was also applied originally to the stream Nant Trefil (1832, ***nant***) and to two hills, later distinguished as Trefil Du (*Trefil-ddu* 1891, ***du*** 'black, dark') and Trefil Glas (*Trefil-lâs* 1891, ***glas*** 'verdant') west and east of the village. The second el. could be ***bil*** 'bill, beak' referring to the shape of the hills. Some later forms seem to show the influence of F ***ville*** (1795), ***tir*** and ***moel*** (*Tirfoel Lime Works* 1814).

TREFILAN Card SN5457

'Ilan's farm', ***tref***, pers.n. ***Ilan***

Trefilan 1234 (late 13cent.), *Trevileyn* 1278-9, *Trevilan* 1282, *Drefylayn* 1298-1300, *Trevillan* 1309, *Trefylan* 1486, *Tref Vilan* 1535, *Trefilan* 1834

The identity of Ilan is unknown, but is almost certainly the same name if not the same person as in Eglwysilan (Glam). Two of the forms seem to suggest an attempt to interpret as ***bilain*** 'villein'.

TRE-FIN Pemb SM8432

?'fortified settlement', ***tref***, ***dynn***

Trefedin 1248-9, *Tredyn* 1293, *Trefdyn* 1274, *Trefdun* 1326 (16cent.), *Trevyn* 1545, *Trevyne* 1554

The forms seem to favour ***dynn*** rather than ***din*** 'fort', and, despite the location on an outcrop, there are no visible remains of a fort. It may be identical to Treuddyn (q.v.) and perhaps Trevethin (q.v.) where ***dynn*** seems to indicate protection by a hedge, fence or even a more substantial wall. However, here -fd- became -fdd- (although not attested in the historical forms) and then assimilated to -f-. In addition, Tre-fin is stressed on the final syllable, probably by analogy with some (but not all) ***tref*** names with a monosyllabic final el. (such as Tre-gib, Trecŵn) especially if, as seems likely here, that el. was perceived to be ***min*** 'edge' (of the sea). A common alternative form is Trevine.

TREFNANT Denb SJ0570
'hamlet on the brook', ***tref***, ***(y)***, ***nant***
Trevenant 1661-2, *Trefnant* 1839
The hamlet developed near Nant Padrig at the junction of roads from Tremeirchion, Henllan, St Asaph and Denbigh. The earlier form represents an original 'Tref-y-nant'.

TREFONNEN see **NASH**

TREFOR Caern SH3746
'(place named after) Trevor', pers.n. ***Trevor***
Trevor 19cent., *Trefor* 20cent.
The village formerly called Yr Hendre (*yr hendre vawr* 1552, *hendre fawr* 1757, *Hendre fawr* 1838) has long been associated with the quarry. In 1839 there were only a few quarrymen's cottages, but by 1880 the *Welsh Granite Company* had established a school there. The modern name is said to have derived from Trevor Jones, manager of the quarry in the 1850s. The spelling as Trefor reflects a standardizing of -v- as -f-, and a perception that the village is the same as other examples of Trefor (such as Trefor Denb, *Trefawr* 1314, *Trevor* 1394) which are ***tref fawr*** 'big hamlet'; cf. the older *hendre vawr* forms.

TREFORGAN see **MORGANSTOWN**

TREFORYS see **MORRISTON**

TREFRIW Caern SH7863
'settlement near the hill', ***tref***, ***rhiw***
Treffruu 1254, *Treurow* 1284, *Treveri* 1291-2, *Tryverew* 1330, *Trefrw* 1352, *trefriw* c.1566, *Trefrew* 1573, *Tre r Rhiw alias Trefrew* 1706, *Trefriw* 1838
The original settlement was near a steep hill now within the village slope where Afon Crafnant meets the floor of the Conwy valley (*Tryverew in Nantkonow* 1330).

TREFWRDAN see **JORDANSTON**

TREFYCLO see **KNIGHTON**

TREFYNWY see **MONMOUTH**

TREGAEAN Angl SH4579
'Caean's farm', ***tref***, pers.n. ***Caean***
Trecgaein 1254, *Trefgaian* 1471-2, *Trefgayan* 1522, *Tregayan* 1583, *Tregaian* 1838

The identity of Caean is unknown. Some of the historical spellings still persist as Tregaian and Plas Tregayan.

TREGARE, TRE'R-GAER Monm SO4110

'settlement near the fort', ***tref, yr, caer***

Tregear 1285, *Tregayr* 1324, *Tregair* 1354, *trer gaer* c.1566

No fort has been identified, despite the late emergence of the def.art. ***yr*** suggesting an identifiable site. The village lies within a roughly oval boundary but the church's position on a fairly low hill may have been the location of a fort. There is a farm or house Henllys 'old court' (***hen, llys***) west of the village.

TREGARON Card SN6759

'settlement in Caron', ***tref***, parish n. ***Caron***

(i) Dre Garon c1485, *tre garon* c.1566, *Caron alias Tre Garon* 1763

Earlier known as Caron (*Karaun* 1281), said to be an older name of Afon Brennig (but lacks conclusive evidence). Caron is usually explained as a pers.n. (as in the church dedication to a saint Caron, for whom evidence is late). However, Caron is best interpreted as a terr. n. from a pers.n. Câr and a terr.suff. -***(i)on***.

TREGARTH Caern SH6067

'hamlet near the ridge', ***tref, yr, garth***

Tre r Garth 1670, *Tre'r Garth* 1789, *Tregarth* 1838

The ridge is an extension of Moelyci above Afon Ogwen. Standardized orthography requires Tre-garth (to conform with final stress) but prevailing usage favours Tregarth.

TREGATWG see **CADOXTON**

TREGEIRIOG Denb SJ1733

'farm on (the river) Ceiriog', ***tref***, r.n. ***Ceiriog***

Tregeriog, Trefkyrac 1277-8, *Tregerioke* 1495, *Tregeiriog* 1571

The village is located where a narrow valley opens out into Dyffryn Ceiriog, some two miles east and down-river of Llanarmon Dyffryn Ceiriog and on the banks of Afon Ceiriog.

TREGELE Angl SH3592

'leech hamlet', ***tref, gele***

Tre-gela 1838

The form -gela is the dial. var. of ***gele***. A quarter-of-a-mile to the west is the croft Tyddyn-gele (*Tyddyn Gela* 1760, *Tyddyn-gela* 1838) near several brooks which may have been the location of leech gathering.

TREGETIN see **KEESTON**

TREGLEMAIS Pemb SM8128

'Clement's farm', ***tref***, pers.n. ***Clemens***

Trefclemens 1326 (16cent.), *Clementiston* 1332, *Trefglemmes* 1483, *Treglemes* 1542, *Tref Glemmeis* 1559, *ville Clementis* 1535

The W form probably represents an established W pers.n. Clemens derived from the var. L Clemens (or F var.) which was assimilated to *Clemes* and then followed names such as Cemais Pemb (q.v.). *Clemens/ Clemais* are independantly recorded as names in late medieval pedigrees. The 1332 form is an anglicized var. (with the E pers.n. Clement and OE ***tūn***) while the 1535 form is latinized, both possibly only documentary; contrast Clementston/Treglement Glam (*Clemenston* 1568, *Clementson* 1631, (*o*) *dre Glement* late 16cent.).

TREGOLWYN see **COLWINSTON**

TRE-GROES Card SN4044

'farm at the crossroads', ***tref***, ***croes***

trer groes 1564, *Tre Grose* 1760, *Tre-groes* 1831

The village is on a crossroads near Afon Cerdin (which was occasionally included in the designation *Tre'r Groes ar gerdin* 16cent., *tre'r groes ar gerdin* 1651). However, it is widely believed that in the 14cent. there was once a chapel-of-ease here on the pilgrim route from Strata Florida to St David's.

TRE-GROES see **WHITCHURCH**

TRE-GŴYR see **GOWERTON**

TREGYNON Mont SO0998

'Cynon's settlement', ***tref***, pers.n. ***Cynon***

Trefkenon 1254, *Trefgenan* 1331-2, *Trefgenon* 1393-4, *Tregonon* 1507, *Tregynnon* 1547, *ll. dref gynon* c.1566, *Tregonen*, *Tregynon* 1583

The church dedication has been ascribed to Cynon (cf. Capel Cynon twice in Card and Croescynon Radn) but it may possibly be a dedication to a saint transferred from a p.n. The pers.n. is also found in Tregynon Pemb (*Trefgenon* 1315).

TREHARRIS Glam ST0997

'Harris's town', ***tref***, pers.n. ***Harris***

The village was initially called *the Huts* which developed after the sinking of the *Harris Navigation Colliery* 1872-3 (later the *Deep Navigation Pit*) by the *Harris Navigation Steam Coal Co.* The Quaker Frederick William Harris (1833-1917) was the main shareholder in the *Deep Navigation*.

TREHERBERT Glam SS9498

'Herbert's town', ***tref***, pers.n. ***Herbert***

Tref Herbert 1851, *Herbert Town* 1854, *Treherbert* 1855

A name bestowed by trustees of the second marquess of Bute (d.1848) and said to have been coined (using one of the favourite Bute family names) after the opening of the first *Bute Merthyr* shaft in Cwmsaerbren begun in 1851.

TREHOPCYN see **HOPKINSTOWN**

TRELAWNYD Flints SJ0879

'slope of Lēofnoth', ***rhiw***, OE pers.n. ***Lēofnoth***

Rivelenoit 1086, *Rywllyfnuyt* 1292-3, *Relevenot* 1312-13, *Riwlyfnoyt* 1339, *Trelawnyd* 1649, *Newmarket* 1711, *Rhylofnydd alias Newmarket* 1719, *Treflawnyd alias Newmarket* 1782

The slope is probably the adjacent Clip y Gop. Lēofnoth is a name which occurs (as *Leuenot*) 14 times in the Cheshire and Flints sections of the Domesday Book. The subsequent development of the p.n. reveals considerable (and frequently conflicting) variation. Some (possibly documentary) forms are distinctly archaic; others show the cymricization of Lēofnoth to Llyfnwyd and the retention of ***rhiw*** (replaced by *Re-* in most forms). The influence of several unrelated els is discernible: ***rhyd*** 'ford', ***llyfn*** 'smooth', ***llyfnwyd*** 'smoothed', ***llawn*** 'full', ***ŷd*** 'corn'. The emergence of *Tref-* in the 17cent. was possibly a conscious change to reflect the emergence of a growing settlement. In 1700 John Wynne of Gop received permission to hold a weekly market and an annual fair and the right to rename the parish *Newmarket*. In 1954 Trelawnyd was accepted as the only official p.n.

TRE-LECH Carm SN3026

?'farm at the slab and the prayer-house', ***tref, llech, a, yr, betws***

Trenleth c.1291, *Treffelegh* 1361, *tre lech* c.1566

From its location on a slope above the stream Dewi Fawr. Occasionally Tre-lech a'r Betws from a former Betws refers to a former chapel-of-ease Capel Betws (*y bettws* c.1566, *Capell Bettus* 1586) (***capel***). Tre-lech is a 19cent. development near a farm here described as *Ty-newydd tre-lech* 1831, 'new house in Tre-lech' (***tŷ, newydd***).

TRELETERT see **LETTERSTON**

TRELEWIS Glam ST1097

'Lewis's town', ***tref***, pers.n. ***Lewis***

Trelewis 1898

William Lewis (1828-1903) of Tir Shag and Y Bontnewydd was a churchwarden of Gelligaer, and is commemorated on a tablet in the church as *founder of Trelewis*. The village developed between *Pontnewydd Colliery* and two bridges Y Bont Newydd (over Nant Bargod Taf) and *Pont-y-Squire* 1833 (over Nant Caeach).

TRELLECK, TRYLEG Monm SO5005

'conspicuous stone', ***try, *lleg***

trylec bechan, Ecclesia Trylec, ecclesiam Trilecc 1136-54, *Trillek* 1254, *Trellek* 1291, *Tryllek* 1316, *Trelec* 1539, *Trelech* 1548, *try leg* c.1566

The -ll- in Trellech represents the E -l- and not the W -ll-, as Tryleg and all the historical forms show. The second el. is probably ****lleg***, an unrecorded var. of ***llech***, and which may be an adaptation of an OIr ***lec*** (as in Trillick Tyrone and Duntreyleague Limerick). The first el. is uncertain, and reveals early variation. It is probably ***try-***, a reinforcing pref. (as in Tryfan Caern 'conspicuous or extraordinary peak' q.v.), a reference to a large stone which once stood on a mound a mile-and-a-half north of the village (possibly near Rock Cottage). The most prominent, surviving topographic features, however, are three prehistoric monoliths arranged in a line on the south-west side of the village called *Harold's Stones* (apparently a 17cent. name., associated by antiquarians with a fictional battle of King Harold before 1066). These three stones probably account for the ***tri*** 'three' of the historical forms (occasionally appearing as ***try-*** in compounds); since ***llech*** is fem. one would expect ***tair*** (fem. of ***tri***) as the qualifier (unless there has been a change of gender). Another influence on the first el. is ***tref***. The first form has been identified with the south part of the village and is ***bechan*** 'little'.

TRELOGAN Flints SJ1380

'farm at (the river) Halogan', ***tref***, r.n. ***Halogan***

Trefvologon 1292-3, *Trevelogan* 1303-4, *Treflogan* 1330, *Trefalogan* 1345, *Trelogan* 1597-8, *Tre Logan* 1632

The village is adjacent to the modern Afon Goch (*Afongoch* 1840, 'red river', ***coch***) supposedly named after a chalybeate iron spring nearby. The earlier name of the river seems to have been an unrecorded *Halogan* from ***halog*** 'dirty, contaminated' and the dim.suff. ***-an***, also an indication perhaps of chalybeate staining. The later phonological development was probably influenced by the desire to eliminate unclean associations, possibly by a fancied link with the Ir and Scots pers.n. Logan, or a logan-stone.

TREMADOG Caern SH5640

'town of Madocks', ***tref***, pers.n. ***Madocks***

Tre-madoc, Tremadock 1810, *Tremadoc* 1838, *Tremadog* 20cent.

The village was developed by William Alexander Madocks who in 1798 had bought the estate of Tanyrallt near Penmorfa and several surrounding farms and was responsible for enclosing Traeth Mawr with the Cob (embankment) and building the harbour of Porthmadog (q.v.). It was built on the northern edge of the enclosed land; the market was first held there in 1805 (having been transferred from Penmorfa). Tremadoc became Tremadog, deliberately recalling the pers.n. Madoc or Madog and more specifically exploits the legend of Madog (allegedly a son of Owain Gwynedd) and said to have discovered America in 1169 or 1170, returning in 1172 to land at Ynys Fadog near the present Tremadog.

TRE-MAIN Card SN2348

'stones farm', ***tref***, ***maen*** pl. ***main***

Tresmaun 1159-81, *Tremeyn* 1241, *Tref Mayne* 1535, *Tremayne* 1559, *trer main* c.1566, *Trermain* 1602, *Tremain* 1719, (*a*) *Threfmaen a elwir yn gyffredin Tremain* 1778, *Tre-maen* 1834

The farm was near stones associated with several prehistoric graves, a standing stone and a large stone Llech yr Ast (the remains of a megalithic tomb). Two of the forms reveal the inclusion of the def.art. ***yr*** (as *-r-*) while others show the influence of the singular ***maen*** and of ***main*** 'narrow, thin'.

TREMARCHOG see **ST NICHOLAS**

TREMEIRCHION Flints SJ0873

'fort of Meirchion', ***din***, pers.n. ***Meirchion***

Dinmersch 1086, *Dymneyrchyvan*, *Dymneychyavn* 1291, *Dimeirchion* 1336, *Dynmerghion* 1344-57, *Demerghion* 1484, *Dynerghion* 1451, *Tremerchion* 1597, *Dymerchion* 1611, *Dimeirchion o. Tremeirchion* 1788, *Dymeirchion* or *Tremeirchion* 1851

The identity of this particular Meirchion is unknown (although the name is still preserved in a stream name in Dyffryn Clwyd). The location of the fort is also uncertain (although there are several prominent hill-sites nearby, Moel-y-gaer hill-fort being the most likely). The intrusion of ***tref*** to oust ***din*** was probably a phonological (rather than a conscious) substitution in an unstressed syllable but nevertheless resisted the usual lenition to 'Trefeirchion', especially as parallel forms (as in 1788 and 1851) were in regular use for some considerable time.

TREOES, TRE-OS Glam SS9478

'goose farm', ***tref***, OE ***gōs***

Goston 1536, *Tress* 1596-1600, *Treos* 1631, *Treoys* 1658, *Tre-Oes* 1748-9, *Treose* 1799, *Treos or Goston* 1833, *Treoes* 2000

The original name was *Goston* (OE ***gōs***, OE ***tūn***), referring to a farm near the marshy area within the Ewenni valley frequented by wild geese. W influence has replaced OE ***tūn*** with W ***tref*** but not ***gōs*** (with W ***gŵydd*** 'goose') because Gos- was neither pronounced as nor understood to be 'goose'. The vowel of Gos-, however, was long which explains its adoption into W as Tre-os with its stressed final long syllable and genitival lenition. Some of the historical forms, as well as most roadsigns and maps, have Treoes reflecting the perception that -ôs was a dial. pronunciation of standard W ***oes*** 'lifetime, age'.

TREORCHY see **TREORCI**

TREORCI, TREORCHY Glam SS9596

'village on (the stream) Gorci', ***tref***, r.n. ***Gorci***

Treorki 1869, *Treorci* 1875, *Treorchy* 1870

A name given to the coal-mining village which developed in the 1860s. The r.n. also appears in Abergorci (*Abergorchwy* 1838, *Abergorki* 1875) and Fforchorci (*fforch Gorky* 1727, *Fforch-orchwy* 1833, *Forchorkay* 1845). The meaning of Gorci is obscure but a similar r.n. possibly occurs in the (lost) name of a messuage *Tall Ardd otherwise Abergorgi* 1782 at Betws Carm. The commonly found form Treorchy may have been influenced by association with the r.n. Orchy, Argyll Scotland but is more likely to be a by-product of the contrived, literary *Abergorchwy* and *Fforch-orchwy*.

TRE'R CEIRI Caer SH3744

'settlements of the giants', ***tref***, ***yr***, ***cawr*** pl. ***cewri*** var. ***ceiri***

Tre'r Caeri, Tre'r Cawri 1810, *Tre yr Caeri* 1816, *Tre'r-Ceiri* 1838

A hill-fort settlement on the eastern peak of Yr Eifl (q.v.). There is literary and modern colloquial evidence for ***ceuri*** and ***ceiri*** as dial. vars of ***cewri*** 'giants' although popular belief interprets Ceiri as an unrecorded var. of ***caerau*** 'forts' (as evidenced in *Tre'r Caeri* 1810). ***cawr*** can mean 'hero, mighty one' which may be appropriate, but it is more likely to be a folk perception of legendary giants who were reputed to inhabit such a site.

TRE'R-DDÔL Card SN6692

'the meadow farm', ***tref***, ***yr***, ***dôl***

Treddole 1572-3, *Tre yr Ddol, Trerddol* 1615, *Tre'rddol* 1780, *Tre'r-ddol* 1837

The meadow is on the bank of Afon Cletwr.

TRE'R-GAER see **TREGARE**

TRE'R-LLAI see **LEIGHTON**

TRE-SAITH Card SN2751

'beach of (the river) Saith', ***traeth***, r.n. ***Saith***

Traeth Saith 1740, *Traeth Saith* 1803, *Traeth Saith* 1811, *Traeth Saeth* 1834, *Tresaith* 1891, *Traethsaith* 1908, *Tresaith* 1958

Afon Saith flows into the sea at the sandy cove here (*Aber Sayth* 1604,

Abersaith 1651). The r.n. appears in several p.ns along its route from its source at Blaen-saith, such as Nant Saith, Penlan-saith and Dyffryn-saith. The r.n. Saith is obscure. It could be the rare ***saith*** 'saint' but is more likely to be an irregular dial. var. of ***saeth*** 'arrow' which, while not straight, could be deemed swift, since it rises at Blaen-saith Fach and reaches the sea after a rapid descent of only two miles. There is also the possibility of an irregular pl. of ***saeth*** but there is no clear reason for a pl. The village itself developed markedly in the late 1890s and 20cent. which seems to have prompted the allegedly deliberate shift from ***traeth*** to ***tref***, although the ***traeth*** was still the prime tourist attraction.

TRESIGIN see **SIGINGSTON(E)**

TRESIMWN see **BONVILSTON**

TRE TALIESIN Card SN6591

'Taliesin's hamlet', ***tref***, pers.n. ***Taliesin***

Treftaliesin 1821, *Tretaliesin* 1827, *Tre' Taliesin* 1837,
Tre Taliesin formerly Common y Dafarn fach 1824

An older name was *Comins-y-Dafarn-bach* c.1700, *Comon of Tafarn fach* 1746, *Commins y Dafarn fach* 1820 ('commons of the little tavern', ***comins, y, tafarn, bach***). The tavern was *Tavarn bach* 1805, *Tafarn fach* 1813, *Tafarn bach* 1824, while the nearby wood was *Coed Tafarn-fâch* 1891. The change of name, probably prompted by Nonconformist sensibilities, linked the village with the Bronze Age cairn (three-quarters-of-a-mile south-east of the village) called Bedd Taliesin (*Gwely Taliesin, or, Taliesin's Bed* 1811, *gwely Taliesin, the bed or grave of Taliesin* 1815). Legend associated the cairn with the 6cent. poet Taliesin. In local usage, the hamlet is generally referred to as Taliesin.

TRETOWER, TRETŴR Brec SO1821

'settlement by the tower', ***tref, (yr), tŵr***

Trevetour 1463, *Tretour* 1479, *tre r twr* late 15cent., *Treretower* 1557,
Tref y Twr 16cent., *Trertowre* 1600-7, *Tretowre* 1578

W ***tŵr***, ME ***tour***, and Modern E are all evidenced in the forms. The tower was the castle, probably established in the late 11cent. by Picard, an Anglo-Norman lord, and its prominence is reaffirmed by the def.art. ***y(r)***.

TRETŴR see **TRETOWER**

TREUDDYN Flints SJ2558

'homestead', ***tref, dynn***

Trefthyn 1275, *Treffdyn* 1372, *trefddyn* 1478-9, *Trythyn* 1539,
Treuthyn 1553, *Tredhyn, Treydhyn, Treudhyn* c.1700, *Treiddyn* 1838

The el. ***dynn*** has several loosely associated meanings such as 'height', 'defence', 'fortification' but in the context of ***tref*** its probable significance is a farm or homestead surrounded by a protective hedge or fence. There is independent evidence of -ef > -eu (as in ***defnydd*** var. ***deunydd***) which appears in at least two other ***tref*** + ***dynn*** names (Treuddyn Caeo Mont and Taltreuddyn Llanenddwyn Mer). The 1539 form reflects the still commonly heard anglicized pronunciation (as if E ***try***) and seen in the spelling and pronunciation of nearby Pontblyddyn (q.v.).

TREVETHIN, TREFDDYN Monm SO2802

'the homestead', ***tref, y, dynn***

Throvethin 1254, *Trevedyn* 1285, *Trevethyn* 1535, *tref ddyn kattwc* c.1566, *Treffdun or Trevethin* 1798, *Trefddyn or Trevethin* 1833

Probably of similar origin as Treuddyn (q.v.) but without the development of -ef > -eu. It is also evident from the early forms that the name included a def.art. suggesting that the protective hedge or fence was of some significance. Most forms, including the modern map form Trevethin and current E pronunciation, retain the three syllables with unusual penultimate stress on the def.art. (cf. Penegoes q.v.). *Trefethin* 1834 in a local W language history of Llanfoist may suggest it was also used by W speakers.

TREWERN Mont SJ2811

'settlement near an alder-grove', ***tref, gwern***

Alretone 1086, *T(re)fwern* 1234, *Alreton* 1245, *Orleton* 1255, *Olorton, Oleretun* 1271, *Trewern* 1287, *Trewern* 1310, *Trefwern* 1354, *Treffwern* 1421-2, *Trewern alias Olarton* c.1558-70

The E name which did not survive is 'settlement near alder-trees' (OE ***alor*** gen. pl. ***alora***, OE ***tūn***) and was long misidentified with Cause castle Shropshire. It is very difficult to say which p.n. is the older since sources are largely E; many places in this area have both W and E names (such as Middletown/Treberfedd). Local pronunciation stresses the initial syllable and is frequently heard as Trowern, Trowen.

TREWYDDEL see **MOYLGROVE**

TRIMSARAN Carm SN4504

'ridge of Sa(e)ran', ***trum***, pers.n. ***Sa(e)ran***

Trymsarren 1564, *Trymsaran* 1570, *trym saran* 1540-77, *Trinsaren* 1586, *Trim-saran* 1833

The modern village name is taken from *Trimsaran Colliery* located near a farm *Trim-saran-fach* (1833) on the east side of the village. The notion that the p.n. contains ***seren*** 'star' probably gave rise to the *Star Inn* (1792) and the *Star T[oll] B[ar]* 1844. Sa(e)ran has not been identified but the pers.n. Saeran is attested in the 12cent.

TRODDI, Afon, TROTHY, River Monm SO4115-4810,

?'river which pushes or penetrates', ***trawdd***, r.n.suff. ***-i***

Trodi c.750 (mid 12cent.), 1292, *Troe* 1465, *Trothy* 1582, *Trodhi* c.1700

The river rises near Craig Syfyrddin and flows through Llyn Troddi to Llanfihangel Troddi (q.v.) to enter Monnow near Monmouth.

TROED-YR-AUR Card SN3245

'Treyr's farm', ***tref***, pers.n. ***Treyr***

Trefdreyr 1158-65 (1308), *Trefdreir* 1288, *Trefdreher* 1291, *Trefdreier* 1408, *Troedyrour* 1547-51, *Tredroyr* 1554, *Troedroyr* 1660, *Troed-yr-aur* 1754

The identity of Treyr is obscure as is the form of the name. The pers.n. was disyllabic which explains some historical forms. The later diphthong -ey- became dial. -ou-, -oy-, which, coupled with the loss of -f-, prompted the popular interpretation as Troed-yr-aur 'foot of gold' (***troed***, ***yr***, ***aur***) and the belief (expressed in 1811) that gold had been found here. Troed-yr-aur is now the name of the hamlet and the parish, but Trefdreyr and Tredreyr are occasionally used in a literary or antiquarian context. The church was very rarely Llanfihangel Tredreyr (*Llanihangel tredyrer* c.1562). Local pronunciation is frequently Troedrour.

TROED-Y-RHIW Glam SO0702

'foot of the slope', ***troed***, ***y***, ***rhiw***

Troedyrhiw 1714, *Troed y rhiw* 1783, *Troedyrhiwgwmrwg* 1813, *Troed-y-rhiw-gwmrwg* 1833

Taken from a former farm Troed-y-rhiw Gwmrwg south of the village in the valley of the river Taf. The meaning of Cwmrwg is obscure; ***cwmwr*** 'foot-bridge' with suff. ***-wg*** makes little sense.

TROFARTH Denb SH8571

?'slope in the hub', ***tor***, ***y***, ***both***

Thorrewothe, *Theirwoch* 1246, *Toronoth* 1311, *Taronoth* 1334, *Trovarth* 1506, *Trofarth* 1630

A difficult p.n. of uncertain etymology. The word ***both*** was used of a hub or ball of a wheel, which here may refer to the location of Trofarth surrounded by hills and between two streams. The slope, ***tor***, is Trofarth's position above a fairly narrow valley leading down to Afon Dulas. The linguistic development (from 'Tor-y-foth') assumes the loss of the ***y*** in the second syllable (to 'Tor-foth'), shift of stress to the first syllable with subsequent change from Tor- to Tro- (to 'Trofoth') (under the influence of ***tro*** 'bend'), and the modification of the last syllable (to 'Trofarth') (under the influence of ***garth*** 'ridge; wooded slope'). Some of the earlier forms show -w- and -n-, both of which could be explained as miscopying -v-.

TRWYN EILIAN see **POINT LYNAS**

TRWYN Y FUWCH see **LITTLE ORME**

TRWYN Y GADAIR see **CARMEL HEAD**

TRYFAN Caern SH6659

'sharp peak', ***try-*, *ban***

Tryvan 1646-7, *Trevaen* 1781, *Tryfan* 1770

The name appears elsewhere in north Wales. The el. ***try-*** is an intensive pref. and the name of this distinctive mountain could be rendered 'conspicuous crest'. Tradition has identified the long-stones on its ridge (popularly Adam and Eve) as two of previously three (***tri*, *try***) such stones (***maen***); however, the ridge does also have three outcrops.

TRYLEG see **TRELLECK**

TRYWERYN, Afon, Llyn Mer SH7838, SH8440

'?considerable soaking (river)', ***afon*, *llyn*, *tra***, ?***gweryn***

Tarwerin 1232-3, *Taraweryn* 1477, *Troweryn* 1578, *Treweryn* 1657-8, *Tryweryn* c.1700

The river leaves Llyn Tryweryn (*Llyn Troweryn* 1645, *Lhyn Trywerin* c.1700, *Llyn Treweryn* 1795, *Llyn Tryweryn* 1796), probably named from the river, and flows through Llyn Celyn (q.v.) and into the river Dee at Bala (q.v.). The first el. seems to be ***tra*** 'extremely, exceedingly' rather than the intensive pref. ***try-*** which emerges in the later forms. In literature, the noun ***gweryn*** 'liquid' is very rare, as is the derivative verb ***gwerynnu*** 'wet, soak, moisten'. The name may refer to a section of the river which was very prone to flooding, perhaps the area near Bala marked on some maps as *Liable to Floods* 1891.

TUDWEILIOG Caern SH2336

'Tudwal's land', pers.n. ***Tudwal*** , ***-iog***

Tut Velliauc 1254, *Tudvaylok* 1291, *Tedwelliock* 1610, *Tidweilioc* 1535, *Tydwellyocke* 1564, *Tudweiliog* 1840

The terr.suff. ***-iog*** (causing -a- > -ei- in the preceding syllable) signifies land associated with Tudwal who is taken to be the saint Tudwal commemorated in the two islands called Ynys Tudwal off the south coast of Llŷn (q.v.). The church at Tudweiliog itself, however, is dedicated to Cwyfen or Cwyfan.

TUFTON Pemb SN0428

?'farm near a cluster of trees', ?ME ***tuft***, ME ***-ton,***

Tufton 1640

Uncertain. Evidence is late and the first el. must be regarded as very speculative. At the end of the 19cent. the area was characterised by a great deal of rough pasturage. The Tufton in Hampshire and the Tuffley in Gloucester contain OE pers.ns as first els (Tucca and Tuffa respectively).

TUMBLE, Y TYMBL Carm SN5412

'a place to tumble', E ***tumble***, W ***y***

Tumble 1831

The name is likely to have been taken directly from the inn here (*New Inn* 1813, *the Tumble Inn* 1875) located on a steep, twisting hill, evidently a humorous allusion to its dangers for travellers. Comparable to a *Tumble beerhouse* located at The Tumble on the steep, western slopes of the Blorenge hill, near Abergavenny, Monm, and to inn names at Tumbledown near Cardiff and near Port Talbot, Glam called Tumbledown Dick (popularly associated with Richard Cromwell but there seems to be no evidence that this was the case here). The use of the def.art. in W (though not always practised) also suggests a specific building. The village developed after the opening of a coal-mine in 1889.

TUSKER ROCK Glam SS8474

'projecting reef', ON ***skot***, ON ***sker***

groundes called Skuttskeeir 1596-1600, *Skuscar I.* 1754, *the Wiskar* 1764, *Skuskar I.* 1777, *Tusker Rock* 1813-4

A prominent isolated rock where the two ON els tend to replicate each other. Sker is common in the area such as Sker Glam (*Skerra* 1173-8, *Skarra, or Sker* 1291). Later forms have been influenced by a fancied resemblance to a ***tusk*** or to ***tusker*** 'elephant, wild boar'.

TWRCH[1], Afon Carm SN6546

'boar river', ***afon, twrch***

twrch c.1170 (c.1400), *Turhc* 1495, *Turch* 1556, *Turghe flu:* 1578, *River Twrch* 1891

The name of several rivers perceived as burrowing or rooting through the land. Also recorded in Blaentwrch (*Tir Blaen Turch* 1675-6, *Blaen Cwm Turch* 1712), Cwmtwrch Uchaf (q.v.) and Cwmtwrch Isaf Glam.

TWRCH[2], Afon Mont SH9714

'boar river', ***afon, twrch***

Twrch 1622, *Afon Twrch* 1836

See Twrch[1]. Also recorded in Pennant Twrch (*pennant turch* 12cent., ***pennant*** 'head of the valley, upland'). The Twrch is a tributary of the river Banw (q.v.) also with an animal name.

TWYMYN, Afon Mont SN8794-8902

'warm river', ***afon, twymyn***

Toymen 1200-4, *Twymyn* 1573, *Twymen, Twymin* 1683-7, *Afon Twymyn* 1836

The river flows from Ffrwd Fawr near Dylife past Llanbryn-mair and Glantwymyn (q.v.) and into Afon Dyfi at Dôl Twymyn. ***twymyn*** 'fever' is also recorded as an adj. 'warm', but here the noun is probably used as a qualifier (as if 'fever river'). The river's temperature is contrasted with that of its tributary Iaen (***iaen*** 'sheet of ice', see Nant-yr-eira) which is in shade.

TWYNLLANNAN Carm SN7524

'hillock at the ?small enclosure', ***twyn, ?llan, -an***

Twyn-llanan 1751, *Twnllaman* 1875, *Twyn Llanan* 1891

A village which developed at crossroads on a promontory above Afon Sawdde. Historical forms are very late but the proximity of two farms Penllanan (*Pen-llanan* 1891) at the eastern top (***pen***) of the village, and Llandre (*Llan-dre* 1891, ***tref***) suggests a specific topographical or structural feature. One possibility is the survival of ***llan*** in the secular sense of 'enclosure', perhaps with a dim.suff. ***-an*** (although there is no other record of such a form) referring to a pound for animals. The road running through the village is possibly Roman, since there is a marching camp about 3 miles away near Talsarn. It was certainly a medieval route, possibly used by drovers. Forms such as *Penlanau* 1831 suggest miscopying or attempts to rationalize *-llanan* as ***llannau*** pl. of ***llan*** 'church'.

TWYNYRODYN Glam ST1173

'hill of the limekiln', ***twyn, yr, odyn***

Twynyrodin 1814, *Twyn-yr-odyn* 1833, *Twynyrodyn* 1839

Identical in meaning to Twynyrodyn, at Lavernock, and at Merthyr Tydfil (*Twyn-yr-odyn* 1845). There were limekilns in the village in 1891 and nearby is *Limekiln Hill* (1846).

TWYN-Y-SHERIFF, TWYN-Y-SIRYDD Monm SO4005

'the sheriff's mound', ***twyn, y, siryf*** var. ***sirydd***, E ***sheriff***

Twyn under Sheriff 1813, *Twyn-sheriff* 1871

The hamlet lies on the south side of a small hill. The significance and identity of the sheriff is uncertain, but may have been associated with Raglan; cf. Shirenewton. A hybrid name of this sort is unusual and it is possible that ***sheriff*** has replaced an earlier W ***siryf*** or ***sirydd*** 'sheriff'.

TWYN-Y-SIRYDD see **TWYN-Y-SHERIFF**

TŶ-CROES[1] Angl SH3472

'cross-shaped house', ***tŷ, croes***

Tŷ-croes 1838

The house is on a junction (***croes***) but the noteworthy feature of the house, apparently, was a wing which made it cross-shaped. After the opening of the railway in 1848, the first station on the Holyhead-Bangor line was located here which helped to consolidate the house name.

TŶ-CROES[2] Carm SN6010

'house at a crossroads', ***tŷ, croes***

Tycross 1716, *Ty crose* 1734-5, *Tŷ-croes* 1831

At the junction of the A483 with lanes leading to Pantyffynnon station and Llanedi.

TYDDEWI see **ST DAVID'S**

TŶ-DU see **ROGERSTONE**

TYLORSTOWN Glam ST0195

'Tylor's town', pers.n. ***Tylor***, E ***town***

Tylorstown 1898, *Tylerstown* 1911

The village developed on the south side of Pendyrys colliery opened in 1873-76 by *Tylor's Colliery Co. Ltd*. The founder of the company was Alfred Tylor (1824-84), a London Quaker who married a daughter of the founder of Treharris (q.v.), and bought the mineral rights of Pendyrys farm in 1872.

TYLWCH Mont SN9780

'?pool', ?***llwch***

Tuluch 1200, *Teleuh* 1241, *Teleuch* 1281, *Tellouch, Towluch* 1781, *Afon Tylwch* 1833

The name seems to have been associated in the earliest records with the confluence of what is now Nant Caegarw with the river Dulas, while later records also refer to a narrow valley (*Glyntollegh* 1360-2, *Glemtologh* 1371-2, *Glyntoloth* 1424-5) possibly the Dulas valley. The second el. is probably ***llwch*** 'pool', at the actual confluence (still referred to in 1809). The first el. is less certain, partly because of the vars in the early forms. ***tŷ*** 'house' been suggested but ***tyle*** '(steep) road' (although more usually associated in later periods with more southerly parts of Wales) could refer to the severe gradients on both approaches to Tylwch, features which have prompted speculation that it could be Ir ***tulach*** 'hill'.

TYMBL, Y see **TUMBLE**

TŶ-NANT Denb SH9944

'croft in the narrow valley', ***tyddyn***, var. ***ty'n***, ***y***, ***nant***

Ty'n-y-nant 1838

The croft is where Nant-y-blodau meets Afon Geirw in the equally narrow valley through which the A5 runs. This is an example of the vars ***ty'n*** and ***tyn*** being interpreted as ***tŷ*** and ***tŷ yn***.

TYNDYRN see **TINTERN**

TŶ-NEWYDD Glam SS9399

'new house', ***tŷ***, ***newydd***

Tynewydd 1813, *Ty-newydd* 1833

Named from a former farm.

TY'N-Y-CEFN Mer SJ0443

'croft in Cefn', ***ty'n***, p.n. ***Cefn***

Ty yn y Cefn 1761, *Ty'n-y-cefn* 1838

Although the first record seems to be ***tŷ yn*** 'house in', it is far more likely to have been ***ty'n*** originally. The ***cefn*** is Cefn Rug, the ridge across the main road from Rug mansion.

TY'N-Y-FFRIDD Denb SJ1130

'croft in the mountain pasture', ***tyddyn*** var. ***ty'n***, ***y***, ***ffridd***

Ty'n-y-ffridd 1838, *Tynyfridd* 1870

The croft is at the junction of two minor roads (from Llanrhaeadr-ym-Mochnant and Llanarmon Dyffryn Ceiriog) in a narrow valley.

TYN-Y-GROES Caern SH7771

'croft at the crossroads', ***tyddyn*** var. ***tyn***, ***y***, ***croes***

Tuthyn y Groes 1553, *Tŷ yn y Groes* 1725, *Tynygroes* 1795, *Ty'n y Groes* 1806, *Ty'n-y-groes* 1838

At Tyn-y-groes, the Conwy-Dolgarrog road intersects the road from the Tal-y-cafn bridge (the only major crossing of Afon Conwy between Llanrwst and Conwy). The 1725 form shows ***tyddyn*** in the contracted var. ***ty'n*** or ***tyn*** being interpreted as ***tŷ yn*** 'house in' contracted as ***tŷ'n***, a development influenced by the size and strategic importance of the building seen to be more of a ***tŷ*** 'house' than a ***tyddyn***. In 1573 the house was a tavern (*Taverne-y-groes* 1578).

TYWI, Afon Carm SN7740-4520

?'swelling river', Br ?****teuā-***

Touios c.150, *tŷwi* 1129, *tigui* c.925 (1136-54), *tiugui* 955 (1136-54), *Tewy* 1280, *Tywye* 1582, *Towi* 1589

The river rises on the moorland of Cors Tywi and flows through Llyn Brianne (q.v.) and Dyffryn Tywi (*Diffrin/vallis Tewe* 1536-9, *Dyffryn Tywy*

1739-40) and westwards to the sea south of Carmarthen. The origin and meaning of the name cannot satisfactorily be resolved, despite the fact that the transliteration of Ptolemy's form c.150 would regularly result in Tywi, and that the el. ****teuā***- 'swell' is probably the root of W ***tyfu*** 'grow'.

TYWYN[1] Mer SH5800

'sea-shore', ***tywyn***

Thewyn 1254, *Tewyn* 1283, 1291, *Tywyn* 1352, *Towen* 1420, *Towyn Meronnygh* 1461, *Towyn Myryonethe* 1592, *Towŷn* 1795

The strand lies between the estuaries of the rivers Dysynni and Dyfi. The addition Meirionnydd to Tywyn was probably to distinguish it from Towyn (Tywyn) Denb. Towyn is also commonly used.

TYWYN[2] see **TOWYN**

U

UNDY, GWNDY Monm ST4386

?'church', ?***gwyndy***

Mundi c.1200, *Wundi* 1254, *Wndi* 1174-1211 (1290), *Wondy* 1314, *Undy* 1535, *gwndi* c.1566, *Wondey* 1798

Of uncertain origin. The absence of early forms with G- cast considerable doubt over the derivation from ***gwyndy***, the precise meaning of which is unclear, as it is rare in early records, but the basic meaning appears to be 'blessed abode, holy house' (***gwyn***, ***tŷ***). Undy has also been explained as the pers.n. ***Gwyndaf***, the alleged founder of the church, and identified with *uillam iunuhic* c.1015, but there is little or no support in historical forms.

UPPER BOAT, GLAN-BAD Glam ST1087

'upper ferry', ' ferry side', E ***upper***, E ***boat***, W ***glan***, ***bad***

Upper Boatside 1769, *the Higher Boat* 1788, *Upper Boat* 1799, *Glanybad* 1887

There were ferries lower down the river Taf at Rhydhelyg near Nantgarw, Taff's Well, Melin Gruffudd and Gabalfa (although there is no certain record of a 'Lower Boat').The later W name, recorded locally, refers more specifically to the landing place on the west shore (*Boatside* 1769) around which the village developed.

USK, River, WYSG, Afon Brec SN9829-ST3283

?'river abounding in fish', E ***river***, W ***afon***, OW ***uisc***

Uscha, *Osce* c.1100, *uisc* 1136-54, *uysc* c.1150, *Husca* 1143-54, *Oschæ flumin* c.1191, *Vsc* 1204-14, Usk 1322, *Wisch*, *Uske* 1536-9

The river rises near a farm Blaenwysg, flows east through Brecon and Abergavenny and south through Usk (q.v.) to the Severn estuary at Newport Mon. *Isca* was the name of the Roman fort beside the Usk at Caerleon (q.v.).

USK, BRYNBUGA Monm SO3700

'(town on the river) Usk', 'hill of Buga', ***bryn***, pers.n. ***Buga***

Uscha 1100, *Uisc* 1150, *Wysc* 13cent., *Usketon* 1322, *Brynbuga* 1450-1500, *Bryn y Buga* 1559

The town of Usk stands on a low hill between the rivers Usk (q.v.) and Olway/Olwy. The identity of Buga is lost. The Roman fort and town at Usk is *Bullaeum* 2cent. (11cent.), *Burrio* 3cent. (8-11cent.) 'place of Burros', with a pers.n. thought to be derived from Br ****burro-*** 'stout, sturdy, big' (as in W ***bwr***).

UWCHMYNYDD Caern SH1525

'further mountain', ***uwch, mynydd***

Uwch Mynydd 1840

This is a prominent area of high ground which rises dramatically from the sea at the south-west tip of Llŷn (notably Mynydd Mawr). Despite its apparently late appearance it is probably the medieval administrative nomenclature where ***uwch*** is 'further', here the furthermost part of Llŷn. The adjectival ***uwch*** 'upper' would regularly result in lenition (to *Uwchfynydd*). The preposition ***uwch*** 'above' might be more appropriate but is extremely difficult to interpret topographically unless it is taken to describe looking down to slightly lower areas of the mountain to the north-east, an interpretation which is more acceptable if ***mynydd*** could be taken as 'common land, moorland, heath' but such a use seems to be restricted to south Wales. Another interpretation is that it was once a navigational name to describe Uwchmynydd as a directional landmark seen from beyond Bardsey island, being 'above and beyond' Bardsey's Mynydd Enlli; cf. Church Bay.

UZMASTON Pemb SM9714

'Osmund's estate', pers.n. ***Osmund***, OE ***tūn***

Villa Osmundi 1176-98 (17cent.), *Osemundeston, Osmondeston* 1295, *Owsmonston* 1543, *Osmonston* c.1594, *Osmaston* c.1602, *Ismeston* 1778

Osmund is an E or Anglo-Scandinavian pers.n. from the Scandinavian pers.n. Ásmundr.

V

VALE OF NEATH see **NEATH**

VALLE CRUCIS, GLYN-Y-GROES Denb SJ2044

'valley of the cross', L ***vallis*** abl. ***valle***, L ***crux*** gen. ***crucis***, W ***glyn***, ***y***, ***croes***
Linneswestel 1236, *Llanegwestl* 1280-3, *Langustle* 1284, *Lynegwestle* 1535, *Llan-Egwest Abbey* 1795, *Valle Crucis* 1275, *Glyn Egwestl* 15 cent., *Llan Egwiste, alias Valle Crucis, an abbay* 1536-9, *the Vale of Llan Egweste or Valle Crucis* 1808, *Glyn Egwest* 1810

The church was dedicated to Egwystl or Egwestl as Llanegwest or Llanegwestl, which also appears in the name of the valley, Glynegwestl, the ***glyn*** through which the river Eglwyseg flows. From early on the (presumably) original ***glyn*** (in its lenited form of ***lyn***) was popularly interpreted as ***llan***. The Cistercian abbey founded there 1200 was known as *Abbatia de Valle Crucis* later translated as Glyn-y-groes (although some maintain that the L was a translation of what was originally a W name); cf. Strata Florida. The cross has traditionally been associated with the nearby Pillar of Elisedd (or Eliseg) (said to have been erected by Cyngen d.855, to commemorate his great-grandfather King Elisedd) in Maes-y-groes (*Maes y groes* 1567), although the pillar is not believed to have been cruciform.

VALLEY, Y FALI Angl SH2979

'(place near the) Valley', E ***valley***, W ***y***
The Valley 1838

The name emerged as a consequence of the building of the Cob or Stanley Embankment in 1822-3 from mainland Angl to Holy Island and the associated Telford post-road to Holyhead. The origin is the valley-like cutting from which rubble was extracted for the Embankment (*the Embankment or Valley* 1825) and a nearby public house called *The Valley* (1838). Soon the hamlet (inhabited mainly by Ir labourers) was called Valley (and occasionally *Pentre Gwyddelod* 'village of the Ir'). Later, the station (opened in 1848), rail-head and cross-roads a little further away to the east came to be called Valley, and the original hamlet became Hen Valley 'old Valley'. The cymricized Fali and Y Fali has long established itself in local and national usage, despite a deliberate attempt in the 70s and 80s to promote a translated Dyffryn (and found in an earlier mansion *Plas Dyffryn*).

VAN see **FAN, Y**

VAYNOR, Y FAENOR Brec SO0410

'the chief residence', *y*, ***maenor***

(parish) *Gwinaw* 1337-8, *Veynor* 1373, *Vaynorweyno* 1402, *maynor wino* c.1566

W ***maenor*** later meant 'group of villein townships' and 'division of a commote' and was later confused with E ***manor***. The second part of the p.n. has been lost, but referred to a saint Gwynno (*Sci. Gwynoci* 1481) to whom the church at nearby Llanwynno is dedicated.

VELINDRE see **FELINDRE**

VYRNWY see **EFYRNWY**

W

WALLIS Pemb SN0125

'walls', ****walis***

Walles 1572, *Upper Wallis* 1834, *Wallis Uchaf* 1839, *Lower Wallis* 1841

This may refer to the walls of Wallis Rath immediately west of the village or *Boystoneswalles* 1360. Another Wallis, Y Walis appears near Fishguard Pemb (*Magwr y Walleys* 1653, *Waleis* 1755, *Wallis* 1793, ***magwyr*** 'wall, fortification'). The cymricized ****walis*** preserves the disyllabic ME pl. ***walles***. ****walis*** appears several times in Pemb and Carm; see Alltwalis.

WALTON Radn SO2559

'settlement near a stream', OE ***wælle***, OE ***tūn***

Walton 1304, *Walltown* 1371-2

The village adjoins the Ridding Brook. However, OE ***wall*** 'wall' is also possible though unexplained; it certainly seems to have influenced the 1371-2 form, a fanciful (if inaccurate) allusion, perhaps, to Offa's Dyke more than a mile away. OE ***walh*** 'Welsh' or 'serf' with the sense of a place distinguished by the presence of distinctively Welsh people (in customs and language) is feasible but Welsh people must have formed a significant part of many other settlements in this area lying on the west side of the dyke.

WALTON EAST Pemb SN0223

'Wale's farm (east)', pers.n. ***Wale***, OE ***tūn***, OE ***ēast***

Waletun 1175, *Waletona* 1181/4, *Waleton* 1338, *Waltown* c.1566, *Wallton* c.1602

Walter son of *Wale* granted the church to the Knights Hospitallers of Slebech in the 12cent. (*ecclesia S[anc]ti Petri de Waletuna* 1230) although the church is now dedicated to Mary. Walton West Pemb (q.v.) is about thirteen miles to the south-west. Walton East is in the hundred of Dungleddy.

WALTON WEST Pemb SM8612

'Wale's farm (west)', pers.n. ***Wale***, OE ***tūn***

Waleton c.1175-76 (c.1600), *Walton* 1307, *Walton in rose* 1539, *Waltwn* c.1566, *Walton West* 1602

See Walton East. Walton West was in the hundred of Rhos.

WALTWN DWYRAIN see **WALTON EAST**

WALTWN GORLLEWIN see **WALTON WEST**

WALWYN'S CASTLE, CASTELL GWALCHMAI

Pemb SM8711

'?Walwayn's castle', 'Gwalchmai's castle', pers.n. ?***Walwayn***, ME ***castel***, W ***castell***, pers.n. ***Gwalchmai***

(de) castro Walwani 1272, *Castle Gaweyn, Castle Walwayn* 1290, *Walweynyscastel* 1349, *Gualwin castel* 1536-9, *Castell gwalchmei* 15cent., *Gualwin castel* 1536-9

Walwayn may well have been an AN settler but the forms show association with the (related) pers.n. E ***Gawayn***, F ***Gawain***, a hero of the Arthurian legends. ***Gwalchmai*** is a distinct W pers.n., replacing Gawain in most Welsh romances; here also it probably reflects a conscious antiquarian substitution for Walwayn.

WARREN

Pemb SR9397

?'restless (river)', OE ***wæfre***

Woveran 1273, *Woueran* 1326 (16cent.), *Overham* 1487, *Oram* 1503, *Waran* 1543, *waram, waran* c.1566, *Warren* c.1557, *Warren* 1684

Highly uncertain. The adj. ***wæfre*** 'wavering, restless' occurs occasionally in p.ns in England such as Woore Shropshire, Wharton Herefordshire and in the r.n. Waver Cumberland. Here it is possibly a lost stream name. The second el. is obscure. Uncertainty has prompted later association with ***over***, ***-ham*** and subsequently ***warren***.

WATERSTON

Pemb SM9305

'Walter's farm', pers.n. ***Walter***, OE ***tūn***

Walterystone 1407, *Walterston* 1546

Walter appears to be unidentified but was presumably an E settler. The loss of -l- is not matched in two other places in Pemb with the same E pers.n., Trewalter Lwyd in Mathri (*Trewallter* 1627, *Wallerston alias Trewalter* 1675) and Trewallter Wen in Llanedrin (*Walterystone* 1406) as well as two in Glam, Walterston Llancarfan and Llanrhidian. Waterston may perhaps represent a particular characteristic of local E dialect but the development is late and may have been precipitated by its location close to the waters of Milford Haven.

WATTSVILLE

Monm ST2091

'ville named after Watts', pers.n. ***Watts***, F ***ville***

Watts Ville 1891, *Wattsville* 1922

Built in the 1880s and 1890s next to a farm (*Dyffryn-isaf* 1891) and named from Edmund Hannay Watts (1830-1902), a partner in the formation of the *London and South Wales Co.* 1873 which purchased the old *Risca Pit* in that year and the *New Risca Pit* in 1875. The village developed rapidly after the opening of the nearby *Nine Mile Point* pits in 1902-5. Watts also gave his name to Wattstown (Rhondda) Glam, a village which appeared about the same period near two collieries sunk by *Watts, Ward and Co.*

WAUN[1] see **GWERNAFFIELD**

WAUN[2] see **CHIRK**

WAUNARLWYDD Glam SS6095

'(the) lord's moor', ***gwaun, yr, arglwydd*** var. ***arlwydd***

Gweine Arlloid 1585, *Weine Arlloid alias Lordes Meade* 1588, *Wain Arglwydd* 1754, *Gwynydd Arllwydd* 1769, *Waun-arlwyd* 1632

The name can be ascribed to persistent lenition following ***i*** 'to' and ***o*** 'from' in speech. The var. ***arlwydd*** is common in Glam. The p.n. has been explained as that part of Portmead (divided during the reign of Henry VII) which was retained by the lords of Gower. Cf. a field name (*Wain yrarlwydd* 1782) in Gabalfa, Cardiff.

WAUNFAWR[1] Caern SH5359

'(the) big moor', (*y*), ***gwaun, mawr***

Y Wyen Vaur 1541, *Wenfawr* 1795, *Waenfawr* 1837

The moor probably extended from Afon Gwyrfai to the slopes of Cefn-du. Convention requires Waun-fawr (to conform with final stress) but usage favours Waunfawr. Locally, it is frequently Y Waun or Y Weun.

WAUN-FAWR[2] Card SN6081

'(the) big moor', (*y*), ***gwaun, mawr***

y Wayen Vawr 1598, *y Wayne-vawr* 1606-7, *Wain* 1814, *Wainfawr* 1815, *Waun-fawr* 1834

The moor is on an exposed and elevated site east of Aberystwyth, now the site of extensive development.

WDIG see **GWDIG**

WELSHPOOL, Y TRALLWNG Mont SJ2207

'Welsh pool', 'the muddy pool', E ***Welsh***, OE ***pōl***, W ***y, trallwng***

yr trallwng c.1200, *Trallūg* 1254, *y Trallwng* 12cent. (14cent.), *y trallwn* c.1566, *Pole* 1196, *la Pole* 1197, *Pola* 1254, *Pole in Wales* 1477, *Walshepole* 1478, *Welshe Poole* 1577, *Pool* 1774

There are many other examples of ***trallwng*** elsewhere in Wales such as Trallwn (Swansea), Trallwng (Pontypridd) Glam, Trallwyn Pemb, and Trallwng (Trallong) Brec, all with a similar topography. 'Pool' is likely to be a loose translation of ***trallwng*** referring to a wet place somewhere along the lower course of the Lledan Brook which flows through the town, though it is traditionally identified with Llyn Du ('black pool') in Powis Castle park. It is interesting to note the use of the def.art.

y, ***la*** and ***the*** which seem to emphasize its association with a specific topographical feature. The town was simply *Pool* or *The Pool* down to the late 15cent. when *Welsh* was prefixed in order to distinguish it from places in England, notably the important borough of Poole Dorset but locally *Pool* survived much later; cf. Pool Quay. Trallwng gave rise to the var. Trallwn (as c.1566) which in turn resulted in the common local var. Trallwm with the common alternation of -n-/-m-.

WELSH ST DONAT'S, LLANDDUNWYD Glam ST0276

'church of Dunwyd', E ***Welsh***, E ***saint***, W ***llan***, pers.n. ***Dunwyd***
Welshe saynt donet c.1545, *Walshe saynte doonetes* 1547,
Welshe Seint Donettes 1559, *ll. dynwyd* c.1566, *Welch Sct. donetes* 1578,
Llandinwd 1678
The church lay in Tal-y-fan, a manor subject to Welsh custom and law in contrast to St Donat's (q.v.) (*Sancto Donato Anglicano* 1341) near Llantwit Major.

WENALLT, Y Mer SH9842

'the white hill', *y*, ***gwen***, ***allt***
Wenallt 1743, *Wennallt* 1783
An inversion of (*yr*) ***allt wen*** here describing a limestone slope. West of the village is Craig y Wenallt. On the inversion, cf. Wenallt/Thornhill Cardiff which has white thorn bushes.

WENTWOOD, COED GWENT Monm ST4394

'wood in (territory of) Gwent', terr.n. ***Gwent***, OE ***wudu***, W ***coed***
Guentuude c.1170, *Wentwode* 1245 (1307), *Wentwode* 1415,
Coed Gwent 1579
A medieval hunting forest and the largest wood in Gwent extending from Cat's Ash to the river Trogi leaving its name in Wentwood Gate and Wentwood Lodge. For Gwent, see Caer-went.

WENVOE, GWENFÔ Glam ST1272

Obscure
Wnfa 1173-83, *Wnuo* late 12cent., *Wunfo* 1254, *Wenvo* c.1262,
Wenfo 13cent., *Wonfo* 1317, *Wenvoe* 1533-8, *Gwenvoo* 1563,
gwenfo c.1566, *Gwenuow* 1578, *Y Wenfoe* 1839
The variation in the first vowel (*Wen-*, *Won-*, *Wun-*) seem to point to W ***gwynfa*** 'the fair land' (with lenition to *wynfa* after the def.art. or a prep.). However, two difficulties are the stress on the long final syllable, and particularly the rarity of forms with a final -a, since most forms (from E sources) before the 16cent. have -o which is difficult to explain unless it be ***bod*** 'abode' with very early loss of final -d. Local W speakers appear to have pronounced it 'Gwaun-fo' but ***gwaun*** only occurs in forms from the late 16cent.

WEPRE, GWEPRA Flints SJ2969

'silted land', OE ***wearpe***

Wepre 1086, *Wapir* 1281, *Weper* 1284, *Wepra* 1299, *Wepper* 1351, *Weppra* 1452, *Gweppra* 1489, *Gwepra* 1601

The Wepre Brook, also known in its higher reaches as Ewloe Brook (*Avon evlo alias Avon Gwepra* c.1700), entered the river Dee to form the Wepre Pool (*Pwlh Gwepra* c.1700), the only deep-water harbour between Flint and Chester until the Dee was canalized in 1737. Silting must have occurred over a long period before this time, and both banks of the Wepre delta were probably 'silted land'. Metathesis of -rp- to -pr- had occurred before 1086; the modern pronunciation is as in the 1284 form. The cymricized form retains the final syllable as a more prominent -a-, while the initial W- was taken as a lenition of Gw- (cf. Gwesbyr).

WEST MOUSE see **MAEN Y BUGAIL**

WEST WILLIAMSTON Pemb SN0305

'(west) William's farm', E ***west***, pers.n. ***William***, OE ***tūn***

Williameston Harvill 1362, *West Williamston* 1366, *Williamston west* 1592

The settlement was distinguished from East Williamston (*Williameston Elnard* 1272, *Williameston Eluard* 1362, *Williamston Elward* 1592, *East Williamston* 1592). Some forms also distinguish them by the names of unknown manorial tenants (*Harvill* and *Eluard*).

WHITCHURCH[1], YR EGLWYS NEWYDD Glam ST1580

'white church', 'the new church', OE ***hwīt***, OE ***cirice***, W ***yr***, ***eglwys***, ***newydd***

Witechurche 13cent., *Album Monasterium* 1296, *Blaunk Moustier* 1315, *Blankmoster* 1322, *Whytechurche* 1376, *Whitchirch* 1401, *Newchurch* 1472, *Newchurche* 1600-7, *Egluis Newith* 1536-9, *yr eglwys newydd* c.1566

The documentary forms have L ***album***, ***monasterium*** and F ***blanc***, ***moustier*** to match the E name, probably with reference to a white-washed or stone-built church. There are no historical forms to indicate whether there was a corresponding W name such as 'Eglwys Wen'. Evidence for the later W name Yr Eglwys Newydd (and its E equivalent, no longer current) refers to the church on the north side of the village, demolished in 1904 and now a small garden. This structure was 'new' (***newydd***, E ***new***) in contrast to an older church on the same site or elsewhere in the same parish (perhaps identifiable with an unlocated chapel Ystum Taf (*Capella de Stuntaf* 1126)).

WHITCHURCH[2], TRE-GROES Pemb SM7925

'white church', 'settlement by the cross', OE ***hwīt***, OE ***cirice***, W ***tref***, ***croes***

Ecclesia Alba c.1291, *Wytchyrch, -church* 1403, *Alba ecclesia, Whitechurch* 1491, *Trefgros* 1551, *Tregroyse* 1618
Identical to Whitchurch[1] (q.v.) and comparable with Eglwyswen/ Whitechurch Pemb (*Alba ecclesia* 13cent., *Whitechurch* 1488, *Egloswen* 13cent. [c.1600]). Later W vars are *Llan Eglwys y Groes* 1513, *y groes* c.1566 (***llan*, *eglwys*, *croes***) and *Pluwy'r Groes* 1637 (***plwyf*, *yr*, *croes***). The cross may be Maen Dewi thought to be the stump of a medieval cross.

WHITEBROOK, GWENFFRWD Monm SO5306
'white brook', OE ***hwīt***, OE ***brōc***, W ***gwyn*** fem. ***gwen***, ***ffrwd***
guenfrut 1136-54, *Wytebrok* 1296, *Whitebroke* 1505
The first form is taken from a copy of a charter thought to be dated c.698. Named from a small tributary of the river Wye which rises near Chapel Farm about three miles north-west of the village. The stream powered several mills. The apparent absence of later W forms probably reflects the predominance of E in historical sources.

WHITEFORD POINT Glam SS4496
'white-ford point', E ***white***, E ***ford***, E ***point***
Whitford poynt 1578, *Whitford Pt.* 1754, *Whiteford point* 1832
The name traditionally refers to stepping-stones crossing part of the Loughor estuary to Pembrey but it may properly refer to some ford over one of the small creeks and streams on the east and south-east side of the promontory, particularly Burry Pill, where there are limestone strata.

WHITESANDS BAY, PORTH MAWR Pemb SM7327
'bay with white sands', 'great bay', E ***white***, E ***sand***, E ***bay***, W ***porth***, ***mawr***
Porthmawr Meneviae id est Portu magno 1194, *Porthmaur, Portmaur* c.1200, *Porthmawr* 1610, *Porthmawre* 1449, *Whitsand Bay* 1578, *Whitesand Bay* 1610
A large sandy bay below the farm Porth-mawr. On *Meneviae* see St David's.

WHITFORD, CHWITFFORDD Flints SJ1478
'white ford', OE ***hwīt***, OE ***ford***
Widford 1086, *Quitfordia* 1240 (1285), *Chwtforth, Chwitforth* 1284, *Chwytford* 1292, *Whitford* 1303-5, *Wittefford* 1315-16, *Chwitford* 1333, *Wytford* 1340, *Chwytffordd* 1373, *Chwitffordd* 1550-62
The water of Afon Dre-lan (*Avon dre-lan* c.1700) above and below the site of the ford is reported still to foam white. The ford was replaced by a bridge (*carreg vawr ar i gorwedh* c.1700, 'a large horizontal stone') later a more modern stone bridge. Cymricization of the name occurred very early possibly prompted by the aspirated OE and ME hw- being very

close to the W chw-; a further development was of -ford to W ***ffordd*** 'road, route'. The earlier meaning of OE ***ford*** was in fact 'way, route'. A translated form Rhyd-wen or Rhydwen (*Rhydwen* 1867) (***rhyd, gwyn***) has been given some literary currency since the 19cent., as with the restored *Whiteford* 1810.

WHITLAND, HENDY-GWYN AR DAF — Carm SN2016

'white glade', 'old white house (on the river Taf)', OE ***hwīt***, OF ***launde***, W ***hen***, ***tŷ***, ***gwyn***, ***ar***, r.n. ***Taf***

(*de*) *Alba domo*, *Albae Landae* c.1191, *Whitland* 1309, *Whiteland* 1352, *albam landam* 1144 (late 13cent.), *Y Ty Gwyn* 1186 (c.1400), *Hendigwyn* 1561, *Alba Domus* c.1191, *la Alba Landa* 1214, *la Blaunchelande* 1318, *Blancalanda* 1329

The name Whitland is taken from that of a Cistercian monastery established initially at *Trefgarn* 1140 (probably Little Trefgarn Pemb) which moved c.1151 to a site next to the river Gronw. It probably acquired its names Whitland and *Tŷ Gwyn* from an existing settlement on the river Taf. Whitland is translated as *Alba Landa* (L ***albus***) and as *Blanchland* (F ***blanc***) and is identical to Blanchland Northumb (*Blanchelande* 1165), with OF ***launde*** then interpreted as E ***land***. *Y Tŷ Gwyn* is latinized as *Alba Domus* (L ***domus***). Both Hendy-gwyn and the qualifier 'ar Daf' (*Teguin ar Taue* 1536-9) seem to occur first in the 16cent. but may have served to emphasise the difference between the small town on the river Taf and the monastic site by the river Gronw. The full name Hendy-gwyn ar Daf seems to occur only in very late sources.

WHITSON — Monm ST3883

?'Wido's farm', OE pers.n. ***Wido***, OE ***tūn***

Villa Widonis 1236-40, *Wydest(ona)* 1240-45, *Wideston* 1241-5 (1290), *Wytteston* c.1291, *Wydeston* 1314, *Wydston* 1495, *y widsone* c.1566

The first form is a latinization, with L ***villa*** with *Widonis* as the gen. of ***Wido***, ***Wida*** or ***Wīd***, a pers.n which is unattested elsewhere. The later development shows the influence of the Whitsun of the Christian calendar.

WHITTON — Radn SO2767

'Hwīta's settlement', pers.n. ***Hwīta***, OE ***tūn***

Whitton 1304, *Whytton* 1332, *Whittyn* 1513, *hwytyn* c.1566

The church dedication to David/Dewi (***llan***, pers.n. ***Dewi***) appears in *ll. ddewi yn hwytyn* c.1566 which may be a literary or ecclestiastical form but is still associated with the church itself (Llanddewi-yn-Hwytyn). For W substitution of -tyn for OE ***tūn***; cf. Prestatyn Flints.

WICK, Y WIG — Glam SS9272

'dairy-farm', OE ***wīc***

Wicam 1148-83, *Wyke* c.1140-80, 1542, *Le Wyke* 1361, *y wig* c.1566, *Greate Wick* 1611, *Wick* 1670, *Y Weeg* 1718

The first form seems to point to a dat. pl. ***wīcan*** ('at the dairy-farms') but subsequent forms have it as a singular; Wick is a common enough place-name in England. W speakers later interpreted it as Y Wig (*y*, ***gwig*** 'the wood') which occurs several times in minor names; in some instances there is some confusion with the E Wick, such as Y Wig, Swansea (*le Weeg, le Wicke* 1583, *the Wicke* 1611, *the Weeg* 1650), aided perhaps by the fact that OE ***wīc*** and W ***gwig*** are cognate.

WIG see **WICK**

WISTOG see **WOODSTOCK**

WISTON, CAS-WIS Pemb SN0218

'Wizo's settlement', 'Wizo's castle', pers.n. ***Wizo***, OE ***tūn***, W ***castell***

Wicestuna 1175, *Wistune* 1319, *Wistune* 1319,

Castell gwiss 1146 (14cent.), *Castel Guys* c.1400, *kastell gwist* c.1566, *Wistonne* 1602

Wizo (d. before 1130) from Flanders was leader of the Flemings in Dungleddy Pembs and established his castle here (*castelli Wytsonis de Dugledin* 1115-47, *Castello Wicii* 1138-48, *Castro Wyz* ?1175-6 [c.1600]). The E name referred to the settlement associated with the castle. The W name referred to the ***castell*** itself (later abbreviated as ***cas-***, see Casnewydd Monm) and the pers.n. was interpreted as a new radical form *Gwiz(o)* which in turn was lenited to -wis. Although the form Cas-wis was not recorded in official documents it evidently survived in local usage.

WNION, Afon Mer SH7418

'(the river named after) Gwnion', ***afon***, pers.n. ***Gwnion***

Wynnion 1765, *Wnion* 1830

The name later given to what was originally the river Mawddach (q.v.). The individual has not been identified here, but Gwynion and its derivative Gwnion appear in several r.ns.

WOLF'S CASTLE, CAS-BLAIDD Pemb SM9526

'Wolf's castle', pers.n. ***Wolf***, OE ***castel***

Castrum Lupi 1293, *Woolfes castell* 1588, *Wolves Castle* 1599, *Wolfes castle* 1602, *Wolfscastle* 1806

There is a motte and bailey south-east of the village. The basis for assuming the pers.n. to have been Wolf rather than the documentary L rendering Lupus is that family name Wolf is well attested in Pemb. Here it has also been translated as W ***blaidd*** appearing in a *Castell Blaidd* with ***castell*** in its later var. ***cas-***.

WOLFSDALE Pemb SM9321

'Wolf's valley', pers.n. ***Wulf***, OE ***dæl***

Wolvedale 1312, *Westwoluedale* 1312, *Wolfedale* 1324,
West Wolfdall 1456, *Estyrwuldall, Westyrwuldall* 1491, *Woldale* 1603

There may be an association with Wolf's Castle (q.v.) less than five miles away which has prompted the modern form Wolfsdale and the popular notion that the valley was the haunt of wolves.

WOLVESNEWTON, LLANWYNNELL Monm ST4599

'Wolf's new settlement ', 'Church of Gwynnell', pers.n. ***Wolf***, OE ***nīwe***, OE ***tūn***, W ***llan***, pers.n. ***Gwynnell***

Nova villa 1148-83, *Wlvesneuton* 1296, *Wolvesneutone* 1311,
(*ecclesia de*) *Noua villa lupi'* c.1348, *Wolveisnewton* 1408,
lann gunnhoill 1136-54, *Languonhoill* 1119, *Llanwennell* 1409,
Llanwonnelch, Llanvennell 1539, *ll. wnell* c.1566

There is evidence of a *Radulfi Lupi* (L ***lupus*** 'wolf') here between 1193 and 1218 and of a *Ralph le Wolf* who held the manor in 1314. The 'old farm' was presumably *Sema Villa* 1291 (=*Sena Villa*, L ***senex***, ***villa***). The earlier ecclesiastical name Llanwynnell has the same pers.n. as St Twynnell's Pemb (with honorific pref. ***ty***- and ***Gwynnell***) and is possibly the same saint; there was a well of *St. Gwynhael* here in 1425. There is also evidence that the W name of the secular settlement was *Drenewydd Dan-y-gaer* 'new town under the fort' (***tref***, ***newydd***, ***tan***, ***y***, ***caer***), the fort possibly being Gaer-fawr (*Kayre* 1409, *Gaiarvaour, le Gayrvaour'* 1480) one-and-a-half miles south-west or, more likely, the small ring motte Cwrt-y-gaer a quarter-of-a-mile west of the village.

WONASTOW, LLANWARW Monm SO4810

'holy place/church of Gwynwarwy', pers.n. ***Gwynwarwy***, OE ***stōw***, W ***llan***

Lanngunguarui 1136-54, *Wonewarstawe* 1292, *Wonewardstowe* 1284,
Wonwarstowe 1293, *Wonewastowe* 1415, *Wonastow* 1483,
Llanwarow 1535, *ll. warw* c.1566

OE ***stōw*** has on occasions been used for W ***llan***, as in the adjoining parish of Dingestow (q.v.), Dewstow Monm (*capella sancti David* 1165-83) and *Dewstow* as an alternative name for St David's (q.v.). Wonastow bore an alternative name recorded as *ecclesiam gurthebiriuc* 'church of *Gurthebiriuc*' c.750 (c.1145) probably standing for *Gwerthefyriwg* 'land of Gwerthefyr' (pers.n. with ***-iwg***), a name found in Worthybrook (*Worthibruht* 1292, *Worthebruck* 1345) and its adjoining stream (*Wortebroke* 1500), clearly influenced by OE ***brōc*** 'stream, brook', a mile north-west of Wonastow. The modern W form Llanwarw probably developed from a **Llanwnwarw* or directly from Llanwynwarwy through loss of the unstressed syllable.

WOODSTOCK, WISTOG, WSTOG Pemb SN0225

'place in the wood', OE ***wudu***, OE ***stōc***

Wodestoke 1176-98 (17cent.), 1377, *Woodestock* 1543, *Woodstock* 1801

There are now no major ancient woods in this area. The development to W Wistog or Y Wystog probably derives from the trisyllabic form (such as *Woddystock* 1287, *Wodystok* 1381) while Wstog derives from the later Woodstock.

WOOLTACK POINT Pemb SM7509

'wild hook', E ***wild***, E ***hook***, E ***point***

Wiltock 1610, *Wilthooke alias Wildhook alias Wildewoke* 1630, *Wooltack* 1729, *Woolake* 1753, *Waltag* 1847

A reference to the exposed headland (on one of the most westerly points of Pemb) which is shaped like a hook.

WORM'S HEAD, PENRHYN GŴYR Glam SS3987

'snake's head', 'promontory of Gŵyr', OE ***wyrm***, OE ***hēafod***, W ***penrhyn***, p.n. ***Gŵyr***

Wormeshed 1400, *insula Wormyshede* 1478, *Wormes hedd* 1562, *Wormesheade Poynt, Wormshead, a little Iland* 1578, (*insula*) *henisweryn* 14cent. (1516)

Frequently Wormshead. This is the OE ***wyrm*** rather than the cognate ON ***ormr*** 'snake' (of Great Orme q.v.). It has been argued that the snake or serpent is an allusion to the prow of a Viking longboat, represented by the long narrow neck of land culminating in a dramatic rocky crag. There was a W form Ynysweryn with similar meaning (***ynys***, ***gweryn*** 'snake' which is probably cognate with OE ***wyrm***). It is not possible to determine which of these two names is the older. Another rendering of the name is Pen-pryf (*Penprys* 1578-84 [c.1700]) with ***pen*** and ***pryf*** (in a specialised sense 'reptile, serpent, snake'). Yet another antiquarian interpretation is Penypyrod (*Pen y Pyrod* 1874) with ****pwr*** pl. ****pyrod*** 'worm' of suspect linguistic provenance. Penrhyn Gŵyr, referring to the Gower peninsula (see Tre-gŵyr/Gowerton), is modern.

WORTHENBURY Flints SJ4246

'manor-house within an enclosure', OE ***worðign***, OE ***burh*** dat. ***byrig***

Hurdingberie 1086, *Worthinbury* 1300, *Wirthinnbury* 1321, *Worddembr'* 1331, *Wrdynbur'* 1346, *Worthumbury* 1386, *Gwrddymbre* 1418, *Gwrthunbre* 1440, *Gwrthynbury* 1441, *Worthenbury* 1527, *Worthembre in Walch Guothumbre* 1536-9

'Fortified place' is one meaning of ***burh*** (or ***byrig*** in the dat. form) but a more appropriate meaning here is 'manor-house' or 'estate', defended by a fence. The enclosure may have been more extensive land around the manor-house, again fenced in for whatever reason. Since Worthenbury is on low-lying land beside the Worthenbury Brook, with the road between Bangor Is-coed and Malpas passing through the village, there may have been strategic significance to the enclosure. The cymricized form *Gwrddymbre* (with loss of final syllable and an initial *Gw-*) did not survive.

WRECSAM see **WREXHAM**

WREXHAM, WRECSAM Denb SJ3350

'water-meadow of Wryhtel', pers.n. ***Wryhtel***, OE ***hamm***

Wristlesha' 1161, *Wrexham* 1186, *wrechtessham* 1200-1, *Wrixham* 1200-7, *Wrechcessam* 1222 (1295), *Gwrexam* 1254, *Gwregsam* 1291, *Wrightesham, Wrechtessham* 1294, *Wrightlesham* 1316, *Wrixham* 1315, *Wrexham treuly caullid Wrightelesham* 1536-9, *gwrek sam c.*1566, *Gwrexam* 1560-90, *Gwrexham* c.1700

The meandering rivers Gwenfro and Clywedog formed the water-meadows which were associated with an unidentified Wryhtel. There were several W versions including some (probably antiquarian and literary vars) which took the initial W- to be a mutation of Gw-. However, the initial W- is not pronounced in either language.

WSTOG see **WOODSTOCK**

WYDDFA, YR see **SNOWDON**

WYDDGRUG, YR see **MOLD**

WYE, River, GWY, Afon

Brec/Her/Monm/Mont/Rad SN8087-ST5497

'winding (river)', Br ?****guo-***

Guoy c.800, (*on*) *Wæge* 956, *Waia, Waie* 1086, *Wai* 1148-83, *Gui, guai* c.1175, *Wye* 1227, *Waye* 1234, *gwye* late 14cent., *Gŵy* 15cent.

The river rises on the east side of Pumlumon and flows south-east to Rhayader, through Builth, Hay, and Hereford, to the Severn estuary at Chepstow. There are various views on the interpretation of a name which may be pre-Celtic but the W forms certainly reinforce a derivation from a root which has given W ***gŵyr*** 'bent'. Cf. (Penrhyn) Gŵyr and the r.n. suff. *-wy*.

WYSG, Afon see **USK, River**

Y

YARDRO Radn SO2258

?'rough ground near an enclosure', OE ***geard***, OE ***rūh***

Kay Lloyd or the Yardro 1715, *Yardro Farm* 1771, *Yardro* 1891

The forms are very late indeed for an OE origin but the name appears to be identical to *le Yardroue* 1325 Cheshire. The otherwise unattested W *Kay Lloyd* has ***cae*** + ***llwyd*** 'grey (or brown) enclosure' probably developed independently of the E name but did not survive.

YERBESTON Pemb SN0609

?'Gerbard's settlement', pers.n. ?***Gerbard***, OE ***tūn***

Villa Gerbaud 1308, *Jerbardeston* 14cent., *Jorbardeston* 1362, *Yerbeston* c.1527, *Yarbaston* 1541

Probably a Continental pers.n. and its forms with J- and Y- may possibly show AN influence. The name certainly influenced the spelling of another Pemb p.n. *Osberneston* 1348, *Iarvaston* 1633 (with the pers.n. *Osbern*); locally pronounced 'Iarbersn'.

YNYS AMLWCH, EAST MOUSE Angl SH4494

'island off Amlwch', 'east little island', W ***ynys***, p.n. ***Amlwch***, E ***east***, E ***mouse***

Ynys Amlwch or East Mouse 1748, *The eastern Mouse* 1818, *Ynys Amlŵch or East Mouse* 1838

Cf. Middle Mouse and especially West Mouse for the meaning of ***mouse***. This island marks the entrance to Porth Amlwch.

YNYS ARW see **NORTH STACK**

YNYS BADRIG, MIDDLE MOUSE Angl SH3895

'island of Padrig', 'middle little island', W ***ynys***, pers.n. ***Padrig***, E ***middle***, E ***mouse***

Ynys Padric 1536-9, *The middle Mouse* 1818, *Middle Mouse/Ynys Badrig* 20cent.

Cf. East Mouse, and see West Mouse for the meaning of ***mouse***, which seems to be a recent addition by analogy with the other two. The island is near Llanbadrig (q.v.) and Porth Padrig (*Porth Badric* 1838), denoting the location of the island rather than any specific association with the saint.

YNYS-BOETH Glam SS0796

'parched river-meadow', ***ynys***, ***poeth***

Ynys boeth issa 1632-3, *Ynysboeth Yssa*, ~ *Ycha* 1636, *ynis both issa*, ~ *ycha* 1782

Named from two farms (***uchaf*** 'upper' and ***isaf*** 'lower') adjacent to the river Cynon. W ***poeth*** may be used here in the sense 'burnt' as in Coed-poeth Denb or 'warm, sunny' or 'scorched, parched, crisp, withered'. Local pronunciation is W 'bôth' and E 'both'.

YNYS BŶR see **CALDEY**

YNYS-DDU Monm ST1892

'black water-meadow', ***ynys, du***

Ynysddy 1649, *Ynysddu* 1715

From its shaded location on the east bank of the river Sirhywi in a narrow part of the valley. It was apparently established as a small model village by FH Moggridge in the 1820s (as he did for Blackwood q.v.).

YNYS DEWI see **RAMSEY**

YNYS DULAS Angl SH5090

'island (off) Dulas', ***ynys***, p.n. ***Dulas***

Carreg y Fran or Ynys Gadarn 1748, *Ynys Gadarn* 1777, *Ynis Gadarn* 1805, *Ynys y Gadern or Carregyfryn* 1818, *Ynys-gadarn or Ynys-dulas* 1841

The older names Carreg y Frân 'the raven rock' (***carreg, y, brân***) and Ynys Gadarn 'steadfast island' (***cadarn*** 'strong, steadfast') were supplanted by a modern reference to its location near Traeth Dulas (q.v.). A popular alias in the mid 20cent. was Seal Island.

YNYS ENLLI see **BARDSEY**

YNYS GYBI, HOLY ISLAND Angl SH2381

'holy island', 'island of Cybi', E ***holy***, E ***island***, W ***ynys***, pers.n. ***Cybi***

Island of Kayrgybi 1522, *Holyhead Isle* 1787, *Ynys Gybi* 1810, *Holyhead Island* 1841

The island which is separated from Angl by a narrow strait from Traeth y Gribin to Cymyran and is joined to it by two major rail and road routes (near Valley q.v.) and the old coach road (at Four Mile Bridge q.v.). The principal settlement of the island, Holyhead/Caergybi (q.v.), preserves the same dedication.

YNYSGYNWRAIDD see **SKENFRITH**

YNYS-HIR Glam ST0292

'long river-meadow', ***ynys, hir***

Ynusshire 1789, *Ynis Hyr* 1799, *Ynyshir* 1833

Named from a former farm on the west bank of the river Rhondda. The village developed around a colliery opened 1871.

YNYS LANNOG see **PRIESTHOLM**

YNYS-LAS Card SN6092

'verdant island', ***ynys, glas***

Ynys Lâs 1748, *Ynis Las* 1772, *Ynys-lâs* 1837

The scattered hamlet is on a sandy promontory between the sea, Afon Leri, the Dyfi estuary and Cors Fochno. ***ynys*** can be interpreted here as land near water. Formerly, there were several patches of dry land in the otherwise very low-lying wet ground, and the same el. also appears in nearby Moel-ynys, Neuadd yr Ynys, Ynys Tachwedd, Ynys Capel, Ynys Hir. Extensive drainage and canalization of Afon Leri permitted reclamation and the development of the area which is crossed by the railway and the road from Tre'r-ddôl.

YNYS LAWD see **SOUTH STACK**

YNYS LLANDDWYN Angl SH3862

'island of the church of Dwyn(wen)', ***ynys, llan, Dwyn(wen)***

Llanddwyn 1349, *ch. St. Donwenna* 1384, *ll.ddwyn* 1480-1,

a little isle caullid Sainct Dunwen 1536-9, *Llanddwyn Abbey* 1795,

Llandwyn Point 1818, *Llanddwyn Island* 1838

The island (at high water) in the south-west of Angl on which stood the church dedicated to Dwyn. Female names were frequently embellished with the suff. ***-gwen*** 'bright, shining' or, here perhaps, 'blessed, holy'. Her well and the church (later destroyed by storms) became centres of pilgrimage, but the island itself was also a harbour, *a barred haven for litle boats* (1548-53).

YNYSMEUDWY see **YNYSYMEUDWY**

YNYS MÔN see **ANGLESEY**

YNYSOEDD Y MOELRHONIAID see **SKERRIES**

YNYS SEIRIOL see **PRIESTHOLM**

YNYS TUDWAL, ST TUDWAL'S ISLAND Caern SH3426

'(St) Tudwal's island', W ***ynys***, E ***island***, pers.n. ***Tudwal***

enys Tudwal 1291, *Inis Tidwale* 1536-9, *Stidwall insula* 1578,

ilands called Stydwall 1638-9, *Ynys Tudwal* 1748, *St. Tudwal's Islands* 1810

Possibly the same 6cent. Tudwal as in Tudweiliog (q.v.). These are two islands east of Abersoch (in St Tudwal's Roads, *The roode of the two Ilondes of stidwall* 16cent., *Stydwalles, a wyld rode and landing place* 1566), which maps tend to distinguish as St Tudwal's Island East (with the remains of a priory, *Prioris de Enys Tudwal* 1291, *St. Tudwals Chap and Island* 1777) and St Tudwal's Island West (with a lighthouse); some documents use the pl. Ynysoedd and Islands.

YNYS-Y-BŴL Glam ST0594

'river-meadow in the hollow', ***ynys, y, bŵl***

Ynys y Bool 1738-9, *ynis y Bool* 1756, *Ynis y Bwl* 1799

W ***bŵl*** is from ME ***boule*** 'bowl, ball' and possibly refers to the shape of the valley at the confluence of the river Clydach and the stream Ffrwd at the north end of the village. It has also been interpreted in late sources as a place where the game of bowls was regularly played.

YNYSYMEUDWY Glam SN7305

'the hermit's river-meadow', ***ynys, y, meudwy***

Ynys Mydo 1529, *Enes e Meydoo* 1558, *Ynys y meydow* 1605, *Ynis y Meidw* 1791

On the west bank of the river Tawe. No hermit's cell has been documented, and the name could be a fanciful desciption of an isolated location. The 1529 form, and local pronunciation (as 'Smitw'), suggest that forms without the definite article *y* were in use, and that the final -wy was reduced to -w and -ow.

YR ORSEDD see **ROSSETT**

YR WYDDGRUG see **MOLD**

YSBYTY IFAN Denb SH8448

'Ifan's hospice', ***ysbyty***, pers.n. ***Ifan***

Spitieeuan 1578, *Spyttie* 1581, *Spyttye* 1621, *Yspytty Evan* 1795

Taken from the travellers' lodging or hospice on the Pentrefoelas-Ffestiniog road belonging to the Knights of St John whose name appears in several W versions (Ieuan, Evan and Ifan). The name of the area became Tir Ifan (*tir Ieuan* 1606, *Tîr Ivan* c.1700, *Tir Evan* 1726, *Tir-Evan or Ifan* 1851), replacing an earlier Dolgynwal (*Yspytty Dolgynwal* 1541, *Spytty dolgynwall* 1632, ***dôl***, pers.n. ***Cynwal***). The village is commonly referred to as Sbyty (as in several of the historical forms).

YSBYTY YSTWYTH Card SN7371

'hospice near (the river) Ystwyth', ***ysbyty***, r.n. ***Ystwyth***

Specerwestic 1277-80, *Spitty Rywistwyth* 1561, *ysbytty Riw ystwyth* c.1566, *Yspittye Istwith* 1578, *Spytty Evan in Rewoystwith alias Rewistwith* 1610, *Spitty Ieuan* 1614, *Spitty Riwystoyth* 1632, *Ysbytty Ystwith* 1798, *Y Spytty Rhiw Ystwith* 1811, *Yspytty Ystwyth* 1834

The hospice was on a hill above Afon Ystwyth, a location once called *Rhiwystwyth* (*Rowestich* 1338) (***rhiw*** 'hill') and incorporated in some of the forms. Omission of the unstressed el. ***rhiw*** occurred sporadically, but has been absent from modern usage. Two of the forms refer to John (of the Knights of St John) in the W var. *Evan* (1610) and *Ieuan* (1614).

YSGEIFIOG Flints SJ1571

'sloping (place)', ***ysgeifiog***

Schinan, Schiviau 1086, *Sceinoc* 1186-1204, *Esceyvauc* 1254, *Skeynyanc* 1291, *Skawyoke* 1302, *Skeiviauc* 1324, *Esgeyfyoc* 1389-91, *Skeyveok* 1451, *Yskeifioc* 1550-62, *Yskeifiog* c.1700

Several of the early documents show -v- miscopied as -n-. There has been a strong belief that ***ysgeifiog*** 'abounding in elder-trees' (***ysgaw*** 'elder-tree') is relevant here, as in *From yskaw because we observed about forty growing within a stone's cast of yᵉ Church and 4 in yᵉ Churchyard, where they observed that there grew formerly many more* (c.1700). However, it is more likely that in the 11cent., ***ysgeifiog*** 'sloping' was the more permanent defining characteristic, as there are several steep slopes north and west of the village. The name also occurs in Angl and Pemb.

YSGIR, Afon Brec SN9933

?'branches', ***ysgwr*** pl. ***ysgyr***

Ischir 11cent., *Eskir, Heskir* c.1143-54, *Heskyr* 1320-1, *Isker* 1578, *Yscir-fawr, Yscir-fechan* 1832

Forms with E- survive down to the 19cent. although it is possible that some are attempts at representing Y- . The interpretation of ***ysgyr*** is very obscure. While the branches could be very small tributaries, other recorded meanings are 'sticks' possibly referring to a place where staves were regularly cut, and 'fragments, bits' possibly fragmented land.

YSTALYFERA Glam SN7608

'the meadow at the end of the short share-land', ***ynys, tâl, y, berran***

Ynys Delvarran 1548, *Ynys Tal y Veran* 1582, *Tir Ynystalverran* 1604, *Staleyfera* 1729, *Stallfera Issaf, ~ uchaf, ~ Genol* 1797, *Ystal-y-fera* 1831

Taken from the name of three farms recorded in the 18cent., located near the river Tawe. On the loss of initial Yny- cf. Skenfrith and Sketty. The el. ***berran*** is not evidenced independently of this p.n.; it appears to be ***ber*** 'short' and ***rhan*** 'part, share' and might have indicated land shared by two or more tenants. On the loss of the final -n cf. Rhosili and Barry. However, it may be misassociated later with ***bere*** 'pile, rick, stack' found in this area. *Ystalyfera* became the name of the ironworks built here in 1831 and then the name of the village.

YSTOG, YR see **CHURCHSTOKE**

YSTRAD Glam SS9895

'vale of (Tyfodwg)', ***ystrad***, pers.n. ***Tyfodwg***

Istradvadok 1375, *Estrad* 1535, *Ystrate* 1536-9, *Ystradavodoge* 1552, *Ystradetyvodoge* 1553, *Istradtevodocke* 1578, *yr Ystrad* 1839, *Ystradyfodwg* 1898

Cf. *Pandy'r Ystrad* 1740. The name is an abbreviated and familiar form of the parish name Ystradyfodwg recalling the church dedication to Tyfodwg (with dedications also at Llandyfodwg and Llantrisant Glam). Some modern maps have *Ystrad Rhondda* from its location in the Rhondda valley but that had very limited currency.

YSTRADAERON — Card SN5256

'vale of (the river) Aeron', ***ystrad***, r.n. ***Aeron***

Estrad 1284, *Estrat* 1302-3, *Ystrath* 1534, *ystrad* c.1566, *Istrad* 1517, *Ystrad* 1679, *Ystrad Aeron* 1936

The village is beside the wide valley of Afon Aeron (q.v.), with an adjacent hamlet of Felin-fach or *Felin-fach-ystrad* (1891). Ystrad was the name of the medieval tnshp. The church was Llanfihangel Ystrad (*Ll. fihangel ynystrad* pre-1569, ***yn*** 'in', *Llanvihangel Istrat* 1590, *Llanfihangell Ystrad* 1632, *Llanfihangel-Ystrad* 1951), a name which occasionally appears as the name of the village.

YSTRADFELLTE — Brec SN9313

'vale of (the river) Mellte', ***ystrad***, r.n. ***Mellte***

Stradmelthin 1230, *Strathvelthly* 1316, *Stradevelth'* 1372, *Stradvellte* 1503, *ystrad felle de* c.1566

The r.n. Mellte (*melltou* 1136-54, *Melldou* 1160-85, *Mellte* 1578) possibly with the el. ***mellt*** 'lightning' (perhaps alluding to the rapid, unpredictable flow of Afon Mellte, notable for its rocky course and waterfalls) and a suff. ***-tou*** or ***-teu*** of uncertain meaning. *Melltou, Mellteu* may also be a pers.n., comparable with Mellte (cf. Bedwellte).

YSTRAD-FFLUR see STRATA FLORIDA

YSTRADGYNLAIS — Brec SN7810

'vale of (the river) Cynlais', ***ystrad***, pers.n. ***Cynlais***

Stradgenles 1372, *Estradgynles* 1493, *ystrat gynleis* late 15cent.

The stream Cynlais (*Cingleis, blayn cygleis* 1129, *Kyn-leic* 1510, *Genles* 1536-9) is probably ***cŷn*** 'chisel' and ***glais*** 'stream'. The stream joins the river Tawe near a farm (*Tyr abar Gynlais* 1729, *Abergynlais* 1831, ***tir, aber***) while another two farms (*Waun-gynlais* and *Wern-gynlais* 1831, ***gwaun, gwern***) take their names directly from the p.n. It has been argued that Cynlais was a pers.n. here.

YSTRADMEURIG — Card SN7067

'vale of (the river) Meurig', ***ystrad***, r.n. ***Meurig***

Stramouric 1148-1176, *Stratmeuric* 1159 (late 13cent.), *Stradmeurich* 1176-98, *Stradmauric* c.1236, *Strat Meuric* 1425, *Ystrad meyryc* c.1566, *Ystrad Meurig* 1831

The present hamlet is a mile west of the original site, the location of a hospice (*hospitium cum horto in Stramouric* 1148-1176, *Ystrad Meiricke alias*

Spytty Evan 1649, where W Evan is a reference to St John of Jerusalem), a church (*ecclesiam de Strotmeurich* 1176-98) and a strategically located castle (*castello Stratmeur* 1137 [late 13cent.]). The r.n. Meurig (*Meuric* 1184 [1285]), allegedly named after Meurig, son of the king Rhodri Mawr (died 878), flows into Afon Aeron at Abermeurig.

YSTRADMYNACH Glam ST1494

'monk's vale', W ***ystrad, mynach***

Ystrad manach 1635, *Ystrad y Mynach* 1833

The name refers to a part of the Rhymni valley. Documentary forms are late (showing the dial. var. ***manach*** or a vestige of the old pl. ***menych***) although there is no conclusive proof of any connection with a monastery. Mynach (Manach) is perhaps a lost r.n. which may have been based on a pers.n.

YSTRADOWEN[1] Carm SN7512

'Owen's vale', ***ystrad***, pers.n. ***Owen***

Ystrad Owen 1831

The village is named from a former farm *Ystrad Owen* 1831 located in the valley of Afon Llynfell near its junction with Afon Twrch. Owen is unidentified.

YSTRADOWEN[2] Glam ST0177

'Owain's vale', ***ystrad***, pers.n. ***Owain***

Stradeuwen 1263, *Stradowayn* 13cent., *Straddouwen* c.1291, *Ystradowen* 1507, *ystrad owain* c.1566

This may also be (chapel of) *sancti Euiani de Cherleton'* 1173-83 if *Euiani* is a latinized form of Owain, Ywain. The parish church is dedicated to a saint Owain but it may well have referred originally to some secular sponsor Owain or Owen. *Charleton'* appears to have been a short-lived E p.n. identical to numerous places called Charlton 'settlement of the freemen or peasants'. The village is located at the head of the stream Nant Dyfrgi in a valley extending over the watershed to tributaries of the river Thaw.

YSTUMTUEN Card SN7378

'bend of (the river) Tuen', ***ystum***, r.n. ***Tuen***

Ystum Tuen 1690, *Istimtean* 1699, *Ystum Ty Hen* 1747, *Ystum-tuen* 1891

The village is near a bend in the Tuen brook which flows into Afon Rheidol, three-quarters-of-a-mile south-east. There was considerable mining in the area which probably prompted the building of a Methodist chapel (*Ebenezer*) there in 1822, but the name of another chapel (*Salem*) appears on the 1834 map, suggesting that Ystumtuen was a fairly late adoption as the name of the village. The r.n. is probably ***tu*** 'side, slope, edge' and the r.n. suff. ***-en***, to refer to the river's precipitous course.

YSTWYTH, Afon Card SN6375-7472

'winding river', ***afon***, Br ****stuctio-***

Στουκκία, Στουκία, Σουκκία 140-150, *Iuctius* before 400 (c.700), *Escud* c.1194, *Yscoyth* before 1282 (1425), *Istuith* 1184 (1285), *Ystwyth* late 14cent., *Ustwith River* 1536-9, *Ystwyth* 1684-5

The river rises on moorland above Cwm Ystwyth, and formerly reached the sea a mile-and-a-half south of the present town of Aberystwyth (q.v.). The Br root meant 'bent, curved' and the MnW derivative ***ystwyth*** still has the meaning 'supple, pliant' referring to the river's curved, winding course.